The Columbia Documentary History
of the Asian American Experience

The Columbia Documentary History of the Asian American Experience

Edited by Franklin Odo

COLUMBIA UNIVERSITY PRESS

NEW YORK

Columbia University Press
Publishers Since 1893
New York   Chichester, West Sussex

Library of Congress Cataloging-in-Publication Data
The Columbia documentary history of the Asian American experience / edited by
Franklin Odo.
    p.   cm.
   Includes index.
   ISBN 0–231–11030–8 (cloth)
    1. Asian Americans—History—Sources. I. Odo, Franklin.
E184.O6 .C63   2002
   973.'0485—dc21   2002019208

Columbia University Press books are printed on permanent and durable acid-free paper.
Printed in the United States of America
c 10 9 8 7 6 5 4 3 2 1

CONTENTS

Expanded Contents vii

Acknowledgments xv

INTRODUCTION

Asian Pacific Americans: An Overview 1

PART ONE

Contact and Conflict: Asia and the Pacific: Through 1900 9

PART TWO

Migration and Settlement: Through 1924 127

PART THREE

Accommodation and Hostility: Through 1941 197

PART FOUR

World War II: Through 1945 247

PART FIVE

The Pacific Ocean: An American Lake?: Through 1975 315

PART SIX

Brave New World: Through 2000 409

Index 567

EXPANDED CONTENTS

PART ONE
Contact and Conflict: Asia and the Pacific: Through 1900   9

1. Naturalization Act, March 26, 1790   13

2. California Foreign Miners Tax, April 13, 1850   15

3. Agreement Between English Merchant and "Chinaman," 1850   17

4. *The People, Respondent, v. George W. Hall, Appellant,* 1854   19

5. Publisher's Remarks on "The Chinese and the Times" in First Chinese
Newspaper in the United States, June 10, 1854   22

6. An Act to Prohibit the "Coolie Trade" by American Citizens in
American Vessels, February 19, 1862   24

7. An Act to Protect Free White Labor Against Competition with
Chinese Coolie Labor, and to Discourage the Immigration of the Chinese
Into the State of California (a.k.a. Police Tax), April 26, 1862   26

8. Amendment 14, U.S. Constitution, 1868   29

9. Burlingame-Seward Treaty, July 28, 1868   31

10. *In re Ah Fong,* September 21, 1874   33

11. An Act Supplementary to the Acts in Relation to Immigration
(a.k.a. The Page Law), March 3, 1875   38

12. "Ah Sin" (Chinese Song), written for and sung by C. T. Parsloe, 1877   41

13. *In re Ah Yup,* April 29, 1878   46

14. Petition from 1,300 Chinese Merchants for Schools, 1878?   49

15. Invalidation of Queue Ordinance, July 7, 1879   51

16. Memorial on Chinatown, Investigating Committee of the Anti-Chinese
Council, Workingmen's Party of California, March 10, 1880   57

17. An Act to Execute Certain Treaty Stipulations Relating to Chinese (a.k.a. Chinese Exclusion Act), May 6, 1882 62

18. Treaty Between the United States and Corea: Peace, Amity, Commerce, and Navigation, May 22, 1882 64

19. Foran Act Prohibiting Contract Labor, February 26, 1885 67

20. California Supreme Court: *Mamie Tape, an Infant, by Her Guardian Ad Litem, Joseph Tape, Respondent, v. Jennie M. A. Hurley et al., Appellants,* March 3, 1885 70

21. Letter from Mary Tape, April 8, 1885 72

22. Saum Song Bo Letter Protesting Fund Raising for Statue of Liberty, October 1885 74

23. Supreme Court: *Yick Wo v. Hopkins,* May 10, 1886 76

24. Hawai'i Constitution (a.k.a. Bayonet Constitution), 1887 81

25. An Act to Prohibit the Coming of Chinese Laborers to the United States (a.k.a. Scott Act), September 13, 1888 84

26. Supreme Court: *Chae Chan Ping v. United States,* May 13, 1889 86

27. An Act to Prohibit the Coming of Chinese Persons Into the United States (a.k.a. Geary Act), May 5, 1892 89

28. Supreme Court: *Nishimura Ekiu v. United States,* January 18, 1892 91

29. Supreme Court: *Fong Yue Ting v. United States, Wong Quan v. Same, Lee Joe v. Same,* May 15, 1893 93

30. Dr. Harvey Saburo Hayashi Admonition to Japanese Immigrants, 1893 97

31. *In re Saito,* June 27, 1894 101

32. Comic Song and Chorus: "The Wedding of the Chinee and the Coon," 1897 104

33. Treaty of Peace Between the United States and Spain, Paris, December 10, 1898 109

34. Supreme Court: *United States v. Wong Kim Ark,* March 1898 112

35. Annexation of Hawai'i, March 16, 1898 115

36. Reverend Eryu Honda, Jodo Shinshu Buddhist Minister, and Japanese Consul Miki Saito, 1898 120

37. Hawai'i Sugar Plantation Wage Policy, March 20, 1899 122

38. Political Cartoons Reflecting U.S. Images of Filipinos, 1899 124

PART TWO
Migration and Settlement: Through 1924   127

39. *Holehole bushi*: Japanese Folk Songs on Hawai'i Sugar
Plantations, 1900   131

40. Samuel Gompers and Mexican/Japanese Farmworkers in Oxnard,
California, June 2, 1903   134

41. Chiura Obata Letter to Family, August 1903   137

42. Sun Yat-sen Application to Enter the United States,
April 21, 1904   139

43. Theodore Roosevelt Executive Order (a.k.a. Gentlemen's Agreement)
March 14, 1907   141

44. Anti-Japanese Laundry League Flyer, 1908   143

45. On Higher Wages for Japanese Laborers, 1909   145

46. Angel Island Poetry, 1910   148

47. Song: "Chinatown, My Chinatown," 1910   150

48. Supreme Court: *Tang Tun v. Edsell*, March 11, 1912   155

49. *Hawaii Hochi*, First Editorial, December 7, 1912   157

50. California Alien Land Law (a.k.a. Webb Act), August 10, 1913   160

51. Immigration Act of 1917 (a.k.a. Barred Zone Act),
February 5, 1917   162

52. Immigration Memorandum re Mrs. Fong See, July 3, 1919   165

53. Federation of Japanese Labor, "The Voice of Labor in
Hawaii," 1920   167

54. Reverend Shiro Sokabe and Japanese Labor, 1920?   170

55. Bishop Koyu Uchida, Testimony to House Immigration
Committee, 1920   172

56. An Ch'angho, "Grand Strategy for Independence" for
Korea, 1920   174

57. The Cable Act, September 22, 1922   179

58. Supreme Court: *Takao Ozawa v. United States*,
November 13, 1922   181

59. Supreme Court: *United States v. Bhagat Singh Thind*,
February 19, 1923   185

60. Supreme Court: *Terrace et al. v. Thompson, Attorney General of the State of Washington*, November 12, 1923   189

61. National Origins Act: An Act to Limit the Immigration of Aliens Into the United States, and for Other Purposes, May 26, 1924   192

PART THREE

Accommodation and Hostility: Through 1941   197

62. Supreme Court: *Hidemitsu Toyota v. United States*, May 25, 1925   199

63. Friendship Dolls to Japan, December 20, 1926   202

64. Supreme Court: *Wallace R. Farrington, Governor of the Territory of Hawaii, et al.v. T. Tokushige et al.*, February 21, 1927   204

65. Supreme Court: *Weedin v. Chin Bow*, June 6, 1927   208

66. Supreme Court: *Gong Lum et al. v. Rice et al.*, November 21, 1927   211

67. Younghill Kang, *The Grass Roof*, 1931   215

68. Hare-Hawes-Cutting Act, January 17, 1933   217

69. California District Court of Appeal: *Salvador Roldan v. Los Angeles County*, January 27, 1933   220

70. Gee Theo Quee Angel Island Interrogation, December 1, 1933   223

71. Tydings-McDuffie Act (Public Law No. 127), March 24, 1934   230

72. Filipino Repatriation Act, July 10, 1935   234

73. A General Staff Study: Plan—Initial Seizure of Orange [Japanese] Nationals, 1936   236

74. International Ladies Garment Workers' Union on Chinese Workers, January 1938   238

75. Chinese Ladies Garment Workers' Union, Local 341, January 1939   240

76. Okinawans in America, 1939   242

PART FOUR

World War II: Through 1945   247

77. Franklin Delano Roosevelt, "Day of Infamy" Speech, December 8, 1941   251

78. *Life* Magazine, "How to Tell Japs from the Chinese,"
December 22, 1941   253

79. Mike Masaoka, "Japanese American Creed," May 9, 1941   256

80. Reverend Tamasaku Watanabe, Appeal for Exemption from
Freezing Assets, August 9, 1941   258

81. Letter from John Steinbeck to John Ford, December 10, 1941   261

82. Petition to Establish Varsity Victory Volunteers, January 30, 1942   263

83. Letter from Charles Hemenway to Ralph Yempuku, Varsity Victory
Volunteers, May 23, 1942   265

84. Executive Order 9066, February 19, 1942   267

85. Army Instructions for Removal of Japanese Americans in
Los Angeles, May 3, 1942   269

86. Letter from Louis Goldblatt to Carol King, May 22, 1942   272

87. Toku Shimomura Diary, 1942   274

88. Repeal of Chinese Exclusion Acts (Public Law 199),
December 17, 1943   281

89. Supreme Court: *Kiyoshi [Gordon] Hirabayashi v. United States,*
June 21, 1943   283

90. Supreme Court: *Minoru Yasui v. U.S. Supreme Court,*
June 21, 1943   288

91. Destruction of Original Relocation Report Documents, 1943   290

92. Carlos Bulosan, *America Is in the Heart,* 1943   292

93. Jimmie Omura on Japanese American Resistance to the Draft,
April 7, 1944   299

94. Supreme Court: *Ex Parte Mitsuye Endo,* December 18, 1944   302

95. Supreme Court: *Korematsu v. United States,* December 18, 1944   306

96. War Brides Act (Public Law 271), December 28, 1945   312

PART FIVE

The Pacific Ocean: An American Lake: Through 1975   315

97. Philippines Veterans Rescission Act, February 18, 1946   320

98. Supreme Court: *Torao Takahashi v. Fish and Game Commission,*
June 7, 1948   322

99. *Honolulu Advertiser* Editorials: Hawaii Dock Strike,
May 5 and 9, 1949   327

100. California Supreme Court: *Fujii Sei v. State of California,*
April 17, 1952   330

101. McCarran-Walter Immigration and Nationality Act,
June 27, 1952   335

102. Supreme Court: *Kwong Hai Chew v. Colding, et al.,*
February 9, 1953   339

103. Supreme Court: *Kimm v. Rosenberg,* June 13, 1960   343

104. Children's Petition on Civil Rights Bill to Senator Hiram Fong,
October 9, 1963   347

105. Immigration and Nationality Act, October 3, 1965   351

106. Nguyen Thanh Trang, "North and South Vietnam Are Not
Two Countries," 1966   355

107. Supreme Court: *Loving et ux. v. Virginia,*
June 12, 1967   358

108. San Francisco State University Third World Liberation
Front Position, 1968   361

109. International Hotel Struggle, Manilatown, San Francisco,
February 1970   365

110. The Need for a United Asian-American Front, 1970   370

111. Preface to *Roots: An Asian American Reader,* 1971   374

112. "Yellow Pearl": Asian American Movement Music,
1972   378

113. Song: "We Are the Children," 1972   381

114. Ramsay Liem, "Some Tasks at Hand," 1972   383

115. Preface to *Aiiieeeee!,* 1973   385

116. Hirabayashi Ethnic Education Statement, 1974   392

117. Supreme Court: *Lau v. Nichols,* January 21, 1974   401

118. Letter, Philip Vera Cruz to Noel Kent re Filipino Farmworkers,
January 17, 1975   404

119. Indochina Migration and Refugee Assistance Act,
May 23, 1975   407

PART SIX
Brave New World: Through 2000   409

120. Asian/Pacific American Heritage Week (Proclamation 4650),
March 28, 1979   413

121. Eric Chock, Writers of Hawaii Conference, 1980   415

122. Recommendations from the Commission on Wartime
Relocation and Internment of Civilians, 1982   419

123. Appeal Letter from Mother of Vincent Chin, 1983   425

124. Resolution on Vincent Chin Decision by Detroit NAACP,
March 1983   427

125. U.S. District Court: *Fred Korematsu v. United States*,
April 19, 1984   429

126. Nobuko Miyamoto, "Yuiyo Bon Odori," 1984   432

127. Southeast Asian Refugee Acts: Resettlement, Amerasian
Homecoming, and Refugees via Thailand, December 22, 1987   434

128. Civil Liberties Act of 1988 (Public Law 100–383),
August 10, 1988   439

129. U.S. Court of Appeals: *William Hohri et al., Plaintiffs-Appellants,
v. United States*, January 21, 1988   444

130. William Hohri/NCJAR Class Action Suit for World War II
Damages, 1988   448

131. Supreme Court: *Wards Cove Packing Company, Inc., et al.
v. Atonio et al.*, June 5, 1989   457

132. Masaru "Pundy" Yokouchi Interview in *Off Center*,
March/April 1990   464

133. Daniel Tsang, "Asians Are Automatically Labeled Gang Members,"
December 12, 1994   467

134. Akaka Legislation to Review for Asian Pacific American
Congressional Medals of Honor (Senate Bill 1026), August 3, 1995   470

135. Peter Hyun, Afterword to *In the New World*, 1995   473

136. Andrew Lam, "Love, Money, Prison, Sin, Revenge," 1995   477

137. "Distant Shores, Common Ground," 1995   487

138. Nobuko Miyamoto, "To All Relations," 1996   494

139. *Washington Post*, Filipino Veterans Editorial,
December 13, 1997   496

140. Revised Office of Management and Budget Directive 15,
December 15, 1997   498

141. Senator Daniel Inouye, Speech on Filipino World War II Veterans,
May 13, 1998   502

142. Statement at Official Close of Japanese American Redress Office,
September 10, 1998   506

143. Vu Nguyen, "Why I Hate Ho Chi Minh,"
February 19–25, 1999   509

144. Le Ly Hayslip Commentary, February 24, 1999   512

145. Executive Order 13125, June 7, 1999   514

146. Senator Daniel Inouye Introduces General Eric Shinseki,
June 9, 1999   518

147. Quang X. Pham, Vietnamese Recognition Luncheon Speech,
August 1999   520

148. Hmong Veterans Naturalization Act (Public Law 106–207),
May 26, 2000   527

149. "On Behalf of Lesbian, Gay, Bisexual, and Transgender [LGBT]
Asian Pacific Islander Individuals and Organizations,"
September 18, 2000   530

150. Celebrating South Asians, September 21, 2000   534

151. Association for Asian American Studies Resolution on Wen Ho Lee,
May 26, 2000   538

152. Committee of 100: American Attitudes Toward Chinese Americans
and Asian Americans, 2001   541

153. 2001 *Obon* Schedule in Hawai'i, May 2001   551

154. Norman Mineta, Speech at National Japanese American Memorial
Foundation, June 29, 2001   555

155. U.S. Catholic Bishops Welcome Asian Pacific Americans,
July 2001   558

ACKNOWLEDGMENTS

I wish to thank a number of individuals who helped me with this volume. The librarians, archivists, students, and scholars who secured particular works are acknowledged separately along with the particular documents they graciously found. Ron Kim helped me to think about the scope of the work in an early stage of this project. Julianna Lee and Grace Lou provided assistance in specific phases of document retrieval while they interned at the Smithsonian's Asian Pacific American Program. But it was a volunteer, Noriko Sanefuji, whose assistance was indispensable in tracking down many citations. I thank her for her diligence and good grace. Jamie Warren, Columbia University Press editor, conceived and proposed the volume and was a constant source of encouragement. My family provided the inspiration: thanks to my parents, Masaru and Betty Masako Odo, and to Enid and our children, David/Jany, Rachel/Tomaso, and Jonathan.

*The Columbia Documentary History
of the Asian American Experience*

Asian-Pacific Americans: An Overview

The field of Asian American studies has expanded steadily and rapidly in the past few decades. Academic departments and programs grace university campuses across the nation, from Hawai'i to Texas, Illinois, and Maryland. Scholarly monographs, collections of essays, and textbooks in various disciplines are available to students and the general public. Literary works have proliferated in spectacular proportions; they include volumes of poetry, best-selling fiction, and a wide range of anthologies. Documentary films and Asian American film festivals feature an extremely diverse set of topics and perspectives. As a result, many people now have at least passing knowledge of the 1882 Chinese Exclusion Act, the U.S. Supreme Court cases involving Japanese Americans during World War II, and the 1965 immigration reforms that dramatically altered the nature and pace of demographic movement from Asia to America.

Asian American history has demonstrated several important principles. First, crucial theoretical insights can be gleaned when research is done from the perspectives of groups being studied. Thus, major contributions have been made in many fields, including western history, feminist studies, immigration history, military history, sociology, anthropology, psychology, and political science. Other fields likely to experience similar growth in the near future are religious studies, education, history of science, and business history. Second, the experiences of this relatively small racial group can be crucial in addressing very large questions, such as the ongoing definition of being or becoming "American." When, how, and why Asians became the only racial group excluded from both immigration and naturalization, for example, lie at the very heart of these issues. Third, solid research results can become important catalysts or supportive evidence for significant policy change involving individuals or entire communities. For example, research on the federal government's own actions during World War II internment litigation revealed sufficient evidence to compel the vacating of several key Supreme Court cases in the 1980s. Research on the relative scarcity of Medals of Honor conferred on Asian American veterans of World War II led to twenty-two additional awards over half a century later. Research reflecting our inability to accommodate refugees from Southeast Asia led to changes in naturalization requirements for Hmong veterans. The list is long and growing.

With the publication of Gary Okihiro's *The Columbia Guide to Asian American History* (New York: Columbia University Press, 2001), we now have a solid volume incorporating narrative and historiographical essays, examples of pointed historical disagreements, and useful bibliographical notes. Readers are encouraged, therefore, to consult that work for further references. But while the immense body of information contained in film, novels, mono-graphs, and textbooks often references major aspects of Asian American history, the majority of interested readers have not had ready access to the actual documents behind these stories. This volume fills that particular gap by providing the relevant sections of those documents for researchers, students, and the general public.

Thus, someone reading about the contemporary federal attempt to "define" race in the United States—the classification of four "races" plus the Hispanic ethnic group in the decennial census—can read Directive 15 from the Office of Management and Budget (1978) as it was amended in 1997. A student intrigued by one of many fine documentaries focusing on Japanese American resistance to mass detention during World War II might read opinions from Supreme Court justices supporting or decrying those landmark decisions. Similarly, scholars curious about the impact of McCarthyism and the Cold War hysteria on Chinese Americans could read the text of legislation designed to "combat" communism.

Documents were selected to illuminate issues and events of lasting historical significance for a range of Asian American ethnic groups. For the period prior to critical immigration pattern changes in the 1960s, most deal with the Chinese and Japanese, with only a few involving Filipinos, Koreans, and South Asians. This imbalance reflects the state of the field into the late twentieth century, and it may be expected to shift as historians explore the experiences of previously ignored groups. But for the post-1965 years, many documents chronicle the influx and experiences of South and Southeast Asian Americans. Many of the choices are obvious, and the critical editorial decisions involved selecting the most relevant portions and determining the length necessary for adequate contextual interpretation. The 1854 *People v. Hall* case and the *coram nobis* cases of the 1980s are good examples. Other choices are less clear, especially the documents from the recent past, and reflect assumptions about the future importance of certain trends.

It is likely, for example, that gender, sexuality, interracial relations, racial profiling, and immigrant-homeland (diasporic) transnational connections will become increasingly important in this field. Included in this volume are speeches from prominent figures who attempt to reflect or set policy agendas as well as define the parameters of our past. But there are also documents that speak to other issues in order to convey the breadth of perspectives reflected among our dozens of ethnic and nationality groupings. As with all periodizing exercises, there is inevitable overlap and apparently arbitrary placement. Part 2, "Migration and Settlements," includes documents that could easily fit into the earlier era of "Contact and Conflict" or later years covered in "Accommodation and Hostility." The framework does, however, provide an intelligible structure through which to comprehend the documents.

Part 1 deals with the late eighteenth and the nineteenth centuries, the period of "Contact and Conflict." Beginning with the Naturalization Act of March 26, 1790 (document number 1), these documents suggest the tentative beginnings of large-scale immigration of the Chinese into the American West (2–7) as well as the first treaty between the United States and China (9). The Burlingame-Seward Treaty of 1868 illustrates the deep and complex ties between domestic race relations and foreign policy. A wide variety of laws and court cases indicates the degree of hostility unleashed against Chinese, Japanese, and Filipinos (19, 20, 27, 28, 38). These official policies were buttressed by private and popular sentiment (12, 16, 32). And national prejudice culminated, for the time, in the Chinese Exclusion Act of 1882 (17). But we do not always appreciate the widespread, courageous resistance to discrimination and racism evident from the beginning (4, 14, 21, 22). The very fact that so many lawsuits were carried to the U.S. Supreme Court indicates the passion with which Asians, especially the Chinese in this period, fought for equal rights (10, 13, 23, 28). Wong Kim Ark, in particular, secured for all time the inviolable right of citizenship for anyone born in U.S. territory (34), a right now taken for granted because of his lawsuit.

Part 2 focuses on continued "Migration and Settlements." The period begins with the momentous impact of the Spanish-American War of 1898 and its open acknowledgment of imperial conquest. But incorporating the Philippines, Guam, and Samoa in the Pacific as well as Puerto Rico and Cuba in the Caribbean (in addition to the separate annexation of Hawai'i) created enormous problems with regard to notions of citizenship and rights. The convoluted ways in which the United States dealt with Filipinos, for example, become evident in part 3. Part 2 ends with the National Origins Act of 1924, defining for later decades an American hierarchy of preferred, tolerated, and excluded groups by nation, race, geography, and ethnicity.

The artist Chiura Obata's letter in 1903 (41) provides an example of a Japanese immigrant who did not come from the usual laboring/peasant/rural background of so many contract and migrant farm workers. People clearly entered the United States for a variety of reasons. Certainly the search for paid employment was critical, since their homelands were caught in the turmoil of modernizing policies that forced governments to extract the maximum amount of cash possible from the rural sectors in order to build engines of commerce and war. Sun Yat-sen left China as a hunted radical, thirsting for knowledge that would allow him to lead his country forward. Sun (42) studied in Hawai'i and

Japan and gained an enormous following in the overseas communities of the Chinese diaspora. Others left for artistic or religious freedom or simply to pursue adventure.

These Asian immigrants quickly found that anti-Asian sentiments were running high. In Hawai'i, Japanese workers in 1909 (45) and 1920 (53) organized massive strikes on the sugar plantations. These threatened the near-total control of society by white leaders, who responded by linking the workers with a rising Japanese military capacity. The strikes were ultimately broken by this appeal to race and nationality—a practice employed successfully until the end of World War II. On the continent, West Coast communities made it clear that Asians were not welcome through lynchings, legal harassment, and the systematic forced expulsion of entire groups from their towns. On the national level, this translated into a 1922 Supreme Court decision denying Takao Ozawa, a Japanese who desperately wanted to assimilate, the right to become a naturalized citizen (58), and a similar case denying naturalization to an Asian Indian, Bhagat Singh Thind (59), the next year.

Asian women were always important in the American construction of this racial grouping. But it was primarily in this second period that they became prominent actors for all to apprehend. At one level, Asian communities were significant features in the national mind—Broadway discovered that songs about Asians could attract audiences. "Chinatown, My Chinatown" became extremely popular in 1910 (47). At the other extreme, Japanese immigrant women composed and sang anonymous field songs (holehole bushi) revealing not only details of work and life on the sugar plantations but also the particular perspectives of their gender (39). And it was clear that Asian women like Mary Tape in an earlier period (21) continued to pursue individual and family mobility and justice (52). Asian women did all this in spite of attitudes and legislation that targeted them as particularly threatening to the prevailing social hierarchy. Thus, the Cable Act of 1922 (57) succeeded, for a decade, in stripping female American citizens of their citizenship if they married foreigners ineligible for naturalization—i.e., Asian immigrants.

Part 3, "Accommodation and Hostility," is all too easy to view as a long prelude to World War II. But the second half of the 1920s and the 1930s also included positive and significant change, often instigated and propelled by Asian immigrants themselves. Since so many Asians were laborers, it was important to convince white unions to incorporate them as working-class partners rather than pawns of the employers. The actions of the International Ladies Garment Workers' Union against Chinese-owned stores were significant victories (74, 75). Perhaps most important, the Supreme Court ruled in 1927 that Hong Kong-born Chin Bow had to be admitted as an American citizen because his grandfather and father were both citizens (65). In the same year, the court also ruled that immigrants had the right to support independent schools to teach the Japanese language (64). Although the decision was reversed in 1925, Hidemitsu

Toyota and other Japanese World War I veterans initially secured the right to become naturalized citizens (62). Even in international relations, some constructive projects emerged, including the sending of "Friendship Dolls" from the United States to Japan in 1926 (63).

Still, it was clear that anti-Asian racism was predominant. The anomalous position of Filipinos, allowed to enter the country as "nationals" while the Philippines remained an American colony, was resolved by encouraging them to return home (72) as well as by passage of the Tydings-McDuffie Act (71). That legislation promised independence for the Philippines after 10 years, partly in order to impose a humiliating annual quota of 50 immigrants. By the mid-1930s, at the highest levels of government in both Japan and the United States, plans were being drafted for war in the Pacific—which in America included the use of concentration camps for Japanese Americans (73).

World War II, covered in part 4, became the historical watershed for most of Asian America. Not until the 1965 immigration reforms would there be another similarly critical era. The most significant event was the mass removal and internment of more than 110,000 Japanese Americans, two-thirds American citizens. While not to be considered on the same human scale as the genocidal treatment of Native Americans or the horrors of slavery and anti-African American racism, the treatment of Japanese Americans is widely considered the single most egregious breach of civil liberties in this country's history. And it was one of the nation's most beloved presidents, Franklin Delano Roosevelt, who authorized the actions through his Executive Order 9066 (84). But even in early 1942, when communities were beginning to be removed and Japanese Americans were a year away from being accepted as volunteers in the U.S. Army, youngsters in Hawai'i were forming the Varsity Victory Volunteers to serve as a volunteer labor unit on a military base (82, 83).

Even before war had been declared by the United States, a young leader of the Japanese American Citizens League, Mike Masaoka, penned an earnest appeal for tolerant treatment based on Japanese American gratitude to their country (79). The critical cases that went to the U.S. Supreme Court involved Gordon Hirabayashi (89), Minoru Yasui (90), Mitsuye Endo (94), and Fred Korematsu (95), all young Japanese Americans who challenged the right of the government to impose curfews, exclusion, and detention, solely on the basis of race. One of the more astonishing discoveries was the fact that the federal administration actually destroyed original documents in order to fabricate evidence to convince the Supreme Court that mass detention was essential to the national defense (91). During World War II and shortly thereafter, however, other Asian Americans—Filipino Americans (92), Korean Americans (98), and Chinese Americans (88)—were gaining a modest measure of sympathy, partly because their homelands were being ravaged by Japan and partly because they served as useful Asian counterpoints to the racial discrimination visited upon Japanese Americans.

Part 5, "An American Lake," takes the story to 1975, a decade after the 1965 Immigration and Nationality Act entirely removed the quota system that had severely restricted immigration from Asia. These three decades saw the emergence of the United States as the most powerful entity in the Pacific Basin and Rim, but with a cold war to contain and destroy communism and several hot wars to stop communism united with nationalism in Korea and Southeast Asia. Internally, the picture was decidedly mixed—with gradual and then dramatic loosening of racial immigration and other legal restrictions coupled with openly hostile anti-Asian American events.

As early as 1946, the United States began to turn its back on Filipinos who had heeded the call to join American forces against the Japanese invaders. In spite of notable sacrifices and heroism, thousands of men were singled out in a Rescission Act (97) to become the only group of foreigners denied veterans' benefits. But for the first time, Filipino American, Chinese American, and Japanese American veterans were able to marry and return home with women from Asia. For Filipinos and Chinese, whose communities included relatively few women, this was an important personal, family, and social opportunity.

Racist laws prohibiting Japanese Americans from fishing (98) or owning land (100) were removed from the books. Finally, in 1952, the McCarran-Walter Act permitted Japanese immigrants to become naturalized citizens (101). But this legislation contained so many elements trampling civil rights that it had to be passed over President Harry Truman's veto. The McCarthy-era or Red Scare hysteria allowed the government to deport Chinese and Koreans suspected of harboring any positive sentiments toward homeland communist regimes (103). And, of course, the brutal war in Vietnam, Laos, and Cambodia produced a national environment in which terms like "gook" could flourish (106).

Partly in response to this challenge and partly influenced by the burgeoning African American civil rights and nationalist movements, Asian Americans began their own series of social, cultural, and political initiatives. Some, like the Filipino migrant workers who partnered with Cesar Chavez and the United Farmworkers Union, built on years of prior organizing and education (118). But it was after the landmark 1968 Third World Liberation Front strike at San Francisco State University (108) that an Asian American movement coalesced. The struggle to save the International Hotel, home of many older Filipino workers, followed soon after, in 1970 (109). UCLA published *Roots: An Asian American Reader*, the first anthology of its kind, in 1971 (111), and popular culture responded with songs like "We Are the Children" in 1972 (113) and a pathbreaking work of Asian American literature, *Aiiieeeee!* (115), in 1973.

By 1975, the United States was forced to leave Southeast Asia, but the effects of the war in terms of refugees and immigrants had only just begun to be felt. There are gaps in this section, as elsewhere; approximately 150,000 Korean children had been adopted, largely by white parents, in the United States since the

Korean War, but they are not addressed here. Where perhaps only half a million people of Asian descent were in the United States at the end of World War II, by the end of the century, there would be about 11 million, almost 4 percent of the total and disproportionately important in key metropolitan areas of California and the Atlantic seaboard.

Part 6, "Brave New World," provides documentary glimpses into the highly complex and diverse universe of Asian Americans in the last quarter of the twentieth century. Problems from earlier periods continued to make the news. Japanese Americans and World War II combined to generate many issues at the time, and several resurfaced in this era. Strategies to secure redress for the internment (122, 130) eventually resulted in President Ronald Reagan's signing of the Civil Liberties Act of 1988 (128), providing official apologies and $20,000 to each survivor. Earlier, Fred Korematsu and Gordon Hirabayashi had had their wartime convictions vacated—largely on the evidence that the executive branch had lied to the judiciary regarding the military necessity of wholesale internment (125). And 22 additional Medals of Honor, the nation's highest award for combat bravery, were awarded to Asian American (mostly Japanese American) veterans who had been incorrectly accorded a lower level of recognition (134).

Some progress was made in correcting earlier mistakes on behalf of Filipino World War II veterans (141) and acknowledging the unusual difficulties faced by Southeast Asian refugees and veterans in acculturating into our extremely different society (148). But the story of Southeast Asians was very complicated; most of the Vietnamese, for example, continue to be strongly anticommunist, and a shopkeeper who dared place a poster of Ho Chi Minh, former leader of North Vietnam, in his shop was hounded out of business (144).

The overwhelming impression at the beginning of the twenty-first century is one of incredible excitement and potential, even though the latter includes altogether too much room for poverty, displacement, prejudice, and oppression among many Asian American groups (133, 152). The final document, from the U.S. Catholic Bishops, is a testament to the need to address these issues (155).

At the same time, folk traditions from Asian homelands continue to flourish—some, like the Japanese *taiko* drumming, have been adapted and transformed into a new American art form, growing from one or two groups in 1970 to more than 100 at present (153). Hundreds of talented writers, artists, filmmakers, and performing artists now grace our cultural scene (135, 138), while our older notions of "Asian American" continue to be stretched to new limits (149, 150).

No single volume can cover the diverse experiences of so many groups, so there will be ample room for disagreement over specific selections and omissions or degree of inclusion. The interpretive essays and the short descriptions accompanying each document attempt to grapple with complex issues in limited space.

These documents reveal some of the negative forces—prejudice, fear, arrogance, and chauvinism—that targeted and constrained so many Asian Americans in the past and that continue to limit our individual and collective human potential. But they also show the positive elements in American society—tolerance, courage, pride, and determination—that mark this history at every step along the way.

PART 1

Contact and Conflict: Asia and the Pacific: Through 1900

Asia has fascinated Europeans for a very long time. Marco Polo was only one in a constant stream of visitors bringing back tales that initially seemed beyond belief. Conversely, people from Asia have been in the Pacific and the Americas for thousands of years. There is interesting evidence to support theories of Asian presence, from linguistic mapping to pottery shards and travel legends. The powerful ocean currents that have helped propel ships westward from the Americas and eastward to the Americas also allowed shipwrecked sailors and merchants to drift from Japan to Hawai'i and North America. The likelihood of early forays or migrations across the relatively narrow Bering Strait separating North America from Asia is a central assumption for anthropologists and archaeologists. It is possible, for example, that the JC virus, carried in the human kidney, demonstrates nearly identical biological links between contemporary Navahos and Japanese.

Travelers from Europe have historically visited and traded with Asia in the northeast, including Siberia, Korea, and Japan; to the east, in Taiwan and China; all along the southeast; southward along the Pacific in the Philippines and Indonesia; and in the southernmost parts of India, Pakistan, and Bangladesh. The Silk Road, linking Europe to China via Central Asia, became a justly fabled artery circulating goods, stories, and other cultural influences over thousands of miles.

The advent of sustained ocean exploration by Western Europeans in the fifteenth century, spurred by the search for a faster and cheaper route to Asian products like spices, generated an entirely new era for movements of goods, capital, ideas, and people. The course of this development radically changed world history. One result was the emergence of monarchies like Portugal and Spain, leading the way to exploration and conquest. In subsequent centuries, other Western European nation-states began competing to create global networks of colonies tied to one another and to metropolitan centers.

One important example, beginning in the 1560s, was the Manila galleon trade conducted by Spain across the Pacific as far as its colony, the Philippines, via another colony, Mexico. These large ships rode southerly currents westward across the Pacific from Mexico and returned following a northern route, reaching the coast of what eventually became the state of California before sailing south to Acapulco. The goods were then trekked across the peninsula for shipment to Spain. These galleons, built in and named for Manila, capital of the Philippines, had crews with many sailors from that archipelago. It is not strange, therefore, that some of the men escaped from the oppressive conditions of life and work aboard ship. They formed communities in areas like the marshes and backwaters of ports; one became the city of New Orleans after the Louisiana Purchase of 1803. Some Filipinos may have been in that region as early as the eighteenth century.

In more recent times, increased contact and communication in the context of European expansion and imperialism fueled both greater understanding between Asians and Europeans and modern racist images. By the eighteenth century, Asian Indians were on the East Coast, and Chinese sailors and merchants had settled in New York City and intermarried with Irish immigrants. Thus, by the time of the better-known migrations of cheap labor from China to the U.S. West Coast in the mid-nineteenth century and subsequent immigration from Japan, Korea, India, and the Philippines, there was already an Asian presence in North America. And there were students as well, including the first group from China, which arrived as early as 1847, just before the California gold rush era.

But large-scale migration from Asia began in response to the need for cheap labor to drive railroad construction, mining, farming, manufacturing, and many other industries. Laborers were concentrated on the West Coast but were also recruited to plantations in Louisiana and shoe factories in Massachusetts. Many workers from China, Japan, Korea, and the Philippines were brought to work on sugar and pineapple plantations in Hawai'i.

As the documents in this section demonstrate, these developments were taking place within two larger contexts. The first was European and American imperialism, which reached into Asia and the Pacific during the nineteenth century; the second was the rapid growth of the United States across North America and the social dislocation created by the need to attract settlers and workers from so many different regions, races, and ethnic groups. To some extent, of course, these two developments were part of the same process, but it is useful to distinguish between them. Both generated fears that the dominant power base of Western European, Protestant core populations might be displaced. Indeed, this became the principal contradiction within both westward expansion across the continent and international contestation over Asia and the Pacific.

In 1853–54, Commodore Matthew Perry "opened" Japan to formal international relationships. One indirect result was the overthrow of the Tokugawa Shogunate and the establishment of the new Meiji government in 1868. That same year, two groups of Japanese were taken to work in California and Hawai'i.

In 1858, the United States established formal relations with China in the Treaty of Tientsin; a year later, the Manchu court broke its long-standing rule against Chinese emigration. In 1868, the Burlingame-Seward Treaty formally permitted the flow of people between China and the United States. The Kingdom of Hawai'i, a sovereign nation, was toppled by a coup in 1893 and annexed in 1898. In that same year, the Treaty of Paris concluded the Spanish-American War, providing the United States with its newest acquisitions in the Pacific, Guam and the Philippines. Samoa had already, in 1896, become part of this far-flung empire. Thus, by the dawn of the twentieth century, the United States had justified its new domain as the will of God in the doctrine "manifest destiny" or evolutionary logic supported by the Social Darwinism of the times.

But rationalizing the extension of American power into the far reaches of the Pacific Ocean and arguing whether the Constitution should therefore also protect the brown peoples newly incorporated was one thing. It was an entirely different matter to contemplate the proper place of those Asian and Pacific peoples who, having been brought as sojourning labor, now seemed all too intent upon creating and maintaining permanent communities in areas where they were not welcome.

As early as 1790, two years after the Constitution was adopted, Congress had declared that only "free white persons" could become naturalized American citizens. In 1870, after the Civil War, people of African descent were also made eligible for citizenship, but it was not until the 1920s that Native Americans would be allowed to naturalize. In the meantime, Asians became the most prominent pawns and players in the debate over this critical question: Who should be allowed or encouraged to become American citizens? It was only in 1898, after all, that the U.S. Supreme Court finally ruled, in *United States v. Wong Kim Ark,* that anyone born in the United States was absolutely and automatically entitled to citizenship. The two major battlegrounds in this monumental struggle then became immigration and naturalization.

The Chinese became the first targets and the first to test the limits of the nation's tolerance. Local and state lawmakers passed a flurry of legislation discriminating against the Chinese almost as soon as they arrived, encouraging them to "go back where they came from." California's series of taxes, like the Foreign Miners Tax of 1850, simultaneously robbed Chinese of their earnings and bankrolled much of the state's budget for many years. Other ordinances focused on the Chinese in order to drive them out of business or out of the region.

As early as 1854, *The People v. George W. Hall* established that Chinese would not be allowed to testify against whites in California. In *Tape v. Hurley* in 1885, California's Supreme Court allowed the San Francisco public school system to prevent a Chinese girl from attending classes with her white peers. Since they were not allowed to become citizens and join the voting public, the Chinese had no representation in the legislative or executive branches of government. The judicial system, designed especially to protect the rights of all minorities, became the last refuge in which justice might be sought. Here the Chinese were active and persistent, often hiring white attorneys to represent them, especially if they were politicians known for their previous anti-Chinese behavior! They lost many of these legal battles, but some of the victories, such as *Yick Wo v. Hopkins* in 1886, broadened American freedoms by declaring unconstitutional laws that were seemingly neutral but clearly had discriminatory impact on specific groups.

While racism on the local scene could not remove Asians from America, the federal and international playing fields yielded more results. As early as 1875, the Page Law successfully prohibited most Asian women—Chinese, Japanese, and other "Mongolians"—from immigrating on the pretext that they were likely to be employed in prostitution. *In re Ah Yup*, in 1878, established that, since the Chinese were not "free white persons," they were not eligible for naturalization. In 1882, for the first time in the nation's history, Congress expressly prohibited the entry of people of a specific country, China (along with the mentally ill, paupers, and felons). Shortly thereafter, labor recruitment began in earnest from Japan, and the courts quickly ruled that the Japanese too were not allowed to become American citizens.

Local, state, and federal political forces were clearly arrayed against Asians who sought to make their livings and homes in the United States on an equal footing with their white counterparts. And many did return to their homelands, content to have earned enough hard cash to help their families, while others were discouraged or cynical as a result of lives worn down with work or gambled away. Untold numbers died here as a result of disease, lynching, accidents, or sheer exhaustion. Some stayed to carve out livelihoods and lives as professionals, entrepreneurs, artists, and white-collar workers. The vast majority of those who remained in America struggled as manual laborers in farming, ranching, mining, industrial agriculture like sugar and pine production, railroads, fishing, restaurants, laundries, and a myriad other jobs to feed, clothe, and service America. As individuals and in growing communities, Asians in America established new frontiers of development and challenge even as the United States was reinventing itself in this turbulent period.

Naturalization Act, March 26, 1790

The first formal attempt by the U.S. government to define who could become "American" was this "Act to establish an uniform Rule of Naturalization." A candidate for naturalization then had to have two years of residence and be "a free white person." This was the fundamental guideline against which centuries of complex struggles would be fought in order to include people of color. Africans and African Americans were the first allowed past this barrier after the Civil War; ironically, American Indians were not qualified until the 1920s, and Asians not until the 1940s and 1950s.

Richard Peters, ed., *The Public Statutes at Large of the United States of America*, vol. 1.
  Boston: Charles Little and James Brown, 1845.

Chap. III. —
An Act to establish an uniform Rule of Naturalization. (a)

Section 1. *Be it enacted by the Senate and House of Representatives of the United States of America in Congress assembled,* That any alien, being a free white person, who shall have resided within the limits and under the jurisdiction of the United States for the term of two years, may be admitted to become a citizen thereof, on application to any common law court of record, in any one of the states wherein he shall have resided for the term of one year at least, and making proof to the satisfaction of such court, that he is a person of good character, and taking the oath or affirmation prescribed by law, to support the constitution of the United States, which oath or affirmation such court shall administer; and the clerk of such court shall record such application, and the proceedings thereon; and thereupon such person shall be considered as a citizen of the United States. And the children of such persons so naturalized, dwelling within the United States, being under the age of twenty-one years at the time of such naturalization, shall also be considered as citizens of the United States. And the children of citizens of the United States, that may be born beyond sea, or out of the limits of the United States, shall be considered as natural born citizens: *Provided*, That the right of citizenship shall not descend to persons whose fathers have never been resident in the United States: *Provided also*, That no person heretofore proscribed by any state, shall be admitted a citizen as aforesaid, except by an act of the legislature of the state in which such person was proscribed. (*a*)

Approved, March 26, 1790.

California Foreign Miners Tax, April 13, 1850

The California State Legislature passed this act requiring "non-natives" (except for native California Indians) who worked in the mines to register and pay monthly fees of $20. While it was ostensibly directed at all foreigners, the state targeted Mexican miners at first, then the Chinese, whose numbers had increased in the early 1850s. This was the first in a long series of laws specifically aimed at the Chinese as racial and economic competitors. The tax provided substantial revenues for California until 1870, when it was declared unconstitutional.

The Statutes of California Passed at the First Session of the Legislature. San Jose: J. Winchester, State Printer, 1850.

Chap. 97
An Act for the better regulation of the Mines, and the government of Foreign Miners

The People of the State of California, represented in Senate and Assembly, do enact as follows:

1. No person who is not a native or natural born citizen of the United States, or who may not have become a citizen under the treaty of Guadalupe Hidalgo (all native California Indians excepted), shall be permitted to mine in any part of this State, without having first obtained a license so to do according to the provisions of this Act.

2. The Governor shall appoint a Collector of Licenses to foreign miners for each of the mining counties, and for the county of San Francisco, who, before entering upon the duties of his office, shall take the oath required by the Constitution, and shall give his bond to the State with at least two good and sufficient sureties, conditioned for the faithful performance of his official duties, which bond shall be approved by the Governor, and filed in the office of the Secretary of State. . . .

6. Every person required by the first section of this Act to obtain a license to mine, shall apply to the Collector of Licenses to foreign miners, and take out a license to mine, for which he shall pay the sum of twenty dollars per month; and such foreigners may from time to time take out a new license, at the same rate per month, until the Governor shall issue his proclamation announcing the passage of a law by Congress, regulating the mines of precious metals in this State.

7. If any such foreigner or foreigners shall refuse or neglect to take out such license by the second Monday of May next, it shall be the duty of the Collector of Licenses to foreign miners of the county in which such foreigner or foreigners shall be, to furnish his or their names to the Sheriff of the county, or to any Deputy Sheriff, whose duty it shall be to summon a posse of American citizens, and, if necessary, forcibly prevent him or them from continuing such mining operations.

8. Should such foreigner or foreigners, after having been stopped by a Sheriff or Deputy Sheriff from mining in one place, seek a new location and continue such mining operations, it shall be deemed a misdemeanor, for which such offender or offenders shall be arrested as for a misdemeanor, and he or they shall be imprisoned for a term not exceeding three months, and fined not more than one thousand dollars.

9. Any foreigner who may obtain a license in conformity with the provisions of this Act, shall be allowed to work the mines anywhere in this State, under the same regulations as citizens of the United States.

3

Agreement Between English Merchant and "Chinaman," 1850

This is an early example of labor contracts between western merchants and Chinese recruiters and laborers. "Ka-la-fo-ne-a" and "Fnh-lan-sze-ko" are phonetic renderings of "California" and "San Francisco." These provisions, including prearranged shipping and travel subsidies as well as the securing of employment and deductions from wages until debt was repaid, became standard practice for tens of thousands of laborers arriving later from China and other parts of Asia. While this arrangement was standard and legal only until the Foran Act of 1885, illicit forms continue for human traffic in the United States and around the globe.

Thanks to the Autry Museum of Western Heritage, which included this document in its exhibit, "On Gold Mountain." Courtesy of Wells Fargo Bank.

Agreement Between The English Merchant & Chinaman

The Tseang Sing Hong having now hired The American ship called the Ah-mah-san for voyaging purposes, the mechanies [sic] and labourers [sic], of their own free will, will put to sea, the ship to proceed to Ka-la-fo-ne-a, and port of Fnh-lan-sze-ko, in search of employment for the said mechanies [sic] and labourers [sic]. For the Time of leaving Shanghae, the expenses of provisions and vessel are all to be defrayed by the head of the Tseang Sing Hong. On Arrival, it is expected that the foreign merchant will search out and recommend employment for the said labourers [sic], and the money he advances on their account, shall be returned when the employment becomes settled. The one hundred and twenty-five dollars passage money, as agreed by us, are to be paid to the said head of the said Hong, who will make arrangements with the employers of the coolies, that a moiety of their wages shall be deducted monthly until the debt is absorbed: after which, they will receive their wages in full every month.

The above is what we agree to, and there must be no differing words; and as evidence, we enter into this contract, a copy of which, each party is to have.
Done in the Moon of the 29th year of Taou Kwang
Courtesy of Wells Fargo Bank
Printed paper 1850

4

The People, Respondent, v. George W. Hall, Appellant, 1854

In 1854, the California Supreme Court ruled that no Chinese person could testify against a white person in a California court. George Hall had been convicted of murder "upon the testimony of Chinese witnesses." Hall appealed, arguing on the basis of a law passed in 1850 that "No Black, or Mulatto person, or Indian, shall be allowed to give evidence in favor of, or against a white man." Chief Judge Hugh Murray delivered the opinion of the court—that the legislation, while not specifying Chinese, really meant the protection of "the White person from the influence of all testimony other than that of persons of the same caste." He then pointed to the "danger" of the Chinese, a clearly inferior race, penetrating all levels of political activity. This ruling stood until 1873, when such prohibitory statutes were repealed.

Reports of Cases Argued and Determined in the Supreme Court of the State of California [microform]. San Francisco: Marvin and Hitchcock, 1851–60.

The People, Respondent, v. George W. Hall, Appellant

Section 394 of the Civil Practice Act provides, "No Indian or Negro shall be allowed to testify as a witness in any action in which a White person is a party."

Section 14 of the Criminal Act provides, "No Black, or Mulatto person, or Indian shall be allowed to give evidence in favor of, or against a White man."

Held, that the words, Indian, Negro, Black and White, are generic terms, designating race. That, therefore, Chinese and all other peoples not white, are included in the prohibition from being witnesses against Whites.

Mr. Ch. J. Murray delivered the opinion of the Court. Mr. J. Heydenfeldt concurred.

The appellant, a free white citizen of this State, was convicted of murder upon the testimony of Chinese witnesses.

The point involved in this case, is the admissibility of such evidence.

The 394th section of the Act Concerning Civil Cases, provides that no Indian or Negro shall be allowed to testify as a witness in any action or proceeding in which a White person is a party.

The 14th section of the Act of April 16th, 1850, regulating Criminal Proceedings, provides that "No Black, or Mulatto person, or Indian, shall be allowed to give evidence in favor of, or against a white man."

The true point at which we are anxious to arrive, is the legal signification of the words, "Black, Mulatto, Indian and White person," and whether the Legislature adopted them as generic terms, or intended to limit their application to specific types of the human species. . . .

Can, then, the use of the word "Indian," because at the present day it may be sometimes regarded as a specific, and not as a generic term, alter this conclusion? We think not; because at the origin of the legislation we are considering, it was used and admitted in its common and ordinary acceptation, as a generic term, distinguishing the great Mongolian race, and as such, its meaning then became fixed by law, and in construing Statutes the legal meaning of words must be presumed.

Again: the words of the Act must be construed in *pari materia*. It will not be disputed that "White" and "Negro," are generic terms, and refer to two of the great types of mankind. If these, as well as the word "Indian," are not to be regarded as generic terms, including the two great races which they were intended to designate, but only specific, and applying to those Whites and Negroes who were inhabitants of this Continent at the time of the passage of the Act, the most anomalous consequences would ensue. The European white man who comes here would not be shielded from the testimony of the degraded and demoralized caste, while the Negro, fresh from the coast of Africa, or the Indian of Patagonia, the Kanaka, South Sea Islander, or New Hollander, would be admitted, upon their arrival, to testify against white citizens in our courts of law.

To argue such a proposition would be an insult to the good sense of the Legislature.

The evident intention of the Act was to throw around the citizen a protection for life and property, which could only be secured by removing him above the corrupting influences of degraded castes. . . .

In using the words, "No Black, or Mulatto person, or Indian shall be allowed to give evidence for or against a White person," the Legislature, if any intention can be ascribed to it, adopted the most comprehensive terms to embrace every known class or shade of color, as the apparent design was to protect the White person from the influence of all testimony other than that of persons of the same caste. The use of these terms must, by every sound rule of construction, exclude every one who is not of white blood. . . .

We are not disposed to leave this question in any doubt. The word "White" has a distinct signification, which *ex vi termini*, excludes black, yellow, and all other colors. It will be observed, by reference to the first section of the second article of the Constitution of this State, that none but white males can become electors, except in the case of Indians, who may be admitted by special Act of the Legislature. On examination of the constitutional debates, it will be found that not a little difficulty existed in selecting these precise words, which were finally agreed upon as the most comprehensive that could be suggested to exclude all inferior races. . . .

We have carefully considered all the consequences resulting from a different rule of construction, and are satisfied that even in a doubtful case we would be impelled to this decision on grounds of public policy.

The same rule which would admit them to testify, would admit them to all the equal rights of citizenship, and we might soon see them at the polls, in the jury box, upon the bench, and in our legislative halls.

This is not a speculation which exists in the excited and over-heated imagination of the patriot and statesman, but it is an actual and present danger.

The anomalous spectacle of a distinct people, living in our community, recognizing no laws of this State except through necessity, bringing with them their prejudices and national feuds, in which they indulge in open violation of law; whose mendacity is proverbial; a race of people whom nature has marked as inferior, and who are incapable of progress or intellectual development beyond a certain point, as their history has shown; differing in language, opinions, color, and physical conformation; between whom and ourselves nature has placed an impassable difference, is now presented, and for them is claimed, not only the right to swear away the life of a citizen, but the further privilege of participating with us in administering the affairs of our Government. . . .

For these reasons, we are of opinion that the testimony was inadmissible.

The judgment is reversed and the cause remanded.

5

Publisher's Remarks on "The Chinese and the Times" in First Chinese Newspaper in the United States, June 10, 1854

The Golden Hills' News *was the first newspaper published in the Chinese language in the United States. "Golden Hills" later became "Gold Mountain," the most common metaphor for America. The San Francisco publication included this English language editorial on page one to promote greater respect for the Chinese and their culture, which extended back thousands of years before Christ; it disparaged, by contrast, not only Negroes but also the Irish and the Germans! The editorial was no doubt written by a non-Chinese and meant to place the Chinese higher in the scale of "races" in order to elicit better treatment in a period when anti-Chinese hostility was increasing all too rapidly. A subscription to* Golden Hills' News *was 75 cents per month—a considerable sum in those days. The paper displayed both a sense of the California Chinese community's positive action orientation at that early stage in immigration history and the beginnings of a pattern of astute use of articulate white advocates on their behalf. Later, the Chinese would consistently turn to white attorneys for assistance in fighting discriminatory legislation and court cases.*

Thanks to Him Mark Lai for providing a copy of this piece. *Golden Hills' News* (San Francisco), June 10, 1854.

The Chinese and the Times

To maximise the area of liberty and minimize that of tyranny has become essentially the principle of the Times. Every effort, of the really liberal, has professedly for its object the improvement of the moral, religious, and legal code of nations and races, but in doing so it is found, that sacred bigotries must be broken into, and vested prejudices be exposed. For instance, a Chinese Mission Chapel, with attached library and school-room, has been opened for the preaching of the gospel to the Chinese race, and for instructing them in the English language in all its branches. The spirit of philantrophy has hailed with unfeigned pleasure the benevolent enterprise. We, too, believing that Civil and

Political knowledge is of infinite importance to the Chinese, both in their individual, social, and relative state, have established "The Golden Hills' News" for that special Mission. The influence of Chapel and Press intended to relieve the pressure of religious ignorance settle and explain our laws, assist the Chinese provide their wants, and soften, dignify, and improve their general character.

And what race of people more deserving of our efforts? They claim a national existence coeval with the most remote antiquity. We read of their virtous sovereigns Fuh-he, and Yaou, reigning in the affection of this people some 2000 years before Christ—of their great philosopher Confucius, who was born 550 before Christ. The doctrines or philosophy of Confucius have obtained a reputation not only national, but have been long celebrated among the literati of Europe, as evidencing a high state of intellectual and moral progress; and in fact, the preceipt of "Do unto others as you would be done unto" has been traced to the Confucian school of Philosophy. Indeed the doctrines of the Chinese sage contain a complete body of rules for the government of one's self, the regulation of social intercourse, the education of a community, the government of an empire, and the management of a complex social machinery.

Yet our Conductors of the Press describe them as "Apes," "Brutes," "social lice"! lower than the Negro-race. Did ever one of these Conductors or Editors see the Negroes as just imported from Africa! If they ever did, and should then compare them with Chinamen, we should consider than [sic] mentality—insanity. The Chinese is also said, to be "unfitted for Caucasian Civilization." Give them a fair trial before condemnation. Why, the Celtic-race have never fairly amalgamated with republican Institutions. In the last papers from the East we read that in every City of America of any size is to be found an "Ireland" and a "Germany." The London Times, and a New York paper say, that in every country the Celtic race wage a war of extermination upon each other and upon Protestantism! While the Germans of Louisville have published a series of resolutions against our present Institutions! We protest against making targets of the poor Chinese, and say, it is only fair, that Republicans should warmly encourage, cherish and protect every effort to diffuse the spirit of Christianity and Republicanism amongst this interesting race.

6

An Act to Prohibit the "Coolie Trade" by American Citizens in American Vessels, February 19, 1862

Enacting this legislation during the American Civil War, Congress pronounced its intent to avoid the excesses of the coolie trade then carried on chiefly by the British, who were seeking an alternative source of cheap labor after having abolished slavery. Technically indentured servants, the coolies were sometimes treated worse than slaves, since employers had no responsibility for them beyond the contract period. Coolie ships from China to the Americas, Cuba, and Australia resembled slave ships bearing Africans, and there were numerous uprisings caused by harsh treatment, including whipping, branding, maiming, and lynching. This international traffic ended in the 1870s when the Chinese government finally became strong enough to resist European attempts to continue exploiting Chinese workers.

George P. Sanger, ed., *The Statutes at Large, Treaties and Proclamations of the United States of America*. Boston: Little, Brown and Company, 1863.

Chap. XXVII. — An Act to prohibit the "Coolie Trade" by American Citizens in American Vessels

Be it enacted by the Senate and House of Representatives of the United States of America in Congress assembled, That no citizen or citizens of the United States, or foreigner coming into or residing within the same, shall, for himself or for any other person whatsoever, either as master, factor, owner, or otherwise, build, equip, load, or otherwise prepare, any ship or vessel, or any steamship or steam-vessel, registered, enrolled, or licensed, in the United States, or any port within the same, for the purpose of procuring from China, or from any port or place therein, or from any other port or place the inhabitants or subjects of China, known as "coolies," to be transported to any foreign country, port, or place whatever, to be disposed of, or sold, or transferred, for any term of years or for any time whatever, as servants or apprentices, or to be held to service or labor. And if any ship or vessel, steamship, or steam-vessel, belonging in whole or in part to citizens of the United States, and registered, enrolled, or otherwise licensed as afore-said, shall be employed for the said purposes, or in the "coolie trade," so called or shall be caused to procure or carry from China or elsewhere, as aforesaid, any subjects of the Government of China for the purpose of transporting or dispos-ing of them as aforesaid, every such ship or vessel, steamship, or steam-vessel, her tackle, apparel, furniture, and other appurtenances, shall be forfeited to the United States, and shall be liable to be seized, prosecuted, and condemned in any of the circuit courts or district courts of the United States for the district where the said ship or vessel, steamship, or steam-vessel, may be found, seized, or carried.

Sec. 2. *And be it further enacted*, That every person who shall so build, fit out, equip, load, or otherwise prepare, or who shall send to sea, or navigate, as owner, master, factor, agent, or otherwise, any ship or vessel, steamship, or steam-vessel, belonging in whole or in part to citizens of the United States, or registered, enrolled, or licensed within the same, or at any port thereof, know-ing or intending that the same shall be employed in that trade or business afore-said, contrary to the true intent and meaning of this act, or in anywise aiding or abetting therein, shall be severally liable to be indicted therefor, and, on con-viction thereof, shall be liable to a fine not exceeding two thousand dollars and be imprisoned not exceeding one year. . . .

Sec. 7. *And be it further enacted*, That this act shall take effect from and after six months from the day of its passage.

Approved, February 19, 1862.

7

An Act to Protect Free White Labor Against Competition with Chinese Coolie Labor, and to Discourage the Immigration of the Chinese Into the State of California (a.k.a. Police Tax), April 26, 1862

Like the 1850 Foreign Miners Tax and a host of other "capitation taxes," this 1862 act was directed against "Mongolians." California's monthly tax of "two dollars and fifty cents" was copied by other states in the West and Midwest. The Chinese vigorously opposed these discriminatory statutes, often with the aid of prestigious white attorneys, and eventually succeeded in overturning them. This process was substantially helped by passage of the Fourteenth Amendment to the U.S. Constitution, guaranteeing due process and equal protection of the laws.

The Statutes of California Passed at the Thirteenth Session of the Legislature, 1862. Sacramento: Benj. P. Avery, State Printer, 1862.

Chap. CCCXXXIX. — An Act to protect Free White Labor against competition with Chinese Coolie Labor, and to discourage the Immigration of the Chinese into the State of California

The People of the State of California, represented in Senate and Assembly, do enact as follows:

Section 1. There is hereby levied on each person, male and female, of the Mongolian race, of the age of eighteen years and upwards, residing in this State, except such as shall, under laws now existing, or which may hereafter be enacted, take out licenses to work in the mines, or to prosecute some kind of business, a monthly capitation tax of two dollars and fifty cents, which tax shall be known as the Chinese Police Tax; *provided*, that all Mongolians exclusively engaged in the production and manufacture of the following articles, shall be exempt from the provisions of this Act, viz: sugar, rice, coffee, tea.

Sec. 2. It shall be the duty of the Controller of State to procure a sufficient number of blank "Police Tax Receipts," which shall be substantially in the following form; these tax receipts shall be numbered consecutively, and a record thereof be made and filed in his office:

CHINESE POLICE TAX.

No..........

.... County, ... 18....

This certifies that .... has this day paid the Tax
Collector of .... County, two dollars and fifty cents,
the same being his police tax for the month commencing
............, and ending ...., both inclusive.

.............., Controller of State.

.............., Collector.

. . . .

Sec. 4. The Collector shall collect the Chinese police tax, provided for in this Act, from all persons liable to pay the same, and may seize the personal property of any such person refusing to pay such tax, and sell the same at public auction, by giving notice by proclamation one hour previous to such sale; and shall deliver the property, together with a bill of sale thereof, to the person agreeing to pay, and paying, the highest therefor, which delivery and bill of sale shall transfer to such person a good and sufficient title to the property. And after deducting the tax and necessary expenses incurred by reason of such refusal, seizure, and sale of property, the Collector shall return the surplus of the proceeds of the sale, if any, to the person whose property was sold; *provided*, that should any person, liable to pay the tax imposed in this Act, in any county in this State, escape into any other county, with the intention to evade the payment of such tax, then, and in that event, it shall be lawful for the Collector to pursue such person, and enforce the payment of such tax in the same manner as if no such escape had been made. . . .

Sec. 5. Any person charged with the collection of Chinese police taxes, who shall give any receipt other than the one prescribed in this Act, or receive money for such taxes without giving the necessary receipt therefor, or who shall insert more than one name in any one receipt, shall be guilty of a felony, and, upon conviction thereof, shall be fined in a sum not exceeding one thousand dollars, and be imprisoned in the State Prison for a period not exceeding one year. . . .

Sec. 7. Any person or company who shall hire persons liable to pay the Chinese police tax, shall be held responsible for the payment of the tax due from each person so hired; and no employer shall be released from this liability on the ground that the employé is indebted to him, (the employer;) and the Collector may proceed against any such employer in the same manner as he might against the original party owing the taxes. . . .

Sec. 8. The Collector shall receive for his service, in collecting police taxes, twenty per cent. of all moneys which he shall collect from persons owing such taxes. And of the residue, after deducting the per centage of the Collector, forty per cent. shall be paid into the County Treasury, for the use of the State, forty per cent. into the general County Fund, for the use of the county, and the remaining twenty per cent. into the School Fund, for the benefit of schools within the county.

8

Amendment 14, U.S. Constitution, 1868

The Fourteenth Amendment has served as the cornerstone of numerous civil rights issues from its ratification in 1868 to the present. Coming just after the Civil War, it was designed to protect the rights of African Americans against racist legislation from individual states but has enjoyed wide use and application. Section 1 was invoked to overturn many West Coast laws that targeted Asian Americans for discriminatory treatment. Because the amendment sheltered "any person," not only citizens, with due process of law and equal protection, Asian immigrants were able to push and clarify the boundaries of constitutional safeguards for everyone in America.

The United States Government Manual 1999/00. Washington, DC: Office of the Federal Register/National Archives and Records Administration, 2000.

The Constitution of the United States

We the People of the United States, in Order to form a more perfect Union, establish Justice, insure domestic Tranquility, provide for the common defence, promote the general Welfare, and secure the Blessings of Liberty to ourselves and our Posterity, do ordain and establish this Constitution for the United States of America. . . .

Amendment 14
Ratified July 9, 1868)

Section 1. All persons born or naturalized in the United States, and subject to the jurisdiction thereof, are citizens of the United States and of the State wherein they reside. No State shall make or enforce any law which shall abridge the privileges or immunities of citizens of the United States; nor shall any State deprive any person of life, liberty, or property, without due process of law; nor deny to any person within its jurisdiction the equal protection of the laws.

Section 2. Representatives shall be apportioned among the several States according to their respective numbers, counting the whole number of persons in each State, excluding Indians not taxed. But when the right to vote at any election for the choice of electors for President and Vice President of the United States, Representatives in Congress, the Executive and Judicial officers of a State, or the members of the Legislature thereof, is denied to any of the male inhabitants of such State, being twenty-one years of age, and citizens of the United States, or in any way abridged, except for participation in rebellion, or other crime, the basis of representation therein shall be reduced in the proportion which the number of such male citizens shall bear to the whole number of male citizens twenty-one years of age in such State.

Section 3. No person shall be a Senator or Representative in Congress, or elector of President and Vice President, or hold any office, civil or military, under the United States, or under any State, who, having previously taken an oath, as a member of Congress, or as an officer of the United States, or as a member of any State legislature, or as an executive or judicial officer of any State, to support the Constitution of the United States, shall have engaged in insurrection or rebellion against the same, or given aid or comfort to the enemies thereof. But Congress may by a vote of two-thirds of each House, remove such disability.

Section 4. The validity of the public debt of the United States, authorized by law, including debts incurred for payment of pensions and bounties for services in suppressing insurrection or rebellion, shall not be questioned. But neither the United States nor any State shall assume or pay any debt or obligation incurred in aid of insurrection or rebellion against the United States, or any claim for the loss or emancipation of any slave; but all such debts, obligations and claims shall be held illegal and void.

Section 5. The Congress shall have power to enforce, by appropriate legislation, the provisions of this article.

9

Burlingame-Seward Treaty, July 28, 1868

Signed on July 28, 1868, this treaty was negotiated between the United States and China by Secretary of State William Seward and Anson Burlingame, formerly an American representative to the Chinese imperial court, who was asked by the emperor to initiate discussions. The Burlingame-Seward version added several important articles to the original treaty of 1858. China and the United States agreed to extend reciprocal most-favored-nation treatment, including "free migration and emigration" and permanent residency. The treaty also mandated freedom of religion and "liberty of conscience." Further, Americans in China and Chinese in America were to enjoy all privileges of public educational institutions, a promise Americans found difficult to honor.

George P. Sanger, ed., *Statutes at Large and Proclamations of the United States of America.* Boston: Little, Brown, and Company, 1871.

By the President of the United States of America: A Proclamation

Whereas certain additional articles to the treaty now in force between the United States of America and the Ta-Tsing Empire, signed at Tientsin the 18th day of June, 1858, were concluded and signed by their plenipotentiaries at Washington, on the 28th day of July, 1868, which additional articles are, word for word, as follows: . . .

Article IV. The twenty-ninth article of the treaty of the 18th of June, 1858, having stipulated for the exemption of Christian citizens of the United States and Chinese converts from persecution in China on account of their faith, it is further agreed that citizens of the United States in China, of every religious persuasion, and Chinese subjects in the United States, shall enjoy entire liberty of conscience, and shall be exempt from all disability or persecution on account of their religious faith or worship in either country. Cemeteries for sepulture of the dead, of whatever nativity or nationality, shall be held in respect and free from disturbance or profanation.

Article V. The United States of America and the Emperor of China cordially recognize the inherent and inalienable right of man to change his home and allegiance, and also the mutual advantage of the free migration and emigration of their citizens and subjects, respectively, from the one country to the other, for purposes of curiosity, of trade, or as permanent residents. The high contracting parties, therefore, join in reprobating any other than an entirely voluntary emigration for these purposes. They consequently agree to pass laws making it a penal offence for a citizen of the United States or Chinese subjects to take Chinese subjects either to the United States or to any other foreign country, or for a Chinese subject or citizen of the United States to take citizens of the United States to China or to any other foreign country, without their free and voluntary consent respectively.

Article VI. Citizens of the United States visiting or residing in China shall enjoy the same privileges, immunities, or exemptions in respect to travel or residence as may there be enjoyed by the citizens or subjects of the most favored nation. And, reciprocally, Chinese subjects visiting or residing in the United States, shall enjoy the same privileges, immunities, and exemptions in respect to travel or residence, as may there be enjoyed by the citizens or subjects of the most favored nation. But nothing herein contained shall be held to confer naturalization upon citizens of the United States in China, nor upon the subjects of China in the United States.

Article VII. Citizens of the United States shall enjoy all the privileges of the public educational institutions under the control of the government of China, and, reciprocally, Chinese subjects shall enjoy all the privileges of the public educational institutions under the control of the government of the United States, which are enjoyed in the respective countries by the citizens or subjects of the most favored nation. The citizens of the United States may freely establish and maintain schools within the Empire of China at those places where foreigners are by treaty permitted to reside, and, reciprocally, Chinese subjects may enjoy the same privileges and immunities in the United States. . . .

In faith whereof, the respective plenipotentiaries have signed this treaty and thereto affixed the seals of their arms.

Done at Washington the twenty-eight day of July, in the year of our Lord one thousand eight hundred and sixty-eight.

[seal.]   WILLIAM H. SEWARD.
                                 ANSON BURLINGAME.

[seal.]   CHIH-KANG.
                                 SUN CHIA-KU.

10

In re Ah Fong, *September 21, 1874*

This important case, decided in the federal Ninth Circuit Court in California in 1874, overturned the State Supreme Court decision and ruled that immigration policy was a national rather than a state prerogative. Ah Fong brought this case to court on a writ of habeas corpus on her behalf as well as that of twenty-one other Chinese women. California's commissioner of immigration refused permission for them to land on the grounds they were in a class that included criminals, paupers, idiots, lunatics, those with incurable diseases, and lewd or debauched women. Justice Field chastised the California courts for exceeding their state powers and ignoring the Fourteenth Amendment. While acknowledging the anti-Chinese hostility in California, Field admonished Californians to seek redress at the federal level. He also invoked the Burlingame-Seward Treaty's promises of equal reciprocal treatment. Californians responded with pressure on Congress. The 1882 Chinese Exclusion Act was a logical consequence of these sentiments and actions.

Power of the State to Exclude Foreigners [*Opinion of Mr. Justice Field of U.S. Supreme Court*]. San Francisco: Edward Bosqui & Company, Printers, 1874.

In the United States Circuit Court, District of California
In the Matter of Ah Fong

1.—The police power of the State may be exercised by precautionary measures against the increase of crime or pauperism, or the spread of infectious diseases from persons coming from other countries. The State may entirely exclude convicts, lepers and persons afflicted with incurable disease; may refuse admission to paupers, idiots and lunatics and others, who from physical causes are likely to become a charge upon the public until security is afforded that they will not become such a charge; and may isolate the temporarily diseased until the danger of contagion is gone.

2.—The extent of the power of the State to exclude a foreigner from its territory is limited by the right of self-defense. Whatever outside of the legitimate exercise of this right affects the intercourse of foreigners with our people, their immigration to this country and residence therein, is exclusively within the jurisdiction of the General Government, and is not subject to State control or interference.

3.—The 6th Article of the Treaty between the United States and China, adopted on the 28th of July, 1868, provides that Chinese subjects visiting or residing in the United States shall enjoy the same privileges, immunities and exemptions in respect to travel or residence as may there be enjoyed by citizens or subjects of the most favored nation, and as the General Government has not seen fit to attach any limitation to the ingress into the United States of subjects of those nations, none can be applied to the subjects of China.

4.—The Fourteenth Amendment to the Constitution declares that no State shall deprive *any person* of life, liberty, or property, without due process of law; nor deny to *any person* the equal protection of the laws; *Held*, that this equality of protection implies not only equal accessibility to the Courts for the prevention or redress of wrongs, and the enforcement of rights, but equal exemption with others of the same class, from all charges and burdens of every kind. Within these limits the power of the State exists, as it did previously to the adoption of the amendment, over all matters of internal police.

5.—On the 31st of May, 1870, Congress passed an Act declaring that "no tax or charge shall be imposed or enforced by any State upon any person immigrating thereto from a foreign country which is not equally imposed or enforced upon every person immigrating to such State from any other foreign country, and any law of any State in conflict with this provision is hereby declared null and void;" *Held*,

1st.—That the term *charge*, as here used, means any onerous condition, and includes a condition which makes the right of an immigrant, arriving in the ports of the State, to land within the State depend upon the execution of a bond by a third party, not under his control, and whom he cannot constrain by any legal proceedings; and,

2d.—That the statute of California, which prohibits foreign immigrants of certain classes, arriving in the State of California by vessel, from landing until a bond shall have been given by the master, owner or consignee of the vessel that they will not become a public charge, and imposes no condition upon immigrants of the same class entering the State in any other way, is in conflict with the Act of Congress.

Opinion of Mr. Justice Field

The petitioner alleges that she is illegally restrained of her liberty by the Coroner of the City and County of San Francisco, and asks to be discharged from such restraint. The facts of the case, as detailed in the proceedings before us, are briefly as follows: The petitioner is a subject of the Empire of China, and came to the port of San Francisco as a passenger on board of the American steamship *Japan*, owned by the Pacific Mail Steamship Company, and under the command as master, of J. H. Freeman. On the arrival of the steamship at this port, which was on the 24th of August last, she was boarded by the Commissioner of Immigration of California, who proceeded under the provisions of a statute of the State, to examine into the character of the petitioner and other alien passengers. Upon such examination, the Commissioner found, and so declared, that the petitioner and twenty-one other persons, also subjects of the Empire of China, arriving as passengers by the same steamship, were lewd and debauched women. He thereupon prohibited the master of the steamship from landing the women, unless he or the owner or consignee of the vessel gave the bonds required by the statute. . . .

The Supreme Court sustained the ruling of the District Court, and denied the application of the parties to be discharged, holding, that the statute of the State, under which they were detained, was valid and binding under the Treaty between the United States and China and the Constitution of the United States, and that the evidence justified the finding of the Commissioner of Immigration as to the character of the women. It therefore made an order directing that the Coroner return the parties to the master or owner or consignee of the steamship *Japan*, on board of the steamship, and requiring such master, owner, or consignee to retain the parties on board of the steamship until she should leave this port, and then to carry them beyond the State. . . .

The petitioner is one of the women thus held by the Coroner, and she now invokes the aid of this Court to be released from her restraint, alleging, as in the other applications, that the restraint is illegal, that the statute which is supposed to authorize it is in contravention of the Treaty with China and the Constitution of the United States, and averring that she is not within either of the classes designated in the statute. . . .

The decision of the District Court, and of the Supreme Court of the State, although entitled to great respect and consideration from the acknowledged ability and learning of their Judges, is not binding upon this Court. The petitioner being an alien, and a subject of a country having treaty relations with the Government of the United States, has a right to invoke the aid of the Federal tribunals for her protection, when her rights, guaranteed by the Treaty, or the Constitution, or any law of Congress, are in any respect invaded; and is, of course, entitled to a hearing upon any allegation in proper form that her rights are thus invaded. . . .

It is undoubtedly true that the police power of the State extends to all matters relating to the internal government of the State, and the administration of its laws, which have not been surrendered to the General Government, and embraces regulations affecting the health, good order, morals, peace and safety of society. . . .

But the extent of the power of the State to exclude a foreigner from its territory is limited by the right in which it has its origin, the right of self-defense. Whatever outside of the legitimate exercise of this right affects the intercourse of foreigners with our people, their immigration to this country and residence therein, is exclusively within the jurisdiction of the General Government, and is not subject to State control or interference. To that Government the Treaty-making power is confided; also, the power to regulate commerce with foreign nations, which includes intercourse with them as well as traffic; also the power to prescribe the conditions of migration or importation of persons, and rules of naturalization; whilst the States are forbidden to enter into any treaty, alliance, or confederation with other nations. . . .

But independent of this consideration, we cannot shut our eyes to the fact that much which was formerly said upon the power of the State in this respect, grew out of the necessity which the Southern States, in which the institution of slavery existed, felt of excluding free negroes from their limits. As in some States negroes were citizens, the right to exclude them from the slave States could only be maintained by the assertion of a power to exclude all persons whom they might deem dangerous or injurious to their interests. But at this day no such power would be asserted, or if asserted, allowed in any Federal Court. And the most serious consequences affecting the relations of the nation with other countries might, and undoubtedly would, follow from any attempt at its exercise. Its maintenance would enable any State to involve the nation in war, however disposed to peace the people at large might be. . . .

I am aware of the very general feeling prevailing in this State against the Chinese, and in opposition to the extension of any encouragement to their immigration hither. It is felt that the dissimilarity in physical characteristics, in language, in manners, religion and habits, will always prevent any possible assimilation of them with our people. Admitting that there is ground for this feeling, it does not justify any legislation for their exclusion, which might not be adopted against the inhabitants of the most favored nations of the Caucasian race, and of Christian faith. If their further immigration is to be stopped, recourse must be had to the Federal Government, where the whole power over this subject lies. The State cannot exclude them arbitrarily, nor accomplish the same end by attributing to them a possible violation of its municipal laws. It is certainly desirable that all lewdness, especially when it takes the form of prostitution, should be suppressed, and that the most stringent measures to accomplish that end should be adopted. But I have little respect for that discriminating virtue which is shocked when a frail child of China is landed on our shores, and yet allows the bedizened and painted harlot of other countries to parade our streets and open her hells in broad day, without molestation and without censure.

By the 5th Article of the Treaty between the United States and China, adopted on the 28th of July, 1868, the United States and the Emperor of China recognize the inherent and inalienable right of man to change his home and allegiance, and also the mutual advantage of the free migration and emigration of their citizens and subjects respectively from the one country to another, for purposes of curiosity, of trade, or as permanent residents. The 6th Article declares that citizens of the United States visiting or residing in China shall enjoy the same privileges, immunities or exemptions in respect to travel or residence as may there be enjoyed by citizens or subjects of the most favored nation. And, reciprocally, that Chinese subjects visiting or residing in the United States shall enjoy the same privileges, immunities and exemptions in respect to travel or residence as may there be enjoyed by citizens or subjects of the most favored nation. . . .

But there is another view of this case equally conclusive for the discharge of the petitioner, which is founded upon the legislation of Congress since the adoption of the Fourteenth Amendment. That Amendment in its first section designates who are citizens of the United States, and then declares that no State shall make or enforce any law which abridges their privileges and immunities. It also enacts that no State shall deprive *any person* (dropping the distinctive designation of citizens) of life, liberty, or property, without due process of law; nor deny to *any person* the equal protection of the laws. The great fundamental rights of all citizens are thus secured against any State deprivation, and all persons, whether native or foreign, high or low, are, whilst within the jurisdiction of the United States, entitled to the equal protection of the laws. Discriminating and partial legislation, favoring particular persons, or against particular persons of the same class is now prohibited. Equality of privilege is the constitutional right of all citizens, and equality of protection is the constitutional right of all persons. *And equality of protection implies not only equal accessibility to the Courts for the prevention or redress of wrongs, and the enforcement of rights, but equal exemption with others of the same class, from all charges and burdens of every kind.* Within these limits the power of the State exists, as it did previously to the adoption of the amendment, over all matters of internal police. . . .

The statute of California which we have been considering imposes this onerous condition upon persons of particular classes on their arrival in the ports of the State by vessel, but leaves all other foreigners of the same classes entering the State in any other way, by land from the British possessions or Mexico, or over the plains by railway, exempt from any charge. The statute is therefore in direct conflict with the Act of Congress.

It follows, from views thus expressed, that the petitioner must be discharged from further restraint of her liberty; and it is so ordered.

11

An Act Supplementary to the Acts in Relation to Immigration (a.k.a. The Page Law), March 3, 1875

This early law, passed by Congress in 1875, noted the Japanese as well as Chinese explicitly. It was designed to deter immigration by Asian women by making the "importation" of women for the purposes of prostitution a felony. Since the vast majority of Chinese in the United States were male, prostitution was clearly an issue, but this law was much more significant in keeping immigration from China at low levels and preventing the development of vibrant Chinese American communities. Indeed, American Chinatowns did become overwhelmingly male "bachelor" societies, and the Chinese American population was artificially truncated over many decades.

The Statutes at Large of the United States, vol. XVIII, part 3. Washington, DC: Government Printing Office, 1875.

Chap. 141. — An act supplementary to the acts in relation to immigration

Be it enacted by the Senate and House of Representatives of the United States of America in Congress assembled, That in determining whether the immigration of any subject of China, Japan, or any Oriental country, to the United States, is free and voluntary, as provided by section two thousand one hundred and sixty-two of the Revised Code, title "Immigration," it shall be the duty of the consul-general or consul of the United States residing at the port from which it is proposed to convey such subjects, in any vessels enrolled or licensed in the United States, or any port within the same, before delivering to the masters of any such vessels the permit or certificate provided for in such section, to ascertain whether such immigrant has entered into a contract or agreement for a term of service within the United States, for lewd and immoral purposes; and if there be such contract or agreement, the said consul-general or consul shall not deliver the required permit or certificate.

Sec. 2. That if any citizen of the United States, or other person amenable to the laws of the United States, shall take, or cause to be taken or transported, to or from the United States any subject of China, Japan, or any Oriental country, without their free and voluntary consent, for the purpose of holding them to a term of service, such citizen or other person shall be liable to be indicted therefor, and, on conviction of such offense, shall be punished by a fine not exceeding two thousand dollars and be imprisoned not exceeding one year; and all contracts and agreements for a term of service of such persons in the United States, whether made in advance or in pursuance of such illegal importation, and whether such importation shall have been in American or other vessels, are hereby declared void.

Sec. 3. That the importation into the United States of women for the purposes of prostitution is hereby forbidden; and all contracts and agreements in relation thereto, made in advance or in pursuance of such illegal importation and purposes, are hereby declared void; and whoever shall knowingly and willfully import, or cause any importation of, women into the United States for the purposes of prostitution, or shall knowingly or willfully hold, or attempt to hold, any woman to such purposes, in pursuance of such illegal importation and contract or agreement, shall be deemed guilty of a felony, and, on conviction thereof, shall be imprisoned not exceeding five years and pay a fine not exceeding five thousand dollars.

Sec. 4. That if any person shall knowingly and willfully contract, or attempt to contract, in advance or in pursuance of such illegal importation, to supply to another the labor of any cooly or other person brought into the United States in violation of section two thousand one hundred and fifty-eight of the Revised Statutes, or of any other section of the laws prohibiting the cooly-trade or of this act, such person shall be deemed guilty of a felony, and, upon conviction thereof, in any United States court, shall be fined in a sum not exceeding five hundred dollars and imprisoned for a term not exceeding one year.

Sec. 5. That it shall be unlawful for aliens of the following classes to immigrate into the United States, namely, persons who are undergoing a sentence for conviction in their own country of felonious crimes other than political or growing out of or the result of such political offenses, or whose sentence has been remitted on condition of their emigration, and women "imported for the purposes of prostitution." Every vessel arriving in the United States may be inspected under the direction of the collector of the port at which it arrives, if he shall have reason to believe that any such obnoxious persons are on board; and the officer making such inspection shall certify the result thereof to the master or other person in charge of such vessel, designating in such certificate the person or persons, if any there be, ascertained by him to be of either of the classes whose importation is hereby forbidden. . . .

If any person shall feel aggrieved by the certificate of such inspecting officer stating him or her to be within either of the classes whose immigration is forbidden by this section, and shall apply for release or other remedy to any proper court or judge, then it shall be the duty of the collector at said port of entry to detain said vessel until a hearing and determination of the matter are had, to the end that if the said inspector shall be found to be in accordance with this section and sustained, the obnoxious person or persons shall be returned on board of said vessel, and shall not thereafter be permitted to land, unless the master, owner, or consignee of the vessel shall give bond and security. . . .

And for all violations of this act, the vessel, by the acts, omissions, or connivance of the owners, master, or other custodian, or the consignees of which the same are committed, shall be liable to forfeiture, and may be proceeded against as in cases of frauds against the revenue laws, for which forfeiture is prescribed by existing law.

Approved, March 3, 1875.

12

"Ah Sin" (Chinese song), written for and sung by C. T. Parsloe, 1877

While legislative actions and court cases vividly recount the anti-Asian, especially anti-Chinese, sentiments of the era, popular culture in the form of newspapers, stories, and songs often captures a sense of the times missing from official documents. When this song was copyrighted by Roe Stephens in 1877, Chinese immigrants and workers had been in America for a quarter century, and in New York City for even longer. These lyrics speak to the long-standing relations between immigrant Chinese men and immigrant Irish women. They also exemplify the widespread use of dialect humor, including Chinese names, for mainstream audiences. Finally, the message is clear: the "Melican" man gets the girl.

Special Collections, Milton S. Eisenhower Library, Johns Hopkins University. Thanks to Kristyn Moon for suggesting and locating this and several other songs in this volume.

"Ah Sin"

"Chinee — Song"

3½

Sung By & Written For

C.T. Parsloe

by

Harry. R. Williams.

Detroit

Published By **Roe Stephens** 184 Woodward Ave.

successor to

Whittemore & Stephens

ENTERED ACCORDING TO ACT OF CONGRESS IN THE YEAR 1876 BY WHITTEMORE & STEPHENS IN THE OFFICE OF THE LIBRARIAN OF CONGRESS AT WASHINGTON.

AH SIN.

CHINESE SONG.

HARRY R. WILLIAMS.

1. My name Ah Sin, come from China, Little wash-y shop me keep down street; No like melican man, too much chin chin, No pay washee bills—him dead beat!

548–3.

Me got Irish gal, she welly nice-y, Me make her some day my wife. We have a nice-y time

go back to Chi-na— Eat much plen ty rats and mice! My name Ah Sin, come from China,

CHORUS.

Me like Irish gal, she like me; Me from Hong Kong, Melican man come 'long, Stealy Irish gal from

poor Chinee!

(Spoken after 2nd verse.) — Me say, "What for you kissee my little gatee?" He get mad and kickee me down stairs, Policeman come along and say What's your name? Then I tellee him.— Chorus.

In re Ah Yup, *April 29, 1878*

Ah Yup petitioned the courts for the right to be naturalized. The Ninth Circuit Court in California denied this request, citing the 1802 naturalization laws (based originally on the 1790 statute) and all Revised Statutes that had been passed since. The "free white person" clause had been amended by the act of July 14, 1870, extending naturalization rights to "aliens of African nativity, and to persons of African descent" (16 Stat. 256, Sec. 7). Judge Sawyer, writing for the court, ruled that a "Mongolian" is not a "white person." The judge provided a brief anthropological exposition of the prevailing classifications of "race" at the time, five major groups: 1) Caucasian or white; 2) Mongolian or yellow; 3) Ethiopian or Negro (black); 4) American or red; and 5) Malay or brown. The only questions entertained by the court, then, were whether Mongolians could be classified as "white" and if the existing provisions precluded all but whites and persons of African nativity or descent from naturalization. The court ruled no in the first instance and yes in the second. The Chinese were forced to wait until 1943 to be eligible for American citizenship.

W. T. Baggett, ed., *Pacific Coast Law Journal*, vol. 1. San Francisco: W. T. Baggett & Co., 1878.

Circuit Court of the United States,
District of California
In the Matter of Ah Yup, Application for Naturalization

1. Naturalization, Chinese. —A native of China, of the Mongolian race, is not entitled to become a citizen of the United States under the Revised Statutes as amended in 1875. (Rev. Stat., Sec. 2169; Amendment Rev. Stat., p. 1435.)

2. A Mongolian is not a "white person" within the meaning of the term as used in the naturalization laws of the United States.

Sawyer, Circuit Judge.

Ah Yup, a native and citizen of the Empire of China, of the Mongolian race, presented a petition in writing, praying that he be permitted to make proof of the facts alleged, and upon satisfactory proof being made, and his taking the oath required in such cases, he be admitted as a citizen of the United States.

The petition stated all the qualifications required by the statute to entitle the petitioner to be naturalized, provided the statute authorizes the naturalization of a native of China of the Mongolian race. . . .

The only question is, whether the statute authorizes the naturalization of a native of China of the Mongolian race.

In all the Acts of Congress relating to the naturalization of aliens, from that of April 14th, 1802, down to the Revised Statutes, the language has been "that any alien, *being a free white person*, may be admitted to become a citizen," etc. After the adoption of the Thirteenth and Fourteenth Amendments to the National Constitution—the former prohibiting slavery, and the latter declaring who shall be citizens—Congress, in the Act of July 14th, 1870, amending the naturalization laws, added the following provision:

"That the naturalization laws are hereby extended to aliens of African nativity, and to persons of African descent." (16 Stat. 256, Sec. 7.) . . .

The questions are:

1. Is a person of the Mongolian race a "white person" within the meaning of the statute?

2. Do those provisions exclude all but white persons and persons of African nativity or African descent?

Words in a statute, other than technical terms, should be taken in their ordinary sense. The words "white person," as well argued by petitioner's counsel, taken in a strictly literal sense, constitute a very indefinite description of a class of persons, where none can be said to be literally white, and those called white may be found of every shade from the lightest blonde to the most swarthy brunette. But these words in this country, at least, have undoubtedly acquired a well-settled meaning in common popular speech, and they are constantly used in the sense so acquired in the literature of the country, as well as in common parlance. As ordinarily used everywhere in the United States, one would scarcely fail to understand that the party employing the words a "white person" would intend a person of the Caucasian race.

In speaking of the various classifications of races, Webster in his dictionary says: "The common classification is that of Blumenbach, who makes five. First, the Caucasian or *white* race, to which belong the greater part of the European nations and those of Western Asia; second, the Mongolian, or *yellow* race, occupying Tartary, China, Japan, etc.; third, the Ethiopian or *negro* [black] race, occupying all Africa, except the north; fourth, the American, or *red* race, containing the Indians of North and South America; and fifth, the Malay, or *brown* race, occupying the islands of the Indian Archipelago," etc. . . .

Thus, whatever latitudinarian construction might otherwise be given to the term "white person," it is entirely clear that Congress intended by this legislation to exclude Mongolians from the right of naturalization. I am, therefore, of the opinion that a native of China, of the Mongolian race, is not a white person within the meaning of the Act of Congress.

The second question is answered in the discussion of the first. . . .

The purpose undoubtedly was to restore the law to the condition in which it stood before the revision, and to exclude the Chinese. It was intended to exclude some classes, and as all white aliens and those of the African race are entitled to naturalization under other words, it is difficult to perceive whom it could exclude unless it be the Chinese.

It follows that the petition must be denied, and it is so ordered.

Petition from 1,300 Chinese Merchants for Schools, 1878?

*Thirteen hundred Chinese merchants, primarily in the San Francisco and Sacra-
mento areas, signed this petition for the establishment of "separate schools" for
more than 3,000 of their children, ages 5 to 17. This appeal notes that more than
$42,000 in real, property, and poll taxes were paid annually by the Chinese in
San Francisco alone. These monies supported public schools for "the children of
negroes and white people," including many foreigners from Europe. At that point
in time, children of Indians (unless with white guardians) and Mongolians were
not included. The petition reveals several important facts: first, like the earlier foreign miners' tax, discriminatory policies against the Chinese forced them to sub-
sidize the state's budget; second, the Chinese community was surprisingly stable
and complex, with a significant number of families and children; and third, the
Chinese regularly advocated for their own rights. In spite of these struggles, the
United States continued its policies of exclusion and denial of civil and human
rights—in 1882, Congress passed the Exclusion Act, and in 1885, Tape v. Hurley
demonstrated that winning court cases did not automatically ensure justice.*

Bancroft Library, University of California, Berkeley. Courtesy of Jean Pfaelzer.

To the Honorable the Senate and the Assembly of the State of California

We respectfully present our petition for the establishment of separate schools for
Chinese children, and for universal education.

We respectfully submit our humble opinion that Chinese merchants and laborers, being here under the protection of your Constitution and laws, are entitled to the same rights and privileges accorded to foreigners generally.

We respectfully represent that we are law-abiding people, and that in our
business as merchants, manufacturers and laborers, we add largely to the prosperity of this State.

We respectfully represent that for many years we have been taxed for the support of Common Schools, and that for the year 1876–77 we paid for this purpose,

in San Francisco alone, in taxes on real and personal property, and in poll taxes, a sum exceeding $42,000; and in other counties of the State a sum, the amount of which we do not know. This money has been used for support of Schools for the education of the children of negroes and white people, many of the latter being foreigners from European countries, while our youth have been excluded from any participation in the benefit. This we hold to be unjust.

We respectfully represent that in the State of California there are more than 3,000 Chinese children between the ages of five and seventeen years, entitled to the benefit of the Public Schools, and who are anxious to learn the English language, but are excluded from these schools, by the laws of the State.

We respectfully represent that the Constitution of the State encourages education in the following terms: Art. IX, Sec. 2. "The Legislature shall encourage, by all suitable means, the promotion of intellectual, scientific moral and agricultural improvement;" and restricts it to no race, color or nationality.

Your petitioners therefore respectfully call your attention to Sec. 1858, of Art. XX, of the School law of this State which reads as follows. "All State School Moneys, apportioned by the Superintendent of Public Instruction must be apportioned to the several counties in proportion to the number of School Census children between five and seventeen years of age, as shown by the returns of the School Census Marshal of the preceding school year: *provided*, that Indian children, who are not living under the guardianship of white persons, and Mongolian children shall not be included in the apportionment." * * * Also Section 1669 of Art. X, which reads: "The education of children of African descent, and Indian children must be provided for in separate schools, *provided*, that if the Directors or Trustees fail to provide such separate schools, then such children must be admitted into the schools for white Children."

We respectfully represent that these sections of the law very clearly exclude our children from the benefits of the public schools, and we humbly approach you with this petition, begging you to change these laws, so that our children may be admitted into the public schools, or what we would prefer, that separate schools may be established for them. We simply ask that our children may be placed upon the same footing as the children of other foreigners so that they may learn the English language, which would be for the advantage of all, and we would be the recipients of your great favor.

Respectfully submitted to the Legislature of California for their deliberation and action.

TRANSLATED BY J. G. KERR, Signed by 1300 Chinese, including the principal Chinese Merchants of San Francisco Sacramento, &c.

15

Invalidation of Queue Ordinance, July 7, 1879

*In 1879, the Circuit Court ruled that San Francisco's Board of Supervisors had vi
olated the equal protection clause of the Fourteenth Amendment when it mandated that every male imprisoned in the county jail must immediately have his
hair "cut or clipped to an uniform length of one inch from the scalp." That 1876
ordinance was part of a long sequence of acts designed to harass Chinese workers
and drive them from the country. Many of these acts were written "facially neutral"—as if they applied to everyone—but clearly were intended solely against the
Chinese. In 1879, Ho Ah Kow appealed his conviction and was rewarded by this
opinion, written by Judge Stephen J. Field. In Qing dynasty China (1644–1911),
the Manchu rulers had decreed that male Han natives must demonstrate acceptance of their "foreign" domination by shaving the forehead and braiding the rest
of the hair in a long "queue." Any Chinese man who contemplated return to
China for any reason had to comply with this on pain of death.*

*This ruling illustrates the fact that the Chinese consistently resisted racist ac-
tions with lawsuits, court cases, and public protests. It also demonstrates that recourse to the Fourteenth Amendment to the Constitution was a major form of securing equal treatment for all residents, not only citizens, of the United States. To
be sure, as Judge Field concluded, the nation had legal recourse to anti-Chinese
sentiment by having the federal government limit or exclude immigrants; three
years later, Congress passed the Chinese Exclusion Act.*

"The Invalidity of the 'Queue Ordinance' of the City and County of San Francisco:
Opinion of The Circuit Court of the United States, For the District of California
in Ho Ah Kow vs. Matthew Nunan, delivered July 7, 1879." San Francisco: J. L.
Rice & Co., Law Printers and Publishers, 1879.

The Circuit Court of the United States, For the District of California
Ho Ah Kow vs. Matthew Nunan

1. The Board of Supervisors of the city and county of San Francisco, the body in which
the legislative power of the city and county is vested, is limited in its authority by the

act which consolidated the government of the city and county, generally known as the Consolidation Act. It can do nothing unless warrant be found for it there, or in a subsequent statute of the State. . . .

3. The general supervision of all matters appertaining to the sanitary condition of the county jail in San Francisco is confided by the act of April 4th, 1870, to the Board of Health of the city and county; and only in exceptional cases would the preservation of the health of the institution require the cutting of the hair of any of its inmates within an inch of his scalp.

4. Accordingly, where an ordinance of the city and county of San Francisco, passed on the 14th of June, 1876, declared that every male person imprisoned in the county jail, under the judgment of any Court having jurisdiction in criminal cases in the city and county, should immediately upon his arrival at the jail, have the hair of his head "cut or clipped to an uniform length of one inch from the scalp thereof," and made it the duty of the Sheriff to have this provision enforced, it was *Held*, that the ordinance was invalid, being in excess of the authority of the Board of Supervisors, whether the measure be considered as an additional punishment to that imposed by the Court upon conviction under a State law, or as a sanitary regulation; and constituted no justification to the Sheriff acting under it.

5. The ordinance being directed against the Chinese only imposing upon them a degrading and cruel punishment, is also subject to the further objection, that it is hostile and discriminating legislation against a class forbidden by that clause of the Fourteenth Amendment to the Constitution, which declares that no State "shall deny to any person within its jurisdiction the equal protection of the laws." This inhibition upon the State applies to all the instrumentalities and agencies employed in the administration of its government; to its executive, legislative and judicial departments; and to the subordinate legislative bodies of its counties and cities.

6. The equality of protection thus assured to every one whilst within the United States, implies not only that the Courts of the country shall be open to him on the same terms as to all others for the security of his person or property, the prevention or redress of wrongs, and the enforcement of contracts, but that no charges or burdens shall be laid upon him which are not equally borne by others, and that in the administration of criminal justice, he shall suffer for his offenses no greater or different punishment.

Mr. Justice Field delivered the opinion of the Court.

The plaintiff is a subject of the Emperor of China, and the present action is brought to recover damages for his alleged maltreatment by the defendant, a citizen of the State of California and the Sheriff of the city and county of San Francisco. The maltreatment consisted in having wantonly and maliciously cut off the queue of the plaintiff, a queue being worn by all Chinamen, and its deprivation being regarded by them as degrading and as entailing future suffering.

It appears that in April, 1876, the Legislature of California passed an act "concerning lodging-houses and sleeping-apartments within the limits of incorporated cities," declaring, among other things, that any person found sleeping or lodging in a room or an apartment containing less than five hundred cubic feet of space in the clear for each person occupying it, should be deemed guilty of a misdemeanor, and on conviction thereof be punished by a fine of not less than ten or more than fifty dollars, or imprisonment in the county jail, or by both such fine and imprisonment. Under this act the plaintiff, in April, 1878, was convicted and sentenced to pay a fine of ten dollars, or in default of such payment to be imprisoned five days in the county jail. Failing to pay the fine, he was imprisoned. The defendant, as Sheriff of the city and county, had charge of the jail, and during the imprisonment of the plaintiff cut off his queue, as alleged. The complaint avers, that it is the custom of Chinamen to shave the hair from the front of the head and to wear the remainder of it braided into a queue; that the deprivation of the queue is regarded by them as a mark of disgrace, and is attended, according to their religious faith, with misfortune and suffering after death; that the defendant knew of this custom and religious faith of the Chinese, and knew also that the plaintiff venerated the custom and held the faith; yet, in disregard of his rights, inflicted the injury complained of; and that the plaintiff has, in consequence of it, suffered great mental anguish, been disgraced in the eyes of his friends and relatives, and ostracised from association with his countrymen; and that hence he has been damaged to the amount of $10,000.

Two defenses to the action are set up by the defendant; the second one being a justification of his conduct under an ordinance of the city and county of San Francisco. It is upon the sufficiency of the latter defense that the case is before us. The ordinance referred to was passed on the 14th of June, 1876, and it declares that every male person imprisoned in the county jail, under the judgment of any Court having jurisdiction in criminal cases in the city and county, shall immediately upon his arrival at the jail have the hair of his head "cut or clipped to an uniform length of one inch from the scalp thereof," and it is made the duty of the Sheriff to have this provision enforced. Under this ordinance the defendant cut off the queue of the plaintiff.

The validity of this ordinance is denied by the plaintiff on two grounds: 1st, that it exceeds the authority of the Board of Supervisors, the body in which the legislative power of the city and county is vested; and, 2d, that it is special legislation imposing a degrading and cruel punishment upon a class of persons who are entitled, alike with all other persons within the jurisdiction of the United States, to the equal protection of the laws. We are of opinion that both these positions are well taken. . . .

The cutting off the hair of every male person within an inch of his scalp, on his arrival at the jail, was not intended and cannot be maintained as a measure of discipline or as a sanitary regulation. The act by itself has no tendency to promote discipline, and can only be a measure of health in exceptional cases. Had the ordinance contemplated a mere sanitary regulation, it would have been limited to such cases and made applicable to females as well as to males, and to persons awaiting trial as well as to persons under conviction. The close cutting of the hair which is practiced upon inmates of the State Penitentiary, like dressing them in striped clothing, is partly to distinguish them from others, and thus

prevent their escape, and facilitate their recapture. They are measures of pre-
caution, as well as parts of a general system of treatment prescribed by the Directors of the Penitentiary under the authority of the State, for parties convicted of and imprisoned for felonies. Nothing of the kind is prescribed or would
be tolerated with respect to persons confined in a county jail for simple misde-
meanors, most of which are not of a very grave character. For the discipline or
detention of the plaintiff in this case, who had the option of paying a fine of ten
dollars, or of being imprisoned for five days, no such clipping of the hair was required. It was done to add to the severity of his punishment. . . .

In the present case, the plaintiff was not convicted of any breach of a municipal regulation, nor of violating any provision of the consolidation act. The
punishment which the Supervisors undertook to add to the fine imposed by the
Court was without semblance of authority. The Legislature had not conferred
upon them the right to change or add to the punishments which it deemed sufficient for offenses; nor had it bestowed upon them the right to impose in any
case a punishment of the character inflicted in this case. They could no more
direct that the queue of the plaintiff should be cut off than that the punishments
mentioned should be inflicted. Nor could they order the hair of any one, Mongolian or other person, to be clipped within an inch of his scalp. That measure
was beyond their power.

The second objection to the ordinance in question is equally conclusive. It
is special legislation, on the part of the Supervisors, against a class of persons,
who, under the constitution and laws of the United States, are entitled to the
equal protection of the laws. The ordinance was intended only for the Chinese
in San Francisco. This was avowed by the Supervisors on its passage, and was so
understood by every one. The ordinance is known in the community as the
"Queue Ordinance," being so designated from its purpose to reach the queues
of the Chinese, and it is not enforced against any other persons. The reason advanced for its adoption, and now urged for its continuance is, that only the
dread of the loss of his queue will induce a Chinaman to pay his fine. That is
to say, in order to enforce the payment of a fine imposed upon him it is necessary that torture should be superadded to imprisonment. Then, it is said, the
Chinaman will not accept the alternative, which the law allows, of working out
his fine by his imprisonment, and the State or county will be saved the expense
of keeping him during the imprisonment. Probably the bastinado, or the knout,
or the thumbscrew; or the rack, would accomplish the same end; and no doubt
the Chinaman would prefer either of these modes of torture to that which entails upon his disgrace among his countrymen and carries with it the constant
dread of misfortune and suffering after death. It is not creditable to the humanity and civilization of our people, much less to their Christianity, that an ordinance of this character was possible.

The class character of this legislation is none the less manifest because of the
general terms in which it is expressed. . . . When we take our seats on the bench

we are not struck with blindness, and forbidden to know as judges what we see as men; and where an ordinance, though general in its terms, only operates upon a special race, sect or class, it being universally understood that it is to be enforced only against that race, sect or class, we may justly conclude that it was the intention of the body adopting it that it should only have such operation, and treat it accordingly. . . .

The complaint in this case shows that the ordinance acts with special severity upon Chinese prisoners, inflicting upon them suffering altogether disproportionate to what would be endured by other prisoners if enforced against them. Upon the Chinese prisoners its enforcement operates as "a cruel and unusual punishment." . . .

During various periods of English history, legislation, general in its character, has often been enacted with the avowed purpose of imposing special burdens and restrictions upon Catholics; but that legislation has since been regarded as not less odious and obnoxious to animadversion than if the persons at whom it was aimed had been particularly designated.

But, in our country, hostile and discriminating legislation by a State against persons of any class, sect, creed or nation, in whatever form it may be expressed, is forbidden by the fourteenth amendment of the Constitution. That amendment in its first section declares who are citizens of the United States, and then enacts that no State shall make or enforce any law which shall abridge their privileges and immunities. It further declares that no State shall deprive *any person* (dropping the distinctive term citizen) of life, liberty, or property, without due process of law, nor deny to *any person* the equal protection of the laws. . . .

It is certainly something in which a citizen of the United States may feel a generous pride that the government of his country extends protection to all persons within its jurisdiction; and that every blow aimed at any of them, however humble, come from what quarter it may, is "caught upon the broad shield of our blessed Constitution and our equal laws."

We are aware of the general feeling—amounting to positive hostility—prevailing in California against the Chinese, which would prevent their further immigration hither, and expel from the State those already here. Their dissimilarity in physical characteristics, in language, manners, and religion would seem, from past experience, to prevent the possibility of their assimilation with our people. And thoughtful persons, looking at the millions which crowd the opposite shores of the Pacific, and the possibility at no distant day of their pouring over in vast hordes among us, giving rise to fierce antagonisms of race, hope that some way may be devised to prevent their further immigration. We feel the force and importance of these considerations; but the remedy for the apprehended evil is to be sought from the general government, where, except in certain special cases, all power over the subject lies. To that government belong exclusively the treaty-making power, and the power to regulate commerce with foreign nations, which includes intercourse as well as traffic, and, with the exceptions presently mentioned, the power to prescribe the conditions of immigration or importation of persons. The State in these particulars, with those exceptions, is powerless, and nothing is gained by the attempted assertion of a control which can never be admitted. The State may exclude from its limits paupers and convicts of other countries, persons incurably diseased, and others likely to become a burden upon its resources. It may perhaps also exclude persons whose presence would be dangerous to its established institutions. But there its power ends. Whatever is done by way of exclusion beyond this must come from the general government. That government alone can determine what aliens shall be permitted to land within the United States, and upon what conditions they shall be permitted to remain; whether they shall be restricted in business transactions to such as appertain to foreign commerce, as is practically the case with our people in China, or whether they shall be allowed to engage in all pursuits equally with citizens. For restrictions necessary or desirable in these matters, the appeal must be made to the general government; and it is not believed that the appeal will ultimately be disregarded. Be that as it may, nothing can be accomplished in that direction by hostile and spiteful legislation on the part of the State, or of its municipal bodies, like the ordinance in question—legislation which is unworthy of a brave and manly people. Against such legislation it will always be the duty of the judiciary to declare and enforce the paramount law of the nation. . . .

Memorial on Chinatown, Investigating Committee of the Anti-Chinese Council, Workingmen's Party of California, March 10, 1880

By the 1870s, anti-Chinese racism had spread across the country, but its epicenter remained California. Both Republicans and Democrats found themselves playing catch-up as more radical groups clamored for an end to immigration from China and the expulsion of Chinese already in their regions. The Workingmen's Party of California, led by Denis Kearney, split from the national Workingmen's Party of the United States when it refused to support a movement based solely on the anti-Chinese mood. The California-based party was successful in galvanizing hostility by portraying the "enemy" as an unholy coalition of greedy monopoly capitalists enriching themselves by employing the Chinese, who embraced despicable lifestyles and with whom honorable white workers could not compete. This "Memorial" was part of a slim packet entitled "Chinatown: Declared a Nuisance!" designed to push the two parties to adopt Chinese exclusion policies. An accompanying piece, by Workingmen's Party member Mayor I. S. Kalloch, warned of "conflagrations" and "bloodshed" if the "corporations and large firms continue to take the bread from their [working people's] children's mouths, and give it to Chinese dogs." Republicans and Democrats determined that sacrificing the Chinese would calm the wrath of the working class and, within two years, passed the Chinese Exclusion Act.

Workingmen's Party of California. "Chinatown: Declared a Nuisance." San Francisco, March 10, 1880. Author's collection.

Memorial on Chinatown
By an Investigating Committee of the Anti-Chinese Council, W. P. C.

To His Honor the Mayor and the Honorable Board of Health of the City and County of San Francisco, Cal.:

Gentlemen:—Within the limits, within the very heart of the city of San Francisco, bounded on the east and west by Kearny and Stockton streets and on the north and south by California street and Broadway, lives a people entirely differing and distinct in custom as well as in manners from the people of this city and State, and the United States, and in such large numbers that, if properly distributed, in accordance with the Cubic Air Ordinance and with the customs and habits of a civilized community, would fill an area as large as the city of Oakland. This alien people, on which our civilization left no impression, who have never changed the habits of their own native soil, though twenty years have passed since their arrival here, belong to the Mongolian race. They are, and have stayed through all this time, contrary to the laws of the United States: practicing slavery, remaining unmarried: obeying the edicts of a foreign potentate, the Emperor of China, etc., and thus menacing the institutions of this free Republic. These Chinese live in the very heart of the city of San Francisco as a distinct colony, violating all laws of hygiene and defying all fire and police ordinances. In their quarters all civilization of the white race ceases, and a locality is created where *lawlessness*, and consequent to it, bribery and corruption, is bred and disseminated through our commonwealth to such an extent that not only the physical condition of our race is endangered, but also the morals of our present and rising generation are corrupted.

Through actual observation (the subscribed committee having inspected Chinatown for the last six weeks), we find there places where thieves and highbinders are sheltered from the law, and tramps and vagabonds are educated. We find there a locality, which, through cheapness by overcrowded habitation, throws a healthy competition of labor out of the question. There we behold dens of iniquity and filth, houses of prostitution of the vilest sort, opium dens, gambling houses, which destroy the very morals, the manhood and the health of our people. There it is from whence leprosy, this inherent factor, this inbred disease of Chinese, is infused into our healthy race by the using, the sucking of opium-pipes, which have been handled by those already afflicted. From thence, from houses of prostitution, grows and steadily infuses itself slowly but surely an incurable and hereditary curse, ultimately destroying whole nations through the instrumentality of Chinese prostitutes, who, in diseasing our young men, implant into them the germs of leprosy and other loathsome, constitutional and hereditary disorders, which will be handed down, through our present and past laxity concerning the enforcement of hygienic laws, to our children and children's children. These diseases are, as yet, foreign to the American people. Furthermore, we have discovered there manufactories of various kinds—of cigars, clothing, etc., even of articles of food, carried on in the filthiest holes imaginable—exposed in such dens to the impregnation of germs of diseases which must be detrimental to the health of the consumer or wearer. Sturdy as the physical condition of the white race is, it must at last succumb to the onslaught of such an evil. For instance, a cigar manufactory is carried on in Ellick alley, in close proximity to a Chinese Hospital, where a case of leprosy and a case of lupus excaedens await dissolution. The surface of a cigar, its filling and cover expose a double surface several feet in length and width, if unrolled and spread out. Upon this large area of raw material, in such dens of filth and disease, in this terrible stench, infectious germs are deposited, which propagate infectious and contagious disorders through inhalation and handling. The "germ" theory of disease is now an acknowledged fact in the science of medicine. The microscope reveals even to the eye a great many of the fungi causing disorders. This theory teaches us that material like cloth, tobacco, food, etc., if exposed to an atmosphere charged with those germs, is infected by them, and thus detrimental to the health of the wearer or consumer of such merchandise. The dangerous result of such evil, we hold, is practically proven by the ravages of diseases like diphtheria, etc., in this city, irrespective of time, season or places. The physician who tries to trace the source of infection of diphtheria in his patients is mostly always unable to do so, and we believe that the existing evils in Chinatown are the proper source. The propagation of these germs of disease and the introduction of them into the fold of private families is, besides this infection through merchandise, greatly assisted through the Chinese wash-houses and Chinese servants of such private families. These Chinese laundrymen and servants have the pernicious habit of visiting almost daily Chinatown, either to partake of the hospitality of their friends, or to buy merchandise, or to revel in the luxury of opium-smoking. Some even sleep in Chinatown, in these filthy holes, every night. Through these means a perfect network of contagion and infection is created, a veritable octopus of disease, having its seat in Chinatown, and its infectious arms thrust into every house of the city, is in existence, which fact must strike a perfect horror to every medical man.

A physician's most sacred duty is to prevent disease. Secondary to this only is to try to cure it. In our perambulations through Chinatown we found, a few feet from Kearny street, on Sacramento, a large colony of Chinese thronged together in the smallest possible compass, smoking opium, cooking at open fires, living in filth and stench and smoke, the floors reeking with slime and filth, water dripping down the wall, whose source (unknown to us) could only be detected by the smell—in short, a veritable stink hole, which gives off and alone breeds disease, enough to endanger the health of the city. This would be an excellent feeding place for any epidemic which might become prevalent in our city. Were it not for the beneficence of Nature providing these severe storms which sweep over the city almost daily, the people could not exist with such a cancer in its very heart. This is a criminal neglect on the part of the proper authorities, to allow such a pest-hole to exist immediately behind the principal stores of Kearny street. Again, there are a number of hospitals in the Chinese quarters in direct violation of all sanitary laws and city ordinances, viz., a hospital on Ellick alley; another on Clay street, between Kearny and Dupont streets; a third hospital on Varennes street, off Union, with Joss-house attached, where the sick are placed to die. This last place is a hole of filth, stench and smoke, in a rickety condition, and unfit for habitation. Several times parties living in its immediate neighborhood have filed complaints against its existence there, but with no avail.

Sickness among children, especially diphtheria and other low typhoid disorders, have appeared and ravaged there ever since the establishment of said hospital—a fact to which parties in the vicinity will testify. Telegraph Hill ought to be one of the healthiest portions of our city; but since the above-named evil exists there its former healthy condition has changed. This same hospital is in close proximity to two of our schools, where the germs of the disease and the utter depravity of the occupants of said hospital endanger the health of the school children, and at the same time destroy the morals of the rising generation. The criminal neglect on the part of the city authorities to not remove said nuisance is hardly pardonable—the complaints have never been listened to.

Another hospital and bone-house is in an alley off Montgomery avenue, near Broadway street, where the remnants of more than 2,000 Chinamen (bones) are stored in satchels. These satchels are there packed in boxes, and thus shipped to China, which practice is in direct violation of our city ordinances. Duncombe alley, off Jackson street, is another place where the most indescribable stink, filth, garbage, etc., exists. Manufactories are carried on there in full blast, as cigars, clothing, etc., and a kitchen thus ventilated and scented regales the hungry stomachs of the Chinamen. Immediately above this alley—entrance through a wood-yard—and above this one, on Mrs. Sheppard's property, near Stockton, is filth in piles everywhere, Chinese living there by the dozen in small, dingy cellars and rooms. Cigars, etc., are manufactured there. Opposite, on the south side of the street, the very paradise of Chinese customs is to be seen, for it reeks in filth and stench.

The same exists adjoining 741 Pacific street, next to a wood-yard. In short, we have in the midst of the city a portion of the empire of China living in open violation of the laws of our State and city, where all laws of hygiene are, as it is seen, successfully defied. Through forbearance, a state of affairs has developed itself there during these last twenty years, which is a shame upon a civilized community. No cleansing or disinfecting can remedy this evil. The reeking filth has sapped through the walls of brick, and permeated wood and stonework. A radical cure alone can do justice to the citizens of San Francisco. The police officers on their beats in Chinatown receive bribes as hush money, so that they shall not disturb their (the Chinese) mode of living. This assertion is proven by the individual wealth of the police officers there on the one side, and the open violation of the law on the part of the Chinese on the other. The special policemen especially should be charged with the above, because they serve only to be subservient to the Chinese, and to guard them against arrest. We pray, therefore, your Honorable Board, as citizens of these United States, as inhabitants of the State of California, and voters and taxpayers of the city and county of San Francisco, to take into consideration the above described existing evil, and to remedy the same as follows:

First—To have Chinatown condemned as a nuisance, because its filth and stench and open lawlessness detroy [sic] the health and morals of the people of this city.

Second—To have the Chinese quartered outside of the city in decent quarters, wherever your Honorable Board may designate, or where the Chinese desire to build and purchase homes.

Third—Whereas the American people are as yet free from such a terrible disease as leprosy—a disease inherent with the Chinese race; and whereas, in accordance with all medical science, constitutional and hereditary or inherent disorders, such as leprosy, lupus, syphilis, etc., are related to and intermingle with each other, so that a contamination with syphilis also carries in its train an inoculation of leprosy or lupus; and whereas, through necessity, on account of the close intercourse existing between the American race and Chinese, the infusion of said incurable and hereditary diseases must follow, and result in the deterioration of our healthy American race; therefore,

We pray—basing also our prayers upon the provisions of the New Constitution, now in force, viz., Article XI., Section 11, to wit; "Any county, city, or town, or township may make and enforce within its limits, all such local, police, sanitary or other regulations as are not in conflict with the general laws"—to have all intercourse cease between Chinese and Americans and vice versa, for sanitary reasons only; and to make it a misdemeanor for any person or citizen to have any business or other relations with the Chinese, for reasons aforesaid, Very respectfully,

GEO. A. REICH, M.D.,
D. McMILLAN, M.D.,
JAMES BARTON,
A. VANINA,
JOHN SHIELDS, *Committee.*

By order of the Anti-Chinese Council.
T. ALLEN, *President.*   W. I. CLARK, *Secretary.*

17

An Act to Execute Certain Treaty Stipulations Relating to Chinese (a.k.a. Chinese Exclusion Act), May 6, 1882

By the 1880s, Americans were concerned about increasing immigration from parts of the globe other than northwestern Europe. The first legislation to exclude immigrants on the basis of nationality, ethnicity, or race, passed in 1882, was directed against the Chinese. The act prohibited Chinese laborers from entering the country for ten years and reversed important sections of the Burlingame-Seward Treaty (1868). It also prohibited the Chinese from becoming naturalized citizens. In 1882, 1884, 1888, and 1902, further legislation extended this anti-Chinese bias, and in 1904, made it indefinite; it was not repealed until 1943. The Exclusion Act established a precedent for excluding or limiting immigration from other Asian countries during the first few decades of the twentieth century and thus successfully halted the development of larger Asian American communities in the United States.

The Statutes at Large of the United States of America, vol. XXII. Washington, DC: Government Printing Office, 1883.

Be it enacted by the Senate and House of Representatives of the United States of America in Congress assembled, That from and after the expiration of ninety days next after the passage of this act, and until the expiration of ten years next after the passage of this act, the coming of Chinese laborers to the United States be, and the same is hereby, suspended; and during such suspension it shall not be lawful for any Chinese laborer to come, or, having so come after the expiration of said ninety days, to remain within the United States.

Sec. 2. That the master of any vessel who shall knowingly bring within the United States on such vessel, and land or permit to be landed, any Chinese laborer, from any foreign port or place, shall be deemed guilty of a misdemeanor, and on conviction thereof shall be punished by a fine of not more than five hundred dollars for each and every such Chinese laborer so brought, and may be also imprisoned for a term not exceeding one year.

Sec. 3. That the two foregoing sections shall not apply to Chinese laborers who were in the United States on the seventeenth day of November, eighteen hundred and eighty, or who shall have come into the same before the expiration of ninety days next after the passage of this act, and who shall produce to such master before going on board such vessel, and shall produce to the collector of the port in the United States at which such vessel shall arrive, the evidence hereinafter in this act required of his being one of the laborers in the section mentioned. . . .

Sec. 6. That in order to the faithful execution of articles one and two of the treaty in this act before mentioned, every Chinese person other than a laborer who may be entitled by said treaty and this act to come within the United States, and who shall be about to come to the United States, shall be identified as so entitled by the Chinese Government in each case, such identity to be evidenced by a certificate issued under the authority of said government, which certificate shall be in the English language or (if not in the English language) accompanied by a translation into English, stating such right to come, and which cerfiticate shall state the name, title, or official rank, if any, the age, height, and all physical peculiarities, former and present occupation or profession, and place of residence in China of the person to whom the certificate is issued and that such person is entitled conformably to the treaty in this act mentioned to come within the United States. Such certificate shall be prima-facie evidence of the fact set forth therein, and shall be produced to the collector of customs, or his deputy, of the port in the district in the United States at which the person named therein shall arrive. . . .

Sec. 13. That this act shall not apply to diplomatic and other officers of the Chinese Government traveling upon the business of that government, whose credentials shall be taken as equivalent to the certificate in this act mentioned, and shall exempt them and their body and household servants from the provisions of this act as to other Chinese persons.

Sec. 14. That hereafter no State court or court of the United Sttaes shall admit Chinese to citizenship; and all laws in conflict with this act are hereby repealed.

Sec. 15. That the words "Chinese laborers," wherever used in this act, shall be construed to mean both skilled and unskilled laborers and Chinese employed in mining.

Approved, May 6, 1882.

18

Treaty Between the United States and Corea:
Peace, Amity, Commerce, and Navigation, May 22, 1882

*By the late nineteenth century, no East Asian nation could avoid direct involve-
ment with rapidly expanding western imperialism. Korea was first forced into the
global arena through the intervention of a modernizing Japan in 1876. In 1882,
the United States became the next country to sign a treaty with Korea, aided by
Chinese encouragement, partly to counter growing Japanese influence in Korean
politics. The treaty was similar to one signed by the United States and Japan nearly thirty years earlier. Japan's influence, however, soon turned into intervention
and colonialism. Until World War II, the Japanese government officially represented Koreans in the United States.*

Treaty Between the United States and Corea: Peace, Amity, Commerce, and Navigation.
Treaty Series, No. 61. Washington, DC: Government Printing Office, 1908. Thanks
to Kim Min-Young of the Consular Section in the Embassy of the Republic of
Korea for securing a copy of this document.

Article I

There shall be perpetual peace and friendship between the President of the
United States and the King of Chosen and the citizens and subjects of their respective Governments.

If other Powers deal unjustly or oppressively with either Government, the
other will exert their good offices, on being informed of the case, to bring about
an amicable arrangement, thus showing their friendly feelings. . . .

Article IV

All citizens of the United States of America in Chosen, peacably [*sic*] attending
to their own affairs, shall receive and enjoy for themselves and everything appertaining to them the protection of the local authorities of the Government of

Chosen, who shall defend them from all insult and injury of any sort. If their dwellings or property be threatened or attacked by mobs, incendiaries, or other violent or lawless persons, the local officers, on requisition of the Consul, shall immediately despatch a military force to disperse the rioters, apprehend the guilty individuals, and punish them with the utmost rigor of the law. . . .

When controversies arise in the Kingdom of Chosen between citizens of the United States and subjects of His Majesty, which need to be examined and decided by the public officers of the two nations, it is agreed between the two Governments of the United States and Chosen, that such cases shall be tried by the proper official of the nationality of the defendant, according to the laws of that nation. . . .

Article VI

Subjects of Chosen who may visit the United States shall be permitted to reside and to rent premises, purchase land, or to construct residences or warehouses in all parts of the country. They shall be freely permitted to pursue their various callings and avocations, and to traffic in all merchandise, raw and manufactured, that is not declared contraband by law.

Citizens of the United States who may resort to the ports of Chosen which are open to foreign commerce, shall be permitted to reside at such open ports within the limits of the concessions and to lease buildings or land, or to construct residences or warehouses therein. They shall be freely permitted to pursue their various callings and avocations within the limits of the port, and to traffic in all merchandise, raw and manufactured, that is not declared contraband by law. . . .

Article XI

Students of either nationality, who may proceed to the country of the other, in order to study the language, literature, laws or arts, shall be given all possible protection and assistance in evidence of cordial good will.

Article XII

This, being the first Treaty negotiated by Chosen, and hence being general and incomplete in its provisions, shall in the first instance be put into operation in all things stipulated herein. As to stipulations not contained herein, after an interval of five years, when the officers and people of the two Powers shall have become more familiar with each others [sic] language, a further negotiation of commercial provisions and regulations in detail, in conformity with international law and without unequal discriminations on either part shall be had.

Article XII

This Treaty, and future official correspondence between the two contracting Governments shall be made, on the part of Chosen, in the Chinese language.

The United States shall either use the Chinese language, or, if English be used, it shall be accompanied with a Chinese version, in order to avoid misunderstanding.

Chosen, May, the 22nd A. D. 1882.

[seal.]   R. W. Shufeldt Commander U. S N.
                                           Envoy of the U. S. to Chosen

[seal.]   [Signatures of Corean Commissioners
                                           in Chinese language.]

19

Foran Act Prohibiting Contract Labor, February 26, 1885

Ohio Congressman Martin Foran sponsored this legislation outlawing the payment of transportation costs for alien contract laborers prior to immigration. The law targeted masters of ships transporting such laborers by imposing fines on those found guilty. This legislation followed closely on the heels of the 1882 Chinese Exclusion Act, which prohibited Chinese laborers from entering the United States. Hawai'i's sugar planters continued paying transportation costs for Japanese contract labor until imposition of U.S. statutes in 1900, two years after the state's annexation. The practice has continued, however, unabated and in secrecy, to the present. Undocumented Chinese immigrants from Fujian, for example, are said to pay their "snakehead" recruiters anywhere from $30,000 to $40,000 for delivery into the United States.

23 Stat. 332; 8 U.S.C. *The Statutes at Large of the United States of America from December, 1883 to March, 1885.* Washington, DC: Government Printing Office, 1885.

Be it enacted by the Senate and House of Representatives of the United States of America in Congress assembled, That from and after the passage of this act it shall be unlawful for any person, company, partnership, or corporation, in any manner whatsoever, to prepay the transportation, or in any way assist or encourage the importation or migration of any alien or aliens, any foreigner or foreigners, into the United States, its Territories, or the District of Columbia, under contract or agreement, parol or special, express or implied, made previous to the importation or migration of such alien or aliens, foreigner or foreigners, to perform labor or service of any kind in the United States, its Territories, or the District of Columbia.

Sec. 2. That all contracts or agreements, express or implied, parol or special, which may hereafter be made by and between any person, company, partnership, or corporation, and any foreigner or foreigners, alien or aliens, to perform labor or service or having reference to the performance of labor or service by any person in the United States, its Territories, or the District of

Columbia previous to the migration or importation of the person or persons whose labor or service is contracted for into the United States, shall be utterly void and of no effect.

Sec. 3. That for every violation of any of the provisions of section one of this act the person, partnership, company, or corporation violating the same, by knowingly assisting, encouraging or soliciting the migration or importation of any alien or aliens, foreigner or foreigners, into the United States, its Territories, or the District of Columbia, to perform labor or service of any kind under contract or agreement, express or implied, parol or special, with such alien or aliens, foreigner or foreigners, previous to becoming residents or citizens of the United States, shall forfeit and pay for every such offence the sum of one thousand dollars, which may be sued for and recovered by the United States or by any person who shall first bring his action therefor including any such alien or foreigner who may be a party to any such contract or agreement, as debts of like amount are now recovered in the circuit courts of the United States; the proceeds to be paid into the Treasury of the United States; and separate suits may be brought for each alien or foreigner being a party to such contract or agreement aforesaid. And it shall be the duty of the district attorney of the proper district to prosecute every such suit at the expense of the United States.

Sec. 4. That the master of any vessel who shall knowingly bring within the United States on any such vessel, and land, or permit to be landed, from any foreign port or place, any alien laborer, mechanic, or artisan who, previous to embarkation on such vessel, had entered into contract or agreement, parol or special, express or implied, to perform labor or service in the United States, shall be deemed guilty of a misdemeanor, and on conviction thereof, shall be punished by a fine of not more than five hundred dollars for each and every such alien laborer, mechanic or artisan so brought as aforesaid, and may also be imprisoned for a term not exceeding six months.

Sec. 5. That nothing in this act shall be so construed as to prevent any citizen or subject of any foreign country temporarily residing in the United States, either in private or official capacity, from engaging, under contract or otherwise, persons not residents or citizens of the United States to act as private secretaries, servants, or domestics for such foreigner temporarily residing in the United States as aforesaid; nor shall this act be so construed as to prevent any person, or persons, partnership, or corporation from engaging, under contract or agreement, skilled workman [sic] in foreign countries to perform labor in the United States in or upon any new industry not at present established in the United States: *Provided,* That skilled labor for that purpose cannot be otherwise obtained; nor shall the provisions of this act apply to professional actors, artists, lecturers, or singers, nor to persons employed strictly as personal or domestic servants: *Provided,* That nothing in this act shall be construed as prohibiting any individual from assisting any member of his family or any relative or personal friend, to migrate from any foreign country to the United States, for the purpose of settlement here.

Sec. 6. That all laws or parts of laws conflicting herewith be, and the same are hereby, repealed.

Approved, February 26, 1885.

20

California Supreme Court: Mamie Tape, an Infant, by Her Guardian Ad Litem, Joseph Tape, Respondent, v. Jennie M. A. Hurley et al., Appellants, *March 3, 1885*

The San Francisco School Board instructed the principal of Spring Valley School, Jennie Hurley, to deny admission to Mamie Tape, a Chinese American girl. Her parents, Joseph and Mary Tape, objected and filed suit. The practice of excluding Chinese and Chinese Americans from California's public schools began in the early 1850s, but after three decades, the insistence of the Chinese was beginning to have an effect. Nonetheless, in this case, although the California Supreme Court ruled that public schools were unequivocally open to all children except "the vicious, the filthy, and those having contagious or infectious diseases," the school board and the principal managed to keep Mamie out. The board then established a segregated institution for "Orientals" and enrolled Mamie there instead of in her neighborhood school.

The Pacific Reporter, vol. V. St. Paul: West Publishing Co., 1885.

Mamie Tape, an Infant, by Her Guardian Ad Litem, Joseph Tape, Respondent, v. Jennie M. A. Hurley et al., Appellants
Supreme Court of California
66 Cal. 473; 6P-129; 1885 Cal

SHARPSTEIN, J.

The main question in this case is whether a child "between six and twenty-one years of age, of Chinese parentage, but who was born and has always lived in the city and county of San Francisco," is entitled to admission in the public school of the district in which she resides.

The language of the code is as follows:

"Every school, unless otherwise provided by law, must be open for the admission of all children between six and twenty-one years of age residing in the district; and the board of trustees, or city board of education, have power to admit adults and children not residing in the district, whenever good reasons exist therefor. Trustees shall have the power to exclude children of filthy or vicious habits, or children suffering from contagious or infectious diseases." (Political Code, 1667.) . . .

As amended, the clause is broad enough to include all children who are not precluded from entering a public school by some provision of law; and we are not aware of any law which forbids the entrance of children of any race or nationality. The legislature not only declares who shall be admitted, but also who may be excluded, and it does not authorize the exclusion of any one on the ground upon which alone the exclusion of the respondent here is sought to be justified. The vicious, the filthy, and those having contagious or infectious diseases, may be excluded, without regard to their race, color or nationality.

This law must be construed as any other would be construed. "Where a law is plain and unambiguous, whether it be expressed in general or limited terms, the legislature should be intended to mean what they have plainly expressed, and consequently, no room is left for construction." (Fisher v. Blight, 2 Cranch, 358, 399.) "When the law is clear and explicit, and its provisions are susceptible of but one interpretation, its consequences, if evil, can only be avoided by a change of the law itself, to be effected by legislative and not judicial action." (Bosley v. Mattingly, 14 B. Mon. 73.) This rule is never controverted or doubted, although perhaps sometimes lost sight of. In this case, if effect be given to the intention of the legislature, as indicated by the clear and unambiguous language used by them, respondent here has the same right to enter a public school that any other child has. It is not alleged that she is vicious, or filthy, or that she has a contagious or infectious disease. As the legislature has not denied to the children of any race or nationality the right to enter our public schools, the question whether it might have done so does not arise in this case.

We think the superintendent of schools was improperly joined as a defendant in this action, and that the court properly dismissed the action as to the board of education. In Ward v. Flood, 48 Cal. 36, the action was against the teacher alone. That it was properly brought, seems to have been conceded.

The board of education has power "to make, establish, and enforce all necessary and proper rules and regulations not contrary to law," and none other. (Stats. 1871-2, p. 846.) Teachers cannot justify a violation of law, on the ground that a resolution of the board of education required them to do so.

The judgment must be modified, so as to make the writ run against the defendant Hurley alone.

In other respects it is affirmed.

21

Letter from Mary Tape, April 8, 1885

Mary and Joseph Tape won the court battle to enroll their daughter, Mamie, in the public school system in San Francisco in 1885. But the school board had the law rewritten to expressly provide segregated schools for "Chinese or Mongolian" children and to prohibit their admission into "any other school." Mary Tape then penned this fierce response, which was printed on page one of the local paper. This version follows both the Alta and Judy Yung, who elected to reprint with imperfect English. Professor Yung wisely chose to do so to highlight the fact that Mary Tape was an extraordinary woman who defied convention to articulate her outrage at this blatantly discriminatory action. As Yung points out, the two Tape children, Mamie and Frank, were among the first to enter the newly established "Chinese Primary School" on April 13, 1885, despite the letter's emphatic protestations. Mamie Tape became a photographer, painter, and telegraph operator.

Alta, April 16, 1885, 1. As noted in Judy Yung, *Unbound Voices: A Documentary History of Chinese Women in San Francisco*. Berkeley: University of California Press, 1999, 171–75.

A Letter from Mrs. Tape

The following is a verbatim copy of a letter received from Mrs. Tape, in regard to her children at present attending the Chinese school:

1769 Green Street.
San Francisco, April 8, 1885.

To the Board of Education—Dear Sirs: I see that you are going to make all sorts of excuses to keep my child out off the Public schools. Dear sirs, Will you please to tell me! Is it a disgrace to be Born a Chinese? Didn't God make us all!!! What right have you to bar my children out of the school because she is a chinese Decend. They is no other worldly reason that you could keep her out, except that. I suppose, you all goes to churches on Sundays! Do you call that a Christian act to compell my little children to go so far to a school that is made in purpose for them. My children don't dress like the other Chinese. They look just as phunny amongst them as the Chinese dress in Chinese look amongst you Caucasians. Besides, if I had any wish to send them to a chinese school I could have sent them two years ago without going to all this trouble. You have expended a lot of the Public money foolishly, all because of a one poor little Child. Her playmates is all Caucasians ever since she could toddle around. If she is good enough to play with them! Then is she not good enough to be in the same room and studie with them? You had better come and see for yourselves. See if the Tape's is not same as other Caucasians, except in features. It seems no matter how a Chinese may live and dress so long as you know they Chinese. Then they are hated as one. There is not any right or justice for them.

You have seen my husband and child. You told him it wasn't Mamie Tape you object to. If it were not Mamie Tape you object to, then why didn't you let her attend the school nearest her home! Instead of first making one pretense Then another pretense of some kind to keep her out? It seems to me Mr. Moulder has a grudge against this Eight-year-old Mamie Tape. I know they is no other child I mean Chinese child! care to go to your public Chinese school. May you Mr. Moulder, never be persecuted like the way you have persecuted little Mamie Tape. Mamie Tape will never attend any of the Chinese schools of your making! Never!!! I will let the world see sir What justice there is When it is govern by the Race prejudice men! Just because she is of the Chinese decend, not because she don't dress like you because she does. Just because she is descended of Chinese parents I guess she is more of a American then a good many of you that is going to prewent her being Educated.

Mrs. M. Tape

22

Saum Song Bo Letter Protesting Fund Raising for
Statue of Liberty, October 1885

In 1882 the United States passed the Chinese Exclusion Act preventing all but a token few from entering the country. Three years later, the nation was preparing to install the Statue of Liberty as a symbol of American welcome for the "huddled masses" of the world. Fund-raising appeals went out to the general public to defray the cost of building the base for the enormous statue. But at least one Chinese, Saum Song Bo, was incensed that he and his countrymen would be solicited in the face of the racism they were confronting. And, of course, there was added insult since the statue was a gift from France, a country that, in the same year, had forced their homeland to give up Indochina to be absorbed into the French empire. It would not be until 1943 that a token 105 Chinese would be allowed to immigrate.

Thanks to Him Mark Lai, dean of Chinese American history, for generously suggesting this document for inclusion. *American Missionary*, October 1885. Reprinted in *East/West Chinese American Journal* (San Francisco), June 26, 1986.

Sir:

A paper was presented to me yesterday for inspection, and I found it to be specially drawn up for subscription among my countrymen toward the Pedestal Fund of the Bartholdi Statue of Liberty. Seeing that the heading is an appeal to American citizens, to their love of country and liberty, I feel that my countrymen and myself are honored in being thus appealed to as citizens in the cause of liberty. But the word liberty makes me think of the fact that this country is the land of liberty for men of all nations except the Chinese. I consider it as an insult to us Chinese to call on us to contribute toward building in this land a pedestal for a statue of Liberty. That statue represents Liberty holding a torch which lights the passage of those of all nations who come into this country. But are the Chinese allowed to come? As for the Chinese who are here, are they allowed to enjoy liberty as men of all other nationalities enjoy it? Are they allowed to go about everywhere free from the insults, abuses, assaults, wrongs, and injuries from which men of other nationalities are free?

If there be a Chinaman who came to this country when a lad, who has passed through an American institution of learning of the highest grade, who has so fallen in love with American manners and ideas that he desires to make his home in this land, and who, seeing that his countrymen demand one of their own number to be their legal adviser, representative, advocate, and protector, desires to study law, can he be a lawyer? By the law of this nation, he, being a Chinaman, cannot become a citizen, and consequently cannot be a lawyer.

And this statue of Liberty is a gift to a people from another people who do not love or value liberty for the Chinese. Are not the Annamese and Tonquinese Chinese, to whom liberty is as dear as to the French? What right have the French to deprive them of their liberty?

Whether this statute against the Chinese or the statue to Liberty will be the more lasting monument to tell future ages of the liberty and greatness of this country, will be known only to future generations.

Liberty, we Chinese do love and adore thee; but let not those who deny thee to us, make of thee a graven image and invite us to bow down to it.

Saum Song Bo

23

Supreme Court: Yick Wo v. Hopkins, May 10, 1886

This was a landmark case establishing that "facially neutral" legislation un-equally applied would be ruled unconstitutional—in conflict with equal protection language in the Fourteenth Amendment. The state of California was relying on a series of requirements for the establishment and operation of laundries to target the Chinese and drive them out of business and out of the country. This was but one in a long series of similar local and state laws. San Francisco's Board of Supervisors passed legislation in 1880 requiring licenses to operate laundries unless they were housed in buildings made of brick or stone. But all the white applicants (about 80) who had laundries made of wood were granted licenses while 200 Chinese were not. Since the Fourteenth Amendment, originally adopted to protect African Americans, protected all persons irrespective of race, color, or nationality, San Francisco's efforts to oppress the Chinese through arbitrary administration of its laws were deemed unconstitutional.

United States Reports, Volume 118, Cases Adjudged in The Supreme Court. New York and Albany: Banks & Brothers, 1886.

Yick Wo v. Hopkins, Sheriff

Error to the Supreme Court of the State of California

Wo Lee v. Hopkins, Sheriff

Appeal from the Circuit Court of the United States for the District of California

In a suit brought to this court from a State court which involves the constitutionality of ordinances made by a municipal corporation in the State, this court will, when necessary, put its own independent construction upon the ordinances.

A municipal ordinance to regulate the carrying on of public laundries within the limits of the municipality violates the provisions of the Constitution of the United

States, if it confers upon the municipal authorities arbitrary power, at their own will, and without regard to discretion in the legal sense of the term, to give or withhold consent as to persons or places, without regard to the competency of the persons applying, or the propriety of the place selected, for the carrying on of the business.

An administration of a municipal ordinance for the carrying on of a lawful business within the corporate limits violates the provisions of the Constitution of the United States, if it makes arbitrary and unjust discriminations, founded on differences of race, between persons otherwise in similar circumstances.

The guarantees of protection contained in the Fourteenth Amendment to the Constitution extend to all persons within the territorial jurisdiction of the United States, without regard to differencs of race, of color, or of nationality.

Those subjects of the Emperor of China who have the right to temporarily or permanently reside within the United States, are entitled to enjoy the protection guaranteed by the Constitution and afforded by the laws.

These two cases were argued as one and depended upon precisely the same state of facts. . . .

The plaintiff in error, Yick Wo, on August 24, 1885, petitioned the Supreme Court of California for a writ of *habeas corpus*, alleging that he was illegally deprived of his personal liberty by the defendant as sheriff of the city and county of San Francisco.

The sheriff made return to the writ that he held the petitioner in custody by virtue of a sentence of the Police Judges Court, No. 2, of the city and county of San Francisco, whereby he was found guilty of a violation of certain ordinances of the board of supervisors of that county, and adjudgcd to pay a fine of $10, and, in default of payment, be imprisoned in the county jail at the rate of one day for each dollar of fine until said fine should be satisfied, and a commitment in consequence of non-payment of said fine.

The ordinances for the violation of which he had been found guilty were set out as follows:

Order No. 1569, passed May 26, 1880, prescribing the kind of buildings in which laundries may be located. . . .

The following facts were also admitted on the record: That petitioner is a native of China and came to California in 1861, and is still a subject of the Emperor of China; that he has been engaged in the laundry business in the same premises and building for twenty-two years last past; that he had a license from the board of fire wardens, dated March 3, 1884, from which it appeared "that the above described premises have been inspected by the board of fire wardens, and upon such inspection said board found all proper arrangements for carrying on the business. . . ."

It was alleged in the petition, that "your petitioner and more than one hundred and fifty of his countrymen have been arrested upon the charge of carrying on business without having such special consent, which those who are not subjects of China, and who are conducting eighty odd laundries under similar conditions, are left unmolested and free to enjoy the enhanced trade and profits arising from this hurtful and unfair discrimination. The business of your petitioner, and of those of his countrymen similarly situated, is greatly impaired, and in many cases practically ruined by this system of oppression to one kind of men and favoritism to all others." . . .

The effect of the execution of this ordinance in the manner indicated in the record would seem to be necessarily to close up the many Chinese laundries now existing, or compel their owners to pull down their present buildings and reconstruct of brick or stone, or to drive them outside the city and county of San Francisco, to the adjoining counties, beyond the convenient reach of customers, either of which results would be little short of absolute confiscation of the large amount of property shown to be now, and to have been for a long time, invested in these occupations. If this would not be depriving such parties of their property without due proces of law, it would be difficult to say what would effect that prohibited result. The necessary tendency, if not the specific purpose, of this ordinance, and of enforcing it in the manner indicated in the record, is to drive out of business all the numerous small laundries, especially those owned by Chinese, and give a monopoly of the business to the large institutions established and carried on by means of large associated Caucasian capital. . . .

But, in deference to the decision of the Supreme Court of California in the case of Yick Wo, and contrary to his own opinion as thus expressed, the circuit judge discharged the writ and remanded the prisoner. . . .

Opinion of the Court

Mr. Justice Matthews delivered the opinion of the court.

In the case of the petitioner, brought here by writ of error to the Supreme Court of California, our jurisdiction is limited to the question, whether the plaintiff in error has been denied a right in violation of the Constitution, laws, or treaties of the United States. The question whether his imprisonment is illegal, under the constitution and laws of the State, is not open to us. And although that question might have been considered in the Circuit Court in the application made to it, and by this court on appeal from its order, yet judicial propriety is best consulted by accepting the judgment of the State court upon the points involved in that inquiry.

That, however, does not preclude this court from putting upon the ordinances of the supervisors of the county and city of San Francisco an independent construction; for the determination of the question whether the proceedings under these ordinances and in enforcement of them are in conflict with the Constitution and laws of the United States, necessarily involves the meaning of the ordinances, which, for that purpose, we are required to ascertain and adjudge.

We are consequently constrained, at the outset, to differ from the Supreme Court of California upon the real meaning of the ordinances in question. That court considered these ordinances as vesting in the board of supervisors a not unusual discretion in granting or withholding their assent to the use of wooden buildings as laundries, to be exercised in reference to the circumstances of each case, with a view to the protection of the public against the dangers of fire. We are not able to concur in that interpretation of the power conferred upon the supervisors. There is nothing in the ordinances which points to such a regulation of the business of keeping and conducting laundries. They seem intended to confer, and actually do confer, not a discretion to be exercised upon a consideration of the circumstances of each case, but a naked and arbitrary power to give or withhold consent, not only as to places, but as to persons. . . .

The ordinance drawn in question in the present case . . . does not prescribe a rule and conditions for the regulation of the use of property for laundry purposes, to which all similarly situated may conform. It allows without restriction the use for such purposes of buildings of brick or stone; but, as to wooden buildings, constituting nearly all those in previous use, it divides the owners or occupiers into two classes, not having respect to their personal character and qualifications for the business, nor the situation and nature and adaptation of the buildings themselves, but merely by an arbitrary line, on one side of which are those who are permitted to pursue their industry by the mere will and consent of the supervisors, and on the other those from whom that consent is withheld, at their mere will and pleasure. . . .

The rights of the petitioners, as affected by the proceedings of which they complain, are not less, because they are aliens and subjects of the Emperor of China. By the third article of the treaty between this Government and that of China, concluded November 17, 1880, 22 Stat. 827, it is stipulated: "If Chinese laborers, or Chinese of any other class, now either permanently or temporarily residing in the territory of the United States, meet with ill treatment at the hands of any other persons, the Government of the United States will exert all its powers to devise measures for their protection, and to secure to them the same rights, privileges, immunities and exemptions as may be enjoyed by the citizens or subjects of the most favored nation, and to which they are entitled by treaty."

The Fourteenth Amendment to the Constitution is not confined to the protection of citizens. It says: "Nor shall any State deprive any person of life, liberty, or property without due process of law; nor deny to any person within its jurisdiction the equal protection of the laws." These provisions are universal in their application, to all persons within the territorial jurisdiction, wihtout regard to any differences of race, of color, or of nationality; and the equal protection of the laws is a pledge of the protection of equal laws. . . .

In the present cases we are not obliged to reason from the probable to the actual, and pass upon the validity of the ordinances complained of, as tried merely by the opportunities which their terms afford, of unequal and unjust discrimination in their administration. For the cases present the ordinances in actual operation, and the facts shown establish an administration directed so exclusively against a particular class of persons as to warrant and require the conclusion, that, whatever may have been the intent of the ordinances as adopted, they are applied by the public authorities charged with their administration, and thus representing the State itself, with a mind so unequal and oppressive as to amount to a practical denial by the State of that equal protection of the laws which is secured to the petitioners, as to all other persons, by the broad and benign provisions of the Fourteenth Amendment ot the Constitution of the United States. Though the law itself be fair on its face and impartial in appearance, yet, if it is applied and administered by public authority with an evil eye and an unequal hand, so as practically to make unjust and illegal discriminations between persons in similar circumstances, material to their rights, the denial of equal justice is still within the prohibition of the Constitution. . . . The fact of this discrimination is admitted. No reason for it is shown, and the conclusion cannot be resisted, that no reason for it exists except hostility to the race and nationality to which the petitioners belong, and which in the eye of the law is not justified. The discrimination is, therefore, illegal, and the public administration which enforces it is a denial of the equal protection of the laws and a violation of the Fourteenth Amendment of the Constitution. The imprisonment of the petitioners is, therefore, illegal, and they must be discharged.

24

Hawai'i Constitution (a.k.a. Bayonet Constitution), 1887

Called the "Bayonet Constitution" because it was forcibly imposed on Hawaii's King Kalakaua, this document enshrined the fundamental shift in economic and political power from the native monarchy to the American business oligarchy. One of the key requirements for retaining power was control of the legislative bodies and the voters who elected them. This constitution limited the franchise to male residents of Hawaiian, American, or European birth. To be eligible to vote, these men had to have paid taxes, and, if younger than 47, be able to read Hawaiian, English, or some European language. The immediate consequence of this constitution, which drastically reduced the power of the native monarchy, was to render immigrants from Asia ineligible to vote. Some Chinese had been imported as laborers beginning in the 1850s, but the primary target in this instance was the growing number of workers from Japan, arriving since 1885. The 1887 constitution may be seen, therefore, as a preemptive strike to keep the Japanese from the polls while Americans and Europeans, equally foreign in the Hawaiian Kingdom, could vote for and become legislators.

U.S. Senate, 55th Cong., 2nd Sess. Senate Document No. 109. Printed in Congressional Serial Set, vol. 3593.

Constitution of 1887

Whereas the constitution of this Kingdom heretofore in force contains many provisions subversive of civil rights and incompatible with enlightened constitutional government;

And whereas it has become imperative, in order to restore order and tranquility and the confidence necessary to a further maintenance of the present Government, that a new constitution should be at once promulgated:

Now, therefore, I, Kalakaua, King of the Hawaiian Islands, in my capacity as sovereign of this Kingdom, and as the representative of the people hereunto by them duly authorized and empowered, do annul and abrogate the constitution promulgated by Kamehameha the Fifth, on the 20th day of August, A. D. 1864, and do proclaim and promulgate this constitution.

Article 1. God hath endowed all men with certain inalienable rights, among which are life, liberty, and the right of acquiring, possessing, and protecting property, and of pursuing and obtaining safety and happiness. . . .

Article 41. The cabinet shall consist of the minister of foreign affairs, the minister of the interior, the minister of finance, and the attorney-general, and they shall be His Majesty's special advisers in the executive affairs of the Kingdom, and they shall be *ex officio* members of His Majesty's privy council of state. They shall be appointed and commissioned by the King, and shall be removed by him only upon a vote of want of confidence passed by a majority of all of the elective members of the Legislature, or upon conviction of felony, and shall be subject to impeachment. No act of the King shall have any effect unless it be countersigned by a member of the cabinet, who, by that signature, makes himself responsible. . . .

Article 48. Every bill which shall have passed the Legislature shall, before it becomes law, be presented to the King. If he approve, he shall sign it and it shall thereby become a law, but if not, he shall return it, with his objections, to the Legislature, which shall enter the objections at large on their journal and proceed to reconsider it. If after such reconsideration it shall be approved by a two-thirds vote of all the elective members of the Legislature, it shall become a law. In all such cases the vote shall be determined by yeas and nays, and the names of the persons voting for and against the bill shall be entered on the journal of the Legislature. If any bill shall not be returned by the King within ten days (Sunday excepted) after it shall have been presented to him, the same shall be a law in like manner as if he had signed it, unless the Legislature by their adjournment prevent its return, in which case it shall not be a law. . . .

Article 59. Every male resident of the Hawaiian Islands of Hawaiian, American, or European birth or descent, who shall have attained the age of twenty years, and shall have paid his taxes, and shall have caused his name to be entered on the list of voters for nobles for his district, shall be an elector of nobles and shall be entitled to vote at any election of nobles; provided,

First. That he shall have resided in the country not less than three years and in the district in which he offers to vote not less than three months immediately preceding the election at which he offers to vote.

Second. That he shall own and be possessed in his own right of taxable property in this country of the value of not less than three thousand dollars over and above all incumbrances, or shall have actually received an income of not less than six hundred dollars during the year next preceding his registration for such election.

Third. That he shall be able to read and comprehend an ordinary newspaper printed in either the Hawaiian, English, or some European language.

Fourth. That he shall have taken an oath to support the constitution and laws, such oath to be administered by any person authorized to administer oaths or by any inspector of elections.

Provided, however, that the requirements of a three years' residence and of ability to read and comprehend an ordinary newspaper printed either in the Hawaiian, English, or some European language shall not apply to persons residing in the Kingdom at the time of the promulgation of this constitution, if they shall register and vote at the first election which shall be held under this constitution. . . .

Article 62. Every male resident of the Kingdom, of Hawaiian, American, or European birth or descent, who shall have taken an oath to support the constitution and laws in the manner provided for electors of nobles, who shall have paid his taxes, who shall have attained the age of twenty years, and shall have been domiciled in the Kingdom for one year immediately preceding the election, and shall know how to read and write either the Hawaiian, English, or some European language (if born since the year 1840), and shall have caused his name to be entered on the list of voters of his district as may be provided by law, shall be entitled to one vote for the representative or representatives of that district: *Provided, however,* That the requirements of being domiciled in the Kingdom for one year immediately preceding the election, and of knowing how to read and write either the Hawaiian, English, or some European language, shall not apply to persons residing in this Kingdom at the time of the promulgation of this constitution if they shall register and vote at the first election which shall be held under this constitution. . . .

25

An Act to Prohibit the Coming of Chinese Laborers to the United States (a.k.a. Scott Act), September 13, 1888

Soon after the passage of the 1882 act preventing Chinese laborers from immigrating, Representative William Scott introduced legislation to prevent the reentry of those Chinese who had temporarily returned to their homeland. It was inspired by competition between Republicans and Democrats in a presidential election year—appealing to rising anti-Chinese sentiment, especially in the western states. The act itself was based on attempts by the United States to alter the 1868 Burlingame-Seward Treaty in order to end Chinese immigration. In the process, thousands of laborers who had complied with regulations to secure certificates allowing them to reenter the country found those guarantees worthless and were forced back to China. The U.S. Supreme Court found the Scott Act constitutional the next year.

The Statutes at Large of the United States of America, vol. 25. Washington, DC: Government Printing Office, 1889.

Chap. 1015—An act to prohibit the coming of Chinese laborers to the United States

Be it enacted by the Senate and House of Representatives of the United States of America in Congress assembled, That from and after the date of the exchange of ratifications of the pending treaty between the United States of America and His Imperial Majesty the Emperor of China, signed on the twelfth day of March, anno Domini eighteen hundred and eighty-eight, it shall be unlawful for any Chinese person, whether a subject of China or of any other power, to enter the United States, except as hereinafter provided.

Sec. 2. That Chinese officials, teachers, students, merchants, or travelers for pleasure or curiosity, shall be permitted to enter the United States, but in order to entitle themselves to do so, they shall first obtain the permission of the Chinese Government, or other Government of which they may at the time be citizens or subjects. . . .

Sec. 3. That the provisions of this act shall apply to all persons of the Chinese race, whether subjects of China or other foreign power, excepting Chinese diplomatic or consular officers and their attendants; and the words "Chinese laborers," whenever used in this act, shall be construed to mean both skilled and unskilled laborers and Chinese employed in mining. . . .

Sec. 5. That from and after the passage of this act, no Chinese laborer in the United States shall be permitted, after having left, to return thereto, except under the conditions stated in the following sections.

Sec. 6. That no Chinese laborer within the purview of the preceding section shall be permitted to return to the United States unless he has a lawful wife, child, or parent in the United States, or property therein of the value of one thousand dollars, or debts of like amount due him and pending settlement. The marriage to such wife must have taken place at least a year prior to the application of the laborer for a permit to return to the Untied States, and must have been followed by the continuous cohabitation of the parties as man and wife.

If the right to return be claimed on the ground of property or of debts, it must appear that the property is bona fide and not colorably acquired for the purpose of evading this act, or that the debts are unascertained and unsettled, and not promissory notes or other similar acknowledgments of ascertained liability.

Sec. 7. That a Chinese person claiming the right to be permitted to leave the United States and return thereto on any of the grounds stated in the foregoing section, shall apply to the collector of customs of the district from which he wishes to depart at least a month prior to the time of his departure, and shall make on oath before the said collector a full statement descriptive of his family, or property, or debts, as the case may be, and shall furnish to said collector such proofs of the facts entitling him to return as shall be required by the rules and regulations prescribed from time to time by the Secretary of the Treasury, and for any false swearing in relation thereto he shall incur the penalties of perjury. . . .

Approved, September 13, 1888

26

Supreme Court: Chae Chan Ping v. United States, *May 13, 1889*

This was a direct challenge to the Scott Act of 1888, which denied reentry into the United States for thousands of Chinese who had complied with earlier regulations to obtain certificates guaranteeing readmission. Chae Chan Ping lived in California for twelve years, from 1875 to 1887, then left for a visit to China. Upon his return, certificate in hand, he demanded permission to land, but the Scott Act had been passed just one week before, and port officials declared his certificate annulled and his right to land abrogated. He argued that his expulsion violated earlier treaties between China and the United States, but the court found that, in spite of such violations, Congress was the final arbiter controlling the nation's borders, which it may do in the face of existing treaties.

United States Reports, Volume 130, *Cases Adjudged in The Supreme Court*. New York and Albany: Banks & Brothers, 1889.

The Chinese Exclusion Case
Chae Chan Ping v. United States

The court stated the case as follows in its opinion:

This case comes before us on appeal from an order of the Circuit Court of the United States for the Northern District of California refusing to release the appellant, on a writ of *habeas corpus*, from his alleged unlawful detention by Captain Walker, master of the steamship Belgic, lying within the harbor of San Francisco. The appellant is a subject of the Emperor of China and a laborer by occupation. He resided at San Francisco, California, following his occupation, from some time in 1875 until June 2, 1887, when he left for China on the steamship Gaelic, having in his possession a certificate, in terms entitling him to return to the United States, bearing date on that day, duly issued to him by the collector of customs of the port of San Francisco, pursuant to the provisions of section four of the restriction act of May 6, 1882, as amended by the act of July 5, 1884. 22 Stat. 58, c. 126; 23 Stat. 115, c. 220.

On the 7th of September, 1888, the appellant, on his return to California, sailed from Hong Kong in the steamship Belgic, which arrived within the port of San Francisco on the 8th of October following. On his arrival he presented to the proper custom-house officers his certificate, and demanded permission to land. The collector of the port refused the permit, solely on the ground that under the act of Congress, approved October 1, 1888, supplementary to the restriction acts of 1882 and 1884, the certificate had been annulled and his right to land abrogated, and he had been thereby forbidden again to enter the United States. 25 Stat. 504, c. 1064. The captain of the steamship, therefore, detained the appellant on board the steamer. Thereupon a petition on his behalf was presented to the Circuit Court of the United States for the Northern District of California, alleging that he was unlawfully restrained of his liberty, and praying that a writ of *habeas corpus* might be issued directed to the master of the steamship, commanding him to have the body of the appellant, with the cause of his detention, before the court at a time and place designated, to do and receive what might there be considered in the premises. A writ was accordingly issued, and in obedience to it the body of the appellant was produced before the court. Upon the hearing which followed, the court, after finding the facts substantially as stated, held as conclusions of law that the appellant was not entitled to enter the United States, and was not unlawfully restrained of his liberty, and ordered that he be remanded to the custody of the master of the steamship from which he had been taken under the writ. From this order an appeal was taken to this court. . . .

Mr. Justice Field delivered the opinion of the court.

The appeal involves a consideration of the validity of the act of Congress of October 1, 1888, prohibiting Chinese laborers from entering the United States who had departed before its passage, having a certificate issued under the act of 1882 as amended by the act of 1884, granting them permission to return. The validity of the act is assailed as being in effect an expulsion from the country of Chinese laborers, in violation of existing treaties between the United States and the government of China, and of rights vested in them under the laws of Congress. . . .

The objection that the act is in conflict with the treaties was earnestly pressed in the court below, and the answer to it constitutes the principal part of its opinion. 36 Fed. Rep. 431. Here the objection made is, that the act of 1888 impairs a right vested under the treaty of 1880, as a law of the United States, and the statutes of 1882 and of 1884 passed in execution of it. It must be conceded that the act of 1888 is in contravention of express stipulations of the treaty of 1868 and of the supplemental treaty of 1880, but it is not on that account invalid or to be restricted in its enforcement. The treaties were of no greater legal obligation than the act of Congress. By the Constitution, laws made in pursuance thereof and treaties made under the authority of the United States are both declared to be the supreme law of the land, and no paramount authority is given to one over the other. A treaty, it is true, is in its nature a contract between nations and is often merely promissory in its character, requiring legislation to carry its stipulations into effect. Such legislation will be open to future repeal or amendment. If the treaty operates by its own force, and relates to a subject within the power of Congress, it can be deemed in that particular only the equivalent of a legislative act, to be repealed or modified at the pleasure of Congress. In either case the last expression of the sovereign will must control. . . .

27

An Act to Prohibit the Coming of Chinese Persons Into the United States (a.k.a. Geary Act), May 5, 1892

California Congressman Thomas Geary introduced this act, another link in the chain of anti-Chinese legislation. It extended all appropriate legislation, including the 1882 Exclusion Act, for another ten years and required all Chinese to acquire certificates of eligibility within one year. Individuals found without certificates were adjudged "to be unlawfully within the United States unless such person shall establish, by affirmative proof, to the satisfaction of such justice, judge, or commissioner, his lawful right to remain in the United States." In 1902, the prohibition was made permanent. It was repealed in 1943 with a token quota of 105 Chinese immigrants per year.

The Statutes at Large of the United States of America, vol. 27. Washington, DC: Government Printing Office, 1893.

Chap. 60.—An act to prohibit the coming of Chinese persons into the United States

Be it enacted by the Senate and House of Representatives of the United States of America in Congress assembled, That all laws now in force prohibiting and regulating the coming into this country of Chinese persons and persons of Chinese descent are hereby continued in force for a period of ten years from the passage of this act.

Sec. 2. That any Chinese person or person of Chinese descent, when convicted and adjudged under any of said laws to be not lawfully entitled to be or remain in the United States, shall be removed from the United States to China, unless he or they shall make it appear to the justice, judge, or commissioner before whom he or they are tried that he or they are subjects or citizens of some other country, in which case he or they shall be removed from the United States to such country: *Provided*, That in any case where such other country of which such Chinese person shall claim to be a citizen or subject shall demand any tax as a condition of the removal of such person to that country, he or she shall be removed to China. . . .

Sec. 6. And it shall be the duty of all Chinese laborers within the limits of the United States, at the time of the passage of this act, and who are entitled to remain in the United States, to apply to the collector of internal revenue of their respective districts, within one year after the passage of this act, for a certificate of residence, and any Chinese laborer, within the limits of the United States, who shall neglect, fail, or refuse to comply with the provisions of this act, or who, after one year from the passage hereof, shall be found within the jurisdiction of the United States without such certificate of residence, shall be deemed and adjudged to be unlawfully within the United States, and may be arrested, by any United States customs official, collector of internal revenue or his deputies, United States marshal or his deputies, and taken before a United States judge, whose duty it shall be to order that he be deported from the United States as hereinbefore provided, unless he shall establish clearly to the satisfaction of said judge, that by reason of accident, sickness or other unavoidable cause, he has been unable to procure his certificate, and to the satisfaction of the court, and by at least one credible white witness, that he was a resident of the United States at the time of the passage of this act; and if upon the hearing, it shall appear that he is so entitled to a certificate, it shall be granted upon his paying the cost. Should it appear that said Chinaman had procured a certificate which has been lost or destroyed, he shall be detained and judgment suspended a reasonable time to enable him to procure a duplicate from the officer granting it, and in such cases, the cost of said arrest and trial shall be in the discretion of the court. And any Chinese person other than a Chinese laborer, having a right to be and remain in the United States, desiring such certificate as evidence of such right may apply for and receive the same without charge. . . .

Approved, May 5, 1892.

28

Supreme Court: Nishimura Ekiu v. United States, *January 18, 1892*

This first Supreme Court case involving someone from Japan established the authority of immigration inspectors to refuse entry, without judicial review, to those seeking it. Nishimura arrived in San Francisco in May 1891 insisting that she had been married for two years but did not know her husband's address and was scheduled to stay at a hotel until he came to meet her. As a matter of immigration history, this was not an unusual arrangement, since so many Japanese men were migrant workers. Using the 1891 statutes that justified exclusion of anyone "liable to become a public charge," the inspector refused to admit her into the country. She argued that allowing an administrative officer to have final authority in her case deprived her of personal liberty without due process. The Supreme Court ruled against her.

United States Reports, Volume 142. Cases Adjudged in The Supreme Court. New York
   and Albany: Banks & Brothers, 1892.

Nishimura Ekiu v. United States

Statement of the Case

Habeas corpus, sued out May 13, 1891, by a female subject of the Emperor of Japan, restrained of her liberty and detained at San Francisco upon the ground that she should not be permitted to land in the United States. The case, as appearing by the papers filed, and by the report of a commissioner of the Circuit Court, to whom the case was referred by that court "to find the facts and his conclusions of law, and to report a judgment therein," and by the admissions of counsel at the argument in this court, was as follows:

The petitioner arrived at the port of San Francisco on the steamship Belgic from Yokohama, Japan, on May 7, 1891. William H. Thornley, commissioner of immigration of the State of California, and claiming to act under instructions from and contract with the Secretary of the Treasury of the United States, refused to allow her to land. . . . "Passport states that she comes to San Francisco in company with her husband, which is not a fact. She states that she has been married two years, and that her husband has been in the United States one year, but she does not know his address. She has $22, and is to stop at some hotel until her husband calls for her."

With this report Thornley sent a letter to the collector, stating that after a careful examination of the alien immigrants on board the Belgic he was satisfied that the petitioner and five others were "prohibited from landing by the existing immigration laws," for reasons specifically stated with regard to each; and that, pending the collector's final decision as to their right to land, he had "placed them temporarily in the Methodist Chinese Mission, as the steamer was not a proper place to detain them, until the date of sailing." . . .

Opinion of the Court

Mr. Justice Gray, after stating the case as above, delivered the opinion of the court. . . .

It is an accepted maxim of international law, that every sovereign nation has the power, as inherent in sovereignty, and essential to self-preservation, to forbid the entrance of foreigners within its dominions, or to admit them only in such cases and upon such conditions as it may see fit to prescribe. . . .

An alien immigrant, prevented from landing by any such officer claiming authority to do so under an act of Congress, and thereby restrained of his liberty, is doubtless entitled to a writ of *habeas corpus* to ascertain whether the restraint is lawful. . . . But, on the other hand, the final determination of those facts may be entrusted by Congress to executive officers; and in such a case, as in all others, in which a statute gives a discretionary power to an officer, to be exercised by him upon his own opinion of certain facts, he is made the sole and exclusive judge of the existence of those facts, and no other tribunal, unless expressly authorized by law to do so, is at liberty to reëxamine or controvert the sufficiency of the evidence on which he acted. . . .

The decision of the inspector of immigration being in conformity with the act of 1891, there can be no doubt that it was final and conclusive against the petitioner's right to land in the United States. The words of section 8 are clear to that effect, and were manifestly intended to prevent the question of an alien immigrant's right to land, when once decided adversely by an inspector, acting within the jurisdiction conferred upon him, from being impeached or reviewed, in the courts or otherwise, save only by appeal to the inspector's official superiors, and in accordance with the provisions of the act. . . .

The result is, that the act of 1891 is constitutional and valid; the inspector of immigration was duly appointed; his decision against the petitioner's right to land in the United States was within the authority conferred upon him by that act; no appeal having been taken to the superintendent of immigration; that decision was final and conclusive; the petitioner is not unlawfully restrained of her liberty, and the *Order of the Circuit Court is affirmed.*

29

Supreme Court: Fong Yue Ting v. United States, Wong Quan v. Same, Lee Joe v. Same, *May 15, 1893*

This ruling validated the 1892 Geary Act mandating the possession of certificates by Chinese in the United States. The case is usually known only by the name of the first of the three men, but all are here listed. The majority determined that Congress rightfully had the power to exclude aliens from the United States and to restrict the rights of those already here. Two justices, Brewer and Fuller, wrote important dissents insisting that exclusion and expulsion were entirely different — and that resident aliens, these Chinese having been here since 1874, 1877, and 1879, were entitled to due process protection under the Fifth Amendment. Substantial sections of these dissenting opinions are included because they transcend the narrow bias of the court and its historic context. It should be noted that, in this as in so many other critical cases, there was immediate and sophisticated legal challenge on the part of the Chinese or Asian community against discriminatory acts.

United States Reports, Volume 149. Cases Adjudged in The Supreme Court. New York and Albany: Banks & Brothers, 1893.

Fong Yue Ting v. United States
Wong Quan v. United States
Lee Joe v. United States
149 U.S. 698

Mr. Justice Gray, after stating the facts, delivered the opinion of the court.

The general principles of public law which lie at the foundation of these cases are clearly established by previous judgments of this court, and by the authorities therein referred to. . . .

In the elaborate opinion delivered by Mr. Justice Field [in Chae Chan Ping v. United States, 130 U.S. 581], in behalf of the court, it was said: "Those laborers are not citizens of the United States; they are aliens. That the government of the United States, through the action of the legislative department, can exclude aliens from its territory is a proposition which we do not think open to contro-versy. Jurisdiction over its own territory to that extent is an incident of every in-dependent nation." . . .

Upon careful consideration of the subject, the only conclusion which ap-pears to us to be consistent with the principles of international law, with the Constitution and laws of the United States, and with the previous decisions of this court, is that in each of these cases the judgment of the Circuit Court, dis-missing the writ of *habeas corpus*, is right and must be *Affirmed*.

Mr. Justice Brewer, dissenting.

I dissent from the opinion and judgment of the court in these cases, and, the questions being of importance, I deem it not improper to briefly state my rea-sons therefor.

I rest my dissent on three propositions: First, that the persons against whom the penalties of section 6 of the act of 1892 are directed are persons lawfully re-siding within the United States; secondly, that as such they are within the pro-tection of the Constitution, and secured by its guaranties against oppression and wrong; and, third, that section 6 deprives them of liberty, and imposes punishment, without due process of law, and in disregard of constitutional guaranties, especially those found in the 4th, 5th, 6th, and 8th articles of the amendments. . . .

But, further, this section 6 recognizes the fact of a lawful residence, and only applies to those who have such; for the parties named in the section, and to be reached by its provisions, are "Chinese laborers within the limits of the United States at the time of the passage of this act, and who are entitled to remain in the United States." These appellants, therefore, are lawfully within the United States, and are here as residents, and not as travelers. They have lived in this country, respectively, since 1879, 1877, and 1874,—almost as long a time as some of those who were members of the Congress that passed this act of punishment and expulsion.

That those who have become domiciled in a country are entitled to a more distinct and larger measure of protection than those who are simply passing through, or temporarily in, it, has long been recognized by the law of nations. It was said by this court in the case of The Venus, 8 Cranch, 253, 278: "The writ-ers upon the law of nations distinguish between a temporary residence in a for-eign country, for a special purpose, and a residence accompanied with an in-tention to make it a permanent place of abode." . . . The rule is thus laid down by Sir Robert Phillimore: "There is a class of persons which cannot be, strictly speaking, included in either of these denominations of naturalized or native cit-izens, namely, the class of those who have ceased to reside in their native coun-try, and have taken up a permanent abode in another. These are domiciled in-habitants. They have not put on a new citizenship through some formal mode enjoined by the law or the new country. They are de facto, though not de jure, citizens of the country of their domicile." . . .

It is said that the power here asserted is inherent in sovereignty. This doctrine of powers inherent in sovereignty is one both indefinite and dangerous. Where are the limits to such powers to be found, and by whom are they to be pronounced? Is it within legislative capacity to declare the limits? If so, then the mere assertion of an inherent power creates it, and despotism exists. May the courts establish the boundaries? Whence do they obtain the authority for this? Shall they look [sic] to the practices of other nations to ascertain the limits? The governments of other nations have elastic powers. Ours are fixed and bounded by a written constitution. The expulsion of a race may be within the inherent powers of a despotism. History, before the adoption of this constitution, was not destitute of examples of the exercise of such a power; and its framers were familiar with history, and wisely, and it seems to me, they gave to this government no general power to banish. Banishment may be resorted to as punishment for crime, but among the powers reserved to the people, and not delegated to the government, is that of determining whether whole classes in our midst shall, for no crime but that of their race and birthplace, be driven from our territory. . . .

It is true this statute is directed only against the obnoxious Chinese, but, if the power exists, who shall say it will not be exercised to-morrow against other classes and other people? If the guaranties of these amendments can be thus ignored in order to get rid of this distasteful class, what security have others that a like disregard of its provisions may not be resorted to? Profound and wise were the observations of Mr. Justice Bradley, speaking for the court in Boyd v. U.S., 116 U.S. 616, 635, 6 Sup. Ct. Rep. 535: "Illegitimate and unconstitutional practices get their first footing in that way, namely, by silent approaches, and slight deviations from legal modes of procedure. This can only be obviated by adhering to the rule that constitutional provisions for the security of person and property should be liberally construed. A close and literal construction deprives them of half their efficacy, and leads to gradual depreciation of the right, as if it consisted more in sound than in substance. It is the duty of the courts to be watchful for the constitutional rights of the citizen, and against any stealthy encroachments thereon. . . .

In the Yick Wo Case, in which was presented a municipal ordinance fair on its face, but contrived to work oppression to a few engaged in a single occupation, this court saw no difficulty in finding a constitutional barrier to such injustice. But this greater wrong, by which a hundred thousand people are subject to arrest and forcible deportation from the country, is beyond the reach of the protecting power of the Constitution. . . .

Mr. Chief Justice Fuller, dissenting.

I also dissent from the opinion and judgment of the court in these cases.

The argument is that friendly aliens, who have lawfully acquired a domicile in this country, are entitled to avail themselves of the safeguards of the constitution only while permitted to remain, and that the power to expel them, and the manner of its exercise, are unaffected by that instrument. It is difficult to see how this can be so, in view of the operation of the power upon the exising rights of individuals; and to say that the residence of the alien, when invited and se-cured by treaties and laws, is held in subordination to the exertion against him, as an alien, of the absolute and unqualified power asserted, is to import a con-dition not recognized by the fundamental law. Conceding that the exercise of the power to exclude is committed to the political department, and that the de-nial of entrance is not necessarily the subject of judicial cognizance, the exer-cise of the power to expel, the manner in which the right to remain may be ter-minated, rests on different ground, since limitations exist or are imposed upon the deprivation of that which has been lawfully acquired. And while the gener-al government is invested, in respect of foreign countries and their subjects or citizens, with the powers necessary to the maintenance of its absolute inde-pendence and security throughout its entire territory, it cannot, in virtue of any delegated power, or power implied therefrom, of a supposed inherent sover-eignty, arbitrarily deal with persons lawfully within the peace of its dominion. But the act before us is not an act to abrogate or repeal treaties or laws in respect of Chinese laborers entitled to remain in the United States, or to expel them from the country, and no such intent can be imputed to congress. As to them, registration for the purpose of identification is required, and the deportation de-nounced for failure to do so is by way of punishment to coerce compliance with that requisition. No euphuism can disguise the character of the act in this re-gard. It directs the performance of a judicial function in a particular way, and inflicts punishment without a judicial trial. It is, in effect, a legislative sentence of banishment, and, as such, absolutely void. Moreover, it contains within it the germs of the assertion of an unlimited and arbitrary power, in general, incom-patible with the immutable principles of justice, inconsistent with the nature of our government, and in conflict with the written constitution by which that gov-ernment was created, and those principles secured.

Dr. Harvey Saburo Hayashi Admonition to Japanese Immigrants, 1893

Saburo Hayashi was born into a prominent samurai family from the Aizu-Wakamatsu clan, defeated in battle by forces that formed the new Meiji government in Japan in 1868. His family went through terrible struggles, but the young Saburo received medical training and went to California in 1885; he eventually received a medical degree in San Francisco. One of his professors dubbed him "Harvey" after the great British physiologist, William Harvey. Hayashi practiced medicine in California but was greatly discouraged by the rampant racism directed against Asians at the time. He went to Hawai'i in 1892 and worked in Kona on the island of Hawai'i until his death in 1943. Hayashi was noted as an uncompromising disciplinarian with a generous soul. He quickly assumed leadership of the Japanese immigrant community and founded the Kona Hankyo (*Kona Echo*) *in 1897, the second Japanese language newspaper to circulate in the islands. In his diary entries for 1893, this essay warned his countrymen that the anti-Chinese hostility that had spawned the 1882 Exclusion Act in Congress would certainly be reincarnated as anti-Japanese hatred unless they changed their ways. Of course, this was a version of blaming the victim, but Hayashi makes clear the brutal and brutish conditions in which these Asian immigrants lived.*

Translated by Jiro Nakano, M.D., in Jiro Nakano, *Kona Echo: A Biography of Dr. Harvey Saburo Hayashi.* Kona, HI: Kona Historical Society, 1990. Reprinted with permission.

My Advice to the Japanese Immigrant Laborers by the Feared
(H. S. Hayashi, M.D.)

Since my birth, I have never written a decent composition of useful discourse. I am not a learned man but will be able to make a judgment by inborn common sense that leads me to good deeds and not intentionally evil conduct. I love my country, Japan, and my countrymen. Hence, with some critique, I attempted to write this composition with a certain anxiety.

America is a general term for the two continents, North America and South America. North America consists of Canada, the United States, Mexico and other Central America countries. The America to which you plan to emigrate is the United States of America. The U.S.A. is a vast country and 30 times as big as Japan. The State of California alone, where San Francisco is located, is almost as big as Japan.

The U.S.A. is a new country which was discovered only 400 years ago. Its population is now 65 millions, so there is an ample space even if 100 millions more people would come to this country. There are many mines where gold and silver are mined and large amounts of minerals are being refined every year. Furthermore, the earth is fertile, and grains, fruits, vegetables, timber and others grow abundantly all over the country. The export of canned fruits and flour amount to large sums of money. There are numerous cattle ranches and abundant fish here. Thus, the U.S.A. is a very rich country.

There is a great demand for laborers in this country and their wages are very high. As a result, every year, a large number of foreigners come to this country; poor aliens keep coming to seek labors here. The steady increase of these uncivilized aliens has caused a corruption of public morals and the outbreak of dreadful diseases (leprosy, tuberculosis, etc.). Furthermore, low paid laborers might disturb the labor situation. The American Government fears that even this most civilized country may become barbaric, and even the rich laborers may become indigent someday. This indiscriminate importation of foreigners would not benefit American citizens. Therefore, the Immigration Law was enacted to examine any potential immigrants and to prevent their easy entry to this country. In particular, the strict Immigration Law prevents entry to this country of Chinese.

It is a very regretable reality. There are several reasons that they hate Chinese in this country: 1) They are a different race from the Caucasian. 2) There are millions of Chinese trying to emigrate to the U.S.A. 3) They bring and maintain their unique customs, and form Chinatowns in the city. They will not change their clothing and life style, and use only tools made in China. They smoke opium, worship the idols and practice gambling, thus, disturbing the American moral life. 4) The Chinese laborers willingly work at much lower wage than most Americans. Thus, most industrialists would like to hire Chinese for farms, ranches, railroad, restaurants and houses.

Because of the entry of the Chinese laborers in the U.S.A., poor Americans suffered from low wages and unemployment, especially in California. These Americans have complained of the Chinese immigrants to the state and to federal legislators. As a result, several years ago the Scott Amendment of the Immigration Law was enacted. In spite of this restriction, numerous Chinese still enter illegally via Canada and Mexico. . . .

It is cruel and unjustified to pass this legal racial discrimination against Chinese. Naturally, it has infuriated Chinese, but, although I regret this law, the Chinese also should bear some responsibility. This is not my prejudice against Chinese.

Lately, like the Chinese, Japanese are hated and mistreated by Americans, and are about to be forbidden entry into the U.S.A. In other words, Japanese are also suffering from racial discrimination. Until recently, most Japanese in the U.S.A have been students who have had good reputations and have received good treatment, with the exception of a few incidents. This limited discrimination did not affect Japanese in general. However, it has become progressively worse. One reason was the influx of Japanese prostitutes in the Western States. Specifically in Seattle and San Francisco, Japanese communities were dishonored by this immoral phenomenon. In addition, since last year, a large number of uneducated Japanese immigrant laborers continuously came to Hawaii and disturbed the Judeo-Christian morality in this country. Because they worked for very cheap wages like the Chinese, Japanese laborers are also hated by the Americans. Many U.S. newspapers have editorialized forbidding future Japanese immigration and expelling those already in this country. It has been rumored that the Japanese Expulsion bill will be presented to the Congress next year. I also believe such a law will be ratified in the near future.

Ah, my dear countrymen! How do we deal with such law if Japanese are refused entry into this country? Should we remain silent and do nothing? Should we send our battleships to have a forceful diplomatic negotiation? I am certain that the Japanese battleship will not stop the passing of such an immigration law. Once enacted, the U.S. Congress would never retract such a law because of the strong public opinion against the Orientals. How should we deal with this problem? I believe the best way to confront this is to prevent the passing of the law by analyzing the reasons why the Americans detest the immigration of orientals in this country.

As stated about Chinese, (1) Japanese have disturbed the morality and customs of this country; (2) they work with very cheap wages, sometimes, their wages are lower than Chinese; (3) most Japanese immigrants have no money, and are poorly clothed, unsanitary and barbaric upon entry to the U.S.A. Many immigrants were sent back to Japan because of poor health reasons.

You may not understand what I mean by barbaric. In Hawaii, Japanese are always compared with Hawaiians and Chinese. The clothes of Japanese immigrants may be as dirty and shabby as those of the Chinese and Hawaiians. Even if Japanese were to walk on the Honolulu streets in kimono without shoes and hats, no one asserts that it would destroy the custom and morals of the society here. No one would criticize women who smoke and drink alcoholic beverages or those who walk naked or urinate on the street because they are in Hawaii. In contrast, things are different in California where citizens resent these careless habits and customs of Japanese.

Furthermore, one of the major causes of the hatred toward Japanese is the fact that they work with lower wages than Chinese. Most Chinese never work with their wages lower than one dollar a day. In contrast, Japanese even work for 25 cents a day if they can not find a decent job. This has resulted in the opinion among employers that they need not pay high wages to Japanese laborers. Of course, the wage depends upon the individual and one may work for low wages if he wishes. But this benefits neither Japanese nor Americans. Most Americans' minimum wage is $1.50 a day and they will never work for lower wages than this. In contrast, Japanese who work for very low wages are hired by employers, resulting in fewer jobs for Americans. They deem that Japanese rob them of their jobs. I believe that Japanese should maintain a reasonable wage scale in order to avoid racial discrimination by the general public.

My next warning concerns the sanitary conditions and habits of Japanese immigrants. I advise all Japanese who enter this country to have some money, wear decent, clean clothes; and keep good hygiene such as nail, skin and mouth care according to American standards. I believe that Japanese immigrants would be respected if they maintain good hygiene, decent clothing and etiquette compatible with those in this country.

My dear countrymen! We are at the most precarious era for Japanese immigration to the U.S.A. and Hawaii. I advise each of you to keep in mind in the above mentioned points. Please keep our honor at the highest degree and behave as a proud subject of the Empire of Japan living in the U.S.A.

31

In re Saito, *June 27, 1894*

This Circuit Court ruling reaffirmed the official American policy of prohibiting Asians from naturalization. The case of Japanese Shebata Saito predated the better-known Takao Ozawa case (1922) by nearly three decades. It reaffirms the "common sense" notion of "whiteness" as well as "scientific" standard anthropological racial categories. The ruling is interesting also because of its clear and concise recourse to legislative intent. It is unusual, like the case of Fong Yue Ting, in pointing to the early existence and experiences of Asians outside the West Coast.

The Federal Reporter, vol. 62. St. Paul, MN: West Publishing Co., 1894.

In re Saito
(Circuit Court, D. Massachusetts. June 27, 1804.)

Aliens—Naturalization of Japanese.

A native of Japan, of the Mongolian race, is not entitled to naturalization, not being included within the term "white persons" in Rev. St. 2169.

Application by Shebata Saito for naturalization.

Colt, Circuit Judge. This is an application by a native of Japan for naturalization.

The act relating to naturalization declares that "the provisions of this title shall apply to aliens being free white persons, and to aliens of African nativity and to persons of African descent." Rev. St. 2169. The Japanese, like the Chinese, belong to the Mongolian race, and the question presented is whether they are included within the term "white persons."

These words were incorporated in the naturalization laws as early as 1802. 2 Stat. 154. At that time the country was inhabited by three races, the Caucasian or white race, the Negro or black race, and the American or red race. It is reasonable, therefore, to infer that when congress, in designating the class of persons who could be naturalized, inserted the qualifying word "white," it intended to exclude from the privilege of citizenship all alien races except the Caucasian.

But we are not without more direct evidence of legislative intent. In 1870, after the adoption of the thirteenth amendment to the constitution, prohibiting slavery, and the fourteenth amendment, declaring who shall be citizens, the question of extending the privilege of citizenship to all races of aliens came before congress for consideration. At that time, Charles Sumner proposed to strike out the word "white" from the statute; and in the long debate which followed the argument on the part of the opposition was that this change would permit the Chinese (and therefore the Japanese) to become naturalized citizens, and the reply of those who favored the change was that this was the very purpose of the proposed amendment. Cong. Globe, 1869–70, pt. 6, p. 5121. The amendment was finally rejected, and the present provision substituted, extending the naturalization laws to the African race.

Again, in the first revision of the statutes, in 1873, the words "being free white persons" were omitted, probably through inadvertence. Under the act of February 18, 1875, to correct errors and supply omissions in the first revision, this section of the statute was amended by inserting or restoring these words. In moving to adopt this amendment in the house, it was stated that this omission operated to extend naturalization to all classes of aliens, and especially to the Asiatics; and reference was made to the fact that, a few years before, the proposition of Mr. Summer, in the senate, to strike out the word "white," had been defeated, and that the committee only proposed, by restoring these words, to place the law where it stood at the time of the revision. The debate which followed proceeded on the assumption that by restoring the word "white" the Asiatics would be excluded from naturalization, and the amendment was adopted with this understanding of its effect. 3 Cong. Rec. pt. 2, p. 1081.

The history of legislation on this subject shows that congress refused to eliminate "white" from the statute for the reason that it would extend the privilege of naturalization to the Mongolian race, and that when, through inadvertence, this word was left out of the statute, it was again restored for the very purpose of such exclusion.

The words of a statute are to be taken in their ordinary sense, unless it can be shown that they are used in a technical sense.

From a common, popular standpoint, both in ancient and modern times, the races of mankind have been distinguished by difference in color, and they have been classified as the white, black, yellow, and brown races.

And this is true from a scientific point of view. Writers on ethnology and anthropology base their division of mankind upon differences in physical rather than in intellectual or moral character, so that difference in color, conformation of skull, structure and arrangement of hair, and the general contour of the face are the marks which distinguish the various types. But, of all these marks, the color of the skin is considered the most important criterion for the distinction of race, and it lies at the foundation of the classification which scientists have adopted. . . .

Whether this question is viewed in the light of congressional intent, or of the popular or scientific meaning of "white persons," or of the authority of adjudicated cases, the only conclusion I am able to reach, after careful consideration, is that the present application must be denied.

Application denied.

32

Comic Song and Chorus: "The Wedding of the Chinee and the Coon," 1897

The earlier song "Ah Sin," from 1877, spoke realistically to interracial relations be-tween Chinese men and white women; this "wedding" is a much more pointed as-sault on African Americans as well as Chinese immigrants. This "unnatural" event takes place "way down in Chinatown," indicating that, by this time, the Chinese presence must have appeared all too permanent for nativists. Worse, the spectacle of race mixing conjured images of an unacceptably hybridized Ameri-ca—"an awful jamble." In fact, the overwhelming numerical superiority of males in the Chinese population made such a union highly improbable; the obverse, a Chinese male forming a bond with an African American woman, was much more likely. Billy Johnson, who wrote the lyrics, would probably have opposed the 1898 Supreme Court decision determining that Wong Kim Ark, like anyone born on U.S. territory, was automatically a citizen.

Archives of American History, National Museum of American History, Smithsonian Institution. Thanks to Krystyn Moon, who discovered this song.

THE WEDDING OF THE
CHINEE AND THE COON.
WORDS BY
BILLY JOHNSON.
MUSIC BY
BOB COLE
AUTHORS OF
"THE BLACK 400s BALL."
"YOU'LL HAVE TO CHOOSE
ANOTHER BABY NOW."
COMIC
SONG & CHORUS
5
NEW YORK.
PUBLISHED BY HOWLEY, HAVILAND & Co. 4. EAST 20TH STREET.
LONDON. CHAS SHEARD & Co

The Wedding of the Chinee and the Coon.

Words by BILLY JOHNSON.

Music by BOB COLE.
(Arr. by THEO. F. MORSE.)

For the Chinese Em-bas-sa-dor has giv-en warning _____ The
Ev-'ry coon's ex-pect-ed to walk stead-y _____ I
The Joss-house Priest or Par-son chick-en feather _____ Chin-

cause of this af-fair _____ Is strange I do de-clare _____ It's the
know there'll be a time _____ And lots of Chin-ee wine _____ Chop-
ese be-gan to stare _____ At ra-zors in the air _____

fun-ni-est thing that's happen'd for man-y a moon _____ Of all
su - ey that will puff you like a bal-loon _____ Don't in-
Ev - 'ry Chin-ee eye look'd like a bal-loon _____ Now what

things beneath the skies _____ This will be a great surprise _____ For a
quire why it is _____ For they'll say it's none your biz _____ When this
were they to do _____ Chinese preacher lost his cue _____ The coon

The wedding of the Chinee &c. 3.

pret-ty Chin-ese girl will wed a coon. ____
pret-ty Chin-ese girl will wed a coon. ____
Par-son joined the Chin-ee and the coon. ____

CHORUS. *not to fast.*

This strange a - mal-ga-ma-tion twixt these two fun-ny na-tions gwine to cause an

awful jamble soon ____ Twill cause a great sensation ov-er the

whole creation The wedding of the Chinee and the coon ____ coon ____

The wedding of the Chinee &c. 3.

33

Treaty of Peace Between the United States and Spain, Paris, December 10, 1898

The Treaty of Paris, signed on December 10, 1898, formally ended the Spanish-American War. While the youthful United States had been aggressively expanding its continental borders in the eighteenth and nineteenth centuries, this war definitively positioned it as a major player among Western European nations in the age of imperialism and quickly demonstrated its industrial and military superiority at the turn of the twentieth century. The United States extended its flag into the Caribbean by acquiring Cuba and Puerto Rico and into the vast Pacific Ocean by taking Guam, in the Marianas Islands, and the Philippines from Spain in exchange for $20 million. Filipinos who had been fighting alongside Americans for liberation from Spain were frustrated and disappointed to learn that they remained subservient to yet another outside force. A serious war between American troops and Filipinos subsequently erupted. It lasted for several years and generated many casualties and much ill will. The Philippines would remain an American territory until 1946, after the end of World War II. The Spanish-American War also caused enormous political turmoil within the United States as many pondered the impact of acquiring an empire, and especially the idea of incorporating large groups of "foreign" people of color. In the end, the lure of an expanded political and business framework prevailed, with consequences that continue to require attention in the twenty-first century.

U.S. Congress, 55th Cong., 3d sess., Senate Doc. No. 62, Part 1. Washington, DC: Government Printing Office, 1899.

Treaty of Peace (Treaty of Paris)

Signed at Paris December 10, 1898

. . .

Entered into force April 11, 1899

The United States of America and Her Majesty the Queen Regent of Spain, in the name of her August Son Don Alfonso XIII, desiring to end the state of war now existing between the two countries, have for that purpose appointed as Plenipotentiaries. [names] . . .

Who, having assembled in Paris, and having exchanged their full powers, which were found to be in due and proper form, have, after discussion of the matters before them, agreed upon the following articles:

Article I

Spain relinquishes all claim of sovereignty over and title to Cuba.

And as the island is, upon its evacuation by Spain, to be occupied by the United States, the United States will, so long as such occupation shall last, assume and discharge the obligations that may under international law result from the fact of its occupation, for the protection of life and property.

Article II

Spain cedes to the United States the island of Porto Rico and other islands now under Spanish sovereignty in the West Indies, and the island of Guam in the Marianas or Ladrones.

Article III

Spain cedes to the United States the archipelago known as the Philippine Islands . . .

The United States will pay to Spain the sum of twenty million dollars ($20,000,000) within three months after the exchange of the ratifications of the present treaty. . . .

Article V

The United States will, upon the signature of the present treaty, send back to Spain, at its own cost, the Spanish soldiers taken as prisoners of war on the capture of Manila by the American forces. The arms of the soldiers in question shall be restored to them.

Spain will, upon the exchange of the ratifications of the present treaty, proceed to evacuate the Philippines, as well as the island of Guam, on terms similar to those agreed upon by the Commissioners appointed to arrange for the evacuation of Porto Rico and other islands in the West Indies, under the Protocol of August 12, 1898, which is to continue in force until its provisions are completely executed.

The time within which the evacuation of the Philippine Islands and Guam shall be completed shall be fixed by the two Governments. Stands of colors, uncaptured war vessels, small arms, guns of all calibres, with their carriages and accessories, powder, ammunition, livestock, and materials and supplies of all kinds, belonging to the land and naval forces of Spain in the Philippines and Guam, remain the property of Spain. Pieces of heavy ordnance, exclusive of field artillery, in the fortifications and coast defences, shall remain in their emplacements for the term of six months, to be reckoned from the exchange of ratifications of the treaty; and the United States may, in the mean time, purchase such material from Spain, if a satisfactory agreement between the two Governments on the subject shall be reached. . . .

Done in duplicate at Paris, the tenth day of December, in the year of Our Lord one thousand eight hundred and ninety eight.

34

Supreme Court: United States v. Wong Kim Ark, *March 1898*

Wong Kim Ark's victory at the U.S. Supreme Court guaranteed the right, under the Fourteenth Amendment, of American citizenship for all individuals born in the United States. Nearly twenty previous court decisions involving Chinese litigants formed part of the legal background. Wong Kim Ark was born in California in 1873; his parents were resident aliens from China who were ineligible for naturalization. He traveled with his parents to China in 1890 and visited briefly in 1894. Upon his return, he was denied reentry since he was a laborer and Chinese—qualities that encouraged many Americans to oppose their presence in the country. He therefore petitioned for a writ of habeas corpus to be released from custody and allowed to reenter the United States as a citizen. The central question was whether the Supreme Court would permit a native-born person to be deprived of his citizenship solely because of his parents' nationality. In a divided opinion, the court ruled that Wong Kim Ark was a citizen and must be allowed to reenter his country. However, in 1905 the Supreme Court (in United States v. Ju Toy) denied an American-born Chinese the right of habeas corpus, the critical legal tool to secure reentry into the United States.

Stephen K. Williams, *Cases Argued and Decided in the Supreme Court of the United States, Book* 42. Rochester, NY: The Lawyers Co-operative Publishing Co., 1926.

United States V. Wong Kim Ark
169 U.S. 649

Mr. Justice Gray delivered the opinion of the court.

The facts of this case, as agreed by the parties, are as follows:

Wong Kim Ark was born in 1873 in the city of San Francisco, in the State of California and and United States of America, and was and is a laborer. His father and mother were persons of Chinese descent, and subjects of the Emperor of China; they were at the time of his birth domiciled residents of the United States, having previously established and still enjoying a permanent residence therein at

San Francisco; they continued to reside and remain in the United States until 1890, when they departed for China; and during all the time of their residence in the United States they were engaged in business, and were never employed in any diplomatic or official capacity under the Emperor of China. Wong Kim Ark, ever since his birth, has had but one residence, to wit, in California, within the United States, and has there resided, claiming to be a citizen of the United States, and has never lost or changed that residence, or gained or acquired another residence; and neither he, nor his parents acting for him, ever renounced his allegiance to the United States, or did or committed any act or thing to exclude him therefrom. In 1890 (when he must have been about seventeen years of age) he departed for China on a temporary visit and with the intention of returning to the United States, and did return thereto by sea in the same year, and was permitted by the collector of customs to enter the United States, upon the sole ground that he was a native-born citizen of the United States. After such return, he remained in the United States, claiming to be a citizen thereof, until 1894, when he (being about twenty-one years of age, but whether a little above or a little under that age does not appear) again departed for China on a temporary visit and with the intention of returning to the United States; and he did return thereto by sea in August, 1895, and applied to the collector of customs for permission to land; and was denied such permission, upon the sole ground that he was not a citizen of the United States, the acts of Congress, known as the Chinese Exclusion Acts, prohibiting persons of the Chinese race, and especially Chinese laborers, from coming into the United States, do not and cannot apply to him.

The question presented by the record is whether a child born in the United States, of parents of Chinese descent, who, at the time of his birth, are subjects of the Emperor of China, but have a permanent domicil and residence in the United States, and are there carrying on business, and are not employed in any diplomatic or official capacity under the Emperor of China, becomes at the time of his birth a citizen of the United States, by virtue of the first clause of the Fourteenth Amendment of the Constitution, "All persons born or naturalized in the United States, and subject to the jurisdiction thereof, are citizens of the United States and of the State wherein they reside."

The 14th Amendment, while it leaves the power where it was before, in Congress, to regulate naturalization, has conferred no authority upon Congress to restrict the effect of birth, declared by the Constitution to constitute a sufficient and complete right to citizenship. . . . The fact, therefore, that acts of Congress or treaties have not permitted Chinese persons born out of this country to become citizens by naturalization, cannot exclude Chinese persons born in this country from the operation of the broad and clear words of the Constitution, "All persons born in the United States, and subject to the jurisdiction thereof, are citizens of the United States." . . .

The evident intention, and the necessary effect, of the submission of this case to the decision of the court upon the facts agreed by the parties, were to present for determination the single question, stated at the beginning of this opinion, namely, whether a child born in the United States, of parents of Chinese descent, who, at the time of his birth, are subjects of the Emperor of China, but have a permanent domicil and residence in the United States, and are there carrying on business, and are not employed in any diplomatic or official capacity under the Emperor of China, becomes at the time of his birth a citizen of the United States. For the reasons above stated, this court is of opinion that the question must be answered in the affirmative.

Order affirmed.

35

Annexation of Hawai'i, March 16, 1898

This report from the Senate Committee on Foreign Relations references the joint resolution that eventually allowed the United States to annex Hawai'i without a treaty requiring the two-thirds Senate majority that was not politically possible. Annexationists successfully argued that it was necessary to take control of Hawai'i because of its strategic location and vulnerability to international competition among imperialist powers. The report asserts that Native Hawaiians simultaneously desire American involvement and, under the tutelage of resident Americans, have created a positive and thriving society even under severe threat from a hostile Japanese population and nation. References to competition with Japan presage worsening conditions for Japanese Americans over the next half century.

Senate Report 681, 55th Congress, 2nd Session. Washington, DC: Government Printing Office, 1899.

Annexation of Hawaii

Mr. Davis, from the Committee on Foreign Relations, submitted the following RE-PORT. [To accompany S. R. 127.]

The joint resolution for the annexation of Hawaii to the United States, herewith reported to the Senate by the Committee on Foreign Relations as a substitute for Senate joint resolution No. 100 and Senate bill No. 2263, which were referred to that committee, brings that subject within reach of the legislative power of Congress under the precedent that was established in the annexation of Texas. . . .

The people of the United States became greatly aroused at the prospect of losing Texas, in consequence of the indignation of her people over the rejection of the treaty, and they demanded immediate annexation by a law that would speak the will of the majority in Congress. Afterwards, and without any further action by the Republic of Texas to signify its consent to annexation to the United States, the following joint resolution, containing two alternate sections, passed both Houses of Congress and was approved by the President on the 7th day of March, 1845. . . .

The policy of annexation, as it applies to Hawaii, has been exceptional and clear since our earliest diplomatic relations with that Government.

From the beginning down to this date the idea and expectation has been constantly entertained by the people and Governments of both countries that whenever the conditions should be such as to make annexation of mutual advantage it should be consummated.

On the part of Hawaii this purpose has been sustained by two facts:

First. That no ruler of Hawaii since the time of Kamehameha I has believed that these islands, that are so tempting to the cupidity of commercial powers, could maintain an autonomous government without the interested support of some great maritime nation.

Second. That the rulers of Hawaii, on each occasion when the islands have been threatened with foreign interference or domestic violence, have at once appealed to some foreign power for help. . . .

There was just cause for the constant reliance of all these kings upon the protection of the United States and upon the Americans in the islands, for the reason that none of them could have been safe at any time in relying for protection or for the enforcement of the laws upon their native subjects.

For like reasons, and because no American called into his counsels ever wronged or deceived a Hawaiian king, they were sought out and were urgently invited to accept leading positions in their cabinets. . . .

That the thoughtful people of Hawaii, who have been thus lifted up to an honorable position among the family of Christian nations, should have a firm faith in the American people and a warm attachment for them, is only an evidence of their gratitude toward their deliverers and of their intelligent appreciation of the great blessings they enjoy through the devoted labors of these Americans. . . .

For many years past the people of the United States and of Hawaii have looked to annexation as a manifest destiny. All legitimate business enterprises there have been based on that recognized fact, and only illegitimate ventures have opposed it.

In the treaty of reciprocity of 1875 the United States demanded, as the consideration of admitting the staple productions of Hawaii free of duty into our ports, that Hawaii should so far renounce her sovereignty over her public domain, her crown lands, and her ports, bays, and harbors, that she could not dispose of them, or of any exclusive or special privileges in them, without the consent of the United States. . . .

To our own people who have emigrated to Hawaii under the open invitation of our national policy and under the pledges given by Congress and our Presidents that no foreign power should disturb their rights we owe all the friendly care that a father can owe to his sons who have with his consent left their home to seek their fortunes in other lands. . . .

We owe it to these people that they should not again be brought into subjection to a monarchy that has lapsed because of its corruptions and its faithless repudiation of solemn oaths. In this obligation our Government is also deeply concerned for the maintenance and enjoyment of our treaty rights in Hawaii.

To these people, and also to the preservation of the native population against a speedy destruction, involving property and life, we owe the duty of rescuing them from the silent but rapid invasion of the pagan races from Asia. This invasion is concerted, and is far more dangerous to Hawaii than if it came on ships of war with the avowed purpose of subjugating the Hawaiian Islands. It is the stealthy approach of a "destruction that wasteth at noonday." The immigrants from Japan retain their allegiance to that Empire, and yet they claim full political rights in Hawaii notwithstanding their alienage.

In this demand they have the undisguised encouragement of the Japanese Government. These privileges are demanded as rights. . . .

Of these subjects of Japan in Hawaii the larger number were soldiers in the war with China, and are still subject to the military orders of the Emperor.

Almost the entire number of Japanese in Hawaii are coolies, who were brought there under the authority of the two Governments, and were to return to Japan at the end of their term of service.

They claim the right to remain in Hawaii under a general treaty which applied only to such persons as came for temporary or permanent residence as voluntary immigrants. This claim is disputed by Hawaii, and there is still trouble over it. Under such circumstances the presence and the constant inflow of Japanese in great numbers is an evil which threatens the native people with the loss of their means of living and the whole country with the overflow of paganism. It also threatens the overthrow of the Republic and the destruction of the lives and property of the republicans through an insurrection or combination of the lower classes of natives, who are for the most part adherents of royalty and are under the control of the Kahunas, who are sorcerers, with the Japanese. . . .

It may be safely assumed that in all respects the white race in Hawaii are the equals of any community of like numbers and pursuits to be found in any country. The success they have achieved in social, religious, educational, and governmental institutions is established in results that are not dwarfed by a comparison with our most advanced communities.

They number 22 per cent in a population of 109,000, the number of Americans being 3,000, British 2,200, Germans 1,400, Norwegians and French 479, and other nationalities 1,055. These white people are so united in the support of good government that there is no political distinction of nationalities among them, and harsh differences of opinion on public questions are seldom found.

This is the supreme governing power in the islands when that power is traced to its origin, as it is in all countries where the white and colored races are admitted, on equal terms, into the exercise of civil rights connected with government. The Portuguese, who are also recognized as white citizens, are included in this estimate of 22 per cent of the entire population of Hawaii. . . .

The Japanese comprise 22 per cent of the whole population, and are equal in numbers to the whites. They do not claim to be permanent residents of Hawaii, and very few of them acquire real estate, except on leases, some of them for as much as five years. They are chiefly laborers and servants; some of them are merchants and fishermen. They are less obedient to law than the people of the other races in Hawaii.

As a rule, they return to Japan at the end of their contract terms of service, so that their numbers fluctuate as the tide of immigration ebbs and flows. They are not trustworthy as laborers, nor honest in their dealings as merchants. They come to Hawaii as coolies, having been collected from the lower classes, and very few of them bringing their wives and children to Hawaii. Their wish to participate in government is evidently inspired by their managers, who are set over them in authority by the Government agents in Japan.

Under our laws the Japanese have the full right of emigration to the United States, but few of them avail of that privilege, because they prefer to return to Japan. The native women seldom intermarry with Japanese, and their association with the natives is not apparently agreeable to either race.

In a community of ignorant people they are a dangerous element and are servile in their obedience to their overseers. It is from this race that the real danger to social order comes in Hawaii, because they act as a unit in obeying the commands of their managers, and are not prone to cowardice.

The Chinese in Hawaii have all resided there for a number of years. They were largely voluntary immigrants, who came to the country prior to 1870, when their coming was prohibited. They are the most industrious and thrifty race that has come to Hawaii. They are a higher class of people, in the main, than those who have come to the United States, and some of them have accumulated considerable estates.

They evince little desire to use the ballot, from which they are excluded. In the culture of rice, taro, and garden stuff they excel, and in fishing they conduct a profitable business. . . .

If the Hawaiian race can be saved from extermination, or, while they exist, from being driven from their homes by the Asiatics, the United States, following up the noble efforts of the Hawaiian Republic, can accomplish that work.

If we do not interpose either to annex Hawaii or to protect her from the influx of Asiatics, the native people will soon be exterminated.

In those islands all the natives who desire homes have them or can freely obtain them under the liberal land laws of the Republic, and the fertility of the country and its abundant fisheries insure a comfortable living to more than tenfold the present population. The efforts of the Republic to fill up the public domain with white people from the United States are being rapidly responded to by a strong tide of such immigrants. The climate, soil, and the agricultural productions invite such immigrants, with inducements that no other country affords. . . .

The colleges are of high grade, and in all the schools the tuition is careful. The people are enterprising, public-spirited, and progressive in all their vocations. The really distinctive feature of society is that it is American in all its traits and habits, and our national holidays are celebrated in Hawaii with the same enthusiasm that is manifested in the United States. The most fatal blow at the spirit of those people and the sorest wound we could inflict upon them would be our refusal to welcome them into the Union.

36

Reverend Eryu Honda, Jodo Shinshu Buddhist Minister, and Japanese Consul Miki Saito, 1898

While various Christian missions had developed active congregations among Japanese immigrants in the United States by the early 1890s, it was not until much later in that decade that Buddhism made its formal entrance. Most of the immigrants had come from regions in which Jodo Shinshu temples predominated, so this form of Buddhism became the most prevalent. Its founder, Shinran, built upon the older Jodo (Pure Land) Buddhism, emphasizing its "true essence" (shinshu) through daily practice, recitation of the nembutsu (calling the name of the Amida Buddha) without meditation, married clergy, and, in general, a direct connection of religious tenets with human social needs and action. This religious ideology reduced the direct importance of clergy to the congregation, but the community required Jodo Shinshu presence for its general well-being, so Honda and Ejun Miyamoto were sent to determine whether Japan should send ministers and money for support. They found positive sentiment among the immigrants but concern from the Consul in Seattle, Miki Saito, who thought introducing this "foreign" religion would add fuel to the growing anti-Japanese racism at the turn of the century. Honda and Miyamoto returned with recommendations to begin serious religious propagation, and the Japanese government continued its guarded stance toward Buddhism for many decades. In this recollection of his conversation with Consul Saito, Reverend Honda reveals that official Japan was hardly an advocate of this religion.

Ryo Munekata, ed., *Buddhist Churches of America: Vol. 1, 75 Year History.* Chicago: Nobart, Inc., 1974, 46. Cited in Tetsuden Kashima, *Buddhism in America: The Social Organization of an Ethnic Religious Institution.* Westport, CT and London: Greenwood Press, 1977, 14.

When I discussed about the proposed Buddhist Missionary work in the United States, Consul Saito with an expression of annoyance on his face and while thumbing through a number of documents, asked whether the United States government would allow the entrance of a "foreign religion." He also expressed his feelings about the numerous problems which might arise from the entrance of a "foreign religion," when the Japanese and Americans are presently coexisting peacefully. Since I felt that such expressions came from an individual who did not know the Buddadharma [Sanskrit term for Buddhism], I took the opportunity to explain some salient points about the religion. Because of such attitudes on the part of the leadership in the Japanese community, I felt that missionary work will be difficult. Yet, somehow, agreement was reached that missionary work may be started. And, since I was able to see the establishment of the San Francisco YMBA [Young Men's Buddhist Association], I returned to Japan with a strong conviction that missionary work must be started in the United States.

37

Hawai'i Sugar Plantation Wage Policy, March 20, 1899

Sugar plantations could be very profitable, but by the 1890s they were also high-ly competitive with one another in Hawai'i and throughout the world. Led by sugar planters, American businessmen orchestrated the overthrow of the Hawaiian Kingdom in 1893, largely to seek annexation by the United States and thus secure its vast domestic sugar market. Competition came in many forms, including advanced technology, transportation, financing, water sources, management techniques, and improved cane stock. But above all else was the need for large numbers of cheap and reliable workers, because cane sugar production was so labor intensive. Allowing a Chinese worker to pit two neighboring plantations against each other in a bidding war would have escalated the cost of labor. Indeed, other notes from this archive indicate that planters anticipated fully 20 percent of their Japanese workers, by then approximately 40 percent of the total labor force, would desert—often heading for Kona on the Big Island of Hawai'i, where a Japanese immigrant community incorporated and hid their countrymen.

Letter, George Renton, Ewa Plantation Manager, to August Ahrens, Manager of the Oahu Sugar Company, March 20, 1899. Oahu Sugar Company Archives.

Honolulu, Oahu, H.I. March 20, 1899

A. Ahrens, Esq.
Manager, Oahu Sugar Co.
Honolulu, Oahu

Dear Sir:

I am given to understand that one of our men has lately left his employ to work with you owing to offers of increased pay. I refer to Ah Hoy a railroad overseer.

It should be perfectly apparent to you that the adoption of a system of competition for overseers between our two estates cannot but be productive of higher rates to employees, and laborers, and will not be of any benefit to the plantations.

And as the Ewa Plantation can probably afford to pay as much for men as the Oahu Sugar Co., it merely means that I will have to pay more and you will not get the men, and vice versa if I attempt the same with you.

Yours truly,

(signed)
George Renton

38

Political Cartoons Reflecting U.S. Images of Filipinos, 1899

It was only through a tortuous process that the United States became a colonial power in 1898. Political cartoons, some of them brilliantly illustrated in gorgeous colors, demonstrate the complex issues at work. Indeed, President William McKinley justified his decision, after much anguished soul-searching, to support annexation of the Philippines by disclosing that "God" had answered his prayers for guidance in the White House. This was high-level documentation of the belief that Filipinos required (and deserved) "civilizing," "uplifting," and "Christianizing" by Americans. This was part of the divine plan—our destiny made "manifest"—and hence, a major rationale for taking over the Philippines. Of course, economic expansion into Asia, in competition with European imperial powers like Great Britain, France, Germany, and, increasingly, even Japan, was another major argument. Providing military protection for these new trade routes would be the role of the new navy, which would require strategic ports in places like Hawai'i, Guam, Samoa, and the Philippines. All four became parts of the American empire in the late 1890s. But there was also vigorous opposition from anti-imperialist forces, including those who used economic arguments, those who read the Bible differently, some who were deeply troubled by territorial expansion and colonization as a contradiction to constitutional democracy, and many frightened by the inclusion of "backward" peoples of color into the national population. Many essays, articles, newspaper editorials, books, and speeches focused on these issues; these cartoons are a vivid and concise example.

1899 political cartoons from *Judge* and *Life* magazines. Abe Ignacio and Helen Toribio kindly provided copies—two from among hundreds they have collected for a forthcoming volume on the subject of American images of Filipinos and the Philippine-American War at the turn of the century.

VOL. 36 NO. 926 JUNE 10 1899 PRICE 10 CENTS

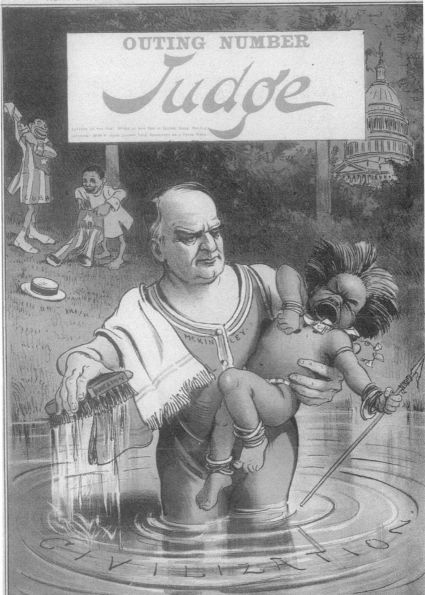

THE FILIPINO'S FIRST BATH.
McKINLEY—" Oh, you dirty boy !"

VOLUME XXXIII. NEW YORK, JUNE 8, 1899. NUMBER 863.

Entered at the New York Post Office as Second-Class Mail Matter.
Copyright, 1899, by LIFE PUBLISHING COMPANY.

Liberty: STOP THIS BLOODY WORK, SAM! HE IS THE ONE WHO IS FIGHTING FOR *ME*.

PART 2

Migration and Settlement: Through 1924

While it is true that there were Asians in the Americas from very early times (however that phrase is defined), it is also a fact that significant migrations only began in the second half of the nineteenth century. Immigration continued into the early twentieth century before being cut off by various treaties and laws. In this period, from the time of the American Civil War to the end of the first quarter of the twentieth century, the United States grew from a young, defiant, recently independent, and struggling nation into one of the major powers in the world. It had embraced and then abolished the enslavement of Africans, presided over the inexorable westward expansion that devastated native tribes, and incorporated new areas as well as vast territories once colonized by other European powers. In the process, the United States had grown into a mighty industrial society that absorbed difficult lessons of economic development at the same time as it subjugated or accommodated complex hierarchies of ethnic, nationality, religious, class, gender, and regional groupings. When Asians became an important element, the nation already had a long history of dealing with "minority" issues. What was different, however, was the sheer breadth and magnitude of the expansion and consolidation taking place. This section takes us to the 1924 Immigration Act, also known as the National Origins Act, certainly one of the key defining documents of American history.

By the 1890s, earlier signs of Asian American presence in the United States had developed into clear indications that they would become permanent features in the American landscape. By then the pattern of immigration and naturalization laws suggested that Asians were not welcome except as sojourning laborers or occasional students or merchants. In the first quarter of the twentieth century, life here was fraught with mixed messages for Asian immigrants and their American-born and, thus, American citizen children. As Wong Kim Ark had definitively established in 1898, the United States would stand by its pledge that anyone born in American territory was an American citizen by virtue of *jus soli*, the law of soil. This was in addition to *jus sanguinis*, the law of blood, which entitled children of U.S. citizen parents, even if born on foreign soil, to be American citizens.

In 1904, Congress permanently halted Chinese immigration by amending the 1882 law. It further extended this exclusion to immigrants from newly acquired insular possessions, including the Philippines, Guam, Samoa, and Hawaiʻi. Then, the federal government turned its attention to a new competitor in the Pacific—Japan—limiting immigration through the Gentlemen's Agreement in 1907. By 1920 the United States had largely ended the practice of importing "picture brides" by which Japanese men already in the United States sent for wives. These men adapted the traditional custom of arranged marriage to new circumstances in order to circumvent laws preventing them from establishing families and communities. Their partial success helps to explain the emergence of a substantial American-born, second-generation Japanese American population, in contrast to largely male, immigrant Chinese communities.

After 1906, thousands of young Chinese males entered the United States as "paper sons" who claimed to be American—offspring sired in China by citizens. Between 1920 and 1940, 71,040 Chinese entered the country, some of whose families had bought rights to immigrate in this fashion. They were known formally as "derivative citizens."

Koreans were treated as Japanese subjects because their country had been colonized in the early twentieth century. There were several thousand Asian Indians in the United States, largely Sikhs from the Punjab, and they too were targeted for exclusion because they came from part of the 1917 "barred zone." As Takao Ozawa discovered in 1922, the United States defined the Japanese as beyond the realm of acceptable groups and refused to allow him to naturalize. Bhagat Singh Thind, an Asian Indian, learned in the following year that he was also prohibited from becoming an American citizen.

The end result was identical: the 1924 National Origins Act set the parameters for desirable, less desirable, and undesirable ethnic and nationality groups. Quotas were established, beginning in 1927, to add no more than 150,000 immigrants from all sources in any single year. Each Asian nation was assigned a nominal quota of 100. But since immigrants were required to be eligible for citizenship and all Asians were ineligible, their quota was effectively zero. Thus, any legal immigrant from China, for example, had to be non-Chinese and non-Asian.

In spite of these immigration restrictions and exclusion acts, there was a growing number of Asian American communities from the beginning of the 1900s. These new immigrants were at once badly needed by a burgeoning industrial economy, whether for sugar plantations in Hawaiʻi, the salmon canneries of Alaska, or the numerous farms growing everything from citrus in Southern California to apples and pears in the Northwest. And while immigration restrictions prevented most new arrivals, nativist fears of contamination from this Asian presence grew apace. Evidence of this racism abounds, ranging from degrading stereotypes in music, film, novels, and cartoons to numerous discriminatory laws and outright mob violence, including lynchings and massacres.

Attempts to force or persuade Asians to leave the United States, or at least the immediate region, assumed many forms. Tang Tun, an American-born Chinese person, for example, was denied reentry into the country. As early as 1902, *Sung v. United States* determined that deportation proceedings allowed practices not permissible in other law enforcement behavior. These included unreasonable searches and seizures, cruel and unusual punishment, and trial without jury. And, while *Kwock Jan Fat v. White* determined, in 1920, that aliens should have a fair hearing, *Ho v. White* maintained that Congress had the right to deport "dangerous" aliens and that they had to "prove" citizenship in order to remain for trial. And even the "paper sons" who awaited hearings to determine whether they might stay in the country were subjected to lengthy incarceration, sometimes lasting for years, in the Angel Island detention center in San Francisco Bay.

One of the more interesting attempts to harass the Asian population was the 1922 Cable Act. Aimed largely at the Japanese, the act stipulated that American women who married "aliens ineligible for naturalization" (only Asians) would lose their citizenship. The only significant group of women in this category was the second-generation Japanese American *nisei*, who were marrying immigrant *issei*.

Except for unusually supportive institutions and individuals, including missionaries returned from Asia, most Americans joined in the anti-Asian crusade. City ordinances often singled out the Chinese to harass them, criminalizing their wearing of long hair braided into queues, required under Manchu dynasty regulations, and levying extra taxes on those who delivered laundry on foot rather than horseback. When the Japanese tried to join Mexican farmworkers in Oxnard, California, in a union, American Federation of Labor leaders, especially Samuel Gompers, blocked the move.

In Hawai'i, the Japanese fared slightly better. The cane sugar industry thoroughly dominated the islands by the time the Japanese were recruited in large numbers, beginning in 1885. But because alternative labor sources outside of Hawai'i were relatively inaccessible to the sugar planters, the Japanese quickly became a critical part of the workforce. By 1900 they were about 40 percent of the total population, and planters feared that the Japanese would become a significant threat to *haole* (Hawaiian for "foreign," specifically white) hegemony. This was not entirely irrational, since increasing numbers of brides meant a new and large generation of American citizens of Japanese descent flowing through the public school system and destined to have a major role in the political system. The first large-scale sugar strike of 1909, organized solely by and for the Japanese, alarmed the planters, who began systematically importing more Filipinos. An early alliance of Japanese and Filipino workers in an even larger strike in 1920 further frightened the planters, but that labor coalition quickly broke down, dashing hopes for class solidarity across ethnic lines until the 1940s.

The emergence of stable communities, especially in Hawai'i and the Chinatowns of the continental United States, created a volatile dynamic for American race relations. The 1924 Immigration Act seemingly ended the flow of immigration from Asia for good—except for Filipinos, who, as their islands were part of the empire, were considered "nationals" with the right to enter. When anti-Filipino agitation became too difficult to contain, Congress passed the Tydings-McDuffie Act in 1934, simultaneously promising independence to the Philippines in a decade and allowing only fifty individuals per year the right to immigrate. In spite of these restrictions, the social and legal contradictions in place sorely tested the ability of the nation to absorb those immigrants already in the country.

39

Holehole bushi: *Japanese Folk Songs on Hawai'i Sugar Plantations, 1900*

By the turn of the twentieth century, Japanese sugar workers comprised about 40 percent of Hawaii's population of 154,000. Their presence, as the single largest ethnic group and as immigrants from a rapidly modernizing and competing Pacific nation, guaranteed a turbulent future. Their experiences in the islands were exceedingly diverse. Among them were entrepreneurs with capitalist dreams; students intent on absorbing cutting-edge lessons from the West; labor leaders imbued with socialism; midwives, nurses, and doctors intent on serving their communities; and laborers oppressed by fearful conditions in the sugar cane fields. In this last group were women who took tunes (bushi) from their native villages and composed lyrics to lament, celebrate, and lampoon their current condition. Many of these women did the relatively lighter work of stripping leaves from the cane stalks (holehole), so that term defined this genre. At least some of the songs predate 1900 and illuminate very specific historical figures or events. The songs were modified to suit drinking parties by the 1910s and nearly disappeared during World War II. Ironically, it was in one of the American internment camps in Hawai'i that a young musician heard stories about the songs and was inspired to record them more than a decade after the end of the war. Harry Minoru Urata collected dozens of lyrics and taped the last surviving immigrants who had actually sung them in the fields. His dedication to preserving the songs led to a revival in the 1980s and 1990s, with younger artists learning old versions and composing new ones.

Harry Minoru Urata collection, in author's possession. Translations by the author.

Holehole Bushi: Japanese Immigrant Songs
from Hawaii's Sugar Heritage

Although a group of 169 Japanese arrived as contract workers in 1868, the first large waves of immigrants came after 1885, a period when Hawai'i was still an independent kingdom. Thus, this song references Hawai'i as *"koku,"* or "country."

Yuko ka Meriken yo	Go on to America?
Kaero ka Nihon	Return to Japan?
Koko ga shian no	This is my dilemma
Hawaii koku	Here in Hawai'i.

Many Japanese saw their government as worse than useless in defending their rights under international law. Japan was intent on securing international status, and her emigrants were hardly a priority. Joji Nakayama, a former high-ranking samurai employed by the Hawaiian government, was Chief Inspector in 1885; he was notorious for exploiting the workers. *Dekasegi* was a traditional Japanese practice of leaving a native village to find wage employment elsewhere in Japan or overseas.

Dekasegi wa kuru kuru	Immigrant workers keep on coming
Hawaii wa tsumaru	Overflowing these islands
Ai no Nakayama	But it's only Inspector Nakayama
Kane ga furu	Who rakes in the dough.

Consul General Taro Ando represented Japan and routinely dismissed workers' complaints about oppressive conditions, poor treatment, and abuse of the contracts. From 1885 to 1900, gambling, violence, drinking, and prostitution were commonplace. This *holehole bushi* uses a traditional Japanese literary device to juxtapose Ando's name with the word for "lantern" and suggest both are in the "dark."

Hizamoto ni bakuchi	Gambling right under your nose
Ameya wa sakan nari	Whorehouses all around
Ome ni mienu ka	Can't see any of this, Consul Ando?
Kuraki Ando	Nothing but a dark lantern.

Even in the midst of a patriarchal society, the gender imbalance could sometimes be used to advantage by Japanese women, who were, in any case, hardly shrinking violets. While they could be victimized by spouses, family members, or others, some used their sexuality on their own terms. "*Kane*" is "male" in Hawaiian—here, "husband," an indication of living and working with native populations.

Asu wa Sande jya yo	Tomorrow is Sunday
Asobi ni oide	Come over and play
Kane ga hanawai	My husband's watering the cane
Washa uchi ni	I'll be at home.

This last song is an example, like the previous one, of women appropriating their own meanings from difficult circumstances. In fact, in the late 1890s, the vast majority of licensed prostitutes in Hawai'i were Japanese. *"Pake"* became a sometimes pejorative term for the Chinese; both *"moi moi"* (sleep) and *"akahi kala"* (one dollar) are Hawaiian. The pay scale for women, always below that for men, for working six days per week put the monthly wage at about eight dollars.

Sanjugosen no	Why settle for thirty-five cents a day
Horehore shiyo yori	Doing *holehole* work
Pake-san to moi moi surya	When I can make a buck
Akahi kala	Sleeping with a Chinaman?

40

Samuel Gompers and Mexican/Japanese Farmworkers in Oxnard, California, June 2, 1903

The American labor movement has a long and complex history of dealing with race and racism. American workers have been told that "foreigners," especially non-Europeans, were willing to work for lower wages and in unacceptable conditions, thus lowering the standard of living for all. A few, like the International Workers of the World (the "Wobblies"), insisted on strategic inclusion of all workers in order to create a stable and effective counterpart to employers. Samuel Gompers, founder of the American Federation of Labor (AFL), was a vocal critic of foreign labor and was especially contemptuous of Asians. In 1903, when the AFL officially chartered a Mexican union of sugar beet and farm laborers in Oxnard, California, Gompers insisted, in a letter dated May 15, that they exclude "any Chinese or Japanese." The Mexicans, led by J. M. Lizarraras, refused the charter, arguing that the Japanese had been among the most steadfast of the striking workers and that the Mexicans would not desert their colleagues and friends. Fred Wheeler was an AFL district and state organizer at the time and reported on the incident to AFL Secretary Frank Morrison, arguing that the Japanese wanted to show "white men" that they were not "cheap" men but stood for the best wages. The incident is cited for the blatant racism demonstrated by conservative labor leaders as well as the courage and principles of other leaders, especially in forging interracial ties.

1903 letter from Fred Wheeler to Frank Morrison, Los Angeles, California, June 2, 1903. John Mitchell Papers, DCU (Catholic University of America, Washington, DC). Thanks to Noriko Sanefuji and Peter Albert, editor of the Gompers Papers at the University of Maryland, College Park, for finding and securing access to this letter. The *American Labor Union Journal*, June 25, 1903, reported on the incident and reproduced the response from Lizarraras ("Lazarraras"), praising the Japanese as brave and generous workers and refusing any charter "except one which will wipe out race prejudices."

Fred Wheeler to Frank Morrison

Los Angeles, Cal., June 2, 1903.

Mr. Frank Morrison,
Sec'y A.F. of L.

Dear Sir and Brother:

Pursuant to your instructions I went to Oxnard to properly install the Sugar Beet and Farm Laborers Union (Mexican), and found an unexpected state of affairs. The large hall was crowded with Mexicans and we had a four hours' session. I was assisted by a member of a Los Angeles union who happened to be in Oxnard that day. After a lengthy discussion in which much feeling was manifest, they read a letter from President Gompers in which he said "That this charter is issued to you (Mexicans) with the express understanding that under no circumstances shall you take into your union any Chinese or Japanese." This was the first intimation I had received that the Japs would be refused admission, as I had written you twice and telegraphed once on this particular point and had received no reply whatsoever. The Japs were much worked up and the Mexicans refused to organize under the conditions. They said this: "That in this valley there are 800 Japs and 400 Mexicans, who work in the beet fields. The Japs were the first to recognize the necessity of organization and asked our help. We as fellow-workers joined in with them. You told us, (and here they quoted various A.F. of L. literature) that you did not discriminate against any wage workers on account of *creed, color* or *nationality*. These men fought with us. Yes, some of them gave up our [their] lives in our defense, — stood guard 24 hours every day for five weeks, divided their food with us, worked with us in the fields, and they went to jail for us, and in the midst of our hard fight when things went hard with us, they were true and brave. The company spent money freely to get outside Japs to come here and take our places, but the union Japs also sent men at their own expense to prevail on their countrymen not to come to Oxnard during the strike. We had a hard bitter fight and now when our victory is absolute and complete you ask us to deny to our Japanese brothers the same right we ask for ourselves. We will not do it. We will stand by the men who stood by us."

This is the substance of what the Mexicans said. Yesterday (May 31) the Japanese in several other localities (some of them 500 miles from Oxnard) met and organized unions. They say "We want to show the white men that we are not *cheap* men, but rather we want and will demand the best wages in our line of work."

I hope you will lay this letter before the Executive Council for their consideration. 150 unions in Southern California have endorsed the Japanese union.

Yours,

(Signed)
F. C. Wheeler,
Organizer A.F. of L.

41

Chiura Obata Letter to Family, August 1903

In August 1903, the young Chiura Obata (1885–1975) booked passage, steerage class, and set sail for America. Widely regarded as among the finest Asian immigrant artists, he had studied painting with his father and in Japan before embarking; he became a professor of art at the University of California, Berkeley. His first letter back to his father and family reveals a very different experience from that of the contract laborers sent to Hawai'i in the 1880s and 1890s, for example, or the men who entered the country illegally from Canada or Mexico. This letter included delightful sketches of sharks apparently racing the ship, seascapes, a Chinese fellow eating from a bowl; first impressions of Vancouver and Seattle; and a caricature of the immigration or customs officials. The letter reveals the relative status of Chinese and Japanese (and women) at the time, both on board the ship (bathing description) and in the eyes of immigration officials.

Original letter courtesy of the Obata family. Translation by Naoko Haruta and Kimi Kodani; edited by Franklin Odo.

First Letter from Chiura Obata to Family from North America, 1903 (excerpts)

August 5: Cloudy, a bit cold. Just after leaving Yokohama. Saw sharks swimming alongside the boat. . . .

August 6: Clear in the morning; later, rain. . . . So interesting to listen to the sound of the Pacific Ocean just beneath the steel plates of the ship and to gaze at the sky while we take our first bath. The Japanese men go first, followed by Japanese women, and then the Chinese. We are told the first- and second-class passengers and crew have bathing facilities available. . . .

August 9: Clear. I feel fine—the waves are calm. I attended morning prayers at 7:30. . . .

August 10: Clear . . . I showed some folks a few of my paintings. I listened to Shida Kotaro discuss modern Japanese painting. . . .

August 11: Clear. First encounter with a foreign country. The fog was very thick and foghorns sounded constantly. . . . We were told we would land in Victoria [Canada]. . . . Seeing endless mountains in Alaska, Vancouver, and Victoria, I could not help myself and shouted *"Yukai!"* [How delightful!] . . . About ten of us fooled the immigration officials into thinking we were not steerage passengers and were able to disembark; we had a good laugh at that. One guy had had some experience in the States and took us from the port boulevard to a baseball game in the park. . . . I had my first western meal and returned to the boat about 10 P.M., very happy. . . .

August 11: Clear. We leave for Seattle. . . . The customs examination wasn't so bad. . . . Arrived in Seattle at 1:30 P.M. and anchored at the pier of the Toyo Kisen Company. . . .

August 13: Rain and mist in the morning; clear later. . . . We went through the medical examination and had to show our medical certificates. . . . The customs official noted that most of my belongings were art supplies. . . . We went into town, had a meal of beef and Japanese cabbage for 10 cents. We got a room for 20 cents each and found it large enough, although we had to turn the light on even in mid-day. But we were set upon by cockroaches as soon as we entered! . . . Later, after going to a Japanese bathhouse, we heard that there was a Baptist minister by the name of Reverend Okazaki who would take us in, so we checked out right away. . . . We celebrated with a Japanese meal for 15 cents. . . . Pretty decent—lots of Caucasians there. Tonight was the first time I had slept in a bed in a house in North America.

42

Sun Yat-sen Application to Enter the United States, April 21, 1904

By 1904 Sun Yat-sen was well on his way to establishing the movement that would bring down the moribund Ching dynasty in China in 1911. Sun inspired this revolution from many places: within China, on its perimeters, in countries like Japan, and in the diaspora communities of Chinese living across the globe. He had attended school in Honolulu, Hawai'i and had enthusiastic followers in America's Chinatowns. This particular document demonstrates the skill and political acumen required of a revolutionary—his assertions of Hawaiian birth are entirely fictitious, but were successful and enabled him to travel extensively in the United States. Sun's statements regarding his status as "an enemy of the Government" are, however, unexceptional. At the time he was born, in 1866, Hawai'i was indeed an independent kingdom—had he actually been born in Hawai'i, he would have become an American citizen when the territory was annexed. This document illustrates the crucial point that much of Asian immigrant politics centered around homeland issues—for the Chinese of this era, reform or overthrow of the Manchus; for the Japanese, rising democratic and socialist movements or pro- or antiemperor sentiments; and for the Koreans, passion for liberating Korea from Japan.

Sworn statement by Sun Yat-sen, April 21, 1904; 9995 Sun Yat Sen; Arrival Investigation Case Files, 1884–1944; National Archives and Records Administration–Pacific Region; FG 85.

Detention Sheds,
Pacific Mail Dock,

April 21, 1904.

As further evidence of my right to enter the United States as a citizen of Hawaii by birth, and that I have never renounced allegiance to that Government, I submit the following additional statement to accompany the other papers in my case on appeal to the Department at Washington:

Some time after the annexation of the Hawaiian Islands to the United States, there was a registration taken of all the residents for the purpose of ascertaining the nationality and birth of such residents. I was registered in the Kula district, in the Island of Maui, as a Hawaiian-born Chinese, about March or April in the year 1901. That is the first thing that I did after the annexation of the Islands to show that I still claimed citizenship there, the next step being that taken just prior to my departure from the Islands for this country, in March of the present year, when I again proved my citizenship and received my passport from the Governor of the Territory. Although a Chinese by blood I never claimed to be a Chinese subject nor in anyway asked the protection of the Chinese Government. On the contrary, my political views have always been opposed to the Chinese Government, and I have been regarded as an enemy of that Government. The student papers I obtained from the official of the Government at Shanghai in order to enable me to enter the United States [handwritten words illegible] was given me merely as an act of personal friendship for me, and was not given me because of any allegiance I bore to the Chinese Government. This officer and myself were personal friends and as such a paper seemed to be necessary in order for me to come to the United States it was granted for that purpose.

[signature of Sun Yat-sen]

Sworn to April 21, 1904.

This additional statement was made by the applicant on finding that his papers had not yet been forwarded to the Department, and is forwarded at his request.

[signature of customs official]

Inspector.

43

Theodore Roosevelt Executive Order
(a.k.a. Gentlemen's Agreement), March 14, 1907

The "Gentlemen's Agreement" between the United States and Japan was not a single document but a series of notes exchanged between the governments. President Theodore Roosevelt brokered the agreement to avoid an international incident precipitated by the San Francisco school board in 1906 when it attempted to remove Japanese children to a segregated school for the Chinese. Roosevelt sought to contain the anti-Japanese racism in California to maintain reasonable relations with Japan, an increasingly powerful force in Asia and the Pacific. The agreement effectively ended the issuing of passports by Japan for laborers who sought to leave for the United States, thus placating Americans who objected to Japanese immigration. The Japanese government was mollified because the United States had not passed specific legislation, as in the case of the Chinese, barring Japanese from immigrating. Parents, spouses, and children of Japanese already in the country were eligible to come here, however; this permitted significant immigration of "picture brides" and children. As a result, the Japanese community never experienced the severe gender imbalance of Chinese and Filipino communities. Some Japanese laborers also entered the United States through Hawai'i, Mexico, and Canada, and Roosevelt issued this executive order to prevent Japanese and Korean laborers with passports for those areas from re-immigrating. Koreans were by then traveling under Japanese passports, as their country had fallen under Japan's control.

CIS Presidential Executive Orders and Proclamations, EO-589, March 14, 1907. Microfiche, Law Library of Congress, Washington, DC.

Executive Order

Whereas, by the act entitled "An Act to regulate the immigration of aliens into the United States," approved February 20, 1907, whenever the President is satisfied that passports issued by any foreign government to its citizens to go to any country other than the United States or to any insular possession of the United

States or to the Canal Zone, are being used for the purpose of enabling the holders to come to the continental territory of the United States to the detriment of labor conditions therein, it is made the duty of the President to refuse to permit such citizens of the country issuing such passports to enter the continental territory of the United States from such country or from such insular possession or from the Canal Zone;

And Whereas, upon sufficient evidence produced before me by the Department of Commerce and Labor, I am satisfied that passports issued by the Government of Japan to citizens of that country or Korea and who are laborers, skilled or unskilled, to go to Mexico, to Canada and to Hawaii, are being used for the purpose of enabling the holders thereof to come to the continental territory of the United States to the detriment of labor conditions therein;

I hereby order that such citizens of Japan or Korea, to-wit: Japanese or Korean laborers, skilled and unskilled, who have received passports to go to Mexico, Canada or Hawaii, and come therefrom, be refused permission to enter the continental territory of the United States.

It is further ordered that the Secretary of Commerce and Labor be, and he hereby is, directed to take, thru the Bureau of Immigration and Naturalization, such measures and to make and enforce such rules and regulations as may be necessary to carry this order into effect.

THEODORE ROOSEVELT.

The White House,
March 14, 1907.

[No. 589.]

44

Anti-Japanese Laundry League Flyer, 1908

This is one of a series of flyers distributed widely in San Francisco about the time that the United States forced Japan to accede to demands formalized in the Gentlemen's Agreement of 1907–8. That agreement ended the immigration of Japanese laborers into the United States, but not the racism that portrayed the existing Japanese American community as unfair competition that would destroy white rule and white civilization. This particular piece was distributed just prior to implementation of the agreement, but subsequent flyers asked, "Will the Japanese Predominate"—urging Caucasians to "successfully combat the inroads of the Japanese [by refusing] to patronize or employ them in any of their industries." Anti-Japanese racism escalated rapidly after significant numbers arrived in the country following the Exclusion Acts, passed beginning in 1882, prohibiting Chinese laborers from entering. Japanese military victory in the Russo-Japanese War of 1904–5 exacerbated this tension because it marked the first time that a non-white nation had defeated a "white" country in modern warfare. The resulting combination of a despised race with military teeth fostered unprecedented fear and loathing.

"White or Jap—Which?" Anti-Japanese Laundry League, San Francisco, n.d. (ca. June 1908). Author's collection.

White or Jap—Which?

FELLOW CITIZENS:—

Japanese competition is a menace to **your** social, industrial and political welfare, as well as to **ours**. Neither we nor you can live like Americans and educate our children for enlightened citizenship on the wages such competition, if continued, will compel us to accept.

Present immigration laws, together with the cunning of the Jap, are resulting in thousands of these Asiatics swarming in upon the industrial market, and Japanese house servants, cooks, waiters, shoemakers, laundry workers, etc., are filling places while white men and women walk the streets in vain in search of work in these and other lines.

This is no idle alarm. The Japanese are not a **future** menace. They are working us great harm **now**.

Do you know that, in the Hawaiian Islands, Japanese do nearly 85 per cent of all plantation work, and 75 per cent of all other work, skilled and unskilled?

Do you know that the Hawaiian Islands are practically orientalized?

Do you know that in California 989 farms aggregating 61,859 acres, are owned or rented by Japs, and worked by a farming population of more than 10,000 Japanese?

Look at the following list, taken from reliable sources, of places of work and kinds of employment invaded by the Jap in San Francisco alone:

Bakeries	Decorating	Grocery stores	Plumbing
Bath Houses	Doctor	House cleaning	Porters
Banks	Employment agencies	Janitors	Restaurants
Bellboy	Florist stores	Jewelry stores	Stationery stores
Barber shops	Fruit stores	Laundries	Tin stores
Billiard parlor	Furnishing stores	Painting	Tailors
Cobblers	Gas-fitting	Photographers	Watchmen
Curio stores			

and all of the thirty odd building trades used in constructing a modern house.

Think over these facts and figures, you citizens of San Francisco who patronize Jap labor and yet hope to live out your lives like white people; think them over, you who expect your children to live here in California after you, and to sustain the social and moral institutions of your country.

There are legal remedies for these evils, and the time will come when the people of California, realizing the seriousness of this menace, will apply them. But, meanwhile, there is a present remedy. There is a remedy that each individual can apply. **HE NEED NOT PATRONIZE.**

Will YOU help the Jap to conquer the industrial field in California—and remember this means social degradation as well—as he has in the Hawaiian Islands? Do you want San Francisco, Oakland, San Jose, Los Angeles, to be overrun with them as are the orchard regions around Vacaville, Watsonville and Fresno?

WE ASK YOU TO BUY FROM WHITES. WE ASK YOU TO BUY GOODS MADE BY WHITES. WE ASK YOU TO HAVE YOUR WORK OF ALL KINDS DONE BY WHITE MEN AND WOMEN WHO LIVE AS YOU LIVE AND PRIZE THE IDEALS AND COUNTRY THAT YOU PRIZE. WE ASK YOU TO PATRONIZE ONLY WHITE LABOR.

ANTI-JAPANESE LAUNDRY LEAGUE,
483 GUERRERO STREET,
SAN FRANCISCO.

45

On Higher Wages for Japanese Laborers, 1909

Japanese workers on Hawaii's sugar plantations organized the first large-scale strike in 1909. There had been numerous work stoppages and several strikes since the beginning of the industry in the 1830s, but this was the first coordinated effort, led by the Higher Wages Association (Zokyu kisei kai); it successfully crippled the industry on the main island of O'ahu. The strategy called for the 7,000 workers on O'ahu plantations to stay off the job while laborers on other islands continued to draw wages and provide support. Japanese language newsmen led the entire community effort, while the Japanese consulate opposed the strike. The Hawaii State Planters Association, with the full array of media, finance, political, and police powers in support, determined to break the strike and refused to negotiate. After four months, the workers were forced to give up, and most returned to the fields and mills. The planters soon implemented reforms including higher wages, better living conditions, and better bonuses. They also imported increasing numbers of Filipinos to weaken the Japanese united front. But in the decade that followed, including World War I, inflation drastically eroded the modest gains and a larger strike ensued, temporarily drawing the Filipinos and Japanese together. This 1920 strike lasted longer and cost the planters more, but it too eventually succumbed to superior power and the blatant use of racist divide-and-rule tactics. In both cases, the Japanese community displayed considerable organizing ability and skill in presenting its side of the case. This particular document from 1909 provided the Japanese laborers' justification for the strike. Excerpts are presented here with typos and mistakes intact.

Higher Wages Association (*Zokyu kisei kai*), "On Higher Wages for Japanese Laborers." Honolulu, HI: Zokyu kiseikai, 1909. Manuscript 42 [Japanese], 20 [English translation] pages. Hamilton Library, University of Hawai'i. Thanks to Joan Hori, head of the Hawai'i Collection, for assistance in locating and duplicating this document.

They say that the planters have money enough and get such a high rate of dividend that they can pay higher wages: but that they have to expend this surplus money for the importation of white labor. We do not mean to say anything about the importation of white labor, nor do we propose to dwell at any length on this phase of question: But we want to say that the argument is not very convincing to us.

As a matter of common justice, we would most politely beg the planters to curtail their own social expenditures; and cut the dividends, establish the special fund for the prosecution and realization of the laudable and patriotic undertaking, to wit the importation of white labor, and that they give the present labor what is justly due to them. Do not sacrifice the labor actually doing work now in the field, for any and all purposes; however high and: laudable they may be. . . .

The planters can pay twenty-two dollars and a half to labor of other nationalities than Japanese and Coreans, and they, also, give them a house and a lot of one acre to each family. And, in view of the fact that the twenty-two dollars and a half wages schedule was established with a view of bringing labor to supplant the entire Oriental working force, the planters can pay the same amount of wages to us, and the same facilities and advantages in the shape of a house and a lot. This shows conclusively the ability of the planters to pay higher wages. . . .

How much a labor spends is no reason for demand for higher wages. But when labor is given only a living wages as in Hawaii, it is one of very potent factor in considering the wages question. The cost of living have increased at least three times as compared with ten years ago, the labor of ten years ago only had to support himself. But now they have to support a family. They must educate children, support educational and religious institutions. They must bear other social expenses, which naturally follows the formation of a family. The price of necessities have doubled, and a labor must buy more of necessities, whose prices have more than doubled, in order to support his wife and children. In addition to this they must contribute to the support of social institutions and bear expenses of social intercourse of advanced type. And yet the labor is paid only at the rate of 69c. per day, which is the wages calculated to suit the condition of a contract labor, — a semi-slavery. The condition has changed. The labor is now free, and they are entitled to soft, humane consideration of the planters. . . .

That the Japanese as plantation hands of Hawaii is equal to any and inferior to none, is attested by all impartial observers. The Japanese merchants and the Japanese who have themselves experience in plantation work, all concur in the opinion that the Japanese labors are doing hardest and dirtiest work in plantation, and that any kind of work at which they are set to work they do with care, skill and quickness which no other labor can equal, and that the present wages schedule is altogether inadequate and antiquated, and that they are sorry to see the labor of such efficiency be paid only 69 cents a day and that they deserve higher wages and that the demand for higher wages came none too soon, if it were too late. . . .

If wages were to be regulated by the price of articles of prime necessity the present wages should be double that which prevailed at the time of the Chino-Japanese war, which will give the laborers $32 a month and if the new wages were to be computed with the present wages as basis, the new schedule should be $22.14 per month. . . .

With the formation of family, there inevitably follows the establishment of churches and schools. These institutions are not unnecessary luxuries. They are just as important as the bread and butter in the life of man. The establishment of these institutions by the laborers are not to be deprecated but it deserves to be encouraged. These institutions will give the planters an intelligent, conscientious and god-fearing labor, instead of lazy, unscrupulous, selfish and savage labor. The Japanese maintains at the present time 59 churches and missions, with 61 ministers and preachers. Of these 33 are of Buddhist denominations; and 26 Christians. These places of worship have remarkably increased in recent years. Down to 1903 there were only 11 Christian missions, but since that year ten were added. The Buddhist missions are only of recent growth. The first mission was established in 1898, and within the last 10 years they have maintained only 23 chapels, but since then they have added 10 more. The Christians do not bear, as a general rule, the expenses of constructing a church or preaching place, they bearing only the ordinary expenses in maintaining the establishment which is between thirty and fifty dollars per month for one place. But the Buddhists bear all expenses themselves.

46

Angel Island Poetry, 1910

In 1910 the United States established an immigration station on Angel Island in San Francisco Bay. Perhaps 200,000 potential immigrants, most from China, were processed and detained there—some for months or years in dehumanizing conditions—until 1940, when the station was transferred. During those three decades, thousands of Chinese were kept in barracks and interrogated to ferret out possible ineligible immigrants. These "paper" sons and daughters claimed American citizenship by virtue of birth in the United States or to American citizens in China; some had bought papers from immigrants who returned to China for visits. Interrogation was often strict and included minute details about the family home and village including, for example, the number of stairs to the door or windows on the east wall or the types of trees in the neighbors' yard. Ironically, the false applicants often memorized detailed "coaching" books to avoid detection, while legitimate citizens might miss a detail and be denied rightful entry or reentry into the country. During detention on Angel Island, some Chinese carved powerful poems into the barracks walls, lamenting their condition or vowing revenge for the personal and national humiliation they faced. Some of these poems have been salvaged and have become extraordinary documents of the times.

Reprinted with permission. Him Mark Lai, Genny Lim, and Judy Yung, eds, *Island: Poetry and History of Chinese Immigrants on Angel Island, 1910–1940.* Seattle and London: University of Washington Press, 1980.

> There are tens of thousands of poems on these walls
> They are all cries of suffering and sadness
> The day I am rid of this prison and become successful
> I must remember that this chapter once existed
> I must be frugal in my daily needs
> Needless extravagance usually leads to ruin
> All my compatriots should remember China

Once you have made some small gains,
you should return home early.

Written by one from Heungshan

In the quiet of night, I heard, faintly, the whistling of wind.
The forms and shadows saddened me;
upon seeing the landscape, I composed a poem.
The floating clouds, the fog, darken the sky.
The moon shines faintly as the insects chirp.
Grief and bitterness entwined are heaven sent.
The sad person sits alone, leaning by a window.

America has power, but not justice.
In prison, we were victimized as if we were guilty.
Given no opportunity to explain, it was really brutal.
I bow my head in reflection but there is
nothing I can do.

I thoroughly hate the barbarians because they
do not respect justice.
They continually promulgate harsh laws to
show off their prowess.
They oppress the overseas Chinese and also
violate treaties.
They examine for hookworms and practice
hundreds of despotic acts.

47

Song: "Chinatown, My Chinatown," 1910

By 1910 the Chinese had been superseded by the Japanese as the most threatening Asian invaders in the popular white imagination. In 1895, the Japanese had defeated the Chinese in a short war, and China's Manchu dynasty was in its death throes, soon to be overthrown in the 1911 Revolution. So, while still derogatory, images of the Chinese evolved into weak, pitiable victims. Like a few other tunes, "Chinatown, My Chinatown" became an enormous hit across the country, both drawing from and creating larger popular stereotypes of Chinese Americans.

Archives of American History, National Museum of American History, Smithsonian Institution. Thanks to Krystyn Moon, whose research has unearthed a wealth of similar songs.

Chinatown, My Chinatown

Words by
WILLIAM JEROME

Music by
JEAN SCHWARTZ

Starts to wink his dream-y eye,
Still thinks he's a mil-lion-aire,

La-zi-ly you'll hear him sigh
Pipe dreams ban-ish ev-'ry care.

CHORUS.

Chi-na-town, my Chi-na-town,— Where the

lights are low,— Hearts that know no

Chinatown my Chinatown 3

48

Supreme Court: Tang Tun v. Edsell, *March 11, 1912*

Tang Tun and his bride, Leung Kum Wui, were denied entry into the United States at the port of Sumas in Washington State in 1906. The "Chinese Inspector," Harry Edsell, ruled that there was insufficient evidence to prove that Tang Tun had been born in 1879 in Seattle and was, therefore, a citizen. They appealed to the district court, which reversed the decision, but the circuit court overruled the reversal. The Supreme Court then heard the case and upheld the decision, thus effectively ordering the couple to be deported in spite of considerable evidence that Tang was in fact born in the United States. One major effect of the decision was to reinforce the authority of the inspectors and, in the absence of egregious misconduct on their part or by the Secretary of Commerce, to whom appeals would be directed, remove the courts from the process. The decision thus effectively denied most Chinese immigrants recourse to the judiciary.

United States Reports, vol. 223. New York: The Banks Law Publishing Co., 1912.

Mr. Justice Hughes delivered the opinion of the court.

On June 22, 1906, Tang Tun and Leung Kum Wui, his wife, Chinese persons, sought entry to the United States at the port of Sumas, State of Washington, and were denied admission by the inspector in charge, whose order was affirmed by the Secretary of Commerce and Labor. Application was then made to the District Court of the United States for a writ of *habeas corpus*.

It was alleged in the petition that Tang Tun was a citizen of the United States, born in 1879, at Seattle, of parents there domiciled; that, in 1884, he went to China, where he remained thirteen years; that, in 1897, he returned to the United States, was admitted by the collector of customs after examination, entered the employ of Wa Chong & Co., in Seattle, and continued with that firm until 1905, when he returned to China for the purpose of marrying; that he was married to Leung Kum Wui in accordance with the laws of China and the consular requirements of the United States; that the officers concerned had improperly conducted the inquiry and had abused their discretion in refusing admission; and that the petitioners were restrained of their liberty without due process of law.

The writ was granted, and the case having been submitted to the District Court upon the record of the proceedings on the application for entry and the appeal to the Secretary of Commerce and Labor, it was held that the petitioners had been denied the hearing for which the act of Congress provided, that Tang Tun had established his citizenship, and that he and his wife were entitled to remain in this country. Accordingly, both were discharged from custody. . . . This decision was reversed by the Circuit Court of Appeals, which reached the conclusion that the requirements of the law had been satisfied and that there was no ground for judicial intervention. . . .

The acts of August 18, 1894, . . . and of February 14, 1903, . . . make the decision of the appropriate immigration officer final unless reversed on appeal to the Secretary of Commerce and Labor. And if it does not affirmatively appear that the executive officers have acted in some unlawful or improper way and abused their discretion, their finding upon the question of citizenship must be deemed to be conclusive and is not subject to review by the court. . . .

The question, however, was whether he was born in the United States. Of the witnesses who professed to testify on this point—other than Tang Tun himself—all save one were shown by their examination to be unworthy of credit; and the knowledge of the one trustworthy witness—a police officer of Seattle— was plainly insufficient to make his testimony controlling. This witness relied upon his identification of the youth of about eighteen years of age, who arrived in 1897, as the same person whom he had last seen as a child some thirteen years before. There remained the testimony of Tang Tun himself, but this, with all the other evidence in the case, was for the consideration of the officers to whom Congress had confided the matter for final decision. The record fails to show that their authority was not fairly exercised, that is, consistently with the fundamental principles of justice embraced within the conception of due process of law. And, this being so, the merits of the case were not open to judicial examination. . . .

Judgment affirmed.

49

Hawaii Hochi, *First Editorial, December 7, 1912*

On December 7, 1912, Frederick Kinzaburo Makino and George Wright published the first copy of the Hawaii Hochi, *soon to become the principal rival to the existing* Nippu Jiji *as leading Japanese language newspaper in the islands. Yasutaro Soga was publisher of the* Nippu Jiji, *and he and Makino had been among the principal leaders in the path-breaking sugar strike by Japanese laborers in 1909. Makino was reportedly unhappy with Soga's journalistic treatment of the events and established his own newspaper, the only one that continues today. As his lead editorial, printed prominently on page one, indicated, the* Hochi *would become his vehicle to establish leadership within the Japanese American community in Hawai'i. A slightly different version appears in a work dedicated to his life:* Life of Kinzaburo Makino, *published in 1965 by the* Hawaii Hochi (four *lines from that version are reprinted here where the original is illegible).*

Makino was born in Japan, the son of a Japanese woman and a British merchant. He moved to Hawai'i at the turn of the century and quickly established himself as a fair but fierce advocate for the Japanese community. Among his major battles were the fight to end Christian wedding ceremonies forced upon Japanese "picture brides" joining their husbands at dockside in Honolulu, support for Japanese language teachers arriving during the period the territory was attempting to abolish the schools, and leadership in the lengthy court fight (1922–27) ending in the U.S. Supreme Court decision establishing the constitutionality of those language schools. His fierce determination to couch Japanese American community advocacy in terms of "American" democratic principles probably saved him from internment during World War II, when Soga and other immigrant leaders were sent to mainland camps.

Reprinted with permission from Paul Yempuku, publisher, *Hawaii Hochi*. From microfilm version of original in *Hawaii Hochi* archives.

The Hawaii Hochi

Editorial in first paper: December 7, 1912, page one.

In making our initial bow to the people of Hawaii, it seems to be proper that we should briefly outline the policy and aims of the Hawaii Hochi.

This paper, to be published daily in the Japanese language, will endeavor, to the utmost of its ability, to further the interests of the Japanese residents of the Territory of Hawaii.

To that end, provision has been made to secure from Japan, full and complete accounts of those matters which are of interest to the Japanese of this Territory, so that the bond existing between Japan and her children in Hawaii will be strengthened.

There are now in Hawaii many children born here of Japanese parents, who, by reason of their birth-place, have all the rights and privileges of citizens of the United States of America. It will be one of the principal aims of this paper, to afford and opportunity to such young people to learn of all the important affairs of the United States, and become familiar with its institutions, so that they may not only enjoy the privileges of citizenship to the fullest extent, but may become patriotic citizens, of intelligence, integrity, and virtue.

Believing that education is the basis of all true prosperity, it will be the policy of this paper to do everything in its power to assist the churches, schools, and other similar institutions conducted by the Japanese here.

In case any disagreement should hereafter arise among the Japanese themselves, or between the Japanese and others, this paper will use its best endeavor to settle such difference or differences in such a manner that the Japanese community as a whole may be benefited thereby, with fairness to all.

This paper recognizes that the principal industry of Hawaii is, and for a long time will be, the Sugar business; and that the sugar planters rely and must rely to a great extent, upon the Japanese for labor. It will almost inevitably follow in the future, that differences of opinion of greater or less importance, will arise between the Japanese on the one hand, and the sugar planters on the other. This paper will do its best in such case to present the actual facts of the case, from the Japanese standpoint.

I believe that the best and only way is to report the truth as truth, and right as right. Regardless of whatever advice I may receive, I will never curry favor with plantation owners. I will never resort to clever deceit and give them a wrong interpretation of the facts. [*]

This paper is not subsidized by the planters, nor, on the other hand, is it exclusively the organ of any Japanese Society or institution, and is therefore free,

---

[*]*These four italicized lines come from the* Life of Kinzaburo Makino *because the original microfilm version is illegible.*

and will always be free to give an unbiased opinion as to any question that may hereafter arise.

With the labor troubles and problems which have arisen in the past, this paper has nothing to do. The strike of 1909 is ended, except as to the matter of criminal acts perpetrated by government officials in those times and as to those acts the proper authorities in Tokio and Washington are now taking steps which will doubtless result, in time, in a satisfactory settlement.

For some years past, Japanese have been leaving Hawaii to return to Japan, and from this cause as well as other natural causes, the supply of laborers has been constantly diminishing. "The gentlemen's agreement" entered into between Tokio and Washington, prevents at the present time the emigration of Japanese to the United States, and, thus, there is no way of filling the places of those laborers who have returned home, and from natural causes have been taken from the labor field. Many Japanese have left the Territory intending to return after a visit to Japan, but have been unable to secure passports for such return after a stay of over eighteen months in Japan. It will be one of the objects of this paper to secure from the Japanese Government a modification of the present rule restricting pass-ports, so that Japanese who formerly resided in Hawaii, but are now staying in Japan, will have the right to return to Hawaii.

It will, at all times be the policy of this paper to encourage the Japanese to remain permanently in Hawaii, and to work together for the benefit of the Territory as a whole.

50

California Alien Land Law (a.k.a. Webb Act), August 10, 1913

California led the way for fifteen states to pass legislation preventing "aliens ineligible to citizenship" from owning land. Although occasionally used against other Asians, these laws were directly aimed at Japanese immigrants, who were perceived as gaining undue economic power through agricultural holdings. Legislation using the words "Asian" or "Japanese" would clearly be unconstitutional, hence the circumlocution. Violators would have their property revert to control by the state. But at least some Japanese managed to evade the law, and the legislature moved in 1920 to strengthen its provisions as well as prohibit the practice of immigrant Japanese (as guardians) placing land in the legal hands of their citizen children. The Supreme Court declared such laws constitutional in 1923, and California's law remained on the books until 1956, although court cases had invalidated the 1920 and 1913 Alien Land Laws in Oyama v. California *(1948) and* Fujii Sei v. State of California *(1952).*

The Statutes of California and Amendments to the Codes Passed at the Fortieth Session of the Legislature, 1913. Sacramento: Superintendent of State Printing, 1913.

Chapter 113

An act relating to the rights, powers and disabilities of aliens and of certain companies, associations and corporations with respect to property in this state, providing for escheats in certain cases, prescribing the procedure therein, and repealing all acts or parts of acts inconsistent or in conflict herewith.

The people of the State of California do enact as follows:

Section 1. All aliens eligible to citizenship under the laws of the United States may acquire, possess, enjoy, transmit and inherit real property, or any interest therein, in this state, in the same manner and to the same extent as citizens of the United States, except as otherwise provided by the laws of this state.

Sec. 2. All aliens other than those mentioned in section one of this act may acquire, possess, enjoy and transfer real property, or any interest therein, in this state, in the manner and to the extent and for the purposes prescribed by any treaty now existing between the government of the United States and the nation or country of which such alien is a citizen or subject, and not otherwise, and may in addition thereto lease lands in this state for agricultural purposes for a term not exceeding three years.

Sec. 3. Any company, association or corporation organized under the laws of this or any other state or nation, of which a majority of the members are aliens other than those specified in section one of this act, or in which a majority of the issued capital stock is owned by such aliens, may acquire, possess, enjoy and convey real property, or any interest therein, in this state, in the manner and to the extent and for the purposes prescribed by any treaty now existing between the government of the United States and the nation or country of which such members or stockholders are citizens or subjects, and not otherwise, and may in addition thereto lease lands in this state for agricultural purposes for a term not exceeding three years. . . .

Sec. 5. Any real property hereafter acquired in fee in violation of the provisions of this act by any alien mentioned in section two of this act, or by any company, association or corporation mentioned in section three of this act, shall escheat to, and become and remain the property of the State of California. . . .

51

Immigration Act of 1917 (a.k.a. Barred Zone Act), February 5, 1917

This was another in the long series of legislation, enacted beginning in 1882, re-stricting immigration into the United States. This particular act established a "zone" including India, Indochina, the Malays, parts of Russia and Arabia, Afghanistan, and island nations of Polynesia and Southeast Asia, from which im-migrants would be barred. It is an excellent example of legislative action follow-ing inconclusive judicial interpretation of prior actions. Congress definitively in-cluded South Asians among those it wished to keep out. The act is an example also of the increasing use of circumlocution—avoiding direct reference to the na-tions and nationalities excluded—by using their precise longitudes and latitudes instead. It retained all restrictions aimed at the Chinese and Japanese, and, for the first time, prohibited entry by anyone over sixteen and illiterate. This act was followed by others, in 1920 and finally in 1924, that more definitively established national policies favoring immigration from Northern and Western Europe. Most of these provisions remained in effect, with minor revisions, until the McCarran-Walter Act of 1952, which included minute quotas for Asian countries. The final removal of racial barriers came in 1965.

The Statutes at Large of the United States of America, vol. XXXIX, part 1. Washington, DC: Government Printing Office, 1917.

Chap. 29.—
An Act To regulate the immigration of aliens to,
and the residence of aliens in the United States

Be it enacted by the Senate and House of Representatives of the United States of America in Congress assembled, That the word "alien" wherever used in this Act shall include any person not a native-born or naturalized citizen of the United States; but this definition shall not be held to include Indians of the United States not taxed or citizens of the islands under the jurisdiction of the United States. . . .

Sec. 3. That the following classes of aliens shall be excluded from admission into the United States: All idiots, imbeciles, feeble-minded persons, epileptics, insane persons; persons who have had one or more attacks of insanity at any time previously; persons of constitutional psychopathic inferiority; persons with chronic alcoholism; paupers; professional beggars; vagrants; persons afflicted with tuberculosis in any form or with a loathsome or dangerous contagious disease; persons not comprehended within any of the foregoing excluded classes who are found to be and are certified by the examining surgeon as being mentally or physically defective, such physical defect being of a nature which may affect the ability of such alien to earn a living; persons who have been convicted of or admit having committed a felony or other crime or misdemeanor involving moral turpitude; polygamists, or persons who practice polygamy or believe in or advocate the practice of polygamy; anarchists, or persons who believe in or advocate the overthrow by force or violence of the Government of the United States, or of all forms of law, or who disbelieve in or are opposed to organized government, or who advocate the assassination of public officials, or who advocate or teach the unlawful destruction of property; persons who are members of or affiliated with any organization entertaining and teaching disbelief in or opposition to organized government, or who advocate or teach the duty, necessity or propriety of the unlawful assaulting or killing of any officer or officers, either of specific individuals or of officers generally, of the Government of the United States or of any other organized government, because of his or their official character, or who advocate or teach the unlawful destruction of property; prostitutes, or persons coming into the United States for the purpose of prostitution or for any other immoral purpose; persons who directly or indirectly procure or attempt to procure or import prostitutes or persons for the purpose of prostitution or for any other immoral purpose; persons who are supported by or receive in whole or in part the proceeds of prostitution; persons hereinafter called contract laborers, who have been induced, assisted, encouraged, or solicited to migrate to this country by offers or promises of employment, whether such offers or promises are true or false, or in consequence of agreements, oral, written or printed, express or implied, to perform labor in this country of any kind, skilled or unskilled; persons who have come in consequence of advertisements for laborers printed, published, or distributed in a foreign country; persons likely to become a public charge; persons who have been deported under any of the provisions of this Act, and who may again seek admission within one year from the date of such deportation, unless prior to their reembarkation at a foreign port or their attempt to be admitted from foreign contiguous territory the Secretary of Labor shall have consented to their reapplying for admission; persons whose tickets or passage is paid for with the money of another, or who are assisted by others to come, unless it is affirmatively and satisfactorily shown that such persons do not belong to one of the foregoing excluded classes; persons whose ticket or passage is paid for by any corporation, association, society, municipality, or foreign Government, either directly or indirectly; stowaways, except that any such stowaway, if otherwise admissible, may be admitted in the discretion of the Secretary of Labor; all children under sixteen years of age, unaccompanied by or not coming to one or both of their parents, except that any such children may, in the discretion of the Secretary of Labor, be admitted if in his opinion they are not likely to become a public charge and are otherwise eligible; unless otherwise provided for by existing treaties, persons who are natives of islands not possessed by the United States adjacent to the Continent of Asia, situate south of the twentieth parallel latitude north, west of the one hundred and sixtieth meridian of longitude east from Greenwich, and north of the tenth parallel of latitude south, or who are natives of any country, province, or dependency situate on the Continent of Asia west of the one hundred and tenth meridian of longitude east from Greenwich and east of the fiftieth meridian of longitude east from Greenwich and south of the fiftieth parallel of latitude north, except that portion of said territory situate between the fiftieth and the sixty-fourth meridians of longitude east from Greenwich and the twenty-fourth and thirty-eighth parallels of latitude north, and no alien now in any way excluded from, or prevented from entering, the United States shall be admitted to the United States.

52

Immigration Memorandum re Mrs. Fong See, July 3, 1919

Diplomats, students, and merchants were the only Chinese allowed into the United States from the 1882 Chinese Exclusion Act until major immigration reform in 1965, except for the token quota of 105 established in 1943. Fong See and his wife, the former Leticie Pruett, had been to China in 1901, and he had gone alone in 1912. But even with substantial prior documentation, immigration officials had difficulty with this early interracial couple. The family was traveling with five children, all American-born and thus citizens, but the negotiations for securing the right to return, given the overt anti-Chinese sentiment then in force, were extremely difficult. Form 431, referenced in the memo, documented the wife of a lawfully domiciled merchant from China. Indeed, Inspector Becktell eventually issued Form 431, but Inspector Harry Blee proceeded to interrogate Ticie See and the children before their passports were issued, only a few days prior to sailing. And, as Lisa See notes in her family memoir, On Gold Mountain *(New York: Vintage, 1995), the family was highly unusual. Of course, the treatment meted out to the merchant See family was far more cordial and favorable than that received by tens of thousands of Chinese detained for weeks or months on Angel Island between 1910 and 1940.*

Thanks to Lisa See and the Autry Museum of Western Heritage for posting this document in the exhibit, "On Gold Mountain." Courtesy National Archives and Records Administration.

U.S. DEPARTMENT OF LABOR
IMMIGRATION SERVICE

IN ANSWERING REFER TO   OFFICE OF THE COMMISSIONER
No. 12017/11940   ANGEL ISLAND STATION
/11946   VIA FERRY POST OFFICE
SAN FRANCISCO, CAL.

JULY 3, 1919

MEMORANDUM FOR THE COMMISSIONER

In re Fong See, merchant departing, and Mrs. Fong See, wife of merchant departing.

The lawful domicile of Fong See is established by certificate of residence No. 130020. There is nothing in the record to indicate that he is not a bona fide merchant. Judging from the photograph attached to Mrs. Fong See's application it seems likely that she is an American-born white person. Her maiden name was Ticia Pruett and her birth place is given as the United States. In July 1912, prior to his departure for China, Fong See testified this his wife was an American. Fong See, his wife Mrs. Fong See and two children departed for china in 1901 and returned on the steamer "Korea" October 28th, 1902. This office had the usual Chinese papers for Fong See and the two children but no papers are on file for Mrs. Fong See. The manifest of the steamer "Korea" shows the following: "Mrs. Fong See, age 24, American."

There appears to be some conflict of opinion as to whether an American-born white woman married to a domiciled Chinese merchant should be given a Form 431, or should be handled strictly under the Immigration Law. In my opinion the latter would be the proper procedure. The Record Room was unable to locate any ruling on this point.

The testimony taken in the present case and the report of the Inspector in Charge [sic] at Los Angeles contain no mention so far as I noted of the race of Mrs. Fong See, and that being the case it might be assumed that in the opinion of the examining officers she is at least part Chinese. In order to obtain definite information as to this it would be necessary to return the record to Los Angeles, and as both applicants are desirous of leaving for China about the middle of this month it would seem that the simplest way of handling her case would be to approve Form 431.

W G Becktell
[signature]
Immigrant Inspector.

WGB:BRW

53

Federation of Japanese Labor,
"The Voice of Labor in Hawaii," 1920

After the serious strike in 1909, wages and conditions improved somewhat on most Hawai'i sugar plantations. But the inflation accompanying World War I seriously eroded the Japanese laborers' purchasing power. Moreover, the arrival of so many wives in the previous decade and the birth of so many children necessitated far greater expenditures for the whole infrastructure of community life. Thus, the amount and nature of bonuses and perquisites became important issues to negotiate. The planters argued that wages and bonuses would be more than adequate if only the Japanese would cease sending hundreds of thousands of dollars back to Japan every year. Besides, planters and major newspapers explained, this was no mere labor-capital dispute but a thinly disguised attempt by the Japanese to take over the islands. Unlike in 1909, when the labor movement had been led by newspapermen in the community, in 1920 more of the leadership appeared to come from the ranks of the workers; more were younger and more militant—indeed, some of the rhetoric suggests familiarity with the worldwide spread of socialism and Marxism as a result of the Bolshevik Revolution in Russia in 1917. The Japanese Federation's articulate leader was Noboru Tsutsumi (whose given name is routinely misread as "Takashi," according to Masayo Duus in The Japanese Conspiracy: The Oahu Sugar Strike of 1920 *[Berkeley: University of California Press, 1999]). The strike was precipitated by Filipino workers, who were then joined by the Japanese, but the former were not as well organized and did not have the large community capable of supporting a long strike. As a result, they fairly quickly returned to the fields. The Japanese stayed off the job for six months, and the strike became a national issue because of price increases for sugar. The planters officially refused to negotiate but raised wages and improved living and working conditions after the workers returned to their jobs.*

The Federation of Japanese Labor in Hawaii, "The Voice of Labor in Hawaii." Pamphlet issued in Honolulu, February 1920. Thanks to Joan Hori for locating this document in Special Collections, Hamilton Library, University of Hawaii at Manoa.

The Voice of Labor in Hawaii.

We are asking that the basic wages of common laborers be increased from 77 cents to $1.25 a day, and that the wages of skilled laborers be increased in some reasonable proportion and we respectfully submit the following points in support of our claims.

We are in favor of a bonus system if reasonably devised and administered, but are desirous of having the number of working days at present required for participation in the bonus reduced, by the number of five days, that is, a reduction from 20 days to 15 days in the case of man laborers and from 15 days to 10 days in the case of woman laborers. . . .

The bonus regulations provide that excuses from work on account of sickness are not approved unless issued by special plantation physicians. Granting that the plantations have fine hospitals under the charge of-highly efficient specialists, can they always be depended upon to protect the health and lives of laborers, especially when the laborers understand little or no English and are unable to tell the doctors exactly what their troubles are, and more especially when such laborers need surgical operations or internal treatments? . . .

The fact is that the twenty-day provision in the bonus regulations exclude about 60 percent of all plantation laborers from participation in the bonus, and that only about forty percent of the laborers actually participate in the ANNUAL, (as distinguished from the monthly) bonus.

In view of these cold facts, we are compelled to regard the present bonus system as a matter of benevolence and not as a source of steady income that will insure our security as the planters seem to think it is. . . .

The rest of our demands bearing on protection of woman labor as well as on work on Sundays and legal holidays and other demands are all in accord with the foregoing.

The planters say that plantation laborers are far better off than laborers in Honolulu because they are given free houses, free fuel and free medical attendance in addition to wages and bonus. . . .

But what kind of houses are they? Many of them are such that they do not permit of sitting space when two beds are put in. How about the kitchen? There are stoves made of empty kerosene tins in them. And how about the toilet? They are hardly endurable. . . .

On some of the plantations, we are aware of, laborers' quarters seem more poorly constructed and less sanitary than stables housing the mules and horses used in the cane fields. This is not a pleasant thing to talk about, but it goes a long way toward strengthening our argument that we are afraid that the planters are saying too much when they prate of free houses furnished their laborers. . . .

Ever since January 20 labor conditions on this island have been in a state of unrest. And during the first week of this labor unrest when tension was high and the situation difficult at its best, the 3000 laborers of this island quietly stopped working and waited for some encouraging news from the Planters. And after one week of patient waiting, when it became definitely known that the planters utterly ignored our demands, we went on strike as a final resort. . . .

54

Reverend Shiro Sokabe and Japanese Labor, 1920?

Shiro Sokabe escaped his rigid samurai family in Fukuoka several years before the 1868 Meiji Restoration. Trained at Doshisha University, he was recruited for mission work in Hawai'i by the famous evangelist Jiro Okabe—these dedicated Japanese Christians were active both in Hawai'i and on the mainland well before their Buddhist counterparts. Sokabe arrived in 1894 and worked quietly in the small sugar plantation town of Honomu near Hilo on the Big Island of Hawai'i. He established the Honomu Gijuku (academy, private school) in 1900 and maintained it as a Christian center, Japanese language school, dormitory for students, orphanage, and refuge for battered women and the homeless. Its fame extended throughout the islands because Sokabe had openly acknowledged the frequent breakdown of moral and civil society among the immigrant Japanese, who suffered from alcoholism, extortion, prostitution, and violence. As this document shows, however, Sokabe seemed incapable of understanding that his community also suffered greatly from economic exploitation and that labor had every right to seek better conditions. Perhaps this was due to Honomu Plantation's relatively benign paternalism. As the holehole bushi (sugar plantation blues) lyrics went:

Honomu gokuraku	If Honomu is heaven
Papaiko jigoku	Then Papaikou is hell
Hiro no Waiakea hitogoroshi	And Waiakea in Hilo is a
	killing field.

Honomu was blessed with relatively level terrain and few rocks, but Papaikou was strewn with large stones and Waiakea had to be cleared of boulders before sugar could be planted.

Translated by Jiro Nakano, M.D. in Jiro Nakano, *Samurai Missionary: The Reverend Shiro Sokabe*. Honolulu: Hawaii Conference of the United Church of Christ, 1984.

Letter to Reverend Scudder

I wished to have a Christian home for them . . .

I can soon include 30 or 40 laborers of whom no need for strike or any troubles because they are always instructed in Christian home.

Servants be obedient unto them that according to the flesh are your masters with fear and trembling in singleness of your heart as unto Christ; . . . doing the will of God from the heart with good will doing service as unto the Lord and not unto men.

Let as many as are servants under the yoke count their own masters worthy of all honour that the name of God and the doctrine be not blasphemed.

Ex[h]ort servants to be in subjection to their own masters and to be well-pleasing to them in all things not gain-saying not purloining but shewing all good fidelity that they may adorn the doctrine of God our Saviour in all things.

Servants be in subjection to your masters with all fear not only to the good and gentle but also to the forward.

From these lines, our principle came forth that to do our labour is to fulfill our duty. Our labour must labour faithfully. Who is excellent in heaven? To go? No! Many heroes? No! One who is faithful in very little and live always in the Lord alone shall live be great in the heaven. O, labourer! Do not neglect yourselves. You may be excellent in heaven more than heroes of this world if you are faithful to your duty even your labour.

Nearly one-third of Honomu sugar mill labourers (not field) are church members. Now thirty-five Christian and ten Christian sided people in three hundred Japanese labourers at Honomu. These are of course the evangelical work but at the same time this is profitable to plantation so I asked Mr. Pullar, Honomu manager, to support some lot and building. It is surely profitable to the plantation to keep always 40 or 50 or some more number of labourers of whom need no fear of strike, nor need anxious if their work well or lazy being those labourers working for their duty and not eyeservice. I am afraid if I make such mistake in this writing but there is no time to write anew after I have finished this long letter. Yours truly,

S. Sokabe

P.S. One thing I forgot to write about the matter of keeping the wives. My home is a refuge for woman and husband; and husband can go to work day or night having no anxious for his wife if he live in my home. Many husbands like to come this home if I do not refuse it but there is no room for them. The labourers of the Christian home will be ideal labourer of the plantation.

Bishop Koyu Uchida, Testimony to House Immigration Committee, 1920

Buddhism became a convenient scapegoat and metaphor for the entire "Yellow Peril" image of the "Oriental Other" in twentieth-century America. By 1920 the U.S. House of Representatives had an active Committee on Immigration with a subcommittee holding hearings in California. That state had led the way in anti-Japanese legislation with its 1906 school board act segregating Japanese students and its 1913 land law prohibiting "aliens ineligible to naturalization" from purchasing real estate. The 1920 hearings provided a forum for anti-Asian xenophobes like Senator James Phelan and publisher Valentine McClatchy to argue that Buddhism incorporated state Shinto, which held the Japanese emperor (the Mikado) to be all-powerful. In response, Jodo Shinshu Bishop Koyu Uchida provided a statement to the committee in which he attempted to disconnect the religious and social mission of Buddhism from the official, government-sponsored Shinto propagated by Japan. The House Committee was constrained by strong American traditions respecting freedom of religion and separation of church and state, but the overall message that Buddhism was inherently foreign and inimical to the well-being of the United States was nonetheless successfully conveyed to the general public. Some of this traditional hostility would diminish after World War II and adoption of Zen Buddhism among artists and intellectuals; it would be many years later before marginal groups like the Soka Gakkai would inspire segments of the general public. After 1964, with major immigration from Buddhist societies in many parts of Asia, the numbers of Buddhists and varieties of practice have increased exponentially.

K. K. Kawakami, *The Real Japanese Question*. New York: Macmillan, 1921, 154. Cited in Tetsuden Kashima, *Buddhism in America: The Social Organization of an Ethnic Religious Institution*. Westport, CT: Greenwood Press, 1977, 32–33.

We wish to strongly emphasize that our Churches have nothing to do whatsoever with Shintoism, politics or any imperialistic policy formulated by the Japanese government. Our mission is to elevate the spiritual life, not to dictate

politics or policies of any government. We should also like to point out that
Buddhism is Democratic, an ideal long held by the citizens of the United States
of America. All the clergy in charge of churches are ordained by Hongwanji as
priests, and authorized to preach our religion, and are duly appointed as missionaries in this country by the Missionary Superintendent who is president of
the Headquarters. The missionaries are required to have sufficient knowledge
and information of America and American customs before being sent here, and
are requested to perfect themselves as soon as possible after their arrival.

An Ch'angho, "Grand Strategy for Independence" for Korea, 1920

The Japanese subjugation and colonization of Korea, officially proclaimed in 1910, was sanctioned by the world powers, including the United States. Both before and after that year, however, there were many Korean patriots who worked to restore their country's sovereignty. Some provided national leadership from several countries, including China and the United States. One of the most important was An Ch'angho (1878–1938), who has been described as the founding father of the modern Republic of Korea. Independence movements gained tremendous momentum after the March 1919 "manse" (long live) Korean independence movement, in which millions of Koreans marched in the streets throughout Korea, provoking vicious oppression from Japanese colonial forces. Leadership and inspiration from the diaspora became, then, ever more crucial. One of the leaders, Yi Sungman (Syngman Rhee) became the first president of South Korea after the end of World War II and the defeat of Japan. But An was one of the principal theoreticians and inspirational leaders who traveled among Korean immigrant communities within the United States and helped organize active resistance to Japanese rule from this country. He was arrested in China in 1932 and was tortured to death in a Japanese prison in Korea in 1938. This document was printed in the January 8, 1920 edition of Tongnip sinmun *(The Independence), an organ of the Korean Provisional Government in Shanghai.*

Translated by Han-Kyo Kim. Reprinted with permission from Peter H. Lee, ed., *Sourcebook of Korean Civilization, Volume II.* New York: Columbia University Press, 1996.

An Ch'angho: Grand Strategy for Independence

There are six major issues on which our people must act resolutely today: military affairs, diplomacy, education, judicial affairs, finance, and unity. Before I get to the main topic, there are a few other things I must mention first.

The Relationship Between Government and People

Isn't there an emperor in our country today? The answer is yes. In the past there was only one emperor in our country, but now every one of the twenty million Koreans is an emperor. Where you are sitting at this moment is the royal throne, and what you are wearing on your head is the royal crown. What is an emperor? He is the one who holds the sovereign power; now all of you have that power. In the past when one person held the sovereign power, the rise and fall of the nation depended on that person; today, they depend on the entire people. Government officials are servants; hence, the president and the prime minister are all your servants. The sovereign people must learn how to guide their servants, and the government officials must learn how to serve the sovereign people. . . .

One more thing that you, as emperors, must know is that if you are divided and act as single individuals, you then lose the sovereign power. Only when you are united as the nation's citizens do you enjoy the sovereign power. In other words, when you are united, you give orders; when you are divided, you have to obey orders.

Some of you resent the ministers of the Provisional Government for assuming an air of importance. But what is wrong when a minister behaves like one? Entrusted by the people with positions of honor, they should properly be proud and conduct themselves with dignity. If the ministers and other government officials, or those persons engaged in various aspects of the independence movement, failed to view their responsibilities with respect and lacked a sense of self-pride and dignity, that would be tantamount to being disrespectful to the nation and being arrogant.

I will tell you another story about the State Council. If things do not work out well when an organization has only new personnel—or, conversely, only old personnel—then it is better to mix some old with some new, or half-new and half-old. There are old, young, and semi-old persons for a good balance in the State Council. In terms of talent, there are civilians and military professionals. . . .

I dare say that, under the present conditions, we cannot have a cabinet better than the one we have now. If you cannot obtain a divorce from your wife, you had better put some powder on her face and be happy with her.

Military Affairs

Let me now discuss the main subject. These six major issues are most crucial. In order to carry out our work, there must first be rational study; this alone produces a clear-cut decision. Our job is to destroy a ferocious Japan and regain our nation. Ours is a huge task, and naturally it needs careful study. Let me ask you, how many times a day do you think about our country? . . .

The big problem we face right now is whether we should conduct our independence campaign in a peaceful way or through war. The advocates of peaceful means as well as those of war are all sincere in their patriotic devotion.

The peace advocates argue that we can only express our thoughts and that war is as useless, when one compares our strength with theirs, as hitting a stone with an egg. It is best, they say, to appeal to the world's opinion.

The war advocates argue that Koreans will not be accused of being extremists even if they should declare war. Others have fought for their independence; isn't it natural that we should fight for ours? Comparing our strength with theirs is folly. We are not to calculate the chances for victory or defeat. Watching one's fellow countrymen being killed, maimed, or dishonored, it is natural to risk one's own death. Moral duty and human feeling compel us to fight. Moreover, Japan today is faced with an unprecedented crisis due to serious foreign complications and internal schism. We therefore can win according to these war advocates.

Considering the circumstances of our time and our moral obligations, we have no other option but to fight. But should we go to battle now or after completing our preparations? Some say that we cannot wait for preparations because a revolution is not like a business venture. Nevertheless, preparations are necessary.

When I say preparations, I do not mean bringing our strength up to the level of the enemy's. But some preparations there must be. Even in a private gang fight, each side prepares its battle plans. To march to battle without preparations is to disparage the significance of the revolutionary war. . . . If we go to war without preparations, we may starve to death before the enemy can kill us.

Therefore, if you should be in favor of war, you must understand that preparations are absolutely necessary. Some say, "Don't talk about preparations. For the last ten years we haven't been able to do anything because we have been preparing." But the truth is that we could not march to war due to lack of preparations caused by incessant talk about marching, not because we were busy with preparations. . . .

Cannons, rifles, airplanes, and many other things are certainly needed, but we must first find out who soldiered in the last dynasty or joined the Righteous Army, thereby acquiring knowledge and experience in military affairs, and organize those people. In order to fight, we must create a new army from scratch — and that requires everyone with military expertise to get together and plan the operations. I will ask those strong men from western and northern Kando: Can you take care of the Japanese all by yourself? If you truly wish to fight Japan, unite. Although people criticize the powerlessness of the government, if you unite, your government will be stronger. Even after we unite, we may still need foreign assistance. . . .

Next comes training. Brave men, some say, go to battle with whatever they happen to have. But they must learn that training is absolutely necessary and that combat tactics must be studied. Above all, spiritual training is important. Spiritual unity is essential even for those who possess superior weapons, not to mention us without such weapons.

Spiritual unity cannot be achieved without a universal conscription system. If the war of independence is not to be a mere fantasy but a reality, every man and woman of the twenty million Koreans must become a soldier. How? Through an effective public information program. We have to travel throughout the country and publicize the universal conscription system through the printed and spoken word. But deeds speak louder than words. Let us all undergo military training, even if only for an hour a day. I too have decided to receive such training. If one studies military science even only for half an hour at a time, then that person is a Korean; if not, he or she is no Korean. Anyone willing to learn can learn. Women, too, must learn. Anyone not undergoing military training is opposed to universal conscription. Anyone opposed to universal conscription is opposed to the war of independence. Anyone opposed to the war of independence is opposed to national independence. Starting tomorrow, let us all register for training. . . .

We often talk about our wish to enter Seoul after winning our independence soon. It will be a joyous occasion indeed. But we shall witness independence only if we resolve not to be alive to witness independence. Everyone speaks of dying for the country, but everyone is likely to panic in fear when death is imminent.

If one fully realizes the shame of enslavement, however, even death may not appear too dreadful. Let us not be too anxious to survive long enough to see the day of independence; rather, let our death build the foundation for national independence. . . .

For the purpose of bringing about a fighting war, we have to continue waging a peaceful war. What is a peaceful war? The *manse* demonstrations would be an example.

Needless to say, *manse* alone will not bring about independence. Yet the power of *manse* has been enormous: it affected the entire population at home and the entire world abroad. In the past, the people of the United States prodded their government and Congress on our behalf; now the government and Congress must prod the people. I have seen a pamphlet being circulated in the Senate on our behalf. Is this not a result of the peaceful war? To induce our fellow coutnrymen who became public officials under enemy rule to leave their positions would be an example of the peaceful war. If the general public should refuse to pay tax to the enemy and pay to the government of the Korean Republic instead, if they should hoist the flag of the Korean Republic instead of the Japanese flag, if they should boycott the Japanese currency, if they should stop dealing with Japanese government agencies for adjudication or other settlements—all these would be examples of the peaceful war. Are these not cases of vigorous warfare?

Even if only a part of our population, not to mention all of the people, should behave in this manner, how effective they would be! Some argue that this would not be enough. Nevertheless we must continue on this course until the outbreak of a major war. The peaceful war may cost hundreds of thousands of lives. It too is a war of independence.

57

The Cable Act, September 22, 1922

*The Cable Act was part of a wave of racialized anti-immigrant sentiment follow-
ing World War I. New legislation and court decisions narrowed the range of protected rights for immigrants from Southern and Eastern Europe, but especially for
those from Asia. Since the concern was not simply who would enter the United
States but how they might change the complexion of American society, marriage
and children became important issues. The Cable Act established that American
citizen women who married aliens ineligible for naturalization would lose their citizenship. Since Asians were the only "racial" group excluded from naturalization,
the act became an important deterrent to marriage between them and women who
were American citizens, and thus to more births of American citizens of Asian descent. Deterring interracial marriage was not the only result—both Chinese American and Japanese American women were penalized if they married immigrants
from their parents' homelands, and it seems that the primary targets were nisei
women, second-generation Japanese Americans. The act was repealed in 1936.*

The Statues at Large of the United States of America, vol. XLII, part 1. Washington,
DC: Government Printing Office, 1923.

Chap. 411.—
An Act Relative to the naturalization and citizenship of married women

*Be it enacted by the Senate and House of Representatives of the United States of
America in Congress assembled,* That the right of any woman to become a naturalized citizen of the United States shall not be denied or abridged because of
her sex or because she is a married woman.

Sec. 2. That any woman who marries a citizen of the United States after the
passage of this Act, or any woman whose husband is naturalized after the passage
of this Act, shall not become a citizen of the United States by reason of such marriage or naturalization; but, if eligible to citizenship, she may be naturalized

upon full and complete compliance with all requirements of the naturalization laws, with the following exceptions:

(a) No declaration of intention shall be required;
(b) In lieu of the five-year period of residence within the State or States and the one-year period of residence within the State or Territory where the naturalization court is held, she shall have resided continuously in the United States, Hawaii, Alaska, or Porto Rico for at least one year immediately preceding the filing of the petition.

Sec. 3. That a woman citizen of the United States shall not cease to be a citizen of the United States by reason of her marriage after the passage of this Act, unless she makes a formal renunciation of her citizenship before a court having jurisdiction over naturalization of aliens: *Provided*, That any woman citizen who marries an alien ineligible to citizenship shall cease to be a citizen of the United States. If at the termination of the marital status she is a citizen of the United States she shall retain her citizenship regardless of her residence. If during the continuance of the marital status she resides continuously for two years in a foreign State of which her husband is a citizen or subject, or for five years continuously outside the United States, she shall thereafter be subject to the same presumption as is a naturalized citizen of the United States under the second paragraph of section 2 of the Act entitled "An Act in reference to the expatriation of citizens and their protection abroad," approved March 2, 1907. Nothing herein shall be construed to repeal or amend the provisions of Revised Statutes 1999 or of section 2 of the Expatriation Act of 1907 with reference to expatriation.

Sec. 4. That a woman who, before the passage of this Act, has lost her United States citizenship by reason of her marriage to an alien eligible for citizenship, may be naturalized as provided by section 2 of this Act: *Provided*, That no certificate of arrival shall be required to be filed with her petition if during the continuance of the marital status she shall have resided within the United States. After her naturalization she shall have the same citizenship status as if her marriage had taken place after the passage of this Act.

Sec. 5. That no woman whose husband is not eligible to citizenship shall be naturalized during the continuance of the marital status.

Sec. 6. That section 1994 of the Revised Statutes and section 4 of the Expatriation Act of 1907 are repealed. Such repeal shall not terminate citizenship acquired or retained under either of such sections nor restore citizenship lost under section 4 of the Expatriation Act of 1907.

Sec. 7. That section 3 of the Expatriation Act of 1907 is repealed. Such repeal shall not restore citizenship lost under such section nor terminate citizenship resumed under such section. A woman who has resumed under such section citizenship lost by marriage shall, upon the passage of this Act, have for all purposes the same citizenship status as immediately preceding her marriage.

Approved, September 22, 1922.

58

Supreme Court: Takao Ozawa v. United States, November 13, 1922

*This case determined that Japanese nationals were not eligible to become natu-
ralized American citizens. They thus were classified with the Chinese and other
Asian immigrants as the only "racial" group excluded from entering the United
States, and from citizenship if in the country. Takao Ozawa was an especially
poignant case because he had staked his life on assimilating into "mainstream"
America. He and his family attended Christian churches, spoke English in their
home, and generally adhered to white middle-class customs. The Ozawa family
moved to Hawai'i, where Takao applied for citizenship in 1914. The courts, in suc-
cession, denied his application on the grounds that Congress had determined that
the right to naturalization was reserved for white people and extended to those of
African descent in 1870, and that Japanese were clearly not "Caucasian." The
Supreme Court even conceded that Ozawa was "well qualified by character and
education." His lawyers argued that Congress's original intent was to exclude
Africans and American Indians—Ozawa was willing to argue that the Japanese
were superior in culture and thus deserving of citizenship—but the court refused
to budge. This case and the subsequent closing of the immigration door in 1924
proved to be devastating blows to many immigrant Japanese who hoped for fuller
participation in American society.*

Cases Argued and Decided in the Supreme Court of the United States, Book 67.
Rochester, NY: The Lawyers Co-operative Publishing Company, 1924.

Mr. Justice Sutherland delivered the opinion of the court:

The appellant is a person of the Japanese race, born in Japan. He applied,
on October 16, 1914, to the United States district court for the territory of
Hawaii to be admitted as a citizen of the United States. His petition was opposed by the United States district attorney for the district of Hawaii. Including the period of his residence in Hawaii appellant had continuously resided
in the United States for twenty years. He was a graduate of the Berkeley, California, High School, had been nearly three years a student in the University
of California, had educated his children in American schools, his family had

attended American churches, and he had maintained the use of the English language in his home. That he was well qualified by character and education for citizenship is conceded.

The district court of Hawaii, however, held that, having been born in Japan, and being of the Japanese race, he was not eligible to naturalization under 2169 of the Revised Statutes (Comp. Stat 4358, 6 Fed. Stat. Anno. 2d ed. p. 944), and denied the petition. Thereupon the appellant brought the cause to the circuit court of appeals for the ninth circuit, and that court has certified the following questions, upon which it desires to be instructed:

"1. Is the Act of June 29, 1906, . . . providing 'for a uniform rule for the naturalization of aliens' [sic] complete in itself, or is it limited by 2169 of the Revised Statutes of the United States?

"2. Is one who is of the Japanese race and born in Japan eligible to citizenship under the Naturalization Laws?

"3. If said Act of June 29, 1906, is limited by 2169, and naturalization is limited to aliens being free white persons, and to aliens of African nativity, and to persons of African descent, is one of the Japanese race, born in Japan, under any circumstances eligible to naturalization?" . . .

It is the duty of this court to give effect to the intent of Congress. Primarily this intent is ascertained by giving the words their natural significance; but if this leads to an unreasonable result, plainly at variance with the policy of the legislation as a whole, we must examine the matter further. We may then look to the reason of the enactment, and inquire into its antecedent history, and give it effect in accordance with its design and purpose, sacrificing, if necessary, the literal meaning in order that the purpose may not fail. . . .

This brings us to inquire whether, under 2169, the appellant is eligible to naturalization. The language of the Naturalization Laws from 1790 to 1870 had been uniformly such as to deny the privilege of naturalization to an alien unless he came within the description "free white person." By 7 of the Act of July 14, 1870 (16 Stat at L. 254, 256, chap. 254, Comp. Stat. 4358, 6 Fed. Stat. Anno. 2d ed. p. 944), the Naturalization Laws were "extended to aliens of African nativity and to persons of African descent." Section 2169 of the Revised Statutes, as already pointed out, restricts the privilege to the same classes of persons; viz.: "To aliens [being free white persons and to aliens] of African nativity and persons of African descent." . . .

On behalf of the appellant it is urged that we should give to this phrase the meaning which it had in the minds of its original framers in 1790, and that it was employed by them for the sole purpose of excluding the black or African race and the Indians then inhabiting this country. It may be true that these two races were alone thought of as being excluded, but to say that they were the only ones within the intent of the statute would be to ignore the affirmative form of the legislation. The provision is not that Negroes and Indians shall be *excluded*, but it is, in effect, that only free white persons shall be *included*. The intention was to confer the privilege of citizenship upon that class of persons whom the fathers knew as white, and to deny it to all who could not be so classified. It is not enough to say that the framers did not have in mind the brown or yellow races of Asia. It is necessary to go farther and be able to say that, had these particular races been suggested, the language of the act would have been so varied as to include them within its privileges. . . .

We have been furnished with elaborate briefs in which the meaning of the words "white person" is discussed with ability and at length, both from the standpoint of judicial decision and from that of the science of ethnology. It does not seem to us necessary, however, to follow counsel in their extensive researches in these fields. It is sufficient to note the fact that these decisions are, in substance, to the effect that the words import a racial, and not an individual, test, and with this conclusion, fortified as it is by reason and authority, we entirely agree. Manifestly the test afforded by the mere color of the skin of each individual is impracticable, as that differs greatly among persons of the same race, even among Anglo-Saxons, ranging by imperceptible gradations from the fair blond to the swarthy brunette, the latter being darker than many of the lighter hued persons of the brown or yellow races. Hence to adopt the color test alone would result in a confused overlapping of races and a gradual merging of one into the other, without any practical line of separation. Beginning with the decision of Circuit Judge Sawyer, in Re Ah Yup (1878) 5 Sawy. 155, Fed. Cas. No. 104, the Federal and state courts, in an almost unbroken line, have held that the words "white person" were meant to indicate only a person of what is popularly known as the Caucasian race. . . .

The determination that the words "white person" are synonymous with the words "a person of the Caucasian race" simplifies the problem, although it does not entirely dispose of it. Controversies have arisen and will no doubt arise again in respect of the proper classification of individuals in border-line cases. The effect of the conclusion that the words "white person" mean a Caucasian is not to establish a sharp line of demarcation between those who are entitled and those who are not entitled to naturalization, but rather a zone of more or less debatable ground outside of which, upon the one hand, are those clearly eligible, and outside of which, upon the other hand, are those clearly ineligible for citizenship. Individual cases falling within this zone must be determined as they arise from time to time by what this court has called, in another connection (Davidson v. New Orleans, 96 U.S. 97, 104, 24 L. ed. 616, 619), "the gradual process of judicial inclusion and exclusion."

The appellant in the case now under consideration, however, is clearly of a race which is not Caucasian, and therefore belongs entirely outside the zone on the negative side. A large number of the Federal and state courts have so decided, and we find no reported case definitely to the contrary. These decisions are sustained by numerous scientific authorities, which we do not deem it necessary to review. We think these decisions are right, and so hold.

The briefs filed on behalf of appellant refer in complimentary terms to the culture and enlightenment of the Japanese people, and with this estimate we have no reason to disagree; but these are matters which cannot enter into our consideration of the questions here at issue. We have no function in the matter other than to ascertain the will of Congress and declare it. Of course, there is not implied—either in the legislation or in our interpretation of it—any suggestion of individual unworthiness or racial inferiority. These considerations are in no manner involved.

The questions submitted are, therefore, answered as follows:

Question No. 1. The Act of June 29, 1906, is not complete in itself, but is limited by 2169 of the Revised Statutes of the United States.

Question No. 2. No.

Question No. 3. No.

It will be so certified.

59

Supreme Court: United States v. Bhagat Singh Thind, *February 19, 1923*

This Supreme Court decision reflected the growing parameters of explicitly racist definitions of those eligible to enter the United States or to become naturalized citizens. It followed by one year the Ozawa case, in which a Japanese immigrant was denied naturalization rights because he was not a "Caucasian." Interestingly, Bhagat Singh Thind, born in Punjab, India, was acknowledged to be a Caucasian but similarly denied citizenship because he did not fit the "common" definition of a "white person." Thind's attorneys argued that high-caste Hindus were "Aryans"—or Caucasians, synonymous to whites. The court went through a convoluted series of arguments essentially rejecting "Caucasian" as a useful racial category and resorting to reliance on "the popular sense" of the word. And, since the framers of the 1790 law restricting citizenship to "free white persons" had come from the British Isles and Northwestern Europe, they must have been thinking of similar immigrants, "bone of their bone and flesh of their flesh." The Immigration and Naturalization Service canceled naturalization certificates of fifty Indians in the following few years. Some white American women who had married Indians thus had their citizenships canceled as well.

United States Reports, Volume 261: Cases Adjudged in the Supreme Court. Washington, DC: Government Printing Office, 1923.

United States v. Bhagat Singh Thind
261 U.S. 204, 43 S.Ct. 338

Mr. Justice Sutherland delivered the opinion of the Court.

This cause is here upon a certificate from the Circuit Court of Appeals, requesting the instruction of this Court in respect of the following questions:

"1. Is a high caste Hindu of full Indian blood, born at Amrit Sar, Punjab, India, a white person within the meaning of section 2169, Revised Statutes?

"2. Does the act of February 5, 1917, (39 Stat. L. 875, section 3) disqualify from naturalization as citizens those Hindus, now barred by that act, who had lawfully entered the United States prior to the passage of said act?"

The appellee was granted a certificate of citizenship by the District Court of the United States for the District of Oregon, over the objection of the naturalization examiner for the United States. A bill in equity was then filed by the United States, seeking a cancellation of the certificate on the ground that the appellee was not a white person and therefore not lawfully entitled to naturalization. The District Court, on motion, dismissed the bill (268 Fed. 683) and an appeal was taken to the Circuit Court of Appeals. No question is made in respect of the individual qualifications of the appellee. The sole question is whether he falls within the class designated by Congress as eligible.

Section 2169, Revised Statutes, provides that the provisions of the Naturalization Act "shall apply to aliens, being free white persons, and to aliens of African nativity and to persons of African descent."

If the applicant is a white person within the meaning of this section he is entitled to naturalization; otherwise not. In *Ozawa v. United States*, 260 U.S. 178, we had occasion to consider the application of these words to the case of a cultivated Japanese and were constrained to hold that he was not within their meaning. As there pointed out, the provision is not that any particular class of persons shall be excluded, but it is, in effect, that only white persons shall be included within the privilege of the statute. "The intention was to confer the privilege of citizenship upon that class of persons whom the fathers knew as white, and to deny it to all who could not be so classified. It is not enough to say that the framers did not have in mind the brown or yellow races of Asia. It is necessary to go farther and be able to say that had these particular races been suggested the language of the act would have been so varied as to include them within its privileges," (p. 195) citing *Dartmouth College* v. *Woodward*, 4 Wheat. 518, 644. Following a long line of decisions of the lower federal courts, we held that the words imported a racial and not an individual test and were meant to indicate only persons of what is *popularly* known as the Caucasian race. But, as there pointed out, the conclusion that the phrase "white persons" and the word "Caucasian" are synonymous does not end the matter. It enabled us to dispose of the problem as it was there presented, since the applicant for citizenship clearly fell outside the zone of debatable ground on the negative side; but the decision still left the question to be dealt with, in doubtful and different cases, by the "process of judicial inclusion and exclusion." Mere ability on the part of an applicant for naturalization to establish a line of descent from a Caucasian ancestor will not *ipso facto* and necessarily conclude the inquiry. "Caucasian" is a conventional word of much flexibility, as a study of the literature dealing with racial questions will disclose, and while it and the words "white persons" are treated as synonymous for the purposes of that case, they are not of identical meaning—*idem per idem*.

In the endeavor to ascertain the meaning of the statute we must not fail to keep in mind that it does not employ the word "Caucasian" but the words "white persons," and these are words of common speech and not of scientific origin. The word "Caucasian" not only was not employed in the law but was probably wholly unfamiliar to the original framers of the statute in 1790. When we employ it we do so as an aid to the ascertainment of the legislative intent and not as an invariable substitute for the statutory words. Indeed, as used in the science of ethnology, the connotation of the word is by no means clear and the use of it in its scientific sense as an equivalent for the words of the statute, other considerations aside, would simply mean the substitution of one perplexity for another. But in this country, during the last half century especially, the word by common usage has acquired a popular meaning, not clearly defined to be sure, but sufficiently so to enable us to say that its popular as distinguished from its scientific application is of appreciably narrower scope. It is in the popular sense of the word, therefore, that we employ it as an aid to the construction of the statute, for it would be obviously illogical to convert words of common speech used in a statute into words of scientific terminology when neither the latter nor the science for whose purposes they were coined was within the contemplation of the framers of the statute or of the people for whom it was framed. The words of the statute are to be interpreted in accordance with the understanding of the common man from whose vocabulary they were taken. . . .

It may be true that the blond Scandinavian and the brown Hindu have a common ancestor in the dim reaches of antiquity, but the average man knows perfectly well that there are unmistakable and profound differences between them today; and it is not impossible, if that common ancestor could be materialized in the flesh, we should discover that he was himself sufficiently differentiated from both of his descendants to preclude his racial classification with either. The question for determination is not, therefore, whether by the speculative processes of ethnological reasoning we may present a probability to the scientific mind that they have the same origin, but whether we can satisfy the common understanding that they are now the same or sufficiently the same to justify the interpreters of a statute—written in the words of common speech, for common understanding, by unscientific men—in classifying them together in the statutory category as white persons. . . .

The eligibility of this applicant for citizenship is based on the sole fact that he is of high caste Hindu stock, born in Punjab, one of the extreme northwestern districts of India, and classified by certain scientific authorities as of the Caucasian or Aryan race. The Aryan theory as a racial basis seems to be discredited by most, if not all, modern writers on the subject of ethnology. A review of their contentions would serve no useful purpose. . . .

The term "Aryan" has to do with linguistic and not at all with physical characteristics, and it would seem reasonably clear that mere resemblance in language, indicating a common linguistic root buried in remotely ancient soil, is altogether inadequate to prove common racial origin. There is, and can be, no assurance that the so-called Aryan language was not spoken by a variety of races living in proximity to one another. Our own history has witnessed the adoption of the English tongue by millions of Negroes, whose descendants can never be classified racially with the descendants of white persons notwithstanding both may speak a common root language. . . .

It does not seem necessary to pursue the matter of scientific classification further. We are unable to agree with the District Court, or with other lower federal courts, in the conclusion that a native Hindu is eligible for naturalization under 2169. The words of familiar speech, which were used by the original framers of the law, were intended to include only the type of man whom they knew as white. The immigration of that day was almost exclusively from the British Isles and Northwestern Europe, whence they and their forbears had come. When they extended the privilege of American citizenship to "any alien, being a free white person," it was these immigrants—bone of their bone and flesh of their flesh—and their kind whom they must have had affirmatively in mind. . . .

It follows that a negative answer must be given to the first question, which disposes of the case and renders an answer to the second question unnecessary, and it will be so certified.

60

Supreme Court: Terrace et al. v. Thompson, Attorney General of the State of Washington, *November 12, 1923*

This Supreme Court case became the principal ruling that validated, until the 1950s, various state anti alien land laws. The state of Washington, along with others, followed California in enacting legislation to prevent Japanese immigrants from owning and leasing land. California's law was passed in 1913, Washington's in 1921. Both would be challenged in the courts, and the U.S. Supreme Court eventually ruled on two issues: first, whether these laws violated due process and equal protection clauses of the Fourteenth Amendment; second, whether they conflicted with provisions of treaties between the United States and Japan. In this case, the Terraces wished to lease land to N. Nakatsuka to farm in King County. The court ruled that, while the federal government controlled immigration and naturalization, states had a legitimate interest in determining land ownership and that prohibiting "aliens ineligible to citizenship" from purchasing or leasing land was constitutional. In spite of these laws, Japanese immigrant farmers continued to develop farming on the West Coast and actually dominated many crops before World War II.

United States Reports, Volume 263: *Cases Adjudged in the Supreme Court.* Washington, DC: Government Printing Office, 1924.

Terrace et al. v. Thompson, Attorney General of the State of Washington
263 U.S. 197

Mr. Justice Butler delivered the opinion of the Court.

Appellants brought this suit to enjoin the Attorney General of Washington from enforcing the Anti-Alien Land Law of that State, *c.* 50, Laws, 1921, on the grounds that it is in conflict with the due process and equal protection clauses of the Fourteenth Amendment; with the treaty between the United States and Japan, and with certain provisions of the constitution of the State.

The appellants are residents of Washington. The Terraces are citizens of the United States and of Washington. Nakatsuka was born in Japan of Japanese parents and is a subject of the Emperor of Japan. The Terraces are the owners of a tract of land in King County which is particularly adapted to raising vegetables, and which for a number of years had been devoted to that and other agricultural purposes. The complaint alleges that Nakatsuka is a capable farmer and will be a desirable tenant of the land; that the Terraces desire to lease their land to him for the period of five years; that he desires to accept such lease, and that the lease would be made but for the act complained of. And it is alleged that the defendant, as Attorney General, has threatened to and will take steps to enforce the act against the appellants if they enter into such lease, and will treat the leasehold interest as forfeited to the State, and will prosecute the appellants criminally for violation of the act; that the act is so drastic and the penalties attached to its violation are so great that neither of the appellants may make the lease even to test the constitutionality of the act, and that, unless the court shall determine its validity in this suit, the appellants will be compelled to submit to it, whether valid or invalid, and thereby will be deprived of their property without due process of law and denied the equal protection of the laws. . . .

Section 33 of Article II of the Constitution of Washington prohibits the ownership of land by aliens other than those who in good faith have declared intention to become citizens of the United States, except in certain instances not here involved. The act provides in substance that any such alien shall not own, take, have or hold the legal or equitable title, or right to any benefit of any land as defined in the act, and that land conveyed to or for the use of aliens in violation of the state constitution or of the act shall thereby be forfeited to the State. . . .

Appellants contend that the act contravenes the due process clause in that it prohibits the owners from making lawful disposition or use of their land, and makes it a criminal offense for them to lease it to the alien, and prohibits him from following the occupation of farmer; and they contend that it is repugnant to the equal protection clause in that aliens are divided into two classes,—those who may and those who may not become citizens, one class being permitted, while the other is forbidden, to own land as defined.

Alien inhabitants of a State, as well as all other persons within its jurisdiction, may invoke the protection of these clauses. *Yick Wo v. Hopkins*, 118 U.S. 356, 360; *Truax v. Raich, supra*, 39. The Fourteenth Amendment, as against the arbitrary and capricious or unjustly discriminatory action of the State, protects the owners in their right to lease and dispose of their land for lawful purposes and the alien resident in his right to earn a living by following ordinary occupations of the community, but it does not take away from the State those powers of police that were reserved at the time of the adoption of the Constitution . . . against eligible aliens who have failed to declare their intention. The classification is based on eligibility and purpose to naturalize. Eligible aliens are free white persons and persons of African nativity or descent. Congress is not trammeled, and it may grant or withhold the privilege of naturalization upon any grounds or without any reason, as it sees fit. But it is not to be supposed that its acts defining eligibility are arbitrary or unsupported by reasonable considerations of public policy. The State properly may assume that the considerations upon which Congress made such classification are substantial and reasonable. Generally speaking, the natives of European countries are eligible. Japanese, Chinese and Malays are not. Appellants' contention that the state act discriminates arbitrarily against Nakatsuka and other ineligible aliens because of their race and color is without foundation. All persons of whatever color or race who have not declared their intention in good faith to become citizens are prohibited from so owning agricultural lands. Two classes of aliens inevitably result from the naturalization laws, — those who may and those who may not become citizens. The rule established by Congress on this subject, in and of itself, furnishes a reasonable basis for classification in a state law withholding from aliens the privilege of land ownership as defined in the act. . . .

The state act is not repugnant to the equal protection clause and does not contravene the Fourteenth Amendment.

3. The state act, in our opinion, is not in conflict with the treaty between the United States and Japan. The preamble declares it to be "a treaty of commerce and navigation," and indicates that it was entered into for the purpose of establishing the rules to govern commercial intercourse between the countries. . . .

The decree of the District Court is affirmed.

61

National Origins Act: An Act to Limit the Immigration of Aliens Into the United States, and for Other Purposes, May 26, 1924

This act defined official U.S. policies toward immigration for much of the twentieth century. It built upon the 1921 act that first quantified numbers of aliens allowed into the United States. Most of the 350,000 total permitted were to be from Northern and Western Europe. The act codified American determination to exclude Asian and Pacific peoples and sharply restrict the large numbers entering from Southern and Central/Eastern Europe. As did so much of this type of legislation, it restricted and excluded specific nationality groups with thinly disguised circumlocution. For unwanted Europeans, national quotas were based on 2 percent of the existing population according to the census of 1890, before the largest influx of these groups. To totally exclude unwanted Asians and Pacific Islanders, the act referenced "aliens ineligible to citizenship." Nonquota status was afforded only to immigrants from the Americans. The act abrogated the 1907–1908 Gentlemen's Agreement with Japan, humiliating and infuriating this modernizing and militarizing Asian nation. Indeed, some see the 1924 act as a principal link in the causal chain of events leading to war between Japan and the United States in 1941. It served as a capstone to congressional and Supreme Court actions that evolved in the previous two decades. The guidelines thus generated would serve, with modest amendments, until the landmark immigration act of 1965.

The Statutes at Large of the United States of America, vol. 42. Washington, DC: Government Printing Office, 1925.

Chap. 190. —
An Act To limit the immigration of aliens into the United States, and for other purposes

Be it enacted by the Senate and House of Representatives of the United States of America in Congress assembled, That this Act may be cited as the "Immigration Act of 1924."

Immigration visas

Sec. 2. (a) A consular officer upon the application of any immigrant (as defined in section 3) may (under the conditions hereinafter prescribed and subject to the limitations prescribed in this Act or regulations made thereunder as to the number of immigration visas which may be issued by such officer) issue to such immigrant an immigration visa which shall consist of one copy of the application provided for in section 7, visaed by such consular officer. Such visa shall specify (1) the nationality of the immigrant; (2) whether he is a quota immigrant (as defined in section 5) or a non-quota immigrant (as defined in section 4); (3) the date on which the validity of the immigration visa shall expire; and (4) such additional information necessary to the proper enforcement of the immigration laws and the naturalization laws as may be by regulations prescribed. . . .

(f) No immigration visa shall be issued to an immigrant if it appears to the consular officer, from statements in the application or in the papers submitted therewith, that the immigrant is inadmissible to the United States under the immigration laws, nor shall such immigration visa be issued if the application fails to comply with the provisions of this Act, nor shall such immigration visa be issued if the consular officer knows or has reason to believe that the immigrant is inadmissible to the United States under the immigration laws.

(g) Nothing in this Act shall be construed to entitle an immigrant, to whom an immigration visa has been issued, to enter the United States, if, upon arrival in the United States, he is found to be inadmissible to the United States under the immigration laws. The substance of this subdivision shall be printed conspicuously upon every immigration visa . . .

Non-Quota Immigrants

Sec. 4. When used in this Act the term "non-quota immigrant" means—

(a) An immigrant who is the unmarried child under 18 years of age, or the wife, of a citizen of the United States who resides therein at the time of the filing of a petition under section 9;

(b) An immigrant previously lawfully admitted to the United States, who is returning from a temporary visit abroad;

(c) An immigrant who was born in the Dominion of Canada, Newfoundland, the Republic of Mexico, the Republic of Cuba, the Republic of Haiti, the Dominican Republic, the Canal Zone, or an independent country of Central or South America, and his wife, and his unmarried children under 18 years of age, if accompanying or following to join him;

(d) An immigrant who continuously for at least two years immediately preceding the time of his application for admission to the United States has been, and who seeks to enter the United States solely for the purpose of, carrying on the vocation of minister of any religious denomination, or professor of a college, academy, seminary, or university; and his wife, and his unmarried children under 18 years of age, if accompanying or following to join him; or

(e) An immigrant who is a bona fide student at least 15 years of age and who seeks to enter the United States solely for the purpose of study at an accredited school, college, academy, seminary, or university, particularly designated by him and approved by the Secretary of Labor, which shall have agreed to report to the Secretary of Labor the termination of attendance of each immigrant student, and if any such institution of learning fails to make such reports promptly the approval shall be withdrawn.

Quota Immigrants

Sec. 5. When used in this Act the term "quota immigrant" means any immigrant who is not a non-quota immigrant. An alien who is not particularly specified in this Act as a non-quota immigrant or a non-immigrant shall not be admitted as a non-quota immigrant or a non-immigrant by reason of relationship to any individual who is so specified or by reason of being excepted from the operation of any other law regulating or forbidding immigration.

Preferences Within Quotas

Sec. 6. (a) In the issuance of immigratior visas to quota immigrants preference shall be given—

(1) To a quota immigrant who is the unmarried child under 21 years of age, the father, the mother, the husband, or the wife, of a citizen of the United States who is 21 years of age or over; and

(2) To a quota immigrant who is skilled in agriculture, and his wife, and his dependent children under the age of 16 years, if accompanying or following to join him. The preference provided in this paragraph shall not apply to immigrants of any nationality the annual quota for which is less than 300. . . .

Numerical Limitations

Sec. 11. (a) The annual quota of any nationality shall be 2 per centum of the number of foreign-born individuals of such nationality resident in continental United States as determined by the United States census of 1890, but the minimum quota of any nationality shall be 100.

(b) The annual quota of any nationality for the fiscal year beginning July 1, 1927, and for each fiscal year thereafter, shall be a number which bears the same ratio to 150,000 as the number of inhabitants in continental United States in 1920 having that national origin (ascertained as hereinafter provided in this section) bears to the number of inhabitants in continental United States in 1920, but the minimum quota of any nationality shall be 100.

(c) For the purpose of subdivision (b) national origin shall be ascertained by determining as nearly as may be, in respect of each geographical area which under section 12 is to be treated as a separate country (except the geographical areas specified in subdivision (c) of section 4) the number of inhabitants in continental United States in 1920 whose origin by birth or ancestry is attributable to such geographical area. Such determination shall not be made by tracing the ancestors or descendants of particular individuals, but shall be based upon statistics of immigration and emigration, together with rates of increase of population as shown by successive decennial United States censuses, and such other data as may be found to be reliable.

(d) For the purpose of subdivisions (b) and (c) the term "inhabitants in continental United States in 1920" does not include (1) immigrants from the geographical areas specified in subdivision (c) of section 4 or their descendants, (2) aliens ineligible to citizenship or their descendants, (3) the descendants of slave immigrants, or (4) the descendants of American aborigines. . . .

(f) There shall be issued to quota immigrants of any nationality (1) no more immigration visas in any fiscal year than the quota for such nationality, and (2) in any calendar month of any fiscal year, no more immigration visas than 10 per centum of the quota for such nationality, except that if such quota is less than 300 the number to be issued in any calendar month shall be prescribed by the Commissioner General, with the approval of the Secretary of Labor, but the total number to be issued during the fiscal year shall not be in excess of the quota for such nationality.

(g) Nothing in this Act shall prevent the issuance (without increasing the total number of immigration visas which may be issued) of an immigration visa to an immigrant as a quota immigrant even though he is a non-quota immigrant.

Nationality

Sec. 12. (a) For the purposes of this Act nationality shall be determined by country of birth, treating as separate countries the colonies, dependencies, or self-governing dominions, for which separate enumeration was made in the United States census of 1890; . . .

(c) No alien ineligible to citizenship shall be admitted to the United States unless such alien (1) is admissible as a non-quota immigrant under the provisions of subdivision (b), (d), or (e) of section 4, or (2) is the wife, or the unmarried child under 18 years of age, of an immigrant admissible under such subdivision (d), and is accompanying or following to join him, or (3) is not an immigrant as defined in section 3. . . .

Approved May 26, 1924

PART 3

Accommodation and Hostility: Through 1941

It may have seemed to most people that the National Origins Act of 1924 and the Tydings-McDuffie Act conclusively sealed the preferred ethnic and racial order for the United States. But the path toward legislating the immigration quota system was tortuous, and implementation proved almost as difficult because the fundamental assumptions of the National Origins Act were so complex: that nation-states were fixed entities (but World War I, for example, changed the map of much of Central Europe), and that ethnicities would never change. Nonetheless, the 1924 quotas were finally implemented in 1929 and remained largely in place for four decades, definitively ending only with the major reforms of 1965.

In some important ways, the United States attempted to accommodate the small numbers of Asians and Asian Americans within its borders after the 1924 act. After all, it appeared that the national course had been set, strictly delimiting the "less desirable" Europeans and nearly eliminating all non-Europeans, including virtually banning all Asian/Pacific immigration. Except in insular possessions, then, the country appeared to have ensured Anglo-Saxon predominance into the foreseeable future.

However, there were a few signs that racism directed against Asians already in the country might diminish. First, several hundred Asian veterans of World War I were naturalized as American citizens, in clear contradistinction to the intent of previous court rulings. A particularly significant group of Japanese immigrants had served in the U.S. Army in Hawai'i. Second, a second-generation citizen cohort, most noticeable in the case of the Japanese community, provided a political base from which more equal rights might be sought. This generation, although still facing enormous challenges in educational and employment discrimination, began to make important inroads in academic circles, graduating from prestigious universities and entering professional occupations.

Third, important gains were made in the labor movement, in terms of both the overall struggle and attempts to integrate Asian workers into the larger unions. In Hawai'i, the brief collaboration of Filipino and Japanese workers in the sugar industry gave hope that some ongoing organization might be possible. The formation of the relatively more inclusive Congress of Industrial Organizations (CIO) in 1938, in competition with the more exclusive American Federation of Labor (AFL), was a major step forward. In many regions, the surge in communist activism, with its own antiracism emphasis, augured well for more working-class racial solidarity. Even the AFL began to relent and, in 1936, granted a charter to fieldworkers who had formed a Filipino-Mexican union. Then, in 1940, the AFL gave a charter to the Filipino Federated Agricultural Laborers Association.

Fourth, some legal and political reforms became possible. The 1931 amendment to the Cable Act ensured that no American-born woman who had lost her citizenship by virtue of having married an alien ineligible for citizenship would be denied the right to naturalization at a later date. And the 1927 Supreme Court ruling in *Farrington v. Tokushige* guaranteed immigrant communities, especially the Germans and the Japanese, the right to support schools to maintain their languages.

But two developments truncated what progress might have been expected. First, the Great Depression, which began in 1929, was used to inflame race baiting as more and more of the working class became mired in poverty. Second, the increasingly hostile stances in Asia and the Pacific, especially between the United States and Japan, fueled anti-Asian stereotyping and prejudice, in spite of some amelioration of anti-Chinese racism with the advent of more sympathetic portrayals in the novels of Pearl Buck and films from Hollywood. It was no surprise, then, that *Hidemitsu v. United States*, in 1925, established again that Japanese could not be naturalized.

The last Asian group still able to immigrate in any numbers was the Filipinos. As an American possession, the Philippines was accorded special status, and its people were allowed to enter as "American nationals." But while their numbers were never large, anti-Filipino riots and movements became significant by the 1920s. In 1933, Filipinos were ruled ineligible for citizenship, and in 1934, the Tydings-McDuffie Act provided for independence in ten years for the Philippines, a measure at least partly designed to allow for excluding Filipinos from the United States. The act also established a token annual quota of 50 until the time of independence. To add insult to injury, subsequent legislation in 1935 encouraged Filipinos already in the country to return to the Philippines at U.S. expense.

Ironically, the fact that Japan was the nation's sole enemy in the Pacific and Asia allowed for some sympathy for other national groups. By the late 1930s, President Roosevelt and top military figures were already planning for an eventual war in the Pacific and concluding that "concentration camps" would be required to intern large numbers of Japanese Americans. For other Asian groups, the picture was different. The public demonstrated support for Koreans and Chinese who raised funds, encouraged educational and propaganda work, boycotted Japanese goods, and even trained military units for eventual service to liberate their homelands. Later, this sentiment led to further erosion of the generally anti-Asian nature of the exclusion laws, beginning with the end of the Chinese Exclusion Act in 1943.

62

Supreme Court: Hidemitsu Toyota v. United States, *May 25, 1925*

The 1922 Ozawa case decided by the U.S. Supreme Court definitively ruled that natives of Japan were not eligible to become naturalized American citizens. But service in wartime was an unusual attribute, and foreigners in America's armed forces during World War I were assisted in becoming citizens by a grateful nation. In the case of the Japanese, however, the Supreme Court held that there was no reason to enlarge the categories of aliens eligible for naturalization under existing statutes. Indeed, the majority opinion devoted significant space to the fact that recent laws related specifically to Filipinos who had served in World War I but not to the Japanese. Hidemitsu Toyota joined the Coast Guard in 1913 and served during the war. He petitioned for naturalization based on a 1918 act allowing alien war veterans who had been honorably discharged to become citizens. His naturalization bid was successful, but the government filed to revoke his citizenship in the First Circuit Court of Appeals. The decision was upheld in the Supreme Court.

United States Reports, *Volume 268,* Cases Adjudged in the Supreme Court. Washington, DC: Government Printing Office, 1926.

Hidemitsu Toyota v. UNITED STATES.
268 U.S. 402, 45, S.Ct. 563

Mr. Justice Butler delivered the opinion of the Court.

Hidemitsu Toyota, a person of the Japanese race, born in Japan, entered the United States in 1913. He served substantially all the time between November of that year and May, 1923, in the United States Coast Guard Service. This was a part of the naval force of the United States nearly all of the time the United States was engaged in the recent war. He received eight or more honorable discharges, and some of them were for service during the war. May 14, 1921, he filed his petition for naturalization in the United States district court for the district of Massachusetts. The petition was granted, and a certificate of naturalization was issued to him. This case arises on a petition to cancel the certificate on the ground that it was illegally procured. . . . It is agreed that if a person of the Japanese race, born in Japan, may legally be naturalized under the seventh subdivision of 4 of the Act of June 29, 1906, as amended by the Act of May 9, 1918, c. 69, 40 Stat, 542, or under the Act of July 19, 1919, c. 24, 41 Stat. 222, Toyota is legally naturalized. The district court held he was not entitled to be naturalized, and entered a decree cancelling his certificate of citizenship. 290 Fed. 971. An appeal was taken to the Circuit Court of Appeals, and that court under 239, Judicial Code, certified to this court the following questions: (1) Whether a person of the Japanese race, born in Japan, may legally be naturalized under the seventh subdivision of 4 of the Act of June 29, 1906, as amended by the Act of May 9, 1918, and (2) whether such subject may legally be naturalized under the Act of July 19, 1919 . . .

It has long been the rule that in order to be admitted to citizenship, an alien is required, at least two years prior to his admission, to declare his intention to become a citizen, and to show that he has resided continuously in the United States for at least five years immediately preceding his admission. . . . But at different times, as to specially designated aliens serving in the armed forces of the United States, Congress modified and lessened these requirements. . . .

The seventh subdivision of 4, of the act of 1918, permits "any native-born Filipino" or "any alien, or any Porto Rican not a citizen of the United States" belonging respectively to the classes there described, on presentation of the required declaration of intention, to petition for naturalization without proof of five years' residence within the United States; and the act permits "any alien" serving in the forces of the United States "during the time this country is engaged in the present war" to file his petition for naturalization without making the preliminary declaration of intention and without proof of five years' residence in the United States. The act of 1919 gave "any person of foreign birth" there mentioned, the benefits of the seventh subdivision of 4. Evidently, a principal purpose of these acts was to facilitate the naturalization of service men of the classes specified. There is nothing to show an intention to eliminate from the definition of eligibility in 2169 the distinction based on color or race. . . .

When the act of 1918 was passed, it was doubtful whether 30 of the act of 1906 extended the privilege of naturalization to all citizens of the Philippine Islands . . . But we hold that until the passage of that act, Filipinos not being "free white persons" or "of African nativity" were not eligible, and that the effect of the act of 1918 was to make eligible, and to authorize the naturalization of, native-born Filipinos of whatever color or race having the qualifications specified in the seventh subdivision of 4.

Under the treaty of peace between the United States and Spain, December 10, 1898, 30 Stat. 1754, Congress was authorized to determine the civil rights and political status of the native inhabitants of the Philippine Islands. And by the act of July 1, 1902, 4, c. 1369, 32 Stat. 691, 692, it was declared that all inhabitants continuing to reside therein who were Spanish subjects on April 11, 1899, and then resided in the Islands, and their children born subsequent thereto, "shall be deemed and held to be citizens of the Philippine Islands and as such entitled to the protection of the United States, except such as shall have elected to preserve their allegiance to the Crown of Spain," according to the treaty. The citizens of the Philippine Islands are not aliens. See *Gonzales* v. *Williams*, 192 U. S. 1, 13. They owe no allegiance to any foreign government. They were not eligible for naturalization under 2169 because not aliens and so not within its terms. . . .

Section 26 of that act repeals certain sections of Title XXX of the Revised Statutes, but leaves 2169 in force. It is to be applied as if it were included in the act of 1906. Plainly, the element of alienage included in 2169 did not apply to the class made eligible by 30 of the act of 1906. The element of color and race included in that section is not specifically dealt with by 30, and, as it has long been the national policy to maintain the distinction of color and race, radical change is not lightly to be deemed to have been intended. "Persons not citizens who owe permanent allegiance to the United States, and who may become residents of any State" may include Malays, Japanese and Chinese and others not eligible under the distinction as to color and race. As under 30 all the applicable provisions of the naturalization laws apply, the limitations based on color and race remain; and the class made eligible by 30 must be limited to those of the color and race included by 2169. As Filipinos are not aliens and owe allegiance to the United States, there are strong reasons for relaxing as to them the restrictions which do not exist in favor of aliens who are barred because of their color and race. And in view of the policy of Congress to limit the naturalization of aliens to white persons and to those of African nativity or descent the implied enlargement of 2169 should be taken at the minimum. The legislative history of the act indicates that the intention of Congress was not to enlarge 2169, except in respect of Filipinos qualified by the specified service. . . .

The answer to the first question is: No.

The answer to the second question is: No.

63

Friendship Dolls to Japan, December 20, 1926

Sidney Gulick was a missionary in Japan for many years after his arrival there in 1888. He returned to the United States in 1913 and attempted to restore sanity in the midst of rampant hostility directed at both Japan and Japanese Americans, through lectures and writing. But anti-Asian racism was impossible to stem, and the 1924 National Origins Act doomed any potential for improved relations until another two decades and the end of World War II. Gulick wrote this letter in December 1926 to Viscount Shibusawa Eiichi, a prominent education, political, and business figure in Japan. The "Doll-Mission of Friendship" was designed to create better United States–Japan relations, especially to end the immigration exclusion policy, through a massive, nationwide project to send dolls from American schoolchildren to their Japanese counterparts. The dolls had to be less than 14" tall and say "mama." Eventually, more than 2.6 million Americans participated and some of the 13,000 dolls, most with blue eyes, reached nearly every school or kindergarten in Japan. They became important parts of the 1927 "Girls' Day" celebration—hinamatsuri (literally, "doll festival"). The Japanese reciprocated with 58 "Dolls of Gratitude" made by top craftsmen. Like their American counterparts, each came with a passport and letters from children. These dolls, fabricated with great care and speed, arrived in time for Christmas 1927. In San Francisco, their arrival was marked by a gathering of 10,000 Japanese Americans who proudly pointed to the dolls sent from prefectures so many of them had come from: Hiroshima, Yamaguchi, Okinawa, Fukuoka, and Wakayama. In spite of generous and well-meaning gestures like these, hostility continued to increase, culminating in the Pacific War.

Letter from Sidney Gulick, Secretary of the Commission on International Justice and Good Will of the Federal Council of the Churches of Christ in America, to Viscount Eiichi Shibusawa, Chairman of the Committee on Japanese American Relations, December 20, 1926. Courtesy of Yoshi Miki, Curator and Director of Education, The Japanese American National Museum.

Committee on World Friendship Among Children
Instituted by The Commission on International Justice and Goodwill of
the Federal Council of the Churches of Christ in America
289 Fourth Avenue
New York, N. Y.

December 20, 1926

My dear Viscount:

I have written a rather full letter of explanations to Vice Minister Matsuura, with regard to the Doll Messenger Project. I am sure you will be glad to see just what I have written to him.

On Saturday we had a Farewell Reception at which 1000 dolls were gathered in, at the Hotel Plaza, where, I think, you stayed when you were in New York. It was a beautiful sight.

On that same day we were shipping over 800 dolls on the Mayebashi Maru. This is the first shipment but from now on, for the next few weeks, we expect to send dolls by every steamer leaving New York.

You will be glad to know that all the steamship lines dispatching vessels to Japan have agreed to share in this gesture of goodwill by carrying these doll Messengers of Friendship free of charge.

With all good wishes for the New Year and with hopes that this doll project may help to change public opinion in America so that, in due time, the exclusion section of the immigration law may be rescinded, I am

Cordially yours,

[signature of Sidney L. Gulick]
Secretary of the Commission

Viscount E. Shibusawa,
Chairman, Committee on Japanese American Relations,
2 Kabutocho, Nihonbashi,
Tokyo, Japan.

64

Supreme Court: Wallace R. Farrington, Governor of the Territory of Hawaii, et al. v. T. Tokushige, et al., *February 21, 1927*

A bitterly divided Japanese American community in Hawai'i took the territory to the Supreme Court to contest blatant attempts to dismantle Japanese language schools. The court ruled that Hawaii's laws went "far beyond mere regulation of privately supported schools where children obtain instruction deemed valuable by their parents and which is not obviously in conflict with any public interest." The case illuminated several important issues. First, Hawaii's ruling oligarchy was determined to eradicate Japanese culture as one strategy of neutralizing the large (nearly 40 percent of the total) Japanese American population. This was especially crucial since about half of the Territory's students, American-born and future voters, were of Japanese descent. Total assimilation into European American culture was the goal. Second, there was profound disagreement within the Japanese immigrant community, evenly split between acceding to the oligarchy's demands and fighting to preserve its rights in court. Third, transcending the limits of "local" rule by recourse to the federal system, up to the U.S. Supreme Court, could be a valuable strategy. The schools had attempted for more than a decade to limit the curriculum to language instruction, but the Territory rejected these reforms as inadequate and began, in 1920, a series of draconian measures to eliminate the schools. The schools were banned after Pearl Harbor and resumed limited operations after the war.

Cases Argued and Decided in the Supreme Court of the United States, Book 71. Rochester, NY: The Lawyers Co-Operative Publishing Company, 1927.

U.S. Supreme Court
Farrington, Governor, et al. v. T. Tokushige et al.
273 U.S. 284

Mr. Justice McReynolds delivered the opinion of the court:

The circuit court of appeals affirmed . . . an interlocutory decree rendered by the United States district court of Hawaii July 21, 1925, which granted a temporary injunction forbidding petitioners—governor, attorney general, and superintendent of public instruction of that territory—from attempting to enforce the provisions of Act 30, Special Session 1920, legislature of Hawaii, entitled, "An Act Relating to Foreign Language Schools and Teachers Thereof," as amended by Act 171 of 1923 and Act 152 of 1925, and certain regulations adopted by the department of public instruction June 1, 1925. The interlocutory decree was granted upon the bill and affidavits presented by both sides. No answer has been filed. In these circumstances we only consider whether the judicial discretion of the trial court was improperly exercised.

Respondents claimed below and maintain here that enforcement of the challenged act would deprive them of their liberty and property without due process of law contrary to the 5th Amendment. Petitioners insist that the entire act and the regulations adopted thereunder are valid; that they prescribe lawful rules for the conduct of private foreign language schools necessary for the public welfare; also that if any provision of the statute transcends the power of the legislature it should be disregarded and the remaining ones should be enforced.

If the enactment is subject to the asserted objections it is not here seriously questioned that respondents are entitled to the relief granted.

There are 163 foreign language schools in the territory. Nine are conducted in the Korean language, seven in the Chinese and the remainder in the Japanese. Respondents are members of numerous voluntary unincorporated associations conducting foreign language schools for instruction of Japanese children. These are owned, maintained and conducted by upwards of five thousand persons; the property used in connection therewith is worth $250,000; the enrolled pupils number 20,000; and 300 teachers are employed. These schools receive no aid from public funds. All children residing within the territory are required to attend some public or equivalent school; and practically all who go to foreign language schools also attend public or such private schools. It is affirmed by counsel for petitioners that Japanese pupils in the public and equivalent private schools increased from 1,320 in 1900 to 19,354 in 1920, and that out of a total of 65,369 pupils of all races on December 31, 1924, 30,487 were Japanese.

The challenged enactment declares that the term, "foreign language school," as used therein, "shall be construed to mean any school which is conducted in any language other than the English language or Hawaiian language, except Sabbath schools." And, as stated by the circuit court of appeals, the following are its more prominent and questionable features:

"No such school shall be conducted in the territory unless under a written permit therefor from the department of public instruction, nor unless the fee therefor shall have been paid as therein provided. . . .

"No person shall teach in a foreign language school unless and until he shall have first applied to and obtained a permit so to do from the department and this shall also be construed to include persons exercising or performing administrative powers at any school. No permit to teach in a foreign language school shall be granted unless and until the department is satisfied that the applicant for the same is possessed of the ideals of democracy; knowledge of American history and institutions, and knows how to read, write and speak the English language. . . .

"No foreign language school shall be conducted in the morning before the school hours of the public schools or during the hours while the public schools are in session, nor shall any pupil attend any foreign language school for more than one hour each day, nor exceeding six hours in any one week nor exceeding thirty-eight weeks in any school year. . . .

The affidavit of T. Iwanaga, in support of motion for temporary injunction, states—

"That in the schools referred to in said bill, which are conducted for each grade for one hour for each school day, nothing contrary to American history and American institutions and principles of democracy is taught, the instruction being confined to the speaking, reading and writing of the Japanese language; . . .

"That in the schools represented by plaintiffs there are about twelve thousand four hundred pupils and said schools employ about one hundred ninety-two teachers; that said teachers are paid and said schools are maintained from voluntary contributions and from the fees of the children attending said schools; that the provisions of said Act 152 of the Session Laws of 1925 are so drastic that the parents of children will be afraid to pay tuition fees and other persons will be afraid to contribute to the funds of said schools lest they be subjected to the pains and penalties provided in said act, and that, therefore, unless immediate relief is afforded by this honorable court, the said schools will be unable to pay the teachers' salaries and the expenses of conducting said schools and the property of plaintiffs in said schools will be utterly destroyed."

An affidavit of the attorney general describes the litigation which has arisen under the legislation concerning foreign language schools. He does not disavow purpose to enforce all provisions of the challenged act and regulations. . . . Also, he says—

"That instruction in said Japanese Language Schools is not and cannot be confined to the speaking, reading and writing of the Japanese language, but extends to many subjects and even in so far as it is intended to have for its object the speaking, reading and writing of said language, the teaching of that is and must be largely through the medium of stories whether of history or fiction and in other ways than the mere teaching of letters and words and sentences. . . .

The foregoing statement is enough to show that the school Act and the measures adopted thereunder go far beyond mere regulation of privately supported schools where children obtain instruction deemed valuable by their parents and which is not obviously in conflict with any public interest. They give affirmative direction concerning the intimate and essential details of such schools, intrust their control to public officers, and deny both owners and patrons reasonable choice and discretion in respect of teachers, curriculum and textbooks. Enforcement of the act probably would destroy most, if not all, of them; and, certainly, it would deprive parents of fair opportunity to procure for their children instruction which they think important and we cannot say is harmful. The Japanese parent has the right to direct the education of his own child without unreasonable restrictions; the Constitution protects him as well as those who speak another tongue. . . .

The general doctrine touching rights guaranteed by the 14th Amendment to owners, parents and children in respect of attendance upon schools has been announced in recent opinions. . . . While that Amendment declares that no *state* shall "deprive any person of life, liberty or property without due process of law," the inhibition of the 5th Amendment—"no person shall . . . be deprived of life, liberty or property without due process of law"—applies to the federal government and agencies set up by Congress for the government of the territory. Those fundamental rights of the individual which the cited cases declared were protected by the 14th Amendment from infringement by the states, are guaranteed by the 5th Amendment against action by the territorial legislature or officers.

We of course appreciate the grave problems incident to the large alien population of the Hawaiian islands. These should be given due weight whenever the validity of any governmental regulation of private schools is under consideration; but the limitations of the Constitution must not be transcended. . . .

We find no abuse of the discretion lodged in the trial court. The decree of the Circuit Court of Appeals must be affirmed.

65

Supreme Court: Weedin v. Chin Bow, *June 6, 1927*

Like the United States v. Wong Kim Ark case in 1898, this was an important constitutional test of equal rights under the law for all people. The Wong Kim Ark decision affirmed that anyone born on U.S. soil was an American citizen by birth (jus soli). Chin Bow was born in China to Chin Dun, an American citizen who had never been in the United States. Chin Dun's father, Chin Tong, was born in the United States, and, therefore, a citizen by birth. When Chin Bow sought admission into the country at Seattle, the Commissioner of Immigration, Weedin, denied his application on the grounds that his father, while admittedly a citizen, had never resided here and therefore could not pass on his citizenship to his son. The bureaucracy agreed, and the Secretary of Labor ordered Chin Bow deported. However, the courts all ruled that under the law of blood (jus sanguinis), *"the rights of citizenship shall descend," and Chin Bow must be admitted.*

Cases Argued and Decided in the Supreme Court of the United States, Book 71. Rochester, NY: The Lawyers Co-operative Publishing Company, 1927.

Luther Weedin, Commissioner of Immigration at the Port of Seattle, Washington, Petitioner, v. Chin Bow

Mr. Chief Justice Taft delivered the opinion of the court:

Chin Bow applied for admission to the United States at Seattle. The board of special inquiry of the immigration bureau at that place denied him admission on the ground that though his father is a citizen, he is not a citizen, because at the time of his birth in China his father had never resided in the United States. Chin Bow was born March 29, 1914, in China. His father, Chin Dun, was also born in China on March 8, 1894, and had never been in this country until July 18, 1922. Chin Dun was the son of Chin Tong, the respondent's grandfather. Chin Tong is forty-nine years old and was born in the United States.

The Secretary of Labor affirmed the decision of the Board of Inquiry, and the deportation of the respondent was ordered. He secured a writ of habeas corpus from the district court. Upon a hearing, an order discharging him was entered without an opinion. On appeal by the United States, the circuit court of appeals affirmed the judgment of the district court, . . . holding him to be a citizen under the provisions of 1993 of the Revised Statutes, U. S. C. title 8, 6, which is as follows:

"All children heretofore born or hereafter born out of the limits and jurisdiction of the United States, whose fathers were or may be at the time of their birth citizens thereof, are declared to be citizens of the United States; but the rights of citizenship shall not descend to children whose fathers never resided in the United States."

The rights of Chin Bow are determined by the construction of this section. The Secretary of Labor, April 27, 1916, asked the opinion of Attorney General Gregory whether a rule of the Chinese regulations of his Department, which denied citizenship to foreign-born children of American Chinese, was a valid one. He advised that it was not, because 1993 applied to all children and therefore included Chinese children as well. The second question was whether foreign-born children of American-born Chinese fathers were entitled to enter the United States as citizens thereof, when they had continued to reside for some time in China after reaching their majorities, without any affirmative action on their part indicating an intention to remain citizens of the United States, and the Attorney General advised that they were, in spite of these circumstances, entitled to enter the United States as citizens thereof, 30 Ops. Atty. Gen. 529.

The United States contends that the proviso of 1993, "but the rights of citizenship shall not descend to children whose fathers never resided in the United States," must be construed to mean that only the children whose fathers have resided in the United States before their birth become citizens under the section. It is claimed for the respondent that the residence of the father at any time in the United States before his death entitles his son whenever born to citizenship. These conflicting claims make the issue to be decided. . . .

In a work by Mr. Borchard, formerly Assistant Counsellor of the State Department, we find this:

"To confer citizenship upon a child born abroad, the father must have resided in the United States. This limitation upon the right of transmitting citizenship indefinitely was intended to prevent the residence abroad of successive generations of persons claiming the privileges of American citizenship while evading its duties. It seems not to have been judicially determined whether the residence of the father in the United States must necessarily have preceded the birth of the child, but by the fact that the statute provides that citizenship shall not 'descend,' it is believed that the residence prescribed must have preceded the birth of the child, and such has been the construction of the Department." . . .

It would seem then that the question before us is one that has really not been authoritatively decided except by two circuit courts of appeals that of the ninth circuit, which is here under review, and that of the circuit court of appeals for the first circuit (Johnson v. Sullivan, 8 F. (2d) 988), which adopted the view of the ninth circuit court and followed it.

The opinion in the ninth circuit says (p. 369):

"The statute refers to the descent of the rights of citizenship. The term 'descend' has a well-defined meaning in law. As defined by Webster, it means: 'To pass down, as from generation to generation, or from ancestor to heir.' If the term 'descend' is given that meaning in this connection, the status of the appellee would not become definitely fixed until his father became a resident of the United States or died without becoming such. In the former event he would become vested with all the rights of citizenship as soon as his father became a resident, while in the latter event his claim to citizenship would be forever lost."

The expression "the rights of citizenship shall descend" can not refer to the time of the death of the father, because that is hardly the time when they do descend. The phrase is borrowed from the law of property. The descent of property comes only after the death of the ancestor. The transmission of right of citizenship is not at the death of the ancestor but at the birth of the child, and it seems to us more natural to infer that the conditions of the descent contained in the limiting proviso, so far as the father is concerned, must be perfected and have been performed at that time.

This leads to a reversal of the judgment of the Circuit Court of Appeals and a remanding of the respondent.

66

Supreme Court: Gong Lum et al. v. Rice et al., November 21, 1927

This 1927 Supreme Court ruling established that segregated, "separate but equal" schools were constitutional as applied to children of Chinese descent, following on the 1896 Plessy v. Ferguson landmark case. Gong Lum was a grocer in Rosedale, Mississippi who insisted that his daughter, Martha, be allowed to attend the white school instead of the blacks-only version with underpaid teachers, inferior books and buildings, and a far shorter school year. Gong Lum sued on behalf of his daughter and her friend, Chew How, to force the trustees and school officials to admit the Chinese students. After all, the plaintiffs argued, if the white race is justified in segregation for its own protection from the "colored race," then it "may not legally expose the yellow race to a danger that the dominant race recognizes." The Supreme Court upheld the state in its determination to segregate the white race from "the brown, yellow, and black" races and insisted that Martha attend the colored public school of her district or select a private school.

United States Reports, Volume 275. Cases Adjudged in The Supreme Court. Washington, DC: Government Printing Office, 1928.

Supreme Court of the United States
Gong Lum et al. v. Rice et al.
275 U.S. 78

Mr. Chief Justice Taft delivered the opinion of the Court.

Gong Lum is a resident of Mississippi, resides in the Rosedale consolidated high school district, and is the father of Martha Lum. He is engaged in the mercantile business. Neither he nor she was connected with the consular service, or any other service, of the government of China, or any other government, at the time of her birth. She was nine years old when the petition was filed, having been born January 21, 1915, and she sued by her next friend, Chew How, who is a nativeborn citizen of the United States and the state of Mississippi. The petition alleged that she was of good moral character, between the ages of 5 and

21 years, and that, as she was such a citizen and an educable child, it became her father's duty under the law to send her to school; that she desired to attend the Rosedale consolidated high school; that at the opening of the school she appeared as a pupil, but at the noon recess she was notified by the superintendent that she would not be allowed to return to the school; that an order had been issued by the board of trustees, who are made defendants, excluding her from attending the school solely on the ground that she was of Chinese descent, and not a member of the white or Caucasian race, and that their order had been made in pursuance to instructions from the state superintendent of education of Mississippi, who is also made a defendant.

The petitioners further show that there is no school maintained in the district for the education of children of Chinese descent, and none established in Bolivar county where she could attend. . . .

The petition alleged that, in obedience to this mandate of the Constitution, the Legislature has provided for the establishment and for the payment of the expenses of the Rosedale consolidated high school, and that the plaintiff, Gong Lum, the petitioner's father, is a taxpayer and helps to support and maintain the school; that Martha Lum is an educable child, is entitled to attend the school as a pupil, and that this is the only school conducted in the district available for her as a pupil; that the right to attend it is a valuable right; that she is not a member of the colored race, nor is she of mixed blood, but that she is pure Chinese; that she is by the action of the board of trustees and the state superintendent discriminated against directly, and denied her right to be a member of the Rosedale school; that the school authorities have no discretion under the law as to her admission as a pupil in the school, but that they continue without authority of law to deny her the right to attend it as a pupil. For these reasons the writ of mandamus is prayed for against the defendants, commanding them and each of them to desist from discriminating against her on account of her race or ancestry, and to give her the same rights and privileges that other educable children between the ages of 5 and 21 are granted in the Rosedale consolidated high school.

The petition was demurred to by the defendants on the ground, among others, that the bill showed on its face that plaintiff is a member of the Mongolian or yellow race, and therefore not entitled to attend the schools provided by law in the state of Mississippi for children of the white or Caucasian race.

The trial court overruled the demurrer and ordered that a writ of mandamus issue to the defendants as prayed in the petition.

The defendants then appealed to the Supreme Court of Mississippi, which heard the case. Rice v. Gong Lum, 139 Miss. 760, 104 So. 105. In its opinion, it directed its attention to the proper construction of section 207 of the state Constitution of 1890, which provides:

"Separate schools shall be maintained for children of the white and colored races."

The court held that this provision of the Constitution divided the educable children into those of the pure white or Caucasian race, on the one hand, and the brown, yellow, and black races, on the other, and therefore that Martha Lum, of the Mongolian or yellow race, could not insist on being classed with the whites under this constitutional division. The court said:

"The Legislature is not compelled to provide separate schools for each of the colored races, and unless and until it does provide such schools, and provide for segregation of the other races, such races are entitled to have the benefit of the colored public schools. Under our statutes a colored public school exists in every county and in some convenient district, in which every colored child is entitled to obtain an education. These schools are within the reach of all the children of the state, and the plaintiff does not show by her petition that she applied for admission to such schools. On the contrary, the petitioner takes the position that, because there are no separate public schools for Mongolians, she is entitled to enter the white public schools in preference to the colored public schools. . . .

"If the plaintiff desires, she may attend the colored public schools of her district, or, if she does not so desire, she may go to a private school. The compulsory school law of this state does not require the attendance at a public school, and a parent under the decisions of the Supreme Court of the United States has a right to educate his child in a private school if he so desires. But plaintiff is not entitled to attend a white public school." . . .

The case then reduces itself to the question whether a state can be said to afford to a child of Chinese ancestry, born in this country and a citizen of the United States, the equal protection of the laws, by giving her the opportunity for a common school education in a school which receives only colored children of the brown, yellow or black races. . . .

The question here is whether a Chinese citizen of the United States is denied equal protection of the laws when he is classed among the colored races and furnished facilities for education equal to that offered to all, whether white, brown, yellow, or black. Were this a new question, it would call for very full argument and consideration; but we think that it is the same question which has been many times decided to be within the constitutional power of the state Legislature to settle, without intervention of the federal courts under the federal Constitution. . . .

In Plessy v. Ferguson, 163 U. S. 537, 544, 545, 16 S. Ct. 1138, 1140, 41 L. Ed. 256, in upholding the validity under the Fourteenth Amendment of a statute of Louisiana requiring the separation of the white and colored races in railway coaches, a more difficult question than this, this court, speaking of permitted race separation, said:

"The most common instance of this is connected with the establishment of separate schools for white and colored children, which has been held to be a valid exercise of the legislative power even by courts of states where the political rights of the colored race have been longest and most earnestly enforced." . . .

Most of the cases cited arose, it is true, over the establishment of separate schools as between white pupils and black pupils; but we cannot think that the question is any different, or that any different result can be reached, assuming the cases above cited to be rightly decided, where the issue is as between white pupils and the pupils of the yellow races. The decision is within the discretion of the state in regulating its public schools, and does not conflict with the Fourteenth Amendment.

The judgment of the Supreme Court of Mississippi is affirmed.

67

Younghill Kang, The Grass Roof, 1931

Published in 1931, Younghill Kang's powerful autobiography focused on the early years of his life (1903–72) before he left for the United States in 1921. He was born just before Japan defeated Russia and just as the Japanese military began solidifying control over Korea, eventually formalizing colonial status in 1910. Kang was reared in a scholarly family with status and means but quickly became aware of the persistent oppression of the peasantry and the intensification of misery by Japan. The March 1, 1919 Korean Independence uprising against the Japanese marked and sparked Korean patriotism both at home and among Koreans in countries like China and the United States until Japan's defeat in 1945. "Mansei" (literally, "ten thousand years"; wan sui in Chinese; banzai in Japanese) became the rallying cry for Kang and thousands of others.

Kang became an influential writer and spokesperson for Korea while a professor at New York University. His story illustrates the range of talent and experiences of Asian immigrants in the United States. The section excerpted here is from chapter 12, "Star of the West." It is melodramatic but represents the heady vision of idealism, modernization, power, and progress embodied in the American dream.

Younghill Kang, *The Grass Roof*. New York: Charles Scribner's Sons, 1931.

At another time he spoke of America to me, America, the home of those queer missionaries of the market-place. Park Soo-San had become a liberal Christian, wishing to turn his back on the past, and his face toward the future; it was a very radical thing to do at that time. An education in America, for the greatest possible number, was the desideratum he always preached. Japan had government students there. China had too. Only Korea had not her quota there, because her national rights had been stolen before she could get the new ways. Yes, now Korea was being punished for her conservatism. Any who could must make their way to America. Others must go by the help of patriotic private citizens who yet had the means in hand. What glamour he cast over the great colleges in America, which held all that the West had ever thought or known, and the latest means for giving it in the diploma packet by the wholesale. An American education was for the few he preached; those few would reap the golden reward. He made me see that the road of a scholar's future prominence lay toward America like the shortest distance between two points . . . in a straight line.

As soon as I understood, my soul had the fixed goal, although I did not speak of it yet to anyone. It seemed too daring. But I studied with all the concentration and enthusiasm of the crazy-poet who would have died at any time for the great poets of the Tang and Sung dynasties; I studied with all the political and social fervor of my uncle *pak-sa* who made his name through pull and scholarship in Seoul; I studied with all the joie-de-vivre and recklessness of the prodigal-son who took his happiness at the expense of others; I studied with all the self-denial and earnestness of my father in slaving for three men's families; I studied with all the brains of my many ancestors who had been scholars and poets and officials beyond count or number.

The old Confucian school receded to the past, in my mind. It seemed to me more and more useless, as a bull-fight or a game of contract bridge, since I began to learn the law of gravitation, and Boyle's law and all the other laws. The study of the lives of Lincoln and Napoleon, and the geography of the World kindled my enthusiasm until sometimes I seemed just to be dazzled by stars in the head.

68

Hare-Hawes-Cutting Act, January 17, 1933

Representative Butler Hayes and Senators Harry Hawes and Bronson Cutting introduced legislation, eventually combined into a single bill, to provide for Philippine independence — although with considerable strings designed to ensure American privileges. The bill passed and was vetoed by President Herbert Hoover; the veto was then overriden by Congress. Eventually, however, the necessary approval from the Philippine legislature was rejected because of immigration, trade, military, and governance policies designed to favor the United States. The depression and mounting anti-Filipino racism encouraged American lawmakers to design this independence act to resolve the problems following the takeover of the Philippines in 1898. Since Filipinos were American "nationals" and could not be lumped together with other Asians for exclusion purposes, and since the increasing hostility against Filipinos in the United States appeared irreversible, the only resolution appeared to be independence. But because the Philippine legislature objected, the act could not be implemented. The next year, 1934, the Tydings-McDuffie Act managed to bring together enough of the elements necessary to provide for independence — and exclusion.

The Statutes at Large of the United States of America, vol. 47. Washington, DC: Government Printing Office, 1933.

An Act
To enable the people of the Philippine Islands
to adopt a constitution and form a government for
the Philippine Islands, to provide for the independence
of the same, and for other purposes

Be it enacted by the Senate and House of Representatives of the United States of America in Congress assembled,

Convention to Frame Constitution for Philippine Islands

Section 1. The Philippine Legislature is hereby authorized to provide for the election of delegates to a constitutional convention, which shall meet in the hall of the house of representatives in the capital of the Philippine Islands, at such time as the Philippine Legislature may fix, within one year after the enactment of this Act, to formulate and draft a constitution for the government of the Commonwealth of the Philippine Islands, subject to the conditions and qualifications prescribed in this Act, which shall exercise jurisdiction over all the territory ceded to the United States by the treaty of peace concluded between the United States and Spain on the 10th day of December, 1898, the boundaries of which are set forth in Article III of said treaty, together with those islands embraced in the treaty between Spain and the United States concluded at Washington on the 7th day of November, 1900. The Philippine Legislature shall provide for the necessary expenses of such convention. . . .

(4) For the purposes of sections 18 and 20 of the Immigration Act of 1917, as amended, the Philippine Islands shall be considered to be a foreign country.

(b) The provisions of this section are in addition to the provisions of the immigration laws now in force, and shall be enforced as a part of such laws, and all the penal or other provisions of such laws, not inapplicable, shall apply to and be enforced in connection with the provisions of this section. An alien, although admissible under the provisions of this section, shall not be admitted to the United States if he is excluded by any provision of the immigration laws other than this section, and an alien, although admissible under the provisions of the immigration laws other than this section, shall not be admitted to the United States if he is excluded by any provision of this section. . . .

Recognition of Philippine Independence and Withdrawal of American Sovereignty

Sec. 10. On the 4th day of July, immediately following the expiration of a period of ten years from the date of the inauguration of the new government under the constitution provided for in this Act, the President of the United States shall by proclamation withdraw and surrender all right of possession, supervision, jurisdiction, control, or sovereignty then existing and exercised by the United States in and over the territory and people of the Philippine Islands, including all military and other reservations of the Government of the United States in the Philippines (except such land or property reserved under section 5 as may be redesignated by the President of the United States not later than two years after the date of such proclamation), and, on behalf of the United States, shall recognize the independence of the Philippine Islands as a separate and self-governing nation and acknowledge the authority and control over the same of the government instituted by the people thereof, under the constitution then in force: *Provided*, That the constitution has been previously amended to include the following provisions: . . .

69

California District Court of Appeal:
Salvador Roldan v. Los Angeles County,
January 27, 1933

Salvador Roldan, a Filipino, sought to marry Marjorie Rogers, a white woman, in 1931, but the Los Angeles County Clerk refused to issue them a marriage license. This was part of the intensifying anti-Filipino hostility across the western states. The issue forced California to clarify its classification of "racial" groups and to categorize Filipinos in antimiscegenation actions. At the time, marriages of whites to "Negroes, Mongolians, or Mulattoes" were considered null and void, and clerks were ordered not to issue licenses for such intermarriages. But it was not clear whether Filipinos were "Mongolians," because a number of "scientific" groupings included a separate category called "Malay." In 1933 the court of appeals upheld a lower court ruling that Filipinos were Malay, not Mongolian, and therefore could marry whites. But this was a very short-lived victory. Within a few months, the California Assembly simply amended the Civil Code to include "Malay" among the races prohibited from marrying whites. This law remained in effect until declared unconstitutional in 1948 by the California Supreme Court.

Reports of Cases Determined in the District Courts of Appeal of the State of California, vol. 129. San Francisco: Bancroft-Whitney Co., 1933.

Solvador Roldan, Respondent, v. Los Angeles County et al., Appellants

ARCHBALD, J., *pro tem.*—Solvador Roldan applied to the county clerk of Los Angeles County for a license to wed a woman of Caucasian descent and was refused such license. On a hearing of his application before the superior court for a writ to compel the issuance thereof he was found to be a "Filipino," viz., "an Illocano, born in the Philippine Islands of Filipino progenitors in whose blood was co-mingled a strain of Spanish," and not a Mongolian. From a judgment making the alternative writ of mandate permanent the defendants have appealed.

[1] Section 69 of the Civil Code, relating to marriage licenses, was amended in 1880 (Code Amendments, 1880, p. 3) to prohibit the issuance of a license au-

thorizing the marriage of a white person "with a . . . Mongolian." Section 60 of the Civil Code was amended in 1905 (Stats. 1905, p. 554) by adding "Mongolians" to the classes whose marriage with a "white" was made "illegal and void." The sole question involved in this appeal is whether or not the legislature in 1880 and 1905 meant to include Filipinos in its use of the word "Mongolian."

We find no dissent to the statement that the Filipino is included among the Malays, although since the time of Huxley, at least, there has been some question among ethnologists as to whether the five grand subdivisions of the races of mankind, as classified by Blumenbach, is the proper classification or whether the Malays are to be included among the "Mongoloid" group and as a branch of the Mongolian family. We are not, however, interested in what the best scientific thought of the day was, but in what was the common use of the word "Mongolian" in California at the time of the enactment of the legislation above mentioned. . . .

In the "Reports of the Immigration Commission" of the United States (1911), vol. 5, "Dictionary of Races or Peoples," p. 94, under "Malay, Malaysian or Brown Race," appears the following, the italics being ours: "One of the five grand divisions of mankind as *commonly* classified since the time of Blumenbach, but the most disputable one in the view of recent ethnologists. Many consider it to be a branch of the Mongolian race, but such admit, at least, that it is the most divergent great branch of the latter. And on page 97 of the same volume, under "Mongolian, etc.," we read: "Many ethnologists so define 'Mongolian' as to include the entire American and Malay races."

We think we have quoted enough to show that, regardless of the fine points of the argument from the ethnologist's standpoint, the early classification of Blumenbach left its impression on the writers from his day to 1905, at least, so that his classification is spoken of as the one "commonly" used; and we venture to think that in the recollection of those whose early schooling was anywhere in the period from 1850 to 1905 his classification of the races into the five divisions, the white, black, yellow, red and brown, still persists.

From 1862 to 1885 the history of California is replete with legislation to curb the so-called "Chinese invasion," and as we read we are impressed with the fact that the terms "Asiatics," "Coolies" and "Mongolians" meant "Chinese" to the people who discussed and legislated on the problem, or at most that they only extended in their thought to natives of China and the inhabitants of adjacent countries having the same characteristics. . . .

Much more could be shown but we think we have set down sufficient to indicate that in 1880, in a group that would compare very favorably with the average legislature, there was no thought of applying the name Mongolian to a Malay; that the word was used to designate the class of residents whose presence caused the problem at which all the legislation was directed, viz., the Chinese, and possibly contiguous peoples of like characteristics; that the *common* classification of the races was Blumenbach's, which made the "Malay" one of the five grand subdivisions, i. e., the "brown race," and that such classification persisted until after section 60 of the Civil Code was amended in 1905 to make it consistent with section 69 of the same code. As counsel for appellants have well pointed out, this is not a social question before us, as that was decided by the legislature at the time the code was amended; and if the common thought of to-day is different from what it was at such time, the matter is one that addresses itself to the legislature and not to the courts.

Judgment affirmed.

70

Gee Theo Quee Angel Island Interrogation, December 1, 1933

After the Angel Island Immigration Station was opened in 1910, hundreds of thousands seeking entry into the United States were processed by inspectors and translators. The 1882 Chinese Exclusion Act halted most immigration from China; the 1906 fire in San Francisco burned the records and created a loophole for many Chinese to claim birth in the United States, and an opportunity to bring immediate family from China or to claim "paper" sons or daughters fathered there. Immigration officials were aware of the widespread practice. Gaining entry then became a deadly contest between inspectors determined to uncover fraud and Chinese anxious to enter the country. As a result, the questioning was severe, sometimes prolonged over months and years, and unfair. In response, many Chinese memorized elaborate details of villages and families entirely fabricated for the inspectors. It was not unusual for true surnames to emerge only after the families were securely anchored by one or more generations of American-born citizens in the 1960s or later. Flo Oy Wong, sister Nellie, and brother Bill uncovered records of their father, Gee Seow Hong's, original entry via Angel Island in 1910 and their mother's subsequent, "paper" arrival in 1933, with three older sisters. These are sections of the transcript from Gee Theo Quee's interrogation. The children lived with the surname Wong because their mother entered as the sister of Gee Seow Hong rather than as his wife. In fact, Gee Seow Hong was an only child, and their mother's testimony was a richly embroidered fable that worked. Their mother referenced her own alleged death in China and reported on several real children, her siblings, and several nonexistent brothers, Gee Hon Ming, Gee Hon Wah, and Gee Hon Keung. The racism of the immigration acts prompted desperate measures for family and community development.

Reprinted with permission from Flo Oy Wong.

HEARING RESUMED, 12/1/33

Inspector Hemstreet replaces Inspector Cole as member of the Board.
By Member Hemstreet: I have familiarized myself with all the evidence so far adduced in this case.

STATEMENT OF APPLICANT 9–5.
ADMONISHED SHE IS STILL UNDER OATH.

Interpreter: Harry Tang.

Q What is your name?

A GEE THEO QUEE.

Q Are you a full blood Chinese person?

A Yes.

Q Of what country are you a citizen or subject?

A I don't know what a citizen means.

Q State your age and date and place of your birth?

A 28 yrs. old, born KS 32–11–24 (Jan. 8, 1907) in Goon Doo Hong Village, Sun Ning dist., China.

Q Did you live in your native village from the time of your birth until you left China to come to this country?

A Yes.

Q What is your occupation?

A I have no occupation.

Q How have you been supported?

A By my parents.

Q Are you able to read any language?

A I have had one year of Chinese schooling; I can read a few Chinese words but cannot write.

Q Who is your nearest relative in China?

A My sister-in-law YEE SHEE, wife of my brother GEE SHOW LEE, now living in my native village.

Q What is your final destination in the U.S.?

A Oakland, Calif.

Q What is your purpose in coming to the U.S.?

A My brother GEE SEOW HONG, asked me to come over to do whatever I could find here because my parents had died and I was lonesome at home.

Q How long do you intend to remain in the U.S.?

A Indefinitely.

Q By whom was your passage to the U.S. paid?

A My father left me $500 to pay my expenses to this country and if that was not enough, my 2nd brother GEE SEOW HONG would furnish the rest.

Q Have you ever been married?

A No.

Q Were you ever in the U.S. previously?

A No.

Q Were you ever confined in a prison or almshouse?

A No.

Q Were you or was either of your parents ever treated as insane?

A No.

Q Are you a polygamist or a believer in the practice of polygamy?

A No.

Q Are you an anarchist?

A No.

Q How much money have you in your possession?

A I have no money.

Q How do you expect to be supported in this country?

A My brother GEE SEOW HONG will look after me.

DESCRIPTION OF APPLICANT 9–3:

    Height, in Chinese slippers, 5 ft 1 3/4 in.

    Hair black, eyes brown, complexion dark.

    Large raised scar on right temple, at hairline.

    Pit scar on right cheekbone.

    Brown mole under right jaw.

    Pit scar outer corner upper left eyelid.

    Deep scar under chin.

Q State just why you believe your self to be admissible to the U.S.?

A I don't know; my parents left a birth paper for me but I do not know what it is.

Q Where is that paper you refer to?

A I do not know.

Q Did you ever see that birth paper?

A I don't know whether I have seen it or not; I wouldn't know it even if I did because I cannot read.

Q Tell us how you know that such a paper exists?

A At the time of my father's death he told me that when I was born he had me reported in Oakland.

Q Do you know where your father was born?

A He was born in the U.S.

Q How did you learn that your father was born in the U.S.?

A When my father was living I heard him say that.

Q What were all the names by which your father was ever known and when and where did he die?

A GEE GING FONG, or GEE KEE JEW, he died in my native village in China last year 10th month, 10th day (Nov. 7, 1932).

Q How many times has your father ever married?

A Only once.

Q Were you born to your father's only wife?

A Yes.

Q What was your mother's name and when and where did she die?

A YEE SHEE, died in my native village in/china, last year, 12th month, 12th day (Jan. 7, 1933).

Q What kind of feet did your mother have?

A Unbound feet.

Q How old was your mother when she died?

A I don't remember.

Q Was she as much as 70 years old?

A No.

Q How old was your father when he died?

A 62.

Q Was your mother as old as your father?

A My father was 1 or 2 yrs. older than my mother.

Q How did you learn that?

A There is a custom in China to celebrate birthdays so in that connection I heard of their ages.

Q When did your father last return to China?

A In CR 17–12th month (Jan. 1929).

Q Previous to his last return to China when was your father last at home?

A On the previous trip my father came home in CR 3 (1914) and left home for the U.S. in CR 9 (1920).

Q Did he remain in the home village all the time during that trip?

A Yes.

Q What occupation did your father follow during those years?

A He had no occupation.

Q How was your family supported during that period?

A My older brothers sent money home from this country.

Q How many children did your parents ever have?

A 6 sons, 1 daughter.

Q Are your brothers all living?

A Yes.

Q State their names, ages and present whereabouts?

A GEE SHOW KING, about 45 yrs. old, now in the U.S., I don't know what city.
GEE SEOW HONG, 38, now in Oakland, Calif.
GEE SHOW LEE, 37, also in Oakland.
GEE SHOW JING, 34, now working in Som Bot Market, S.N.D., China.
GEE SHOW KOON, 32, also employed in Som Bot Market.
GEE SHOW HONG, 30, now employed in Sun Ning City.

Q Did you ever have a brother or sister who died?

A No.

Q Which of your brothers are married?

A GEE SHOW KING, GEE SEOW HONG and SHOW LEE.

Q How many times was GEE SHOW KING married?

A Once.

Q What is his marriage name?

A GEE KUEY NAM.

Q What family has GEE SHOW KING?

A His wife is dead, and he has a son, no daughter.

Q What was the name of his wife and when and where did she die?

A HONG SHEE, died in about CR 8 (1919) in Goon Doo Hong Village, China.

Q Describe the son of your 1st brother?

A GEE HING TEUNG, about 20 yrs. old, now in the Straits Settlements.

Q When did he first go abroad?

A I don't remember but he went there a good many years ago.

Q Has he ever visited the home village since he first went abroad?

A No.

Q When did you last see GEE SHOW KING?

A Either in CR 6 or 7 (1917 or 1918), I was pretty small then.

Q Do you remember seeing GEE SHOW KING?

A Yes.

Q How many times has your 2nd brother been married?

A Twice.

Q When, where and to whom was he married the 1st time?

A The 1st time he was married in CR 8–12 (Jan. 1920), in Goon Doo Hong Village, China, to YEE SHEE.

Q When and where did SEOW HONG's first wife die?

A She died in CR 13–1 (Feb. 1924) in Goon Doo Hong Village, China.

Q Did GEE SEOW HONG have any children by his 1st wife?

A Yes, 1 son and 1 daughter.

Q Describe those children?

A GEE HON KING, 14 yrs. old, now attending school in his maternal grandmother's village, the Ai Leung Village, S.N.D, China.
Dau.: GEE LI HONG, 12 yrs. old, applicant.

Q When, where and to whom was GEE SEOW HONG married the 2nd time?

A The 2nd time he was married in CR 13–7 (Aug. 1924), in Goon Doo Hong Village, China, to YEE SHEE.

Q Is GEE SEOW HONG's 2nd wife living?

A No, she is dead.

Q When and where did she die?

A She died this year, 2nd month, 2nd day (Feb. 25, 1933).

Q How many children did GEE SEOW HONG have by his 2nd wife?

A 2 sons, 2 daughters.

Q Are those children all living?

A Yes.

Q Describe them?

A Sons: GEE HON WAH, 9, now attending school in his maternal grandmother's village, the Ai Leung Village, S.N.D., China.
GEE HON KEUNG, 5, now living with his maternal grandmother in Ai Leung Village.
Daus: GEE LI KENG, 8, applicant.

GEE LI WAH, 4, applicant. . . .

Q What was the native place of GEE SEOW HONG's first wife?

A Lin Hong Village, S.N.D.

Q Do you know if her parents are living?

A I do not know that.

Q Did you ever see the father or mother of GEE SEOW HONG's first wife?

A No.

Q Where is GEE SEOW HONG's first wife buried?

A Also buried in Foo Hong Hill.

Q About how far is her grave from those of your parents?

A I don't know because according to the custom in the Sun Ning District only male members of the family visit the graves.

Q Did you attend the funerel of GEE SEOW HONG's first wife?

A Yes.

Q Was GEE SEOW HONG's 2nd wife a native of the Ai Leung Village?

A Yes.

Q Is her father living?

A No.

Q What was his name and when did he die?

A YEE JUNG SIK, I heard that he died before his daughter married my brother.

Q Describe the wife of YEE JUNG SIK?

A I don't know her name, she is 60 odd yrs. old, and has natural feet.

Q Has any of the children here with you ever visited the Ai Leung Village?

A They all have.

Q Have they been there with you?

A No, I have never been to the Ai Leung Village but I just went with them as far as Som Bot Market where their paternal grandmother came to meet them.

Q Did SEOW HONG's 2nd wife have any brothers or sisters?

A No.

Q Did any of these children here with you ever remain in the Ai Leung Village for as long as several days at a time?

A No, only this year they stayed in their grandmother's home overnight.

Q Who accompanied them on their return to Goon Doo Hong Village on that occasion?

A Their grandmother accompanied them to Som Bot Market and I went there to meet them.

Q What caused the death of GEE SEOW HONG's 2nd wife?

A She died from sickness, she had a cough.

Q Was she confined to bed for some time prior to her death?

A Yes, she was sick in bed for a little over one month.

Q Did any doctor treat her in your house during that illness?

A Yes,

Q Did GEE LI HONG attend her stepmother's funeral?

A Yes.

Q How large is the Goon Doo Hong Village?

A It has 30 odd houses.

Q How many rows of houses has the village?

A 9 rows.

Q In what direction does the village face and which and is considered the head?

A It faces southwest; the head is on the right hand side where our house is located.

Q Has the village had the same number of houses as far back as your memory extends?

A Yes.

Q Are you certain that no new houses have been built in your village within your memory?

A Yes, because those that had money moved away, to some other place. . . .

Q Was there a dining table which was always kept in the parlor of your house?

A Yes, that was the same table that we used to worship.

Q Did your single brothers generally spend the New Year vacation in your home village?

A Yes.

Q Where would they sleep when they were in the village?

A In the schoolhouse.

Q Did they always have their meals at home during those periods?

A Yes. . . .

Q Were any of GEE SEOW HONG's sons in the village any time while he was home last?

A Yes, they came home each Sunday to see him.

Q Did they ever remain overnight in the village during that time?

A Yes, once they stayed overnight and returned to their school Monday morning.

Q Do you know where they slept that night?

A They slept in the schoolhouse with their father.

Q What schools have you attended?

A I have attended the girl's private school in Ow How Village, that's all.

Q When did you attend that school?

A The year before last.

Q Didn't you learn how to write your own name when you attended school?

A Yes, I did at that time, but on account of death and other trouble in my family I have forgotten how to write it now.

NOTE: Applicant demonstrates that she knows a few of the simpler characters written in Chinese on form 430.

Q Do you know how GEE SEOW HONG learned of the his 2nd wife's death?

A I sent him a letter and told him.

Q Did you yourself write that letter?

A I had someone to write it for me and my other brothers at at home also wrote him a letter about his wife's death. . . .

71

Tydings-McDuffie Act (Public Law No. 127), March 24, 1934

This legislation is also known as the "Philippines Independence Act." Congress finally succeeded, after nearly two decades of attempts, at crafting legislation acceptable to the Philippine legislature that would halt immigration from the Philippines, establish a timetable for its independence, and secure sufficient privileges for American business and strategic purposes. As American nationals, Filipinos had been free to enter the United States. While some came as students or businessmen, the vast majority were laborers on sugar or pineapple plantations in Hawai'i or migrant workers on farms and fish canneries on the West Coast. Anti-Filipino rhetoric suggested they were unfair competition to white workers and sexual threats to white women. Providing independence for the Philippines became the sole means of prohibiting further immigration. This act included an annual immigration quota of fifty Filipinos per year, the lowest assigned to any nation, except for Hawaii's plantation needs—and it prohibited re-migration from Hawai'i to the mainland United States. It also gave the Philippines status as a commonwealth, with independence to follow in ten years. World War II intervened, and independence was finally achieved on July 4, 1946.

The Statutes at Large of the United States of America, vol. 48, part 1. Washington, DC: Government Printing Office, 1934.

An Act
To provide for the complete independence of the Philippine Islands, to provide for the adoption of a constitution and a form of government for the Philippine Islands, and for other purposes

Be it enacted by the Senate and House of Representatives of the United States of America in Congress assembled,

Convention to Frame Constitution for Philippine Islands

Section 1. The Philippine Legislature is hereby authorized to provide for the election of delegates to a constitutional convention, which shall meet in the hall of the house of representatives in the capital of the Philippine Islands, at such time as the Philippine Legislature may fix, but not later than October 1, 1934, to formulate and draft a constitution for the government of the Commonwealth of the Philippine Islands, subject to the conditions and qualifications prescribed in this Act, which shall exercise jurisdiction over all the territory ceded to the United States by the treaty of peace concluded between the United States and Spain on the 10th day of December 1898, the boundaries of which are set forth in article III of said treaty, together with those islands embraced in the treaty between Spain and the United States concluded at Washington on the 7th day of November 1900. The Philippine Legislature shall provide for the necessary expenses of such convention.

Character of Constitution — Mandatory Provisions

Sec. 2. (a) The constitution formulated and drafted shall be republican in form, shall contain a bill of rights, and shall, either as a part thereof or in an ordinance appended thereto, contain provisions to the effect that, pending the final and complete withdrawal of the sovereignty of the United States over the Philippine Islands—

(1) All citizens of the Philippine Islands shall owe allegiance to the United States.

(2) Every officer of the government of the Commonwealth of the Philippine Islands shall, before entering upon the discharge of his duties, take and subscribe an oath of office, declaring, among other things, that he recognizes and accepts the supreme authority of and will maintain true faith and allegiance to the United States.

(3) Absolute toleration of religious sentiment shall be secured and no inhabitant or religious organization shall be molested in person or property on account of religious belief or mode of worship.

(4) Property owned by the United States, cemeteries, churches, and parsonages or convents appurtenant thereto, and all lands, buildings, and improvements used exclusively for religious, charitable, or educational purposes shall be exempt from taxation. . . .

(8) Provision shall be made for the establishment and maintenance of an adequate system of public schools, primarily conducted in the English language.

(9) Acts affecting currency, coinage, imports, exports, and immigration shall not become law until approved by the President of the United States.

(10) Foreign affairs shall be under the direct supervision and control of the United States.

(11) All acts passed by the Legislature of the Commonwealth of the Philippine Islands shall be reported to the Congress of the United States.

(12) The Philippine Islands recognizes the right of the United States to expropriate property for public uses, to maintain military and other reservations and armed forces in the Philippines, and, upon order of the President, to call into the service of such armed forces all military forces organized by the Philippine government. . . .

Submission of Constitution to Filipino People

Sec. 4. After the President of the United States has certified that the constitution conforms with the provisions of this Act, it shall be submitted to the people of the Philippine Islands for their ratification or rejection at an election to be held within four months after the date of such certification, on a date to be fixed by the Philippine Legislature, at which election the qualified voters of the Philippine Islands shall have an opportunity to vote directly for or against the proposed constitution and ordinances appended thereto. Such election shall be held in such manner as may be prescribed by the Philippine Legislature, to which the return of the election shall be made. . . .

Sec. 8. (a) Effective upon the acceptance of this Act by concurrent resolution of the Philippine Legislature or by a convention called for that purpose, as provided in section 17—

(1) For the purposes of the Immigration Act of 1917, the Immigration Act of 1924 (except section 13(c)), this section, and all other laws of the United States relating to the immigration, exclusion, or expulsion of aliens, citizens of the Philippine Islands who are not citizens of the United States shall be considered as if they were aliens. For such purposes the Philippine Islands shall be considered as a separate country and shall have for each fiscal year a quota of fifty. This paragraph shall not apply to a person coming or seeking to come to the Territory of Hawaii who does not apply for and secure an immigration or passport visa, but such immigration shall be determined by the Department of the Interior on the basis of the needs of industries in the Territory of Hawaii.

(2) Citizens of the Philippine Islands who are not citizens of the United States shall not be admitted to the continental United States from the Territory of Hawaii (whether entering such Territory before or after the effective date of this section) unless they belong to a class declared to be nonimmigrants by section 3 of the Immigration Act of 1924 or to a class declared to be nonquota immigrants under the provisions of section 4 of such Act other than subdivision (c) thereof, or unless they were admitted to such Territory under an immigration visa. The Secretary of Labor shall by regulations provide a method for such exclusion and for the admission of such excepted classes. . . .

(4) For the purposes of sections 18 and 20 of the Immigration Act of 1917, as amended, the Philippine Islands shall be considered to be a foreign country.

(b) The provisions of this section are in addition to the provisions of the immigration laws now in force, and shall be enforced as a part of such laws, and all the penal or other provisions of such laws not inapplicable, shall apply to and be enforced in connection with the provisions of this section. An alien, although admissible under the provisions of this section, shall not be admitted to the United States if he is excluded by any provision of the immigration laws other than this section, and an alien, although admissible under the provisions of the immigration laws other than this section, shall not be admitted to the United States if he is excluded by any provision of this section. . . .

Recognition of Philippine Independence and Withdrawal of American Sovereignty

Sec. 10. (a) On the 4th day of July immediately following the expiration of a period of ten years from the date of the inauguration of the new government under the constitution provided for in this Act the President of the United States shall by proclamation withdraw and surrender all right of possession, supervision, jurisdiction, control, or sovereignty then existing and exercised by the United States in and over the territory and people of the Philippine Islands, including all military and other reservations of the Government of the United States in the Philippines (except such naval reservations and fueling stations as are reserved under section 5), and, on behalf of the United States, shall recognize the independence of the Philippine Islands as a separate and self-governing nation and acknowledge the authority and control over the same of the government instituted by the people thereof, under the constitution then in force. . . .

Immigration After Independence

Sec. 14. Upon the final and complete withdrawal of American sovereignty over the Philippine Islands the immigration laws of the United States (including all the provisions thereof relating to persons ineligible to citizenship) shall apply to persons who were born in the Philippine Islands to the same extent as in the case of other foreign countries. . . .

Effective Date

Sec. 17. The foregoing provisions of this Act shall not take effect until accepted by concurrent resolution of the Philippine Legislature or by a convention called for the purpose of passing upon that question as may be provided by the Philippine Legislature.

Approved, March 24, 1934.

72

Filipino Repatriation Act, July 10, 1935

Although the 1934 Tydings-McDuffie Act provided a negligible annual quota of 50 Filipino immigrants in exchange for independence in 10 years, there remained approximately 45,000 Filipinos in the various states whose presence was resented by nativist whites. This legislation provided free transportation for Filipinos, except those in Hawai'i, willing to return to Manila. Support came from anti-Asian groups who simply wanted to remove the Filipinos as well as those who claimed that the depression had created a large group desiring return but too poor to afford the transportation costs. Anyone accepting repatriation would only be able to return to the United States as part of the annual quota of 50 individuals. Thus, both exclusionists and advocates could support the legislation. President Franklin D. Roosevelt signed this act into law, but fewer than 2,200 men accepted the offer, perhaps because of embarrassment, lack of opportunity in the Philippines, or concern about returning to the United States.

Statutes at Large of the United States of America, vol. 49, part 1. Washington, DC: Government Printing Office, 1936.

An Act
To provide means by which certain Filipinos can emigrate from the United States

Be it enacted by the Senate and House of Representatives of the United States of America in Congress assembled, That any native Filipino residing in any State or the District of Columbia on the effective date of this Act, who desires to return to the Philippine Islands, may apply to the Secretary of Labor, upon such form as the Secretary may prescribe, through any officer of the Immigration Service for the benefits of this Act. Upon approval of such application, the Secretary of Labor shall notify such Filipino forthwith, and shall certify to the Secretary of the Navy and the Secretary of War that such Filipino is eligible to be returned to the Philippine Islands under the terms of this Act. Every Filipino who is so certified shall be entitled, at the expense of the United States, to transportation and maintenance from his present residence to a port on the west coast of the United States, and from such port, to passage and maintenance to the port of Manila, Philippine Islands, on either Navy or Army transports, whenever space on such transports is available, or on any ship of United States registry operated by a commercial steamship company which has a contract with the Secretary of Labor as provided in section 2.

Sec. 2. The Secretary of Labor is hereby authorized and directed to enter into contracts with any railroad or other transportation company, for the transportation from their present residences to a port on the west coast of the United States of Filipinos eligible under section 1 to receive such transportation, and with any commercial steamship company, controlled by citizens of the United States and operating ships under United States registry, for transportation and maintenance of such Filipinos from such ports to the port of Manila, Philippine Islands, at such rates as may be agreed upon between the Secretary and such steamship, railroad, or other transportation company. . . .

Sec. 4. No Filipino who receives the benefits of this Act shall be entitled to return to the continental United States except as a quota immigrant under the provisions of section 8 (a) (1) of the Philippine Independence Act of March 24, 1934, during the period such section 8 (a) (1) is applicable. . . .

Sec. 6. No application for the benefits of this Act shall be accepted by any officer of the Immigration Service after December 1, 1936; and all benefits under this Act shall finally terminate on December 31, 1936, unless the journey has been started on or before that date, in which case the journey to Manila shall be completed.

Sec. 7. Nothing in this Act shall be construed as authority to deport any native of the Philippine Islands, and no Filipino removed from continental United States under the provisions of this Act shall hereafter be held to have been deported from the United States.

Approved, July 10, 1935.

73

A General Staff Study: Plan—Initial Seizure
of Orange [Japanese] Nationals, 1936

Drafted by Lt. Col. George Patton, this plan listed the 126 individuals who were to be arrested and detained immediately once the anticipated war between the United States and Japan began. Patton, who would become the famous World War II Commander of the Third Army, was in Hawai'i from 1935 to 1937. Orange was the color assigned to Japan in war preparations from early in the twentieth century. It is clear from documents like these that the highest levels of the U.S. government were preparing for summary detention of preselected immigrants and their American-born children if they were considered "inimical to American interests," or useful as "hostages." Moreover, officials from President Roosevelt on down used the term "concentration camp" to describe the places where these individuals were to be secured.

"A General Staff Study: Plan—Initial Seizure of Orange Nationals," n.d. [1936]. Records of the Hawaiian Department, Record Group 338, National Archives. Thanks to Michael Slackman for leads to this document. He is the author of *Target: Pearl Harbor* (Honolulu: University of Hawaii Press and Arizona Memorial Museum Association, 1990).

SECRET

I. THE PLAN:

1. To arrest and intern certain persons of the Orange [Japanese] race who are considered most inimical to American interests, or those whom, due to their position and influence in the Orange community, it is desirable to retain as hostages. Lists of these persons are prepared, showing name, occupation, address, and telephone number, as inclosures as follows:

Inclosure 1: Honolulu Sector (by zones)
Inclosure 4: Schofield Sector
Inclosure 5: Other islands (by island)

2. To dismantle or collect on M/R all amateur radio sending and receiving sets belonging to persons of Orange race. Inclosure 2 is a list of owners of these sets with addresses and telephone numbers.

3. (a) To close, through cooperation with the Navy, all harbors to the egress of Orange vessels regardless of size.

(b) To sieze [sic] and intern all Orange steamships in port.

4. To sieze [sic] and close all Orange banks, trust companies, and travel or ticket agencies as listed on Inclosure 7. Hotels will be continued under military supervision.

5. To remove all persons of Orange race, including servants, from all military posts, stations, and establishments.

6. To close all Orange language schools.

7. To establish press, mail, cable, and radio censorship under plan on file in the office of Assistant Chief of Staff, G-2.

8. To establish a Military Commission for the trial of persons accused of military offenses.

9. To issue a proclamation declaring martial law and specifying rules and regulations to be followed. Inclosure 8 is a draft of same.

10. To intern all Orange-owned or Orange-operated automobiles and taxicabs. . . .

/S/ G. S. Patton, Jr.
Lieut. Colonel, Gen Staff Corps,
Asst. Chief of Staff, G-2.

74

International Ladies Garment Workers' Union on Chinese Workers, January 1938

The American organized labor movement, with a few exceptions, had considerable difficulty dealing with workers of color, especially African Americans and Asians. The ILGWU took a major step forward in encouraging and supporting Chinese workers in their 1938 attempt to organize a union in the dozens of retail stores established by Joe Shoong, himself of Chinese origin. The nation was still in the throes of the Great Depression, but San Francisco was a hotbed of labor organizing, with feelings running extremely high on all sides. The fact that a major union like the ILGWU would incorporate the Chinese as comrades rather than denounce them as unfit labor meant that one traditional "divide and rule" tactic had become a bit more difficult for management to implement against the workforce. This was an important lesson for white workers, who had been told that Asian labor would not fight for better pay or conditions, thus creating an unfair competitor pool.

Thanks to Him Mark Lai for providing this document. *ILGWU Union Bulletin*, January 1938.

GOOD NEWS . . .
CHINESE WORKERS ARE IN THE UNION!

*IT IS CERTAINLY A FACT THAT THE
EMANCIPATION OF A PEOPLE
MUST BE THE CONCERN OF THE
PEOPLE THEMSELVES!*

Finally, finally, the Chinese workers themselves awakened to the realization that Chinese workers, like any other workers must organize if they wish to get decent working conditions, and wages by which they can live in some degree of comfort.

We welcome our Chinese fellow workers! We pledge them all the support a Union can give in their struggle for a better economic life! We greet the new Chinese Local No. 341, and wish them well!

The Chinese Local was hardly born when it was put to the test! As soon as it became known that the workers were organising, the National Dollar Store factory fired four Union workers,—men who had been with the firm for years! The membership was ready to walk out if the discharged workers were not reinstated! The Retail Department Store Employees Union advised the firm that it was wiser to reinstate the workers than to put the people to the test;—their members would not go through a picket line! Our Union counseled the firm that unless the men were put back on the job they would have a strike on their hands. The men were put back!

Now the new Chinese Local is working out an agreement to present to the firm. We trust the firm will be as reasonable in meeting the demands of its workers as other manufacturers in San Francisco have been. We hope that shortly the Dollar factory will be a Union shop, and that every garment made therein will bear a Union label! It will be a pleasure to advertise the Dollar Store as carrying Union made garments,—just as soon as a Union contract is consummated! The wives and families of Union men will gladly throw their buying power to the Dollar store when they know the Dollar factory is 100% Union!

Should the firm, however, choose to take a different course, the workers are ready to meet the challenge,—and our Union is ready to back them to the fullest!

On the opposite page is the appeal of the Chinese Local to all other Chinese workers in our trade to join the Union! Translated in part it is as follows:

"Obviously, it is impossible for any single person to make demands for better conditions for all, and be successful. So, fellow-workers, we must unite and make these demands as one body. Even then, the employers may still refuse to concede. If such be the case, our next step shall be to STRIKE AND PICKET, and to continue these tactics until OUR PURPOSES SHALL BE OBTAINED! . . . ."

Such spirit and intelligence must succeed! The new local has started off admirably. Nearly all the workers in the Dollar factory are in the Union now. Many Chinese workers in the contracting shops are in the Union, also! We hope it will not be long before every worker in our trade in Chinatown will be a Union worker, working under Union conditions!

Good luck to our Chinese Local No. 341! With your efforts and ours we will wipe out cheap labor in San Francisco! We are proud to have you with us!

75

Chinese Ladies Garment Workers' Union,
Local 341, January 1939

Local No. 341 of the International Ladies Garments Workers' Union was organized in January 1938 and soon found itself in a difficult strike to organize the garment factory for the National Dollar Stores. The workers won pay raises and better working conditions after a strike lasting 105 days. They had to endure many difficulties, including an attempt by the owners to scuttle the union agreement by a bogus sale and name change of the company. In this "greetings" extended in January 1939, a year after it was organized, Local 341, ILGWU, expresses gratitude for the support it enjoyed from across the country. For many of the women, especially the younger and American-born, the 1930s became a decade of empowerment in choice of careers and lifestyles.

Thanks to Him Mark Lai for this document, along with several others in this volume.
   ILGWU Union Bulletin, January 1939.

THE CHINESE LOCAL EXTENDS GREETINGS

The following is a translation of the Chinese Greeting on the opposite page, which besides being in our Bulletin, was distributed among a thousand Chinese Workers in Chinatown. The Chinese, as well as the English translation, was written by the Chinese members, themselves.

"WE GREET THE NEW YEAR WITH NEW HOPES. A YEAR HAS PASSED SINCE OUR LOCAL WAS ORGANIZED. IN THE LAST YEAR WE WON OUR FIRST STRIKE FOR UNION RECOGNITION, AND BETTER WAGES. OUR STRIKE LASTED 105 DAYS. WE OWED OUR SUCCESS TO THE SOLIDARITY AND DETERMINATION OF OUR MEMBERS TO FIGHT 'TO THE END' TO RAISE OUR LIVING STANDARD.

"WE ARE GRATEFUL TO OUR INTERNATIONAL FOR THE FULLEST MORAL AND FINANCIAL SUPPORT WHICH IT GAVE US SO GENEROUSLY. WE ARE GRATEFUL TO THE S.F. JOINT BOARD AND THEIR OFFICERS FOR THEIR GENEROUS HELP, ALSO.

"WE ARE ALSO GRATEFUL TO LOCAL 1100 FOR THE FULL SUP-
PORT THEY GAVE US IN OUR STRIKE. WE SHALL NEVER FORGET IT.

"WE ENJOYED THE PRIVILEGE OF A UNION SHOP FOR OVER
HALF A YEAR, AND WE WISH THE REST OF THE CHINESE GAR-
MENT WORKERS WERE WITH US. WITH THE BEGINNING OF THE
NEW YEAR, WE HOPE THAT THEY WILL REALIZE, AS WE HAVE RE-
ALIZED, THAT A UNION WILL HELP THEM WIN BETTER LIVING
CONDITIONS IN ALL CHINATOWN.

"WE GREET EVERYONE OF OUR FRIENDS IN THE ILGWU, AND
WISH YOU ALL A HAPPY AND PROSPEROUS NEW YEAR."

CHINESE LADIES' GARMENT WORKERS' UNION

LOCAL NO. 341 I. L. G. W. U.

76

Okinawans in America, 1939

The Japanese who came from Okinawa (prefecture) have a history, language, and culture distinct from that of "mainstream" Japan. Until Okinawa, or the Ryukyu Islands, was absorbed into the Japanese empire in 1879, it had maintained flexible relations, triangulating itself with both China and the Japanese feudal system through the Satsuma (Kagoshima prefecture) domain. Okinawans thereafter found themselves a colonized minority, and they were treated as such when they emigrated with other Japanese to various parts of the world, including Hawai'i and the mainland United States. Today there is a major resurgence of Okinawan pride and identity, but at the time this essay was penned there was still considerable prejudice and discrimination against the "Uchinanchu" (in their language) by the "Yamatonchu."

Kenden Yabe, "Zaibei Okinawa Kenjin Gaishi" [An unofficial history of Okinawans in America], *Ryukyu*, 1939. Translated by Ben Kobashigawa and reprinted here with permission. Also published in *History of the Okinawans in North America*, compiled by The Okinawa Club of America, translated by Ben Kobashigawa (Los Angeles: UCLA Asian American Studies Center and The Okinawa Club of America, 1988).

Introduction

When I let it be known that I meant to write a history of the Okinawans in America, some laughed at the idea. They wondered whether we as Okinawans had much to pass on to future generations. In my view history is not a story of heroic events or the biographies of great self-made men; it is a record of the life of a society. History exists wherever there is civilization. The thousand or more Okinawans who passed through the gate inscribed with the words *"Shurei no kuni"* (Land of Courtesy) went abroad in a spirit of adventure. Can they truly live without their history?

Pioneers have always etched their history in blood and sweat, and this is no less true for our Okinawan issei.[1] Sad as it may be, few of the old-timers were blessed with any material success—"made it," as people say here—and it was bound to be so. For it is a general truth that behind all bright tales of success there is a dark shadow, "the skeletons of the many who died for one general's fame," as the old saying goes. The old-timers unstintingly paved the way for those of us who have come after, and the price they paid for the sake of Okinawan progress was their own lack of material success.

The nisei[2] are everywhere coming to the fore with the decline of the issei in America. Shall they who are now gone be forgotten? Many have become mere names of the past, and the story of their struggle has not yet been recorded. If nothing is done about this, their history will probably be lost altogether. It lies with us to preserve it.

My aim in compiling this history is not simply to eulogize the ordinary successes of individuals. History is a process of development. Who can say whether that issei who merely hummed songs to himself in a gloomy San Francisco basement might not have emerged into the bright light of day to lead the entire chorus? You can see the signs of such promise in the faces of our growing nisei. My decision to compile this history occurs at a point of transition between ourselves and the issei, on the one side, and the nisei, on the other. As I gathered the material of what I now know of the struggles of our predecessors from the still living issei, I have come to realize what a need exists to transmit this record of immigrant life beyond our own nisei. The deeply felt sense of triumph should be conveyed to the 600,000 Okinawans back home, 4,000 miles away. Unfortunately, I am not so great a writer. My abilities and time are limited, but I have begun this history in the hope that someday someone better may come along to take up the pen and complete it.

January 1936

The first Okinawan immigrant to reach the United States was Tōki Higa in the 29th year of Meiji (1896). He was followed by Tokutā Nishime, Chōkō Hyakuna, Chōsuke Nago, and Jittoku Yasumoto, who all sailed about the same time in the 31st year of Meiji (1898). They are the ones who should be counted as the first even if a certain Keizō Kawatsu from Naha did enter the United States through Canada in the 22nd year of Meiji (1889). As nothing is known about his life in the subsequent ten years, and no one else came over during that time, his arrival is of little significance for Okinawan immigration.

A whole group emigrated in the 32nd year of Meiji (1899). They were twenty-seven young men who sailed for Hawaii, followed in the 35th year of Meiji (1903) by forty others who were led by Kyūzō Tōyama, a pioneering contributor to Okinawan emigration. . . .

---

[1]*issei = "first generation," "immigrants"*
[2]*nisei = "second generation"*

Creation of the Okinawan Kenjinkai

In the 35th year of Meiji (1902), the fifty or so Okinawans scattered over Northern California were organized for the first time by Nishime, Nakayoshi, and others into an Okinawan *kenjinkai* (prefectural association). It was based in San Francisco and was just what the early Okinawans needed. The office functioned more like a boarding house. People left from there to seek work and returned there when they were out of work. The Okinawans gathered there at night from their places of work and, like lovers meeting, did not count the many miles of travel involved. They talked over their successes and mistakes, set up short courses in English or cooking, and held debates or listened to lectures. Occasionally, a recent arrival from Japan would be given a welcome. The guests had all their needs seen to and, at night, with mattresses laid out for beds, everyone got involved in the night-long reminiscences of life back home. . . .

They came to work in America as penniless workers with visions of easy money, but could find no avenues of escape from the net of exploitation so skillfully laid down by the capitalists. Life consisted of a never-ending pursuit of the mirage, and one after another they fell by the wayside. Some fell into debt, and others were dragged down trying to help them out. . . .

The creation of the Okinawa Kenjinkai manifested the early immigrant's instinct for mutual aid. The sick were brought to the *kenjinkai* to be taken care of, funeral services were performed for those who died, and help in returning home was given to those who could no longer work. They even shared a single slice of bread there. The kenjinkai provided the only comfort in this weary immigrant life, which was more often sad than happy. . . .

Ban on Picture Brides

In 1920 (the 9th year of Taishō) Tamekichi Ōta, the consul general in San Francisco, and someone in the executive of the Zaibei Nihonjinkai (Japanese Association of America), without consulting the views of the resident Japanese, halted the practice of picture bride marriages. They gave as their reason the evident strangeness of the picture bride practice in the eyes of the non-Japanese (*hakujin*), who followed the principle of free marriage. They considered the practice a contributory cause of exclusion. And besides, all manner of scandal could arise between husband and wife under the system. Behind their move, however, was a shallow concept of mutual interest aimed at a softening of the Alien Land Law. The resident Japanese were outraged by the arbitrariness of this action, which had come as a complete surprise. There was a great uproar everywhere at the general meetings held by the resident Japanese.

Truthfully speaking, the picture bride system was not an ideal system of marriage. It was really a last resort. But among Japanese, accustomed to the *omiai* (arranged) marriage system of their parents, there were fewer abuses than the *hakujin* believed. The various scandals that did occur among the men and women in the immigrant areas were not due to the defects of their mode of marriage; rather, marital problems arose from the disproportion in the numbers of men and women. The ban on picture brides became itself the source of the most extreme marriage problem for unmarried youths by trapping them in an unnatural life. And what of the intended softening of the land bill? That turned out to be a mere fool's dream. . . .

The Reimeikai

The young Okinawans were excellent in their outlook as workers. They were incapable of indifference to the currents of thought prevailing in that period of transformation in the cultures of the world. With the end of the Great War in Europe, humankind stood at a major crossroad: a resettling of accounts in politics, philosophy, and the arts. The emergence of soviet republics in European Russia, in particular, rang the alarm for the world's proletariat. The idea of a proletarian movement establishing a proletarian culture shook the whole world. Such a world-wide current couldn't help but find its way into the impressionable hearts of young Okinawan workers who were just then searching for a purposeful life. . . .

The Reimeikai ("New Dawn" Club) was founded in Los Angeles in 1921 by this group of young men. They met every Saturday evening at a hotel run by Chōshirō Tamaki on Banning street and studied philosophy, religion, science, art, social issues, and so forth. Because most of the members of the Reimeikai were farm hands who wandered from one area to another following the season, the Reimeikai tended to be carried with them and thus became a travelling society. It was held in Imperial Valley during the cucumber season and in Fresno during the grape-picking season. . . .

During the brief period of the Reimeikai restaurant, Seikan Higa, a Methodist minister from Honolulu, made a tour of inspection of America. During his visit, he was a guest of the Reimeikai, where he was surrounded by the group of young Okinawans and vigorously criticized for his views. By the time he was ready to go back his beliefs had changed. On his return to Honolulu, he abandoned his robe and, single-handedly, set up a Reimei Kyōkai (Reimei Church). Thus, did the little flame of the Reimeikai create a spark which flew all the way to Hawaii.

Organizing the Zaibei Okinawa Seinenkai

The creation of the Reimeikai out of the initiative solely of the younger people provoked the antagonism of the older Okinawans, and tension gradually emerged between the two. It took the form of an ideological opposition to the Reimeikai, which came to be viewed as delinquent and dangerous. Although some of the older Okinawans, such as Seijūrō Uyema and Seishū Aniya, sometimes did come to the Reimeikai meetings and gave lectures, they were branded in the harshest terms as heretics by two officers of the Okinawa Kenjinkai, Rinshō Matayoshi and Kamado Ōta. The latter two arranged to have someone they trusted, Bukyū Arakaki, nominated to create the "Zaibei Okinawa Seinenkai" (Okinawan Young People's Association of America). Their idea was that the safest group, in terms of the possibility of guiding the thinking of the Okinawan youth generally, was to be found among the most recent, idealistic young immigrants from Japan.

The older issei expected the Seinenkai to develop according to their desires, considering its backing by the Okinawa Kenjinkai. However, when the Kenjinkai later reorganized itself as the Southern California Branch of the Okinawa Kaigai Kyōkai (Okinawa Overseas Association) and proposed inclusion of the Seinenkai in the change, the latter adamantly refused. The previous schism reemerged, this time pitting the Seinenkai and the Kaigai Kyōkai against each other. This parallelism of ill-feeling and schism recreated the old antagonism between the Kenjinkai and the Reimeikai.

Such antagonism between older and younger Okinawans was hardly a matter for rejoicing from the broader perspective of Okinawans living in America. We refrained at the time from making this criticism in the hope of improving the chances for establishing unity. . . .

PART 4

World War II: Through 1945

World War II was the single most critical historical era for Asian Americans in the century since immigration had begun. The war exacerbated existing tensions created by hostilities in the homelands. Japan had colonized Korea in the early twentieth century and was ravaging much of China's coastline and its major cities, as well as most of the Philippines and many islands in the Pacific. In the United States, immigrants from Korea, China, and the Philippines engaged in efforts to liberate their countries, sometimes in the form of political lobbying or financial support, but even in paramilitary training in the countrysides of California and Hawai'i. At the same time, their children were in the American military, fighting fascism abroad and racism at home.

The United States entered World War II in December 1941 as a result of Japan's attacks on Pearl Harbor in Hawai'i and on the Philippines, but hostilities had begun long before, in the mid-1930s in China. And the United States had long anticipated military confrontation with Japan. There were dramatic shifts in the fortunes of Asian Americans, both on battlefields and and on the home front, as the war highlighted issues of race and nationality. More than 50,000 Asian Americans, primarily sons and daughters of Japanese, Chinese, Filipino, and Korean immigrants, fought in nearly every theater of the war and in every military service. But that record was accomplished only with great difficulty and after overcoming a variety of barriers. President Franklin Roosevelt had set the tone on January 19, 1942, by signing Executive Order 9066, paving the way for mass removal of Japanese Americans from their homes into concentration camps in the interior.

The selective internment of 2,000 Japanese Americans from Hawai'i (out of 160,000) and complete "evacuation" of all 120,000 individuals of Japanese descent on the West Coast became the single worst case of civil rights violations perpetrated by the U.S. government in American history. Coupled with a long record of anti-Asian racism, these actions provided substantial ammunition for Japan's military to convince Asian leaders that the war was being fought on their behalf against European and American white racist oppressors. To counter these claims, the United States finally began to reverse laws and policies excluding Asians and preventing them from becoming naturalized citizens. In 1943, most notably, Chinese were given a token annual quota of 105 immigrants—although, unlike with any other ethnic group, anyone of Chinese descent from anywhere in the world was counted against that number.

In early 1942, the army began removing all those of Japanese descent, two-thirds of them American citizens, from the western portions of California, Washington, and Oregon, and the southern tip of Arizona. Through much of 1942, they were forced into assembly centers, often commandeered racetracks and fairgrounds, and then into hastily constructed camps confined by barbed wire and armed guards. Hundreds left to continue college on the few campuses willing to accept a few of the internees, while others were able to find sponsors and employment in the Midwest or East before the end of the war.

But most of the internees endured several years in humiliating circumstances: numbered for identification, living in cramped barracks, taking all meals in central cafeterias, doing their laundry and bathing in communal facilities without privacy, all in desolate areas subject to severe cold in the winters and blistering heat in the summers. There were no hearings, no trials, no due process; no one was even accused of espionage or sabotage. Dozens of camps were scattered around the Midwest, as far east as Arkansas and south into Texas, close to the Mexican border. Some internees were employed, but with minimal compensation. The highest paid were doctors, for example, who received $21 per month.

The community responded to these conditions in a wide variety of ways. Schools were maintained; elections were held to provide a small measure of democratic self-determination; newspapers, albeit seriously censored, were published; and cultural events like plays and concerts were performed. The internees formed Boy Scout troops and organized serious baseball and football leagues, as well as art and civics courses. But there were suicides and depression; the immigrant generation had lost nearly everything, including authority over their families, and despair was palpable. Young men faced the problem of deciding, at first, whether to volunteer to fight and, even more wrenching, how to respond when the draft was imposed.

Within the American military itself, the war provided the context for major changes. This would be the last war fought by racially segregated—Japanese American, Filipino American, and African American—units. For most of 1942, almost every American of Japanese descent was declared "4C"—enemy alien unfit to serve. In the meantime, volunteer and draftee Japanese Americans were already serving as American spies in the Pacific, translators and interpreters with the Military Intelligence Service, and combat soldiers in the 100th Infantry Battalion. Frustrated by their nation's lack of trust, 169 Japanese Americans in Hawai'i formed the "Varsity Victory Volunteers" to support the war effort by doing manual labor on an army base.

Chinese Americans joined the volunteer "Flying Tigers" in China, battling the Japanese before Pearl Harbor, and many more, including women, volunteered or were drafted during the war. The First and Second Filipino Regiments, formed by Filipino Americans, were trained and sent to the Philippines to help liberate that country. In January 1943, Japanese Americans were finally allowed to form the voluntary, segregated, 442nd Regimental Combat Team, commanded at first by all-white officers. Amazingly, one of its GIs, Young Oak Kim, a Korean American, became a highly decorated veteran. Fewer than 2,000 left the concentration camps to volunteer for the 442nd or the Military Intelligence Service, where they used their Japanese language skills against the Japanese empire. In 1944, in a highly controversial move, the draft was extended to Japanese Americans, including those already imprisoned in the camps, precipitating resistance efforts by several hundred internees.

Nearly 30,000 Japanese Americans served in World War II, compiling a remarkable record of tenacity and bravery. The 442nd RCT became the most highly decorated army unit of its size in American history. One of its members, Sadao Munemori, was awarded a Medal of Honor. A review conducted half a century after the war revealed that bias in the original process justified the awarding of 22 more Medals of Honor to one Chinese/Hawaiian, one Filipino, and 20 Japanese Americans. Fighting in the military was one way of trying to secure full citizenship rights; resisting the draft until their families were released from concentration camps was another; a third was recourse to the judicial system, and several notable cases remain on the books.

Gordon Hirabayashi, then a student at the University of Washington at Seattle, deliberately violated curfew regulations applied only to Japanese Americans. He was convicted, and appeals to the U.S. Supreme Court resulted in a prison sentence in 1943. Minoru Yasui met a similar fate that same year. Fred Korematsu defied the order to move from the West Coast and was caught—in 1944 the Supreme Court ruled that forcible relocation on the basis of race was constitutional. But, also in 1944, the court determined that Mitsuye Endo's *habeas corpus* petition was justified and ordered her released from camp. These four Supreme Court cases are among the most important in American constitutional and racial history.

The Japanese American community was sharply divided over the appropriate reaction to the government's decision to detain them in concentration camps. The "official" response came from the Japanese American Citizens League, barely a decade old, comprised of the *nisei*, American-born children of the immigrants. Their leaders urged cooperation with the internment and criticized dissenters, including those who took the government to court or who resisted the draft.

The situation in Hawai'i was very different. One reason was the imposition of martial law on December 7, immediately after the attack on Pearl Harbor. Military control, lasting into 1944, ensured tight security and less concern over the fact that 160,000 individuals, almost 40 percent of Hawaii's population, were of Japanese descent. But the need for this ethnic community's manpower, more than half of the entire labor force, as well as a tradition of relative racial tolerance allowed a multiracial civilian/military leadership to adroitly harness the potentially dangerous mix of ethnic and racial tensions in the islands.

The end of World War II had one immediate impact on Asian American communities. Approximately 200,000 women arrived as "war brides" from various countries. A modest number of Japanese American GIs returned with brides from Japan. In some cases, as with the Chinese and Filipino servicemen, these women were critically important because anti-Asian laws had created communities overwhelmingly male. In an era when interracial marriages were illegal — at least with whites — many mature Chinese and Filipino men were seemingly destined to live out their lives as bachelors; the war dramatically changed their personal lives. Some of the women returned with white or African American veterans, and their children became the first significant generation of multiracial "Amerasians."

The first half of the twentieth century was marked by escalating anti-Asian racism, leading to numerous restrictions on immigration, naturalization, and the freedom to find employment, own land, seek education, and marry whom they chose. But Asian Americans were hardly passive victims, as the enormous numbers of lawsuits and work actions indicated. Further, "paper sons" and "picture brides" indicated how the restrictive laws were manipulated or evaded in order to continue building communities in the United States.

The end of World War II left the United States as the uncontested power in the entire Pacific. The next half century would bring enormous tensions throughout the globe, with the contest between the United States and the Soviet Union. Asia and the Pacific became one major battlefield of the "Cold War," certainly a term inappropriate to describe a region that would see China emerge as a Communist nation in 1949, Korea become a very "hot" battlefield in 1950, the Pacific become a nuclear testing ground soon after the war, and Southeast Asia become a quagmire for the French, and then the United States, after the 1950s. This context emerged as a central motif for Asian Americans in the period 1945–75, when some observers saw the Pacific Ocean as an "American lake."

77

Franklin Delano Roosevelt, "Day of Infamy" Speech, December 8, 1941

The day after Japan attacked Pearl Harbor and other Pacific targets, President Franklin Roosevelt addressed Congress, delivering this speech denouncing the "unprovoked and dastardly attack by Japan" and asking that Congress declare that "a state of war has existed" since December 7. Since then historians have debated the origins of this war, including whether FDR, determined to bring the United States into the war against Germany, indeed "provoked" Japan into an attack to justify American participation. While the war had been raging for years in Asia and Europe, the entry of the United States finally tipped the balance against the Axis powers, Germany, Japan, and Italy.

Congressional Record, 77th Cong, vol. 87, part 9. Washington, DC: Government Printing Office, 1941.

To the Congress of the United States:

Yesterday, December 7, 1941—a date which will live in infamy—the United States of America was suddenly and deliberately attacked by naval and air forces of the Empire of Japan.

The United States was at peace with that nation and, at the solicitation of Japan, was still in conversation with its Government and its Emperor looking toward the maintenance of peace in the Pacific. Indeed, 1 hour after Japanese air squadrons had commenced bombing in Oahu, the Japanese Ambassador to the United States and his colleague delivered to the Secretary of State a formal reply to a recent American message. While this reply stated that it seemed useless to continue the existing diplomatic negotiations, it contained no threat or hint of war or armed attack.

It will be recorded that the distance of Hawaii from Japan makes it obvious that the attack was deliberately planned many days or even weeks ago. During the intervening time the Japanese Government has deliberately sought to deceive the United States by false statements and expressions of hope for continued peace.

The attack yesterday on the Hawaiian Islands has caused severe damage to American naval and military forces. Very many American lives have been lost. In addition American ships have been reported torpedoed on the high seas between San Francisco and Honolulu.

Yesterday the Japanese Government also launched an attack against Malaya.

Last night Japanese forces attacked Hong Kong.

Last night Japanese forces attacked Guam.

Last night Japanese forces attacked the Philippine Islands.

Last night the Japanese attacked Wake Island.

This morning the Japanese attacked Midway Island.

Japan has, therefore, undertaken a surprise offensive extending throughout the Pacific area. The facts of yesterday speak for themselves. The people of the United States have already formed their opinions and well understand the implications to the very life and safety of our Nation.

As Commander in Chief of the Army and Navy I have directed that all measures be taken for our defense.

Always will we remember the character of the onslaught against us.

No matter how long it may take us to overcome this premeditated invasion, the American people, in their righteous might, will win through to absolute victory.

I believe I interpret the will of the Congress and of the people when I assert that we will not only defend ourselves to the uttermost but will make very certain that this form of treachery shall never endanger us again.

Hostilities exist. There is no blinking at the fact that our people, our territory, and our interests are in grave danger.

With confidence in our armed forces—with the unbounded determination of our people—we will gain the inevitable triumph—so help us God.

I ask that the Congress declare that since the unprovoked and dastardly attack by Japan on Sunday, December 7, a state of war has existed between the United States and the Japanese Empire.

Franklin D. Roosevelt.
The White House, December 8, 1941.

78

Life *Magazine, "How to Tell Japs from the Chinese," December 22, 1941*

Within two weeks of Pearl Harbor, there were enough incidents of vigilante hate crime attacks on Japanese Americans and other Asians assumed to be Japanese to require an organized response. Chinese groups actually produced pins declaring I am Chinese to deflect anti-Japanese hostility. This article, often reproduced in later years, reflects the awkwardness of relying on pseudo-scientific notions of anthropological representation to "inform" the public how to distinguish friend from foe. Life failed, however, to mention that most Chinese would be indistinguishable from most Japanese. It also failed to alert readers to the fact that most Japanese immigrants were permanent residents of long standing and that two-thirds of the population was American-born. Then, assuming that accurate ethnic distinctions could be made, Life left untouched the moral and legal questions of assault.

"How to Tell Japs from the Chinese," *Life* Magazine, December 22, 1941.

How to Tell Japs from the Chinese

Angry Citizens Victimize Allies with Emotional Outburst at Enemy

In the first discharge of emotions touched off by the Japanese assaults on their nation, U.S. citizens have been demonstrating a distressing ignorance on the delicate question of how to tell a Chinese from a Jap. Innocent victims in cities all over the country are many of the 75,000 U.S. Chinese, whose homeland is our stanch ally. So serious were the consequences threatened, that the Chinese consulates last week prepared to tag their nationals with identification buttons. To dispel some of this confusion, LIFE here adduces a rule-of-thumb from the anthropometric conformations that distinguish friendly Chinese from enemy alien Japs.

To physical anthropologists, devoted debunkers of race myths, the difference between Chinese and Japs is measurable in millimeters. Both are related to the Eskimo and North American Indian. The modern Jap is the descendant of

Mongoloids who invaded the Japanese archipelago back in the mists of prehistory, and of the native aborigines who possessed the islands before them. Physical anthropology, in consequence, finds Japs and Chinese as closely related as Germans and English. It can, however, set apart the special types of each national group.

The typical Northern Chinese, represented by Ong Wenhao, Chungking's Minister of Economic Affairs (*left, below*), is relatively tall and slenderly built. His complexion is parchment yellow, his face long and delicately boned, his nose more finely bridged. Representative of the Japanese people as a whole is Premier and General Hideki Tojo (*right, below*), who betrays aboriginal antecedents in a squat, long-torsoed build, a broader, more massively boned head and face, flat, often pug, nose, yellow-ocher skin and heavier beard. From this average type, aristocratic Japs, who claim kinship to the Imperial Household, diverge sharply. They are proud to approximate the patrician lines of the Northern Chinese.

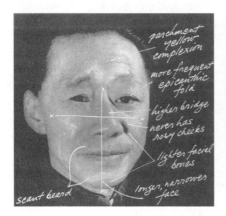 

Chinese public servant, Ong Wen-hao, is representative of North Chinese anthropological group with long, fine-boned face and scant beard. Epicanthic fold of skin above eyelid is found in 85% of Chinese. Southern Chinese have round, broadfaces, not as massively boned as the Japanese. Except that their skin is darker, this description fits Filipinos who are often mistaken for Japs. Chinese sometimes pass for Europeans; but Japs more often approach Western types.

Japanese warrior, General Hideki Tojo, current Premier, is a Samurai, closer to type of humble Jap than highbred relatives of Imperial Household. Typical are his heavy beard, massive cheek and jaw bones. Peasant Jap is squat Mongoloid, with flat, blob nose. An often sounder clue is facial expression, shaped by cultural, not anthropological, factors. Chinese wear rational calm of tolerant realists. Japs, like General Tojo, show humorless intensity of ruthless mystics.

Chinese journalist, Joe Chiang, found it necessary to advertise his nationality to gain admittance to White House press conference Under Immigration Act of 1924, Japs and Chinese, as members of the "yellow race," are barred from immigration and naturalization.

Tall Chinese brothers, full length, show lanky, lithe build of northern anthropological group that has suffered most in China's recent history from flood, famine and war with Japs. Average height of Northern Chinese is 5 ft. 7 in., sometimes exceeds 6 ft. Most Chinese in America come from southern and coastal cities, Canton and Shanghai. They are shorter than Northern Chinese, but retain the slight proportions of the young men shown here. When middle-aged and fat, they look more like Japs.

Short Japanese admirals, full length, exhibit the squat, solid, long torso and short stocky legs of the most numerous Japanese anthropological group. Since Navy is relatively new and junior service, Jap naval officer corps numbers fewer Samurai, has more of the round-faced, flat-nosed peasant type. Over 6 ft. tall, Admiral Nomura shows traits of the big, fair-skinned hairy Ainu, aborigines who still live on reservations in Northern Japan. Special Emissary Kurusu, also atypical, looks European.

79

Mike Masaoka, "Japanese American Creed," May 9, 1941

The pressures to assimilate into mainstream America created a unique, highly articulate leader among American-born children of Japanese immigrants. Mike Masaoka, from Utah, emerged as the government-sanctioned spokesperson for the Japanese American community after war broke out between the United States and Japan. But even before Pearl Harbor, Masaoka had developed an ideology and strategy to cope with the anti-Japanese racism of the times—to incorporate and trumpet the "highest" ideals of American nationalism and shape them as the core values of Japanese America. Perhaps this was an American version of the Japanese martial arts—the ancient jujitsu or modern judo—which transformed an antagonist's strength into one's own advantage. This creed took on a life of its own because of its eloquent hyperbole. It helped fashion a strategy for many Japanese Americans to get ahead in society but deeply alienated others to whom it appeared a caricature of their own beliefs, the reality of their history, and the proper approach to securing equal and dignified treatment in America. As late as 2000, Masaoka's creed stirred considerable controversy as one of the inscriptions in a Washington, DC memorial dedicated to the World War II patriotism of Japanese Americans.

Mike Masaoka, "The Japanese American Creed." As read before the U.S. Senate and printed in *Congressional Record,* May 9, 1941. Salt Lake City, Utah: Japanese American Citizens League, n.d.

The Japanese American Creed

I am proud that I am an American of Japanese ancestry, for my very background makes me appreciate more fully the wonderful advantages of this nation. I believe in her institutions; ideals, and traditions; I glory in her heritage; I boast of her history; I trust in her future; She has granted me liberties and opportunities such as no individual enjoys in this world today. She has given me an education befitting kings; She has entrusted me with the responsibilities of the franchise.

She has permitted me to build a home, to earn a livelihood, to worship, think, speak, and act as I please—as a free man equal to every other man.

Although some individuals may discriminate against me, I shall never become bitter or lose faith, for I know that such persons are not representative of the majority of the American people. True, I shall do all in my power to discourage such practices but I shall do it in the American way; above board; in the open, through courts of law, by education, by proving myself to be worthy of equal treatment and consideration. I am firm in my belief that American sportsmanship and attitude of fair play will judge citizenship and patriotism on the basis of action and achievement, and not on the basis of physical characteristics.

Because I believe in America, and I trust she believes in me and because I have received innumerable benefits from her, I pledge myself to do honor to her at all times and in all places; to support her Constitution; to obey her laws; to respect her Flag; to defend her against all enemies, foreign or domestic, to activity assume my duties and obligations as a citizen cheerfully and without any reservations whatsoever, in the hope that I may become a better American in a greater America.

[signature of Mike Masaoka]

80

Reverend Tamasaku Watanabe, Appeal
for Exemption from Freezing Assets, August 9, 1941

On the road to Pearl Harbor, both the United States and Japan engaged in hostile acts designed to intimidate or retaliate. One American action, in summer 1941, froze the assets of Japanese nationals, thus penalizing Japanese immigrants who were not able to become naturalized citizens. Ironically, this group included those most anxious to Americanize, such as Christian ministers from Japan. Reverend Tamasaku Watanabe learned English well and supported American efforts to assimilate his fellow Japanese immigrants. On August 12, the General Secretary of the Board of the Hawaiian Evangelical Association, Norman Scheuch, wrote to advise that the "Governor's special committee dealing with the freezing of assets of citizens of China and Japan who are in this territory" elected to have these ethnic/immigrant churches operate under "General License A," as referenced in Reverend Watanabe's affidavit. While this exemption may have saved the churches, Watanabe himself was not as fortunate—he was arrested and sent to Kilauea Military Reservation, then to Honolulu's Sand Island before shipment to Angel Island and finally to Santa Fe, New Mexico's Internment Center operated by the Justice Department.

Collection of Gail Okawa, Reverend Watanabe's granddaughter. Reprinted with permission.

Reverend Tamasaku Watanabe Affidavit
for Japanese Christian Church

AFFIDAVIT OF OWNERSHIP, PURPOSES, ACTIVITIES, FINANCES, AND OPERATIONS OF THE OLAA JAPANESE CHRISTIAN CHURCH AT OLAA, HAWAII, IN THE TERRITORY OF HAWAII FILED FOR THE INFORMATION OF THE GOVERNOR OF HAWAII AND OFFICIALS OF THE UNITED STATES TREASURY DEPARTMENT IN COMPLIANCE WITH THE STIPULATION OF "GENERAL LICENSE A."

Date: August 9, 1941

I, Tamasaku Watanabe, being the Minister of the Olaa Japanese Christian Church at Olaa, District of Puna, County and territory of Hawaii and
representing that institution, being duly sworn do hereby make the following
affidavit:

That I, Rev. Tamasaku Watanabe, am the head of the Olaa Japanese
Christian Church and am empowered by the members of said Church to
submit the following information to the officials of the United States Treasury Department and the Governor of the Territory of Hawaii, to wit:

The Olaa Japanese Christian Church is governed by the Hawaiian Board
of Missions, whose principal office is located at Honolulu, T.H.;

That the said Olaa Japanese Christian Church was organized in 1912 and
it has a total of 91 members, consisting of 50 aliens and 41 American Citizens, in which 33 families are representing;

That the executive committee of said Church is composed of the following members:

Sekigo Tanioka,	Olaa, Hawaii,	Japanese Nationality
Tsuto Hata	"	"
Mitsutaro Fujisaki	"	"
Tokio Funaki	"	"
Kotaro Kaneshiro	"	"
Shosaburo Fujiyoshi	"	"
Paul Fukuo Sakamaki	"	Citizen

All of said committee members have been continuously residing in the Territory of Hawaii at all times on and since June 17, 1940;

That I, as Minister and head of said Olaa Japanese Christian Church received the following yearly income: $690.00 from the Hawaiian Board of
Missions and $900.00 from the Church members, which sums include trav-
eling and administrative expenses;

That I am informed and upon such information and belief state that the
value of the personal property of the Olaa Japanese Christian Church consisting of Church building and parsonage is worth about $8500.00

[one paragraph illegible]

That I, Reverend Tamasaku Watanabe, came from California to the Territory of Hawaii on November 27, 1922, and have been residing in the Territory of Hawaii ever since said time and have been the Minister of the Olaa
Japanese Christian Church for approximately 6 years;

The purposes of maintaining the Church are:

To teach them the Christian Gospel and the fundamentals of Christianity; and to train them in the fundamentals of the Christian moral and ethical code.

The Church does not teach Japanese Nationalism or any political, religious, economic, or social theories subversive to or at variance with the highest ideals of Americanism.

The Church does not receive any subsidy or support from any agency connected with the Japanese government or from any source outside of the United States.

The Church is exclusively a local institution and is operated by local people for the benefit of the people of Olaa.

(signed) Rev. Tamasaku Watanabe
Subscribed and sworn to before me
this ninth day of August, 1941
(signed) ? Marden
Notary Public, 4th Judicial Circuit,
Territory of Hawaii
My commission expires June 30, 1945

81

Letter from John Steinbeck to John Ford, December 10, 1941

When World War II began for the United States, John Steinbeck was a highly re-garded writer and John Ford (Jack) an accomplished filmmaker. Ford became "Co-ordinator of Information" and developed considerable American Hollywood World War II propaganda. It is interesting, therefore, to note the early correspon-dence between the two. Here, Steinbeck is in the midst of scripting a play but re-sponds to his old friend, and to an inquiry about whether Japanese Americans were loyal from William Donovan, who headed the Office of Strategic Services (OSS), precursor to the Central Intelligence Agency (CIA). Steinbeck had grown up in Salinas, California, and knew the Japanese community fairly well. When Ford offered him formal appointment as an officer in the military, Steinbeck, in a telephone conversation, said he preferred the navy over the army—"The uni-forms are better." Note the date—three days after Pearl Harbor—and the broad-ness of inquiry proceeding at high levels. It was not long, however, before media and political pressure made mass internment inevitable.

National Archives, RG 226, Folder 534. Thanks to Noriko Sanefuji for initial search and to Lawrence McDonald, Modern Military Records, Textual Archives Services Division, for assistance in locating this and related documents.

New York

December 10, 1941

Dear Jack: I keep writing suggestions. Here is one which might be of some value. It may well be that this has been done.

1. The Nisei or native born Japanese have condemned the action of Japan and have reiterated their loyalty.

2. In every community the Nisei have very close organizations.

3. Every Japanese foreign born or native born is known to these organi-zations.

4. There is no reason so far to suspect the loyalty of Japanese-American citizens.

IT IS SUGGESTED:

1. That local civilian defense authorities make contact with these Japanese.
2. That they be given auxiliary status in controlling sabotage.
    (1) They know the language.
    (2) They would be more likely to know of illegal gatherings plans than whites.
    (3) They have very close check on unknown or strange Japanese.
    (4) Such evidence of trust would be likely to cement the loyalty of inherently loyal citizens.
3. No information need be given them. It can all come from them.
4. Any valuable information coming from them would do much to over turn a distrust of themselves.
5. This can all be done by local authorities.
6. A failure to cooperate would be indicative of disloyalty.

CONCLUSION:

A. By instituting this cooperation, some actual information may be gained and since the Japanese community is settled, such a plan would in effect make the loyal Japanese responsible for the disloyal.

B. In case valuable work were done by the Nisei, it should be published, thus cementing loyalties and driving a wedge between loyal and disloyal Japanese.

C. Organization of this cooperation by the local Civil defense organizations should be very easy to accomplish.

D. It would constitute a test of loyalty.

That's all.

/s/ *John Steinbeck*

I suggest this because, as you will remember, Col Donovan asked me whether I thought the native born Japanese were loyal

J.S.

82

Petition to Establish Varsity Victory Volunteers,
January 30, 1942

In Hawai'i, site of the Pearl Harbor attack and far closer to Japan than the rest of the United States, the vast majority of Japanese Americans were never detained or interned. Why were they treated so differently from their West Coast cousins? Part of the answer lies in different histories and demographics, but the story of the Varsity Victory Volunteers helps explain the multiracial determination to avoid demonizing Japanese Americans. On January 21, 1942, the Military Governor of Hawai'i dismissed from the Hawai'i Territorial Guard nearly 400 men of Japanese descent. The armed guardsmen had been protecting strategic areas against sabotage. The Japanese Americans were demoralized by this action, but a small group met to address the crisis. Led by several key civilian leaders, about 130 university students petitioned the Military Governor to use them as "you may see fit." In February, 155 of them formed the Varsity Victory Volunteers, an auxiliary unit of the 34th Engineers at Schofield Barracks, to perform all manner of serious labor designed to further the war effort. Eleanor Roosevelt and Assistant Secretary of War John McCloy visited Hawai'i in 1942 and were impressed with this show of patriotism and perseverance. In all, 169 Japanese Americans worked in the VVV until disbanding in January 1943, when the United States resumed accepting them for combat duty. One consequence of this different treatment was the eagerness with which Hawaii's Japanese Americans volunteered for the military, as opposed to the rancor caused within the camps when volunteers were recruited and, later, the draft was imposed.

Yutaka Nakahata, ed., "The Volunteer." Honolulu: n.p., n.d. (1943).

Honolulu, T. H.

January 30, 1942

Lt. Gen. Delos C. Emmons
Commanding General, Hawaiian
Department, U.S.A.
Fort Shafter, T. H.

Sir:

We, the undersigned, were members of the Hawaii Territorial Guard until its recent inactivation. We joined the Guard voluntarily with the hope that this was one way to serve our country in her time of need. Needless to say, we were deeply disappointed when we were told that our services in the Guard were no longer needed.

Hawaii is our home; the United States, our country. We know but one loyalty and that is to the Stars and Stripes. We wish to do our part as loyal Americans in every way possible and we hereby offer ourselves for whatever service you may see fit to use us.

Respectfully yours,

83

Letter from Charles Hemenway to Ralph Yempuku, Varsity Victory Volunteers, May 23, 1942

This letter was written some three months after the VVV started working as a volunteer labor unit at the army's Schofield Barracks on O'ahu. The VVV formed both to offer war service on behalf of the Japanese American community and to protest their exclusion from military enlistment, and it operated until January 1943, when the War Department created the segregated 442nd Regimental Combat Team. The VVV became a major symbol of Japanese American dedication to the war effort. Charles Hemenway was a regent of the University of Hawaii and a major corporate figure; his support of these young men was crucial to the climate of relative tolerance in Hawai'i, radically different from the increasingly hostile racism directed at the 120,000 Japanese Americans interned from the West Coast—ironically, in precisely the time frame the VVV was at work. Ralph Yempuku was the civilian supervisor of the group.

Ralph Yempuku Collection. Author's possession.

Hawaiian Trust Company, Limited
Honolulu, Hawaii
U.S.A

May 23, 1942

My dear Ralph:

Many thanks for your letter and the copy of "The Volunteer" which I have found very interesting. Unfortunately I have been laid up at home for the past six weeks so I haven't been able to keep as closely in touch with the general situation as I would like but from the reports I have had the VVVs have continued to make a fine record and deep impression on the rest of the community and are making a real contribution to our war effort. More and more of our fellow citizens are beginning to understand that your loyalty to our country is just as real as theirs and are also beginning to see that it is given under conditions which are definitely hard and unfair. You are fighting for an ideal and that is worth all the personal sacrifices which you are making. This war can only be won by those who are fighting for liberty and justice to all—and all means everyone.

The old notion of superior and inferior races has been proved wrong and must be discarded in the thinking of all of us. No individual and no race has any monopoly of those traits of character which in combination make good citizens. Understanding, tolerance, integrity, justice and friendliness always win in the end, as they always have and will again. You men are in my thoughts every day and you probably do not realize how deeply I appreciate the daily proof you are giving that my confidence in you has been more than justified.

Aloha to you all!
Sincerely,

[signature]
C. R. Hemenway

84

Executive Order 9066, February 19, 1942

President Roosevelt issued this order authorizing the Secretary of War to place cer-
tain areas under military authority in order to remove people of Japanese descent.
It was the first in a series of official acts required to provide a cover of due process
while interning the entire Japanese American population on the West Coast.
These actions were arguably reminiscent of wholesale forced removals of Native
Americans from much of the North American continent. In March, Congress
passed Public Law 503, making it a felony for anyone resisting compliance with
military action authorized by EO 9066. This freed the army to begin issuing Pub-
lic Proclamations clearing out the Japanese from the prescribed areas, a process
that continued into fall 1942.

United States Code Congressional Service, Acts of 77th Congress, 1942. St. Paul, MN:
West Publishing Co. and Brooklyn, NY: Edward Thompson Co., 1943.

EXECUTIVE ORDER
AUTHORIZING THE SECRETARY OF WAR
TO PRESCRIBE MILITARY AREAS

WHEREAS the successful prosecution of the war requires every possible protection against espionage and against sabotage to national-defense material,
national-defense premises, and national-defense utilities as defined in Section
4, Act of April 20, 1918, 40 Stat. 533, as amended by the Act of November 30,
1940, 54 Stat. 1220, and the Act of August 21, 1941, 55 Stat. 655 (U. S. C., Title
50, Sec. 104):

NOW, THEREFORE, by virtue of the authority vested in me as President of
the United States, and Commander in Chief of the Army and Navy, I hereby authorize and direct the Secretary of War, and the Military Commanders whom he
may from time to time designate, whenever he or any designated Commander
deems such action necessary or desirable, to prescribe military areas in such
places and of such extent as he or the appropriate Military Commander may

determine, from which any or all persons may be excluded, and with respect to which, the right of any person to enter, remain in, or leave shall be subject to whatever restrictions the Secretary of War or the appropriate Military Commander may impose in his discretion. The Secretary of War is hereby authorized to provide for residents of any such area who are excluded therefrom, such transportation, food, shelter, and other accommodations as may be necessary, in the judgment of the Secretary of War or the said Military Commander, and until other arrangements are made, to accomplish the purpose of this order. The designation of military areas in any region or locality shall supersede designations of prohibited and restricted areas by the Attorney General under the Proclamations of December 7 and 8, 1941, and shall supersede the responsibility and authority of the Attorney General under the said Proclamations in respect of such prohibited and restricted areas.

I hereby further authorize and direct the Secretary of War and the said Military Commanders to take such other steps as he or the appropriate Military Commander may deem advisable to enforce compliance with the restrictions applicable to each Military area hereinabove authorized to be designated, including the use of Federal troops and other Federal Agencies, with authority to accept assistance of state and local agencies.

I hereby further authorize and direct all Executive Departments, independent establishments and other Federal Agencies, to assist the Secretary of War or the said Military Commanders in carrying out this Executive Order, including the furnishing of medical aid, hospitalization, food, clothing, transportation, use of land, shelter, and other supplies, equipment, utilities, facilities, and services.

This order shall not be construed as modifying or limiting in any way the authority heretofore granted under Executive Order No. 8972, dated December 12, 1941, nor shall it be construed as limiting or modifying the duty and responsibility of the Federal Bureau of Investigation, with respect to the investigation of alleged acts of sabotage or the duty and responsibility of the Attorney General and the Department of Justice under the Proclamations of December 7 and 8, 1941, prescribing regulations for the conduct and control of alien enemies, except as such duty and responsibility is superseded by the designation of military areas hereunder.

[signature of Franklin Delano Roosevelt]
THE WHITE HOUSE,
February 19, 1942.

85

Army Instructions for Removal of Japanese Americans in Los Angeles, May 3, 1942

FDR's Executive Order 9066 paved the way for laws allowing the army to forcibly remove Japanese Americans from their homes along the West Coast and in southern Arizona. Through much of 1942, even after the threat of invasion by Japanese forces had abated, the army removed entire communities to "Assembly Centers" and then to more permanent concentration camps in the interior. This exclusion order was one of many—often prominently nailed to telephone poles—that removed and interned more than 110,000 individuals without benefit of any constitutional safeguards. Eventually, more than 120,000 Japanese Americans and a few non-Japanese spouses were placed in dozens of camps run by the federal government. At least 2,000 were detained in Latin American countries, notably Peru, then transported into the United States and held for potential hostage exchange with Japan. Note that none of those interned knew where they were going or how long they might be detained. The World War II Japanese American story is the best-researched and published of any in Asian American history, with numerous books and documentary films describing the internment experiences; the military exploits of the segregated 100th Battalion, 442nd Regimental Combat Team, and 1399th Engineers; and the 6,000 who served as interpreters and translators for the Military Intelligence Service. There are also many publications dealing with those who challenged the government in the courts. The roles and experiences of Japanese American women in the military have not yet been addressed, but more attention recently has been devoted to those who became draft resisters of principle from within the camps.

Presidio of San Francisco, "Instructions to all Persons of Japanese Ancestry." San Francisco: U.S. Army, May 3, 1942.

Presidio of San Francisco, California
May 3, 1942

INSTRUCTIONS TO ALL PERSONS OF
JAPANESE ANCESTRY

Living in the Following Area:

All of that parties of the City of Los Angeles, State of California, within that boundary beginning at the past at which North Figueroa Street meets a line following the middle of the Los Angeles River: thence southerly and following the said line to East First Street: thence westerly on East First Street to Alameda Street; thence southerly on Alameda Street to East Third Street; thence northwesterly on East Third Street to Main Street; thence northerly on Main Street to First Street; thence north westerly on First Street to Figueroa Street; thence northeasterly on Figueroa Street to the point of beginning.

Pursuant to the provisions of Civilian Exclusion Order No. 33, this Headquarters, dated May 3, 1942, all persons of Japanese ancestry, both alien and non-alien, will be evacuated from the above area by 12 o'clock noon, P. W. T., Saturday, May 9, 1942.

No Japanese person living in the above area will be permitted to change residence after 12 o'clock noon, P. W. T., Sunday, May 3, 1942, without obtaining special permission from the representative of the Commanding General, Southern California Sector, at the Civil Control Station located at:

> Japanese Union Church,
> 120 North San Pedro Street,
> Los Angeles, California.

Such permits will only be granted for the purpose of uniting members of a family, or in cases of grave emergency.

The Civil Control Station is equipped to assist the Japanese population affected by this evacuation in the following ways:

1. Give advice and instructions on the evacuation.
2. Provide services with respect to the management, leasing, sale, storage or other disposition of most kinds of property, such as real estate, business and professional equipment, household goods, boats, automobiles and livestock.
3. Provide temporary residence elsewhere for all Japanese in family groups.
4. Transport persons and a limited amount of clothing and equipment to their new residence.

The Following Instructions Must Be Observed:

1. A responsible member of each family, preferably the head of the family, or the person in whose name most of the property is held, and each individual living alone, will report to the Civil Control Station to receive further instructions. This must be done between 8:00 A. M. and 5:00 P. M. on Monday, May 4, 1942, or between 8:00 A. M. and 5:00 P. M. on Tuesday, May 5, 1942.

2. Evacuees must carry with them on departure for the Assembly Center, the following property:

    (a) Bedding and linens (no mattress) for each member of the family;.

    (b) Toilet articles for each member of the family;

    (c) Extra clothing for each member of the family;

    (d) Sufficient knives, forks, spoons, plates, bowls and cups for each member of the family;

    (e) Essential personal effects for each member of the family.

    All items carried will be securely packaged, tied and plainly marked with the name of the owner and numbered in accordance with instructions obtained at the Civil Control Station. The size and number of packages is limited to that which can be carried by the individual or family group.

3. No pets of any kind will be permitted.

4. No personal items and no household goods will be shipped to the Assembly Center.

5. The United States Government through its agencies will provide for the storage, at the sole risk of the owner, of the more substantial household items, such as iceboxes, washing machines, pianos and other heavy furniture. Cooking utensils and other small items will be accepted for storage if crated, packed and plainly marked with the name and address of the owner. Only one name and address will be used by a given family.

6. Each family, and individual living alone, will be furnished transportation to the Assembly Center or will be authorized to travel by private automobile in a supervised group. All instructions pertaining to the movement will be obtained at the Civil Control Station.

Go to the Civil Control Station between the hours of 8:00 A.M. and 5:00 P.M., Monday, May 4, 1942, or between the hours of 8:00 A.M. and 5:00 P.M., Tuesday, May 5, 1942, to receive further instructions.

J. L. DeWITT
Lieutenant General, U. S. Army
Commanding

86

Letter from Louis Goldblatt to Carol King, May 22, 1942

Louis Goldblatt was Secretary-Treasurer of the California State Industrial Union Council, CIO, one of the few who testified in support of Japanese American civil rights before the House Committee on Interstate Migration on February 23, 1942. These "Tolan Committee Hearings" provided considerable testimony demonstrating the racism rampant in California—increasing pressure to intern the entire Japanese American community. The testimony itself has been cited and quoted often to demonstrate labor solidarity with minority rights struggles. Interestingly, Dillon Myer, head of the Wartime Relocation Authority in charge of the federal internment centers, wrote to Goldblatt to congratulate him on his "understanding and courage" at the time. But Goldblatt's testimony in February poignantly demonstrated that even supporters had reluctantly agreed that mass internment was necessary. Few labor or other leaders were willing to speak for Japanese Americans at this point. Some of the strongest support came from the leadership of the International Longshoremen's and Warehousemen's Union, based in San Francisco. The ILWU was making great strides in organizing the docks and the sugar and pineapple plantations of Hawai'i, where Japanese American union leaders were abundant. Goldblatt's letter to Carol King, in New York City, demonstrates a personal side to his professional commitment.

ILWU Library, ILWU Archives (San Francisco), Folder: "Minorities—Japanese-Americans." The letter from Myer to Goldblatt is undated but probably from 1946, as the WRA final report was being written. Thanks to Eugene Vrana, Librarian and Archivist, for uncovering the letters, and to Rae Shiraki in the Hawaii ILWU offices, who referred me to Gene.

May 22, 1942

Carol King
100 Fifth Avenue
New York, New York

Dear Carol:

I am enclosing some letters and newspaper clippings from the San Francisco Chronicle on the Japanese evacuation procedure. These were forwarded to me by a Japanese girl employed by the Labor-Herald who has been sent to one of the assembly centers. This girl is a citizen and is married to a white American. However, no exception is made in her case and she too has been evacuated.

I don't know how far along you have come on this problem, but it seems to me some action should be taken with the War Relocation Authority to remedy the conditions outlined in the enclosed letters. You will note from the clippings that while they are evacuating the Japanese from their own farms, they have no objection to sending them back to work as agricultural laborers in restricted districts. The other plan to set up Japanese work corps on an army volunteer basis smacks of forced labor and could be an important factor in breaking down wage scales. A drive to set up these labor corps will materially forestall any genuine effort to relocate the Japanese in regular industry in inland regions and would add to the hardships of evacuation [and] the segregation of Japanese in labor colonies. At no time is provision made for distinguishing between fascist and anti-fascist Japanese.

All in all, I think the manner in which the Japanese have been handled stinks to the high heavens and I am very happy to see people in the East taking an interest in working out some solution.

Would you please let me know whether you think anything can be done to straighten out these difficulties and alter the policy that has been initiated by the War Relocation Authority. While we will undoubtedly take action on our own initiative, I would like to get word on what is being done in the East on the problem.

Terry and Ann send their love. Regards to John.

As ever,

                                              [S] LOUIS GOLDBLATT

87

Toku Shimomura Diary, 1942

Toku Machida was a nurse in Japan before agreeing to an arranged marriage to Yoshitomi Shimomura, who was in the United States. She became an active midwife in the Seattle area, delivering more than 1,000 babies. In 1939, she came out of retirement to deliver her first grandchild, Roger. Roger became a celebrated artist who created a remarkable series of paintings based on entries from diaries she kept while detained at the Puyallup fairgrounds beginning April 28 and interned in Camp Minidoka, Idaho, beginning August 17, 1942. Other portions of diaries Toku maintained through the 56 years she lived in the United States have been used in various works, including a chapter in Donald Keene's Modern Japanese Diaries. *An unusually diligent and articulate diarist, Toku captured the monotony of most days in camp, interspersed with occasions of despair and joy. She used the traditional Japanese device of noting the weather to introduce, in a fully empathetic fashion, the brutal realities of the environment and living conditions.*

Toku Shimomura Diaries. Reprinted with permission from Roger Shimomura.

Feb. 9

Rain at dawn. Clear during the day.

I energetically did laundry . . .

In the afternoon I went to the [Japanese American] Citizen's League with Papa to go through the formalities of property registration. After all of these procedures were finished we were told that the Citizen's League would send us notifications later. We felt relieved and entrusted ourselves to them with a sense of security. We returned home.

I felt tormented by the news concerning the serious disaster in Singapore. Once again I felt restless over the debate about removing coastal Japanese 500 miles to the hinterlands. I can only leave everything to providence and be thankful for today.

Again, at night, we had a heavy rain. . . .

Mar. 19

The newspaper reported that the evacuation of California Japanese Americans started. The first 1,000 will begin leaving.

Mar. 28

We reluctantly sold our Ford for $350. We deposited the money into Kazuo's bank account.

Apr. 4

Clear.

I went to the bank with Papa. We received permission to transfer our $3,500 account at Washington Mutual Bank to Kazuo's name.

We paid the balance of $845 left from the painting of the house.

This house now belongs completely to Kazuo.

During the afternoon I attended Mrs. Okumura's funeral.

Apr. 18

Today most of the Japanese stores in the traditional shopping areas marked the end and closed down. In this fashion our brethren, residents of America for 40 years, experienced a profound end. I have high blood pressure again so I received a second injection. I stayed in bed and rested but my heart was full of deep emotions thinking about our future. Looking back over our past, my eyes filled with tears.

Apr. 21

At last the order was issued. An order for the evacuation was given formally by General DeWitt. The first move had limitations. Kazuo and others will leave here on the 28th as an advanced party. We hurriedly started to prepare for the leave. . . .

Apr. 27

I went downtown because I still had some things to shop for.

Yoichi and Fumi came over and helped us do various things.

I felt very busy and became very tired. We spent all day in a rush. Finally I went for a final farewell at Hart's Drugstore. When I heard the kind words "please come back quickly and return to work," tears again overflowed.

At night we said goodbye to our neighbor Americans. Everybody cried for us. There should not be a difference in human hearts. Tears flowed. I pray from the bottom of my heart that peace will come as early as possible.

Apr. 28

Enter the Camp

The rain cleared up since last night. At last the day has arrived. It is time to leave Seattle, the city where we have lived for such a long time. During the morning Tsuboi san borrowed an automobile to come to see us. Rikio also came by automobile to help. Yoichi and Fumi came. In this fashion it was a merry departure for our journey. Even though I tried not to cry, the tears flowed. Our group of 370 working people departed at 9:30 in a long string of cars and buses. We arrived in Puyallup at 11:30. We settled into our assigned place; A-2, Apt. 27. At 3 p.m. we received another physical examination and smallpox vaccinations. We all felt dissatisfied with out army cots and cotton mattresses. Until late at night we heard a mixture of hammering and the crying voices of children. With some difficulty I finally fell asleep. . . .

May 10

Rainy weather. Rained on and off.

It was an unusual lunch. Roast beef. This is the first time we had meat since we were interned in this camp.

At 2:30 p.m. there was Dr. Warren's sermon. I felt lonesome because there was no special gathering for Mother's Day. I shared "onigiri" [rice balls] with everyone. This was made by Fumi and entrusted to Reverend Thompson. After this I visited Ogishima san. I was treated with "oshiruko" (red bean sweet soup with rice cakes) and went to supper with them. After supper Ogishima visited our place. All of us talked together. . . .

I asked Reverend Thompson for a bucket and two chairs.

May 11

Cloudy & cold.

I woke up early in the morning. Around 10 a.m. we received more internees from Seattle. When we greeted the buses the people looked like they were in "tomaru kago" (bamboo cage for transporting criminals) which were used in the old years. When I looked at the wire fences next to the buses my eyes filled with tears and my heart suffered. I prayed that I could believe in the wartime treaty and forget that I was captive and maintain my morale.

Today Matsuda's whole family was interned. They delivered the articles which I asked them to bring for me.

Sasaki and Obasawa san also were interned today. I heard that all of these people were staying in Area D. I will not be able to meet them. Kazuo and Michio supplied me with this news.

At night I wrote a letter to Tsuboi san and asked her to bring the articles that I left behind. . . .

Jun. 29

Clear.

I did the laundry in the early morning. . . .

I heard that there was going to be a "Bon Odori" (Festival dance) practice today. I feel that these people are being insensitive to our current situation.

They are, however, unbelieving friends and from that standpoint their actions are predictable.

Jun. 30
    Clear.
    The heat is severe from the morning. I don't have the energy to do anything. I did finish the laundry during the morning. I spent the afternoon protecting myself from the heat. Even during coffee time nobody came over.
    The heat made me drowsy and I could not get to sleep.

Jul. 1
    Clear.
    The heat is severe and there is no breeze.
    I heard that some rooms never got below 110° yesterday. It seems that today is hotter than yesterday.
    I did not have any appetite. At noon I ate an o-nigiri with Fumiko instead of lunch.
    Also during the noon I stood under the grandstand to avoid the sun. . . .
    At night I went to bed exhausted.
    I heard that the temperature in the sickbed rooms went up to 120°.
    This is certainly unbearable heat.

Jul. 2
    Clear. The heat today is as hot as it was yesterday.
    After lunch I stayed cool by sitting under the grandstand. . . .

Aug. 15
    The heat was severe. The temperature was 107°.
    I was concerned over Ayako and Roger who left early this morning. The whole day was difficult to bear because of the heat.
    I went to bed with a feeling of relief after we sent out our baggage.
    I was annoyed by the noise from the neighbors as well as all around.
    Dawn came without sleep because of this.
    When I think that tonight is the last night I will be here I somewhat regret leaving this barrack which was home to us.

Aug. 16
    We gathered at the gate at 7:30 a.m. with "obento" (boxed lunch) given to us from Tamura san and Kazuo. We left the area at 9:30 a.m.
    We, the brethren of 500, departed to the hinterlands, locked in 16 old passenger train cars.
    We arrived in Portland at 2:30 p.m. After a one hour break we departed at 3:30 and arrived at The Dalles at 5:50. After a three minute stop our train continued toward the Cascades.

It was difficult and hot for those two and a half hours before sunset! I felt more dead than alive. The nurses and soldiers checked on us hourly to see if we needed anything. Around 2:30 a.m. I fell into a doze after going crazy with suffering and fatigue.

Aug. 17

We arrived at Arlington, Idaho, unnoticed, at 5:30 a.m. Everybody looked "deep black." They were no longer the same people as they were yesterday. After we had a chicken dinner for lunch, the heat increased. Half dead and half alive our bodies continued on. We arrived at Rock Mountain at 2:30. Finally, at 4 p.m., we arrived at the newly built camp after taking a bus journey, by bus, of 8 ri (ri = 2.44 miles).

Though it was unfinished we could see the grand scale of this city near the mountains. We were simply amazed.

I was assigned to Block 5 B. 6, Apt. A. After we roughly cleaned the dust from the room we went to bed. I fell into a deep sleep.

We had roast beef for our first supper in this camp. . . .

Sep. 9

It was cloudy in the morning but the weather changed into the usual dusty conditions around noon. We could not open our eyes and mouth. . . .

The speed of the wind increased and we were not able to see in front of us. I didn't want to mention this but I would like to offer a grudge word to the government. I heard that during the process of internment of the Portland people, a mother was seen crying, holding her child.

Sep. 10

It was a comfortable day; like the calm after the storm.

I finished laundering the sheets. I was a little tired. Surprisingly, Sasaki and Watanabe sans came.

We had a nice chat over tea. What a day! Even Beppu san came. She stayed and talked till around 8 p.m. Sato sans came and said that they came to this camp for business. They left with Beppu san. Kazuo and Roger came. They made a bench for us and we had a nice time together. . . .

Nov. 17

It rained continuously.

I went to choir practice in the afternoon.

At night a memorial service was held at recreation hall number 34 for Shig Tanabe's mother who passed away last November 5th. I attended it taking advantage of the use of the hospital automobile. I returned at 9:30 and was tremendously fatigued and could not sleep.

The rain created puddles that rippled around the 21 and 34 area just like a small pond. I became concerned about the inconvenience of moving about.

Nov. 18

Rain and more rain.

We had received permission to go to Twin Falls so 6 of us, Hamamoto, Kazuo, Nomura and I, departed by auto at 9 a.m. in the rain. When we arrived on the open road, Roger's expressions of joy moved me to tears. We arrived at city center at 9:30 and shopped. We rested at Reverend Thompson's home after lunch. We then walked around town again. We met Michio, had supper, then returned home. I was worn out. . . .

Dec. 25

The muddy ground was completely covered by snow which fell last night. It was a beautiful cover of white cloth. It was a suitable sight for Christmas. Around noon it turned into a snow storm which lead to some extreme coldness.

The dinner treat for us in number 6 was at mess hall number 7 at 4:30. The waiters and cooks were all dressed up in the beautifully decorated dining room. The radio emitted melodies of Christmas carols. For a moment I forgot where I was. We happily sat at our family table. A Christmas program was held at mess hall number 6 at 7 p.m. Nearly ten performances were shown with Kazuo acting as emcee. Our three person choir act was included. At 9 p.m. Santa Claus appeared and gave presents to all of us.

There was a severe storm outside and we were not able to walk with our heads up. But the gathering inside suited the day of the birth of the child of peace. It was a memorable Christmas day and we spent it joyfully.

Dec. 26

I was not feeling well probably due to mental fatigue.

I went to the placement office during the early morning to receive my unemployment allowance. It was postponed for two weeks because there was a shortage of workers.

I heard that Sister Sasaki was in bed with a cold. I made udon for her. Meals became increasingly worse because of the rationing. We had sandwiches in the room.

Dec. 27

The snow fell continuously.

I rested leisurely. The snow fall turned into a snow storm.

The time for the meeting at church changed to 1:30 p.m. We gathered at recreation hall number 8. Reverend Hashimoto was in charge.

I heard that Sister Sasaki entered the hospital for a rest.

A heavy rain started from the evening. The condition of the road became grave.

I read a book in the room.

Dec. 28

Cloudy weather.

The temperature abated a bit but the surface of the road was frozen like a mirror. We had to be careful to walk on it.

Probably because I slept well last night I felt good today.

I spent time doing the ironing and cleaning the room.

I made a call on Sister Sasaki's sickbed. I also visited Mrs. Kimura and Mrs. Tsugawa's sickbed.

I received greens and berries from Mrs. Mimbu. Mrs. Tanagi visited us.

I checked my blood pressure at night and it was 170.

Dec. 29

Fine weather.

I heard that Mrs. Sasaki had an operation during the early morning.

88

Repeal of Chinese Exclusion Acts
(Public Law 199), December 17, 1943

During World War II Japan had some success convincing leaders of other Asian countries that it was waging a struggle for justice against the imperialist white races of Europe and the United States. Largely to counter these propaganda claims, Congress repealed the 1882 Exclusion Act and subsequent laws that had extended the official prohibition of Chinese immigration over the intervening sixty years. President Franklin Roosevelt, in a proclamation issued February 8, 1944, denied the propaganda element, insisting that the quota was "designed solely for the purpose of compliance with the pertinent provisions" of the 1924 and 1943 acts and did not have "any significance extraneous to this purpose." The section designating the quota for the Chinese based on the 1924 Immigration Act allowed for a total of 105 individuals to enter per year. In addition, unlike other national quotas, this included Chinese coming from countries other than China (which was to provide 75 percent of the total). So this was an insignificant number. Nonetheless, Public Law 199 was a historic break in a long chain of legislation restricting or prohibiting Asian immigration. It also allowed for naturalization of Chinese immigrants, a privilege extended to Filipinos and Indians in 1946 and to Japanese and Koreans only in 1952.

United States Statutes at Large Containing the Laws and Concurrent Resolutions Enacted During the First Session of the Seventy-eighth Congress of the United States, 1943, vol. 57. Washington, DC: Government Printing Office, 1944.

An Act
To repeal the Chinese Exclusion Acts,
to establish quotas, and for other purposes

Be it enacted by the Senate and House of Representatives of the United States of America in Congress assembled, That the following Acts or parts of Acts relating to the exclusion or deportation of persons of the Chinese race are hereby repealed: May 6, 1882 (22 Stat. L. 58); July 5, 1884 (23 Stat. L. 115); September 13,

1888 (25 Stat. L. 476); October 1, 1888 (25 Stat. L. 504); May 5, 1892 (27 Stat. L. 25); November 3, 1893 (28 Stat. L. 7); that portion of section 1 of the Act of July 7, 1898 (30 Stat. L. 750, 751), which reads as follows: "There shall be no further immigration of Chinese into the Hawaiian Islands except upon such conditions as are now or may hereafter be allowed by the laws of the United States; and no Chinese, by reason of anything herein contained, shall be allowed to enter the United States from the Hawaiian Islands." . . .

Sec. 2. With the exception of those coming under subsections (b), (d), (e), and (f) of section 4, Immigration Act of 1924 (43 Stat. 155; 44 Stat. 812; 45 Stat. 1009; 46 Stat. 854; 47 Stat. 656; 8 U. S. C. 204), all Chinese persons entering the United States annually as immigrants shall be allocated to the quota for the Chinese computed under the provisions of section 11 of the said Act. A preference up to 75 per centum of the quota shall be given to Chinese born and resident in China.

Sec. 3. Section 303 of the Nationality Act of 1940, as amended (54 Stat. 1140; 8 U. S. C. 703), is hereby amended by striking out the word "and" before the word "descendants," changing the colon after the word "Hemisphere" to a comma, and adding the following: "and Chinese persons or persons of Chinese descent:."

Approved December 17, 1943.

89

Supreme Court: Kiyoshi [Gordon]
Hirabayashi v. United States, *June 21, 1943*

Gordon Hirabayashi deliberately violated the curfew imposed only on those of Japanese descent in order to challenge the constitutionality of race-based special treatment of citizens. Hirabayashi, a Quaker committed to independent action in the face of official misconduct, was a student at the University of Washington in May 1942 when he refused to obey the curfew order and simultaneously refused to report to the Civil Control Station for instructions for removal from the West Coast exclusion zone. His court case presented two major challenges: first, whether civilian elected officials in Congress had unconstitutionally delegated authority to the military, which then wielded this power over civilians; second, whether the military had then unconstitutionally used this power to discriminate against people of Japanese descent. The court decided the first question by allowing wide latitude in wartime, declaring the delegation of authority constitutional. While lower courts had convicted Hirabayashi of both curfew and exclusion violations, the Supreme Court ruled only on the curfew case, arguing that the sentences ran concurrently and that there was no need to rule on exclusion. (That would be done in the Fred Korematsu case in 1944.) Hirabayashi v. United States was a critical case because it established the government's insistence that, in the war between the United States and Japan, no ready means could be found to separate "loyal" from potentially disloyal Japanese Americans and, therefore, that separate treatment was justified. The reasoning included notions of an "alien" race whose true sentiments were unknowable but also the idea that decades of discrimination against them might have nurtured antagonistic feelings about the United States. A curious conclusion—that current discrimination was justified by prior discrimination! Two justices, Douglas and Murphy, expressed discomfort about the transparent use of differential racial treatment, but the decision was unanimous. One year later, these justices would change their minds and write powerful dissenting opinions in the Korematsu case. Forty years later, the Hirabayashi decision was vacated through the little-known legal procedure called coram nobis *(our error), in which the executive branch admits to having substantially lied to the judiciary.*

Supreme Court Reporter, vol. 63. St. Paul, MN: West Publishing Co., 1943.

Mr. Chief Justice STONE delivered the opinion of the Court.

Appellant, an American citizen of Japanese ancestry, was convicted in the district court of violating the Act of Congress of March 21, 1942, 56 Stat. 173, 18 U.S.C.A. 97a, which makes it a misdemeanor knowingly to disregard restrictions made applicable by a military commander to persons in a military area prescribed by him as such, all as authorized by an Executive Order of the President.

The questions for our decision are whether the particular restriction violated, namely that all persons of Japanese ancestry residing in such an area be within their place of residence daily between the hours of 8:00 p.m. and 6:00 a.m., was adopted by the military commander in the exercise of an unconstitutional delegation by Congress of its legislative power, and whether the restriction unconstitutionally discriminated between citizens of Japanese ancestry and those of other ancestries in violation of the Fifth Amendment.

The indictment is in two counts. The second charges that appellant, being a person of Japanese ancestry, had on a specified date, contrary to a restriction promulgated by the military commander of the Western Defense Command, Fourth Army, failed to remain in his place of residence in the designated military area between the hours of 8:00 o'clock p.m. and 6:00 a.m. The first count charges that appellant, on May 11 and 12, 1942, had, contrary to a Civilian Exclusion Order issued by the military commander, failed to report to the Civil Control Station within the designated area, it appearing that appellant's required presence there was a preliminary step to the exclusion from that area of persons of Japanese ancestry.

By demurrer and plea in abatement, which the court overruled (D.C., 46 F. Supp. 657), appellant asserted that the indictment should be dismissed because he was an American citizen who had never been a subject of and had never borne allegiance to the Empire of Japan, and also because the Act of March 21, 1942, was an unconstitutional delegation of Congressional power. . . .

The evidence showed that appellant had failed to report to the Civil Control Station on May 11 or May 12, 1942, as directed, to register for evacuation from the military area. He admitted failure to do so, and stated it had at all times been his belief that he would be waiving his rights as an American citizen by so doing. The evidence also showed that for like reason he was away from his place of residence after 8:00 p.m. on May 9, 1942. The jury returned a verdict of guilty on both counts and appellant was sentenced to imprisonment for a term of three months on each, the sentences to run concurrently. . . .

Appellant does not deny that he knowingly failed to obey the curfew order as charged in the second count of the indictment, or that the order was authorized by the terms of Executive Order No. 9066, or that the challenged Act of Congress purports to punish with criminal penalties disobedience of such an order. His contentions are only that Congress unconstitutionally delegated its legislative power, to the military commander by authorizing him to impose the challenged regulation, and that, even if the regulation were in other respects lawfully authorized, the Fifth Amendment prohibits the discrimination made between citizens of Japanese descent and those of other ancestry. . . .

The challenged orders were defense measures for the avowed purpose of safeguarding the military area in question, at a time of threatened air raids and invasion by the Japanese forces, from the danger of sabotage and espionage. As the curfew was made applicable to citizens residing in the area only if they were of Japanese ancestry, our inquiry must be whether in the light of all the facts and circumstances there was any substantial basis for the conclusion, in which Congress and the military commander united, that the curfew as applied was a protective measure necessary to meet the threat of sabotage and espionage which would substantially affect the war effort and which might reasonably be expected to aid a threatened enemy invasion. . . .

There is support for the view that social, economic and political conditions which have prevailed since the close of the last century, when the Japanese began to come to this country in substantial numbers, have intensified their solidarity and have in large measure prevented their assimilation as an integral part of the white population. In addition, large numbers of children of Japanese parentage are sent to Japanese language schools outside the regular hours of public schools in the locality. Some of these schools are generally believed to be sources of Japanese nationalistic propaganda, cultivating allegiance to Japan. . . .

Congress and the Executive, including the military commander, could have attributed special significance, in its bearing on the loyalties of persons of Japanese descent, to the maintenance by Japan of its system of dual citizenship. Children born in the United States of Japanese alien parents, and especially those children born before December 1, 1924, are under many circumstances deemed, by Japanese law, to be citizens of Japan. . . .

The large number of resident alien Japanese, approximately one-third of all Japanese inhabitants of the country, are of mature years and occupy positions of influence in Japanese communities. . . .

As a result of all these conditions affecting the life of the Japanese, both aliens and citizens, in the Pacific Coast area, there has been relatively little social intercourse between them and the white population. The restrictions, both practical and legal, affecting the privileges and opportunities afforded to persons of Japanese extraction residing in the United States, have been sources of irritation and may well have tended to increase their isolation, and in many instances their attachments to Japan and its institutions.

Viewing these data in all their aspects, Congress and the Executive could reasonably have concluded that these conditions have encouraged the continued attachment of members of this group to Japan and Japanese institutions. . . .

But appellant insists that the exercise of the power is inappropriate and unconstitutional because it discriminates against citizens of Japanese ancestry, in violation of the Fifth Amendment. The Fifth Amendment contains no equal protection clause and it restrains only such discriminatory legislation by Congress as amounts to a denial of due process. . . .

Distinctions between citizens solely because of their ancestry are by their very nature odious to a free people whose institutions are founded upon the doctrine of equality. For that reason, legislative classification or discrimination based on race alone has often been held to be a denial of equal protection. . . . We may assume that these considerations would be controlling here were it not for the fact that the danger of espionage and sabotage, in time of war and of threatened invasion, calls upon the military authorities to scrutinize every relevant fact bearing on the loyalty of populations in the danger areas. Because racial discriminations are in most circumstances irrelevant and therefore prohibited, it by no means follows that, in dealing with the perils of war, Congress and the Executive are wholly precluded from taking into account those facts and circumstances which are relevant to measures for our national defense and for the successful prosecution of the war, and which may in fact place citizens of one ancestry in a different category from others. "We must never forget, that it is a constitution we are expounding," "a constitution intended to endure for ages to come, and, consequently, to be adapted to the various crises of human affairs." . . .

The conviction under the second count is without constitutional infirmity. Hence we have no occasion to review the conviction on the first count since, as already stated, the sentences on the two counts are to run concurrently and conviction on the second is sufficient to sustain the sentence. For this reason also it is unnecessary to consider the Government's argument that compliance with the order to report at the Civilian Control Station did not necessarily entail confinement in a relocation center.

Affirmed.

Mr. Justice DOUGLAS concurring.

While I concur in the result and agree substantially with the opinion of the Court, I wish to add a few words to indicate what for me is the narrow ground of decision. . . .

But I think it important to emphasize that we are dealing here with a problem of loyalty not assimilation. Loyalty is a matter of mind and of heart not of race. That indeed is the history of America. Moreover, guilt is personal under our constitutional system. Detention for reasonable cause is one thing. Detention on account of ancestry is another.

In this case the petitioner tendered by a plea in abatement the question of his loyalty to the United States. I think that plea was properly stricken; military measures of defense might be paralyzed if it were necessary to try out that issue preliminarily. But a denial of that opportunity in this case does not necessarily mean that petitioner could not have had a hearing on that issue in some appropriate proceeding. Obedience to the military orders is one thing. Whether an individual member of a group must be afforded at some stage an opportunity to show that, being loyal, he should be reclassified is a wholly different question. . . .

Mr. Justice MURPHY, concurring.

It is not to be doubted that the action taken by the military commander in pursuance of the authority conferred upon him was taken in complete good faith and in the firm conviction that it was required by considerations of public safety and military security. Neither is it doubted that the Congress and the Executive working together may generally employ such measures as are necessary and appropriate to provide for the common defense and to wage war "with all the force necessary to make it effective." . . .

Distinctions based on color and ancestry are utterly inconsistent with our traditions and ideals. They are at variance with the principles for which we are now waging war. We cannot close our eyes to the fact that for centuries the Old World has been torn by racial and religious conflicts and has suffered the worst kind of anguish because of inequality of treatment for different groups. There was one law for one and a different law for another. Nothing is written more firmly into our law than the compact of the Plymouth voyagers to have just and equal laws. To say that any group cannot be assimilated is to admit that the great American experiment has failed, that our way of life has failed when confronted with the normal attachment of certain groups to the lands of their forefathers. As a nation we embrace many groups, some of them among the oldest settlements in our midst, which have isolated themselves for religious and cultural reasons.

Today is the first time, so far as I am aware, that we have sustained a substantial restriction of the personal liberty of citizens of the United States based upon the accident of race or ancestry. Under the curfew order here challenged no less than 70,000 American citizens have been placed under a special ban and deprived of their liberty because of their particular racial inheritance. In this sense it bears a melancholy resemblance to the treatment accorded to members of the Jewish race in Germany and in other parts of Europe. The result is the creation in this country of two classes of citizens for the purposes of a critical and perilous hour—to sanction discrimination between groups of United States citizens on the basis of ancestry. In my opinion this goes to the very brink of constitutional power. . . .

90

Supreme Court:
Minoru Yasui v. U.S. Supreme Court,
June 21, 1943

Along with the Hirabayashi case, this was the first of the constitutional challenges to the mass removal and internment of Japanese Americans during World War II to be decided by the U.S. Supreme Court. Minoru Yasui, an American citizen, deliberately challenged the right of the government to impose curfew restrictions directed solely against Japanese Americans. He walked into a police station in Portland, Oregon on March 28, 1942 and demanded to be arrested. He was a lawyer and a second lieutenant in the Infantry Reserve, and had been employed by the Japanese Consulate in Chicago until the day after Pearl Harbor, when he resigned and unsuccessfully tried to volunteer for military duty. The district court ruled that the curfew order was unconstitutional with regard to Americans, but that Yasui's conviction was reasonable since he had renounced his citizenship by taking employment with the Japanese government. Yasui appealed to the circuit court, but the government, anxious to have his case heard before its almost certain habeas corpus defeat in the Mitsuye Endo case, hurried the appeal to the U.S. Supreme Court. It decided that Yasui had not renounced his citizenship, that the curfew order singling out the Japanese community was constitutional, and that the original sentence of one year's imprisonment and $5,000 fine was excessive. The government convinced the court to use this case as preliminary justification for the entire internment. At this point in time, the Japanese American Citizens League, the government-acknowledged leadership group for the community, strongly opposed constitutional challenges to the curfew and internment.

Supreme Court Reporter, vol. 63. St. Paul, MN: West Publishing Co., 1943.

Minoru Yasui v. United States, 320 U.S. 115

Decided June 21, 1943

Mr. Chief Justice STONE delivered the opinion of the Court. . . .

Appellant, an American-born person of Japanese ancestry, was convicted in the district court of an offense defined by the Act of March 21, 1942, 56 Stat. 173, 18 U.S.C.A. 97a. The indictment charged him with violation, on March 28, 1942, of a curfew order made applicable to Portland, Oregon, by Public Proclamation No. 3, issued by Lt. General J. L. DeWitt on March 24, 1942. 7 Federal Register 2543. The validity of the curfew was considered in the Hirabayashi case, and this case presents the same issues as the conviction on Count 2 of the indictment in that case. From the evidence it appeared that appellant was born in Oregon in 1916 of alien parents; that when he was eight years old he spent a summer in Japan; that he attended the public schools in Oregon, and also, for about three years, a Japanese language school; that he later attended the University of Oregon, from which he received A.B. and LL.B degrees; that he was a member of the bar of Oregon, and a second lieutenant in the Army of the United States, Infantry Reserve; that he had been employed by the Japanese Consulate in Chicago, but had resigned on December 8, 1941, and immediately offered his services to the military authorities; that he had discussed with an agent of the Federal Bureau of Investigation the advisability of testing the constitutionality of the curfew; and that when he violated the curfew order he requested that he be arrested so that he could test its constitutionality.

[1] The district court ruled that the Act of March 21, 1942, was unconstitutional as applied to American citizens, but held that appellant, by reason of his course of conduct, must be deemed to have renounced his American citizenship. D.C., 48 F.Supp. 40. The Government does not undertake to support the conviction on that ground, since no such issue was tendered by the Government, although appellant testified at the trial that he had not renounced his citizenship. Since we hold, as in the Hirabayashi case, that the curfew order was valid as applied to citizens, it follows that appellant's citizenship was not relevant to the issue tendered by the Government and the conviction must be sustained for the reasons stated in the Hirabayashi case.

[2] But as the sentence of one year's imprisonment—the maximum permitted by the statute—was imposed after the finding that appellant was not a citizen, and as the Government states that it has not and does not now controvert his citizenship, the case is an appropriate one for resentence in the light of these circumstances. See Husty v. United States, 282 U.S. 694, 703, 51 S.Ct. 240, 242, 75 L.Ed. 629, 74 A.L.R. 1407. The conviction will be sustained but the judgment will be vacated and the cause remanded to the district court for resentence of appellant, and to afford that court opportunity to strike its findings as to appellant's loss of United States citizenship.

So ordered.

Conviction sustained; cause remanded for resentence.

91

Destruction of Original Relocation
Report Documents, 1943

Aiko Yoshinaga-Herzig discovered this deceptively simple document that was one key to the ultimate vacating of several World War II U.S. Supreme Court cases. Minoru Yasui, Fred Korematsu, and Gordon Hirabayashi were all convicted of defying some aspect of orders for curfew in or exclusion from their West Coast homes in 1942. The final report on this "Japanese Evacuation" was used to justify the government's actions on the basis of military necessity because there was no way to determine the loyal and the disloyal among the 120,000 residents of Japanese descent. But the 10 copies of the draft of the final report contained racist language that would have compromised the pending cases. Therefore, Assistant Secretary of War John J. McCloy insisted that important changes be made. The key edit modified General John DeWitt's insistence that it was "impossible" for the government to determine loyal and disloyal to a statement that emphasized difficulty due to "insufficient time." Karl Bendetsen, the architect of the report, ordered the files cleansed—including all 10 draft copies. The document here, from Theodore E. Smith, attests to the remarkable task of preparing the Justice Department to mislead the Supreme Court. The War Department submitted the revised version as if it were the original, and it was used before the court. Aiko and her husband, Jack, tirelessly combed the National Archives for documents regarding this series of events and uncovered this as well as one miraculously surviving original report to document this unsavory history. Later, in the coram nobis *cases, evidence provided by documents like this was decisive.*

National Archives, RG 338—Army Commands, Western Defense Command. Courtesy Jack Herzig and Aiko Yoshinaga-Herzig.

Headquarters Western Defense Command and Fourth Army
Presidio, San Francisco, California
Civil Affairs Division

29 June 43

I certify that this date I witnessed the destruction by burning of the galley proofs, galley pages, drafts and memorandums of the original report of the Japanese Evacuation.

[signature]
THEODORE E. SMITH

WOJG   AUS

92

Carlos Bulosan, America Is in the Heart, 1943

Carlos Bulosan was a gifted Filipino American writer whose work here is a fictionalized memoir of his life in the Philippines and in the United States from the time he immigrated, about 1930, until the beginning of World War II. The title is a ringing affirmation of his dedication to the ideals of this country, but there is savage and poignant exploration of his decadelong confrontation with the violence inhering in the intersections of race, class, and gender. As he says in one section: "I feel like a criminal running away from a crime I did not commit. And this crime is that I am a Filipino in America." America Is in the Heart has become a classic exposition of the trials faced by Filipino American men who worked the fields and factories of the West Coast and the ideas and ideologies they entertained or embraced. By the time Bulosan arrived in Seattle, there were approximately 50,000 Filipinos on Hawaii's sugar plantations and another 50,000 scattered along the West Coast, mostly in California. They inherited the xenophobic racism that had been directed against Chinese and Japanese and absorbed the colonialist contempt directed against their homeland, still squarely within the American empire. At the same time, they had grown up in that context and believed they were good Americans at heart. The antimiscegenation law, the exploitation, the discrimination, and the ostracism were, as a result, all the more difficult to understand or accept.

Carlos Bulosan, *America Is in the Heart*. 1943; reprint, Seattle and London: University of Washington Press, 1973. Reprinted with permission.

Chapter XIV

When I landed in Seattle for the second time, I expected a fair amount of money from the company. But the contractor, Max Feuga, came into the play room and handed us slips of paper. I looked at mine and was amazed at the neatly itemized expenditures that I was supposed to have incurred during the season. Twenty-five dollars for withdrawals, one hundred for board and room, twenty for bedding, and another twenty for something I do not now remember. At the bottom was the actual amount I was to receive after all the deductions: *thirteen dollars!*

I could do nothing. I did not even go to the hotel where I had left my suitcase. I went to a Japanese dry goods store on Jackson Street and bought a pair of corduroy pants and a blue shirt. It was already twilight and the cannery workers were in the crowded Chinese gambling houses, losing their season's earnings and drinking bootleg whisky. They became quarrelsome and abusive to their own people when they lost, and subservient to the Chinese gambling lords and marijuana peddlers. They pawed at the semi-nude whores with their dirty hands and made suggestive gestures, running out into the night when they were rebuffed for lack of money.

I was already in America, and I felt good and safe. I did not understand why. The gamblers, prostitutes and Chinese opium smokers did not excite me, but they aroused in me a feeling of flight. I knew that I must run away from them, but it was not that I was afraid of contamination. I wanted to see other aspects of American life, for surely these destitute and vicious people were merely a small part of it. Where would I begin this pilgrimage, this search for a door into America?

I went outside and walked around looking into the faces of my countrymen, wondering if I would see someone I had known in the Philippines. I came to a building which brightly dressed white women were entering, lifting their diaphanous gowns as they climbed the stairs. I looked up and saw the huge sign:

MANILA DANCE HALL

The orchestra upstairs was playing; Filipinos were entering. I put my hands in my pockets and followed them, beginning to feel lonely for the sound of home.

The dance hall was crowded with Filipino cannery workers and domestic servants. But the girls were very few, and the Filipinos fought over them. When a boy liked a girl he bought a roll of tickets from the hawker on the floor and kept dancing with her. But the other boys who also liked the same girl shouted at him to stop, cursing him in the dialects and sometimes throwing rolled wet papers at him. At the bar the glasses were tinkling, the bottles popping loudly, and the girls in the back room were smoking marijuana. It was almost impossible to breathe.

Then I saw Marcelo's familiar back. He was dancing with a tall blonde in a green dress, a girl so tall that Marcelo looked like a dwarf climbing a tree. But the girl was pretty and her body was nicely curved and graceful, and she had a way of swaying that aroused confused sensations in me. It was evident that many of the boys wanted to dance with her; they were shouting maliciously at Marcelo. The way the blonde waved to them made me think that she knew most of them. They were nearly all oldtimers and strangers to Marcelo. They were probably gamblers and pimps, because they had fat rolls of money and expensive clothing.

But Marcelo was learning very fast. He requested one of his friends to buy another roll of tickets for him. The girl was supposed to tear off one ticket every three minutes, but I noticed that she tore off a ticket for every minute. That was ten cents a minute. Marcelo was unaware of what she was doing; he was spending his whole season's earnings on his first day in America. It was only when one of his friends shouted to him in the dialect that he became angry at the girl. Marcelo was not tough, but his friend was an oldtimer. Marcelo pushed the girl toward the gaping bystanders. His friend opened a knife and gave it to him.

Then something happened that made my heart leap. One of the blonde girl's admirers came from behind and struck Marcelo with a piece of lead pipe. Marcelo's friend whipped out a pistol and fired. Marcelo and the boy with the lead pipe fell on the floor simultaneously, one on top of the other, but the blonde girl ran into the crowd screaming frantically. Several guns banged at once, and the lights went out. I saw Marcelo's friend crumple in the fading light.

At once the crowd seemed to flow out of the windows. I went to a side window and saw three heavy electric wires strung from the top of the building to the ground. I reached for them and slid to the ground. My palms were burning when I came out of the alley. Then I heard the sirens of police cars screaming infernally toward the place. I put my cap in my pocket and ran as fast as I could in the direction of a neon sign two blocks down the street.

It was a small church where Filipino farm workers were packing their suitcases and bundles. I found out later that Filipino immigrants used their churches as rest houses while they were waiting for work. There were two large trucks outside. I went to one of them and sat on the running board, holding my hands over my heart for fear it would beat too fast. The lights in the church went out and the workers came into the street. The driver of the truck in which I was sitting pointed a strong flashlight at me.

"Hey, you, are you looking for a job?" he asked.

"Yes, sir," I said.

"Get in the truck," he said, jumping into the cab. "Let's go, Flo!" he shouted to the other driver.

I was still trembling with excitement. But I was glad to get out of Seattle—to anywhere else in America. I did not care where so long as it was in America. I found a corner and sat down heavily. The drivers shouted to each other. Then we were off to work.

It was already midnight and the lights in the city of Seattle were beginning to fade. I could see the reflections on the bright lake in Bremerton. I was reminded of Baguio. Then some of the men began singing. The driver and two men were arguing over money. A boy in the other truck was playing a violin. We were on the highway to Yakima Valley.

After a day and a night of driving we arrived in a little town called Moxee City. The apple trees were heavy with fruit and the branches drooped to the ground.

It was late afternoon when we passed through the town; the hard light of the sun punctuated the ugliness of the buildings. I was struck dumb by its isolation and the dry air that hung oppressively over the place. The heart-shaped valley was walled by high treeless mountains, and the hot breeze that blew in from a distant sea was injurious to the apple trees.

The leader of our crew was called Cornelio Paez; but most of the oldtimers suspected that it was not his real name. There was something shifty about him, and his so-called bookkeeper, a pockmarked man we simply called Pinoy (which is a term generally applied to all Filipino immigrant workers), had a strange trick of squinting sideways when he looked at you. There seemed to be an old animosity between Paez and his bookkeeper.

But we were drawn together because the white people of Yakima Valley were suspicious of us. Years before, in the town of Toppenish, two Filipino apple pickers had been found murdered on the road to Sunnyside. At that time, there was ruthless persecution of the Filipinos throughout the Pacific Coast, instigated by orchardists who feared the unity of white and Filipino workers. A small farmer in Wapato who had tried to protect his Filipino workers had had his house burned. So however much we distrusted each other under Paez, we knew that beyond the walls of our bunkhouse were our real enemies, waiting to drive us out of Yakima Valley. . . .

Mr. Malraux, our employer, had three daughters who used to work with us after school hours. He was a Frenchman who had gone to Moxee City when it consisted of only a few houses. At that time the valley was still a haven for Indians, but they had been gradually driven out when farming had been started on a large scale. Malraux had married an American woman in Spokane and begun farming; the girls came one by one, helping him on the farm as they grew. When I arrived in Moxee City they were already in their teens.

The oldest girl was called Estelle; she had just finished high school. She had a delightful disposition and her industry was something that men talked about with approval. The other girls, Maria and Diane, were still too young to be going about so freely; but whenever Estelle came to our bunkhouse they were always with her. . . .

When we came back from hunting we would go to the Malraux house with some of the men who had musical instruments. We would sit on the lawn for hours singing American songs. But when they started singing Philippine songs their voices were so sad, so full of yesterday and the haunting presence of familiar seas, as if they had reached the end of creation, that life seemed ended and no bright spark was left in the world.

But one afternoon toward the end of the season, Paez went to the bank to get our paychecks and did not come back. The pockmarked bookkeeper was furious.

"I'll get him this time!" he said, running up and down the house. "He did that last year in California and I didn't get a cent. I know where to find the bastard!"

Julio grabbed him by the neck. "You'd better tell me where to find him if you know what is good for you," he said angrily, pushing the frightened bookkeeper toward the stove.

"Let me alone!" he shouted.

Julio hit him between the eyes, and the bookkeeper struggled violently. Julio hit him again. The bookkeeper rolled on the floor like a baby. Julio picked him up and threw him outside the house. I thought he was dead, but his legs began to move. Then he opened his eyes and got up quickly, staggering like a drunken stevedore toward the highway. Julio came out of the house with brass knuckles, but the bookkeeper was already disappearing behind the apple orchard. Julio came back and began hitting the door of the kitchen with all his force, in futile anger.

I had not seen this sort of brutality in the Philippines, but my first contact with it in America made me brave. My bravery was still nameless, and waiting to express itself. I was not shocked when I saw that my countrymen had become ruthless toward one another, and this sudden impact of cruelty made me insensate to pain and kindness, so that it took me a long time to wholly trust other men. As time went by I became as ruthless as the worst of them, and I became afraid that I would never feel like a human being again. Yet no matter what bestiality encompassed my life, I felt sure that somewhere, sometime, I would break free. This faith kept me from completely succumbing to the degradation into which many of my countrymen had fallen. It finally paved my way out of our small, harsh life, painfully but cleanly, into a world of strange intellectual adventures and self-fulfillment.

The apples were nearly picked when Paez disappeared with our money. We lost interest in our work. We sat on the lawn of the Malraux's and sang. They came out of the house and joined us. The moonlight shimmered like a large diamond on the land around the farm. The men in the bunkhouse came with their violins and guitars. Julio grabbed Diane and started dancing with her; then the two younger girls were grabbed by other men.

It was while Estelle was singing that we heard a gun crack from the dirt road not far from the house. Malraux saw them first, saw the clubs and the iron bars in their hands, and yelled at us in warning. But it was too late. They had taken us by surprise.

I saw Malraux run into the house for his gun. I jumped to the nearest apple tree. I wanted a weapon—anything to hit back at these white men who had leaped upon us from the dark. Three or four guns banged all at once, and I turned to see Maria falling to the ground. A streak of red light flashed from the window into the crowd. Estelle was screaming and shouting to her father. Diane was already climbing the stairs, her long black hair shining in the moonlight.

I saw Julio motioning to me to follow him. Run away from our friends and companions? No! *Goddamn you, Julio!* I jumped into the thick of fight, dark with fury. Then I felt Julio's hands pulling me away, screaming into my ears:

"Come on, you crazy punk! Come on before I kill you myself!"

He was hurting me. Blinded with anger and tears, I ran after him toward our bunkhouse. We stopped behind a pear tree when we saw that our house was burning. Julio whispered to me to follow him. . . .

We followed a narrow footpath and, to our surprise, came to the low, uninhabited, wide desert of the Rattlesnake Mountains. The stars were our only guide. . . .

After a while we crossed the plain again, hiding behind the trees whenever we saw anyone approaching us. I was too exhausted to continue when we reached Zillah, where some children stoned us. We hid in an orange grove and rested. At sunset we started again. When we were nearing the town of Granger, I heard the sudden tumult of the Yakima River. Julio started running again, and I followed him. Suddenly we saw the clear, cool water of the river. We sat in the tall grass, cooling our tired bodies beside the bright stream.

I was the first to enter the water. I washed my shirt and spread it to dry on the grass. Sunnyside was not far off. I could hear the loud whistle of trains running seaward.

"This is the beginning of your life in America," Julio said. "We'll take a freight train from Sunnyside and go to nowhere."

"I would like to go to California," I said. "I have two brothers there—but I don't know if I could find them."

"All roads go to California and all travelers wind up in Los Angeles," Julio said. "But not this traveler. I have lived there too long. I know that state too damn well. . . ."

"What do you mean?" I asked.

Suddenly he became sad and said: "It is hard to be a Filipino in California."

Not comprehending what he meant, I began to dream of going to California. Then we started for Sunnyside, listening eagerly to the train whistle piercing the summer sky. It was nearly ten in the evening when we reached Sunnyside. We circled the town, and then we saw the trains—every car bursting with fruit—screaming fiercely and chugging like beetles up and down the tracks. The voices of the trainmen came clearly through the night.

We stopped in the shadow of a water tower. Julio disappeared for a moment and came back.

"Our train leaves in an hour," he said. "I'll go around for something to eat. Wait for me here."

I waited for him to come back for several hours. The train left. Then I began to worry. I went to town and walked in the shadows, looking into the darkened windows of wooden houses. Julio had disappeared like a wind.

I returned to our rendezvous and waited all night. Early the next morning another train was ready to go; I ran behind the boxcars and climbed inside one. When the train began to move, I opened the door and looked sadly toward Sunnyside. Julio was there somewhere, friendless and alone in a strange town.

"Good-bye, Julio," I said. "And thanks for everything, Julio. I hope I will meet you again somewhere in America."

Then the train screamed and the thought of Julio hurt me. I stood peering outside and listening to the monotonous chugging of the engine. I knew that I could never be unkind to any Filipino, because Julio had left me a token of friendship, a seed of trust, that ached to grow to fruition as I rushed toward another city.

93

Jimmie Omura on Japanese American Resistance to the Draft, April 7, 1944

Japanese American military service during World War II went through several key phases. Before Pearl Harbor was attacked on December 7, 1941, the second-generation nisei were treated like other citizens and accepted as volunteers or drafted subsequent to Selective Service procedures implemented in late 1940. For a few months after the attack, there was a period of indecision when nisei were turned away from enlistment offices, although some of them were armed and guarding vital installations in Hawai'i. After spring 1942, however, in spite of their American citizenship, they were designated "enemy aliens." In January 1943, the War Department formally recruited nisei for a segregated combat unit. Then, in early 1944, the U.S. government imposed the draft on nisei still interned in the various concentration camps across the West. The volunteer enlistments evoked controversy within families and camps; the draft provoked resistance, and many nisei actively protested. Jimmie Omura, a columnist for the independent Rocky Shimpo *newspaper in Colorado, supported the draft resisters—but only in terms of their petition to have their status clarified. His actions displeased the leaders of the Japanese American Citizens League and the U.S. government, which accused him of seditious behavior, bordering on treason. This column references an earlier one in which he reminds the draft resisters that "unorganized draft resistance is not the proper method to pursue our grievances." After the war, the JACL leaders treated Omura as a pariah.*

Jimmie Omura, "Nisei America: Know the Facts." *The Rocky Shimpo*, April 7, 1944.

Nisei America
Know the Facts

By Jimmie Omura

The Rocky Shimpo Affirms Its Stand

In consideration of the various public charges leveled against the editorial policy of The Rocky Shimpo and the wholly unfounded cry of sedition raised by the national leaders of the JACL and sustained in part by the W.R.A., it would seem pertinent here today to restate our position on the matter of Nisei selective service in accordance with our editorial enunciation of Feb. 28th.

It was on the date—in an editorial entitled "Let Us Not Be Rash"—that we emphatically and unequivocally stated our position upon this great question, foreseeing as we did the probable attacks, which have now materialized, from quarters inimical to our interest.

We said:

"We further agree that the government should restore a large part of those rights BEFORE asking us to contribute our lives to the welfare of the nation—to sacrifice our lives on the field of battle."

We feel confident that we have been neither derelict in our duties or inconsistent in our policy on this much-discussed issue of selective service. Our words are plain. We have stood forthrightly on proper clarification of the disputed legal implication involved. The JACL and the WRA have contended that no issue exists. We do not agree.

In our mind, we hold a serious doubt that the Army can legally subject to military obligation citizens whose constitutional guarantees are under technical suspension and denial in the same manner as those whose rights are recognized and fully granted. The Rocky Shimpo has urged and supported any action seeking a clarification on this point.

However, we have not been amiss in exploring the various other facets of this question. In that same editorial, we seriously cautioned the Nisei public on any adverse action.

We said:

"We cannot conscientiously believe that by these sporadic actions anything concrete and fundamental can be achieved . . . We should think the matter through and in the ultimate end retain a proper regard for the implications and repercussions that in all probability would arise from our acts."

In no way have we attempted to present a lop-sided viewpoint as the JACL and others have contended. We think that we have been most fair in our presentation. We are not one bit troubled about sedition, for we see no seditious implication in our editorial demand for full restoration of constitutional rights as a prelude to military service.

The support we accord the Fair Play Committee as Heart Mountain is predicated simply upon our desire for authentic and authoritative clarication of the legal status of the Nisei as citizens. We have at no time supported that organization on any other point. We make no apologies for our stand now. We affirm once more our support of that body in seeking judicial and/or legislative clarification.

We fully comprehend that interests inimical to the welfare of this publication would attempt by whatever means available to discredit and injure our journalistic sovereignty simply because such persons are not in accord with our policy. Wherever no good causes exist, such people will employ that artful weapon of indirection and misrepresentation—generalities, innuendos and insinuations. These people seek to condemn us purely on implication—Implication as they interpret it to their own design and not as we state it.

94

Supreme Court: Ex Parte Mitsuye Endo,
December 18, 1944

This was a habeas corpus *case, the "ideal" test case selected by the Japanese American Citizens League in mid-1942. Endo was a Methodist and a U.S. citizen who did not speak Japanese. She had never been to Japan, and her brother was in the U.S. Army. Designed to force the government to release loyal American citizens from internment camps, Endo's case was filed on July 12, 1942 in San Francisco. The court took a year to dismiss the petition, apparently convinced by the government's argument that there was no way to separate the loyal from the disloyal among Japanese Americans. But the delay may also have been influenced by federal pressure to delay the inevitable decision to release Endo, which would force the closing of the camps. There was evidently partisan politics at work— Franklin Roosevelt, seeking his fourth presidential term in the 1944 election, felt that releasing the Japanese might weaken his support among the general population. When the case reached the U.S. Supreme Court, government lawyers realized there was no justification for the continued internment of admittedly loyal citizens like Endo, and the justices ruled unanimously in favor of the petition. As in the Korematsu case, it is instructive to review the opinions by Justices Murphy and Roberts (included here). Roberts agrees that Endo must be released but criticizes his colleagues for failing to confront the great constitutional questions generated by the case. For example, Endo was freed from internment but refused entry into the state of California, which continued to enforce exclusion laws. This is the least studied of the World War II constitutional cases and deserves more attention.*

Cases Argued and Decided in the Supreme Court of the United States, Book 89.
  Rochester, NY: The Lawyers Co-operative Publishing Co., 1945

Mr. Justice Douglas delivered the opinion of the Court:
    This case comes here on a certificate of the Court of Appeals for the Ninth Circuit. . . .
    Mitsuye Endo, hereinafter designated as the appellant, is an American citizen of Japanese ancestry. She was evacuated from Sacramento, California, in

1942, pursuant to certain military orders which we will presently discuss, and was removed to the Tule Lake War Relocation Center located at Newell, Modoc County, California. In July, 1942, she filed a petition for a writ of habeas corpus in the District Court of the United States for the Northern District of California, asking that she be discharged and restored to liberty. That petition was denied by the District Court in July, 1943, and an appeal was perfected to the Circuit Court of Appeals in August, 1943. Shortly thereafter appellant was transferred from the Tule Lake Relocation Center to the Central Utah Relocation Center located at Topaz, Utah, where she is presently detained. The certificate of questions of law was filed here on April 22, 1944, and on May 8, 1944, we ordered the entire record to be certified to this Court. . . .

Her petition for a writ of habeas corpus alleges that she is a loyal and law-abiding citizen of the United States, that no charge has been made against her, that she is being unlawfully detained, and that she is confined in the Relocation Center under armed guard and held there against her will.

It is conceded by the Department of Justice and by the War Relocation Authority that appellant is a loyal and law-abiding citizen. They make no claim that she is detained on any charge or that she is even suspected of disloyalty. Moreover, they do not contend that she may be held any longer in the Relocation Center. They concede that it is beyond the power of the War Relocation Authority to detain citizens against whom no charges of disloyalty or subversiveness have been made for a period longer than that necessary to separate the loyal from the disloyal and to provide the necessary guidance for relocation. But they maintain that detention for an additional period after leave clearance has been granted is an essential step in the evacuation program. . . .

First. We are of the view that Mitsuye Endo should be given her liberty. In reaching that conclusion we do not come to the underlying constitutional issues which have been argued. For we conclude that, whatever power the War Relocation Authority may have to detain other classes of citizens, it has no authority to subject citizens who are concededly loyal to its leave procedure. . . .

We do not mean to imply that detention in connection with no phase of the evacuation program would be lawful. The fact that the Act and the orders are silent on detention does not of course mean that any power to detain is lacking. Some such power might indeed be necessary to the successful operation of the evacuation program. At least we may so assume. Moreover, we may assume for the purposes of this case that initial detention in Relocation Centers was authorized. But we stress the silence of the legislative history and of the Act and the Executive Orders on the power to detain to emphasize that any such authority which exists must be implied. If there is to be the greatest possible accommodation of the liberties of the citizen with this war measure, any such implied power must be narrowly confined to the precise purpose of the evacuation program.

A citizen who is concededly loyal presents no problem of espionage or sabotage. Loyalty is a matter of the heart and mind, not of race, creed, or color. He who is loyal is by definition not a spy or a saboteur. When the power to detain is derived from the power to protect the war effort against espionage and sabotage, detention which has no relationship to that objective is unauthorized.

Nor may the power to detain an admittedly loyal citizen or to grant him a conditional release be implied as a useful or convenient step in the evacuation program, whatever authority might be implied in case of those whose loyalty was not conceded or established. If we assume (as we do) that the original evacuation was justified, its lawful character was derived from the fact that it was an espionage and sabotage measure, not that there was community hostility to this group of American citizens. The evacuation program rested explicitly on the former ground not on the latter as the underlying legislation shows. The authority to detain a citizen or to grant him a conditional release as protection against espionage or sabotage is exhausted at least when his loyalty is conceded. . . . As the President has said of these loyal citizens:

"Americans of Japanese ancestry, like those of many other ancestries, have shown that they can, and want to, accept our institutions and work loyally with the rest of us, making their own valuable contribution to the national wealth and well-being. In vindication of the very ideals for which we are fighting this war it is important to us to maintain a high standard of fair, considerate, and equal treatment for the people of this minority as of all other minorities." . . .

The judgment is reversed and the cause is remanded to the District Court for proceedings in conformity with this opinion.

Reversed.

Mr. Justice Murphy, concurring:

I join in the opinion of the Court, but I am of the view that detention in Relocation Centers of persons of Japanese ancestry regardless of loyalty is not only unauthorized by Congress or the Executive but is another example of the unconstitutional resort to racism inherent in the entire evacuation program. As stated more fully in my dissenting opinion in Korematsu v. United States, decided this day [323 U.S. 233, ante, 208, 65 S. Ct. 193] racial discrimination of this nature bears no reasonable relation to military necessity and is utterly foreign to the ideals and traditions of the American people.

Moreover, the Court holds that Mitsuye Endo is entitled to an unconditional release by the War Relocation Authority. It appears that Miss Endo desires to return to Sacramento, California, from which Public Proclamations Nos. 7 and 11, as well as Civilian Exclusion Order No. 52, still exclude her. . . .

Mr. Justice Roberts:

I concur in the result but I cannot agree with the reasons stated in the opinion of the court for reaching that result.

As in Korematsu v. United States, No. 22 of this Term [323 U.S. 214, ante, 194, 65 S. Ct. 193] the court endeavors to avoid constitutional issues which are necessarily involved. The opinion, at great length, attempts to show that neither the executive nor the legislative arm of the Government authorized the detention of the relator.

1. With respect to the executive, it is said that none of the executive orders in question specifically referred to detention and the court should not imply any authorization of it. This seems to me to ignore patent facts. As the opinion discloses, the executive branch of the Government not only was aware of what was being done but in fact that which was done was formulated in regulations and in a so-called handbook open to the public. . . . I think it inadmissible to suggest that some inferior public servant exceeded the authority granted by executive order in this case. Such a basis of decision will render easy the evasion of law and the violation of constitutional rights, for when conduct is called in question the obvious response will be that, however much the superior executive officials knew, understood, and approved the conduct of their subordinates, those subordinates in fact lacked a definite mandate so to act. It is to hide one's head in the sand to assert that the detention of relator resulted from an excess of authority by subordinate officials. . . .

3. I conclude, therefore, that the court is squarely faced with a serious constitutional question, —whether the relator's detention violated the guarantees of the Bill of Rights of the federal Constitution and especially the guarantee of due process of law. There can be but one answer to that question. An admittedly loyal citizen has been deprived of her liberty for a period of years. Under the Constitution she should be free to come and go as she pleases. Instead, her liberty of motion and other innocent activities have been prohibited and conditioned. She should be discharged.

95

Supreme Court: Korematsu v. United States, December 18, 1944

Fred Toyosaburo Korematsu did not intend to become a constitutional test case. His decision to avoid removal from his home area, even to the extent of plastic surgery on his face, rested on his determination to remain with his Italian American fiancée. But he was arrested and decided to fight the order excluding him from San Leandro, California. The case was bitterly contested within the U.S. Supreme Court; by the time it was argued (October 11–12, 1944) and determined (December 18, 1944), several justices had changed their minds about the constitutionality of the drastic removal and internment of an entire ethnic group in the name of military necessity. Historians have long looked to the dissenting opinions of Justices Murphy and Jackson to find redeeming strands in the tangled web of judicial reasoning that constitutionally validated America's concentration camps. Jackson, in particular, warned that the decision rationalized a "principle of racial discrimination" that "lies about like a loaded weapon ready for the hand of any authority that can bring forward a plausible claim of an urgent need." And Murphy astutely raised serious concerns about Lt. General John L. DeWitt's "Final Report" on the evacuation—relied upon by the Supreme Court majority—in which the executive branch of the government suppressed vital evidence disputing the military necessity argument. Korematsu was convicted and, for years after the war, was ignored by the world. In the 1980s, as part of the Asian American civil rights movement, attorneys and researchers, including Jack Herzig and Aiko Yoshinaga-Herzig, uncovered evidence of suppression. That and the use of an obscure legal device, the writ of error coram nobis that allowed for reopening cases after the statute of limitations had run out, allowed Minoru Yasui, Gordon Hirabayashi, and Fred Korematsu to successfully return to court to have their cases vacated.

United States Reports, Volume 323: Cases Adjudged in the Supreme Court. Washington, DC: Government Printing Office, 1945.

Mr. Justice Black delivered the opinion of the Court.

The petitioner, an American citizen of Japanese descent, was convicted in a federal district court for remaining in San Leandro, California, a "Military

Area," contrary to Civilian Exclusion Order No. 34 of the Commanding General of the Western Command, U. S. Army, which directed that after May 9, 1942, all persons of Japanese ancestry should be excluded from that area. No question was raised as to petitioner's loyalty to the United States. . . .

It should be noted, to begin with, that all legal restrictions which curtail the civil rights of a single racial group are immediately suspect. That is not to say that all such restrictions are unconstitutional. It is to say that courts must subject them to the most rigid scrutiny. Pressing public necessity may sometimes justify the existence of such restrictions; racial antagonism never can. . . .

In *Hirabayashi* v. *United States*, 320 U. S. 81, we sustained a conviction obtained for violation of the curfew order. The Hirabayashi conviction and this one thus rest on the same 1942 Congressional Act and the same basic executive and military orders, all of which orders were aimed at the twin dangers of espionage and sabotage. . . .

We upheld the curfew order as an exercise of the power of the government to take steps necessary to prevent espionage and sabotage in an area threatened by Japanese attack.

In the light of the principles we announced in the *Hirabayashi* case, we are unable to conclude that it was beyond the war power of Congress and the Executive to exclude those of Japanese ancestry from the West Coast war area at the time they did. True, exclusion from the area in which one's home is located is a far greater deprivation than constant confinement to the home from 8 p.m. to 6 a.m. Nothing short of apprehension by the proper military authorities of the gravest imminent danger to the public safety can constitutionally justify either. But exclusion from a threatened area, no less than curfew, has a definite and close relationship to the prevention of espionage and sabotage. The military authorities, charged with the primary responsibility of defending our shores, concluded that curfew provided inadequate protection and ordered exclusion. They did so, as pointed out in our *Hirabayashi* opinion, in accordance with Congressional authority to the military to say who should, and who should not, remain in the threatened areas. . . .

Like curfew, exclusion of those of Japanese origin was deemed necessary because of the presence of an unascertained number of disloyal members of the group, most of whom we have no doubt were loyal to this country. It was because we could not reject the finding of the military authorities that it was impossible to bring about an immediate segregation of the disloyal from the loyal that we sustained the validity of the curfew order as applying to the whole group. In the instant case, temporary exclusion of the entire group was rested by the military on the same ground. . . .

It is now argued that the validity of the exclusion order cannot be considered apart from the orders requiring him, after departure from the area, to report and to remain in an assembly or relocation center. The contention is that we must treat these separate orders as one and inseparable; that, for this reason, if detention in the assembly or relocation center would have illegally deprived the petitioner of his liberty, the exclusion order and his conviction under it cannot stand.

We are thus being asked to pass at this time upon the whole subsequent detention program in both assembly and relocation centers, although the only issues framed at the trial related to petitioner's remaining in the prohibited area in violation of the exclusion order. . . . These separate requirements were that those of Japanese ancestry (1) depart from the area; (2) report to and temporarily remain in an assembly center; (3) go under military control to a relocation center there to remain for an indeterminate period until released conditionally or unconditionally by the military authorities. Each of these requirements, it will be noted, imposed distinct duties in connection with the separate steps in a complete evacuation program. . . .

The *Endo* case, *post*, p. 283, graphically illustrates the difference between the validity of an order to exclude and the validity of a detention order after exclusion has been effected. . . .

Since the petitioner has not been convicted of failing to report or to remain in an assembly or relocation center, we cannot in this case determine the validity of those separate provisions of the order. It is sufficient here for us to pass upon the order which petitioner violated. . . .

Korematsu was not excluded from the Military Area because of hostility to him or his race. He *was* excluded because we are at war with the Japanese Empire, because the properly constituted military authorities feared an invasion of our West Coast and felt constrained to take proper security measures, because they decided that the military urgency of the situation demanded that all citizens of Japanese ancestry be segregated from the West Coast temporarily, and finally, because Congress, reposing its confidence in this time of war in our military leaders—as inevitably it must—determined that they should have the power to do just this. There was evidence of disloyalty on the part of some, the military authorities considered that the need for action was great, and time was short. We cannot—by availing ourselves of the calm perspective of hindsight— now say that at that time these actions were unjustified.

Affirmed.

Mr. Justice Murphy, dissenting.

This exclusion of "all persons of Japanese ancestry, both alien and non-alien," from the Pacific Coast area on a plea of military necessity in the absence of martial law ought not to be approved. Such exclusion goes over "the very brink of constitutional power" and falls into the ugly abyss of racism.

In dealing with matters relating to the prosecution and progress of a war, we must accord great respect and consideration to the judgments of the military authorities who are on the scene and who have full knowledge of the military facts. The scope of their discretion must, as a matter of necessity and common sense, be wide. And their judgments ought not to be overruled lightly by those whose training and duties ill-equip them to deal intelligently with matters so vital to the physical security of the nation.

At the same time, however, it is essential that there be definite limits to military discretion, especially where martial law has not been declared. Individuals must not be left impoverished of their constitutional rights on a plea of military necessity that has neither substance nor support. . . .

The judicial test of whether the Government, on a plea of military necessity, can validly deprive an individual of any of his constitutional rights is whether the deprivation is reasonably related to a public danger that is so "immediate, imminent, and impending" as not to admit of delay and not to permit the intervention of ordinary constitutional processes to alleviate the danger. . . .

It must be conceded that the military and naval situation in the spring of 1942 was such as to generate a very real fear of invasion of the Pacific Coast, accompanied by fears of sabotage and espionage in that area. The military command was therefore justified in adopting all reasonable means necessary to combat these dangers. In adjudging the military action taken in light of the then apparent dangers, we must not erect too high or too meticulous standards; it is necessary only that the action have some reasonable relation to the removal of the dangers of invasion, sabotage and espionage. But the exclusion, either temporarily or permanently, of all persons with Japanese blood in their veins has no such reasonable relation. And that relation is lacking because the exclusion order necessarily must rely for its reasonableness upon the assumption that *all* persons of Japanese ancestry may have a dangerous tendency to commit sabotage and espionage and to aid our Japanese enemy in other ways. It is difficult to believe that reason, logic or experience could be marshalled in support of such an assumption.

That this forced exclusion was the result in good measure of this erroneous assumption of racial guilt rather than bona fide military necessity is evidenced by the Commanding General's Final Report on the evacuation from the Pacific Coast area. In it he refers to all individuals of Japanese descent as "subversive," as belonging to "an enemy race" whose "racial strains are undiluted," and as constituting "over 112,000 potential enemies . . . at large today" along the Pacific Coast. In support of this blanket condemnation of all persons of Japanese descent, however, no reliable evidence is cited to show that such individuals were generally disloyal, or had generally so conducted themselves in this area as to constitute a special menace to defense installations or war industries, or had otherwise by their behavior furnished reasonable ground for their exclusion as a group.

Justification for the exclusion is sought, instead, mainly upon questionable racial and sociological grounds not ordinarily within the realm of expert military judgment, supplemented by certain semi-military conclusions drawn from an unwarranted use of circumstantial evidence. . . .

The military necessity which is essential to the validity of the evacuation order thus resolves itself into a few intimations that certain individuals actively aided the enemy, from which it is inferred that the entire group of Japanese Americans could not be trusted to be or remain loyal to the United States. No one denies, of course, that there were some disloyal persons of Japanese descent on the Pacific Coast who did all in their power to aid their ancestral land. Similar disloyal activities have been engaged in by many persons of German, Italian and even more pioneer stock in our country. But to infer that examples of individual disloyalty prove group disloyalty and justify discriminatory action against the entire group is to deny that under our system of law individual guilt is the sole basis for deprivation of rights. Moreover, this inference, which is at the very heart of the evacuation orders, has been used in support of the abhorrent and despicable treatment of minority groups by the dictatorial tyrannies which this nation is now pledged to destroy. To give constitutional sanction to that inference in this case, however well-intentioned may have been the military command on the Pacific Coast, is to adopt one of the cruelest of the rationales used by our enemies to destroy the dignity of the individual and to encourage and open the door to discriminatory actions against other minority groups in the passions of tomorrow. . . .

I dissent, therefore, from this legalization of racism. Racial discrimination in any form and in any degree has no justifiable part whatever in our democratic way of life. It is unattractive in any setting but it is utterly revolting among a free people who have embraced the principles set forth in the Constitution of the United States. All residents of this nation are kin in some way by blood or culture to a foreign land. Yet they are primarily and necessarily a part of the new and distinct civilization of the United States. They must accordingly be treated at all times as the heirs of the American experiment and as entitled to all the rights and freedoms guaranteed by the Constitution.

Mr. Justice Jackson, dissenting.

Korematsu was born on our soil, of parents born in Japan. The Constitution makes him a citizen of the United States by nativity and a citizen of California by residence. No claim is made that he is not loyal to this country. . . .

Now, if any fundamental assumption underlies our system, it is that guilt is personal and not inheritable. Even if all of one's antecedents had been convicted of treason, the Constitution forbids its penalties to be visited upon him, for it provides that "no attainder of treason shall work corruption of blood, or forfeiture except during the life of the person attainted." But here is an attempt to make an otherwise innocent act a crime merely because this prisoner is the son of parents as to whom he had no choice, and belongs to a race from which there is no way to resign. . . .

In the very nature of things, military decisions are not susceptible of intelligent judicial appraisal. They do not pretend to rest on evidence, but are made on information that often would not be admissible and on assumptions that could not be proved. Information in support of an order could not be disclosed to courts without danger that it would reach the enemy. Neither can courts act on communications made in confidence. Hence courts can never have any real alternative to accepting the mere declaration of the authority that issued the order that it was reasonably necessary from a military viewpoint.

Much is said of the danger to liberty from the Army program for deporting and detaining these citizens of Japanese extraction. But a judicial construction of the due process clause that will sustain this order is a far more subtle blow to liberty than the promulgation of the order itself. A military order, however unconstitutional, is not apt to last longer than the military emergency. Even during that period a succeeding commander may revoke it all. But once a judicial opinion rationalizes such an order to show that it conforms to the Constitution, or rather rationalizes the Constitution to show that the Constitution sanctions such an order, the Court for all times has validated the principle of racial discrimination in criminal procedure and of transplanting American citizens. The principle then lies about like a loaded weapon ready for the hand of any authority that can bring forward a plausible claim of an urgent need. . . .

96

War Brides Act (Public Law 271), December 28, 1945

This legislation provided for nonquota admission of foreign women who married American servicemen overseas during and after World War II. While this was a boon to many whose wives came from Europe, much more dramatic impact was felt in Asian American communities, where immigration had been almost nonexistent for many years.* There were many Japanese "war brides" married to Japanese Americans (especially those who had been in the Military Intelligence Service) and to others. These women were important culture bearers who helped the United States continue a tradition of linkages to Japan and its heritage. But the critical impact was on Chinese American communities, where the gender imbalance caused by immigration restrictions had stunted family and community development. In the years immediately after World War II and the Korean War, about 7,000 Chinese women accompanied American husbands to the United States. Most of them had married Chinese American servicemen—thus dramatically adding both numbers and cultural influence to these communities.

United States Statutes at Large Containing the Laws and Concurrent Resolutions Enacted During the First Session of the Seventy-ninth Congress of the United States of America, 1945, vol. 59. Washington, DC: Government Printing Office, 1946.

An Act
To expedite the admission to the United States
of alien spouses and alien minor children of citizen
members of the United States armed forces

Be it enacted by the Senate and House of Representatives of the United States of America in Congress assembled, That notwithstanding any of the several clauses of section 3 of the Act of February 5, 1917, excluding physically and mentally de-

---

**This law, through an amendment in 1947, opened the door to substantial immigration of women from Asia.*

fective aliens, and notwithstanding the documentary requirements of any of the immigration laws or regulations, Executive orders, or Presidential proclamations issued thereunder, alien spouses or alien children of United States citizens serving in, or having an honorable discharge certificate from the armed forces of the United States during the Second World War shall, if otherwise admissible under the immigration laws and if application for admission is made within three years of the effective date of this Act, be admitted to the United States: *Provided*, That every alien of the foregoing description shall be medically examined at the time of arrival in accordance with the provisions of section 16 of the Act of February 5, 1917, and if found suffering from any disability which would be the basis for a ground of exclusion except for the provision of this Act, the Immigration and Naturalization Service shall forthwith notify the appropriate public medical officer of the local community to which the alien is destined: *Provided further*, That the provisions of this Act shall not affect the duties of the United States Public Health Service so far as they relate to quarantinable diseases.

Sec. 2. Regardless of section 9 of the Immigration Act of 1924, any alien admitted under section 1 of this Act shall be deemed to be a nonquota immigrant as defined in section 4 (a) of the Immigration Act of 1924.

Sec. 3. Any alien admitted under section 1 of this Act who at any time returns to the United States after a temporary absence abroad shall not be excluded because of the disability or disabilities that existed at the time of that admission.

Sec. 4. No fine or penalty shall be imposed under the Act of February 5, 1917, except those arising under section 14, because of the transportation to the United States of any alien admitted under this Act.

Sec. 5. For the purpose of this Act, the Second World War shall be deemed to have commenced on December 7, 1941, and to have ceased upon the termination of hostilities as declared by the President or by a joint resolution of Congress.

Approved December 28, 1945.

PART 5

The Pacific Ocean: An American Lake?: Through 1975

The crushing defeat of the Japanese empire, punctuated by the detonation of atomic bombs over Hiroshima and Nagasaki on August 6 and 9, 1945, confirmed the status of the United States as the preeminent military and political power throughout the Pacific—both Rim and Basin. The subsequent Cold War between the United States and the Soviet Union would dominate global politics for the rest of the century. In Asia and the Pacific, this confrontation had critical ramifications that directly affected Asian American communities. The heightened presence of America in Asia was neither unchallenged nor unlimited, but America's foreign policies continued to play a major role in defining Asian American fortunes. This was a period of intense change and radically new developments on the home front. The total number of Asian Americans would grow from perhaps half a million at the end of World War II to about three million in 1975, and from a group dominated by those of Japanese, Chinese, and Filipino descent to one diversified by a large influx of immigrants and refugees from China, the Philippines, Korea, Southeast Asia, and South Asia.

In Asia, the twin forces of nationalism and communism, sometimes inseparably linked, combined to heighten confrontation with this new American frontier. Even in the Philippines, which received its independence in 1946, the United States continued to maintain a crucial military presence through Clark Air Force Base and Subic Bay Naval Base. Many Filipinos continued to join the U.S. Navy, especially as service personnel such as stewards in mess halls, both on ships and at bases in California, Maryland, and Virginia. The 1949 victory of the Chinese Communist Party over the American-supported Kuomintang was immediately followed by a vicious war on the Korean peninsula in 1950. When Vietnamese Communists defeated the French in the 1950s, the United States was inexorably drawn into an ultimately disastrous war in Southeast Asia that did not end until 1975. In the meantime, Japan became America's most important ally in Asia and almost immediately began receiving substantial aid to re-develop its shattered economy.

All these events in Asia and the Pacific had direct and critical impact on the development of Asian American communities. Some changes had begun during

World War II, including the lifting of absolute restrictions against Chinese immigration and naturalization. Within a year of the war's end, the Luce-Celler Bill allowed for a token number (100) of Asian Indians to enter the country. Congress extended naturalization rights to Filipinos who had arrived before March 24, 1943. The War Brides Act provided the mechanism for more than 700 Chinese and 2,000 Japanese women to immigrate between 1947 and 1953. The Korean War, 1950–53, and subsequent American occupation intensified interaction between U.S. troops and local women, with intermarriages and adoptions increasing the numbers of Asian Americans.

These shooting wars—and the Cold War—routinely generated more Asian immigrants. After the Communist victory in 1949, some 5,000 Chinese were granted special refugee status. In 1959, Chinese who could not prove they had immigrated legally were allowed to participate in a "confession" program that pardoned undocumented aliens and granted residency privileges. Our anticommunist fervor resulted in large communities of immigrants from similar countries like Cuba and Hungary. But one long-term result of this unending stream of major wars in Asia was the exacerbation of historical stereotypes of Asians as fanatical, desperate, sneaky enemies who had little or no respect for human life, especially coming from societies where numbers were so great and individuality was so denigrated. Following hard on the heels of the half century of anti-Japanese bias was hostility toward a more generic "Asian" enemy. It was in this period that the term "gook" became widely used and commonly accepted. One concrete result of the complexity of these concurrent developments was that growing numbers of GIs were willing to marry and bring home Asian women, but there were increasing reports of serious abuse, including racist outbursts, by their husbands.

Unfortunately, official acts of rejection did not end with the war. Perhaps the most egregious example was the 1946 Rescission Act targeting thousands of men in the Philippines who responded to Roosevelt's call to serve in the U.S. Army. Filipino veterans alone were denied financial and other benefits promised to foreign nationals who served in the American military during World War II. Congress accomplished this by appropriating $200 million for the Philippine military and making the newly independent Philippine government responsible for subsequent support. The anticommunist "witch hunts" also targeted Chinese and some Koreans, forcing many promising scientists back to their Asian homelands. For example, in *Kimm v. Rosenberg* in 1960, a Korean national was deported because, like many others, he asserted his rights guaranteed by the Fifth Amendment to the Constitution and refused to answer when asked whether he was a communist.

But this was also a period of general progress on many other fronts for Asian Americans. The fact that Japan had quickly become an ally led gradually to improved treatment of Japanese Americans. Japan was providing a critical staging area for the United States in all Asian military conflicts after World War II and had become its crucial ideological partner. By 1948 the Japanese American Claims Act was beginning to produce modest redress payments to compensate for losses incurred as a result of removal from the West Coast. No more than 10 cents on the dollar (in 1942 dollars), the payments were pitifully inadequate, but they pointed to a changed climate. In that same year, the courts ruled that Japanese aliens could not be barred from fishing, an occupation in which many had flourished before World War II. In 1952, Sei Fujii successfully sued California to end its alien land law that since 1913 had prevented purchase of real property by Japanese immigrants. Securing civil and human rights for Japanese Americans accompanied progress toward the signing of the peace treaty, finally, between the United States and Japan in San Francisco in 1951.

There were some ironies. Even as some Chinese were being forced back to China as potentially sympathetic to the Communist regime, others were admitted as refugees from the mainland. At the same time, larger historical forces were being unleashed, including global initiatives to push back the borders of colonialism and imperialism. Those efforts inevitably led to more intense domestic movements for equality and justice, especially since World War II had demonstrated the bankruptcy of Nazism. President Harry Truman finally ordered an end to segregation of military troops in 1948. In 1952 the McCarran-Walter Immigration and Nationality Act finally established an immigration quota for Japan and provided naturalization rights for Japanese immigrants. This was a significant step forward for Japanese Americans, partly due to improved international conditions, skillful use of their World War II military exploits in segregated units in Europe, and the lobbying efforts of the Japanese American Citizens League. In 1956, Dalip Singh Saund became the first Asian American elected to Congress. Born in India, Saund was a scholar and businessman who served three terms in the House of Representatives until disabled by a stroke.

The admission of Hawai'i as the fiftieth state in the union came in 1959, when many of these positive steps had weakened the most virulent manifestations of anti-Asian racism. Opponents of statehood for Hawai'i often pointed to the fact that two thirds of the population was nonwhite and that the plurality was of Japanese descent. Thus, statehood would almost surely bring "Japs" into Congress. They were correct: in the very first election, Japanese American Daniel Inouye became a Congressman, while Chinese American Hiram Fong was sent to the U.S. Senate. In 1964, Patsy Takemoto Mink became America's first Asian American woman elected to Congress. These individual political victories were the tip of a surfacing iceberg in Hawai'i, major breakthroughs in social, economic, and political spheres. The most visible sign of change came with the election of 1954, when the Democratic Party, dominated by Asian Americans, for the first time controlled territorial politics. The emergence of many Americans of Japanese ancestry (AJAs) as elected Democrats, many of whom were World War II veterans, was dramatic.

Probably more fundamentally important, however, was the momentum created by organizing victories on the plantations and the docks by the International Longshoremen's and Warehousemen's Union (ILWU) immediately after the war. The strategies developed in the late 1930s and during the war, when organizing was prohibited, released enormous pent-up energies, and Hawaii's agricultural labor soon became the best compensated in the world. The process of creating the multiethnic labor movement sowed the seeds for Democratic Party electoral success nearly a decade later. One indication of the ILWU threat to Republican/business elite hegemony was the red-baiting unleashed during the longshoremen's strike in 1949.

But the crucial change for all Asian Americans came in 1965, with the watershed legislation eliminating the old "national origins" quota system established in the 1920s to favor immigration from Anglo-Saxon Europe. Although designed primarily to facilitate reunification of families from those same countries, the act inadvertently opened the gates to a dramatically different form of increase from Latin America and Asia. Growth for Asian American communities to that point had been slow and tortured because of massive racist obstacles. These new regulations encouraged immigration by family members and people with skills required for postwar economic development. Large numbers began arriving from China, Taiwan, the Philippines, Vietnam, India, and Korea. With the U.S. retreat from Southeast Asia and our obligations to those in jeopardy because they had supported American military and political efforts, refugees from Vietnam, Cambodia, and Laos began arriving after the fall of Saigon in 1975.

Domestically, the civil rights movement continued apace with voting rights acts, desegregation policies, and affirmative action efforts on a broad array of fronts. Even antimiscegenation walls crumbled as California ended its ban in 1948 and the U.S. Supreme Court declared, in the 1967 Loving v. Virginia ruling, that state law criminalizing interracial marriage was unconstitutional. When the civil rights movement seemed to be faltering, after the assassinations of John and Robert Kennedy as well as Martin Luther King, Jr., Asian Americans established their own "Yellow Power" movement in urban centers like New York City, San Francisco, Berkeley, Honolulu, and Los Angeles as well as on university campuses.

Liberal and left-wing groups worked in ethnic-specific communities like Chinatowns while others created pan-Asian American or multiracial groups and coalitions. Many specifically referred to political and ideological affinity with anticolonial forces in Asia, including the communist forces in the Philippines and the People's Republic of China as well as the Viet Cong and the North Vietnamese. Channeling the surge of energy from a marginalized racial minority, groups like Basement Workshop in NYC created dynamic clusters of artist-activists. In Los Angeles, young filmmakers established Visual Communications ("VC") intent on energizing Asian American communities through cutting-edge technologies. On campuses, led by demands for an Ethnic Studies curriculum by San Francisco State University students in their celebrated 1968 strike, a movement to incorporate the history and heritage of Asian Americans spread across the country and has continued into the present.

By the 1970s, these movements had penetrated mainstream institutions well beyond university campuses. In 1971, *Gooey Hung Lee v. Johnson* forced desegregation of all public schools serving Chinese American students, while *Lau v. Nichols* in 1974 mandated bilingual education services for immigrant children with limited English backgrounds. At exactly the same time, the rise in Asian immigrant numbers created Asian American communities in which the foreign-born outnumbered the American-born, and technology and culture shifts were changing our very notions of acculturation and assimilation into "America."

The confluence of challenges to American hegemony in Asia and to racism at home created, by 1975, a highly unstable context for Asian Americans in the next quarter century. The three decades between the end of World War II and American defeat in Southeast Asia were marked by serious reforms in immigration, refugee, and naturalization policies as well as civil and human rights advances in many areas. At the same time, the new influx of Asians, including the undocumented, created conditions for ongoing exploitation, especially at the hands of those from their own ethnic groups.

97

Philippines Veterans Rescission Act, February 18, 1946

In 1941, months before the Japanese military attacked Pearl Harbor, President Franklin Roosevelt issued an order incorporating Filipino troops into the American armed forces. Many of these soldiers fought with the understanding that they would accrue benefits as a result of this formal relationship with the United States. But in 1946, after the war had ended and before the Philippines had been granted independence, Congress passed legislation that singled out Filipinos, among the many foreigners who had served the United States in World War II, to be denied a variety of benefits, including mustering-out pay, back pay under the Missing Persons Act, benefits from the Terminal Leave Act, and disability support. The Washington Post of June 17, 1947 issued an editorial condemning this action. One rationale was the fact that these soldiers were fighting for their own country, even though that was true of most other foreign soldiers as well. Another justification argued that the newly independent government of the Philippines should assume this burden, but it seemed clear that the major reason was the presumed cost, perhaps in excess of $1 billion, of dealing with approximately 400,000 veterans, and the fact that they were Asians. This discriminatory action has prompted responses, including civil disobedience at the White House, through the decades, and especially in the late 1990s when the veterans were entering their seventies and eighties.

United States Statutes at Large Containing the Laws and Concurrent Resolutions Enacted During the Second Session of the Seventy-ninth Congress of the United States of America, 1946, vol. 60. Washington, DC: Government Printing Office, 1947.

Army of the Philippines, $200,000,000: *Provided*, That service in the organized military forces of the Government of the Commonwealth of the Philippines, while such forces were in the service of the armed forces of the United States pursuant to the military order of the President of the United States dated July 26, 1941, shall not be deemed to be or to have been service in the military or naval forces of the United States or any component thereof for the purposes of any law of the United States conferring rights, privileges, or benefits upon any person by reason of the service of such person or the service of any other person in the military or naval forces of the United States or any component thereof, except benefits under (1) the National Service Life Insurance Act of 1940, as amended, under contracts heretofore entered into, and (2) laws administered by the Veterans' Administration providing for the payment of pensions on account of service-connected disability or death: *Provided further,* That such pensions shall be paid at the rate of one Philippine peso for each dollar authorized to be paid under the laws providing for such pensions: *Provided further,* That any payments heretofore made under any such law to or with respect to any member of the military forces of the Government of the Commonwealth of the Philippines who served in the service of the armed forces of the United States shall not be deemed to be invalid by reason of the circumstances that his service was not service in the military or naval forces of the United States or any component thereof within the meaning of such law.

98

Supreme Court: Torao Takahashi v. Fish and Game Commission, *June 7, 1948*

Torao Takahashi, a Japanese immigrant fisherman, sued California to issue him a commercial fishing license. Prior to World War II, Japanese fishermen played leading roles in developing commercial fishing on the West Coast and were routinely issued licenses. In 1943, with the Japanese in concentration camps, the Fish and Game Commission amended its code by prohibiting licenses to "alien Japanese." Then, in 1945, concerned that such explicit language might render them vulnerable to court challenges, the commissioners altered the amendment to target any "person ineligible to citizenship." For most Japanese who had lost boats, gear, buildings, profits, and careers, this latest move was gratuitous; they had already been driven out of the industry for good. Takahashi, however, decided to pursue the issue and won in June 1948.

Supreme Court Reporter, Volume 68. Cases Argued and Determined in the Supreme Court of the United States. St. Paul, MN: West Publishing Co., 1948.

U.S. Supreme Court
Torao Takahashi v. Fish and Game Commission, 334 U.S. 410

Mr. Justice BLACK delivered the opinion of the Court.

The respondent, Torao Takahashi, born in Japan, came to this country and became a resident of California in 1907. Federal laws, based on distinctions of "color and race," Hidemitsu Toyota v. United States, 268 U.S. 402, 411, 412, 565, 566, have permitted Japanese and certain other nonwhite racial groups to enter and reside in the country, but have made them ineligible for United States citizenship. The question presented is whether California can, consistently with the Federal Constitution and laws passed pursuant to it, use this federally created racial ineligibility for citizenship as a basis for barring Takahashi from earning his living as a commercial fisherman in the ocean waters off the coast of California. Prior to 1943 California issued commercial fishing licenses to all qualified persons without regard to alienage or ineligibility to citizenship. From

1915 to 1942 Takahashi, under annual commercial fishing licenses issued by the State, fished in ocean waters off the California coast, apparently both within and without the three-mile coastal belt, and brought his fresh fish ashore for sale. In 1942, while this country was at war with Japan, Takahashi and other California residents of Japanese ancestry were evacuated from the State under military orders. See Korematsu v. United States, 323 U.S. 214. In 1943, during the period of war and evacuation, an amendment to the California Fish and Game Code was adopted prohibiting issuance of a license to any "alien Japanese." Cal.Stats. 1943, ch. 1100. In 1945, the state code was again amended by striking the 1943 provision for fear that it might be "declared unconstitutional" because directed only "against alien Japanese"; the new amendment banned issuance of licenses to any "person ineligible to citizenship," which classification included Japanese. Cal.Stats. 1945, ch. 181.3 Because of this state provision barring issuance of commercial fishing licenses to persons ineligible for citizenship under federal law, Takahashi, who met all other state requirements, was denied a license by the California Fish and Game Commission upon his return to California in 1945.

Takahashi brought this action for mandamus in the Superior Court of Los Angeles County, California, to compel the Commission to issue a license to him. That court granted the petition for mandamus. It held that lawful alien inhabitants of California, despite their ineligibility to citizenship, were entitled to engage in the vocation of commercial fishing on the high seas beyond the three-mile belt on the same terms as other lawful state inhabitants, and that the California code provision denying them this right violated the equal protection clause of the Fourteenth Amendment. The State Supreme Court, three judges dissenting, reversed, holding that California had a proprietary interest in fish in the ocean waters within 3 miles of the shore, and that this interest justified the State in barring all aliens in general and aliens ineligible to citizenship in particular from catching fish within or without the three mile coastal belt and bringing them to California for commercial purposes. 30 Cal.2d 719, 185 P.2d 805, 808.4 To review this question of importance in the fields of federal-state relationships and of constitutionally protected individual equality and liberty, we granted certiorari. . . .

The contention is this: California owns the fish within three miles of its coast as a trustee for all California citizens as distinguished from its noncitizen inhabitants; as such trustee-owner, it has complete power to bar any or all aliens from fishing in the three-mile belt as a means of conserving the supply of fish; since migratory fish caught while swimming in the three-mile belt are indistinguishable from those caught while swimming in the adjacent high seas, the State, in order to enforce its three-mile control, can also regulate the catching and delivery to its coast of fish caught beyond the three mile belt under this Court's decision in Bayside Fish Co. v. Gentry, 297 U.S. 422. Its law denying fishing licenses to aliens ineligible for citizenship, so the state's contention goes, tends to reduce the number of commercial fishermen and therefore is a proper fish conservation measure; in the exercise of its power to decide what groups will be denied licenses, the State has a right if not a duty, to bar first of all aliens, who have no community interest in the fish owned by the State. Finally, the legislature's denial of licenses to those aliens who are "ineligible to citizenship" is defended as a reasonable classification, on the ground that California has simply followed the Federal Government's lead in adopting that classification from the naturalization laws.

First. The state's contention that its law was passed solely as a fish conservation measure is vigorously denied. The petitioner argues that it was the outgrowth of racial antagonism directed solely against the Japanese, and that for this reason alone it cannot stand. . . .

Second. It does not follow, as California seems to argue that because the United States regulates immigration and naturalization in part on the basis of race and color classifications, a state can adopt one or more of the same classifications to prevent lawfully admitted aliens within its borders from earning a living in the same way that other state inhabitants earn their living. The Federal Government has broad constitutional powers in determining what aliens shall be admitted to the United States, the period they may remain, regulation of their conduct before naturalization, and the terms and conditions of their naturalization. . . .

The Fourteenth Amendment and the laws adopted under its authority thus embody a general policy that all persons lawfully in this country shall abide 'in any state' on an equality of legal privileges with all citizens under non-discriminatory laws.

All of the foregoing emphasizes the tenuousness of the state's claim that it has power to single out and ban its lawful alien inhabitants, and particularly certain racial and color groups within this class of inhabitants, from following a vocation simply because Congress has put some such groups in special classifications in exercise of its broad and wholly distinguishable powers over immigration and naturalization. The state's law here cannot be supported in the employment of this legislative authority because of policies adopted by Congress in the exercise of its power to treat separately and differently with aliens from countries composed of peoples of many diverse cultures, races, and colors. For these reasons the power of a state to apply its laws exclusively to its alien inhabitants as a class is confined within narrow limits.

Third. We are unable to find that the "special public interest" on which California relies provides support for this state ban on Takahashi's commercial fishing . . . To whatever extent the fish in the three-mile belt off California may be "capable of ownership" by California, we think that "ownership" is inadequate to justify California in excluding any or all aliens who are lawful residents of the State from making a living by fishing in the ocean off its shores while permitting all others to do so. This leaves for consideration the argument that this law should be upheld on authority of those cases which have sustained state laws barring aliens ineligible to citizenship from land ownership. Assuming the continued validity of those cases, we think they could not in any event be controlling here. They rested solely upon the power of states to control the devolution and ownership of land within their borders, a power long exercised and supported on reasons peculiar to real property. They cannot be extended to cover this case.

The judgment is reversed and remanded for proceedings not inconsistent with this opinion.

Reversed.

Mr. Justice MURPHY, with whom Mr. Justice RUTLEDGE agrees, concurring.

The opinion of the Court, in which I join, adequately expresses my views as to all but one important aspect of this case. That aspect relates to the fact that 990 of the California Fish and Game Code, barring those ineligible to citizenship from securing commercial fishing licenses, is the direct outgrowth of antagonism toward persons of Japanese ancestry. Even the most cursory examination of the background of the statute demonstrates that it was designed solely to discriminate against such persons in a manner inconsistent with the concept of equal protection of the laws. Legislation of that type is not entitled to wear the cloak of constitutionality.

The statute in question is but one more manifestation of the anti-Japanese fever which has been evident in California in varying degrees since the turn of the century. See concurring opinion in Oyama v. California, 332 U.S. 633, 650, 277 and dissenting opinion in Korematsu v. United States, 323 U.S. 214, 233, 201. That fever, of course, is traceable to the refusal or the inability of certain groups to adjust themselves economically and socially relative to residents of Japanese ancestry. For some years prior to the Japanese attack on Pearl Harbor, these protagonists of intolerance had been leveling unfounded accusations and innuendoes against Japanese fishing crews operating off the coast of California. These fishermen numbered about a thousand and most of them had long resided in that state. It was claimed that they were engaged not only in fishing but in espionage and other illicit activities on behalf of the Japanese Government. As war with Japan approached and finally became a reality, these charges were repeated with increasing vigor. Yet full investigations by appropriate authorities failed to reveal any competent supporting evidence; not even one Japanese fisherman was arrested for alleged espionage. Such baseless accusations can only be viewed as an integral part of the long campaign to undermine the reputation of persons of Japanese background and to discourage their residence in California. . . .

Mr. Justice REED, dissenting.

The reasons which lead me to conclude that the judgment of the Supreme Court of California should be affirmed may be briefly stated. As fishing rights have been treated traditionally as a natural resource, in the absence of federal regulation, California as a sovereign state has power to regulate the taking and handling of fish in the waters bordering its shores. It is, I think, one of the natural resources of the state that may be preserved from exploitation by aliens. The ground for this power in the absence of any exercise of federal authority is California's authority over its fisheries.

The right to fish is analogous to the right to own land, a privilege which a state may deny to aliens as to land within its borders. Terrace v. Thompson, 263 U.S. 197.3 It is closely akin to the right to hunt, a privilege from which a state may bar aliens, if reasonably deemed advantageous to its citizens. A state's power has even been held to extend to the exclusion of aliens from the operation of pool and billiard halls when a city deemed them not as well qualified as citizens for the conduct of a business thought to have harmful tendencies. Clarke v. Deckebach, 274 U.S. 392.5

The Federal Government has not pursued a policy of equal treatment of aliens and citizens. Citizens have rights superior to those of aliens in the ownership of land and in exploiting natural resources. Perhaps Congress as a matter of immigration policy may require that states open every door of opportunity in America to all resident aliens, but until Congress so determines as to fisheries, I do not feel that the judicial arm of the Government should require the states to admit all aliens to this privilege. . . .

99

Honolulu Advertiser *Editorials:*
Hawaii Dock Strike, May 5 and 9, 1949

*The International Longshoremen's and Warehousemen's Union (ILWU) made sig-
nificant strides organizing Hawaii's workers on the docks and in plantation fields
beginning in the 1930s. The war stopped official organizing, but momentum increased rapidly after 1945. In 1949, the ILWU struck the docks, fighting for wage
parity with West Coast workers. In the prewar period, the newspapers, especially*
The Honolulu Advertiser, *weighed in on behalf of employers by relying on racial
scare tactics, as in the anti-Japanese editorials on and reporting of the 1909 and
1920 sugar strikes. But in the postwar, Cold War period, it made more sense to attack the union as subversive and responsive to "Joe" Stalin in the Soviet Union.
The shift from racism to ideology fit with the McCarthyism of that period. These
fabricated, heavy-handed "letters to Joe" became a staple on the front pages, creating a bizarre mix of red-baiting and antiunion sloganeering. "Pau" in the May
5 version is Hawaiian for "completed." "Wahines" in the May 9 "letter" is "female." The latter refers to the women, primarily upper class and white, who temporarily formed a "broom brigade" to "sweep" the rascals of the ILWU out and end
the strike. The strike ended with a solid union victory, marking the beginning of a
long period of working-class gains in Hawai'i.*

The Honolulu Advertiser (Honolulu, Hawai'i), May 5 and 9, 1949, 1. Thanks to Joan
Hori for retrieving these from Special Collections, Hamilton Library, University of
Hawai'i at Manoa.

Honolulu Advertiser
Hawaii's Territorial Newspaper
May 5, 1949

A Report to Joe . . . . . Progress!!

We're not Communists, you know—but just thought you'd like a report.

Things are going great down here in Hawaii, Joe. Employers are getting sore
and Joe Public's wondering what to do.

We've put a lot of guys on the bricks up at Crockett. The sugar gang is going nuts because before long all their warehouses will be full to busting and they'll have to shut down a bunch of plantation mills.

They'll be next—but we're stalling on sugar talks till they give in on the waterfront. Going to pull a stop work meeting on 23 plantations later on in the month—to keep 'em worried.

No kidding—We're going to have a first class mess going very shortly. You'd really be proud.

Some groups are getting scared and are hoarding rice. Same old story—somebody else goes hungry—but NOT ME!

A lot of little guys in business, who we say have been "starving their help" with low wages, will be out of business in a few weeks and you should hear them holler!

Not a thing in the world they can do but gripe and we're of course telling 'em like you do your boys, its rich guys who are back of it—and they believe it.

We scared the American President Lines into keeping the Cleveland outside all yesterday. That hit the taxi boys and the lei sellers—no business and a full ship. About 3,000 bucks wasn't spent in Honolulu. Tough, ain't it?

Boy—are they going to need tourists before we get finished.

Guess we ought to have asked for 62 cents an hour across the board instead of 32 cents—Then the guys in Frisco could strike for parity, too—and we'd tie these guys up again.

That's a good word—parity. Most of our group don't know what it means—but it sure sounds good.

Divide and rule! Does it work! We're dividing '

em fast. We'll rule 'em before too long.

P. S.

A bunch of guys at the Legislature just pau had us scared for a bit. Thought they might try and get a law to "protect" the community. But votes mean plenty—so there's nothing on the books to cause us trouble. And did we tell 'em what we'd do next time!

See you in China.

The Honolulu Advertiser
Hawaii's Territorial Newspaper
May 9, 1949

The Blockade Is Working, Joe!

People Are Beginning to Holler.

Berlin. Hawaii. Same thing, Joe! Blockade 'em! Starve 'em out. Bust 'em! Don't let them get things they got to have. Make 'em realize we ain't kidding. Not this time.

Thought you'd be glad to know about the Bakers' Association. Everyone of them is squawking and HOW!

They say in two weeks there'll be no more bread—or darn little. People will have to stand in breadlines.

Now ain't that really tough? Let's cry about it. Some bird suggested an "Operation Vittles" to save people in Hawaii.

Well, all we got to say is Congress is too busy and there ain't any International complications to get 'em interested—so we're safe. Hawaii's forgotten these days. No one in Washington gives a damn.

Canned milk is getting scarce, too, Joe. If some babies die, it'll raise hell, but why should these lousy business men moan about losing the profits on some canned milk?

You've showed us, Joe. We got to be tough in this racket. Well, all we got to say is "nuts." This is a showdown, Joe, and we don't think the employers got the guts to fight it out—cause they'll lose too much money.

We have preached that to the boys for years and proved it to 'em by getting raises each time.

You know, Joe, there's just one thing we ain't sure of—that's those little business guys.

Many of 'em are going bust and they don't like it. "Can't take it"—we tell the boys.

The big companies are a cinch—rules, regulations, lawyers, Boards of Directors—policies, ethics—all that sort of thing. But them little guys might be a pain in the neck.

And the wahines. The boys don't mind busting up scabs—and such guys. That's fun. But they ain't so dumb as to bust up wahines that's trying to protect their kids and homes.

P. S.

About 50 guys tieing up the whole island of Kauai. Ain't that a joke?

100

California Supreme Court:
Fujii Sei v. State of California, *April 17, 1952*

Like the Oyama v. California *U.S. Supreme Court case in 1948, this State Supreme Court case repealed previous alien land laws.* Oyama *forced the court to rule unconstitutional the 1920 law prohibiting immigrant Japanese from buying land in their minor children's names.* Fujii *went back to the original 1913 Webb Act that prohibited purchase of land by aliens "ineligible to naturalization" and challenged it directly. Interestingly, he did so first on the basis of the recently acknowledged United Nations Charter pledging member nations to promote the "observance of human rights and fundamental freedoms without distinction as to race." The court politely observed the "humane and enlightened objectives" of the charter but insisted that its provisions could not supersede existing domestic legislation. On the second point, however, the constitutionality of the alien land law itself, the court was divided but ruled in favor of the plaintiff. By 1949, as dissenting justice Schauer pointed out, Chinese, Filipinos, and Indians were eligible for naturalization; only Japanese and Polynesians remained ineligible. Moreover, as his opinion makes clear, there was still considerable hostility toward the Japanese, "the people of this late enemy nation, though perhaps unwillingly rescued from totalitarianism." In 1956, Californians finally voted to repeal the alien land laws, although the* Oyama *and* Fujii *cases, along with the* Masaoka *case (1952), effectively ended the discrimination against Japanese immigrants owning land. But, as the dissenting opinion by Justice Schauer indicates, there remained a significant reservoir of anti-Japanese hostility.*

Pacific Reporter, Second Series, Vol. 242 P. 2d: Cases Argued and Determined in the Courts of AZ, CA, etc. St. Paul, MN: West Publishing Co., 1952.

GIBSON, Chief Justice.

Plaintiff, an alien Japanese who is ineligible to citizenship under our naturalization laws, appeals from a judgment declaring that certain land purchased by him in 1948 had escheated to the state. There is no treaty between this country and Japan which confers upon plaintiff the right to own land, and the sole question presented on this appeal is the validity of the California alien land law.

United Nations Charter

It is first contended that the land law has been invalidated and superseded by the provisions of the United Nations Charter pledging the member nations to promote the observance of human rights and fundamental freedoms without distinction as to race. . . .

The humane and enlightened objectives of the United Nations Charter are, of course, entitled to respectful consideration by the courts and Legislatures of every member nation, since that document expresses the universal desire of thinking men for peace and for equality of rights and opportunities. The charter represents a moral commitment of foremost importance, and we must not permit the spirit of our pledge to be compromised or disparaged in either our domestic or foreign affairs. We are satisfied, however, that the charter provisions relied on by plaintiff were not intended to supersede existing domestic legislation, and we cannot hold that they operate to invalidate the alien land law.

Fourteenth Amendment of the Federal Constitution

The next question is whether the alien land law violates the due process and equal protection clauses of the Fourteenth Amendment. Plaintiff asserts, first, that the statutory classification of aliens on the basis of eligibility to citizenship is arbitrary for the reason that discrimination against an ineligible alien bears no reasonable relationship to promotion of the safety and welfare of the state. He points out that the land law distinguishes not between citizens and aliens, but between classes of aliens, and that persons eligible to citizenship are given all the rights of citizens regardless of whether they desire or intend to become naturalized. Secondly, he contends that the effect of the statute, as well as its purpose, is to discriminate against aliens solely on the basis of race and that such discrimination is arbitrary and unreasonable.

[9, 10] The issue of the constitutionality of the alien land law is thus again presented to this court, and we are met at the outset with the contention that a reexamination of the question is foreclosed by decisions of the United States Supreme Court rendered in 1923 upholding the statute. . . .

This objection is a serious one, and we have rejected it only after the most careful deliberation. . . .

The holding of the United States Supreme Court in the Oyama case was that a presumption declared by section 9 of the alien land law violated the rights of citizens who were children of ineligible aliens and discriminated against such citizens solely because of their parents' ancestry. . . .

By its terms the land law classifies persons on the basis of eligibility to citizenship, but in fact it classifies on the basis of race or nationality. This is a necessary consequence of the use of the express racial qualifications found in the federal code. Although Japanese are not singled out by name for discriminatory treatment in the land law, the reference therein to federal standards for naturalization which exclude Japanese operates automatically to bring about that result. . . .

Subsequent to the Oyama case the Supreme Court condemned the enforcement by state courts of covenants which restrict occupancy of real property on the basis of race or color, and it expressly pointed out that statutes incorporating such restrictions would violate the Fourteenth Amendment. . . .

It is well established that all aliens lawfully in this country have a right "to work for a living in the common occupations of the community." . . .

The truth is that the right to earn a living in many occupations is inseparably connected with the use and enjoyment of land. Farming, for example, is one of the most ancient and common ways of making a living, but the rule of the Porterfield case permits a state, in the absence of treaty, to so restrict an ineligible alien resident that he can farm land only in the capacity of an employee or hired hand. . . .

The California alien land law is obviously designed and administered as an instrument for effectuating racial discrimination, and the most searching examination discloses no circumstances justifying classification on that basis. There is nothing to indicate that those alien residents who are racially ineligible for citizenship possess characteristics which are dangerous to the legitimate interests of the state, or that they, as a class, might use the land for purposes injurious to public morals, safety or welfare. Accordingly, we hold that the alien land law is invalid as in violation of the Fourteenth Amendment.

The judgment is reversed. . . .

CARTER, Justice.

I concur in the judgment of reversal. . . .

[citing article by Blake Clark in *The Freeman*, July 16, 1951] "Before the end of World War II, the United States and Nazi Germany were the only two major nations that used race as a test for naturalization. Now, *we alone* maintain this discrimination. In Asia we face a well-organized minority attempting to unite the East against us. We can show the people of the Orient we stand back of our national pledge of 'liberty and justice for all' by welcoming worthy persons and providing them equality under our naturalization and immigration laws. From a purely selfish standpoint, wiping discrimination off the books as well as out of our hearts would be worth more to us in the Orient than a dozen army divisions." . . .

SCHAUER, Justice (dissenting and concurring).

This case is remarkable and regrettable in judicial annals for this reason: A majority of the justices of this court join in an opinion which recognizes the law as it is but refuses to follow it.

There is no question as to what the law is. It was enacted in the year 1920 by the people of California through the initiative (Deering's Gen. Laws, Act 261); it is based, as to the classification established, on an act of the Congress of the United States; for the past thirty-two years this law, as will appear more fully in the cases hereinafter cited and discussed, has been consistently upheld by this court and by the Supreme Court of the United States as against the precise attack now made on it. But now, say the majority, upon an elaborate analysis of the trend of recent decisions of the Supreme Court of the United States, they think that that court, if the question were to be again presented to it might or would change its holding. The most careful study of the majority opinion discloses no other legal basis for their holding than this conjecture. . . .

The majority opinion, I think, is not motivated by an effort to find the law, and to uphold it as found. I think it stems more from the strong social views of the justices who write it and from their desire to make the law what they think it should be. But whether this law should be modified or repealed or continued in force is not, I think, a proper subject for our debate or ruling. The people enacted it and, as already noted, the only classification it makes is created by an act of the Congress of the United States. By constitutional processes the people, if they will, can amend or repeal it or the Congress can abolish the classification. But until and unless the people or the Congress act by the constitutional process, the law should not unnecessarily be stricken down by judicial intervention.

That the justices who join in striking down this law find it obnoxious to their personal social views and to their concepts of desirable international relations is quite understandable, and that they shall examine the law in the light of their personal views and concepts is of course a part of our judicial process. But our legitimate judicial process likewise requires that we indulge every reasonable presumption in favor of the validity of a law whether we like it or not; that, when personal views and public law differ, we subjugate our personal social views and concepts to the law adopted by the people; and that we not strike down as unconstitutional any law which, consistently with constitutional precepts, can be sustained. That this law can be sustained is indubitably demonstrated by the plain fact that for twenty-two years it has been sustained both by this court and the United States Supreme Court. . . .

This case today is probably not of such immediately grave importance to the citizens of California, and to the United States as a nation, as it would have been prior to the events of the period between December 7, 1941, and August 14, 1945. The long-planned occupation and conquest of California by Japan has been at least for the foreseeable future averted. That nation, finally defeated at horrible cost to the United States and to other freedom-loving peoples of the world, as well as to itself, is now building a new government. It is to be hoped that this new government may in time prove its right to, and thereupon be welcomed in, the family of nations as a champion of peace and good will and a defender against aggressors, their stealth, their devices, their cunning and their violence. It is indeed to be fervently hoped that the people of this late enemy nation, though perhaps unwillingly rescued from totalitarianism, may espouse the principles of democracy, and of forthrightness, honesty, reason and gentleness for their own government and in their dealings with all. . . .

101

McCarran-Walter Immigration and Nationality Act, June 27, 1952

This legislation eliminated all restrictions on naturalization, finally allowing Japanese immigrants to become American citizens. It followed earlier legislation permitting Chinese, Filipinos, and Asian Indians to naturalize. It also equalized policies dealing with gender. Its major limitation was the retention of the quota system that severely limited immigration from Asian and Pacific nations. The act also broadened definitions of deportable and excludable aliens and those of potentially subversive intent, creating language to validate possible mass detention. And, while the elimination of the 1917 "barred zone" was positive, a new term, "the Asia Pacific triangle," permitted a maximum of only 2,000 immigrants from the nineteen countries included. One further limitation was the section requiring any immigrant who traced half or more of her or his ancestry to the Asia-Pacific triangle nations to be counted against that country's meager quota, no matter where the actual locus of emigration. Thus, third-generation Portuguese, in Portugal, of Indian descent were assigned to the Indian quota. This practice was restricted to Asian-Pacific peoples. President Harry Truman, feeling the act did not go far enough to remove objectionable elements, vetoed the bill, but he was overriden by Congress. In later years, Truman, Eisenhower, Kennedy, and Johnson worked to eliminate the racially restrictive quota system.

United States Statutes at Large, 1952, vol. 66. Washington, DC: Government Printing Office, 1953.

TITLE II — IMMIGRATION

Chapter 1 — Quota System

Numerical Limitations; Annual Quota Based Upon National Origin; Minimum Quotas
Sec. 201. (a) The annual quota of any quota area shall be one-sixth of 1 per centum of the number of inhabitants in the continental United States in 1920,

which number, except for the purpose of computing quotas for quota areas within the Asia-Pacific triangle, shall be the same number heretofore determined under the provisions of section 11 of the Immigration Act of 1924, attributable by national origin to such quota area: *Provided*, That the quota existing for Chinese persons prior to the date of enactment of this Act shall be continued, and, except as otherwise provided in section 202 (e), the minimum quota for any quota area shall be one hundred.

(b) The determination of the annual quota of any quota area shall be made by the Secretary of State, the Secretary of Commerce, and the Attorney General, jointly. Such officials shall, jointly, report to the President the quota of each quota area, and the President shall proclaim and make known the quotas so reported. Such determination and report shall be made and such proclamation shall be issued as soon as practicable after the date of enactment of this Act. Quotas proclaimed therein shall take effect on the first day of the fiscal year, or the next fiscal half year, next following the expiration of six months after the date of the proclamation, and until such date the existing quotas proclaimed under the Immigration Act of 1924 shall remain in effect. . . .

Determination of Quota to Which an Immigrant Is Chargeable

Sec. 202. (a) Each independent country, self-governing dominion, mandated territory, and territory under the international trusteeship system of the United Nations, other than the United States and its outlying possessions and the countries specified in section 101 (a) (27) (C), shall be treated as a separate quota area when approved by the Secretary of State. All other inhabited lands shall be attributed to a quota area specified by the Secretary of State. . . .

(5) notwithstanding the provisions of paragraphs (2), (3), and (4) of this subsection, any alien who is attributable by as much as one-half of his ancestry to a people or peoples indigenous to the Asia-Pacific triangle defined in subsection (b) of this section, unless such alien is entitled to a nonquota immigrant status under paragraph (27) (A), (27) (B), (27) (D), (27) (E), (27) (F), or (27) (G) of section 101 (a), shall be chargeable to a quota as specified in subsection (b) of this section. . . .

(b) With reference to determination of the quota to which shall be chargeable an immigrant who is attributable by as much as one-half of his ancestry to a people or peoples indigenous to the Asia-Pacific triangle comprising all quota areas and all colonies and other dependent areas situate wholly east of the meridian sixty degrees east of Greenwich, wholly west of the meridian one hundred and sixty-five degrees west, and wholly north of the parallel twenty-five degrees south latitude —

1. there is hereby established, in addition to quotas for separate quota areas comprising independent countries, self-governing dominions, and territories under the international trusteeship system of the United Nations situate wholly within said Asia-Pacific triangle, an Asia-Pacific quota of one

hundred annually, which quota shall not be subject to the provisions of subsection (e);

2. such immigrant born within a separate quota area situate wholly within such Asia-Pacific triangle shall not be chargeable to the Asia-Pacific quota, but shall be chargeable to the quota for the separate quota area in which he was born;

3. such immigrant born within a colony or other dependent area situate wholly within said Asia-Pacific triangle shall be chargeable to the Asia-Pacific quota;

4. such immigrant born outside the Asia-Pacific triangle who is attributable by as much as one-half of his ancestry to a people or peoples indigenous to not more than one separate quota area, situate wholly within the Asia-Pacific triangle, shall be chargeable to the quota of that quota area;

5. such immigrant born outside the Asia-Pacific triangle who is attributable by as much as one-half of his ancestry to a people or peoples indigenous to one or more colonies or other dependent areas situate wholly within the Asia-Pacific triangle, shall be chargeable to the Asia-Pacific quota;

6. such immigrant born outside the Asia-Pacific triangle who is attributable by as much as one-half of his ancestry to peoples indigenous to two or more separate quota areas situate wholly within the Asia-Pacific triangle, or to a quota area or areas and one or more colonies and other dependent areas situate wholly therein, shall be chargeable to the Asia-Pacific quota.

(c) Any immigrant born in a colony or other component or dependent area of a governing country for which no separate or specific quota has been established, unless a nonquota immigrant as provided in section 101 (a) (27) of this Act, shall be chargeable to the quota of the governing country, except that (1) not more than one hundred persons born in any one such colony or other component or dependent area overseas from the governing country shall be chargeable to the quota of its governing country in any one year, and (2) any such immigrant, if attributable by as much as one-half of his ancestry to a people or peoples indigenous to the Asia-Pacific triangle, shall be chargeable to a quota as provided in subsection (b) of this section.

(d) The provision of an immigration quota for a quota area shall not constitute recognition by the United States of the political transfer of territory from one country to another, or recognition of a government not recognized by the United States.

(e) After the determination of quotas has been made as provided in section 201, revision of the quotas shall be made by the Secretary of State, the Secretary of Commerce, and the Attorney General, jointly, whenever necessary, to provide for any change of boundaries resulting in transfer of territory from one sovereignty to another, a change of administrative arrangements of a colony or other dependent area, or any other political change, requiring a change in the list of quota areas or of the territorial limits thereof, but any increase in the number of minimum quota areas above twenty within the Asia-Pacific triangle shall result in a proportionate decrease in each minimum quota of such area in order that the sum total of all minimum quotas within the Asia-Pacific triangle shall not exceed two thousand. In the case of any change in the territorial limits of quota areas, not requiring a change in the quotas for such areas, the Secretary of State shall, upon recognition of such change, issue appropriate instructions to all consular offices concerning the change in the territorial limits of the quota areas involved. . . .

102

Supreme Court: Kwong Hai Chew v. Colding, et al., *February 9, 1953*

Kwong Hai Chew brought suit against the Attorney General because he had been ordered permanently excluded from the United States as an alien whose entry was deemed prejudicial to the public interest. Chew was refused the right to a hearing on the ground that the order was based on confidential information that should not be disclosed lest the public interest be compromised. Given the circumstances, the information was likely to involve China and communism. In this case, the Supreme Court ruled against the federal government because the plaintiff was a permanent resident who was a merchant seaman on a ship of American registry, home ported in the United States. The fact that his ship had entered ports in the "Far East" undoubtedly contributed to official suspicions. The court had permitted fairly wide latitude for immigration or justice officials to deny foreigners seeking first entry into the country. But it cited the due process clause of the Fifth Amendment, assuring protection to all lawful permanent residents, in insisting that he was at least entitled to know the nature of the charges before being expelled and deported. Chew had served during World War II in the U.S. Merchant Marine. The government's action in this case was consistent with a wholesale assault on Chinese American political and intellectual freedoms after the victory of Mao Tse-tung and the Communist Party in China.

United States Reports Volume 344: Cases Adjudged in the Supreme Court. Washington, DC: Government Printing Office, 1953.

Kwong Hai Chew v. Colding et al.
Certiorari to the United States Court of Appeals for the Second Circuit

Petitioner is an alien and a lawful permanent resident of the United States, who currently maintains his residence in the United States and usually is physically present there. While returning from a voyage to foreign ports as a seaman on a vessel of American registry with its home port in the United States, he was detained on board by an order of the Attorney General and ordered "temporarily excluded" from the United States under 8 CFR 175.57 (b). . . .

Mr. Justice Burton delivered the opinion of the Court.

A preliminary consideration that is helpful to the solution of this litigation is whether, under 8 CFR 175.57 (b), the Attorney General has authority to deny to a lawful permanent resident of the United States, who is an alien continuously residing and physically present therein, the opportunity to be heard in opposition to an order for his "permanent exclusion" and consequent deportation, provided the Attorney General determines that the order is based on information of a confidential nature, the disclosure of which would be prejudicial to the public interest. Assuming, as seems to be clear, that the Attorney General does not have such authority, the critical issue then presented is whether he has that authority under the following additional circumstances: the resident alien is a seaman, he currently maintains his residence in the United States and usually is physically present there, however, he is returning from a voyage as a seaman on a vessel of American registry with its home port in the United States, that voyage has included scheduled calls at foreign ports in the Far East, and he is detained on board by order of the Attorney General. For the reasons hereafter stated, we hold that these additional circumstances do not change the result and that the Attorney General does not have the authority suggested.

Petitioner, Kwong Hai Chew, is a Chinese seaman last admitted to the United States in 1945. Thereafter, he married a native American and bought the home in which they reside in New York. Having proved his good moral character for the preceding five years, petitioner secured suspension of his deportation. In 1949, he was admitted to permanent residence in the United States as of January 10, 1945. In World War II, he served with credit in the United States Merchant Marine. He never has had any difficulty with governmental authorities. In April, 1950, he filed a petition for naturalization which is still pending. In November, 1950, he was screened and passed by the Coast Guard for employment as a seaman on a merchant vessel. In the same month he signed articles of employment as chief steward on the S. S. *Sir John Franklin*, a vessel of American registry with its home port in New York City. The voyage was to include calls at several foreign ports in the Far East. He remained aboard the vessel on this voyage but, at San Francisco, in March, 1951, the immigration inspector ordered him "temporarily excluded," under 8 CFR 175.57, as an alien whose entry was deemed prejudicial to the public interest.

On the vessel's arrival in New York, March 29, petitioner's "temporary exclusion" was continued and he was not permitted to land. March 30, he sought a writ of habeas corpus from the United States District Court for the Eastern District of New York, charging that his detention was arbitrary and capricious and a denial of due process of law in violation of the Fifth Amendment to the Constitution of the United States. Purporting to act under 8 CFR 175.57 (b), the Attorney General directed that petitioner be denied a hearing before a

Board of Special Inquiry and that his "temporary exclusion be made permanent." The Attorney General continues to deny petitioner all information as to the nature and cause of any accusations against him and all opportunity to be heard in opposition to the order for his "exclusion." He is detained at Ellis Island "for safekeeping on behalf of the master of the S. S. 'Sir John Franklin.'"

The writ was issued but, after a hearing, it was dismissed by the District Court. 97 F. Supp. 592. The Court of Appeals for the Second Circuit affirmed. 192 F. 2d 1009. Both courts relied upon *Knauff v. Shaughnessy*, 338 U. S. 537. We granted certiorari because of the doubtful applicability of that decision and the importance of the issue in the administration of the Nation's immigration and naturalization program. 343 U. S. 933. . . .

The issue is petitioner's detention, without notice of any charge against him and without opportunity to be heard in opposition thereto. Petitioner contends that such detention is not authorized by 8 CFR 175.57 (b). He contends also that, if that regulation does purport to authorize such detention, the regulation is invalid as an attempt to deprive him of his liberty without due process of law in violation of the Fifth Amendment. Agreement with petitioner's first contention makes it unnecessary to reach his second.

The case of *Knauff v. Shaughnessy, supra*, relied upon below, is not in point. It relates to the rights of an alien entrant and does not deal with the question of a resident alien's right to be heard. For purposes of his constitutional right to due process, we assimilate petitioner's status to that of an alien continuously residing and physically present in the United States. . . .

It is well established that if an alien is a lawful permanent resident of the United States and remains physically present there, he is a person within the protection of the Fifth Amendment. He may not be deprived of his life, liberty or property without due process of law. Although it later may be established, as respondents contend, that petitioner can be expelled and deported, yet before his expulsion, he is entitled to notice of the nature of the charge and a hearing at least before an executive or administrative tribunal. Although Congress may prescribe conditions for his expulsion and deportation, not even Congress may expel him without allowing him a fair opportunity to be heard. For example, he is entitled to a fair chance to prove mistaken identity. At the present stage of the instant case, the issue is not one of exclusion, expulsion or deportation. It is one of legislative construction and of procedural due process. . . .

Petitioner's final contention is that if an alien is a lawful permanent resident of the United States and also is a seaman who has gone outside of the United States on a vessel of American registry, with its home port in the United States, and, upon completion of such voyage, has returned on such vessel to the United States and is still on board, he is still, from a constitutional point of view, a person entitled to procedural due process under the Fifth Amendment. We do not regard the constitutional status which petitioner indisputably enjoyed prior to his voyage as terminated by that voyage. From a constitutional point of view, he is entitled to due process without regard to whether or not, for immigration purposes, he is to be treated as an entrant alien, and we do not now reach the question whether he is to be so treated. . . .

While it may be that a resident alien's ultimate right to remain in the United States is subject to alteration by statute or authorized regulation because of a voyage undertaken by him to foreign ports, it does not follow that he is thereby deprived of his constitutional right to procedural due process. His status as a person within the meaning and protection of the Fifth Amendment cannot be capriciously taken from him. . . .

This preservation of petitioner's right to due process does not leave an unprotected spot in the Nation's armor. Before petitioner's admission to permanent residence, he was required to satisfy the Attorney General and Congress of his suitability for that status. Before receiving clearance for his foreign cruise, he was screened and approved by the Coast Guard. Before acceptance of his petition for naturalization, as well as before final action thereon, assurance is necessary that he is not a security risk. . . .

For the reasons stated, we conclude that the detention of petitioner, without notice of the charges against him and without opportunity to be heard in opposition to them, is not authorized by 8 CFR 175.57 (b). Accordingly, the judgment of the Court of Appeals is

Reversed and the cause remanded to the District Court.

103

Supreme Court: Kimm v. Rosenberg, June 13, 1960

In 1960, John F. Kennedy was elected president, partly by proclaiming a suspect (actually nonexistent) "missile gap" with the Soviet Union. And while there were many potential confrontations in Europe because of the Berlin Wall and in the Americas, especially over Cuba, a series of crises occurred in Asia, eventually culminating in the wars involving Vietnam, Cambodia, and Laos. The Korean War in the early 1950s was an integral part of this global confrontation—indeed, it is sometimes forgotten that the last three major military commitments in which significant numbers of American lives were lost were World War II, the Korean War, and the war in Southeast Asia; in all of these conflicts, Asians were often indiscriminately cast as enemies. In 1960, Korean immigrant Kimm was ordered deported; he did not contest the order but petitioned for suspension at the discretion of the Attorney General under 19 (c) of the Immigration Act of 1917. This provision allowed for exceptions based on evidence of good moral character. Kimm had entered the United States in 1928 and studied and worked here for several decades, and was generally found to be of good character. The immigration officer, for some unknown reason, asked whether he was a member of the Communist Party. Being a Communist was prima facie evidence of bad character. Kimm refused to answer, claiming Fifth Amendment privilege against self-incrimination. The U.S. Supreme Court upheld lower court rulings that Kimm failed to provide evidence as to the Communist Party question and thus was automatically ineligible for suspension of deportation. Justice Douglas criticized the majority for thus making the use of the Fifth Amendment the basis of inferring guilt. Among the largely unasked questions is why, in all the Supreme Court documents, we never find reference to Mr. Kimm's full name.

United States Reports, Volume 363, Cases Adjudged in the U.S. Supreme Court at October Term, 1959. Washington, DC: Government Printing Office, 1960.

Kimm v. Rosenberg, District Director, Immigration and Naturalization Service
363 U.S. 405

Petitioner applied for suspension of an order directing his deportation to Korea or permitting his voluntary departure. He does not question the validity of the deportation order, but contends that he is within the eligible statutory class whose deportation may be suspended at the discretion of the Attorney General. 19 (c) of the Immigration Act of 1917, as amended. Relief on this score was denied on the basis that the Attorney General has no power to exercise his discretion in that regard since petitioner failed to prove his eligibility under that section and the Internal Security Act of 1950.

Before the hearing officer, petitioner was asked if he was a member of the Communist Party. He refused to answer, claiming the Fifth Amendment privilege against self-incrimination. The officer refused the suspension on the grounds that petitioner had failed to prove that he was a person of good moral character and that he had not met the statutory requirement of showing that he was not a member of or affiliated with the Communist Party. The Board of Immigration Appeals affirmed on the latter ground, as did the Court of Appeals. 263 F. 2d 773.

Petitioner contends that he presented "clear affirmative evidence" as to eligibility which stands uncontradicted and that the burden was on the Government to show his affiliations, if any, with the Party. He contends that the disqualifying factor of Communist Party membership is an exception to 19 (c) which the Government must prove. We think not. Rather than a proviso, it is an absolute disqualification, since that class of aliens is carved out of the section at its very beginning by the words "other than one to whom subsection (d) of this section is applicable." Subsection (d) referred to aliens deportable under the Act of October 16, 1918. Section 22 of the Internal Security Act of 1950 amended the 1918 Act to include Communists, and thus terminated the discretionary authority under 19 (c) as to any alien who was deportable because of membership in the Communist Party. Petitioner offered no evidence on this point, although the regulations place on him the burden of proof as to "the statutory requirements precedent to the exercise of discretionary relief." 8 CFR, 1949 ed., 151.3 (e), as amended, 15 Fed. Reg. 7638. This regulation is completely consistent with 19 (c). The language of that section, in contrast with the statutory provisions governing deportation, imposes the general burden of proof upon the applicant.

It follows that an applicant for suspension, "a matter of discretion and of administrative grace," *Hintopoulos v. Shaughnessy*, 353 U. S. 72, 77 (1957), must, upon the request of the Attorney General, supply such information that is within his knowledge and has a direct bearing on his eligibility under the statute. The Attorney General may, of course, exercise his authority of grace through duly delegated agents. *Jay v. Boyd*, 351 U. S. 345 (1956). Perhaps the petitioner was justified in his personal refusal to answer—a question we do not pass upon—but this did not relieve him under the statute of the burden of establishing the authority of the Attorney General to exercise his discretion in the first place.

Affirmed.

Mr. Justice Douglas, with whom The Chief Justice and Mr. Justice Black concur, dissenting.

It has become much the fashion to impute wrongdoing to or to impose punishment on a person for invoking his constitutional rights. Lloyd Barenblatt has served a jail sentence for invoking his First Amendment rights. See *Barenblatt v. United States*, 360 U. S. 109. As this is written, Dr. Willard Uphaus, as a consequence of our decision in *Uphaus v. Wyman*, 360 U. S. 72, is in jail in New Hampshire for invoking rights guaranteed to him by the First and Fourteenth Amendments. So is the mathematician, Horace Chandler Davis, who invoked the First Amendment against the House Un-American Activities Committee. *Davis v. United States*, 269 F. 2d 357 (C. A. 6th Cir.). Today we allow invocation of the Fifth Amendment to serve, in effect though not in terms, as proof that an alien lacks the "good moral character" which he must have under 19 (c) of the Immigration Act in order to become eligible for the dispensing powers entrusted to the Attorney General.

The import of what we do is underlined by the fact that there is not a shred of evidence of bad character in the record against this alien. The alien has fully satisfied the requirements of 19 (c) as shown by the record. He entered as a student in 1928 and pursued his studies until 1938. He planned to return to Korea but the outbreak of hostilities between China and Japan in 1937 changed his mind. Since 1938 he has been continuously employed in gainful occupations. That is the sole basis of his deportability. The record shows no criminal convictions, nothing that could bring stigma to the man. His employment since 1938 has been as manager of a produce company, as chemist, as foundry worker, and as a member of O. S. S. during the latter part of World War II. He also was self-employed in the printing business, publishing a paper "Korean Independence." No one came forward to testify that he was a Communist. There is not a word of evidence that he had been a member of the Communist Party at any time. The only thing that stands in his way of being eligible for suspension of deportation by the Attorney General is his invocation of the Fifth Amendment.

The statute says nothing about the need of an alien to prove he never was a Communist. If the question of Communist Party membership had never been asked and petitioner had never invoked the Fifth Amendment, can it be that he would still be ineligible for suspension? It is for me unthinkable. Presumption of innocence is too deeply ingrained in our system for me to believe that an alien would have the burden of establishing a negative. What the case comes down to is simply this: invocation of the Fifth Amendment creates suspicions and doubts that cloud the alien's claim of good moral character.

Imputation of guilt for invoking the protection of the Fifth Amendment carries us back some centuries to the hated oath *ex officio* used both by the Star Chamber and the High Commission. Refusal to answer was contempt. Thus was started in the English-speaking world the great rebellion against oaths that either violated the conscience of the witness or were used to obtain evidence against him. . . .

We therefore today make a marked departure from precedent when we attach a penalty for reliance on the Fifth Amendment. The Court in terms does not, and cannot, rest its decision on the ground that by invoking the Fifth Amendment the petitioner gave evidence of bad moral character. Yet the effect of its decision is precisely the same. In so holding we disregard history and, in the manner of the despised oath *ex officio*, attribute wrongdoing to the refusal to answer. It seems to me indefensible for courts which act under the Constitution to draw an inference of bad moral character from the invocation of a privilege which was deemed so important to this free society that it was embedded in the Bill of Rights. . . .

104

Children's Petition on Civil Rights Bill to Senator Hiram Fong, October 9, 1963

Hiram Fong, born into a family of poor immigrants from China, graduated from Harvard Law School in 1935 and became one of the first senators from the new state of Hawai'i and the first Chinese American senator (1959–77). He was a staunch Republican and a fiscal conservative but supported civil rights initiatives, including the landmark 1965 immigration reforms. He also championed the Civil Rights Act of 1964 that transformed race relations in the nation and probably helped to end President Lyndon Johnson's political career by alienating his southern supporters. Fong proudly presented this petition to the Senate and had it inserted in the Congressional Record. *The petition, written on a scroll 10 feet long by 2 feet wide and signed by 64 schoolchildren, 9 to 11 years old, was sent from Manoa Elementary School in Honolulu, Hawai'i. It urged passage of the bill, marrying the multicultural backgrounds of the signers to the urgency of the "Negro" issue. While clearly a product of teacher intervention, the petition did reflect the idealism of Asian American and other youths in Hawai'i and the impact upon their politicians in Washington, DC.*

Petition dated October 9, 1963. Thanks to Michaelyn Chou for providing reference to this petition. *Congressional Record*, October 16, 1963.

Honolulu, Hawaii,
October 9, 1963

Hon. Hiram Fong and Senators, U.S. Senate, Washington, D.C.

Honorable Sirs: May we have a moment of your precious time to discuss a matter of extreme consequence to us?

We are 64, 9- to 11-year-olds from Manoa Elementary School in Honolulu, Hawaii. In this nice school of ours we have all kinds of faces.

There are Filipino, Japanese, Chinese, Irish, Korean, Norwegian-German, Scottish-Irish, French-Japanese, and Hawaiian-Chinese faces. Religiously we represent Episcopalians, Buddhists, Friends, Baptists, Methodists. Protestants, and Catholics. We have fun learning and living together. (We have disagreements, too.) We would miss the different races and religions if they were gone. Today we play together, tomorrow we earn together.

How grateful we are to our country, the United States of America, for such equal opportunities. We have always been proud of our country. Now that we are a State, our pride and love are overflowing.

The civil turmoil that is presently afflicting America deeply troubles us. When you love a thing very much and it is in trouble you feel a need to help.

We are aware that our brains cannot encompass the entire problem. We have tried to read as much available material as possible and have carried on numerous discussions in school, with friends and at home. But of these reasons we are certain, and upon these principles therefore we urge you, the lawmakers of our land, for the passage of the civil rights bill.

In the beginning there was little difference between man and animal. When man hungered, he hunted and ate food without preparation and without fork or spoon. He roamed the earth with little clothing and shelter. He thought only of himself. He had little time for anything else.

Man has risen slowly from this crude form of living. In many ways he has become superior to other animals. He has made remarkable advances in communication and transportation. In only one way has he failed to keep pace with his scientific achievements. In the one sphere which should be of most concern—human needs—he has seemingly failed.

Numerous wars attest this fact. Since the early Egyptians, wars have been fought. Almost always the reason has been man's desire to suppress another idea, or thought or belief because it threatened, or differed from his own. He was responsible for brutal, regrettable action. He thought himself right but failed to see many times that right does not necessarily equal the truth.

We must believe in man. In what other species can we trust? The task of the human race is to lift ourselves and our brothers, not to subjugate them. Progress should not be measured at the price of human defeat.

We read of hungering children and thank our lucky stars we are born Americans. How thankful we are that our parents chose the United States as their country—or did they?

Even if we are only fifth and sixth graders, we know how we would choose if we had to make the choice today. But oftentimes children have no part in making such choices. The Negro child did not ask to be born Negro—he was born one.

Long ago our forefathers knew food was not the only substance for which man hungers. They knew of human needs, just as important as physical needs, human dignity, human worth, and friendship. So they endowed the American citizen with unalienable rights—liberty and the pursuit of happiness.

The goal of our country is in a way similar to the goals our parents have in raising us. They guide us to maturity so we can become independent individuals, economically, socially, and politically. As we grow we depend upon them for counsel and unconsciously or perhaps deliberately try to imitate them, because we are proud of them.

The democratic society to perpetuate itself must maintain a citizenship with deep maturity, intelligence, and a fearlessness for independent thought and action. To achieve this schools are provided.

We are members of such schools today. We are preparing for the future. How effective we become will depend in a large measure on the type of schooling we receive.

If a society provides inferior education and poor social adjustment for a group of its people the following will result: It will need to support continuously, at great expense financially and in heartaches "the educated and social cripples" it has helped to raise.

We have grandpas and grandmas at home. They once worked on plantations. They hardly speak English. However our fathers and mothers were permitted to attend the public schools in Hawaii.

Today we are proud of them. Some are nurses, accountants, Government workers, teachers, counselors, engineers, and architects. We feel our parents are really contributing to our State of Hawaii. There is still much to be done—but we have come a long way since 1855—when oriental laborers came to Hawaii.

This is one reason why we had to write this letter. The majority of the people of Hawaii are learning to become better citizens, because we have the opportunities to become such.

We were all a bit scared to even begin to write this letter. The task seemed too large for our small brains. But after our teacher read parts of J. S. Mill's essay "On Liberty," our duties and obligations were spelled out. We had to have inclinations and not bow to what is customary. We felt the need for our minds to escape the yoke of accepting what is commonly done or has been done for years and therefore regarded as right and truthful.

In today's world too many people are oppressed and unhappy. Many are merely struggling to exist day by day. Let democracy radiate hope for all men.

Let us begin at home. Let us begin with something as fundamental as civil rights. Let us begin to lift all men upward. Let us make real democracy, as P. W. Bridgman writes: "For, of course, the true meaning of a term is to be found by observing what a man does with it, not by what he says about it."

Then truly can we sing; our hearts lifted in pride, our minds unconfused, our voices singing true:

"This is my country
Grandest on earth . . . !"

Thank you for your time.
Sincerely yours.

Karen Yamamoto, Rayna Katekaru, Eloise Motonaga,
Beverlyn Nagaue, Carla Mizumoto, Terryl Leong, Rae Shiraki,
Elizabeth Hokada, Ruth Kaneshiro, Clesson Kawaski, Ronald Lee,
Clyan Ayabe, Tommy Lockhart, Charlotte Sonoda, Jay Komatsu,
Dwight Kono, Jo Ann Arakaki, Jocelyn Takaki, Karen Iwamoto,
Michelle Imata, Angela In, Heather Rognstad, Lani Joy Niino,
Debra Johnstone, Cheryl Ling, Joan Matsuzaki, Leslie Ogawa,
Dennis Hara, Roger Kuwahara, Rodney Leong, Brian Lee,
Mrs. Winifred Chang Young, Mark Rognstad, Carlton Shiraki,
Dale Oda, Stephen Nishimoto, Bonnie Katayama, Jane Miyake,
Aileen Komagome, Nori Kiyosaki, Elleen Yee, David Cox,
James Yano, Michael Nugent, Barbara Liner, Lynette Nishimura,
Leslie Harakawa, Allyn Miyashiro. Tina Tsuyemura, Samuel Cox,
Amy Kiriu, Howard Walker, Isaac Ishihara, Patricia Shimazu,
Danette Kong, Thomas Tomai, Michal Hong, Russel Yamashita,
Mason Chung, Oscar Ocopan, Susan Muramoto,
Susan Toyama, Wendy Suyetsugu.

105

Immigration and Nationality Act, October 3, 1965

This was by far the most important and far-reaching revision of American immigration policy since the 1924 Immigration Act. It is directly responsible for the dramatic growth in Asian American communities from less than one percent of the U.S. population in 1970 to about four percent in 2000 and significantly more in states like California, where approximately 10 percent of the population now traces its ancestry to Asia. The 1965 reform was intended to remove internationally embarrassing elements that dramatically discriminated against people of color outside the Western Hemisphere. But proponents of reform never expected major changes in the racial makeup of the country. The new law provided for 20,000 immigrants from each of the nations in the Eastern Hemisphere, with a total cap of 170,000 per year. Its basic features favored family unification—thus, immediate relatives of U.S. citizens were not subject to any quotas or limitations. The second big change was intended to meet the nation's business and social needs for people in specific occupations such as the professions or with special skills in the arts. But the designers of the preference system, outlined below, failed to understand the pent-up demands of the Asian nations/communities and the mechanisms by which immigration from that region might soar. There were seven categories or "preferences":

First preference: adult, unmarried sons and daughters of citizens.

Second preference: spouses and unmarried sons and daughters of lawful permanent resident aliens. Green card holders (permanent residents) may send for relatives in this category only.

Third preference: members of the professions or those with exceptional ability in the sciences or the arts—who can benefit the economy, cultural interests, or welfare of the United States.

Fourth preference: married sons or daughters of citizens.

Fifth preference: brothers or sisters of citizens.

Sixth preference: skilled or unskilled workers, not temporary, for which a shortage of employable persons exists.

Seventh preference: persons fleeing the Middle East, uprooted by natural calamity, and because of persecution due to race, religion, or political opinion from Communist or Communist-dominated countries.

United States Statutes at Large, 1965, vol. 79. Washington, DC: Government Printing Office, 1966.

An Act
To amend the Immigration and Nationality Act,
and for other purposes

Be it enacted by the Senate and House of Representatives of the United States of America in Congress assembled, That section 201 of the Immigration and Nationality Act (66 Stat. 175; 8 U.S.C. 1151) be amended to read as follows:

"Sec. 201. (a) Exclusive of special immigrants defined in section 101 (a) (27), and of the immediate relatives of United States citizens specified in subsection (b) of this section, the number of aliens who may be issued immigrant visas or who may otherwise acquire the status of an alien lawfully admitted to the United States for permanent residence, or who may, pursuant to section 203 (a) (7) enter conditionally, (i) shall not in any of the first three quarters of any fiscal year exceed a total of 45,000 and (ii) shall not in any fiscal year exceed a total of 170,000.

"(b) The 'immediate relatives' referred to in subsection (a) of this section shall mean the children, spouses, and parents of a citizen of the United States: *Provided,* That in the case of parents, such citizen must be at least twenty-one years of age. The immediate relatives specified in this subsection who are otherwise qualified for admission as immigrants shall be admitted as such, without regard to the numerical limitations in this Act.

"(c) During the period from July 1, 1965, through June 30, 1968, the annual quota of any quota area shall be the same as that which existed for that area on June 30, 1965. . . .

"(d) Quota numbers not issued or otherwise used during the previous fiscal year, as determined in accordance with subsection (c) hereof, shall be transferred to an immigration pool. Allocation of numbers from the pool and from national quotas shall not together exceed in any fiscal year the numerical limitations in subsection (a) of this section. The immigration pool shall be made available to immigrants otherwise admissible under the provisions of this Act who are unable to obtain prompt issuance of a preference visa due to oversubscription of their quotas, or subquotas as determined by the Secretary of State. Visas and conditional entries shall be allocated from the immigration pool within the percentage limitations and in the order of priority specified in section 203 without regard to the quota to which the alien is chargeable.

"(e) The immigration pool and the quotas of quota areas shall terminate June 30, 1968. Thereafter immigrants admissible under the provisions of this Act who are subject to the numerical limitations of subsection (a) of this section shall be admitted in accordance with the percentage limitations and in the order of priority specified in section 203."

Sec. 2. Section 202 of the Immigration and Nationality Act (66 Stat. 175; 8 U.S.C. 1152) is amended to read as follows:

"(a) No person shall receive any preference or priority or be discriminated against in the issuance of an immigrant visa because of his race, sex, nationality, place of birth, or place of residence, except as specifically provided in section 101 (a) (27), section 201 (b), and section 203: *Provided*, That the total number of immigrant visas and the number of conditional entries made available to natives of any single foreign state under paragraphs (1) through (8) of section 203 (a) shall not exceed 20,000 in any fiscal year: *Provided further*, That the foregoing proviso shall not operate to reduce the number of immigrants who may be admitted under the quota of any quota area before June 30, 1968.

"(b) Each independent country, self-governing dominion, mandated territory, and territory under the international trusteeship system of the United Nations, other than the United States and its outlying possessions shall be treated as a separate foreign state for the purposes of the numerical limitation set forth in the proviso to subsection (a) of this section when approved by the Secretary of State. All other inhabited lands shall be attributed to a foreign state specified by the Secretary of State. . . .

"(c) Any immigrant born in a colony or other component or dependent area of a foreign state unless a special immigrant as provided in section 101 (a) (27) or an immediate relative of a United States citizen as specified in section 201 (b), shall be chargeable, for the purpose of limitation set forth in section 202 (a), to the foreign state, except that the number of persons born in any such colony or other component or dependent area overseas from the foreign state chargeable to the foreign state in any one fiscal year shall not exceed 1 per centum of the maximum number of immigrant visas available to such foreign state.

"(d) In the case of any change in the territorial limits of foreign states, the Secretary of State shall, upon recognition of such change, issue appropriate instructions to all diplomatic and consular offices."

Sec. 3. Section 203 of the Immigration and Nationality Act (66 Stat. 175; 8 U.S.C. 1153) is amended to read as follows:

"Sec. 203. (a) Aliens who are subject to the numerical limitations specified in section 201 (a) shall be allotted visas or their conditional entry authorized, as the case may be, as follows:

"(1) Visas shall be first made available, in a number not to exceed 20 per centum of the number specified in section 201 (a) (ii), to qualified immigrants who are the unmarried sons or daughters of citizens of the United States.

"(2) Visas shall next be made available, in a number not to exceed 20 per centum of the number specified in section 201 (a) (ii), plus any visas not required for the classes specified in paragraph (1), to qualified immigrants who are the spouses, unmarried sons or unmarried daughters of an alien lawfully admitted for permanent residence.

"(3) Visas shall next be made available, in a number not to exceed 10 per centum of the number specified in section 201 (a) (ii), to qualified immigrants who are members of the professions, or who because of their exceptional ability in the sciences or the arts will substantially benefit prospectively the national economy, cultural interests, or welfare of the United States.

"(4) Visas shall next be made available, in a number not to exceed 10 per centum of the number specified in section 201 (a) (ii), plus any visas not required for the classes specified in paragraphs (1) through (3), to qualified immigrants who are the married sons or the married daughters of citizens of the United States.

"(5) Visas shall next be made available, in a number not to exceed 24 per centum of the number specified in section 201 (a) (ii), plus any visas not required for the classes specified in paragraphs (1) through (4), to qualified immigrants who are the brothers or sisters of citizens of the United States.

"(6) Visas shall next be made available, in a number not to exceed 10 per centum of the number specified in section 201 (a) (ii), to qualified immigrants who are capable of performing specified skilled or unskilled labor, not of a temporary or seasonal nature, for which a shortage of employable and willing persons exists in the United State.

"(7) Conditional entries shall next be made available by the Attorney General, pursuant to such regulations as he may prescribe and in a number not to exceed 6 per centum of the number specified in section 201 (a) (ii), to aliens who satisfy an Immigration and Naturalization Service officer at an examination in any non-Communist or non-Communist-dominated country, (A) that (i) because of persecution or fear of persecution on account of race, religion, or political opinion they have fled (I) from any Communist or Communist-dominated country or area, or (II) from any country within the general area of the Middle East, and (ii) are unable or unwilling to return to such country or area on account of race, religion, or political opinion, and (iii) are not nationals of the countries or areas in which their application for conditional entry is made; or (B) that they are persons uprooted by catastrophic natural calamity as defined by the President who are unable to return to their usual place of abode. For the purpose of the foregoing the term 'general area of the Middle East' means the area between and including (1) Libya on the west, (2) Turkey on the north, (3) Pakistan on the east, and (4) Saudi Arabia and Ethiopia on the south: *Provided,* That immigrant visas in a number not exceeding one-half the number specified in this paragraph may be made available, in lieu of conditional entries of a like number, to such aliens who have been continuously physically present in the United States for a period of at least two years prior to application for adjustment of status. . . .

106

Nguyen Thanh Trang, "North and South Vietnam Are Not Two Countries," 1966

Most Americans apprehend a Vietnamese presence in this country only after 1975, with the fall of Saigon and the influx of South Vietnamese officials and, later, refugees. But a small group was here earlier, and they were important in providing some measure of intelligent commentary on conditions in Vietnam even as the United States was assuming the major anticommunist role abandoned by the French after their defeat in 1954. This essay by a Vietnamese student in the United States tried to alert Americans to the fact that anticommunism could too easily morph into anti-Vietnamese ideology, especially if directed at splitting Vietnam into north versus south. At the time, in the mid-1960s, there continued to be official U.S. optimism that an anticommunist South Vietnam could be sustained with limited infusions of American troops buttressed with massive technological and military superiority. In the end, however, Trang was correct in predicting that any U.S. attempt to divide Vietnam into two countries would be defeated "sooner or later like the French in 1954." The document is unedited.

From bilingual Vietnamese student newsletter, "*Giao Dan*," vol. II, no. 2, March 1966. Published by The Vietnamese Students Group in New England. Thanks to Vu Hong Pham for providing a copy.

North and South Vietnam Are Not Two Countries

During the last few months the American people have been very much concerned about the situation in Viet Nam. More American soldiers have been sent to South Viet Nam, month after month and hundreds of them have been killed since 1957.

To help the public to understand President Johnson's policy and the war in Viet Nam, Television add Radio have given many special programs on Viet Nam, and many intellectuals have written articles about Viet Nam. But it seems to me very few of them have fully understood The People and The History of Viet Nam.

In an article on December 15, 1965 The Editor of the Washington Post has written:

"The assortment of different peoples in Viet Nam never was a country until the French tried to amalgamate them: and to say that the South is "one" with the North is like saying that Germany is part of France because Napoleon conquered it."

With almost the same tone, William C. Marlow on his article "History Lesson" published on December 16, 1965 in the DiamondBack (University of Maryland), made the following statements:

. . . "Raising the issue of Vietnamese nationalism is deceptive. Demographically, there are four nations in Viet Nam, the Tonkinese, the Anamese, the Chochinese and so-called montagnards."
. . . "If we were to support Nationalism in Viet Nam, we must support the dissolution of that country, not its reuniting."

When the American public is so concerned and so confused about the war going on in Viet Nam, such statements are serious and intolerable mistakes.

The truth is that the Vietnamese people, both North and South, are very proud of their united nationalistic spirit.

To say that Viet Nam has never been a country before is ridiculous and contrary to the History of Viet Nam. If the Viets have never unified, how could they defeat the Mongol Hordes of Genghis Khan in 1257? (We would like to remind the readers that Genghis Khan at that time has conquered most of territories in Asia and more than half of that of Europe). If the Viets have never unified, how could they defeat the French in 1954, when the French had tremendous supports from many countries in The Free World (and The United States was also France's ally)?

To say that the French tries to amalgamate and unify the Viets is just like saying that the Ku-Klux-Klan is helping to unify the Negroes with the White Americans! The opposite is true that the French have tried to "separate the Viets for domination and repression." In fact, those names Tonkinese, anamese and Chochinese were named by French colonists. If the American people do not believe that the South is "one with North, why does The United States support the present government of Gen. Nguyen Cao Ky in South Viet Nam, since he is from the North? No one in Viet Nam, communist or non-communist, living in the North or in the South would tolerate those people who consider that North and South Viet Nam are two countries. As Tran Quang Tri, a Vietnamese student answered in an interview given to American reporters, "We are intensely anti-communist but also intensely nationalistic."

To say that North and South Viet Nam are two countries is just like saying Sen. Edward Kennedy and Sen. Robert Kennedy are not brothers simply because one is living in Masachussetts and the other in New York.

The U.S.-GI's are fighting now in Viet Nam only against communist Vietnamese, if The United States attempts to make Viet Nam into two countries, American soldiers will have to fight communist Vietnamese and non-communist Vietnamese as well. Were this to happen there is no doubt that the U.S. will be defeated in Viet Nam sooner or later like the French in 1954.

Nguyen Thanh Trang
Vietnamese Student

107

Supreme Court: Loving et ux. v. Virginia, *June 12, 1967*

While this particular case, in which a white man and an African American woman were convicted for having been married, did not directly involve an Asian American, its resolution was very important to the equal protection clause as related to all people of color. Virginia was then one of sixteen states that continued to maintain statutes prohibiting interracial marriages with whites. Virginia argued that it did not violate the equal protection clause of the Fourteenth Amendment because it called for equal punishment for all parties regardless of race. William Marutani argued for reversal on behalf of the Japanese American Citizens League, as amicus curiae. In his opinion, Chief Justice Earl Warren cited the Hirabayashi and Korematsu cases to emphasize the need for the "most rigid scrutiny" when racial classifications are used in criminal cases, and that they then must be "necessary to the accomplishment of some permissible state objective." While many white-Asian couples lived outside the sixteen states, this decision freed them to live, legally, anywhere in the United States for the first time since antimiscegenation laws were implemented against them beginning in the nineteenth century.

United States Reports, Volume 388: Cases Adjudged in The Supreme Court at October Term, 1966. Washington, DC: Government Printing Office, 1968.

Loving et ux. v. Virginia
388 U.S. 1

Mr. Chief Justice Warren delivered the opinion of the Court.

This case presents a constitutional question never addressed by this Court: whether a statutory scheme adopted by the State of Virginia to prevent marriages between persons solely on the basis of racial classifications violates the Equal Protection and Due Process Clauses of the Fourteenth Amendment. For reasons which seem to us to reflect the central meaning of those constitutional commands, we conclude that these statutes cannot stand consistently with the Fourteenth Amendment.

In June 1958, two residents of Virginia, Mildred Jeter, a Negro woman, and Richard Loving, a white man, were married in the District of Columbia pursuant to its laws. Shortly after their marriage, the Lovings returned to Virginia and established their marital abode in Caroline County. At the October Term, 1958, of the Circuit Court of Caroline County, a grand jury issued an indictment charging the Lovings with violating Virginia's ban on interracial marriages. On January 6, 1959, the Lovings pleaded guilty to the charge and were sentenced to one year in jail; however, the trial judge suspended the sentence for a period of 25 years on the condition that the Lovings leave the State and not return to Virginia together for 25 years. He stated in an opinion that:

> "Almighty God created the races white, black, yellow, malay and red, and he placed them on separate continents. And but for the interference with his arrangement there would be no cause for such marriages. The fact that he separated the races shows that he did not intend for the races to mix."

After their convictions, the Lovings took up residence in the District of Columbia. On November 6, 1963, they filed a motion in the state trial court to vacate the judgment and set aside the sentence on the ground that the statutes which they had violated were repugnant to the Fourteenth Amendment. The motion not having been decided by October 28, 1964, the Lovings instituted a class action in the United States District Court for the Eastern District of Virginia requesting that a three-judge court be convened to declare the Virginia antimiscegenation statutes unconstitutional and to enjoin state officials from enforcing their convictions. On January 22, 1965, the state trial judge denied the motion to vacate the sentences, and the Lovings perfected an appeal to the Supreme Court of Appeals of Virginia. On February 11, 1965, the three-judge District Court continued the case to allow the Lovings to present their constitutional claims to the highest state court.

The Supreme Court of Appeals upheld the constitutionality of the antimiscegenation statutes and, after modifying the sentence, affirmed the convictions. The Lovings appealed this decision, and we noted probable jurisdiction on December 12, 1966, 385 U. S. 986.

The two statutes under which appellants were convicted and sentenced are part of a comprehensive statutory scheme aimed at prohibiting and punishing interracial marriages. . . .

Virginia is now one of 16 States which prohibit and punish marriages on the basis of racial classifications. Penalties for miscegenation arose as an incident to slavery and have been common in Virginia since the colonial period. The present statutory scheme dates from the adoption of the Racial Integrity Act of 1924, passed during the period of extreme nativism which followed the end of the First World War. The central features of this Act, and current Virginia law, are the absolute prohibition of a "white person" marrying other than another "white person," a prohibition against issuing marriage licenses until the issuing official is satisfied that the applicants' statements as to their race are correct, certificates of "racial composition" to be kept by both local and state registrars, and the carrying forward of earlier prohibitions against racial intermarriage. . . .

There can be no question but that Virginia's miscegenation statutes rest solely upon distinctions drawn according to race. The statutes proscribe generally accepted conduct if engaged in by members of different races. Over the years, this Court has consistently repudiated "[d]istinctions between citizens solely because of their ancestry" as being "odious to a free people whose institutions are founded upon the doctrine of equality." *Hirabayashi v. United States*, 320 U. S. 81, 100 (1943). At the very least, the Equal Protection Clause demands that racial classifications, especially suspect in criminal statutes, be subjected to the "most rigid scrutiny," *Korematsu v. United States*, 323 U. S. 214, 216 (1944), and, if they are ever to be upheld, they must be shown to be necessary to the accomplishment of some permissible state objective, independent of the racial discrimination which it was the object of the Fourteenth Amendment to eliminate. . . .

There is patently no legitimate overriding purpose independent of invidious racial discrimination which justifies this classification. The fact that Virginia prohibits only interracial marriages involving white persons demonstrates that the racial classifications must stand on their own justification as measures designed to maintain White Supremacy. We have consistently denied the constitutionality of measures which restrict the rights of citizens on account of race. There can be no doubt that restricting the freedom to marry solely because of racial classifications violates the central meaning of the Equal Protection Clause. . . .

Marriage is one of the "basic civil rights of man," fundamental to our very existence and survival. *Skinner v. Oklahoma*, 316 U. S. 535, 541 (1942). See also *Maynard v. Hill*, 125 U. S. 190 (1888). To deny this fundamental freedom on so unsupportable a basis as the racial classifications embodied in these statutes, classifications so directly subversive of the principle of equality at the heart of the Fourteenth Amendment, is surely to deprive all the State's citizens of liberty without due process of law. The Fourteenth Amendment requires that the freedom of choice to marry not be restricted by invidious racial discriminations. Under our Constitution, the freedom to marry, or not marry, a person of another race resides with the individual and cannot be infringed by the State.

These convictions must be reversed.

It is so ordered.

108

San Francisco State University Third World
Liberation Front Position, 1968

*The movement for ethnic studies, including African American, Latino, Native
American, and Asian Pacific American studies, began with an interracial coalition
of students at San Francisco State University in the late 1960s. By June 1968 the
"Third World Liberation Front" had drafted position papers in order to press demands on both faculty and administration. Student demands reflected the rapid
growth of mass hostility toward the U.S. role in Southeast Asia and escalating support for the Black Power movement in light of diminishing returns from the more
moderate civil rights movement. At San Francisco State, the confrontation evolved
into a serious strike, capturing nationwide attention and encouraging students at
many urban universities to follow suit. While many universities, including the
most prestigious, now offer "ethnic studies" of various stripes, this earliest version
was deeply grounded in community advocacy, militant confrontational tactics,
and student control of serious administrative and educational issues. Chinese, Filipino, and Japanese ethnic groups comprised the Asian American unit. Eventually, San Francisco State established a College of Ethnic Studies.*

San Francisco State College Archives, n.p., n.d. Thanks to Professor Ben Kobashigawa
at San Francisco State University for providing a copy.

Third World Liberation Front: School of Ethnic Area Studies

Throughout the entire educational systems in California, a complete and accurate representation of minority peoples' role in the past and the present conditions of this state is nonexistent. In every aspect from lectures to literature the
educational facilities do not contain the information necessary to relate any
facet of minority peoples' history and/or culture. Such an institutionalized condition of negligence and ignorance by the state's educational systems is clearly
an integral part of the racism and hatred this country has perpetuated upon
nonwhite peoples. The consistent refusal of State Education to confront its inadequacies and attain an equitable resolution between our peoples, makes it

mandatory for minority people to initiate and to maintain educational programs specifically based upon their people's background and present situation at intra and international levels.

The Third World Liberation Front is demanding a school of Ethnic Area Studies specifically organized to establish area studies of nonwhite peoples within the United States. At the present there are being developed area studies of Mexican American, Latin American, Filipino American, Chinese American, and Japanese American peoples.

The school's function is as a resource and an educational program for those minority peoples actively concerned with the lack of their peoples' representation and participation in all levels of California's educational institutions.

The school clearly intends to be involved in confronting the racism, poverty and misrepresentation imposed on minority peoples by the formally recognized institutions and organizations operating in the State of California. The process of such clarification and exposure will be developed through the collection, organization and presentation through ethnic area studies of all information relevant to the historical and contemporary positions of the minority peoples throughout local, state, national and international levels.

As assurance against the reoccurence of education's traditional distortion and misrepresentation of Third World people's cultures and histories, the School of Ethnic Area Studies is to be developed, implemented, and controlled by Third World people. Whether an area study is at a developmental or a departmental level within the school, the people of an area study will have sole responsibility and control for the staffing and curriculum of their ethnic area study. The operation and development of the School of Ethnic Area Studies is the responsibility and the control of those programs and departments within the School of Ethnic Area Studies.

Intercollegiate Chinese for Social Action
Position Paper

San Francisco State, a community college, exists in a moral vacuum, oblivious to the community it purports to serve. It does not reflect the pluralistic society that is San Francisco; it does not begin to serve the 300,000 people who live in this urban community in poverty, in ignorance, in despair. The Chinese ghetto, Chinatown, is a case in point.

1. SF State has a Chinese language department that isolates the "Chinese Experience" as a cultural phenomenon in a language that 83% of the Chinese in the United States do not speak. Realistically, we can expect that a Chinese woman, living in the ghetto, who speaks Cantonese, cannot explain to the scholar that she is dying to tuberculosis because she speaks a "street language" while

the scholar mutters classical poetry in Mandarin. San Francisco State College does not teach Cantonese.

2. Chinatown is a *ghetto*. In San Francisco there are approximately 50,000 Chinese of whom the vast majority live in Chinatown. It is an area of old buildings, narrow streets and alleys, and the effluvia of a great number of people packed into a very small space. At present, more that 5000 new Chinese immigrants stream into this overpopulated ghetto every year, an area already blessed with a birth rate that is rising, and will rise more. Chinatown is basically a tenement. Tuberculosis is endemic, rents are high and constantly rising, city services are inadequate to provide reasonable sanitation, and space is at such a premium as to resemble the Malthusian ratio at its most extreme conclusion.

There are no adequate courses in any department or school at SF State that even begin to deal specifically with the problems of the Chinese people in this exclusionary and racist environment.

WE, THEREFORE, SUPPORT THE ESTABLISHMENT OF A SCHOOL OF ETHNIC AREA STUDIES and further submit (under separate cover) our proposal for the establishment of a Chinese Ethnic Studies Department within that school that will begin to attack the problems that exist in the Chinese Community and address itself to the problems that exist in the Chinese Community at large—to the problems of acculturation and identity for Chinese people in these United States.

Phillipine [sic] American Collegiate Endeavor

We, the Filipino-American students of San Francisco State College support those demands made by the Third World Liberation Front.

We, the Filipinos, have come to the realization, along with our Third World brothers, that the struggle for self-determination is the struggle of all Third World peoples; that the neutrality, a neutrality which for the most part kept our community from progressing in this racist society, can not be tolerated or practiced any longer. There have been too many situations in which our people have denied to themselves the rights and opportunities to determine their future. There have been too many situations in which our people were given jobs as busboys, clerks, and janitors, even though they may have had college degrees. It is therefore evident to Filipinos at SF State that racism is not only levelled at our Black brother, but at us as well, when we consider the prevailing inadequacies (small number of Filipinos in college, opportunities denied to Filipino professionals in this country, exploitation of Filipino farm workers in Delano working for a few dollars a day). Seeing that these inadequacies should and must be eliminated for the betterment of our community, WE DEMAND:

1. That there be established in the School of Ethnic Studies a Department of Filipino Studies, and that within this department individuals who comprise the Department of Filipino Studies will have complete control of its business, including faculty practices and course material.

2. That the college fulfill their contract by filling the unused slots in the Special Admissions Program with an agreeable number of Filipino students from the community in the Spring of '68.

3. That any Filipino who desires to go to college would be admitted in the Fall of 1969.

109

International Hotel Struggle, Manilatown, San Francisco, February 1970

The historical forces that helped create ethnic studies at universities like San Francisco State and the University of California campuses at Berkeley and Los Angeles found their way back into some of the communities from which that energy was generated. In cities like Honolulu, Los Angeles, San Francisco, and New York, Chinatowns became immediate metaphors for the historic injustices that had bred poverty and social isolation for elderly bachelors. One volatile example was the Manilatown of San Francisco, where elderly Filipino men were living out difficult lives. Community, faculty, and students who now had access to research and courses that explained the plight of these men mobilized to support them in the streets. This pamphlet, dated February 1970, was a call to action that drew thousands of advocates to the International Hotel. These coordinated movements inspired a generation of students to move into social services, political activism, and cultural advocacy. At the dawn of the twenty-first century, the International Hotel continues its work.

Save International Hotel. San Francisco, CA: n.p., February 1970. Thanks to Frank Celada for a copy of the pamphlet.

History of International Hotel

The history of the International Hotel is essentially a history of a unique, often forgotten people. The hotel today is a symbol of their past and their future. Located at Kearny and Jackson in San Francisco, the small Filipino community of 1000 known as Manilatown, faces probable death and extinction.

The International hotel rests on the periphery of old, crowded Chinatown and of the towering ominous financial district of San Francisco. These clearly visual contradictions surrounding the hotel are merely part of the contradictions implicit within the Hotel crisis, itself.

Manilatown carefully eyes the ex-skyline, as one by one the hotels business that have been the home of Manilatowns elderly residents for twenty and thirty years are replaced by parking lots and office buildings.

Manilatown is just one example of an impoverished minority community in which the guise of redevelopment has displaced the poor, damaged traditional organizations and uprooted their cultural heart. Residents are separated, forced into often worse conditions, and acculturated—a massive blow to the identity and culture of a minority.

The Residents

The majority of the residents are elderly men without families, living on welfare checks or pensions. Reminiscing about "old times," they are bleakly aware about their invisible status in America . . . After decades of menial labor the plight of poverty makes it unlikely that they will ever return to their homelands or families.

Half are in need of medical care. Their rooms average 40–69 square ft; sparsely furnished with a basin, bed, bureau, and chair. Weekly linen is included in the typical $38 monthly rent. Common kitchen facilities exist only in the International and one other hotel. Recreation is too often limited to the local pool hall.

These elderly men are living out their lives in a country which has been historically hostile to them, a country which has exploited the labor of their youth and once again threatens their lives by the destruction of the last vestiges of their community.

Brutal History

The Philippines became a possession of the United States in 1898 as a settlement of the Spanish American War. Taking advantage of the cheap labor source Hawaiian plantation owners recruited young uneducated Filipino laborers under 4 years contracts. They worked 12 hours a day, seven days a week at a dollar a day with room and board. Poor living conditions and violations of the minimum wage caused periodic escapes; most were unsuccessful and ended in prison.

The exploitation of Filipinos ended with the coming of other victims—Chinese and Japanese immigrants. Leaving Hawaii, many of these men were attracted by hopes of better opportunities in California. In cities like San Francisco, San Diego, Los Angeles these men settled in places like Kearny St. because of discrimination, poverty, cultural companionship and the cheap hotels.

The pattern of the Filipinos is similar to those of other Asian groups in America: As immigrants they were confined to menial labor as domestics, sailors, field workers. *Prohibition of interracial marriage combined with the scarcity of Filipino women resulted in extreme loneliness and hardship for many of these men. Furthermore immigrants were limited to a quota of 50 persons annually from the Philippines in a compromise that gave those islands independence in 1934. Filipinos were limited from owning land until 1945.*

Meanwhile during the 1920's and 1930's the area on Kearny St. began to thrive with restaurants and Filipino business. The area expanded to ten blocks as it became a tourist spot and sentimental stop for homesick Filipinos in the American military.

During the depression era (1930–41) Manilatown was a well-knit and well-organized community. To help one another, they used the *bayanihan* system — the sharing of food, housing, and money with those who had none.

With the importation of cheaper Mexican labor and job opportunies in war industries (less discrimination) Filipinos began to return to the city. This weakened the efforts of the Filipino farm workers union who first began activities in 1939. A strong union did not regain strength until Filipino workers were the first to walk out in the 5 year old Delano strike.

Dying Community

Today most Filipino Americans have shared to a degree in the prosperity of the post war days. Large numbers of women have recently been able to immigrate, and the increasing phenomena of Filipino families have increased the population.

With new affluence the young and recent educated immigrant has moved into the suburbs. Many of the poorer have returned to the valley as farm-workers.

Yet the area still serves as a center for those who seek lost relatives, as a launching pad for the new immigrant, as a community for the old and a historic site in the history of Filipinos in America.

Taking a Stand

Growing concern over the fate of Manilatown has sparked some Bay Area Filipino groups into action. In the recent dispute the United Filipino Association with the support of several student groups was in the forefront.

In December 1968, UFA began negotiations to purchase the hotel's lease from the management of International. Then in March 1968 just before the contract was signed a mysterious fire, which many feel was an arson attempt, destroyed one wing on its top floor and killed three elderly persons. Negotiation stopped and the owner refused to negotiate the lease. Eviction notices and plans for a new parking lot on the site of the Hotel suddenly appeared.

Community protests and demonstrations centered around the historic nature of the hotel, the impossibility of finding new homes in a city where the vacancy for low-cost housing is 1%, and human necessity of keeping this community of elderly gentlemen intact.

The controversy which flared led to picketing the offices of Walter Shorenstein, head of the Milton-Meyer Company which owns the property. When tenants were harassed by deteriorating conditions, lack of service and repairs . . . public pressure increased.

The community accused the mayor's office of being hostile, because of Shorenstein's large donations to the Democratic funds.

After months of struggle, the United Filipino Association finally reached a settlement with the reluctant Milton-Meyer Company. *Most see the settlement as extremely unfair.* The $40,000 rent/year, the $23,000 yearly property taxes, the rehabilitation of the hotel, and fire damage repairs were fully assumed by UFA.

Despite the financial debts, volunteers have been able to rehabilitate much of the hotel, set up a recreational activities for the tenants.

While much of the continuing renovation takes place during "work sessions" each weekend, more emphasis is now being placed on fundraising.

The fate of the Hotel, Manilatown and low-cost housing for the elderly poor now hangs once more in limbo as the International faces its financial crisis.

Why?: Student Volunteers

By Loreto Almazol

What does the crisis of the International Hotel signify to the student? How does it arouse? There are undoubtedly many interpretations of the issues behind this crisis, but there are three that are paramount:

Parking Lot or Human Lives?

Which has more importance, a parking lot or the lives of the aged tenants of the Hotel who would have been forced to seek other housing in areas of the city totally unfamiliar and potentially dangerous to their well-being?

The Hotel and the community of which it is a part are all that these elderly men have. To demolish the Hotel and disperse its tenants would be inhuman. The question arises, "What right does progress or urban renewal under the gulse of a parking lot and high-rise buildings have to destroy a community?"

Shortage of Low-Cost Housing

The Hotel is one of the few remnants of low-cost housing in the city. Demolition of the Hotel for construction of a parking lot would seem to compound the housing need. The Hotel stands a couple of blocks away from San Francisco's glorified ghetto—Chinatown. Would not low-cost housing be more essential to this area than a parking lot? (Unless, of course, the real interest is private gain.)

Historic Significance

Finally, the symbolism behind the crisis of the Hotel for the Filipino community transcends any interpretation.

For the Filipino, the Hotel is the last remaining landmark of what was once a flourishing ethnic community. It would complete the dispersement of the Filipino in the Bay Area.

The crisis of the Hotel is the vanguard. It is the first major overt threat to the Filipino and his community which has knocked him (especially the youth) from his seat of complacency.

The efforts of the student volunteers are prolonging the life of the Hotel. The students, through picketing and leafletting, helped to bring the hotel crisis into the public awareness. Because of the lack of financial resources, volunteers have contacted businesses that donated materials for renovation of the Hotel. Furthermore, students have repainted, repaired, and refurnished more than half of the rooms, with the remaining rooms awaiting renovation. *The role of the student volunteer is a crucial one.*

Efforts to attract the student volunteer have been handicapped by the stereotype that the Hotel is a "Filipino project" because of its location in the heart of Manilatown. Consequently, the majority of student volunteers have been Filipino while the Filipino tenants are actually outnumbered by Chinese, black and white tenants.

Students, regardless of their ethnic backgrounds, can provide this community with impetus. But, involvement in this struggle is by no means a one-sided affair. The student will benefit just as much, if not more. The mere participation in nitty social action is more than any textbook could ever offer.

There is an urgent need for more student volunteers. Any person (student or otherwise) who would like to freak out on something real and who would like to see things as they really are, are urged to contact the International Hotel, Emil deGuzman, 982–1783.

110

The Need for a United Asian-American Front, 1970

Alex Hing founded the Red Guard party in 1969 in San Francisco. It assumed the name of the ultraradical youth groups formed as shock troops in Mao Tsetung's Cultural Revolution. At the time, radical youth in the Chinese American community interpreted the movement in China as one they could adopt and adapt to the American scene, even though, as Hing here asserts, the Asian American minority collectively formed less than one percent of the total population. In San Francisco, the Red Guards acted much more like the Black Panther Party than their namesakes in China. They relied on "serve the people" strategies built on astute observation of the real social service needs of Chinatown, where the immigrant elderly were mired in poverty. They also used direct confrontation with established authorities like the police, generating a measure of admiration from people who had been treated with disrespect for decades. Hing referred to the "apparent contradiction" in the use of Marxist-Leninist ideologies for revolutionary work among people who had fled communism in China. But the Red Guards predicted that imperialism abroad and fascism at home would force Americans, beginning with Asian Americans and other people of color, to work together. While the party itself was ephemeral, it is interesting for its very early evocation of at least three separate ideas with lasting consequences: first, it called on Asian Americans to look to Asia for guidance and support rather than assimilate into the white mainstream ("learn our native tongues"); second, it attempted to tie its racial politics to an incipient ecological movement, predicting disaster "within thirty years" unless the affluent lifestyle of America could be changed; third, it called for coalition building—a United Front of Asians in America.

Alex Hing, "The Need for a United Asian-American Front," *Aion* Magazine. San Francisco: Asian American Publications, 1970. Reprinted with permission.

The Need for a United Asian-American Front

By Alex Hing

The most politically aware of the Asians in America are usually those who have reached a high level of assimilation into the White Mother Country's culture. This is because of two reasons: 1) The frustrations which Asian-Americans encounter while trying to assimilate have educated them on the impossibility of attaining entry into the so-called "American mainstream" because of the racism inherent in this society. 2) The most assimilated of the Asians in America are usually native born citizens and, as such, they cannot be deported by the immigration authorities for political reasons.

On the other hand, the large masses of Asians in America are totally unassimilated into American culture. 70% of the population of San Francisco's Chinatown can speak no English, with the majority of its inhabitants being recent immigrants from Hong Kong and Formosa. These people are the most exploited and most oppressed segment of the Asians in America. These are the workers who earn as little as 70¢ an hour toiling 12 hours a day, 6 days a week. These are the families who are crammed into one or two room apartments with kitchen and toilet facilities shared with the other occupants of their building. These are the people with the highest suicide and tuberculosis rates in the nation. These are the people who take all of this shit without one cry of outrage so that their children can go to college and be successful in business.

Most of the politically aware Asians are students who are undergoing identity crises. They realize that they cannot fit into White society, yet at the same time they are also rebelling against the strict, Confucian ideas instilled into them by their parents. The contradiction caused by trying to assimilate into two cultures at one time can be resolved not by rejecting one and assimilating more into the other; but by rejecting the bad elements in both cultures and building a revolutionary culture from the best elements of both.

It has become apparent, however, that the so-called "American culture" is so decadent that it is totally beyond salvation. It has the blood of the Third World and the now more recent blood of the Mother Country's own young on her hands. We must become Asians and we should be clear on exactly what that means. First of all, Asians have the longest unbroken civilization in history. Secondly, Asia is the vanguard of the Third World Liberation Struggle against Yankee Imperialism.

The situation in the Asian communities is so deplorable that a Marxist-Leninist Party must begin to take firm root among the people. It is necessary that this party does not alienate the people or create any factions among the budding Asian-American Movement as we do not even make up 1% of the total population of America. The purpose of this party is to educate the people on the fact that the Asian communities in America are included in the genocidal American foreign policy in Asia. If America ever enters into a war with China, the Asians in America will pay the price in blood.

In respect to the Chinese community in San Francisco, there is an apparent contradiction between organizing a Marxist-Leninist Party in an area where the population consists of refugees from a Socialist Revolution. This contradiction will resolve itself as the people realize that the desperate imperialist policies of the United States in Asia are reflected by the ever-increasing fascism at home.

The universities must be made to respond to the needs of the community. Therefore, Asian Studies programs are necessary. Also, the campuses provide a mass base for organizing Asians to fight imperialism. But students should realize that their knowledge must be used as a weapon for the masses to wield in their struggle for liberation — that their knowledge is genuine only if it is put into practice in order to serve the people. There has been very little research on the power structures of the Asian communities, particularly in Chinatown. This research is best handled by students and should be made available for mass distribution.

Also, as Asians, we must become more sensitive to our environment. We must realize that the affluency of American society is nothing but a joy ride on nature, and that within thirty years, unless we are able to sanely control our environment, ecological disaster will occur. Given expert ecological data on the amount of time we, as human beings, have left to save our environment from total collapse, we must realize the urgency of our task and begin to work much harder.

Because of the San Francisco Bay Area's political climate and because San Francisco's Chinatown is the largest Asian community outside of Asia, the Bay Area is the most logical place for a massive Asian-American Movement to begin. In fact, the Bay Area has already made steps in that direction with the formation of the Asian-American Political Alliance (AAPA), the Inter-Collegiate Chinese for Social Action (ICSA), the Pilipino-American Collegiate Endeavor (PACE) and the Red Guard. There are also a few Asian-Americans in the Bay Area with a revolutionary perspective who do not belong to any organized group. It is extremely important that these diverse elements of political Asians in America come together to fight our common oppressor.

In other words, a United Front of Asians in America must be formed to combat fascism and imperialism. This United Front must be led by Marxists-Leninists and develop into a strong organization which serves the Asian people. The United Front should bring forth a program which relates to the needs of Asians in America and not become issue oriented. The United Front should not rely on demonstration-type, symbolic confrontations but build mass support through hard, thorough work among the people, which is not as glamorous as demonstrating but a lot more rewarding in terms of building a revolution.

Communications must develop on two levels. We must build an efficient communications system among the various Asian groups and we must have a smooth flow of information between the masses and the Asian-American

Movement. One possible way to further develop communications would be to combine our efforts into producing one community oriented newspaper. This would also avoid duplication of labor and conserve our resources which are scarce. We must also begin to learn our native tongues and put our knowledge of it into practice in the community.

The main emphasis of all Asian-American political groups must be intensive political education. The lack of such an education, is unfortunately, characteristic of the whole Asian-American Movement. Without painstaking study we will not be able to properly analyze our situation and develop the proper strategy and tactics for it. Without political education, a general political line for the Asian-American Movement will not be developed; and as a result, factionalism will occur. We must all become teachers and pupils at the same time.

Every Asian in the Movement should also be educated on first-aid and self-defense—which includes fire arms handling and safety. Qualified teachers and materials are available providing each cadre is willing to accept the discipline of studying and attending classes. This knowledge is necessary for survival in America's urban environment.

A legal defense program must be set up in order to provide legal assistance for those of us who will be ripped off by the pigs. At this stage of American fascism it would be foolish for us to disregard this task. The Red Guards have experienced over thirty arrests since they began to organize a scant nine months ago. The legal defense program must include a bail fund, bail contacts, legal defense fund and lawyer contacts.

In our relations with other groups, we must always make a class analysis to determine who are our friends and who are our enemies. It would be absurd to believe that Asians alone could seize state power in America. We must link up with the Third World and White revolutionaries throughout the country and establish international contacts, especially in Asia, with those who are struggling against Yankee Imperialism.

The time has come for us to break out of the sterotypes imposed upon us by the racists. We are not docile, complacent, obedient and self-sufficient Orientials. We are Asians, and as such, identify ourselves with the baddest motherfuckers alive. We can no longer be a witness to the daily slaughter of our people in Asia nor to the oppression of the Asians here in America and be afraid of death or prison. We must fight because that's what Asians are all about.

111

Preface to Roots: An Asian American Reader, 1971

This was the first published anthology dealing with Asian Americans and intended for college classroom use. After three decades, it remains in print and may be useful both for the pieces it assembles and for the perspectives that illuminate the historical context in an early part of the "Asian American Movement." The principal editors, Amy Tachiki and Eddie Wong, were graduate and undergraduate students, respectively. Buck Wong was also an undergraduate; Franklin Odo was a junior faculty member. All were at UCLA in the midst of initial enthusiasm for major change in race relations both on campus and in the society at large. Opposition to the war in Southeast Asia was spawning large demonstrations as well as more deliberate movements; continuing revelations of official wrongdoing generated waves of anger and cynicism. The assassinations of the Kennedys and of the moderate civil rights leader Martin Luther King, Jr. deeply affected this generation; they began to look to more radical figures, like Malcolm X at home and Mao Tse-tung abroad, for inspiration. The anthology includes sections on "Identity," "History," and "Community," with a mix of poems, essays, scholarly pieces, and political tracts.

Franklin Odo, "Preface" to *Roots: An Asian American Reader.* Los Angeles: UCLA Asian American Studies Center, 1971. Reprinted with permission of the Center.

As the title indicates, this volume was written and edited with the intent of going to the "roots" of the issues facing Asians in America. It may, therefore, strike the reader as "radical"—a term which derives from the latin [*sic*] *radix,* meaning, appropriately enough, roots. Fair enough. The selections were chosen to encourage readers to consider and compare the experiences of Asian Americans, individually and collectively, within the context of the human condition. Our work is designed to meet the particular needs of Asian Americans. At this point in time, the lack of appropriate materials in readily accessible form is one of the greatest immediate problems. Asian Americans who have tried to serve their communities as social workers, organizers, lawyers, businessmen, workers, housewives and students have long expressed the need for a convenient anthology focusing on the lives of our people. Equally important is the increasing number of people who have sought a convenient book with which to begin their reading on this neglected subject.

Several points need to be made about this work. It contains a variety of materials written from a multitude of perspectives. There are scholarly pieces which rely on traditional, academic sources for information and present a mixed sociological and historical picture of Asian Americans. There is, however, equal emphasis on the contemporary expression of the Asian American condition by the people themselves. ROOTS is, therefore, not only a handy repository of secondary writings on the subject but a documentary collection from our time.

These are critical times for Asian Americans and it is imperative that their voices be heard in all their anger, anguish, resolve and inspiration. Many selections have not been edited at all; others only to avoid undue repetition. We have felt it important to preserve something of the person who wrote the piece—thus insisting that the reader make a positive effort to understand the author's intent and examine it critically. The wide variety of styles and viewpoints have helped create a work which, we hope, suggests the riches awaiting those who pursue an interest in the experiences of Asian Americans.

One of the first things to note is the magnitude of interest already exhibited. Asian American studies classes and student groups have formed across the country and a national conference on the subject attracted several hundred participants to Los Angeles in April, 1971. There is a long tradition of interest in the academic uses of Asian Americans—here, limited to Chinese, Japanese, Filipinos, and Koreans—as sociological "case studies" to test (and usually to "prove") the validity of American society as a largely open and democratic one. As the section on identity indicates, however, that type of analysis has done serious disservice to all Asian Americans and has been part of the self-delusion white America has suffered.

Amy Tachiki notes, in her important opening remarks to the section on identity, the range of misconceptions, the mechanisms through which they operate, and the consequences thereof. Identity is a question to which we return time and again. It is never neatly solved and incorporated into the computation of other variables. Identity is crucial to ideology and action—central to the problem of self-determination at any level. The Asian who "identifies" white (or *anything* other than what he is) faces the insurmountable problem of his physical makeup. Any individual of talent who is "skimmed" from his generally oppressed group faces a lifetime of ambivalence—increasingly regarded as a turncoat by them and as an exception by others.

A few, tortured by their inability to make sense of a crazy world of color, choose to destroy themselves in drugs and/or blind hostility. The rest of us, workers and professionals alike, endure a lifetime of alienation and uncertainty marked by an intuitive sense of powerlessness. Until, that is, some sequence of events forces us to turn to the problem of identity—with whom are we to identify? That turn forces increasing numbers to look to their "roots."

The central section of this volume deals with the history of Asian Americans, from the emigration period to the present. This was another facet of the title's significance—our "roots" go deep into the history of the United States and they can do much to explain who and what we are and how we became this way. Buck Wong's opening section is properly critical of the bland *pap* that has masqueraded as history—the number of new articles and their various styles should convince all of us that much important work remains to be done in this area. Interestingly, some of the features of the "generation gap" unique to Japanese Americans seem to disappear when the youth talk to parents and grandparents about the World War II concentration camp experience, or the "picture bride" practice. This should be true for all ethnic groups.

Disregarding or misinterpreting the historical background of the particular group is one of the most important reasons for the failure to make meaningful changes in the ethnic community. All Asians have much in common: the history of their exploitation as migrant farm labor is but one significant theme that continues to this day with the Filipino laborers in Delano. But there are unique qualities to each of the ethnic groups which make united struggles difficult—they need to be understood and discussed rather than shaded or wished away.

Many of those qualities are discussed in the section on Asian American communities. Eddie Wong's introduction sets the articles and interviews in the all-important context—without it they might easily be read as merely interesting reflections on the present state of affairs. The notion of "community" is an elusive one—for decades now social scientists have thought that Asian Americans would be geographically dispersed as they were culturally assimilated. Instead, as the 1970 census will probably show, even those who have achieved middle class economic status are congregating in suburban pockets. Some of the same features from the central city ghetto areas accompany them—an ethnic church, food stores and a few cultural centers offering instruction in the various Asian arts. Why this phenomenon if our assumptions about the gradual assimilation of Asians in the "majority" society are accurate? In fact, the yellow bourgeoisie may be discovering what his black brothers did long ago—racism exists at all levels of American society.

Even Asians who advance to managerial level positions find themselves bound by restrictions on the basis of race. The case of Los Angeles County Coroner Dr. Thomas Noguchi is instructive (see document by J.U.S.T. in the community section). A recent survey of personnel decision-making executives in 50 top corporations in metropolitan California areas (San Francisco, Los Angeles, San Diego) revealed considerable anti-Asian racism.[1] The fifty companies, each with at least twenty executives, were selected from 1700 available

---

[1]*Student paper submitted to course on "Asians in America" (Occidental College, December, 1970).*

by means of a chi-square test to ensure a random and representative sample. A surprising number of these executives (39–79%) had served in the Pacific Theater in World War II, Korea or Vietnam. Thirty four (67%) had seen combat against Asians. This preliminary questioning established the strong probability of U.S. foreign policies in Asia serving as a major contributor to anti-Asian racism.

As expected, only two (4%) had ever employed Asians at the executive level while the others rejected the possibility on the basis of one or another function of mistrust. "Sneaky," "conniving," "shifty," are terms they used to express their reservations about hiring or promoting at the executive level. In a tight, competitive situation, the personal prejudices of potential customers are considered important and 35 (70%) of the sample felt they shared personal perspectives with other business associates. The point should be clear—success on any but the basest of material levels will continue to be elusive and even that remains subject to events beyond our control and related to race.

This volume focuses considerable attention, perhaps disproportionately on Asian American youth; their attitudes, their problems, their movements. That focus should be interpreted in two contexts: first, as part of the long and rich heritage of generations of Asian American struggles for equality and justice and, second, in light of contemporary Third World movements. Several writers and interviews allude to problems of conflicts of emphasis and limited vision even among those who see themselves at the forefront of the movement. Two questions of importance have not received adequate attention: one is the relationship of any ethnically based struggle to others such as other ethnic groups or economic class-oriented ones, while a second one is, if anything, even more complex. What should be a "proper" stance toward the inculcation or maintenance of a cultural heritage? How closely, if at all, and in what ways should Asian Americans relate to Asia? Responses vary from "back to Asia" types to a strictly Americanist, localized, point of view. There are no hard and fast solutions to these problems but the evidence suggests a few guidelines.

Any "answer" which treats symptoms and fails to look to the roots of the condition will be woefully inadequate. Our questioning and thinking must relate directly to the issue of Asian ethnicity in a racist society but they must move from the particular to the universal, from personal identity to the identity of larger groups, to the nature of human experience and the human condition. And in all of this, an essential identification with the people and a redistribution of power must be seen as both possible and necessary; that is, after all, what is meant by the demand for power to the people.

112

"Yellow Pearl": Asian American Movement Music, 1972

"Yellow Pearl" became one of the signature songs by a young trio of musicians based in New York City in the early 1970s. "Chris, Joanne, and Charlie" were the Asian American political/social movement's equivalent of medieval European troubadours who traveled across the country singing news unavailable through mainstream media. Self-consciously activist, they called for a revolutionary consciousness among Asian American communities. Chris Iijima, Joanne (now Nobuko) Miyamoto, and Charlie Chin joined activists protesting the wars in Southeast Asia as well as the grassroots struggles by Native American, black, and Latino leaders. They were cultural leaders furthering recent moves to combine the disparate communities of Asian descent in the United States to assert a renewed claim to self-determination and antiracist action. This song, "Yellow Pearl," was written and composed by Miyamoto and Iijima and spoke to the need for subverting the oppressive system that weighed so heavily on communities of color. It also insisted that there was a capacity for resistance, albeit in this metaphor, a passive version, for the struggle.

Reprinted by permission. New York: Basement Workshop, 1972.

YELLOW PEARL

MIYAMOTO — IIJIMA

A grain
a grain of sand
landing in the belly
in the belly of the monster

and time is telling
only how long it takes
layer after layer
as its beauty unfolds
until its captor
it holds in peril

a grain
a tiny grain of sand

Now you might say I'm just a dream - er
pearls like you just don't ap - pear
and I re - fuse to grant you schem - er
rec - og - ni - tion that you're here

now you can say just what you want
but my hurt has ceased
I see signs of my - self
come drift - ing in from the East

Chorus

and time is telling
only how long it takes
layer after layer
as our beauty unfolds
until our captor
we'll hold in peril

a grain
a tiny grain of sand.

Song: "We Are the Children," 1972

Another popular song by Chris Iijima and Joanne (Nobuku) Miyamoto. Its lyrics directly appropriate the working-class backgrounds of most Asian Americans of the era. It takes the sometimes stereotypically treated historical genealogy and makes it a point of ethnic pride—thus using the best known and most denigrated elements of Asian America, including migrant workers, railroad builders, waiters, and gardeners as well as former internees of the World War II concentration camps. These images helped instill pride in specific Filipino, Chinese, and Japanese American populations while seeking to forge a pan-Asian ideology for political activism. Moreover, the song called for Asian Americans to acknowledge themselves as "a part of the Third World Peoples," even to the extent, when confronted with cowboy-and-Indian movies, of "secretly rooting for the other side." Songs and performances influenced generations of youths as they attempted to place themselves in the turbulent years of the civil rights and antiwar struggles.

Reprinted with permission from Chris Iijima and Nobuko Miyamoto.

WE ARE THE CHILDREN

MIYAMOTO - IIJIMA

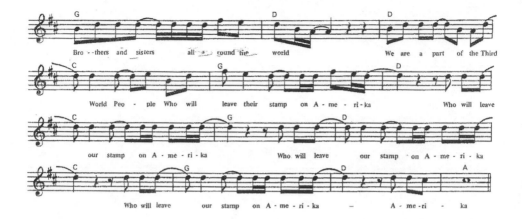

Bro - -thers and sisters all a-round the world We are a part of the Third

World Peo - ple Who will leave their stamp on A - me - ri - ka Who will leave

our stamp on A - me - ri - ka Who will leave our stamp on A - me - ri - ka

Who will leave our stamp on A - me - ri - ka — A - me - ri - ka

We are the children of the Chinese waiter

Born and raised in the laundry rooms

We are the offspring of the Japanese gardener

Who leave their stamp on Amerika

Chorus

Foster children of the Pepsi generation

Cowboys and Indians — ride redmen ride!

Watching war movies with the next door neighbors

Secretly rooting for the other side

Chorus

114

Ramsay Liem, "Some Tasks at Hand," 1972

In the spring of 1972, a group of Korean Americans started a journal to publish their thoughts. Insight was a bimonthly, edited by Brenda Paik Sunoo, with poetry, critiques of the Korean War, and many pieces on identity issues. Ramsay Liem's piece, originally published in 1972 and reprinted in a collection of works from Insight, is an early example of the newly awakened but quite sophisticated reflection then occurring in Asian American circles. He suggests that first-, second-, and third-generation Korean Americans met originally to share personal experiences and that the next developmental stage involves Korean history and culture. Liem then says they must move on to broad comparative study ("Asians, Blacks, Browns etc.") to understand the totality of race relations in America through a focus on the institutional rather than the accidental or incidental. Further, he argues, this is the sort of analysis needed to pursue "real and permanent change" in the actual living conditions of Korean Americans.

Ramsay Liem, "Some Tasks at Hand." *Insight, Korean American Bimonthly* (New York), May 1972. Reprinted with permission.

Some Tasks at Hand

As the result of several get togethers of Korean Americans in New York City and Boston, some thoughts have occurred to me which might be of interest to those who attended as well as other Korean Americans. One of the major outcomes of these meetings seemed to be a fuller awakening on our part to being Korean as well as American. At first it seemed as if we were discovering something new, something perhaps once a part of ourselves but somehow lost or taken away. Being a Korean, however, is not something one is at one moment in time, and then is no longer, at another. We are Koreans as well as Americans and, if only one part is public, it is so because of the effects of the particular arrangements of society at this moment in time.

The awakening, then, is to something that has always been a part of ourselves but denied—by self or other. And just as I find I need persistent help in the morning to awaken from one kind of sleep, so it is true for this other sleep. Through our individual desire to be as we are, Korean Americans without hyphens or special explanations, we offer each other that nudge from sleep. In this sense our individual interests bind us together; our meeting together is no[t] artificial but necessitated by individual needs that cannot be satisfied in isolation.

Our initial meetings seemed to be occupied with sharing of personal experiences and attempts to find common ground. A future direction for us has been suggested in the interest shown in study groups directed at Korean history, culture, and language. This knowledge is important not simply for its inherent interest or exchange value, but because history; culture, and language serve to sharpen the character of a people and to maintain it. They are what continue to hold an identity firm when individuals are separated by distance and time. Our study of Korean history and culture must be conducted with an understanding of how this endeavor is directly related to the immediate concerns of Korean Americans.

I have been writing largely in terms of some of the impressions I have had during the first few meetings of one group of Korean Americans. There is, however, another order of business which has yet to emerge which constitutes a second important reason for Korean Americans to join together; a reason that hopefully will become more apparent in the near future. Beyond awakening from our own sleep we have the responsibility to arrive at an understanding of how minorities are put to sleep in this country in the first place. What forces operate to erase from our minds the fact that we are Asians, Blacks, Browns etc.? Without this kind of analysis we can never contribute to a real and permanent change in the living conditions of Koreans in the United States in a way which will insure a future for us as *Korean* Americans.

We need to study the political, economic, educational, and social institutions in this country to understand the program which is operating against all minorities. For example, what happens in the schools to deny Korean American children knowledge of themselves? Is it simply the insensitivity of a particular teacher or the oversight of a curriculum planner; in a word, the accidents of one's circumstances? Certainly we are led to believe that this is the case. However, many of us have discovered that we experienced the same kinds of "accidents" in our separate educational careers. None of us was encouraged to study Korean history; there were always the teachers who could not pronounce Korean names and consequently shortened them or changed them; and; there was always praise for acquiescence, a noble Oriental characteristic. In as much as many of us have experienced the same "accidents," one is hard pressed not to wonder why. This questioning should bring us to a study of the many social institutions which shape life in the United States, and in particular the experience of Korean Americans. This task is perhaps considerably more formidable than awakening from our own sleep, but it must be assumed if we are to achieve a lasting solution to the problems which initially brought us together only so recently.

115

Preface to Aiiieeeee!, *1973*

Aiiieeeee! hit the Asian American community with incredible force when it was first published by Howard University Press. Indeed, the fact that only a historically black university press would accept the manuscript became part of its mythology. The editors, all accomplished writers, compiled this anthology of literary writings, fiction, and drama to highlight the richness of Chinese, Japanese, and Filipino American experience. But, they insisted, these had to be "authentic" expressions, as opposed to the huge outpouring of works accepted by the mainstream culture as a result of "legislative racism and euphemized white racist love." The former was relatively simple to recognize; the latter became their primary target—because it had cast most Asian Americans adrift in a state of "self-contempt, self-rejection, and disintegration." Reprinted here almost in its entirety, the preface remains a powerful document. While not all scholars or students accepted this grim analysis, many recognized the power of the call to active reflection and the will to creative energy. In later years, the volume was criticized for its "macho" cast and perspective, but it had clearly taken a stark position in the literary world, which would never be the same again. Nearly three decades later, the authors "revisited" Aiiieeeee! in a 1997 Meridian edition and defiantly denounced their "yellow critics [who] all ignore history and literary scholarship in their histories of Asian American writing."

Reprinted with permission of the authors. Frank Chin, Jeffery Paul Chan, Lawson Inada, and Shawn Hsu Wong, "Preface" to *Aiiieeeee!*. Copyrighted by authors in 1974. Originally published Washington, DC: Howard University Press, 1975.

Preface

Asian-Americans are not one people but several—Chinese-Americans, Japanese-Americans, and Filipino-Americans. Chinese-and Japanese-Americans have been separated by geography, culture, and history from China and Japan for seven and four generations respectively. They have evolved cultures and sensibilities distinctly not Chinese or Japanese and distinctly not white American. Even the

Asian languages as they exist today in America have been adjusted and developed to express a sensitivity created by a new experience. In America, Chinese- and Japanese-American culture and history have been inextricably linked by confusion, the popularization of their hatred for each other, and World War II.

Filipino America differs greatly from Chinese and Japanese America in its history, the continuity of culture between the Philippines and America, and the influence of western European and American culture on the Philippines. The difference is definable only in its own terms, and therefore must be discussed separately.

Our anthology is exclusively Asian-American. That means Filipino-, Chinese-, and Japanese-Americans, American born and raised, who got their China and Japan from the radio, off the silver screen, from television, out of comic books, from the pushers of white American culture that pictured the yellow man as something that when wounded, sad, or angry, or swearing, or wondering whined, shouted, or screamed "aiiieeeee!" Asian America, so long ignored and forcibly excluded from creative participation in American culture, is wounded, sad, angry, swearing, and wondering, and this is his AIIIEEEEE!!! It is more than a whine, shout, or scream. It is fifty years of our whole voice.

Seven generations of suppression under legislative racism and euphemized white racist love have left today's Asian-Americans in a state of self-contempt, self-rejection, and disintegration. We have been encouraged to believe that we have no cultural integrity as Chinese- or Japanese-Americans, that we are either Asian (Chinese or Japanese) or American (white), or are measurably both. This myth of being either/or and the equally goofy concept of the dual personality haunted our lobes while our rejection by both Asia and white America proved we were neither one nor the other. Nor were we half and half or more one than the other. Neither Asian culture nor American culture was equipped to define us except in the most superficial terms. However, American culture, equipped to deny us the legitimacy of our uniqueness as American minorities, did so, and in the process contributed to the effect of stunting self-contempt on the development and expression of our sensibility that in turn has contributed to a mass rejection of Chinese and Japanese America by Chinese- and Japanese-Americans. The Japanese-American Citizens League (JACL) weekly, the *Pacific Citizen*, in February, 1972, reported that more than 50 percent of Japanese-American women were marrying outside their race and that the figure was rising annually. Available statistics indicate a similar trend among Chinese-American women, though the 50 percent mark may not have been topped yet. These figures say something about our sensibility, our concept of Chinese America and Japanese America, our self-esteem, as does our partly real and partly mythical silence in American culture.

The age, variety, depth, and quality of the writing collected here proves the existence of Asian-American sensibilities and cultures that might be related to but are distinct from Asia and white America. American culture, protecting the sanctity of its whiteness, still patronizes us as foreigners and refuses to recognize Asian-American literature as "American" literature. America does not recognize Asian America as a presence, though Asian-Americans have been here seven generations. For seven generations we have been aware of that refusal, and internalized it, with disastrous effects.

Asian-American sensibility is so delicate at this point that the fact of Chinese or Japanese birth is enough to distinguish you from being American-born, in spite of the fact that you may have no actual memories of life in Asia. However, between the writer's actual birth and birth of the sensibility, we have used the birth of the sensibility as the measure of being an Asian-American. Victor Nee was born in China and came to the United States when he was five. Novelist Louis Chu came when he was nine. For both, Chinese culture and China are not so much matters of experience as they are of hearsay and study. Victor and his wife Brett have written the first Chinese-American history of Chinese America, *Longtime Californ': A Documentary Study of an American Chinatown* (1973). Louis Chu's *Eat a Bowl of Tea* (1961) is the first Chinese-American novel set in Chinese America. Here we get sticky, however, for the first novel published by an American-born Chinese-American is *The Frontiers of Love* (1956), by Diana Chang, a Eurasian. She was born in America but moved to China before her first birthday, to be raised in the "European Compound" of Shanghai as an American in China. She writes of that experience, while Chu writes of Chinatown, New York. Between them so many questions are raised as to what is or is not Chinese-American that to save, and in another sense encourage, confusion (our criterion of Asian-American literature and identity is not a matter of dogma or party line), we have included them both. Chu's book honestly and accurately dramatizes the Chinese-American experience from a Chinese-American point of view, and not from an exclusively "Chinese or Chinese-according-to-white" point of view. Diana Chang in her protagonists of mixed blood and their single-blooded parents provides us with a logical dramatic metaphor for the conflict of cultures. Her protagonist, Sylvia, cannot choose between her parents or identify her blood as one thing or the other. The question of choice is shown to be a phony one imposed on her by outside forces.

Sensibility and the ability to choose differentiate the Asian-American writers in this collection from the Americanized Chinese writers Lin Yutang and C. Y. Lee. They were intimate with and secure in their Chinese cultural identity in an experiential sense, in a way we American-born can never be. Again, unlike us, they are American by choice. They consciously set out to become American, in the white sense of the word, and succeeded in becoming "Chinese-American" in the stereotypical sense of the good, loyal, obedient, passive, law-abiding, cultured sense of the word. It is no surprise that their writing is from whiteness, not from Chinese America. Becoming white supremacist was part of their consciously and voluntarily becoming "American." Lin Yutang's *A Chinatown Family* (1948) and C. Y. Lee's *Flower Drum Song* affected our sensibility but did not express it. They come from a white tradition of Chinese novelty literature, would-be Chinese writing about America for the entertainment of Americans in books like As a Chinaman Sees Us, Chinaman's Chance, and A Chinaman Looks at America. These travel books were in the tradition not so much of de Tocqueville as of Gulliver's Travels. Their attraction was comic. The humor derived from the Chinese mangling of the English language and from their comic explanations of American customs and psychology. These books appeared in the early twentieth century after almost fifty years of travel books on China written by Christian missionaries and "world travelers" who cited missionaries as authorities on China. The reversal of the form, books of American adventures by Chinese travelers, was a comic inevitability. During this period the exploitation of the comic potential of Asian dialect became, forever, a part of popular American culture, giving rise to Earl Derr Biggers' series of Charlie Chan novels and Wallace Irwin's Hashimura Togo stories. The Hashimura Togo stories were featured in Good Housekeeping magazine and described the adventures of a Japanese house servant who is both unintelligible and indispensable in an American household. A sample of the wit and wisdom of Hashimura Togo, from "Togo Assists in a Great Diamond Robbery," (Good Housekeeping, March, 1917):

> With occasional oftenness she approached up to me and report with frogged voice, "Togo where did you put my diamond broach and Mother Hubbard chamois ring when you stole it?"

The substance and imagery of these books and stories were reinforced by the whining, apologetic tone of books done by Chinese government officials giving the official explanations of Chinese culture and the nonthreatening, beneficial, humble motivations of the Chinese presence and immigration to America. Books were written as The Real Chinese in America (1923) by J. S. Tow, secretary of the Chinese Consulate at New York, with the rank of Consul-Eleven. The subservient character of the Chinese and the inferiority of China were major themes in works by Chinese converts to white supremacy and Christianity. Yung Wing's My Life in China and America (1909) is the outstanding example of early yellow white supremacy.

In 1925 Earl Derr Biggers, a distinctly non-Chinese, non-Chinese-American, and subtly racist writer, created the modern Chinese-American: Charlie Chan, the Chinese detective, who first appears in "The House Without a Key" walking with "the light dainty step of a woman." The travel format, going from one nation to another, became in Biggers' immensely popular Charlie Chan novels, an interior journey from one culture to another. Thus, the form evolved into the Chinatown book itself reinforced, and clearly articulated today's popular notion of being an Asian-American. The concept of the dual personality, of going from one culture to another, emerged. . . .

The Charlie Chan model of Chinese-Americans was developed in books like Pardee Lowe's *Father And Glorious Descendant*, Lin Yutang's novel *A Chinatown Family*, Jade Snow Wong's *Fifth Chinese Daughter*, *Inside Chinatown* by Garding Lui, and two books titled *Chinatown, U.S.A.*, one by Calvin Lee and the other by a white, Elizabeth Coleman.

Chinatown Inside Out was obviously a fraud. The author's name, "Leong Gor Yun," means "two men" in Cantonese. The book consists of items cribbed and translated from the Chinese-language newspapers of Chinatowns in San Francisco and New York tied together with Charlie Chan/Fu Manchu imaginings and the precise logic of a paranoid schizophrenic. Part exposé, part cookbook, the book was supremacist in its overlooking of the effect of racism on our psychology and its never missing a chance to brown-nose the white man with Charlie Chan-like observations.

Far from giving America a big yuk, and celebrated as a classic of American humor, *Chinatown Inside Out* was accepted by everyone as the first book about Chinese America by a Chinese-American. No one, not even the scholars of Chinese America, noticed the awkward changes of voice and style, the differences between the outright lies and the rare facts. The clue of the author's pen name "two men" escaped all. *Chinatown Inside Out* was the source of Lin Yutang's 1948 novel *A Chinatown Family*. In 1962 S. W. Kung from China published *Chinese in American Life* and cited the work of another foreigner to Chinese America, Lin Yutang's *A Chinatown Family*. In 1965 Calvin Lee, a former assistant dean at Columbia University and the author of Chinese cookbooks, saw the light and testified to his successful conversion to utter white supremacy in *Chinatown U.S.A.* in which he cited Leong Gor Yun and S. W. Kung. Betty Lee Sung loosed *Mountain of Gold* in 1967. She praised the "Chinese in America" for never being "overly bitter about prejudice." In this book, she told us, "If you make yourself obnoxious . . . that is a hindrance to acceptance." *Mountain of Gold* cited the gospel according to S. W. Kung, Lin Yutang, and Calvin Lee. In 1971 the gospel of Leong Gor Yun became hilarious self-parody in Francis L. K. Hsu's *The Challenge of the American Dream*:

> The Chinese in America, in common with other minority groups, will have a continuing problem of double identity. But the effective way of dealing with it is not to deny its existence but to face it squarely. The first step is to realize that the double identity of a minority group is not dissimilar to that of the professional woman. She is a woman and a professional. Some American professional women have tended to forget their sex identity but most have kept some sort of balance between it and their profession. In the latter case, their sex identity sometimes becomes an advantage rather than a disability.

> . . . The period from the late twenties through the thirties that spawned Charlie Chan, Fu Manchu, and Leong Gor Yun also produced a rash of popular

songs, Charlestons, and fox trots about "China boys" being stranded in America without their women. Such a song was "So Long Oolong (How Long You Gonna Be Gone)," that tells of a girl, "Ming Toy," pining for her sweetheart, "Oolong," stranded in America. Songs with titles like "Little Chinky Butterfly," "Hong Kong Dream Girl," and dozens of others appeared to be Tin Pan Alley's way of celebrating America's closing of the last loopholes in the Chinese Exclusion Act of 1923 by finding ways to exclude entry to Chinese women into the country. Also, a series of popular novels and movies involving passive Chinese men, worshiping white women and being afraid to touch them, appeared in *Son of the Gods, East is West,* and the Fu Manchu and Charlie Chan series.

In the meantime Japanese-Americans cranked up an underground press and literary movement in English, publishing their own poetry magazines, literary quarterlies, and newspapers that featured, as they still do, creative writing supplements in their holiday issues. . . .

During World War II the inside books became more personal and more manipulated. Patriotic Chinese-Americans wrote anti-Japanese propaganda disguised as autobiography. Pardee Lowe's *Father and Glorious Descendant* was the first. Though *Fifth Chinese Daughter* was published in 1950, it fits the propaganda-as-autobiography mold perfectly. There is reason to believe work on it actually began during the war. Chapters of it appeared in magazines in 1947. America's "anti-Jap" prejudice, as indicated by the release of new anti-Japanese war movies, continued strong until the mid-fifties, when the first sign of a change in white attitude was an announcement disclaiming prejudice against loyal Japanese-Americans before the airing of World War II "anti-Jap" movies on television.

In travel books and in music, Japanese America was indiscriminately linked in confusion with Chinese America. In America's pop mind, Japan and China, as well as Japanese America and Chinese America, were one in exotica. China and Japan and Japanese America became distinguished from each other by hatred. That hatred was not explained in the terms of culture and politics, but in the terms of the Hatfields and McCoys—we were all some kind of silly, but civilized hillbillies feuding in the hills of jade. Chinese-Americans became America's pets, were kept and groomed in kennels, while Japanese-Americans were the mad dogs who had to be locked up in pounds. The editors and writers of the Japanese-American community papers were thrown ever closer to Japanese-American artists, poets, and storytellers. The Japanese-American writing in English that had been an activity was now welded into a movement.

The tradition of Japanese-American verse as being quaint and foreign in English, established by Yone Noguchi and Sadakichi Hartman, momentarily influenced American writing with the quaintness of the Orient but said nothing about Asian America, because, in fact, these writers weren't Asian-Americans but Americanized Asians like Lin Yutang and C. Y. Lee.

The first serious creative writing by an Asian-American to hit the streets was Miné Okubo's *Citizen 13660*, an autobiographical narrative in drawings and words, describing the relocation and camp experience from an artist's point of view. It was a remarkable book given the time of its appearance, 1946, when anti-Japanese sentiment was still high. Toshio Mori's collection of stories, *Yokohama, California*, appeared in 1949. It had been scheduled for release in 1941, but World War II "anti-Jap" prejudice worked against Japanese-Americans appearing in print; however, it also spared their being shaped, used, and manipulated as Chinese-Americans.

After the war, the best way to rehabilitate Japanese America, from the white point of view, was to link it up and get it inextricably confused with Chinese America again, so from *Fifth Chinese Daughter* came son of *Fifth Chinese Daughter*, Monica Sone's *Nisei Daughter*, a book remarkable for maintaining its Japanese-American integrity in spite of its being, in the publisher's eyes, blatantly modeled on Wong's snow job.

None of the Chinese-, Japanese-, and Filipino-American works in this volume are snow jobs pushing Asian-Americans as the miracle synthetic white people that America's proprietors of white liberal pop, like Tom Wolfe, ABC television ("If Tomorrow Comes," "Kung Fu," "Madame Sin"), and such racist henchmen passing for scholars as Gunther Barth and Stuart Miller, make us out to be.

The Asian-American writers here are elegant or repulsive, angry and bitter, militantly anti-white or not, not out of any sense of perversity or revenge but of honesty. America's dishonesty—its racist white supremacy passed off as love and acceptance—has kept seven generations of Asian-American voices off the air, off the streets, and praised us for being Asiatically no-show. A lot is lost forever. But from the few decades of writing we have recovered from seven generations, it is clear that we have a lot of elegant, angry, and bitter life to show. We know how to show it. We are showing off. If the reader is shocked, it is due to his own ignorance of Asian-America. We're not new here. Aiiieeeee!!

The editors extend a special note of thanks of Kay Boyle, The Combined Asian-American Resources Project, Inc., Kai-yu Hsu, David Ishii, H. Mark Lai, Dorothy Okada, Glenn Omatsu, Ishmael Reed, Leslie Silko, Ben R. Tong, Richard Wada, and Connie Young Yu for their help and encouragement in the preparation of this anthology. Grateful acknowledgement is also made to authors, publishers, and agents for their permission to reprint the following selections.

San Francisco, 1973

Frank Chin
Jeffery Paul Chan
Lawson Fusao Inada
Shawn Hsu Wong

Hirabayashi Ethnic Education Statement, 1974

By the beginning of the twenty-first century, ethnic studies (including Asian American studies) has proliferated across the nation at many universities, including several of the most elite. But there was (and is) ongoing doubt about the field's appropriateness and its rigor, and resistance is strongly rooted, if not always easily detectable. James Hirabayashi was in a unique position to note the personal and idiosyncratic opposition as well as the structural and ideological barriers to ethnic studies from its inception. Already a full professor of anthropology at San Francisco State University, he was at professional risk identifying himself with this new venture. He accepted a position as Dean of the School of Ethnic Studies, 1971–76, and found himself in the difficult position of simultaneously representing the administration of this large university and advocating for the radical demands of the minority students and their communities. After several years of intense, on-the-job experience, he presented this paper at the Second Annual Conference on Emerging Programs at the University of Washington, Seattle, November 7–9, 1974, describing the inherent conflicts between the assumptions of the prevailing society and academy and the requirements of authentic ethnic education for America's minority groups of color. This thoughtful statement concludes, sadly, that the field is destined never to achieve its basic aims. A quarter of a century later, Hirabayashi's essay remains an important stimulus for ongoing reflection and reevaluation.

Reprinted by permission of the author. The essay was also published in *On Common Ground: A Journal of Ethnic Thought* 1 (3) (October 24, 1979). San Francisco: School of Ethnic Studies at San Francisco State University.

Ethnic Education: Its Purposes and Prospects

In this essay I will focus on some basic assumptions underlying the education of certain ethnic minorities in this country, the problems of articulation with traditional educational systems and future prospects given this condition. When

I say certain ethnic minorities, I make a distinction between all ethnic minorities which refer to: "any group which is defined or set off by race, religion, or national origin, or some combination of these categories, and those ethnic groups who consistently experience forms of social and economic discrimination in our society. Specifically, I will relate to Black, Mexican, Latin, Asian, and Native Americans. . . .

I am an advocate of separate ethnic studies programs and am an active participant in one such program. My direct experience in program development has been primarily with the Asian American Studies program and as an administrator of the School of Ethnic Studies at San Francisco State University. As a result, the following analysis will rely heavily upon the events at San Francisco State University, the site of one of the initial confrontations to start an independent ethnic studies program. Finally, I am formally trained in the field of anthropology.

Ethnic Experience and Ethnic Education

Given the fundamental principles underlying our society, it seems inevitable that certain ethnic minorities in this country should ultimately rise in protest of the existing conditions. After years of adapting to a situation of inequity and noting the discrepancies between the society's ideal values and behavioral norms and attitudes in regard to many phases of their lives, it is surprising that they should have waited so long. Perhaps in terms of a long historical perspective it will not be assessed so, but the events of the tumultuous Sixties appear to be culmination of pent-up emotions exploding into action. Undoubtedly one related factor was the push for gradual social change during the Fifties on the part of the liberals with the ultimate goal of integration of the ethnic minorities into the mainstream of American life. There was a certain style used, characterized by legal analyses, deliberate strategies and the mobilization of people for nonviolent confrontations. However, these events were quickly to be followed by spontaneous and more extreme forms of direct confrontations in the urban centers where there were concentrations of low income populations. For them, conditions had become too drastic: it became a matter of survival to act for the changes in economic and social conditions were too slow in evolving and emotions could no longer be contained. . . .

Most of the early essays concerning the need for development of Ethnic Studies based their rationale upon an emotional assessment of the life conditions of ethnic groups in our society. This was certainly legitimate in view of the situation as outlined above when the development of concerns about the plight of the ethnic minorities was intricately interwoven with concrete events such as discrimination in housing, employment and other forms of inequity. These events relate essentially to a question of racism and therefore an emotional evaluation was a natural outcome of the situation. However, it is not the fact of racism per se that gives us the rationale for Ethnic Studies, it only gives us the reason for the development of the rationale. The correct way of developing a rationale for Ethnic Studies is to recognize its legitimacy and to create a positive base from which to construct a meaningful program for the people it is to serve. To build a rationale on the basis of racism results in negativism, and this is not a healthy base upon which to develop a creative program.

The recognition of the legitimacy of Ethnic Studies essentially rests upon an assessment of American society as a pluralistic society. Public and social science ideologies and theories concerning the relations of ethnic groups to American culture and society can be classified into three main types: 1) conformity to dominant society standards (assimilation); 2) biological, cultural and social blending into a new synthesis (acculturation); and 3) preservation of significant portions of the original culture and society within the context of the American society (pluralism). It would appear, from a cursory assessment of the literature, that the majority of the public and social science view are either explicitly or implicitly formulated in terms of the first type with an underlying assumption of an eventual assimilation to "middle class standards." It would seem that this goal motivated the actions of the liberals of the Forties bent upon easing the ethnic minorities into the mainstream of American life. This view and the second view, i.e., the "melting pot synthesis," both postulate a unitary model with the expectation that people conform to the model. Of the two, the second type is much more palatable to the ethnic minorities, for at least there is some attention paid to the variety of unique cultural experiences which are a part of their lives. . . .

When the conceptualization is made in terms of a unitary model, regardless of the sources of the model, ethnic groups are seen as assimilating from divergent cultural backgrounds to some single uniform American culture. Let us examine the case of the migrant ethnic groups for illustrative purposes. A large number of social scientists' assessments of the adjustments of the migrant ethnic groups in America have used a particular type of the acculturation-assimilation model. Briefly, an ideal type is postulated for the original culture and society and likewise an ideal type is conceptualized for the American Culture and society. Ethnic groups are then studied in the new setting and their adjustments assessed in terms of "how far they have diverged from the original culture and society" and "how close they have come to the American culture and society." Some ethnic groups are then considered "more progressive" than others because they have assimilated more rapidly. Consider the assessments made of the Japanese-Americans where they have often been lableled "model minorities." They are assessed as having made good adjustments to the degree that they have conformed closely to the ideals of middle class society. . . .

The conceptualization of the original culture and society of the migrants is usually an over-generalization which disregards the special situation and conditions of the migrants. The expectation that everyone moves along a continuum is based on the assumption that we have had in the past, do have in the present, and will have in the future a uniform culture and society.

Thus we have migrants bringing their "cultural baggage," whatever segments of the original society from whence they come, and whatever conceptualizations of the ideal values of the original society, and adapting creatively to the new environment as they assess it. They do not recreate the original culture and society in totality for that is impossible. What they do is to develop new meanings and relationships adapting old forms where they can, but in novel ways. . . .

I have used the example of recent migrant ethnic groups to illustrate the adaptive process to the general society. The migration of the Black people is quite distinct. They were torn from their social and cultural contexts in Africa and forceably resettled, by and large and consciously, in a socially fragmentary fashion. The slave traders and plantation owners broke up social groups in order to maintain an oppressive social and economic control over them. . . .

The Native Americans, of course, were not migrants but the original settlers of this continent. In spite of long-term governmental policies which were designed either to eliminate or to assimilate them (the ultimate goal of the Bureau of Indian Affairs was to work themselves out of a job after assimilation was complete), the Native Americans who were not completely decimated by social and cultural genocide through wars, disease, social and economic oppression continued to evolve their own unique distinct life styles. . . .

As it has been one of the functions of educational institutions to facilitate the discovery and internalization of a "correct." model for individuals in our society, it becomes necessary to challenge traditional education which has generally been based on a normative philosophy with an assumption of assimilation to a single uniform society. To the extent that the traditional educational system assumes a unitary model for all members of the society and to the extent that it does not relate directly to the perceptions and conceptions of the ethnic minorities, the ethnic minorities cannot readily find meaning for themselves if a positive understanding of their primary experience is prevented. Moreover, racism compounds their problem for their primary experiences are judged negatively.

There are those who contend that the traditional educational system no longer holds assumptions which prevent the ethnic minorities from dealing with primary issues of their ethnicity because certain corrections have been made now, and ethnic content is being added to the traditional curricula; but I will argue that basic changes have not been made. Moreover, the traditional educational system is resisting changes which will allow ethnic studies to develop the postulates needed to serve the primary needs of ethnic education. The main thesis of this essay is that the basic assumptions underlying traditional education do not accommodate concepts and perceptions of the ethnic minorities without immediately distorting them. And without fundamental changes in traditional education. I remain an advocate of separate ethnic studies programs.

The University Setting

The university, in its broadest definition, is characterized as a place for learning where knowledge and new ideas are developed, where students are prepared for useful lives in our society, and a place where self-awareness and intellectual development are promoted. Although there are many sources we may use for an assessment of the university and its purposes, I shall take one by my colleagues at San Francisco State University for not only do they review the meaning of the university experience for students, but they do so in the context of the events which led to the strike of 1968. . . .

In a traditional educational institution, if we assume as an objective a uniform culture and society, a single uniform culture and society, a single uniform normative ideology would suffice as there would be compatible assumptions underlying the ideology. However, because of the diversity of the life styles of the people who make up this nation, the assumptions underlying the ideology of middle class society must be called into question. Let us isolate one of the assumptions contained in their definition of a mature ideology, the nature of man and his relation to his fellows, and view it in conjunction with one of the "lives" of the university experience, life as a place for self-discovery. If the life styles for the ethnic minorities are at variance with that of "middle class" America, as has been argued above, it follows that the ethnic minorities cannot achieve self-understanding if they approach self discovery with assumptions and perceptions other than their own. Unless ethnic education sees the development of a rationale based on their own assumptions, all other goals become diverted. The "lives" of the university as an institution, if they rest on middle class assumptions, do not serve the basic needs of the students from ethnic communities.

Given these differences, the issue of control of ethnic studies programs becomes paramount. The irony of the strike at San Francisco State is that the very people who were forced to recognize Ethnic Studies are the self same people who now sit in judgment of everything that is done. All programmatic developments, all staff appointments require ultimate approval by those in charge of the institution. If we isolate the assumptions underlying the "ideal goals and purposes of individuals to be nurtured by institutions and society," . . . and take that in conjunction with one of the lives of the institution as a corporation, we can readily determine what administrators are charged to do, and there is immediate and basic conflict. Specifically, the conflicts come out explicitly in almost all decision making procedures in the development of the program. Questions such as: Do all of the courses meet the academic standards? Are the teachers qualified to teach? Does the format in terms of which the course is conceptualized fit into existing curriculum? All are judged in terms of standardized traditional criteria and ultimately fit into the general educational system. Here I am not necessarily charging administrators with conscious and malevolent intent, I am merely pointing out that the pervasive nature of the basic assumptions underlying the system are never made explicit, but they affect the nature and kind of adjustments forced upon ethnic studies at every turn. Thus, the issue of control is not simply a Machiavellian grab for power, as many have characterized those who press for ethnic studies, but it is an insistence upon the fundamental necessity of defining ethnic education on its own terms. . . .

To illustrate the pervasiveness of the assumptions underlying traditional education, it may be instructive for us to examine the relation between traditional education, conventional research, and ethnic education. Conventional education and research rest upon certain assumptions which have resulted in a total disregard of the particular needs of the ethnic minorities to understand themselves and they have not contributed a body of data for the explicit purpose of the education of the ethnic minorities either individuals or as members of their communities. Why is this so? The answer comes from the inquiry: What motivates a conventional researcher to do research?

One of the primary motives is the validation of his activities in the eyes of his peers. Consider those activities. The basic conceptual framework which he uses, the theories which are based on the framework, the hypotheses he derives from those theories, the methodology which he uses to generate these data to test the hypotheses, all are based upon certain specialized assumptions underlying that particular discipline. The results of any research are then evaluated in terms of what contribution it makes to the further clarification and development of the conceptual framework and the associated body of data of that discipline. Central to the motivations of any given researcher is that he contributes to the goals of that discipline and the structure of the conventional research community demands this kind of accountability. If this is so, then those who are "researched" necessarily remain "objects" to be used as sources of "data," data based on their conceptualizations, for those academicians to further the development of their own discipline. . . .

The way in which the people of the community remain "objects" becomes clearer when we examine how the "data" about the people are used. Since the results of the research are presented in terms of conventional social science disciplines, as browsing in any university library will readily show, these data are primarily available to the very academicians who give it validation, due to an elitist bias on the part of the same academicians. Further, when we examine the funding of applied social science research and any implementation of these in action programs, we must question the role of values and motivations of those supplying the funds. Those values, inasmuch as they as based on "outside" perspectives, cannot be the same as those of the community members. As stated above, even if the welfare of the community is claimed as a motive their perception of this is in terms of persons other that the members of the community so that at best it becomes arbitrary, imposed and paternalistic.

Rationale for an Ethnic Studies

In the redefinition of Ethnic Studies and research we must look at the issues both in terms of the content and the process. For not only do we challenge the relevancy of the basic conceptualizations made of us by traditional academia, but also the very processes of discovery and education which have become alienated from the people concerned. . . .

We learn and come to understand ourselves and our world views, i.e., the way we see ourselves in relation to all else, only when we undertake this process of understanding as active participants. To the extent that we relinquish being active participants in this task, we become alienated from ourselves: for what we are talking about is not the objective world as such but our perception of it. . . . Moreover, if we accept norms imposed on us and if we use those norms to pattern our behavior regardless of our life experiences, we will estrange ourselves from those very experiences and this process leads ultimately to our dehumanization. Thus when our cultural context is penetrated by outsiders, and their descriptions are then imposed on us (as in negative stereotyping) in disrespect of our own views, this imposition inhibits our self-awareness by curbing it. Therefore, it is absolutely essential that self-understanding be based on an active participation in the process itself. . . .

Ethnic education must be relevant for the ethnic minorities and their communities. The codification of reality must be made in terms of symbols derived from the people themselves which begins with the language and the universe of the participants. It follows that this process must be tied closely to community involvement and research: community people involved in education and the education community involved in the ethnic community.

Ethnic education must include the following foci in research and studies: a re-examination of the historical experiences of the people concerned, a thorough study of the community and its culture, and the articulations of the lives of those people with the total society of which they are a part. It is particularly crucial in its initial stages that we give free rein to the development of the humanities and creative arts, for free expression of the life experiences is the basis upon which ethnic education must build new knowledge and self-understanding. . . .

Conclusions: Summary and Prospects

To summarize the basic necessities of ethnic education: it must deal directly with the life experiences of the ethnic minorities and deal with it by codifying that reality in terms of the conceptions and perceptions of those who are living that life. It must take care that in the process of abstraction, it does not destroy the linkage between the primary experience and the conceptualizations that follow from it. To ensure relevance for the ethnic minorities, and to ensure the proper linkage in this process, it is necessary for ethnic education and the community to engage in this process together. An ethnic community must be an integral part of the process of research and studies and the results must be directly relevant and applicable to that community.

As long as the university as an educational institution continues to operate in terms of its existing set of assumptions, the successful implementation of ethnic studies programs is seriously curtailed from the outset. . . .

Although I count among my non-ethnic colleagues many who have been sympathetic and have gained a measure of understanding of our position, I remain rather pessimistic of the prospects of ethnic education within the context of traditional educational systems. There are inevitable and overwhelming forces represented by consistent and persistent articulations with the operations of traditional education which mitigate against the implementation of the fundamental precepts of ethnic education, making the outlook for change discouraging. I do not say, thereby, that the effort has been for naught, for there have been some changes, not only in the minds of the ethnic population, but in challenges which have forced adjustments on the part of traditional systems. Perhaps enough of these adjustments may call into question the basic assumptions underlying their operations, but that is yet to come. My perceptions of the situation as an administrator of an ethnic studies program is that the odds are overwhelming, and that gradually the total forces of the system will wear us down. . . .

Since this resistance to accommodate is implicit and disguised, the adjustments of traditional educational systems to ethnic education have been inadequate. Various responses to pressure brought by ethnic minorities include piecemeal and token accommodations as for example the requirement of primary and secondary teachers to take a few units in ethnic studies so that they can then "relate" to students coming from that cultural background. Were it so simple, we could have long since solved many of the educational issues for the ethnic minorities. To take another example, university administrators "solved the problem" by assembling enough of these courses for a major in ethnic studies. This is no solution at all, for the fundamental concepts and perceptions are still those of the traditional disciplines which I have argued do not address the basic issue of codification of reality into symbols based on the perceptions of the ethnic minorities. Often the failure of those programs is pointed to with delight on the part of the detractors of ethnic studies as proof that they did not have substance, quality, or standards. To the extent that forces in the dominant society have been able to divert the purpose of ethnic education, such factors guarantee failure for the ethnic minorities are quick to recognize that it does not serve their needs at all.

It is not correct to merely lay all blame on those outside of ethnic education. To the extent that we who are involved fail to recognize the fact that, after all, we are also creatures of the total society and that we have internalized those implicit assumptions in terms of which this society operates, we often neglect to question the assumptions underlying traditional education and thus, we do not need outside oppressors. We function very well in that respect ourselves.

So our task is difficult and will take time. Perhaps my pessimism concerning the educational system is justified, and ultimately it will grind us down to the point where ethnic studies will be indistinguishable from any traditional department or program. When that time comes, the battle will have been lost and we will only be able to gain solace in the fact that there may have been some overall effect upon the system and upon those ethnic minorities who have been involved in its development. But when that time comes, and if the situation for the ethnic minorities is not such that they are able to relate in a positive way to their own life experiences, it will be time to do something else.

117

Supreme Court: Lau v. Nichols, *January 21, 1974*

By the early 1970s, increased immigration, especially the groups entering as a result of the 1965 immigration policy reforms, caused significant growth in Chinese
communities, with concomitant rises in school populations. The San Francisco
Unified School District, for example, enrolled more than 2,800 students of Chinese descent, about 1,000 of whom spoke no English and were receiving special
English language instruction. About 1,800, however, had limited English and
found themselves falling behind in classes where English language competence
was presumed. Their families filed a class action suit, claiming that the students'
civil rights were being denied, specifically section 601 of the Civil Rights Act of
1964 prohibiting discrimination based on "race, color, or national origin." The
district and the California state courts rejected their appeal, but the U.S.
Supreme Court ruled unanimously that the district had violated the 1964 act. The
court ordered the school district to respond to the Chinese community's needs by
providing the English language support required to ensure "equality of educational opportunity." The case encouraged many others throughout the nation to
attend to bilingual issues in their districts.

Supreme Court Reporter, Volume 94: Cases Argued and Determined in the Supreme
    Court of the United States, October Term, 1973. St. Paul, MN: West Publishing
    Co, 1975.

U.S. Supreme Court

Lau v. Nichols

414 U.S. 563

MR. JUSTICE DOUGLAS delivered the opinion of the Court.

The San Francisco, California, school system was integrated in 1971 as a result of a federal court decree, 339 F. Supp. 1315. See Lee v. Johnson, 404 U.S.
1215. The District Court found that there are 2,856 students of Chinese ancestry
in the school system who do not speak English. Of those who have that language

deficiency, about 1,000 are given supplemental courses in the English language. About 1,800, however, do not receive that instruction.

This class suit brought by non-English-speaking Chinese students against officials responsible for the operation of the San Francisco Unified School District seeks relief against the unequal educational opportunities, which are alleged to violate, inter alia, the Fourteenth Amendment. No specific remedy is urged upon us. Teaching English to the students of Chinese ancestry who do not speak the language is one choice. Giving instructions to this group in Chinese is another. There may be others. Petitioners ask only that the Board of Education be directed to apply its expertise to the problem and rectify the situation.

The District Court denied relief. The Court of Appeals affirmed, holding that there was no violation of the Equal Protection Clause of the Fourteenth Amendment or of 601 of the Civil Rights Act of 1964, 78 Stat. 252, 42 U.S.C. 2000d, which excludes from participation in federal financial assistance, recipients of aid which discriminate against racial groups, 483 F.2d 791. One judge dissented. A hearing en banc was denied, two judges dissenting. Id., at 805.

We granted the petition for certiorari because of the public importance of the question presented, 412 U.S. 938.

The Court of Appeals reasoned that "every student brings to the starting line of his educational career different advantages and disadvantages caused in part by social, economic and cultural background, created and continued completely apart from any contribution by the school system," 483 F.2d, at 797. Yet in our view the case may not be so easily decided. This is a public school system of California and 71 of the California Education Code states that "English shall be the basic language of instruction in all schools." That section permits a school district to determine "when and under what circumstances instruction may be given bilingually." That section also states as "the policy of the state" to insure "the mastery of English by all pupils in the schools." And bilingual instruction is authorized "to the extent that it does not interfere with the systematic, sequential, and regular instruction of all pupils in the English language."

Moreover, 8573 of the Education Code provides that no pupil shall receive a diploma of graduation from grade 12 who has not met the standards of proficiency in "English," as well as other prescribed subjects.

Moreover, by 12101 of the Education Code (Supp. 1973) children between the ages of six and 16 years are (with exceptions not material here) "subject to compulsory full-time education."

Under these state-imposed standards there is no equality of treatment merely by providing students with the same facilities, textbooks, teachers, and curriculum; for students who do not understand English are effectively foreclosed from any meaningful education.

Basic English skills are at the very core of what these public schools teach. Imposition of a requirement that, before a child can effectively participate in the educational program, he must already have acquired those basic skills is to make a mockery of public education. We know that those who do not understand English are certain to find their classroom experiences wholly incomprehensible and in no way meaningful.

We do not reach the Equal Protection Clause argument which has been advanced but rely solely on 601 of the Civil Rights Act of 1964, 42 U.S.C. 2000d, to reverse the Court of Appeals.

That section bans discrimination based "on the ground of race, color, or national origin," in "any program or activity receiving Federal financial assistance." The school district involved in this litigation receives large amounts of federal financial assistance. The Department of Health, Education, and Welfare (HEW), which has authority to promulgate regulations prohibiting discrimination in federally assisted school systems, 42 U.S.C. 2000d-1, in 1968 issued one guideline that "school systems are responsible for assuring that students of a particular race, color, or national origin are not denied the opportunity to obtain the education generally obtained by other students in the system." . . .

Discrimination among students on account of race or national origin that is prohibited includes "discrimination . . . in the availability or use of any academic . . . or other facilities of the grantee or other recipient."

Discrimination is barred which has that effect even though no purposeful design is present: a recipient "may not . . . utilize criteria or methods of administration which have the effect of subjecting individuals to discrimination" or have "the effect of defeating or substantially impairing accomplishment of the objectives of the program as respect individuals of a particular race, color, or national origin."

It seems obvious that the Chinese-speaking minority receive fewer benefits than the English-speaking majority from respondents' school system which denies them a meaningful opportunity to participate in the educational program—all earmarks of the discrimination banned by the regulations. . . .

We accordingly reverse the judgment of the Court of Appeals and remand the case for the fashioning of appropriate relief.

Reversed and remanded.

118

Letter, Philip Vera Cruz to Noel Kent
Re Filipino Farmworkers, January 17, 1975

Philip Vera Cruz was one of several Filipino farmworkers who led the original grape pickers' strike in Coachella-Delano, California, beginning in 1965. The strike generated national interest and catapulted Chicano leaders César Chavez and Dolores Huerta into international prominence. The Filipino leaders, partly because they were fewer in number than their Chicano counterparts, were largely obscured, but as Vera Cruz makes clear in this letter to Kent, a professor of ethnic studies at the University of Hawai'i at Manoa, their contributions were significant. Agbayani Village, named for a worker who died during the strike struggle, was built to house elderly Filipino workers and encouraged hundreds of students to join in work camps and to listen to the workers' stories. Vera Cruz was not highly educated but was an eloquent speaker. His letter is unedited. Later, there was a falling out between Filipino and Chicano leaders, partly because Chavez accepted an award from then Philippine President Ferdinand Marcos. Marcos's corruption and political repression inspired a massive popular movement demanding his resignation; it included many Filipino Americans and was successful.

Letter, Philip Vera Cruz to Noel Kent, January 17, 1975. Philip Vera Cruz Collection, Box 8, Folder: PVC Correspondence, 1974–75, Wayne State University Archives of Labor and Urban Affairs. Thanks to Dorothy Fujita Rony for alerting me to this collection. Reprinted with permission.

UNITED FARM WORKERS of AMERICA AFL-CIO
P.O. BOX 62 KEENE, CALIFORNIA 93531 (805) 822–5571

Jan. 17, 1975

Noel Kent
2142 Atherton Rd.
Honolulu, Hawaii 96822

Dear Noel,

While you were with us in the Agbayani Village last Summer, we had a few short conversations leading to the Filipino role as workers and unions in relation to the Farm Workers Movement in Hawaii and in the U S mainland, particularly in California. I honestly revealed to you that my knowledge of the past history of Filipino agricultural labor here and there was wanting, or very inadequate, for a more definite and clearer picture to relate it to the present. Very seldom a writer took notice of the Filipino farm workers and their union activities. Unfortunately, not much of their struggle was even mentioned or written.

In the Coachella-Delano Grape Strike of 1965, the Filipino role is missing in its history. Yet, not just a matter of opinion, but of fact, that the Filipino decision and action for a strike had set the spark, or triggered the explosion for the Farm Workers Revolution. In the Agbayani Village Dedication last Summer (and maybe you were here then at the time), John Henning, Secretary-Treasurer of the AFL-CIO California State Federation, said: Without those retired Filipino original strikers, you don't have a union today.

No one cared to find out what was happening to Filipino strikers, holding the labor camps—with their light, gas and water turned off; their personal belongings thrown outside the building; and doors padlocked. They were hungry, but stood firmly behind their union. Filipino pickets in the fields, in front of cold storages and railroad tracts were harrassed and insulted by Growers, security guards and the sherifs. Those who had to work for their families left the Delano area struct fields and got lost elsewhere. Mostly green carders and illegals took their jobs. But those contributions to the Movement were ignored or not appreciated and mistakes in the Hiring Hall made matters worse. It led to more dissatisfaction and disappointment, and gave a psychological incentive to a dissastrous collusion of Growers and Teamsters for "Sweetheart Contracts," costing the UFW millions of dollars to recover them. We are still in the process of doing so.

This missing link in the chains of events in the Farm Workers Movement must be filled up. But, for almost ten years now in the union, I've not seen one writer interested enough to do the job. Some friends expect me to do it, but I know I am not a journalist. I don't even know how and where to start.

Anyway, I've been trying to gather relevant materials to Filipino union activities in Agriculture both in Hawaii and in the mainland. Then I hope to reconstruct them into a factual story from their initial participation in unionism to their role in the 1965 Delano Grape Strike.

I would like to help revive the Filipino fighting spirit in youths to reenforce the flame of World Liberation. But being a minority within a minority, I feel deeply compelled to advise the Filipino youths to get more serious in their studies and later, more effectively help the Liberation Movement in their capacities as technicians and professionals. Their acquired status might tend to make them more conservative than progressive, but at least if thrown out of the union by the leadership, they have a better chance to survive. This has been my personal observation and experiences to a certain extent in the internal union politics. It could be more ruthless and dirtier as practised by other unions. . . .

With best wishes to all our friends, brothers and sisters in Aloha State, I am

As always,

[*signature*]
[*S*] *Philip Vera Crus*

119

Indochina Migration and Refugee
Assistance Act, May 23, 1975

The ill-fated war in Southeast Asia officially ended with the retreat of the United States in 1975. With this withdrawal, however, came immense responsibility for the hundreds of thousands of Vietnamese, Cambodians, and Laotians we had recruited in the war against communism. Indeed, many of them paid a fearful price when South Vietnam fell and American protection disappeared. In partial recompense, the United States began a refugee program to admit some of the populations displaced. One of the first significant acts of Congress to acknowledge this responsibility came the year the United States left. The actual policy of dispersing Vietnamese and Cambodian refugees into all states except Alaska was a disaster, however, and subsequent legislation such as the Refugee Act of 1980 attempted to improve the situation. In the decade after this act, more than 750,000 refugees entered the country from Southeast Asia. Their communities have become among the largest and most complex of Asian Americans in the nation, especially with regard to extreme gaps in status, education, and wealth.

United States Statutes at Large Containing Laws and Concurrent Resolutions Enacted During the First Session of the Ninety-fourth Congress, 1975, vol. 89. Washington, DC: Government Printing Office, 1977.

An Act
To enable the United States to render assistance to,
or in behalf of, certain migrants and refugees

Be it enacted by the Senate and House of Representatives of the United States of America in Congress assembled, That this Act may be cited as "The Indochina Migration and Refugee Assistance Act of 1975."

Sec. 2. (a) Subject to the provisions of subsection (b) there are hereby authorized to be appropriated, in addition to amounts otherwise available for such purposes, $455,000,000 for the performance of functions set forth in the Migration and Refugee Assistance Act of 1962 (76 Stat. 121), as amended, with respect to aliens who have fled from Cambodia or Vietnam, such sums to remain available in accordance with the provisions of subsection (b) of this section.

(b) None of the funds authorized to be appropriated by this Act shall be available for the performance of functions after June 30, 1976, other than for carrying out the provisions of clauses (3), (4), (5), and (6) of section 2(b) of the Migration and Refugee Assistance Act of 1962, as amended. None of such funds shall be available for obligation for any purpose after September 30. 1977.

Sec. 3. In carrying out functions utilizing the funds made available under this Act, the term "refugee" as defined in section 2(b) (3) of the Migration and Refugee Assistance Act of 1962, as amended, shall be deemed to include aliens who (A) because of persecution or fear of persecution on account of race, religion, or political opinion, fled from Cambodia or Vietnam; (B) cannot return there because of fear of persecution on account of race, religion, or political opinion; and (C) are in urgent need of assistance for the essentials of life.

Sec. 4. (a) The President shall consult with and keep the Committees on the Judiciary, Appropriations, and International Relations of the House of Representatives and the Committees on Foreign Relations, Appropriations and Judiciary of the Senate fully and currently informed of the use of funds and the exercise of functions authorized in this Act.

(b) Not more than thirty days after the date of enactment of this Act, the President shall transmit to such Committees a report describing fully and completely the status of refugees from Cambodia and South Vietnam. Such report shall set forth, in addition—

1. a plan for the resettlement of those refugees remaining in receiving or staging centers;
2. the number of refugees who have indicated an interest in returning to their homeland or being resettled in a third country, together with (A) a description of the plan for their return or resettlement and the steps taken to carry out such return or resettlement, and (B) any initiatives that have been made with respect to the Office of the High Commissioner for Refugees of the United Nations; and
3. a full and complete description of the steps the President has taken to retrieve and deposit in the Treasury as miscellaneous receipts all amounts previously authorized and appropriated for assistance to South Vietnam and Cambodia but not expended for such purpose, exclusive of the $98,000,000 of Indochina Postwar Reconstruction funds allocated to the Department of State for movement and maintenance of refugees prior to the date of enactment of this Act. . . .

Approved May 23, 1975

PART 6

Brave New World: Through 2000

The last quarter of the twentieth century was a time of truly startling changes for Asian America. Most important, disparate groups began solidifying the idea and practice of a pan-Asian identity, first on college campuses and then in urban centers. This has led to greater visibility and participation in local and national society and politics as well as intensified tensions and stresses. According to the 1970 census, there were only 1.5 million Asian Americans, less than one percent of the population. Japanese Americans were the largest single ethnic group, followed by Chinese and Filipinos, and very small numbers of other nationalities. The 2000 census revealed an entirely different landscape, with more than 10 million Asian Americans, about 4 percent of the total U.S. population. Filipino and Chinese American communities grew to about 2 million each, while Koreans and Asian Indians, as well as Vietnamese, also outnumbered the Japanese. Further, as a consequence of the large influx of immigrants in this period, the majority of Asian Americans will continue to be foreign born well into the twenty-first century.

Where previous generations may have envisioned acculturation or "progress" as a steady march toward assimilation and economic improvement, there are growing indications that linear notions of "Americanization" have become fuzzier and national boundaries count for much less. Some of this is the result of advances in transportation and information technology. Immigrants use long-distance telephone lines and the Internet to communicate daily with family and friends in the homeland; those with means fly regularly between, for example, Korea and Los Angeles or New York City. Here, they can access shopping centers that provide almost everything available in Seoul, including current soap operas on videotape.

More significant, the presence of many immigrants who are highly educated or trained, including doctors, nurses, researchers, academics, entrepreneurs, and engineers, has created a class of Asian Americans who are unwilling to accept notions of gradual acculturation with deferred gratification. Many see no reason to give up their cultures, traditions, and lifestyles. They also, often without fully realizing it, stand on the foundations of cultural renaissance efforts of an older, activist generation from the late 1960s and the 1970s, when new Asian American theater and film groups challenged the mainstream and new writers began explicitly dismantling "outsider" constructions of their communities. In the '70s, community social service and cultural centers were developed for the elderly in urban Little Tokyos and for Filipino farmworkers in rural areas of California. Students and activists organized to create ethnic studies courses and programs on campuses and defended housing for the Chinese and Filipinos in cities ranging from Honolulu, Los Angeles, San Francisco, and Seattle to Boston and New York. The end result of these large movements for educational change and social services is a very significant increase in the sheer volume and the diversity and vitality of "ethnic" cultural activities among Asian American groups.

There have been two basic sets of responses from the larger American public. First is continued abuse of a "model minority" interpretation that sees Asian Americans as uniformly successfully assimilated, despite ongoing evidence of immense social dislocation. Second is growing concern over competition for resources, including admission into elite universities. Some of these are public research units like the University of California campuses, many of which now have entering classes that are more than half Asian American. Others are prestigious private colleges like the Ivies or Stanford, where 15–30 percent of the student body may be Asian American. Since Asian Americans comprise about 4 percent of the total population, this "overrepresentation" is remarkable. At the same time, glass-ceiling issues continue to abound—particularly at upper levels of management in both public and private sectors. On the same elite campuses showcasing so many Asian American students, for example, there are very few faculty or administrators from similar backgrounds.

At the other extreme, there is competition for diminishing resources in the social service arena, especially with cuts in welfare and assistance programs. Generations of Asian Americans, especially from Southeast Asia, have become welfare-dependent, with school dropout/pushout rates, poverty, drug abuse, and gang involvement at similar levels as in depressed Native American, Latino, and black communities.

This volume has deliberately focused on Asian Americans, omitting reference to Pacific Islander Americans, including Native Hawaiians, Samoans, and Guamanians (Chamorros). In fact, from the U.S. government's point of view, Pacific Islanders were lumped together with Asian Americans only briefly, as a result of OMB Directive No. 15, issued in 1977. Initiatives from Native Hawaiians led to disaggregation exactly twenty years later, and the 2000 census affirmed this separation. The process was difficult and complex. For Native Hawaiians, there were two major issues: first, conflating the two groups misreprented them as "immigrants" when they were, in fact, indigenous peoples, like Native Americans; second, they were incorporated to increase the total numbers of the umbrella Asian Pacific American group, yet often marginalized within the group itself. Separate data gathering would highlight the need for federal economic and educational resources and create the political base for empowerment. On the other hand, Asian American advocates feared that Native Hawaiian and Pacific Islander numbers were simply too small in the first place, and that the loss of numbers by disaggregation would weaken the overall movement to secure resources and representation.

In a similar vein, concerns have been raised about Chinese and Japanese Americans dominating the leadership of political, academic, media, and civil rights arenas. Challenges to apparent marginalization come from mixed-race individuals, South and Southeast Asians, Filipinos, and groups with different lifestyles, including gay, lesbian, bisexual, and transgendered individuals of Asian descent. A Korean, lesbian, immigrant sweatshop worker, for example, would have difficulty finding support from any one of the groups that theoretically exists to help her: ethnic, gay rights, immigrant rights, or labor agencies.

The sheer diversity contained within this rubric is daunting. Examining an issue like religion is illuminating. There are, of course, many different types of Buddhists, ranging from the esoteric sects of Nepal to the groups inhabiting expansive Taiwanese temples in Southern California. The introduction of Laotian monks to small-town Illinois was at least unsettling for immigrants and residents alike. Many Korean immigrants are Protestants; most Filipinos are Catholics, although some are Muslim. And few Americans realize that Indonesia is the most populous Muslim nation in the world. Animists, Confucians, Hindus, Sikhs, and Jews are also represented. Immigrants bring their cultures with them, and the potential for mischief is great unless American society's parameters for tolerance are expanded.

The numbers of new immigrants and their diverse languages and lifestyles have regenerated concerns over the very old stereotype of Asians as "perpetual foreigners." Ironically, some of the positive developments allowing immigrant communities to nurture cultural practices such as the use of their languages, including in signage on storefronts, and traditional dress have provoked more nativist reaction. One of the more vicious consequences of increased anti-Asian hostility is the rise in hate crimes, a new category—legally recognized in 1990 — of incidents that are manifestations of antagonism directed at whole groups of people, based on race, ethnicity, religion, or lifestyle. Statistics on hate crimes, including those perpetrated against Asian Americans, continue to climb even though many go unreported. In an especially vicious and notorious incident, Vincent Chin was clubbed to death by unemployed auto workers in Detroit in 1982, during industry downsizing that incorporated anti-Japan propaganda. There were also deadly assaults against Southeast Asian schoolchildren by a Vietnam war veteran, Latino youths in New Jersey calling themselves "dot busters" against Asian Indians, and a white supremacist killing a Filipino postal carrier after shooting into a Jewish community center in 1999.

Hate crimes are among the few tragedies that bring together various groups, perhaps because many can identify with the victims and the assaults are often so random and vicious. A similar response was generated by high-level racial profiling such as that directed toward Dr. Wen Ho Lee, a nuclear weapons scientist publicly accused of delivering critical secrets to the People's Republic of China. His case combined the "perpetual foreigner" element and the inscrutable enemy image with partisan attacks on the Democratic National Committee for accepting illegal political donations from noncitizen Chinese. He became a classic scapegoat, although eventually 59 of 60 charges against him were dropped. The remaining one, to which he pled guilty, was a misdemeanor for mishandling classified data, and he was released for time served. It should be noted that many of Lee's colleagues, and top officials at government labs and in the Central Intelligence Agency, were also discovered to have downloaded secret data for unauthorized use at home but were never prosecuted. Lee's case revealed the degree to which both major political parties succumbed to temptation to scapegoat Asian Americans.

At the same time, old injustices were more easily addressed. The 1988 Civil Liberties Act apologized for the mass internment of Japanese Americans during World War II and provided $20,000 redress payments for approximately 60,000 still alive when President Ronald Reagan signed the legislation. The three men convicted of disobeying World War II exclusion-related orders, Minoru Yasui, Fred Korematsu, and Gordon Hirabayashi, had their convictions vacated, although their cases remain on the books at the U.S. Supreme Court. While refugees from Laos, Vietnam, and Cambodia continue to face enormous problems, Congress has passed legislation making it easier for Hmong veterans to become naturalized American citizens. And while Filipino veterans who were cut off from benefits continued to die without justice, some survivors experienced incremental gains from a reluctant Congress.

As the fastest-growing "racial" group in the United States, Asian Americans illuminate some of the basic ways in which the nation is changing. Perhaps the most important shift is rapid globalization—capital, goods, information, and people moving across borders at such increasing rates of speed that the very notion of boundaries is being fundamentally challenged. Definitions of who or what constitutes an "American" will be subject to greater stress. And, while some old traditions deserve to be shelved, there will be enormous dislocations as more immigrants arrive, adding their cultures to and changing the size of Asian American communities, and more native-born Asian Americans strive to assert and improve their position in society. Asian Americans will be at the center of many serious issues, and will have great opportunity for innovation and creativity.

120

Asian/Pacific American Heritage Week
(Proclamation 4650), March 28, 1979

President Jimmy Carter signed this proclamation designating a week, beginning May 4, 1979, celebrating the presence of Asian Pacific Americans (APAs). Since then the annual week has turned into a month (May) devoted to APAs and their heritages. Throughout much of the United States, individuals and organizations present films, performances, lectures, and other events reflecting Asian or Pacific Islander "home country" cultures and/or the evolving cultures of these groups in America. While these specially designated periods are sometimes criticized because they can encourage society to ignore the group the rest of the year, it is true that many regions and institutions would never address APA heritages without this encouragement.

Special Edition of the Federal Register, 3: The President, 1979 Compilation. Washington, DC: National Archives and Records Service, Revised as of January 1, 1980.

Proclamation 4650 of March 28, 1979
Asian/Pacific American Heritage Week, 1979

By the President of the United States of America
A Proclamation

America's greatness—its ideals, its system of government, its economy, its people—derives from the contribution of peoples of many origins who come to our land seeking human liberties or economic opportunity. Asian-Americans have played a significant role in the creation of a dynamic and pluralistic America, with their enormous contributions to our science, arts, industry, government and commerce.

Unfortunately, we have not always fully appreciated the talents and the contributions which Asian-Americans have brought to the United States. Until recently, our immigration and naturalization laws discriminated against them. They were also subjected to discrimination in education, housing, and employment. And during World War II our Japanese-American citizens were treated with suspicion and fear.

Yet, Asians of diverse origins—from China, Japan, Korea, the Philippines, and Southeast Asia—continued to look to America as a land of hope, opportunity, and freedom.

At last their confidence in the United States has been justified. We have succeeded in removing the barriers to full participation in American life, and we welcome the newest Asian immigrants to our shores—refugees from Indochina displaced by political, and social upheavals. Their successful integration into American society and their positive and active participation in our national life demonstrates the soundness of America's policy of continued openness to peoples from Asia and the Pacific.

The Ninety-fifth Congress has requested the President by House Joint Resolution 1007, approved October 5, 1978, to designate the seven-day period beginning on May 4, 1979, as "Asian/Pacific American Heritage Week."

NOW, THEREFORE, I, JIMMY CARTER, President of the United States of America, declare the week beginning on May 4, 1979, as Asian/Pacific American Heritage Week. I call upon the people of the United States, especially the educational community, to observe this week with appropriate ceremonies and activities.

IN WITNESS WHEREOF, I have hereunto set my hand this twenty-eighth day of March, in the year of our Lord nineteen hundred seventy-nine, and of the Independence of the United States of America the two hundred and third.

JIMMY CARTER

121

Eric Chock, Writers of Hawaii Conference, 1980

Hawai'i has always had a serious body of literature. Prior to the arrival of west-erners and literacy, there was a long and masterly oral tradition among Native Hawaiians. Later, Hawaiians and other arrivals created a singular literature crafted from a unique series of experiences. But aside from the writings be-queathed by the largely white (haole in Hawaiian) elite, there was little acknowl-edged as literature until a movement of "local" writers coalesced in the 1970s. An early manifestation was the 1978 "Talk Story: Words Bind, Words Set Free" con-ference in Honolulu. Bamboo Ridge Press was founded shortly thereafter, and many volumes of poetry and prose have been published since. Darrell Lum and Eric Chock were the founding coeditors of Bamboo Ridge: The Hawaii Writers Quarterly, *and the latter opened the 1980 Writers of Hawaii Conference with this introduction. Chock refers to HLAC, the Hawaii Literary Arts Council, and Al-fred Preis, the first executive director of the Hawaii State Foundation on Culture and the Arts, the state arts council. Note here the sense that the early movement sought recognition both within the state for local writing as a distinct genre and as a unique literature apart from "mainland" hegemony.*

Reprinted with permission from Bamboo Ridge Press. *The Best of Bamboo Ridge: The Hawaii Writers' Quarterly*, ed. Eric Chock and Darrell H.Y. Lum. Honolulu: Bam-boo Ridge Press, 1986.

On Local Literature

In October 1980, the Writers of Hawaii Conference convened at the Hawaii State Capitol Auditorium for six nights to an audience of 200 people each night. It was sponsored by the Hawaii Literary Arts Council and Talk Story, Inc. with support from the Hawaii Committee for the Humanities and the State Foundation on Culture and the Arts. The following is an edited version of the opening night in-troduction, most of which is still relevant today. It is excerpted from Writers of

Hawaii: A Focus On Our Literary Heritage, *edited by Eric Chock and Jody Manabe (Bamboo Ridge Press, 1981).*

I

Welcome everybody, to "Writers of Hawaii: A Focus On Our Literary Heritage." I am Eric Chock, president of the Hawaii Literary Arts Council. It was almost a year ago when the director of the State Foundation on Culture and the Arts, Mr. Preis, congratulated me on winning the HLAC presidency. And only half-jokingly he asked me, "Was this an election, or was it a revolution?" Must be my long hair, I guess. Some people are still afraid that the hippies are gonna take over.

Well, for Mr. Preis and everyone else, a late answer: I believe that this is part of not a revolutionary process, but an evolutionary process. And I hope that this is a process that will eventually lead to local literature being taught in the schools in Hawaii. Sounds a little strange, I know, to some people—local literature—Hawaii stories, written by Hawaii people, and taught to Hawaii's children in the schools. Sounds almost redundant.

But I hope that it will happen someday, in the schools, even at the college level. Because it will lead to more pride among Hawaii's people, and an awareness of Hawaii's directions, past and present. And also it will provide more opportunities for people, like me, who grew up here and want to be writers and who need clear models for exactly what that is—a Hawaii writer.

This process, this goal for the Hawaii Literary Arts Council, is as Mr. Preis once said, "To bring before the people of Hawaii the great importance of literature." And this process is what we're continuing tonight.

But literature, and especially Modern Hawaiian Literature, what is that? And why is it so important? Literature is an activity that happens in a society, a culture, a group, any group. It is a shared sense of belonging and identity, expressed in words. Like any other kind of art, it is a way to understand life, to appreciate living and therefore to participate in life to the fullest of your potential. It should make you feel inspired about your life.

And how can it do that? Well, theoretically, literature helps you intensify your sense of individual identity in such a way that you feel like a so-called "universal being." What that means is that, in literature, the range of human experiences specific to your group is demonstrated to be characteristic of all people. Human traits are shown to occur naturally in all humans.

While the theory sounds simple, it's not so easily achieved. You would expect that in Hawaii, the world's most celebrated melting pot of cultures, we would have developed a literature which emphasizes and focuses on the humanity in people of all races. You would expect that with Hawaii's cultural blending, a literature would naturally emerge which expressed the infinite variety of ways in which people can share their lives, develop common goals, and achieve a sense of community pride. A literature which, in effect, expressed a sense of the word "aloha."

But what do we in Hawaii have as "our literature"? In Hawaii, which as John Dominis Holt said, "gave the world the word 'aloha,' " it is ironic that the most commonly held notion of our literature is that it is non-existent.

It is no secret that language has always been a crucial factor in Hawaii's history. It's no secret that the so-called "blending of cultures" often manifested itself in a clash of languages, sometimes in a competition for sovereignty. It's no secret that our own government, through its various organs, has attempted to suppress varying forms of languages in favor of one common language. And that ain't pidgin they talking about.

And though it may be a practical necessity—and I believe it is—it is again ironic that this chosen form of a common language is seemingly unable—seemingly unable—to produce a literature expressing a common Hawaiian life. And what indicators do we have of a lack of common literature?

If we did have a clearly defined common literature, a Hawaii literary tradition, wouldn't Hawaii's educational systems teach it and use it for educational purposes? They don't. And we wonder why they have problems teaching our kids to read and write. The answer is the problem, obviously. If there is no such thing as a Hawaii writer, how can you teach a Hawaii kid to write?

Should we also ask, why is it that there is so little emphasis in Hawaii's public educational systems placed on Hawaii's history? That is, of our sense of common background, our sense of common experiences—that sense of community again? Or should we take that a step higher and ask, why is it that in Hawaii's colleges and universities, in English departments and colleges of education, there is practically no mention, much less the study, of literature in Hawaii? In fact, there is denial that Hawaii literature of value exists.

And if you want statistics, take the Hawaii State Foundation on Culture and the Arts Report for fiscal year 1979. It reports that $1.7 million was spent on the arts: painting, dance, music, theater, literature. Why is it that out of over 1.7 million dollars, just over 2% of that sum is for literature? Just over 2%.

In all these factors, the main underlying point is that we in Hawaii are expected to believe that we are subordinate to the mainland. At best, we are expected to believe that we are really no different here and can even be *like* the mainland if we try hard enough. We are asked to reject the feeling that Hawaii is special. And when we become numbed and lose the feeling, it then becomes possible to accept mainland history and mainland culture as our own.

We are asked to accept mainland literature as the norm. In the process, our own literature loses its cohesiveness, our writings are categorized according to the framework of mainland, mainstream literary history, if at all. And without having had the chance to establish its own integrity and unique qualities, the literature of Hawaii is dissipated.

But there are those of us who believe *Hawaii no ka oi* ["Hawaii is the best"]. We know there exists a body of writings which we identify as the Modern Hawaiian Literary Tradition. We admit that it's a confusing conglomeration of writers representing a variety of cultures and viewpoints. We admit that much research must be done, much scholarship completed, before a working understanding of the literature becomes common knowledge here. But that's what scholars and universities are for, aren't they?

We know the literature exists. The art of writing has always occurred in Hawaii. And this conference is an attempt to make this tradition more visible, to clarify the different voices which contribute to the overall picture of the Hawaii we love.

122

Recommendations from the Commission on Wartime Relocation and Internment of Civilians, 1982

After exhaustive research and hearings held across the nation, the Commission on Wartime Relocation and Internment of Civilians, established by Congress, issued its Final Report (Part One) in 1982 and Recommendations (Part Two) in 1983. The end result was the Civil Liberties Act of 1988 incorporating most of the recommendations listed here. There was related but separate consideration of World War II treatment of the Aleuts in Alaska, who were also forcibly removed from their homes. For some activists, the process vindicated the strategy of establishing the injustices of the World War II internment before attempting direct legislative action or going directly to the courts, as the Hohri case was doing. The hearings had another, perhaps unintended consequence: they elicited hundreds of emotional testimonies from Japanese Americans, presented in person or submitted in writing to the commission. Many revealed experiences never before divulged, even to family members. Thus, the recommendations were crucial to the redress effort itself and to the massive recovery of an entire community's collective memory of wartime experiences.

Commission on Wartime Relocation and Internment of Civilians, *Personal Justice Denied, Part Two: Recommendations.* Washington, DC: Government Printing Office, 1983. Thanks to Aiko Yoshinaga-Herzig both for her assiduous research efforts for the CWRIC and for locating the documents. She and husband, Jack Herzig, have been of enormous assistance to many researchers.

Recommendations

In 1980 Congress established a bipartisan Commission on Wartime Relocation and Internment of Civilians, and directed it to:

1. review the facts and circumstances surrounding Executive Order Numbered 9066, issued February 19, 1942, and the impact of such Executive Order on American citizens and permanent resident aliens.

2. review directives of United States military forces requiring the relocation and, in some cases, detention in internment camps of American citizens, including Aleut civilians, and permanent resident aliens of the Aleutian and Pribilof Islands; and

3. recommend appropriate remedies.

The Commission fulfilled the first two mandates by submitting to Congress in February 1983 a unanimous report, *Personal Justice Denied*, which extensively reviews the history and circumstances of the fateful decisions to exclude, remove and then to detain Japanese Americans and Japanese resident aliens from the West Coast, as well as the treatment of Aleuts during World War II. The remedies which the Commission recommends in this second and final part of its report are based upon the conclusions of that report as well as upon further studies done for the Commission, particularly an analysis of the economic impact of exclusion and detention.

In considering recommendations, the Congress and the nation therefore must bear in mind the Commission's basic factual findings about the wartime treatment of American citizens of Japanese ancestry and resident Japanese aliens, as well as of the people of the Aleutian Islands. A brief review of the major findings of *Personal Justice Denied* is followed by the Commission's recommendations.

I. American Citizens of Japanese Ancestry and Resident Japanese Aliens

On February 19, 1942, ten weeks after the Pearl Harbor attack, President Franklin D. Roosevelt signed Executive Order 9066, empowering the Secretary of War and the military commanders to whom he delegated authority to exclude any and all persons, citizens and aliens, from designated areas in order to secure national defense objectives against sabotage, espionage and fifth column activity. Shortly thereafter, on the alleged basis of military necessity, all American citizens of Japanese descent and all Japanese resident aliens were excluded from the West Coast. A small number—5,000 to 10,000—were removed from the West Coast and placed in "relocation centers"—bleak barrack camps in desolate areas of the Western states, guarded by military police.

People sent to relocation centers were permitted to leave only after a loyalty review on terms set, in consultation with the military, by the War Relocation Authority, the civilian agency that ran the camps. During the course of the war, approximately 35,000 evacuees were allowed to leave the camps to join the Army, attend college outside the West Coast or take whatever private employment might be available to them. When the exclusion of Japanese Americans and resident aliens from the West Coast was ended in December 1944, about 85,000 people remained in government custody. . . .

The federal government contended that its decision to exclude ethnic Japanese from the West Coast was justified by "military necessity." Careful review of the facts by the Commission has not revealed any security or military threat from the West Coast ethnic Japanese in 1942. The record does not support the claim that military necessity justified the exclusion of the ethnic Japanese from the West Coast, with the consequent loss of property and personal liberty.

The decision to detain followed indirectly from the alleged military necessity for exclusion. No one offered a direct military justification for detention; the War Relocation Authority adopted detention primarily in reaction to the vocal popular feeling that people whom the government considered too great a threat to remain at liberty on the West Coast should not live freely elsewhere. . . .

In sum, Executive Order 9066 was not justified by military necessity, and the decisions that followed from it—exclusion, detention, the ending of detention and the ending of exclusion—were not founded upon military considerations. The broad historical causes that shaped these decisions were race prejudice, war hysteria and a failure of political leadership. . . .

The excluded people suffered enormous damages and losses, both material and intangible. To the disastrous loss of farms, businesses and homes must be added the disruption for many years of careers and professional lives, as well as the long-term loss of income, earnings and opportunity. . . .

Less tangibly, the ethnic Japanese suffered the injury of unjustified stigma that marked the excluded. There were physical illnesses and injuries directly related to detention, but the deprivation of liberty is no less injurious because it wounds the spirit rather than the body. . . .

These facts present the Commission with a complex problem of great magnitude to which there is no ready or satisfactory answer. No amount of money can fully compensate the excluded people for their losses and sufferings. Two and a half years behind the barbed-wire of a relocation camp, branded potentially disloyal because of one's ethnicity alone—these injustices cannot neatly be translated into dollars and cents. . . .

It is well within our power, however, to provide remedies for violations of our own laws and principles. This is one important reason for the several forms of redress recommended below. Another is that our nation's ability to honor democratic values even in times of stress depends largely upon our collective memory of lapses from our constitutional commitment to liberty and due process. Nations that forget or ignore injustices are more likely to repeat them.

The governmental decisions of 1942 were not the work of a few men driven by animus, but decisions supported or accepted by public servants from nearly every part of the political spectrum. Nor did sustained or vocal opposition come from the American public. The wartime events produced an unjust result that visited great suffering upon an entire group of citizens, and upon resident aliens whom the Constitution also protects. . . .

The belief that we Americans are exceptional often threatens our freedom by allowing us to look complacently at evil-doing else-where and to insist that

"It can't happen here." Recalling the events of exclusion and detention, en-
suring that later generations of Americans know this history, is critical immu-
nization against infection by the virus of prejudice and the emotion of wartime
struggle. . . .

In proposing remedial measures, the Commission makes its recommendations in light of a history of postwar actions by federal, state and local governments to recognize and partially to redress the wrongs that were done:

- In 1948, Congress passed the Japanese-American Evacuation Claims Act;
  this gave persons of Japanese ancestry the right to claim from the government real and personal property losses that occurred as a consequence of
  the exclusion and evacuation. . . .
- In 1972, the Social Security Act was amended so that Japanese Americans
  over the age of eighteen would be deemed to have earned and contributed
  to the Social Security system during their detention.
- In 1978, the federal civil service retirement provisions were amended to
  allow the Japanese Americans civil service retirement credit for time spent
  in detention after the age of eighteen.
- In four instances, former government employees have received a measure
  of compensation. In 1982, the State of California enacted a statute permitting the few thousand Japanese Americans in the civil service, who
  were dismissed or who resigned during the war because of their Japanese
  ethnicity, to claim $5,000 as reparation. . . .

Each measure acknowledges to some degree the wrongs inflicted during the
war upon the ethnic Japanese. None can fully compensate or, indeed, make the
group whole again.

The Commission makes the following recommendations for remedies in several forms as an act of national apology.

1. The Commission recommends that Congress pass a joint resolution, to
be signed by the President, which recognizes that a grave injustice was done
and offers the apologies of the nation for the acts of exclusion, removal and
detention.

2. The Commission recommends that the President pardon those who were
convicted of violating the statutes imposing a curfew on American citizens on
the basis of their ethnicity and requiring the ethnic Japanese to leave designated areas of the West Coast or to report to assembly centers. The Commission
further recommends that the Department of Justice review other wartime convictions of the ethnic Japanese and recommend to the President that he pardon
those whose offenses were grounded in a refusal to accept treatment that discriminated among citizens on the basis of race or ethnicity. . . .

3. The Commission recommends that Congress direct the Executive agencies to which Japanese Americans may apply for the restitution of positions, status or entitlements lost in whole or in part because of acts or events between December 1941 and 1945 to review such applications with liberality, giving full consideration to the historical findings of this Commission. For example, the responsible divisions of the Department of Defense should be instructed to review cases of less than honorable discharge of Japanese Americans from the armed services during World War II over which disputes remain. . . .

4. The Commission recommends that Congress demonstrate official recognition of the injustice done to American citizens of Japanese ancestry and Japanese resident aliens during the Second World War, and that it recognize the nation's need to make redress for these events, by appropriating monies to establish a special foundation.

The Commissioners all believe a fund for educational and humanitarian purposes related to the wartime events is appropriate, and all agree that no found would be sufficient to make whole again the lives damaged by the exclusion and detention. . . .

Such a fund should sponsor research and public educational activities so that the events which were the subject of this inquiry will be remembered, and so that the causes and circumstances of this and similar events may be illuminated and understood. A nation which wishes to remain just to its citizens must not forget its lapses. . . .

5. The Commissioners, with the exception of Congressman Lungren, recommend that Congress establish a fund which will provide personal redress to those who were excluded, as well as serve the purposes set out in Recommendation 4. Appropriations of $1.5 billion should be made to the fund over a reasonable period to be determined by Congress. This fund should be used, first, to provide a one-time per capita compensatory payment of $20,000 to each of the approximately 60,000 surviving persons excluded from their places of residence pursuant to Executive Order 9066. . . . After per capita payments, the remainder of the fund should be used for the public educational purposes discussed in Recommendation 4 as well as for the general welfare of the Japanese American community. . . .

Finally, the Commission recommends that a permanent collection be established and funded in the National Archives to house and make available for research the collection of government and private documents, personal testimony and other materials which the Commission amassed during its inquiry.

The Commission believes that, for reasons of redressing the personal injustice done to thousands of Americans and resident alien Japanese, and to the Aleuts—and for compelling reasons of preserving a truthful sense of our own history and the lessons we can learn from it—these recommendations should be enacted by the Congress. In the late 1930's W. H. Auden wrote lines that express our present need to acknowledge and to make amends:

> We are left alone with our day, and the time is short and
> History to the defeated
> May say Alas but cannot help or pardon.

It is our belief that, though history cannot be unmade, it is well within our power to offer help, and to acknowledge error.

123

Appeal Letter from Mother of Vincent Chin, 1983

Vincent Chin was brutally murdered in Detroit, Michigan, on June 19, 1982 by two white men who started a fight with him by lumping him with the Japanese auto industry that was responsible, in their eyes, for the slump in the American manufacturing sector. Ronald Ebens was an unemployed auto worker out for an evening of drinking with his stepson, Michael Nitz. Vincent Chin was celebrating his wedding, the next day, with his friends. Unfortunately, both parties were at the Fancy Pants Tavern in a suburb of Detroit at the same time. Ebens and Nitz taunted Chin with racial slurs, including, according to Ebens: "It's because of you motherf-ckers that we're out of work." Both parties were ejected; Ebens and Nitz got a baseball bat and stalked Chin for blocks before finding him and bludgeoning him to death. The defense attorneys negotiated a manslaughter charge, and Wayne County Circuit Court Judge Charles S. Kaufman gave the defendants each a $3,000 fine and probation, saying they "weren't the kind of people you send to jail." Subsequent efforts by a community group, American Citizens for Justice, and the federal government ended in failure to convict, although a civil suit ordered Ebens to pay $1.5 million to Chin's estate. The entire affair was documented in a film by Christine Choy and Renee Tajima, Who Killed Vincent Chin. This letter was an effort by Chin's mother to solicit support. She was devastated by the outcome and returned to China.

Translation of letter originally addressed to The Chinese Welfare Council of Detroit. Helen Zia Collection. Reprinted with permission.

A Letter of Appeal

[translation of original addressed to The Chinese Welfare Council of Detroit]

I, King Fong Yu (the wife of Bing Heng Chin), grieve for my son, Vincent Chin, who was brutally beaten to death by two assailants with a baseball bat. The two killers were apprehended by police and prosecuted in court. During the court proceedings, I, because I am widowed and poor, with no money in my bed, could not retain legal counsel to press the case for my deceased son. As a result, the murderers' attorneys had the say. Yesterday, I read in the newspaper, the sentence was only a fine and probation; and the killers were set free. There was also no compensation for the victim's family. This is injustice to a terrible extreme. My son's blood had been shed; how unjust could this be? I grieve in my heart and shed tears of blood. Yes, my son cannot be brought back—and I can only wait for death. It is just that my deceased son, Vincent Chin, was a member of your council. I therefore plead to you to please help me. Please let the Chinese American community know about this case so they can help me raise funds to hire legal counsel for an appeal. You must help put the killers in prison so my son's soul may rest and my grief be vindicated. This old woman will be forever grateful.

I, King Fong Yu, respectfully submit this letter of appeal.
March 18, 1983.

124

Resolution on Vincent Chin Decision
by Detroit NAACP, March 1983

The 1982 slaying of Vincent Chin and Judge Charles Kaufman's sentencing of his assailants, Ronald Ebens and Michael Nitz, to a fine and probation angered many people, especially Asian Americans and other people of color. The Detroit Chapter of the National Association for the Advancement of Colored People issued a resolution condemning the arbitrary judgment in Kaufman's reported statements, including the judge's decision to make the punishment fit the criminal and not the crime. The Detroit Chapter decided to speak out on the case because "we infer the elements of racism in Judge Kaufman's reported statements, which elements helped to bring our movement into being. Black people know that when punishment is meted out to fit the perpetrator, rather than the crime itself, we as victims become the ultimate, unrequited losers." Thus, in solidarity with the Asian American community, the chapter sought to focus African American attention on the broader racial cast of the case. While the larger injustices of the federal case in Cincinnati were not to happen until several years later, the case galvanized large segments of the Asian American community to focus on racial bias, race baiting, and race-based hate crimes that had, until then, occurred without public scrutiny.

Detroit Chapter, National Association for the Advancement of Colored People, March 1983. Helen Zia Collection. Reprinted with permission.

RESOLUTION

WHEREAS the Detroit Branch of the NAACP has been active in the Detroit area for over 50 years; and

   WHEREAS the Detroit Branch of the NAACP has fought for civil rights and justice for all minorities; and

   WHEREAS the Detroit Branch of the NAACP is aware of the brutal and senseless death of Chinese-American Vincent Chin; and

WHEREAS Judge Charles Kaufman has sentenced those responsible for Vincent Chin's death to probation; and

WHEREAS a probationary sentence for the brutal killing of any human by the Court is reprehensible;

NOW, THEREFORE, BE IT RESOLVED that the Detroit Branch of the NAACP deplores the probationary sentence pronounced by Judge Charles Kaufman for the killers of Vincent Chin and support all efforts to have said sentence rescinded and a new sentence rendered mandating appropriate incarceration.

DETROIT BRANCH OF THE NATIONAL ASSOCIATION FOR THE ADVANCEMENT OF COLORED PEOPLE

125

U.S. *District Court*: Fred Korematsu v. United States, *April 19, 1984*

Forty years after the U.S. Supreme Court upheld his conviction, Fred Korematsu sued the federal government in order to have this judgment vacated. But the statute of limitations had long run out, and the only legal remedy at hand was the little-known or -used writ of coram nobis (our error), through which cases may be heard when there is substantial evidence that the government deliberately provided misleading information and/or omitted relevant information in papers before the court. Dale Minami and several lawyers, including law professor Peter Irons, led the Korematsu team in the case before the U.S. District Court in Northern California. The "smoking gun" document was unearthed by researchers Aiko Yoshinaga-Herzig and Jack Herzig, who had made second careers as volunteer experts on World War II Japanese American internment files in the National Archives. While this case, like the Hirabayashi and Yasui cases, vacated the defendant's conviction, the Supreme Court rulings still stand as the only ones in modern times validating racial classification as constitutional.

Federal Supplement, Volume 584: Cases Argued and Determined in the U.S. District Courts. St. Paul, MN: West Publishing Co., 1984.

United States District Court,
N.D. California.
Fred Korematsu, Plaintiff, v. United States
of America, Defendant.
584 F. Supp. 1406

Petition granted and countermotion denied.
Opinion
Patel, District Judge
Fred Korematsu is a native born citizen of the United States. He is of Japanese ancestry. On September 8, 1942 he was convicted in this court of being in a place from which all persons of Japanese ancestry were excluded pursuant to

Civilian Exclusion Order No. 34 issued by Commanding General J.L. DeWitt. His conviction was affirmed. . . .

Mr. Korematsu now brings this petition for a writ of coram nobis to vacate his conviction on the grounds of governmental misconduct. . . .

It was uncontroverted at the time of conviction that petitioner was loyal to the United States and had no dual allegiance to Japan. He had never left the United States. He was registered for the draft and willing to bear arms for the United States.

In his papers petitioner maintains that evidence was suppressed or destroyed in the proceedings that led to his conviction and its affirmance. He also makes substantial allegations of suppression and distortion of evidence which informed Executive Order No. 9066 and the Public Proclamations issued under it. While the latter may be compelling, it is not for this court to rectify. However, the court is not powerless to correct its own records where a fraud has been worked upon it or where manifest injustice has been done.

The question before the court is not so much whether the conviction should be vacated as what is the appropriate ground for relief . . .

The Petition for a Writ of Coram Nobis

A writ of coram nobis is an appropriate remedy by which the court can correct errors in criminal convictions where other remedies are not available. Although Rule 60(b), Fed.R.Civ.P., abolishes various common law writs, including the writ of coram nobis in civil cases, the writ still obtains in criminal proceedings where other relief is wanting. . . .

Where, as here, the government offers no opposition and, in effect, joins in a similar request for relief, an expansive inquiry is not necessary. In fact, the government agrees petitioner is entitled to relief and concedes: "There is, therefore, no continuing reason in this setting for the court to convene hearings or make findings about petitioner's allegations of governmental wrongdoing in the 1940's." . . . However, even where the government has acknowledged that the conviction should be set aside, albeit on different grounds, the court must conduct some review to determine whether there is support for the government's position.

Ordinarily, in cases in which the government agrees that a conviction should be set aside, the government's position is made clear because it confesses error, calling to the court's attention the particular errors upon which the conviction was obtained. A confession of error is generally given great deference. Where that confession of error is made by the official having full authority for prosecution on behalf of the government it is entitled to even greater deference. . . .

In this case, the government, joining in on a different procedural footing, is not prepared to confess error. Yet it has not submitted any opposition to the petition, although given ample opportunity to do so. Apparently the government would like this court to set aside the conviction without looking at the record in an effort to put this unfortunate episode in our country's history behind us. . . .

Conclusion

The Supreme Court has cautioned that coram nobis should be used "only under certain circumstances compelling such action to achieve justice" and to correct "errors of the most fundamental character." . . . It is available to correct errors that result in a complete miscarriage of justice and where there are exceptional circumstances.

Coram nobis also lies for a claim of prosecutorial impropriety. This Circuit noted in United States v. Taylor, 648 F.2d at 573, that the writ "strikes at the veracity vel non of the government's representations to the court" and is appropriate where the procedure by which guilt is ascertained is under attack. The Taylor court observed that due process principles, raised by coram nobis charging prosecutorial misconduct, are not "strictly limited to those situations in which the defendant has suffered arguable prejudice; . . . [but also designed] to maintain public confidence in the administration of justice." . . .

Thus, the Supreme Court's decision stands as the law of this case and for whatever precedential value it may still have. Justices of that Court and legal scholars have commented that the decision is an anachronism in upholding overt racial discrimination as "compellingly justified." "Only two of this Court's modern cases have held the use of racial classifications to be constitutional." . . . referring to Korematsu and Hirabayashi v. United States, 320 U.S. 81, 63 S.Ct. 1375, 87 L.Ed. 1774 (1943). . . .

Korematsu remains on the pages of our legal and political history. As a legal precedent it is now recognized as having very limited application. As historical precedent it stands as a constant caution that in times of war or declared military necessity our institutions must be vigilant in protecting constitutional guarantees. It stands as a caution that in times of distress the shield of military necessity and national security must not be used to protect governmental actions from close scrutiny and accountability. It stands as a caution that in times of international hostility and antagonisms our institutions, legislative, executive and judicial, must be prepared to exercise their authority to protect all citizens from the petty fears and prejudices that are so easily aroused.

In accordance with the foregoing, the petition for a writ of coram nobis is granted and the counter-motion of the respondent is denied.

IT IS SO ORDERED.

126

Nobuko Miyamoto, "Yuiyo Bon Odori," 1984

Bon odori *are dances celebrating the return of souls of the departed, who are welcomed back to their neighborhoods in festivals—obon—in late summer throughout Japan. Immigrant groups re-created this tradition after establishing families and communities, adapting the practice to their new environments. This particular piece was the first in a series commissioned by the Senshin Buddhist Temple in Los Angeles and was first danced by 2,000 people from 18 temples throughout Southern California. It was even used in a scene in the popular film,* Karate Kid II. Yuiyo *is a Japanese term simply adding emphasis.* "Namuamidabutsu" *is used by some Buddhist groups to invite the attention of Amida Buddha. At the turn of the twenty-first century, Buddhism and Islam were the fastest-growing religions in the United States. Senshin Buddhist Temple, led by the Reverend Masao Kodani, began in the 1970s to try to engage younger Japanese Americans in new ways, encouraging them to embrace their religious and ethnic identities. Composing songs for obon in English was one way to make the tradition accessible to generations untrained in the language of their ancestors.*

Words and music: Nobuko Miyamoto. Japanese lyrics: Rev. Masao Kodani. Copyright 1984. Reprinted with permission.

Yuiyo Bon Odori

Ureshii kai?	(Are you happy?)
Kanashii kai?	(Are you sad?)
Kekko, Kekko, Odore, Odore!	(Wonderful, its all right, dance, dance!)
Namuamidabutsu, *tada odore*	(Namuamidabutsu, just dance!)

Sunset . . .
Sky turning indigo

Moon and stars begin their evening dance
Circle in the sky
Voice of wind—*Yuiyo!*
Rhythm of trees—*Yuiyo!*
You can feel it if you dance
Just dance

  Anno Mamma—Yuiyo!   (Like that over there—
             just dance)

  Sonno Mamma—Yuiyo!   (Like that—just dance)
  Konno Mamma—Yuiyo!   (Like this—just dance)
  Tada Odore   (Just dance)

Obon . . .
Gathering of joy
Joy in remembering the past
In embracing the sorrow
Close your eyes—*Yuiyo!*
Let it go—*Yuiyo!*
From your Kokoro (from your whole being)
Just dance

  Anno Mamma—Yuiyo!
  Sonno Mamma—Yuiyo!
  Konno Mamma—Yuiyo!
  Tada Odore

Isshoni . . . (all together)
Moving as one
Forget the self and join in celebration
Why look at life go by?
Don't be shy—*No Hazukashil*
Don't make a show—*No Shibai!*
Let your Kokoro
Just dance

  Anno Mamma—Yuiyo!
  Sonno Mamma—Yuiyo!
  Konno Mamma—Yuiyo!
  Tada Odore

Southeast Asian Refugee Acts: Resettlement, Amerasian Homecoming, and Refugees via Thailand, December 22, 1987

Coming a dozen years after the 1975 Refugee Act that recognized the responsibility of the United States to accommodate some of the Southeast Asians displaced as a result of the Vietnam War, these acts attempted to address the issue of continuing disruption and population movements. Section 904 calls for renewed attention to the needs of refugees from Vietnam, Cambodia, and Laos, many of whom made their way to asylum camps in Thailand and other Southeast Asian countries. Section 906 specifically addresses the issues raised by the horrors of the Khmer Rouge rule in Cambodia and the subsequent deployment of 140,000 Vietnamese troops in that beleaguered country, facilitating Cambodians' entry into the United States. Section 905 is especially interesting because it acknowledges U.S. responsibility, finally, to provide entry to thousands of people born to Vietnamese mothers and American fathers. These individuals and their families were abandoned by both American and Vietnamese societies and faced unusually harsh conditions. Their migration to the United States added more complexity to the existing difficulties of refugees within this country.

United States Statutes at Large, 1987, vol. 101, part 3. Washington, DC: United States Government Printing Office, 1989.

Public Law 100–204

Sec. 904. Indochinese Refugee Resettlement

(a) Findings.—It is the sense of the Congress that—

1.   the continued occupation of Cambodia by Vietnam and the oppressive conditions within Vietnam, Cambodia, and Laos have led to a steady flight of persons from those countries, and the likelihood for the safe repatriation of the hundreds of thousands of refugees in the region's camps is negligible for the foreseeable future;

2. the United States has already played a major role in responding to the Indochinese refugee problem by accepting approximately 850,000 Indochinese refugees into the United States since 1975 and has a continued interest in persons who have fled and continue to flee the countries of
Cambodia, Laos, and Vietnam;

3. Hong Kong, Indonesia, Malaysia, Singapore, the Philippines, and Thailand have been the front line countries bearing tremendous burdens
caused by the flight of these persons;

4. all members of the international community bear a share of the responsibility for the deterioration in the refugee first asylum situation in Southeast
Asia because of slow and limited procedures, failure to implement effective
policies for the region's "long-stayer" populations, failure to monitor adequately refugee protection and screening programs, particularly along the
Thai-Cambodian and Thai-Laotian borders, and the instability of the Orderly Departure Program (ODP) from Vietnam which has served as the
only safe, legal means of departure from Vietnam for refugees, including
Amerasians and long-held "reeducation camp" prisoners;

5. the Government of Thailand should be complimented for allowing the
United States to process ration card holders in Khao I Dang and potentially qualified immigrants in Site 2 and in Khao I Dang;

6. given the serious protection problem in Southeast Asian first asylum countries and the need to preserve first asylum in the region, the United States
should continue its commitment to an ongoing, generous admission and
protection program for Indochinese refugees, including urgently needed
educational programs for refugees along the Thai-Cambodian and Thai-
Laotian borders, until the underlying causes of refugee flight are addressed
and resolved;

7. the executive branch should seek adequate funding levels to meet United States policy objectives to ensure the well-being of Indochinese
refugees in first asylum, and to process 29,500 Indochinese refugees within the overall refugee admissions level of 68,000 as determined by the
President; and

8. the Government of Thailand should be complimented for the progress
that has been made in implementing an effective antipiracy program.

(b) Recommendations.—The Congress finds and recommends the following with respect to Indochinese refugees:

1. The Secretary of State should urge the Government of Thailand to allow
full access by highland refugees to the Lao Screening Program, regardless of
the method of their arrival or the circumstances of their apprehension, and
should intensify its efforts to persuade the Government of Laos to accept the
safe return of persons rejected under the Lao Screening Program. . . .

(c) Allocations of Refugee Admissions.—Given the existing connection between ongoing resettlement and the preservation of first asylum, the United States and the United Nations High Commissioner for Refugees should redouble efforts to assure a stable and secure environment for refugees while dialog is pursued on other long-range solutions, it is the sense of the Congress that—

1. within the worldwide refugee admissions ceiling determined by the President, the President should continue to recommend generous numbers of admissions from East Asia first asylum camps and from the Orderly Departure Program sufficient to sustain preservation of first asylum and security for Indochinese in Southeast Asia, consistent with worldwide refugee admissions requirements and the consultative processes of the Refugee Act of 1980;

2. within the allocation made by the President for the Orderly Departure Program from Vietnam, the number of admissions allocated for Amerasians and their immediate family members should also be generous;

3. renewed international efforts must be taken to address the problem of Indochinese refugees who have lived in camps for 3 years or longer; and

4. the Secretary of State should urge the United Nations High Commissioner for Refugees to organize immediately an international conference to address the problems of Indochinese refugees . . .

Sec. 905. Amerasian Children in Vietnam

(a) Findings and Declarations.—The Congress makes the following findings and declarations:

1. Thousands of children in the Socialist Republic of Vietnam were fathered by American civilians and military personnel.

2. It has been reported that many of these Amerasian children are ineligible for ration cards and often beg in the streets, peddle black market wares, or prostitute themselves.

3. The mothers of Amerasian children in Vietnam are not eligible for government jobs or employment in government enterprises and many are estranged from their families and are destitute.

4. Amerasian children and their families have undisputed ties to the United States and are of particular humanitarian concern to the United States.

5. The United States has a longstanding and very strong commitment to receive the Amerasian children in Vietnam, if they desire to come to the United States.

6. In September 1984, the United States informed the Socialist Republic of Vietnam that all Amerasian children in Vietnam, their mothers, and qual-

ifying family members would be admitted as refugees to the United States during a three-year period.

7. Amerasian emigration from Vietnam increased significantly in fiscal year 1985 under the Orderly Departure Program of the United Nations High Commissioner on Refugees.

8. On January 1, 1986, the Socialist Republic of Vietnam unilaterally suspended interviews of all individuals seeking to leave Vietnam legally under the auspices of the Orderly Departure Program for resettlement in the United States.

9. On the 19th and 20th of October 1987, the Socialist Republic of Vietnam permitted the United States to resume interviewing Amerasians and their families.

(b) Sense of the Congress. — It is the sense of the Congress that —

1. the United States should maintain its strong commitment to receive the Amerasian children in the Socialist Republic of Vietnam and their families;

2. the Socialist Republic of Vietnam should cooperate fully in facilitating the processing of all Amerasians who desire to be resettled in the United States; and

3. the Socialist Republic of Vietnam should cooperate fully in the processing of Amerasians for emigration.

Sec. 906. Refugees from Southeast Asia

(a) Findings. — The Congress finds that —

1. the United States remains firmly committed to the security of Thailand and to improving relations between our two nations;

2. the United States refugee resettlement and humanitarian assistance programs constitute an important factor in bilateral relations between the United States and Thailand;

3. the preservation of first asylum for those fleeing persecution is one of the primary objectives of the United States refugee program;

4. the actions of another government in labeling refugee populations as "displaced persons" or closing its borders to new arrivals shall not constitute a barrier to the United States considering those individuals or groups to be refugees;

5. it is in the national interest to facilitate the reunification of separated families of United States citizens and permanent residents, and the Congress will look with disfavor on any nation which seriously hinders emigration for such reunifications;

6. the persecution of the Cambodian people under the Khmer Rouge rule
   from 1975–1979, which caused the deaths of up to two million people and
   in which the bulk of the Khmer people were subjected to life in an Asian
   Auschwitz, constituted one of the clearest examples of genocide in recent
   history; and

7. the invasion of Cambodia by Vietnam and the subsequent occupation of
   that country by 140,000 Vietnamese troops backing up the Heng Samrin
   regime, which itself continues to seriously violate the human rights of
   Cambodians, and the presence of 40,000 heavily armed troops under the
   control of the same Khmer Rouge leaders, overwhelmingly demonstrate
   that the life or freedom of any Cambodian not allied with the Khmer
   Rouge or supporting Heng Samrin would be seriously endangered if such
   individual were forced by a country of first asylum to return to his or her
   homeland.

(b) Statement of Policy. — It is the sense of the Congress that—

1. any Cambodians who are, or had been, at Khao I Dang camp should be
   considered and interviewed for eligibility for the United States refugee
   program, irrespective of the date they entered Thailand or that refugee
   camp;

2. any Cambodian rejected for admission to the United States who can
   demonstrate new or additional evidence relating to his claim should have
   his or her case reviewed;

3. the United States should work with the United Nations High Commissioner for Refugees, the International Committee of the Red Cross, and
   the Government of Thailand to improve the security of all refugee facilities in Thailand and to prevent the forced repatriation of Cambodian
   refugees;

4. the United States should treat with utmost seriousness the continued reports of forced repatriations to Laos of would-be asylum seekers, and
   should lodge strong and continuous protests with the Thai Government to
   bring about an end to these repatriations, which endanger the life and
   safety of those involuntarily returned to Laos; and

5. within the Orderly Departure Program the United States will give high
   priority consideration to determining the eligibility of serious health cases
   and cases involving children separated from both parents . . .

Civil Liberties Act of 1988 (Public Law 100–383), August 10, 1988

This legislation culminated nearly two decades of efforts by the Japanese American community to secure an official government apology for the World War II internment of 120,000 Japanese Americans and redress payments of $20,000 for each internee alive at the time of the signing. More than 80,000 individuals received apologies and checks. Aleut Indians, from the Aleutian and Pribilof islands of Alaska, were also removed from their homes during the war to live in desolate camps in order to clear strategic areas. Their "evacuation" was badly mismanaged, and the lack of consideration led to much suffering. Surviving Aleuts received $12,000 each. The Office of Redress Administration was established within the Justice Department to implement the program and managed to find and pay nearly all of the survivors. It closed its doors in February 1999. While it was making the redress payments, a lawsuit was filed on behalf of Japanese Latin Americans who had been forcibly removed from countries like Peru and confined in U.S. camps during the war; these individuals were not included in the 1988 legislation. After the war the United States attempted to deport them to Japan, a country to which many had never gone, because they were illegally in the United States. Mochizuki v. United States provided for apologies and $5,000 payments. The act also included a provision for educational funds, although they proved to be modest because most of the money went to individuals.

United States Statutes at Large, 1988, vol. 102, part 1. Washington, DC: Government Printing Office, 1990.

Public Law 100–383
An Act
To implement recommendations of the Commission
on Wartime Relocation and Internment of Civilians

Be it enacted by the Senate and House of Representatives of the United States of America in Congress assembled,

Section 1. Purposes.

The purposes of this Act are to —

1. acknowledge the fundamental injustice of the evacuation, relocation, and internment of United States citizens and permanent resident aliens of Japanese ancestry during World War II;
2. apologize on behalf of the people of the United States for the evacuation, relocation, and internment of such citizens and permanent resident aliens;
3. provide for a public education fund to finance efforts to inform the public about the internment of such individuals so as to prevent the recurrence of any similar event;
4. make restitution to those individuals of Japanese ancestry who were interned;
5. make restitution to Aleut residents of the Pribilof Islands and the Aleutian Islands west of Unimak Island, in settlement of United States obligations in equity and at law, for —

   (A) injustices suffered and unreasonable hardships endured while those Aleut residents were under United States control during World War II;
   (B) personal property taken or destroyed by United States forces during World War II;
   (C) community property, including community church property, taken or destroyed by United States forces during World War II; and
   (D) traditional village lands on Attu Island not rehabilitated after World War II for Aleut occupation or other productive use;

6. discourage the occurrence of similar injustices and violations of civil liberties in the future; and
7. make more credible and sincere any declaration of concern by the United States over violations of human rights committed by other nations.

Sec. 2. Statement of the Congress

(a) With Regard to Individuals of Japanese Ancestry. — The Congress recognizes that, as described by the Commission on Wartime Relocation and Internment of Civilians, a grave injustice was done to both citizens and permanent resident aliens of Japanese ancestry by the evacuation, relocation, and internment of civilians during World War II. As the Commission documents, these actions were carried out without adequate security reasons and without any acts of espionage or sabotage documented by the Commission, and were motivated largely by racial prejudice, wartime hysteria, and a failure of political leadership. The excluded individuals of Japanese ancestry suffered enormous damages, both material and intangible, and there were incalculable losses in education and job training, all of which resulted in significant human suffering for which appropriate compensation has not been made. For these fundamental violations of the basic civil liberties and constitutional rights of these individuals of Japanese ancestry, the Congress apologizes on behalf of the Nation.

(b) With Respect to the Aleuts. — The Congress recognizes that, as described by the Commission on Wartime Relocation and Internment of Civilians, the Aleut civilian residents of the Pribilof Islands and the Aleutian Islands west of Unimak Island were relocated during World War II to temporary camps in isolated regions of southeast Alaska where they remained, under United States control and in the care of the United States, until long after any potential danger to their home villages had passed. The United States failed to provide reasonable care for the Aleuts, and this resulted in widespread illness, disease, and death among the residents of the camps; and the United States further failed to protect Aleut personal and community property while such property was in its possession or under its control. The United States has not compensated the Aleuts adequately for the conversion or destruction of personal property, and the conversion or destruction of community property caused by the United States military occupation of Aleut villages during World War II. There is no remedy for injustices suffered by the Aleuts during World War II except an Act of Congress providing appropriate compensation for those losses which are attributable to the conduct of United States forces and other officials and employees of the United States.

Title I — United States Citizens of Japanese Ancestry and Resident Japanese Aliens

Sec 101. Short Title

This title may be cited as the "Civil Liberties Act of 1988."

Sec. 102. Remedies with Respect to Criminal Convictions

(a) Review of Convictions. — The Attorney General is requested to review any case in which an individual living on the date of the enactment of this Act was, while a United States citizen or permanent resident alien of Japanese ancestry, convicted of a violation of —

1. Executive Order Numbered 9066, dated February 19, 1942;
2. the Act entitled "An Act to provide a penalty for violation of restrictions or orders with respect to persons entering, remaining in, leaving, or committing any act in military areas or zones," approved March 21, 1942 (56 Stat. 173); or

3. any other Executive order, Presidential proclamation, law of the United States, directive of the Armed Forces of the United States, or other action taken by or on behalf of the United States or its agents, representatives, officers, or employees, respecting the evacuation, relocation, or internment of individuals solely on the basis of Japanese ancestry; on account of the refusal by such individual, during the evacuation, relocation, and internment period, to accept treatment which discriminated against the individual on the basis of the individual's Japanese ancestry.

(b) Recommendations for Pardons. — Based upon any review under subsection (a), the Attorney General is requested to recommend to the President for pardon consideration those convictions which the Attorney General considers appropriate.

(c) Action by the President. — In consideration of the statement of the Congress set forth in section 2(a), the President is requested to offer pardons to any individuals recommended by the Attorney General under subsection (b). . . .

Sec. 104. Trust Fund

(a) Establishment. — There is established in the Treasury of the United States the Civil Liberties Public Education Fund, which shall be administered by the Secretary of the Treasury.

(b) Investment of Amounts in the Fund. — Amounts in the Fund shall be invested in accordance with section 9702 of title 31, United States Code.

(c) Uses of the Fund. — Amounts in the Fund shall be available only for disbursement by the Attorney General under section 105 and by the Board under section 106. . . .

(e) Authorization of Appropriations. — There are authorized to be appropriated to the Fund $1,250,000,000, of which not more than $500,000,000 may be appropriated for any fiscal year. Any amounts appropriated pursuant to this section are authorized to remain available until expended.

Sec. 105. Restitution

(a) Location and Payment of Eligible Individuals. —

1. In general. — Subject to paragraph (6), the Attorney General shall, subject to the availability of funds appropriated to the Fund for such purpose, pay out of the Fund to each eligible individual the sum of $20,000, unless such individual refuses, in the manner described in paragraph (4), to accept the payment.
2. Location of eligible individuals. — The Attorney General shall identify and locate, without requiring any application for payment and using records

already in the possession of the United States Government, each eligible individual. . . .

3. Notice from the attorney general.—The Attorney General shall, when funds are appropriated to the Fund for payments to an eligible individual under this section, notify that eligible individual in writing of his or her eligibility for payment under this section. Such notice shall inform the eligible individual that—

(A) acceptance of payment under this section shall be in full satisfaction of all claims against the United States arising out of acts described in section 108(2)(B), and

(B) each eligible individual who does not refuse, in the manner described in paragraph (4), to accept payment under this section within 18 months after receiving such written notice shall be deemed to have accepted payment for purposes of paragraph (5).

4. Effect of refusal to accept payment.—If an eligible individual refuses, in a written document filed with the Attorney General, to accept any payment under this section, the amount of such payment shall remain in the Fund and no payment may be made under this section to such individual at any time after such refusal.

5. Payment in full settlement of claims against the United States.—The acceptance of payment by an eligible individual under this section shall be in full satisfaction of all claims against the United States arising out of acts described in section 108(2)(B). This paragraph shall apply to any eligible individual who does not refuse, in the manner described in paragraph (4), to accept payment under this section within 18 months after receiving the notification from the Attorney General referred to in paragraph (3). . . .

129

U.S. *Court of Appeals:* William Hohri et al., Plaintiffs-Appellants, v. United States, *January 21, 1988*

The "et al." are often omitted from the historical record. In this important case, they are listed, including the organization known as the National Council for Japanese American Redress (NCJAR). Redress for Japanese Americans who were interned during World War II came with congressional action to provide an official apology and $20,000 to each person alive at the time the act was signed in August 1988. This was a parallel case making its way through the judicial system that sought a class-action remedy to the wartime injustice. William Hohri led a group of nineteen plaintiffs in this strategy. They were organized, with many supporters, as NCJAR. Their suit ultimately failed but generated considerable interest and may have directly aided the legislative momentum by posing a separate and far more expensive resolution. At the U.S. Supreme Court, the suit received no hearing on the issues — instead, the court remanded it to the U.S. Court of Appeals, which ruled here, on the narrow grounds that the statute of limitations had expired. As in so many cases, the dissenting opinion often provides useful information on the significance of the issue.

West's Federal Reporter, Volume 847 F.2d: Cases Argued and Determined in the U.S. Courts of Appeals and Temporary Emergency Court of Appeals. St. Paul, MN: West Publishing Co., 1988.

William HOHRI; Hannah Takagi Holmes; Chizuko Omori, Ind. and Rep. for Haruko Omori; Midori Kimura; Merry Omori; John Omori, Ind. and Rep. for Juro Omori; Gladyce Sumida; Kyoshiro Tokunaga; Tom Nakao; Harry Ueno; Edward Tokeshi; Rentaro Hashimoto; Nelson Kitsuse, Ind. and Rep. for Takeshi Kitsuse; Eddie Sato; Sam Ozaki, Ind. and Rep. for Kyujiro Ozaki; Kumao Toda, Ind. and Rep. for Suketaro Toda; Kaz Oshiki; George R. Ikeda; Tim Takayoshi; Cathy Takayoshi; National Council for Japanese Amer. Redress, Plaintiffs-Appellants, v. The UNITED STATES of America, Defendant-Appellee.

United States Court of Appeals, Federal Circuit.
847 F.2d 779

PER CURIAM.

This appeal comes to this court following the decision of the Supreme Court in *United States v. Hohri*, 482 U.S.—, 107 S.Ct. 2246, 96 L.Ed.2d 51 (1987) (vacating judgment of District of Columbia Circuit and remanding with instructions to transfer to this court pursuant to 28 U.S.C. 1631 (1982)). . . .

The appeal here is from the judgment of the United States District Court for the District of Columbia, 586 F.Supp. 769 (D.D.C.1984) (Oberdorfer, J.), dismissing the claims of nineteen individuals and an organization of Japanese-Americans which sought damages and declaratory relief for injuries resulting from the internment of Japanese-Americans during World War II. The district court held, *inter alia*, that appellants' claims were barred by applicable statutes of limitations.

Each of the numerous issues raised to this court is fully addressed in the opinion of Judge Oberdorfer. After a meticulous review of that opinion, we are unpersuaded of any error. We see no need to restate or elaborate on the district court's careful and scholarly analysis, nor to burden appellants with further delay. Accordingly, we affirm for the reasons stated in the district court opinion.

AFFIRMED.

BALDWIN, Senior Circuit Judge, dissenting-in-part.

The majority adopts, *in toto*, the District Court's opinion, *Hohri v. United States*, 586 F.Supp. 769 (D.D.C.1984). Although I agree with much of what the trial judge says, I respectfully dissent because I believe he erred in concluding that appellants' takings claims are barred by the statute of limitations. . . .

The trial judge rejected appellants' contention that the statute of limitations was tolled as a result of the government's fraudulent concealment of information relating to the military necessity for relocating and interning Japanese-Americans during World War II. 586 F.Supp. at 786–91. Instead, he found that appellants failed to exercise due diligence in asserting their claims. *Id.* at 790–91. He found that a reasonably diligent plaintiff would have discovered sufficient evidence to state a claim as early as the late 1940's. *Id.* I cannot agree that the government's fraudulent concealment of vital information did not toll the statute. . . .

As a general rule, a statute of limitations is tolled where a defendant fraudulently or deliberately conceals material facts relevant to a plaintiff's claim. . . . As the trial judge pointed out, 586 F.Supp. at 787–88, the parties do not dispute that appellee concealed various intelligence reports which contradicted the claim of military necessity raised in *Hirabayashi* and *Korematsu*. The parties do dispute, however, the effect this concealment had on the accrual of appellants' claims, and the duration of the effective concealment of sufficient matter to delay such accrual. . . .

Appellants' position is that the Supreme Court erected an insurmountable legal barrier with its decisions in *Hirabayashi v. United States*, 320 U.S. 81, 63 S.Ct. 1375, 87 L.Ed. 1774 (1943) and *Korematsu v. United States*, 323 U.S. 214, 65 S.Ct. 193, 89 L.Ed. 194 (1944), when it upheld the internment policy in deference to the military. This barrier could be removed they assert only by an affirmative statement by one of the "war-making" branches that military necessity did not require the internment policy. They argue that the creation of CWRIC [Commission on Wartime Relocation and Internment of Civilians] and the publication of *Personal Justice Denied* is the first event constituting such a statement. This conclusion is premised upon the disclosure in *Personal Justice Denied* that the government fraudulently concealed significant and vital information concerning its role in the *Korematsu* and *Hirabayashi* decisions. . . .

Where a defendant fraudulently conceals information, and that concealment has the effect of dooming a plaintiff's claims at the outset, the statute of limitations should be tolled until such time as the plaintiff discovers or should have discovered, through due diligence, the facts concealed. Under this standard, it would not matter whether the information concealed went to a claim or an affirmative defense. If it can be said that a plaintiff's claim would not survive a motion to dismiss on the pleadings *because* the defendant fraudulently concealed information relevant to an *essential* element of the claim, I would find the statute tolled until such time as a plaintiff, exercising due diligence, could discover the information.

Appellee's actions during the War clearly constituted fraudulent concealment. The district court found, based on the pleadings and the historical evidence, that appellee did, in fact, conceal critical evidence during the prosecution of *Hirabayashi* and *Korematsu* before the Supreme Court. 586 F.Supp. at 787–88. But the court found that once the Hoover, Fly, and Ringle documents, all objects of concealment, were leaked, the statute began to run. *Id.* I disagree that these documents were sufficient to rebut the presumption of military deference provided by the Supreme Court in *Hirabayashi* and *Korematsu*. These documents constituted only a small portion of the information concealed, and by no means the most important information. . . .

The statute having been tolled by appellee's fraudulent concealment, the question remaining is when did it begin to run? The traditional standard applied by this court is that appellants "must either show that [appellee] has concealed its acts with the result that [appellants were] unaware of their existence or [appellants] must show that [their] injury was 'inherently unknowable' at the accrual date." . . .

Before the statute could begin to run against appellants, there had to be sufficient evidence in the public domain to permit appellants to state a claim. In the peculiar facts of this case, this means that appellants needed enough facts to potentially rebut the Supreme Court's presumption of deference. Thus, the evidence concealed by appellee must have been sufficient to provide appellants with enough facts to make a good faith determination that they could *potentially* rebut this presumption. The leaked documents, as noted earlier, could not suffice to defeat the presumption erected. It was not until CWRIC exposed and declassified a wealth of intelligence information that appellants became aware of the existence of adequate facts indicating that sufficient concealment had occurred to cast sincere doubt upon the Supreme Court's *Hirabayashi* and *Korematsu* holdings. . . .

Our nation has evolved tremendously since the incidents which gave rise to this action occurred. So, too, our government institutions have matured since that time. Unfortunately, we have not yet erased the possibility of abuse of individual citizens or groups of citizens. Fortunately, we have adequate means in our laws and our Constitution for those harmed by governmental actions to seek recompense in the courts. While the statute of limitations seeks justly to protect the United States from endless claims that may be age old, it does not behoove our society to sanction the perpetration of fraud by the sovereign. Appellants are, I believe, entitled to their day in court to attempt to prove their allegations that their property was taken, and that they are entitled to relief for that taking. Whether they will succeed is irrelevant at this point. In my opinion, appellee's actions before this nation's highest Court, and its long concealment of the factual basis of appellants' claims entitles appellants to the opportunity to try. I would therefore reverse that portion of the trial judge's opinion dismissing the takings clause claims for those appellants who did not receive payment under the American-Japanese Evacuation Claims Act.

130

William Hohri/NCJAR Class Action Suit
for World War II Damages, 1988

In 1979, William Hohri and 19 others established the National Council for Japanese American Redress for the sole purpose of securing monetary restitution for Japanese Americans who had been placed in American concentration camps during World War II. The suit sought damages of $10,000 for each of 22 separate counts of government misconduct (total $220,000) to be provided to the 125,000 individuals or their heirs—a total of $27 billion. This document is part of a book, Repairing America: An Account of the Movement for Japanese-American Redress, *written by Hohri and published before the final court decision ruled that the statute of limitations had expired, thus extinguishing the lawsuit forever. Soon after its publication, however, Congress passed and President Reagan signed legislation providing for $20,000 in redress to every survivor of the World War II camps still alive on the date of the signing. The total would amount to slightly more than $1.2 billion. This legislation culminated the Japanese American Citizens League-led effort to create a Commission on Wartime Relocation and Internment of Civilians that would make recommendations for congressional action. A third advocacy group, the National Coalition for Redress/Reparations, was also intensely involved in the redress movement. While the NCJAR class-action suit ultimately failed in the courts, it was important for its stark presentation of the adversarial nature of the* World War II *experience: the U.S. government had wrongfully imprisoned an entire class of people solely on the basis of race. Pursued concurrently with the legislative strategy, the court case may have prompted some politicians to "settle" for the lesser amount.*

Reprinted with permission of the author.

The Complaint

NCJAR's lawsuit was filed on March 16, 1983. For the first time in the history of the mass exclusion and detention of Japanese-Americans and their aftermath, the defendant is identified and the plaintiffs defined. For the first time in this history, we, the plaintiffs, spell out our injuries from our perspective, as the injured parties. . . . We shed official euphemisms such as "evacuation" and "relocation centers" and replace them with "forced exclusion" and "prison camps." Our causes of action, the formal statement of charges, specify each constitutional and legal right that was violated. Nor are the remedies gratuitous as they were in the Evacuation Claims Act. We seek the maximum compensation allowed for our causes of action. . . . Instead of repressing our outrage for want of focus, we victims now have a lawsuit against the United States; we now have the proper means by which to channel our grievances and our demands for redress.

Twenty-Seven Billion

We are suing the United States of America for an unambiguously adversarial sum of twenty-seven billion dollars. The ante has been raised since 1979. The first Lowry Redress Bill had a projected cost of around three billion dollars. The ninefold increase of our action came not from a motive to sensationalize, but from the cumulative effect of the detailed allegations of facts and injuries embedded in our Complaint. These allegations coalesce into twenty-two causes of action. The magnitude of our prayer for relief, to use the legal expression, results from the multiplication of the class of 125,000 victims by twenty-two causes of action. We seek compensation of at least $10,000 for each cause of action. Twenty-two of them yield $220,000 per victim. Given the nature of the injuries, the individual claim is modest. This claim multiplied by 125,000 victims yields 27.5 billion dollars. Our Complaint is not addressing merely property losses. We are addressing injuries we sustained through the government's violation of our constitutional and civil rights. . . .

This is a point which many Americans fail to understand. We Americans have forgotten the hard lessons learned by the founders of our nation and the framers of the United States Constitution. Many of us think of the Constitution as the rules of self-governance, much like the bylaws of a corporation or organization. While it does specify the requirements for being president and the manner of popular representation in the two houses of Congress, the Constitution is much more than bylaws: it guarantees our individual freedoms by placing limitations on government. It mandates, for example, that the privilege of the writ of *habeas corpus* shall not be suspended "unless when in cases of rebellion or invasion the public safety may require it." Such suspension, moreover, requires an explicit act of government, such as an act of Congress. There is no constitutional provision for *ignoring* the writ as was done with Japanese-Americans. . . . It should be an inviolable right. Its violation withdraws the protection of the courts. The establishment of an exception to this rule of protection may easily enable the exception to overtake the rule, especially when the protection of the courts blocks the misguided will of citizens' inflamed passions or a government's will to abuse its power. . . . When those rights and privileges are breached by the government, the government must be held accountable. And the victims have the responsibility to demand the accounting.

Defendant United States of America

The Complaint names as adversary and defendant the United States of America. The naming of defendant United States of America is disturbing for most Americans, as it is enlightening and liberating for the Americans who were the victims. Many Americans resist being held accountable for their sins, or those of their parents, of forty years ago, even though the Ten Commandments warn us of the long-term effects of our failure to obey God's ethical laws. Many of us would deny knowledge of the events; we would deny malicious intent. Why should we have to pay for someone else's mistakes? The questioners are not mollified when they are told that even the victims themselves will have to pay their share of the redress. Nor will the questioners' resistance lessen when informed that the United States Court of Claims regularly accepts judgments against the United States for which we all must pay.

The distress, I suspect, is really an averted look, an unwillingness to look at the enormity of the charges delineated. The victims charge that the rights guaranteed within the Constitution of the United States were violated by the government of the United States. Many Americans avoid looking at this. They would avoid the implication that the violation of constitutional rights of Japanese-Americans could be inflicted on any other group of Americans or to all Americans. They try to hide behind the fact that they are not of Japanese ancestry, as if one's ancestry circumscribed susceptibility. They do not see the violation as a violation of *their* rights. . . .

Just as many Americans fail to recognize the preciousness of our constitutionally guaranteed freedoms, many lack any strong sense of identity with Americans of Japanese ancestry. They want to identify Japanese-Americans as Japanese from Japan. They ask with revealing indignation, "What about Pearl Harbor? What about the Bataan Death March?" Japanese-Americans remain "those people" and "they," not "we." Many Americans fail to realize that the movement for Japanese-American redress is a gift to America: the repairing of damages to the constitutional foundations of America's freedoms.

For us, the victims, the naming of defendant United States of America is enlightenment and liberation. We never knew quite what had hit us. Of course, we had grown up with racism. We had heard about Lieutenant General DeWitt's outlandish remark, "A Jap's a Jap." We knew the term "Jap" as one that was particularly hostile and hate-filled as well as demeaning. To us in that time, the term was an obscenity like "fuck," differing only as an obscenity accepted in polite and public language by leaders of government and teachers of our children, in newspaper editorials and comic strips, by radio commentators and standup comedians. We victims were mired in our "Japness." And we have been overwhelmed with a variety of theories of why mass exclusion and detention happened to us, and of who the culprits were. We were told of public racism, commercial greed, political opportunism, media excesses, military paranoia, and stupidity. This diversity of explanations tends to diffuse and confuse the source of our injuries. The naming of the defendant as the United States of America clarifies reality and brings it into focus. . . .

The Complaint becomes our liberation. Instead of bowing and yielding to a government which deprived us of our liberties, instead of taking an oath of unqualified allegiance and subscribing to a creed of sycophantic obedience, we are identifying the government as our adversary in our effort to remedy the injuries we had sustained from the government's abuse of privilege and power. . . .

Plaintiffs: Japanese America

NCJAR selected twenty-five persons, living and dead, to represent the class of 125,000 victims and plaintiffs. These twenty-five represent Issci who had been interned in Department of Justice camps; Issei, Nisei, and Sansei who had been excluded and detained in one of the ten prison camps; a Buddhist priest for the special religious discrimination applied to leaders of Eastern religious faiths; veterans of the 442nd Regimental Combat Team, volunteers and draftees; a deaf person for those disabled; a dissident who doubly suffered in the isolation camps of Moab and Leupp; a draft resister who resisted because he was denied entrance to branches of the armed forces other than the U.S. Army; mothers and fathers, sons and daughters, children, adults, and the elderly. The representation is geographical as well. Several were selected from the District of Columbia because we filed our lawsuit in that federal district court. The rest came from New York, Chicago, Seattle, San Jose, and Los Angeles. . . .

Allegations

The *Factual Allegations* of the Complaint open with numbered paragraph 43:

> 43. Following the outbreak of World War II, defendant maliciously and unlawfully conspired to and did deprive plaintiffs of their constitutional rights by subjecting them to forcible segregation, arrest, exclusion, and imprisonment solely on the basis of their Japanese ancestry. Defendant intentionally concealed and misrepresented the illegal nature of its actions by fabricating claims of "military necessity."

The allegations extend for sixty-eight paragraphs through paragraph 110, establishing the character of the defendant. They then describe in chronological order the events and actions preceding Pearl Harbor, the exclusion order, expulsion and detention, life in the camps, the constitutional test cases, release and relocation—all implicating defendant United States in twenty-two causes of action.

Establishing the Character of the Defendant

The allegations covering the years before Pearl Harbor establish the character of the defendant United States by describing them as "years of racial hostility and invidious discrimination" towards the plaintiffs. They refer to anti-Japanese laws which forbade immigration of all persons of Japanese ancestry, regardless of nationality, and prohibited permanent resident aliens of Japanese ancestry from applying for naturalized citizenship. They describe the secondary effect of alien land laws passed by state governments prohibiting land ownership by persons ineligible for naturalized citizenship. Government-sanctioned racism led to other forms of racism, such as discrimination in housing, employment, business practices, and public schools.

The Complaint points to a specific interest of defendant United States in establishing concentration camps. On October 9, 1940, Secretary of Navy Frank Knox sent a memorandum to President Roosevelt which recommended building concentration camps in order to impress Japan with the seriousness of United States preparations for war. The Complaint's allegations describe the monitoring and investigations conducted by the government of a suspect Japanese-American population, including a secret break-in at the Japanese Consulate in Los Angeles in March 1941. The result of these intelligence activities refuted the foregone conclusion of mass internment. Official intelligence reports recommended that only a limited number of persons were suspect and that Japanese-Americans as a whole were "loyal to the United States or, at worst, hope that by remaining quiet they can avoid concentration camps . . ."

During the early weeks of the war, the government did conspire and concoct a devious plan to exclude and imprison Japanese-Americans, paying special attention to avoid violation of the Constitution. The government planned to designate military areas from which "any and all persons" would be excluded, thereby not discriminating racially and then, through a system of permits, to allow "everyone but the Japs" to return.

Also during this period, the case for military necessity was fabricated. Reports of illegal signals and radio transmissions had occurred. These had been investigated by the FBI and the Federal Communications Commission and found to be without substance. Nevertheless, these reports, plus the patently racist notion of a Japanese affinity for espionage and sabotage, were used to establish the existence of military necessity, setting the stage for mass exclusion and imprisonment. . . .

Life in the Prison Camps

If one was blessed with a healthy body and mind, life in the prison camps was spartan but tolerable. "The housing construction," the Complaint alleges, "was designed according to specifications . . . for temporary housing for seasoned combat units." Unfortunately, we were hardly "seasoned combat units." Even the healthy suffered from the severe deprivations of privacy through the communalization of sleeping, eating, bathing, and toileting. If one could tolerate this for three uninterrupted years, there remained other obstacles to survival. We had to withstand a diet which "fell below the standards required for prisoners of war by international convention." We had to cope with "deprivations of liberty" made real by barbed wire. We were forced to work at jobs prohibited by international convention for prisoners of war, and were compensated at six to eight cents an hour, approximating involuntary servitude. (As a teenage gardener in 1941, I earned sixty cents an hour.) The Complaint alleges further restrictions on liberty by the prohibition on speaking Japanese in public meetings, censorship of mail, warrantless searches and seizures of person and property, limitations of religious freedom, substandard education, and inadequate medical services.

Continued Exclusion and Segregation

The allegations take defendant United States to task for its failure to release inmates for the cowardly reason of " unfavorable community sentiment" and for continuing the prison camps long after the War Department itself had determined that military necessity no longer required the exclusion of Japanese-Americans from their homes on the West Coast. . . .

The Complaint also alleges that Public Law 405 was passed to enable imprisoned American citizens of Japanese ancestry to renounce their citizenship. As Wayne Collins, wartime attorney for renunciants, said, "You can no more resign citizenship in time of war than you can resign from the human race." The Complaint characterizes this law as "forcible deportation" of over 4,700 plaintiffs. These renunciants are another group of Japanese-Americans who in the past were relegated to the scrap heap of history for their "disloyalty." . . .

Illegalities in the Judicial Process

The Complaint points to recently declassified documents as demonstrating affirmative misrepresentations and suppression of evidence by the government in the legal battles of the period. It alleges that the government was "shielding its illegal acts from judicial scrutiny, and denying plaintiffs access to a fair trial and to any form of fair judicial redress for the injuries inflicted on them." . . .

The Complaint alleges that the defendant conspired "to prevent plaintiffs from adjudicating their legal claims against defendant's actions . . . [and] sought numerous delays, raised frivolous procedural disputes, claimed in bad faith that plaintiffs failed to exhaust nonexistent administrative remedies, removed plaintiffs from the jurisdiction of the courts, and released selected individual litigants from its custody in order to avoid an adjudication of defendant's illegal conduct." The Complaint highlights the seriousness of this conspiracy by citing the defendant United States' response to Mitsuye Endo's appeal for her freedom under the writ of *habeas corpus*. The defendant threatened to suspend the writ of *habeas corpus* and to revoke citizenship and residency status. . . .

Twenty-Two Causes of Action

Our lawsuit is impelled by twenty-two causes of action or counts. Like punch lines, they are the distillate of the dozens of allegations. Most are quite straightforward and easily understood. The first is entitled Due Process and states that what Japanese-Americans suffered they suffered "without individual hearings or the opportunity to be heard, in violation of the Fifth Amendment's guarantee that individuals shall not be deprived of life, liberty, or property without due process of law." The second, Equal Protection, is equally clear: Equal Protection was violated because the defendant acted "solely on the basis of race and national ancestry."

But the third, Unjust Taking, is more subtle. The Fifth Amendment states, "nor shall private property be taken for public use, without just compensation." This cause of action attempts to extend the idea of unjust taking from the destruction of our "real and personal property, commercial interests, livelihood, reputation, liberty, and other property rights," to "privileges, and entitlements secured by federal, state, and local law," charging that the defendant "failed to compensate or has provided grossly inadequate compensation for plaintiffs' losses of property rights." Our attorneys were anticipating the legal defense of sovereign immunity, whereby one may sue the government, the "sovereign," for monetary damages, only when the government consents to be sued. This Fifth Amendment clause mandates compensation. By this attempt to extend its meaning to encompass constitutional rights, our attorneys hoped to find a way around sovereign immunity.

The fourth count is based upon the Fourth Amendment's protection against unreasonable arrest, search, and seizure, an obvious violation. The fifth is based upon the privileges and immunities clause of Article 4, Section 2 of the Constitution:

> The citizens of each state shall be entitled to all privileges and immunities of citizens in the several states . . .

This little-used clause is much like equal protection, and was plainly violated.

The sixth through the thirteenth counts are again quite direct. The sixth, based on the Sixth Amendment, is Right to Fair Trial and Representation by Counsel. It is difficult to believe that this failed to occur 125,000 times. The seventh states that the Eighth Amendment's protection from cruel and unusual punishment was violated, in that our treatment was "grossly disproportionate to any security risk . . . and, in light of the absence of the commission of any crime."

The eighth through eleventh counts are based upon the First Amendment. In the eighth count, we state that our First Amendment right to freedom of religion was violated with respect to the practice of Eastern religious beliefs. In the ninth, we state our denial of the Amendment's guarantee of freedom of speech and press. This refers to the prohibition of using the Japanese language in public meetings and censorship of camp newspapers. In the tenth, we state that we were not free to associate, again in violation of the First Amendment. In the eleventh, it is the Amendment's guarantee of Freedom of Petition for Redress of Grievances that is violated. When the WRA deemed inmates to be "troublemakers" and sent them to the Moab or Leupp isolation camps, these "troublemakers" were often no more than American citizens who demanded the redress of grievances.

The twelfth count, Privacy, Travel, and other Constitutional Rights, summarizes the absence of privacy and the reality of confinement. The thirteenth count, Protection from Involuntary Servitude is based upon the Thirteenth Amendment and refers to the inadequate compensation received for labor.

I was at first confused by the fourteenth count. It cites Presidential Proclamation 2525, Presidential Orders 9066 and 9102 and Public Laws 503 and 405 as Bills of Attainder and Ex Post Facto Laws. Bills of Attainder and Ex Post Facto laws are enactments of the legislative branch of government. The count includes presidential proclamation and executive order. Why are these executive branch acts included as laws? When we examine Executive Order 9066 and Public Law 503, we see that 503 "gave teeth" to 9066 by providing penalties for violations of 9066. Taken together, the two constitute a Bill of Attainder as "a legislative enactment against a person pronouncing him guilty without trial," to cite the term's dictionary definition.

The fifteenth count is the final constitutional one: denial of *habeas corpus*, the right of a detained person to challenge the legality of his or her imprisonment. Not only was this right violated, but the government made a serious attempt to suspend *habeas corpus* through legislation in response to Mitsuye Endo's petition for freedom under *habeas corpus*.

The sixteenth through nineteenth counts are again straightforward: conspiracy to deprive plaintiffs of their civil rights, assault and battery, false arrest and imprisonment, and abuse of process and malicious prosecution.

The twentieth, Negligence, needs elaboration. The Complaint states that the defendant "failed to exercise reasonable care to protect plaintiffs' property from loss, destruction, and vandalism during plaintiffs' exclusion and imprisonment. Defendant negligently failed to feed, house, and otherwise care for plaintiffs adequately during their incarceration in the prison camps."

The twenty-first count, Contract, is explained by the Complaint:

> 133. Defendant secured plaintiffs' cooperation in peacefully leaving their homes, businesses, and property, on the basis of defendant's promises (1) that plaintiffs would be free to relocate to inland communities, and there pursue normal life, work, and schooling; (2) that defendant would protect plaintiffs and their property during relocation; (3) that plaintiffs would be permitted to return to their homes as soon as the alleged temporary military emergency subsided; (4) and that plaintiffs would not be deprived of their constitutional rights.

The twenty-second and final count, Breach of Fiduciary Duty, was added on August 8, 1983 in order to take advantage of a Supreme Court decision, *United States v. Mitchell*, rendered in June 1983. This count states that since defendant United States assumed "comprehensive and pervasive control, management, and supervision of every aspect of plaintiffs' daily lives during the period of detention," fiduciary duties were assumed as well. Given this, the "defendant breached its fiduciary duties to plaintiffs and is accountable for damages resulting therefrom."

The Complaint was a solid achievement. It was a product of heart, mind, and soul. The monetary contributions from hundreds of supporters, including *ronin* supporters, made it possible. Many of these checks were as much from the heart as from checking accounts. Aiko and Jack Herzig had left to their posterity and ours the allegations resting on documents they had retrieved. Ellen Godbey Carson, the "young attorney," and Benjamin Zelenko, together with their colleagues at Landis, Cohen, Singman and Rauh, had forged a powerful, compelling document, making the case for Japanese-American redress unmistakably clear, comprehensive, and specific. But it had to undergo the twisting and tearing of adversarial challenge and judicial scrutiny. What would survive? Would anything?

131

Supreme Court: Wards Cove Packing Company, Inc., et al. v. Atonio et al., *June 5, 1989*

The Civil Rights Act of 1964 was a major advance in the struggle for racial equality and the end to outright discrimination in the workplace. Workers' rights quickly assumed an important role in the overall civil rights movement in the decades that followed. This particular case reflected the general national trend of the late 1980s of reversing gains in the labor movement by making it far more difficult to prove discrimination. Here, "unskilled" workers, predominantly Filipino Americans and Alaskan natives, claimed that nepotism and other hiring practices caused racial stratification in which the lower-paid cannery positions paid less while the largely white noncannery jobs paid more. Further, there was a plantationlike environment, with largely segregated housing and dining facilities. The suit reached the U.S. Supreme Court, which ruled that the fact of vastly different racial composition of the two workforces did not provide prima facie *evidence of racial bias. With this, the court remanded the case to the Court of Appeals and removed a major constraint on employers to attend to issues of racial diversity and equity. The case is an excellent example of the way in which conservative currents fundamentally diverted the civil rights movement.*

United States Reports, Volume 490: Cases Adjudged in the Supreme Court at October Term, 1988. Washington, DC: Government Printing Office, 1992.

Wards Cove Packing Co., Inc., et al. v. Atonio et al.
490 U.S. 642

Jobs at petitioners' Alaskan salmon canneries are of two general types: unskilled "cannery jobs" on the cannery lines, which are filled predominantly by nonwhites; and "noncannery jobs," most of which are classified as skilled positions and filled predominantly with white workers, and virtually all of which pay more than cannery positions. Respondents, a class of nonwhite cannery workers at petitioners' facilities, filed suit in the District Court under Title VII of the Civil Rights Act of 1964, alleging, *inter alia,* that various of petitioners'

hiring/promotion practices were responsible for the work force's racial stratification and had denied them employment as noncannery workers on the basis
of race. The District Court rejected respondents' claims, finding, among other
things, that nonwhite workers were overrepresented in cannery jobs because
many of those jobs were filled under a hiring hall agreement with a predominantly nonwhite union. The Court of Appeals ultimately reversed in pertinent
part, holding, *inter alia*, that respondents had made out a prima facie case of
disparate impact in hiring for both skilled and unskilled noncannery jobs, relying solely on respondents' statistics showing a high percentage of nonwhite
workers in cannery jobs and a low percentage of such workers in noncannery
positions. The court also concluded that once a plaintiff class has shown disparate impact caused by specific, identifiable employment practices or criteria,
the burden shifts to the employer to prove the challenged practice's business
necessity.

Held:

1. The Court of Appeals erred in ruling that a comparison of the percentage
of cannery workers who are nonwhite and the percentage of noncannery workers who are nonwhite makes out a prima facie disparate-impact case. Rather, the
proper comparison is generally between the racial composition of the at-issue
jobs and the racial composition of the qualified population in the relevant labor
market. . . . Under the Court of Appeals' method of comparison, any employer
having a racially imbalanced segment of its work force could be haled into court
and made to undertake the expensive and time-consuming task of defending
the business necessity of its selection methods. For many employers, the only
practicable option would be the adoption of racial quotas, which has been rejected by this Court and by Congress in drafting Title VII. . . .

2. On remand for a determination whether the record will support a prima
facie disparate-impact case on some basis other than the racial disparity between
cannery and noncannery workers, a mere showing that nonwhites are underrepresented in the at-issue jobs in a manner that is acceptable under the standards set forth herein will not alone suffice. Rather, the courts below must also
require, as part of respondents' prima facie case, a demonstration that the statistical disparity complained of is the result of one or more of the employment
practices respondents are attacking here, specifically showing that each challenged practice has a significantly disparate impact on employment opportunities for whites and nonwhites. This specific causation requirement is not undu-
ly burdensome, since liberal discovery rules give plaintiffs broad access to
employers' records, and since employers falling within the scope of the Uniform Guidelines on Employee Selection Procedures must maintain records disclosing the impact of tests and selection procedures on employment opportunities of persons by identifiable race, sex, or ethnic group.

3. If, on remand, respondents establish a prima facie disparate-impact case
with respect to any of petitioners' practices, the burden of producing evidence

of a legitimate business justification for those practices will shift to petitioners, but the burden of persuasion will remain with respondents at all times.
This rule conforms with the usual method for allocating persuasion and production burdens in the federal courts and with the rule in disparate-treatment
cases that the plaintiff bears the burden of disproving an employer's assertion
that the adverse employment practice was based solely on a legitimate, neutral consideration. . . .

Justice White delivered the opinion of the Court.

Title VII of the Civil Rights Act of 1964, 78 Stat. 253, as amended, 42 U. S.
C. 2000e *et seq.*, makes it an unfair employment practice for an employer to
discriminate against any individual with respect to hiring or the terms and condition of employment because of such individual's race, color, religion, sex, or
national origin; or to limit, segregate, or classify his employees in ways that
would adversely affect any employee because of the employee's race, color, religion, sex, or national origin. 2000e-2(a). *Griggs v. Duke Power Co.*, 401 U. S.
424, 431 (1971), construed Title VII to proscribe "not only overt discrimination
but also practices that are fair in form but discriminatory in practice." Under
this basis for liability, which is known as the "disparate-impact" theory and
which is involved in this case, a facially neutral employment practice may be
deemed violative of Title VII without evidence of the employer's subjective intent to discriminate that is required in a "disparate-treatment" case.

I

The claims before us are disparate-impact claims, involving the employment
practices of petitioners, two companies that operate salmon canneries in remote
and widely separated areas of Alaska. The canneries operate only during the
salmon runs in the summer months. They are inoperative and vacant for the
rest of the year. In May or June of each year, a few weeks before the salmon runs
begin, workers arrive and prepare the equipment and facilities for the canning
operation. Most of these workers possess a variety of skills. When salmon runs
are about to begin, the workers who will operate the cannery lines arrive, remain as long as there are fish to can, and then depart. . . .

The length and size of salmon runs vary from year to year, and hence the
number of employees needed at each cannery also varies. Estimates are made
as early in the winter as possible; the necessary employees are hired, and when
the time comes, they are transported to the canneries. Salmon must be
processed soon after they are caught, and the work during the canning season
is therefore intense. For this reason, and because the canneries are located in
remote regions, all workers are housed at the canneries and have their meals in
company-owned mess halls.

Jobs at the canneries are of two general types: "cannery jobs" on the cannery
line, which are unskilled positions; and "noncannery jobs," which fall into a va-

riety of classifications. Most noncannery jobs are classified as skilled positions. Cannery jobs are filled predominantly by nonwhites: Filipinos and Alaska Natives. The Filipinos are hired through, and dispatched by, Local 37 of the International Longshoremen's and Warehousemen's Union pursuant to a hiring hall agreement with the local. The Alaska Natives primarily reside in villages near the remote cannery locations. Noncannery jobs are filled with predominantly white workers, who are hired during the winter months from the companies' offices in Washington and Oregon. Virtually all of the noncannery jobs pay more than cannery positions. The predominantly white noncannery workers and the predominantly nonwhite cannery employees live in separate dormitories and eat in separate mess halls.

In 1974, respondents, a class of nonwhite cannery workers who were (or had been) employed at the canneries, brought this Title VII action against petitioners. Respondents alleged that a variety of petitioners' hiring/promotion practices—e. g., nepotism, a rehire preference, a lack of objective hiring criteria, separate hiring channels, a practice of not promoting from within—were responsible for the racial stratification of the work force and had denied them and other nonwhites employment as noncannery workers on the basis of race. Respondents also complained of petitioners' racially segregated housing and dining facilities. All of respondents' claims were advanced under both the disparate-treatment and disparate-impact theories of Title VII liability.

The District Court held a bench trial, after which it entered 172 findings of fact. . . . It then rejected all of respondents' disparate-treatment claims. It also rejected the disparate-impact challenges involving the subjective employment criteria used by petitioners to fill these noncannery positions, on the ground that those criteria were not subject to attack under a disparate-impact theory.

On appeal, a panel of the Ninth Circuit affirmed, 768 F. 2d 1120 (1985), but that decision was vacated when the Court of Appeals agreed to hear the case en banc, 787 F. 2d 462 (1985). . . . The Ninth Circuit also concluded that in such a case, "[o]nce the plaintiff class has shown disparate impact caused by specific, identifiable employment practices or criteria, the burden shifts to the employer," id., at 1485, to "prov[e the] business necessity" of the challenged practice, id., at 1486. Because the en banc holding on subjective employment practices reversed the District Court's contrary ruling, the en banc Court of Appeals remanded the case to a panel for further proceedings.

On remand, the panel applied the en banc ruling to the facts of this case. 827 F. 2d 439 (1987). It held that respondents had made out a prima facie case of disparate impact in hiring for both skilled and unskilled noncannery positions. The panel remanded the case for further proceedings, instructing the District Court that it was the employer's burden to prove that any disparate impact caused by its hiring and employment practices was justified by business necessity. Neither the en banc court nor the panel disturbed the District Court's rejection of the disparate-treatment claims.

Petitioners sought review of the Court of Appeals' decision in this Court, challenging it on several grounds. . . .

II

In holding that respondents had made out a prima facie case of disparate impact, the Court of Appeals relied solely on respondents' statistics showing a high percentage of nonwhite workers in the cannery jobs and a low percentage of such workers in the noncannery positions. Although statistical proof can alone make out a prima facie case, see *Teamsters* v. *United States*, 431 U. S. 324, 339 (1977); *Hazelwood School Dist.* v. *United States*, 433 U. S. 299, 307–308 (1977), the Court of Appeals' ruling here misapprehends our precedents and the purposes of Title VII, and we therefore reverse. . . .

It is clear to us that the Court of Appeals' acceptance of the comparison between the racial composition of the cannery work force and that of the noncannery work force, as probative of a prima facie case of disparate impact in the selection of the latter group of workers, was flawed for several reasons. Most obviously, with respect to the skilled noncannery jobs at issue here, the cannery work force in no way reflected "the pool of *qualified* job applicants" or the "*qualified* population in the labor force." Measuring alleged discrimination in the selection of accountants, managers, boat captains, electricians, doctors, and engineers—and the long list of other "skilled" noncannery positions found to exist by the District Court, . . . —by comparing the number of nonwhites occupying these jobs to the number of nonwhites filling cannery worker positions is nonsensical. If the absence of minorities holding such skilled positions is due to a dearth of qualified nonwhite applicants (for reasons that are not petitioners' fault), petitioners' selection methods or employment practices cannot be said to have had a "disparate impact" on nonwhites. . . .

The Court of Appeals also erred with respect to the unskilled noncannery positions. Racial imbalance in one segment of an employer's work force does not, without more, establish a prima facie case of disparate impact with respect to the selection of workers for the employer's other positions, even where workers for the different positions may have somewhat fungible skills (as is arguably the case for cannery and unskilled noncannery workers). As long as there are no barriers or practices deterring qualified nonwhites from applying for noncannery positions, see n. 6, *supra*, if the percentage of selected applicants who are nonwhite is not significantly less than the percentage of qualified applicants who are nonwhite, the employer's selection mechanism probably does not operate with a disparate impact on minorities. Where this is the case, the percentage of nonwhite workers found in other positions in the employer's labor force is irrelevant to the question of a prima facie statistical case of disparate impact. As noted above, a contrary ruling on this point would almost inexorably lead to the use of numerical quotas in the workplace, a result that Congress and this Court have rejected repeatedly in the past. . . .

Consequently, we reverse the Court of Appeals' ruling that a comparison between the percentage of cannery workers who are nonwhite and the percentage of noncannery workers who are nonwhite makes out a prima facie case of disparate impact. Of course, this leaves unresolved whether the record made in the District Court will support a conclusion that a prima facie case of disparate impact has been established on some basis other than the racial disparity between cannery and noncannery workers. This is an issue that the Court of Appeals or the District Court should address in the first instance. . . .

As a general matter, a plaintiff must demonstrate that it is the application of a specific or particular employment practice that has created the disparate impact under attack. Such a showing is an integral part of the plaintiff's prima facie case in a disparate-impact suit under Title VII.

Here, respondents have alleged that several "objective" employment practices (e.g., nepotism, separate hiring channels, rehire preferences), as well as the use of "subjective decision making" to select noncannery workers, have had a disparate impact on nonwhites. Respondents base this claim on statistics that allegedly show a disproportionately low percentage of nonwhites in the at-issue positions. However, even if on remand respondents can show that nonwhites are underrepresented in the at-issue jobs in a manner that is acceptable under the standards set forth in Part II, *supra*, this alone will *not* suffice to make out a prima facie case of disparate impact. Respondents will also have to demonstrate that the disparity they complain of is the result of one or more of the employment practices that they are attacking here, specifically showing that each challenged practice has a significantly disparate impact on employment opportunities for whites and nonwhites. To hold otherwise would result in employers being potentially liable for "the myriad of innocent causes that may lead to statistical imbalances in the composition of their work forces." . . .

Though we have phrased the query differently in different cases, it is generally well established that at the justification stage of such a disparate-impact case, the dispositive issue is whether a challenged practice serves, in a significant way, the legitimate employment goals of the employer. . . . The touchstone of this inquiry is a reasoned review of the employer's justification for his use of the challenged practice. A mere insubstantial justification in this regard will not suffice, because such a low standard of review would permit discrimination to be practiced through the use of spurious, seemingly neutral employment practices. At the same time, though, there is no requirement that the challenged practice be "essential" or "indispensable" to the employer's business for it to pass muster: this degree of scrutiny would be almost impossible for most employers to meet, and would result in a host of evils we have identified above. . . .

In this phase, the employer carries the burden of producing evidence of a business justification for his employment practice. The burden of persuasion, however, remains with the disparate-impact plaintiff. To the extent that the Ninth Circuit held otherwise in its en banc decision in this case, see 810 F. 2d, at 1485–1486, or in the panel's decision on remand, see 827 F. 2d, at 445, 447 — suggesting that the persuasion burden should shift to petitioners once respondents established a prima facie case of disparate impact — its decisions were erroneous. . . . The persuasion burden here must remain with the plaintiff, for it is he who must prove that it was "because of such individual's race, color," etc., that he was denied a desired employment opportunity. . . .

For the reasons given above, the judgment of the Court of Appeals is reversed, and the case is remanded for further proceedings consistent with this opinion.

It is so ordered.

Justice Blackmun, with whom Justice Brennan and Justice Marshall join, dissenting.

I fully concur in Justice Stevens' analysis of this case. Today a bare majority of the Court takes three major strides backwards in the battle against race discrimination. It reaches out to make last Term's plurality opinion in Watson v. Fort Worth Bank & Trust, 487 U.S. 977 (1988), the law, thereby upsetting the longstanding distribution of burdens of proof in Title VII disparate-impact cases. It bars the use of internal work force comparisons in the making of a prima facie case of discrimination, even where the structure of the industry in question renders any other statistical comparison meaningless. And it requires practice-by-practice statistical proof of causation, even where, as here, such proof would be impossible.

The harshness of these results is well demonstrated by the facts of this case. The salmon industry as described by this record takes us back to a kind of overt and institutionalized discrimination we have not dealt with in years: a total residential and work environment organized on principles of racial stratification and segregation, which, as Justice Stevens points out, resembles a plantation economy. This industry long has been characterized by a taste for discrimination of the old-fashioned sort: a preference for hiring nonwhites to fill its lowest level positions, on the condition that they stay there. The majority's legal rulings essentially immunize these practices from attack under a Title VII disparate-impact analysis.

Sadly, this comes as no surprise. One wonders whether the majority still believes that race discrimination — or, more accurately, race discrimination against nonwhites — is a problem in our society, or even remembers that it ever was. . . .

132

Masaru "Pundy" Yokouchi Interview in Off Center, March/April 1990

Yokouchi was the driving force behind the creation of the Hawaii State Foundation on Culture and the Arts, the state component receiving support from the National Endowment of the Arts, beginning in the mid-1960s. His nickname, "Pundy," referred to his family's bakery—noted for its production of Portuguese sweet bread, pao doce *(pronounced "pun deuce"). A second-generation Japanese American, Yokouchi was appointed the first chairman of the foundation by Governor John Burns (1962–73), whom Pundy had convinced of the centrality of the arts for Hawaii's people. Two years later, in 1967, Hawai'i became the first state to require that one percent of funds appropriated for new buildings be allocated to purchase works of art. Since then, more than half of the states have followed suit. For Yokouchi, it was crucial for "local" residents (meaning the two thirds who were people of color) to appreciate that art was not only for the white elite but also for the enrichment of all other groups. Moreover, he understood that, after the political and economic gains made by nonwhites in the 1950s, Euro-American notions of superiority would finally fall only when the artistic and cultural barriers had been successfully breached.*

Interview by Rita Golden, *Off Center* (Maui Community Arts and Cultural Center)(March/April 1990): 15–18.

I had Tadashi Sato's painting hung in my living room. It's an abstract of an ocean scene, and [Gov. Burns] asked me. "What's that?" In a kind of uncomplimentary way. That's when I set into him. I told him, "How dare you, as a champion of education, ask me something like that in that way?"

He said, "No, explain to me what it is." And I told him, "That's an artist who takes a scene and in his own mind creates something—in this case it was serenity—but he doesn't do it in a representational form. He does it in his own way." . . .

I became the first chairman of the State Foundation on Culture and the Arts! People obviously thought it was a political appointment, but the essence of it was that I had told the governor that art should be universal.

I walked in [to his office] one day, and the secretary smiled at me and went to the door and said, "Your chairman is here." Then he said, "Come right in, Mr. Chairman. You're going to Chicago."

I said, "Okay. Chairman of what?"

"State Foundation, Culture and the Arts." And he had the bill in front of him. I said, "What's the joke?"

He said, "It's no joke. You're going to Chicago in ten days."

Finally I realized the guy was serious. I said, "You want me to represent the State of Hawaii in this first national conference for the arts in Chicago, and I don't know anything about the arts. You've got to be out of your cotton-pickin' mind!"

So he said, "You gotta accept, because your name is already sent up to the national council."

I said, "You're crazy! Guys gonna laugh at you—you have a nobody in the arts! In [Honolulu] you have very prominent people involved with the arts who would give their right arm to be there. Those are the people you should select. I just came out of the bakery!"

He said, "Didn't you tell me the arts belong to the common man? Well, what better way can the common man identify with the arts than if its chairman is cut from the same cloth?" . . .

My fundamental goal was, how do we get the people involved in the arts in a universal way? Just at that time there was an experiment known as the Model Cities Program for economically and socially deprived people. It had some federal funds to help uplift those people. In Honolulu, it was Kalihi/Palama and Wai'anae Nanakuli. I insisted our foundation set up a program in there also, on our own, for the arts. People said, "What are you doing? Must be some political exploitation."

But to prove our point that the arts belong to everybody, we wanted to start our own experiment. And it worked. Until today, those two communities still have very active councils. . . .

We also started an arts in the schools program. You know, in Hawaii, the state controls all the public schools. So it was a good vehicle to introduce the arts. And we've been trying for the last 20 years to get them to expand the arts. It still didn't really happen, but at least there's more introduction to the arts. . . .

One of the most severely downtrodden people, people that were treated very, very cheaply, was the native Hawaiian. Society said, "The Hawaiian culture is pagan. They need to be converted to Western culture." And the Hawaiians themselves believed it more strongly than the rest of society.

Our first year as a foundation, 1966, we formed a governor's conference for the arts. We had people from across the state, and even some of our friends from the Mainland. That's when we found out the weakness of the arts, especially the skills of the Hawaiian people; their arts and crafts were almost forgotten. We made a priority of rescuing the Hawaiian arts. . . .

We started in a very small way: We wanted to give money to Hawaiian organizations to perpetuate and protect the arts. There were no takers. There was nobody! Can you believe that? There was one individual at the University of Hawaii who was starting to put together the Hawaiian language, a Hawaiian professor, and he was already ready to retire. If he died, a vast knowledge would have gone with him. . . .

When you restore the culture, now the person knows what he is. Then he has confidence, and realizes that he has a richer background than he thought he had. We're starting to finally find out that everybody had something: they have to develop that to understand what they are. You have to know yourself first before you can understand the other guy, so the individual culture for all the different ethnic groups is very important.

I used to work in a bakery. It was the family bakery, and I probably, at that time, was earning about $300 a month, or $250. Those days, already, I was involved in real estate. We used to have a *hui*, have the people get together and pool our few dollars. And I had a check for $1,000, which was a lot of money I heard of Tadashi Sato returning home from the Mainland. He was located in Lahaina, so I went to see him one day. I bought three paintings for $1,000. I spent it all up. I didn't mean to, I just loved the paintings.

So I came home with these paintings, and my wife cried. "You spent $1,000!" A thousand dollars, you could buy a car in those days. So she cried and got carried away, but I loved the paintings. . . .

I like all kinds of paintings, but I lean more to impressionistic . . . some abstraction. I've got some non-objective paintings, and some representational paintings, too. I don't go out looking for something or trying to make a collection. My paintings are all by accident. I walk in a gallery, and pick up something. Nothing done in a systematic way. . . .

I think I'm much more aware, not just because of age, either, but because of this exposure to the arts. I think I'm a better person. And if I didn't have that, at this age, I think something would be lacking in me.

133

Daniel Tsang, "Asians Are Automatically Labeled Gang Members," December 12, 1994

At the turn of the twenty-first century, there were two stark and contrasting images of Asian Americans. One was the "model minority" picture of an overachieving racial group crowding out others in elite universities and occupations. The other was that of Asian immigrant youth involved in gangs—dealing drugs, battling over turf, extorting money from merchants, and assassinating one another. In this essay, Daniel Tsang examines this phenomenon in one Orange County, California, incident but suggests that it has widespread application in many Vietnamese American and other Asian American communities where gang activity may be prevalent. The "racial profiling" by some law enforcement personnel included random photographing of Asian youths who simply dressed the part. In this particular case, Tu Anh Tran may have been a gang member. Some years later he was again involved with the law and became a fugitive. Tu may have been wrongly persecuted and later turned to crime, or Tsang and other community advocates may have mistakenly come forward on his behalf. Regardless, the issue of random racial profiling remains thorny for all of American society.

Daniel Tsang, "Asians Are Automatically Labeled Gang Members." *Los Angeles Times*, December 12, 1994, B5.

Community Essay

'Asians Are Automatically Labeled Gang Members'

Critics say cultural bias figures into the case against a Vietnamese student. Propositions 187 and 184 could exacerbate the problem.

By Daniel C. Tsang

The bobbing shaved heads in a sea of orange, for one fleeting moment, brought me back to Southeast Asia, reminding me of Buddhist monks going about their routine in their saffron robes. But reality struck. I am in the waiting room at Orange County Men's Jail.

I am here to see Tu Anh Tran, 22, who legally immigrated from Vietnam in 1988. He is charged with murder, attempted murder and robbery. His public defender, Jeff Lund, says Tu is a victim of being in the "wrong place at the wrong time." Tu says tattoos and cigarette burns on his arm and hand, inflicted years ago as a memorial to his dead mother, have caused police to label him a gangbanger. Others, including Li Ren Fong, Tu's math instructor at Rancho Santiago College and his mentor, firmly believe police are mistaken. Lund believes that without the gang assumption, Tu, who was shot in the back during the incident, would not have been charged.

On April 2, Tu was a student at Rancho Santiago College in Santa Ana. It was spring break. Tu and a friend ate at a Little Saigon restaurant in Westminster. As Tu was paying the bill, a fight broke out, he says. As Tu tried to break up the fight, he says, on off-duty security guard shot and killed his friend, and wounded Tu. The next thing Tu knew, he was taken from the hospital to jail.

Even though he has no prior convictions, Tu faces a possible life sentence if convicted. The man who did the shooting is free, claiming self-defense, that he was attacked by a group of people in the crowded cafe.

Tu believes his predicament is due to cultural misinterpretation of his tattoos and cigarette burns. Tu has a tattoo of an eagle on his arm and the words, in Vietnamese, "bird without its flock." He says it speaks to his loneliness after his mother's death when he was 17 and living in Iowa. According to Tu, the police told him the tattoo is proof he is in a Chinese gang, even though he is Vietnamese.

Tu says the faded burns on his hands were also to show his pain at his mother's passing. Dr. Hoang Van Duc, who teaches pathology at USC, says Tu's actions may have been an adaptation of old Vietnamese religious tradition—when monks are initiated into Buddhism, their skulls are seared with burning incense to prove they can handle pain through meditation. But the 1993 Southeast Asian Gangs manual from the California Commission on Peace Officer Standards and Training states that cigarette burn marks are "without a doubt" the "most common form of marking found on Asian gang members."

John Song, an associate professor of criminal justice at Buffalo State who wrote his dissertation on the conflict between law enforcement and Southern Californians of Vietnamese and Chinese descent, disputes that view. Police are incorrectly generalizing from a small sample of arrestees with body markings, says Song. He believes that such flawed gang profiles perpetuate stereotypes of Asians as criminals.

Many in the Orange County Asian American community fear that too many youths are automatically labeled gang members, based on little evidence. They note that even though the 1990 census put Westminster's population at less than 23% Asian Pacific, 72% of those stopped by police as part of the Tri-Agency Resource Gang Enforcement Team program crackdown on gangs have been Asian, according to the program's 1993 year-end report.

Tu's fate will be decided at his trial in Santa Ana Superior Court, scheduled to begin this week. But his case raises questions about the future of recent immigrants. Passage of Proposition 187 and "three-strikes" Proposition 184 will exacerbate an already bad situation in which immigrants are singled out for discriminatory treatment, further dividing our society. If so, we are condemning them—especially our youth—to *bui doi,* or "a life like dust."

Daniel C. Tsang, a social sciences lecturer at UC Irvine, co-founded the Alliance Working for Asian Rights and Empowerment in Orange County. He also hosts "Subversity," a weekly interview show, on KUCI, 88.9 FM.

134

Akaka Legislation to Review for Asian Pacific American Congressional Medals of Honor (Senate Bill 1026), August 3, 1995

Senator Daniel Akaka (D-HI) introduced this amendment to order a review of the World War II Asian Pacific American recipients of the Distinguished Service Cross (DSC), the nation's second highest combat award. Congress had authorized a study to determine whether some African American World War II veterans had been awarded DSCs and thus denied the highest award, the Congressional Medal of Honor (CMH), due to the prevailing climate of racial hostility. Akaka wanted a similar review for Asian Pacific Americans. In 2000, after a rigorous study by the army, 21 men were awarded Medals of Honor, most posthumously, by President William J. Clinton. One other person was separately found to be deserving. Thus, 22 Medals of Honor were conferred upon Asian Pacific Americans, over half a century after they had been earned. In this group, 21 were Japanese Americans, including Senator Daniel Inouye of Hawai'i, and one was of Filipino-Mexican descent. In addition to the very high honor, CMH recipients receive substantial material benefits—benefits denied these veterans and their families for more than five decades.

Congressional Record, Vol. 141, No. 128, August 3, 1995.

Amendment No. 2100 to S. 1026

Mr. NUNN. Mr. President, I have another amendment by the Senator from Hawaii, Senator Akaka. This amendment would require a review of awards to Asian-Americans and native American Pacific Islanders during World War II. It requires the review of awards to African-Americans to determine whether they should be upgraded.

The Army has undertaken a review of World War II awards of the Distinguished Service Cross to determine whether any should be upgraded to the Medal of Honor. The review is requested based on a concern that some awards may have been downgraded due to prejudice.

The amendment requests a similar review of awards to native American Pacific Islanders in view of the possible prejudice at that time against these groups. . . .

Sec. 544. *Review Regarding Awards of Distinguished-Service Cross to Asian-Americans and Pacific Islanders for Certain World War II Service*

(a) Review Required.—The Secretary of the Army shall—

(1) review the records relating to the award of the Distinguished-Service Cross to Asian-Americans and Native American Pacific Islanders for service as members of the Army during World War II in order to determine whether the award should be upgraded to the Medal of Honor; and

(2) submit to the President a recommendation that the President award a Medal of Honor to each such person for whom the Secretary determines an upgrade to be appropriate.

(b) Waiver of Time Limitations.—The President is authorized to award a Medal of Honor to any person referred to in subsection (a) in accordance with a recommendation of the Secretary of the Army submitted under that subsection. . . .

Mr. AKAKA. Mr. President, I rise to offer an amendment to S. 1026, the fiscal year 1996 Department of Defense authorization bill. The amendment directs the Secretary of the Army to review the service records of Asian-Americans and Native American Pacific Islanders who received the Distinguished Service Cross to determine whether the award should be upgraded to the Medal of Honor.

Under the direction of then-Acting Secretary John Shannon, the Army is reviewing all Distinguished Service Cross [DSC] awards given to African-American soldiers during World War II to determine whether any of these cases merited an upgrade to the Congressional Medal of Honor [CMH].

Mr. President, I offer my amendment to ensure that the Army conducts a similar study for Asian-Americans and Pacific Islanders who served during World War II. I am deeply concerned that this group of Americans may have also been discriminated against in the awarding of the CMH. The internment of Japanese-Americans during World War II is a clear indication of the bias that existed at the time. This hostile climate may have impacted the decision to award the military's highest honor to Asians, particularly Japanese-Americans.

The famed 100th Infantry Battalion/ 442 Regimental Combat Team, which performed extraordinary deeds in Europe, still has the unique distinction of being the most highly decorated unit of its size in American history. In fact, 47 individuals of the 442d Regimental Combat Team received the DSC. However, only one Japanese-American who served during World War II received the CMH; this award was given post-humously after the war only when concerns were raised that not one American of Japanese descent who served in World War II had received the medal.

Mr. President, my amendment only serves to ensure fairness for Asian-Americans and Pacific Islanders who so gallantly served their country during World War II. As we celebrate the fiftieth anniversary of the Allied victory over the Axis powers. I think it is timely and appropriate that we undertake such an initiative. I hope that my colleagues will support this important amendment.

135

Peter Hyun, *Afterword to* In the New World, 1995

Peter Hyun was born in Hawai'i in 1906, the first son of a highly unusual couple who joined the first group of Korean workers sent to the sugar plantations beginning in 1903. The Hyun family traced its lineage back to generations of important officials in Korea. Peter's father, Soon Hyun, was an important leader of the Korean independence movement. After the March 1, 1919 uprising against Japanese colonial rule, the family lived in exile in China and the United States, where the Korean liberation forces fought on diplomatic, political, military, cultural, and financial fronts. Peter had a rich and varied life. He attended college in Indiana and became one of a handful of artists of color working in theater companies in many major cities, including New York, Massachusetts, and California. His writings reflect rare glimpses of minority, especially Asian, presence in mainstream art circles in prewar America. These early years were depicted in Man Sei!: The Making of a Korean American *(Honolulu: University of Hawaii Press, 1986). This selection, the afterword to the sequel,* In the New World: The Making of a Korean American, *which brings his story into the 1990s, is a commentary on the privileges and problems of being the first-born son in a traditional family. It is also a thoughtful and ultimately optimistic reminiscence about the challenges faced by a Korean American who lived through much of the twentieth century (Peter Hyun died in 1993).*

From Peter Hyun, *In the New World: The Making of a Korean American*. Honolulu: University of Hawaii Press, 1995, 276–79. Reprinted with permission.

Afterword

In the age-old Korean tradition, the family name, the family property, and all honor and responsibility are entrusted to the oldest son. And I had the misfortune to be the firstborn son. Not only my parents and grandparents, but all the members of the clan regarded me as the heir to the family tradition and lavished on me limitless indulgence. I was allowed to sit at the table of the elders and partake of the special food prepared for them. I always received the first new suit of clothes and sandals. Only after that, new clothes for my younger brothers. On special holidays such as my uncle's birthday, I would be taken to the festivities by Papa and Umma; younger ones—they stayed at home.

These traditional discriminations were openly displayed not only on special occasions, but even more openly in daily activities at home. There was distinction between the manner of speaking to the oldest son and to the rest of the children. Papa always took me with him when he went to the public baths where hot water was abundant. The rest of the family first had to heat the water in a kerosene can over an open fire and bathe in a tub. For my younger brothers, it was most tantalizing and aggravating at mealtimes. They had to sit and wait and watch the big helping of choice bits of food passed to me. Then they received their bowls, but not with too many choice bits. How such a Korean way of life must have hurt my brothers.

The status of my sisters was even one step lower than my brothers. Except for my oldest sister Alice, who was a little mother to all of us, the three other sisters had little recognition. Sister Soon-Ok, one year younger than I, was given more attention by virtue of the fact that she was an invalid; she had been bedridden from age ten until her death in Shanghai at sixteen.

Enjoying to the full all the privileges of a number one son, I was totally unaware of the anger and jealousy bordering on hatred felt by all my sisters and brothers. These stored animosities did not surface until our adult lives nearly a half century later. I was mortified and horrified to realize the hurts and pains my family role must have heaped on them when we were all young. The full impact of this did not fully crystallize until after Papa and Umma had both died. In vain attempts to redeem myself and to earn their forgiveness, I tried in many ways to belittle my place in the family and encourage my younger brothers to assume the leadership. But, alas, it was too late. Neither would their frozen hearts thaw nor their memories of pain ever quite disappear.

Having spent my childhood in a semifeudal society, and having transplanted myself into an industrialized democratic society, I was conscious and aware of the advantages and drawbacks of both. Living in America, I witnessed and cringed at the sight of some youngster cursing and attacking an older person. At the same time, the traditional confines and restrictions placed on Korean children restricted their ability to develop their talents. While I enjoyed as a young boy the privileges of being the number-one son, I can see how confining the traditional way was to my brothers and sisters.

The making of a Korean American is essentially a story of a cultural marriage. Such a marriage is consummated only after a prolonged period of engagement—ten years, twenty, or even longer.

At seventeen, a son of the ancient Korean culture, I was propelled into the New World called America. It was unreal: The streets, the buildings, the people and the language they spoke, all seemed like a scene in a dream. After living in Korea and China, once again I had to change my life drastically in this New World, or perish.

The immensity of the challenge dawned on me when I began to study the English language; it was a nightmare! I had studied and lived with three Asian languages—Korean, Japanese, and Chinese. I had also dabbled in Russian. But English, I discovered, was the most unreasoning language. The more I studied, the more complicated it became. Learning the grammar and memorizing the rules were of little help, for there were always exceptions to every rule. I was a prisoner of my own choosing. It was clear that I would never be free until I had conquered this devilish language.

Fortunately, I was born with the Korean stubborn streak: I refused to give up. For ten years, I struggled in agony, and suddenly one day, English was no longer a foreign language. The final testimonial of the long engagement between the Korean and the American cultures appeared in my sleep. In my dream, I was speaking not Korean as usual, but English. I awoke with a great sigh of relief and a feeling of overwhelming elation.

However, the trials and tribulations of the engagement did not cease. Learning and accepting the language of the American people was one thing; but accepting and being accepted as one of them was quite something else. The thousands of years of man's struggle for survival must have implanted instinctive suspicion, hostility, and hate of others. And the walls among people persist today.

"Hey! Chinaman!"

"Hey! Charlie!"

"Hey! Chink!"

These names were hurled at me at odd moments and at odd places—by a workman digging ditches, by a vendor selling apples on the street, by college students, artists, and professionals. How can such deep chasms in human minds be bridged? Will they ever be bridged? The tragedy is that these chasms dwell in the minds of all people; some carefully hidden, some disguised in polite smiles, and some bluntly exposed.

It took many more years for me to understand that the hostility and the hate came from two sources: ignorance and fear—the ignorance of another culture, and the fear of being exposed to it. The most effective weapon was laughter. People of different cultures laughing at and with each other could more quickly dispel their hostility.

"You think the Koreans speak funny English? You should hear the American missionaries speaking Korean!"

Laughter!

"Oh, yeah? You think Orientals with slanted eyes are funny looking? Ask a Korean farmer to tell you how the American missionaries look: Watery eyes, yellow hair, long nose!"

Laughter!

The sharing of laughter more than any books or lectures could draw us together and open the door for communication. Only communication can eventually wipe out prejudice, enlighten the ignorant, and neutralize hostility. True,
it has taken more than thirty years for me to reach a state of mutual respect. Perhaps, with a little more patience and with a little more time, we might finally
achieve mutual acceptance and the ultimate fruition of our cultural marriage.

Nearly half a million Koreans live in the state of California, and that many
also live in all major cities throughout the country. How many of them will become fully integrated? And when? Let's add to the Koreans all the other newcomers from Asia, Latin America, Europe, and Africa.

To succeed, cultural marriage has to travel on a two-way street. Why must
the world's peoples come and adopt the American way of life? Can't American
people, too, learn and understand the cultures and languages of other lands?
The study of foreign cultures could and should be part of the basic educational program from kindergarten through college. This is not only feasible, but
may be essential to human survival.

Today, we have the capability to destroy the world as we know it. Some believe such a holocaust is inevitable. And in another million years, out of the
ashes, a new living species with greater intelligence than the extinct Homo sapi-
ens may emerge to build a new and more rational world. That is the most tragic and cynical view of man's future. I would rather cling to my faith that the
human race is endowed with the potential to construct a world of peace and
tolerance that our own sons and daughters will inherit.

136

Andrew Lam, "Love, Money, Prison, Sin, Revenge," 1995

Southeast Asian American writers may be a unique cohort. Most Vietnamese Americans, for example, who have become prominent writers, like Andrew Lam, were natives of Vietnam and mastered English as a second language. But while their styles may be different, the sense of writing in exile and the awesome heritage of the war are of critical importance. Lam is a commentator for National Public Radio's "All Things Considered" and an editor for the Pacific News Service. He was born in Saigon, now Ho Chi Minh City, and arrived in the United States in 1975 at the age of 11. He has published numerous short stories and essays in a wide variety of venues. This particular piece is redolent with the painful awareness that the war will never go away for his generation. And he deftly explores the enormous gap between the Vietnamese families and their children who arrived in 1975 or shortly thereafter and were educated and professional—largely those intimately associated with the South Vietnamese government and the U.S. war effort—and the "boat people" arriving from refugee camps in the 1980s, peasants or workers subjected to unspeakable horrors. Their children all too often ended in tragic circumstances, like the four youths in this account.

Andrew Lam, "Love, Money, Prison, Sin, Revenge," in De Tran, Andrew Lam, and Hai Dai Nguyen, ed., *Once Upon a Dream . . . The Vietnamese—American Experience*. Kansas City: Andrews and McMeel, 1995. Reprinted with permission.

Love, Money, Prison, Sin, Revenge

by Andrew Lam

On the afternoon of April 4, 1991, fifteen years, eleven months and twenty-seven days after the end of the Vietnam War, four Vietnamese youths armed with semiautomatic pistols stormed into a Good Guys electronic store on Stockton Boulevard in Sacramento and held forty-one people hostage. Speaking heavily accented and broken English, they issued what the *Sacramento Bee* described as "a series of bizarre demands." They wanted a helicopter to fly to Thailand so they could fight the Vietcong, four million dollars, four bulletproof vests, and forty pieces of 1,000 year-old ginseng roots.

While a crowd, some enthusiasts equipped with their own camcorders, gathered across the street, TV reporters informed viewers that three of the gunmen were brothers—Loi Khac Nguyen, twenty-one; Pham Khac Nguyen, nineteen, and Long Khac Nguyen, seventeen—and that the last, Cuong Tran, sixteen, was Long Nguyen's best friend. The Nguyen brothers had come from a poor Vietnamese Catholic family headed by an ex-sergeant of the South Vietnamese army. All four were altar boys. Three of the youths had dropped out of school or had been expelled. None had been able to find a steady job.

The gunmen could be seen on live television behind the store's glass doors, strolling back and forth with their firearms, bound hostages at their feet. Sacramento County Sheriff Glen Craig, who had implanted listening devices in the store, reported that the gunmen were jubilant at seeing themselves and hearing their names on TV—"Oh, ah, we're going to be movie stars!" The sheriff had also told reporters that the gunmen belonged to a loosely knit gang called Oriental Boys—an error, as it turned out, since the police couldn't prove membership in any gang.

As the siege wore on, negotiations between the gunmen and the taut-faced, gray-haired sheriff reached a stalemate. The gunmen, for their part, had grown increasingly edgy and refused to negotiate after authorities met only part of one demand, providing them with a single bulletproof jacket. Sheriff Craig, on the other hand, later told reporters that the four would not "focus on any single demand. They were attempting to gain notoriety, attention and, perhaps, some transportation out of the country."

Eight and a half hours later, after the gunmen wounded two of the hostages, a SWAT team raided the store on live television. Three of the young men were killed immediately, but not before one of them sprayed the hostages with bullets, killing two employees—John Lee Fritz and Kris Sohne—and a customer—Fernando Gutierrez—and wounding eight more. Loi Nguyen, the oldest, and the one who wore the bulletproof jacket, was seriously wounded. His trial on forty-nine felony counts and three counts of murder is set for July 11. He is pleading not guilty.

As I watched this tragedy unfold on my TV set that night, I remember being overwhelmed by an irrational fear. It was the fear that the Vietnam War had somehow been renewed by those gunmen and by those helicopters hovering over the store. And though I was on the safe side of the TV screen now and judging their barbaric acts, I was not without this singular sense of foreboding: Six years ago I could have been one of them.

If the story of the Good Guys ended in carnage on the linoleum floor of an electronics store, it began an ocean and an epic journey away, nourished by numerous subterranean streams. It is those streams I am foundering in. I am at once too close and too far from their story. Though an American journalist now, I came to this country as a Vietnamese refugee, the son of a South Vietnamese army officer. The young men and I, through our fathers, are veterans of a civil war we never actually fought. In their demands, I hear the thematic echo of vengeance, which forms and shapes all Vietnamese youths who grow up in America. Perhaps all this binds me to the Good Guys hostage-takers nearly two decades after the last U.S. helicopter hovered over a burning Saigon before heading toward the South China Sea.

When I asked for directions, the blond kid on Stockton Boulevard rattled off names of generic American landmarks in an amiable tone: Midas . . . Shakey's Pizza . . . Carl's Jr. . . . Man, you can't miss it. . . . Turn left at the House of Fabrics. Next to it, you'll see the Good Guys.

Inside, the first thing you noticed was yourself. Walk through the glass door and a dozen camcorders gave you back your reflections on the various TV sets. For as little as $549, you could be (oh, ah) your own movie star.

I saw but tried not to look at my own faces on those TV screens. The faces, my faces, appeared expressionless, the thick brows slightly raised, touched perhaps by a tinge of skepticism. I do not believe in instant fame, had always thought Andy Warhol's prediction an odd American curse. . . .

A few who watched the siege recall a dangerous combination of arrogance and confusion among the TV reporters and, especially, the authorities. "They ran around like chickens without heads," said one Vietnamese man who volunteered to help the police but was turned away. "The boys were Vietnamese Catholics and the sheriff initially had a Laotian monk at the scene," he said.

Yet clues that would have helped the sheriffs and the journalists unlock the gunmen's psyches were just minutes from the Good Guys, in Little Saigon. In a mini-mall a mile or so away, a video store called Ngoc Thao (Precious Herb) catered to a Vietnamese clientele. Colorful posters of gangsters and cops holding Uzis and of ancient swordsmen in silk brocades flying above temple rooftops covered the walls and glass windows. Here, as in many other video stores frequented by local Vietnamese in Sacramento, one can find 1,000-year-old ginseng roots—the precious cure-all usually discovered by the lucky hero in kung-fu epics—or other magical panaceas and cursed swords.

They're in hundreds of Hong Kong videos, dubbed in Vietnamese, that line the shelves. The cashier, a heavily made-up woman, was having a busy day. Like a high priestess with holy water, she dispensed pieces of Asia's fabled past to hordes of homesick Vietnamese. . . .

Two days after the Good Guys Siege, a *Sacramento Bee* photo that ran the length of the page showed the Nguyen brothers' parents standing in their living room as if facing a firing squad. Though stricken with grief, Bim Khac and Sao Thi Nguyen admitted journalists into their tiny two-bedroom unit in the Laura Dawn Manor Apartments, a two-story structure rented out mostly to Southeast Asian families.

The photo shows a sagging sofa, a VCR and, of course, a large TV set. On top of the TV stands a South Vietnamese flag—three red horizontal stripes against a gold background—representing a country that no longer exists. On the opposite wall, a three-tier shrine displays crucifixes, statues of Mary, Joseph, and Jesus and various martyred saints, all with mournful faces.

The Nguyens and their six children spent four months in a refugee camp in Indonesia before coming to the United States in the early 1980s. In Sacramento, they were receiving Aid to Families with Dependent Children. The ex-sergeant from the South Vietnamese army, who is active in church, said through an interpreter that he was no help to his children when it came to explaining American things such as homework or news on TV. Still, wasn't what he wanted for his children the same as what any Vietnamese parent wants—that they do well in school and keep "Vietnamese traditions"?

"Please tell the people of Sacramento I am very sorry for what my sons have done," the patriarch offered. Asked how his quiet obedient boys wound up becoming hostage-takers, Nguyen and his wife provided only a miserable silence. . . .

For Loi, Pham and Long Nguyen and Cuong Tran, who failed school and grew up between the Good Guys electronics store and the Ngoc Thao, there existed two separate notions—notoriety and revenge, revenge being the stronger impulse. One encourages public displays (i.e., confessing on "Oprah," or holding shoppers hostage and giving incoherent speeches) that may lead mainstream America to acknowledge that they exist. The other fulfills the old man's extraterritorial passion—"helicopters to Thailand to kill Viet Cong"—and rejects America as the wasteland.

To grow up Vietnamese in America, after all, is to grow up with the legacy of belonging to the loser's side and to endure all that entails. To grow up in America is to desire individual fame and glory, a larger sense of the self. Driving on Stockton Boulevard, it suddenly occurs to me that, while I myself might have learned to walk that strange Vietnamese-American hyphen, it continues to hurl young and hapless Vietnamese down into a dark and bottomless pit.

After the Good Guys, the media offered a variety of explanations. One had to do with the chronology of waves, as in waves of Vietnamese immigrants. The first wave of refugees who came to America in 1975, my wave comprised intellectuals, educators, army officers, skilled civil servants, professionals—Vietnam's best and brightest—those who had not experience Vietnam under Communist rule. This wave adjusted readily to American life to an America of the 1970s that was economically stable and motivated, partly by guilt, to be generous to the newly arrived: There were English-as-a-Second-Language teachers, low-interest loans, job-training programs.

The later wave, the boat people who came in the '80s, were a different group—people who had been traumatized by re-education camps, cannibalism, rape, robbery, drowning at the hands of sea pirates, people who had suffered a chaotic and broken society back home under Communist hand. These less-skilled, less-educated refugees were ill-equipped to adjust to a less generous America.

But there were deeper currents that fed this second-wave refugee family that the media failed to detect. According to one Vietnamese who has been their social worker and knows the family well, the Nguyen parents had been burned not once but twice by communism. They fled to the South in 1954, when Catholics were persecuted by Ho Chi Minh and his army, and they fled Saigon as boat people a few years after the communists ransacked the South in 1975. Communist crimes, Vietcong crimes, human-rights abuses by the Hanoi regime—all are meticulously documented by Vietnamese Catholic newspapers and magazines in the United States. The Vietcong, whom the eldest Nguyen boy barely remembered, nevertheless figured as the prime villains in the household cosmology—the chief cause of their family's suffering in America, the robbers of their father's dignity, the blasphemers of the crucifix in their church, called the Vietnamese Catholic Martyrs.

The Nguyen brothers and Cuong Pham (whose more affluent Chinese-Vietnamese parents, unlike the Nguyens, refused to open their doors to journalists) were reportedly Hong Kong movie fanatics. All four youths watched the highly stylized films whose sword crossing heroes and gun-toting detectives and gangsters duked it out amid Hong Kong highrises, filling their waking dreams with homilies to honor, fraternal loyalty, betrayal and, of course, revenge. . . .

I try but cannot reach Loi Nguyen. His defense lawyer, Linda M. Parisi, refuses to answer my letters and phone calls. She traveled to Vietnam at her own expense to better understand the case and is known to be extremely protective of her client.

Then I go to interview his parents, both under psychiatric care. Although I imagine myself to be an American journalist, the closer I come to their home, the more I realize this has been a false assumption. Sitting in my car outside the Laura Dawn Manor, I am overwhelmed by fear and guilt. Once the door opens and the old couple welcomes me in, in my mother's language, I know I will lose all perspective. An American journalist would ask the old couple, "How do you feel?" but I can't. Among Vietnamese, a collective understanding assumes that we have all suffered an epic loss, so it is pointless to ask. Once inside, I might as well put away the notepad and declare my loyalty to the old couple, whatever their shortcomings.

I am also aware that I will somehow benefit from their tragedy. If the youths were inarticulate and failed to become stars, I, the one who has a public voice, am about to gain a measure of notoriety as the teller of their sensational tale. Irrational as it may be, I feel like a cannibal. And this, perhaps more than any other reason, is why I can't bring myself to knock on their door.

Defeated, I return to San Francisco, the city of glassy highrises and rolling hills, where I live. It is, I realize, a different narrative that I am after now, one that moves from the incidental toward the historical. I go to Tu Lan, a Vietnamese coffee shop in the Tenderloin area where Vietnamese men wearing unkempt army jackets argue about Vietnamese politics in low voices on a weekday afternoon. Cigarette smoke hangs in the air like a white mosquito net. A song entitled "Mother Vietnam: We Are Still Here" echoes from the stereo. . . .

I remember that day when my father, the South Vietnamese general, remained behind in Vietnam while my family and I escaped to Guam. We sat on a beach near our refugee camp with a hundred or so Vietnamese countrymen, listening to the British Broadcasting Corp. detail Saigon's fall. I heard screams, saw wailing women tear their hair, saw men beat the sand with their fists, saw children weep. Then as the sun set, an old man stood up and sang our national anthem. "Let's go to the battlefields together, why regret one's life? National blood debts must be avenged by blood . . . Oh, citizens, sacrifice your lives for the flag . . ."

And so on. But no one joined the old man in the song. There was only silence. Then my mother whispered a challenge: "We are no longer citizens, we are now *ma troi* (wandering ghosts)." And the sun, blood red, dissolved into the horizon where Vietnam was, behind my mother's words.

Silence enshrouded the two-bedroom apartment in San Francisco where ten of us—two others, six grandchildren, two struggling sisters—made our new home. Our bodies hurtled through the narrow, dark corridors like bats, avoiding the tiny kitchen where only the women were allowed entrance (and the smell of fish sauce seeped out). We ate in silence (but always with the television turned on) in the dining room that served as another bedroom at night; waited silently in line for the bathroom, took showers together, slept together, yet we negotiated these intimate acts with the gestures of mimes. Why talk at all if everything to be voiced would only invoke sorrow? Where once we had been lively, upper-middle-class families in that tropical land now so far away, here were mousy, impoverished, miserable exiles living in a deep, dark hole.

The Vietnamese refugee's first self-assessment in America is, inevitably, of his own helplessness. It is characterized by blushing, by looking down at one's feet, by avoiding eye contact and by waiting: for welfare and food stamps, for the free clinic exam, for free jackets donated by charity, for green cards. As for the Vietnamese child, at some point he comes to the brutal realization that "his" side has lost, and "his" nation is gone; that his parents are inarticulate fools in a new country called America, and he must face the outside world alone.

As I did. One autumn morning in the locker room of my junior high, Johnny M., the blond and blue-eyed boy standing gloriously naked, asked, "Refugee boy, which side were you on? The winner's or the loser's?"

English still an unbendable language on my tongue, I answered, "Me: Loser's side!" The locker room immediately erupted into a chorus of laughter, and I felt Johnny's wet towel on my face—the white flag, I supposed, to surrender with. In geography class, Mrs. Collier brought out the new map of East Asia. Vietnam, that country coiling in the voluptuous shape of an S, was no longer mine. It was repainted now in a uniform color—red—the South flooded with blood. Mrs. Collier didn't know why, exactly, that strange Asian kid, so quiet, suddenly buried his face in his arms and wept.

It was my father's passion that I was feeling. A couple of months after our arrival, my father, the defeated general, made it to America. He and Aunty Tuyet's husband, a Ranger captain, had commandeered a ship and escaped from Vietnam. The defeated warriors shattered the silence with tales of battles. The women evacuated to other corners of the apartment, but we boys sat and listened, half in rapture, half in fright. Late at night, over Johnnie Walker whiskey, the living room warriors recounted the time when they were young and brave and most alive.

The Captain: "I remember going up Cambodia, brother, in '71. We killed so many Vietcong up there, we lost count. There was this Mien, and he would kill and kill, crazy for blood, and take out the VC livers and eat them raw . . . I swear in front of my ancestral grave I know no one more loyal than that guy." . . .

How can such language not stir a child's imagination? America is dull by comparison; it is too real, too impersonal outside the window—a parking lot, a supermarket, Coke machines; the fog drifting harsh and cold. But inside, napalm fire, helicopters exploding, para-troopers landing, bombs oozing out of a drunken warriors' fragmented sentences, transforming the dilapidated apartment into a battleground. Did I not hear the wailing voices of Vietcong under fire? Did I not see a helicopter burst into flame? Smell the burnt flesh? . . .

In this way the dynamic of the exiled Vietnamese family is formed. So I still understand my brother in the coffee shop. But while he speaks of vengeance, I have learned a different lesson, the American lesson: the knack of reinventing oneself. To survive in the New World, we must, likewise, challenge the old world's blood-for-blood ethos and search for a new story line.

I am no longer simply Vietnamese. I have changed. I have, like many I know, driven down that hyphen that stretches like a freeway from the mythological kingdom with its 1,000-year-old ginseng roots toward the cosmopolitan city, the wind in my hair and Springsteen on the radio. English is a bendable language now, English my own song.

I am, for that matter, no longer moved by the old man's martial words on that Guam beach. I believe instead in self-liberation, in American rebirth. But never mind. I am thinking now of those four boys and their fatal gestures and what distinguishes good guys from bad guys in the new Vietnamese-American fable.

I am not a Catholic. There is no three-tiered shrine in my family's living room for martyred saints. My mother is a Buddhist but she stopped praying for a time when we lost the war. My father, born a French citizen when Vietnam was a colony, was given a Christian name but never went to church. Unlike the Nguyen brothers, I am only half a Northerner, and I take my cardinal points from the South, from Saigon, my birthplace, where bourgeois sensibilities and

Southern irreverence replaces Northern pieties. I have been to Paris and Nice, where my father's relatives live and where—for the first time since leaving Vietnam—I felt, shamelessly, somehow I had come home.

"The Northerners are fanatics," my father said at dinner one night after the Good Guys incident. My father had lived in Paris and liked wine more than jasmine tea; within five years of his arrival in America, he obtained an MBA and lifted us out of poverty into a suburban middle-class life. "The Northerners immolate themselves and talk too readily of martyrdom. They don't think rationally. They think emotionally. *Tu sais, comme ta mere!* Those boys must have ingested all the plots for tragedy from their Northern Catholic parents."

My mother dropped her chopsticks and feigned anger. "We Northerners defeated the French while you drank their wine," she said, but we all laughed. She was, like the rest of us, also drinking French wine. As the entire family sat there under the gaudy faux-crystal chandelier, in my parent's five-bedroom house with its kidney-shaped swimming pool, the irony did not escape us: Historical tragedy had come to seem beside the point.

How did this happen? Perhaps only a loser knows real freedom. Forced outside of history away from home and hearth he can choose to remake himself. One night America seeps in, and out goes the Vietnamese soul of sorrow. For the Vietnamese refugee family, the past is an enigma best left (at least temporarily) alone. Didn't I see America invade the household when the conversation at dinner in our new home leaned slowly but surely toward real estate and escrow, toward jobs and cars and GPAs and overtime and vacation plans—the language of the American dream? Even my father's dinner conversation had shifted to memories of an earlier time, a time before the war, when B-52 bombs were not falling and Vietnam was a lush tropical paradise or when he was living in Paris as a young man, tempestuously in love.

But I suspect irony was a luxury unavailable to those young men. Without the warriors-turned-businessmen, the pool, the chandelier above the dining room table to anchor them in a more complex reality, their passions remained colored by old-world vehemence. . . .

I did not, because of my father's help, fail school. That singularly most important American-making institution embraced me and rejected those boys. I am also nearly seven years older than Loi Nguyen, old enough to record the actual war in my memories as an army brat. I do not need John Woo's slo-mo gore. Because I thought it through myself years ago, I know the illogic of killing Vietcong from helicopters in peacetime—how would you distinguish them from ordinary Vietnamese? Which conical-hatted figure would you shoot?

A friend who works in Palawan refugee camp in the Philippines recently sent me a poem he found carved on a stone under a tamarind tree. Written by an unknown Vietnamese boat person, it tells how to escape tragedy.

"Your mind is like a radio that you can dial to a different voice. It depends on you. So do not keep your mind always tuned to sorrow. If you want, just change the channel."

When I turned thirty recently, years after I switched the dial, as it were, my father said, "At your age I was already a colonel."

"We are very different now, Dad," I snapped, a little irritated. "I don't have a need to be a warrior here in America." My father smiled a sad, knowing smile. What relevant words of wisdom can an exiled general pass down to his fully grown American son, the one whom he sometimes introduces to his ex-army buddies as "traitor"?

As I think about those young men and what they did, I realize that I, in Vietnamese eyes, haven't been a very good son. I had denounced my father's passion for his homeland as parochialism, had learned to listen to his war stories as tales of nostalgia, had, in fact, taken the private angst of his generation and disseminated it in public light—an unfilial act.

I imagine the Nguyen brothers adoring their father, the ex-sergeant of the South Vietnamese army. They must have loved and trusted his war stories. According to the *Sacramento Bee*, the Nguyen brothers had folded their arms, the Vietnamese filial pious gesture, and asked their parents for permission to leave the house that fateful day. This image haunts me. They tried to bring dignity to their father by fighting his war. They coveted being good Vietnamese sons: To assuage the old man's grief, the young man must defeat his old man's enemy.

But Hamlet's unfocused vehemence is not to my taste, his bloody rampage to be his father's son inappropriate to the New World. I am more intrigued by the complicated character of Indar in V.S. Naipaul's *A Bend in the River*, who has lost his family home and fortune to political upheavals and been forced outside of territorial boundaries. "I am lucky," he said, "I carry the world within me. . . . I'm tired of being on the losing side. I want to win and win and win."

"To be or not to be" is no longer the question, for some of us Vietnamese children in America have learned to escape the outdated passions. These days, after a weekend visit I hug my mother but cannot approach my father. We regard each other instead from a distance, nod, and no more. We are veterans from different wars, and I have won mine.

A mile or so from the Good Guys store, at the newest plot in St. Mary's Cemetery, flanked by a large statue of St. Pius and an American flag, Long and Pham Nguyen are buried side by side. It takes a while to find their tombstones behind the pink mausoleum. It is late afternoon, and a few birds chirp as the sprinklers spray mist that forms rainbows. The only other visitors at St. Mary's are a Vietnamese family busy burning incense sticks. The smoke, blown by a warm breeze, wavers alluringly.

This desert-like landscape, with its sandalwood fragrance, is not part of Joan Didion's California anymore. The dark epic journeys that end in California have new players. Searching for the Nguyen brother's tombstones, I find names that leave a kind of phosphorescence on my mind—names like Le, Tran, Vuong, Nguyen—Vietnamese last names that once belonged to emperors of millennia passed, etched on new tombstones on plots where the grass has not yet fully grown.

Between the two brother's tombstones I place ginseng roots, $10.99 a box in a Vietnamese grocery store. The box has a plastic cover with the American Stars and Stripes painted on it. And printed in the lower right hand corner was the word U.S.A.

137

"Distant Shores, Common Ground," 1995

This essay comes from a catalogue created for an unusual art exhibit organized by the Smithsonian Institution Traveling Exhibition Service (SITES). When SITES began exploring the subject in 1991, director Anna Cohn understood that this was potentially politically explosive. The Vietnamese American community still includes many people unable to deal with contemporary Vietnam. But it was fifteen years since the United States had left the Southeast Asian battleground, and the large numbers of refugees and immigrants from that region had to be acknowledged. Bringing Vietnamese and Vietnamese American artists together, at least symbolically, was a major statement. The idea for the exhibition came from art professor C. David Thomas. Jeffrey Hantover, an art critic based in Hong Kong, has a distinguished list of publications on contemporary Vietnamese art. The exhibit itself has been dismantled, but its impact was immediate and appreciated.

From *An Ocean Apart: Contemporary Vietnamese Art from the United States and Vietnam*. Washington, DC: Smithsonian Institution Traveling Institution Service in association with Roberts Rinehart Publishers, Boulder, Colorado and Dublin, Ireland, 1995. Reprinted with permission.

Distant Shores, Common Ground

Jeffrey Hantover

In a Vietnamese home on either side of the ocean, you are likely to find an ancestral altar, on it faded photographs of the dead—a visible reminder of the past's living presence. Visit the home of almost any artist in Vietnam and among the ancestral photographs will be ancient ceramics, and polychrome and lacquered figures from temples and pagodas. In a country where economic and social change until recently has been slow, Vietnamese artists have lived surrounded by visible expressions of their past, from weathered pagodas to the repetitive rhythms of village life.

Vietnamese artists engage in an ongoing, almost osmotic dialogue with the past. It is not a dialogue of rejection or ironic appropriation as it is in other Asian countries and the West. Rather, it is a comfortable embrace of traditional arts and aesthetics that reaches well beyond the short history of oil painting in Vietnam.

A telling example of how past and present mingle harmoniously was evident at the first national abstract painting exhibition held in May 1992 in Ho Chi Minh City. During the opening, singers and musicians performed traditional Quan Ho folk songs unique to the region north of Hanoi. On the walls hung once-forbidden abstract paintings, while families sat cross-legged on mats and listened to women, wearing traditional costumes and hiding with demure coquetry behind straw hats, trade songs of love with their suitors. People smiled and shook their heads in appreciation of old musical favorites. It was as if at an opening of cutting-edge American art at The Museum of Modern Art, musicians from the mountains of Appalachia performed eighteenth-century ballads.

Vietnamese art of both sides of the ocean cannot be understood outside the currents of Vietnam's past. The history in which the art is embedded, the soil which gives it sustenance, is deeper, richer, and more layered than most Americans, conditioned only by images of war, might imagine. Contemporary Vietnamese art is more than the child of colonialism and war. Without understanding its cultural lineage, we run the risk of dismissing Vietnamese art as derivative, as wan copies of Western modernism. Vietnamese art has its own integrity and expressive character: the modernity of the best of contemporary Vietnamese painting flows more from the traditional art of the village than from the ateliers of turn-of-the-century Paris.

On the other side of the ocean, Vietnamese American artists, facing the physical and emotional hardships of migration and building new lives and identities, have in the last decade also found in their Vietnamese past a sense of identity, a cultural anchorage, and a source of artistic inspiration. While artists in Vietnam remain more conservative in approach and more constrained from experimenting due to lack of resources, artists on both shores are fashioning a modern vision that continues to draw sustenance from a shared cultural heritage.

Cultural Colonialism and the Living Legacy of the Village

Demographics, ideology, and cultural history have kept the village at the center of social and cultural life for most of Vietnamese history. Even today, Vietnam remains a rural country with almost 80 percent of the population living outside its cities. In the past, more literati lived in the villages as teachers and scholars than served the central authority as mandarins. Unlike Europe, where culture flowed outward from the cities, the Vietnamese village was, until the twentieth century, home to the highest cultural achievements, from literature and theater to Confucian scholarship.

While there were court craftsmen at the imperial capital of Hue in the nineteenth century, there was no painting academy. Without the royal court as a dominant cultural center, there never developed a sharp division between fine art or the high art of the court and folk art of the village, its Tet woodblock prints, pagoda and temple sculpture, and communal house carving. The Vietnamese adage applied to art as well as politics: "The laws of the Emperor are less than the customs of the village."

The Vietnamese literati, unlike their Chinese counterparts, did not widely practice or highly value painting as a scholarly pursuit. When the French introduced oil painting to the Vietnamese at the end of the nineteenth century, they did not have to dislodge an entrenched indigenous painting tradition. Until the August Revolution of 1945, oil painting in Vietnam followed French academic painting—but with a Vietnamese accent.

The vehicle for the export of French aesthetics and art was the Ecole des Beaux-Arts de l'Indochine, founded in Hanoi in 1925 and the only fine art academy established by a colonial power in Southeast Asia. Based on the prejudiced premise that the Vietnamese as a race were not capable of being artists, the purpose of the school was to train Vietnamese craftsmen who would then export their handicrafts back to France. Instead, before the Japanese coup against the French in March 1945 forced it to close, the school unintentionally created a self-conscious class of professional painters. From its 128 graduates came Bui Xuan Phai, Nguyen Tu Nghiem, Nguyen Gia Tri, To Ngoc Van, Nguyen Do Cung, Nguyen Sang, and other major figures in the development of Vietnamese painting. Unlike the traditional craftsmen and artisans of Vietnam, they were a class of urban professional painters, who, using mostly modern techniques and media, produced works for an urban audience.

Most importantly, a combination of sympathetic staff who appreciated traditional forms of artistic expression and those who dismissed Vietnamese artistic originality and capability propelled students to search for a distinct cultural identity and sowed the seeds of modern Vietnamese painting based on traditional imagery and aesthetics. The first director was Victor Tardieu, an academic painter who supported the study of indigenous art forms and allowed graduate examinations to be held in lacquer painting, colored woodcuts, and silk painting. With his encouragement, students applied Western concepts of color and composition, experimented with new methods, and revitalized traditional art forms.

When the second director, Evariste Jonchère, reduced the academic course in oil painting and instituted other curricula changes to train "art craftsmen not artists," students protested. They defended the vigor and originality of their own traditions and challenged Jonchere to compare his own sculpture to that found in village pagodas and communal houses.

Two Roads to Modernism

With the Revolution of 1945 marking Vietnamese independence from the French and the partition of the country in 1954, Northern and Southern artists took divergent paths from French academic painting to modernism. The artistic differences that emerged go beyond novelist Graham Greene's observation that one sees in the South the colors of green and gold and in the North, brown and black.

In the South, artists looked outward to the currents of twentieth-century Western art. Cubism, futurism, and abstraction could all be found in the flourishing gallery scene in Saigon in the 1960s and 1970s. Artists in the South were invited to exhibit their works in Europe, Asia, and North and South America. While lip service was given to Vietnamese traditions, the government promoted Saigon as, an official of the Directorate of Fine Arts Education enthused in 1962, "a centre of transcendental creative spirit of both the Eastern and Western worlds."

In the North, the West was the cultural as well as the military enemy. "Art for art's sake" was seen as a colonial effort to dampen revolutionary fervor. Later, the melting pot theory of Western and Eastern cultures was branded a neo-colonialist trap. Political realities made it dangerous to embrace "capitalist" artists such as Matisse and Cézanne. As early as 1945, Ho Chi Minh chided artists for subject matter distant from the "reality of everyday life." Nudes, still lifes, and abstraction were at best frivolous and self-absorbed, at worst subversive acts against the Revolution.

Cut off from contemporary currents in Western art by a half-century of war, poverty, repression, and cultural campaigns against the "poisonous vestiges of U.S. neocolonialist culture," artists in the North were forced to look inward and backward. Nguyen Do Cung, formerly a student at the Ecole des Beaux-Arts de l'Indochine, where he had been a leader in the protests against Jonchere, served as director of the Hanoi Museum of Fine Arts in the 1960s and early 1970s. There he documented and exhibited traditional Vietnamese art—folk paintings, ancient ceramics, the sculpture of the village communal house, and the arts of ethnic minorities. These exhibitions exposed artists to the fullness of their village artistic inheritance, to its motifs and modernist aesthetics.

The central painter in the movement to a tradition-based modernity was Nguyen Tu Nghiem, who, after serving the Resistance and teaching at the art college in the Viet Bac, began to look in the mid-1950s to indigenous village art rather than Western models for inspiration. His paintings of village dances and festivals, national myths and literature, and zodiac animals have the chiselled geometry, flatness, immediacy, energy, and childlike innocence of popular sculpture and woodblock prints. Following his lead, Northern artists found in Tet woodblock prints and seventeenth-century communal house carving an aesthetic that both rejected Renaissance rules of perspective, symmetry, and order, and the stultifying straitjacket of Socialist Realism.

On the trusses, beams, columns, and partitions of communal houses were dense, lyrical, and expressive relief carvings that were secular, sometimes erotic, celebrations of rural life. In these centers of village life and on prints that hung on almost every door was an art that celebrated village communalism and ridiculed the feudal order. Here was an art that possessed the modernist spirit of multiple perspectives, expressive distortion, and vivid colors chosen for emotional effect, not naturalistic representation.

Nghiem's work dramatically demonstrated the shared essence of Western modernism and Vietnamese traditional aesthetics. It is too simplistic to say Vietnamese artists copied or borrowed from the West. Vietnamese artists, primed by their own village traditions, felt an aesthetic kinship to the early masters of modernism, who, like Picasso, Derain, and Matisse, found inspiration and affirmation of their new directions in the villages of Africa and Oceania. These Western modernists rejected the Renaissance aesthetic to which the anonymous artists of the Vietnamese village had never been exposed and which for the students of the Ecole des Beaux-Arts de l'Indochine posed a new way of looking at the world. The artists of the North discovered in their own villages the politically safe path to modernity: they could be modernists and cultural patriots at the same time.

The Primacy of Personal Vision

Doi moi (or renovation), proclaimed in 1986, gave official approval in Vietnam to a movement toward self-expression that had begun to emerge in the early 1980s. The first public display of nudes since the August Revolution was held in 1982, and Bui Xuan Phai, the country's most famous and respected artist, was allowed his first one-person exhibition in 1984, almost thirty years after running afoul of the government. After a half-century of serving the agendas of Party and power—revolution, national solidarity, cultural autonomy, and national integration—visual artists are now free to serve the self.

Regardless of gender, age, and region, Vietnamese artists have embraced the primacy of private vision with an invigorating passion. They are more interested in making visible this inner vision than playing with the definitional boundaries of what a painting is or making art historical references to other works and movements. In Vietnam, there is no hothouse atmosphere of artists talking only to other artists. Without the fine art/popular art division and without an entrenched academy, there is no self-conscious avant-garde.

Paintings in the last decade have become more exploratory, personal, expressive, and colorful (aided by better quality paint and canvas from abroad). Nudes are commonplace, perhaps too commonplace. The abstract art exhibition in 1992 was a cultural watershed, an affirmation and legitimation of the primacy of individual expression. As abstract artist Dao Minh Tri commented recently, "Much time in the past was lost fighting over what was right art and wrong art, now we are fighting whether it is good or bad art."

The Art of Remembrance and Rediscovery

For Vietnamese American artists, Vietnam is an object of remembrance and re-discovery. Those who came of artistic age during the heady internationalism of Saigon in the 1960s and 1970s use their art to recapture the mood and feel of the country they once knew. Younger artists educated in America sift through the past of others, familial and historical, trying to better understand their own bi-cultural present.

An Ocean Apart marks an artistic reunion for members of the Young Painters Association, an independent group of artists active in Saigon in the late 1960s and early 1970s. Once in America, Dinh Cuong, Ho Thanh Duc, Nguyen Thi Hop, Nguyen Khai, and Nguyen Trong Khoi could study first-hand what they had only seen reproduced (often poorly) in magazines and books. Clearer in their understanding of where they came from than younger, American-educated Vietnamese American artists, theirs is an art not of ques-tioning and exploration but a gentle memory work evoking the spirit of the land they reluctantly left.

For Vietnamese artists who came to this country as children, art is a vehicle for self-understanding. More expansive in their definition of what art can be, more comfortable with mixed media, they use bits and pieces of the present to reconnect with the past. Issues of gender, and family and ethnic identity, cur-rent in the air all contemporary American artists breathe, take on special mean-ing for first-generation Vietnamese American artists whose familial break with their homeland was abrupt and whose stay in the United States has been rela-tively short. Perhaps even more important, unlike other young transplanted artists, they have a more urgent need to understand the culture and history of their native land because it has so dramatically shaped contemporary American culture and history.

The Vietnamese Poetic Vision

A contemporary Vietnamese painter has said that half the country is composed of painters and the other half poets. Many, it seems, on both sides of the ocean are both. With few exceptions, Vietnamese artists are not interested in the prose of descriptive realism. Art for the Vietnamese is expression, not repre-sentation. Even when their art is rooted in the objective world around them, Vietnamese artists reject descriptive realism for a more subjective and expres-sive art, for what the symbolists called the "subjective deformation of nature." At its best, Vietnamese painting has the fluid, allusive associations of poetry. Whether it is the lyrical expressionism of the North or the resurgent abstrac-tion of the South, Vietnamese painting is surprisingly free of anguish, anger, or avant-garde irony.

Though more experimental, more attuned to international art trends, Vietnamese American artists also speak with a poet's soul. Having the luxury of sufficient materials, Vietnamese Americans mix objects and images, more interested in creating emotional moods than mirroring external reality. Talk of national character can sometimes be a slippery exercise, but Vietnamese artistic expression, though an ocean apart, gives support to the Roman poet Horace's observation two thousand years ago: "They change their sky, not their soul, who run across the sea."

138

Nobuko Miyamoto, "To All Relations," 1996

Nobuko Miyamoto has been a performing artist/spokesperson for human and civil rights since the early 1970s. She is among those leaders who insisted, from the inception of the Asian American movement, that serious working relationships had to be forged not only with progressive whites but especially with other communities of color. In early work with Chris Iijima and Charlie Chin, she often put this credo into practice; the trio performed with artists of color and occasionally composed and sang in Spanish in New York City's Latino barrios. This song, she explains, "came through me after a gathering of Native American elders in San Pedro, California. Before it they spoke, 'Mitake Oyasin,' 'to all my relations' in the Lakota language. It captured my heart with its simple and profound truth." The lyrics to this song reference the group's earlier compositions in the 1970s, in which "a tiny grain of sand" was a major metaphor for the political movement harbored within the United States, like the tiny irritant that becomes a pearl within a large oyster.

From the album *To All Relations*. Binda Records. Words and music: Nobuko Miyamoto. Copyright 1996. Reprinted with permission.

To All Relations

To all relations . . . . mother earth and father sky
To all relations . . . . every nation, every tribe
Every family, every stranger, every friend & every foe
Every form and every creature
To all relations

Mitake Oyasin . . . to all relations

From the borders of the madness
From the edges of our fear

From the canyons of our sadness
From the well of our tears
To the womb of our beginning
To the place of our return
To the circle of oneness . . . where the fire burns

In the circle of oneness
Illusion is unmasked
In the circle of oneness
There's no first and there's no last

One drop of water
One link in the chain
One note, one kernel
One . . . tiny grain

A grain, a tiny grain of sand
A world, a universe, a new beginning
A grain, alone and yet a part
A heart within a heart
Ever changing

Mitake Oyasin . . . To all relations

In the circle of oneness
We dance a simple prayer
Feel the beauty, know the wonder
Of the circle that we share
In the circle of oneness
A sound that each one knows
In the circle of oneness
A song . . . from where the river flows . . .

Mitake Oyasin . . . to all relations

139

Washington Post, *Filipino Veterans Editorial,*
December 13, 1997

More than forty years after the Filipino Rescission Act, there was much unfinished business regarding government obligations to Filipinos brought into the U.S. armed forces. Some progress was made in piecemeal fashion, but these remain the only unpaid debts to foreign nationals who fought during World War II under American auspices. As the editorial makes clear, these veterans are a rapidly dwindling group. In November 2000, Congress authorized $6 million as part of H.R. 4635 to provide for full medical care, access to Veterans Administration hospitals, and compensation of up to $2,000 per month for those still living. There would also be $500,000 allocated for burial in national cemeteries, including $300 for each family with funeral expenses, and $500,000 for hospital and nursing home care for veterans permanently disabled as a result of war-related illnesses or injuries. These benefits accrue to the 17,000 surviving Filipino World War II vets now residing in the United States.

Editorial, *The Washington Post*, December 13, 1997.

Under the American Flag

In 1941, as Japan prepared for War, the United States folded the armed forces of its then-territory the Philippines into its own. Promises of onerous [*sic*] individual military benefits followed. Fighting to liberate their homeland, the Filipinos conducted themselves, it is established, with valor. But no sooner was the War over and independence bestowed than Congress reneged on important benefits. Now some of the American citizens among the 70,000 aging survivors of those Filipino heroes are petitioning for review. Considerations of equity and honor commend their cause, but the benefits remain frozen.

As it happens, a couple of American Pacific War veterans loom over the Washington political terrain in which this issue is being fought. Chairman Ben A. Gilman (R-NY) of International Relations Committee introduced the Filipino Veterans Equity Act. Chairman Bob Stump (R-Ariz) of the Veterans' Affairs Committee thinks it costs too much. For one thing, the new congressional pay-as-go rule would require his committee to take up the nearly half-billion-dollar annual cost of pension matching those given to American servicemen. The Filipino former soldiers swore an oath to American authority and fought side by side with American soldiers, but Mr. Stump questions whether they are American veterans. So as not to raise their expectations, he has resisted the hearings they seek to promote their appeal.

It is demeaning to Americans as well as to Filipinos for the United States to continue denying benefits that were pledged at the highest level, then abundantly earned on the battlefield, then denied, then withheld through decades of Filipino entreaty. Surely, this is an issue begging to full-fledged comrades who fought under the American flag. It would ease the declining years of survivors' ranks that are shrinking by the day. A Senate version of this bill would leave the Filipino veterans with funeral and burial expenses only. We would not like to be the ones to tell these fading old soldiers they must die for the government they served to pay.

140

Revised Office of Management and Budget Directive 15, December 15, 1997

Directive 15, originally issued by the Office of Management and Budget (OMB) in 1978, fundamentally shaped definitions of race and ethnicity in the United States. It was developed in order to create consistency in the vast reporting requirements throughout the federal government. Because the numbers assigned to each "race" determine amounts of money, power, and other resources allocated to each group, who is counted in which category is extremely important. The original categories included "American Indian or Alaska Native," "Asian or Pacific Islander," "Black," "Hispanic," and "White." The group advising OMB recommended that Asian Indians, because they are "Caucasian," be included among whites. The Association of Indians in America successfully lobbied to be included in the Asian or Pacific Islander group. This 1997 revision is here used because it established a new category: "Native Hawaiian or Other Pacific Islander," disaggregating it from the "Asian or Pacific Islander" category of the past two censuses. The effort to create a new "mixed race" category failed, but individuals can now mark more than one response. The actual numbers influencing public policy and resources will be very important; figures from the 2000 census demonstrate this vividly. But the more critical point of this document is that it demonstrates yet again the ways in which "race" and/or "ethnicity" can shift so dramatically over time and space.

Federal Register, vol. 62, no. 210, Thursday, October 30, 1997. The original Directive No. 15 appeared in *Federal Register*, vol. 43, no. 19 (1978).

Standards for Maintaining, Collecting and Presenting Federal Data on Race and Ethnicity

This classification provides a minimum standard for maintaining, collecting, and presenting data on race and ethnicity for all Federal reporting purposes. The categories in this classification are social-political constructs and should not be interpreted as being scientific or anthropological in nature. They are not to be used as determinants of eligibility for participation in any Federal program. The standards have been developed to provide a common language for uniformity and comparability in the collection and use of data on race and ethnicity by Federal agencies.

The standards have five categories for data on race: American Indian or Alaska Native, Asian, Black or African American, Native Hawaiian or Other Pacific Islander, and White. There are two categories for data on ethnicity: "Hispanic or Latino," and "Not Hispanic or Latino."

1. Categories and Definitions

The minimum categories for data on race and ethnicity for Federal statistics, program administrative reporting, and civil rights compliance reporting are defined as follows:

American Indian or Alaska Native. A person having origins in any of the original peoples of North and South America (including Central America), and who maintains tribal affiliation or community attachment.

Asian. A person having origins in any of the original peoples of the Far East, Southeast Asia, or the Indian subcontinent including, for example, Cambodia, China, India, Japan, Korea, Malaysia, Pakistan, the Philippine Islands, Thailand, and Vietnam.

Black or African American. A person having origins in any of the black racial groups of Africa. Terms such as "Haitian"or "Negro" can be used in addition to "Black or African American."

Hispanic or Latino. A person of Cuban, Mexican, Puerto Rican, Cuban, South or Central American, or other Spanish culture or origin, regardless of race. The term, "Spanish origin," can be used in addition to "Hispanic or Latino."

Native Hawaiian or Other Pacific Islander. A person having origins in any of the original peoples of Hawaii, Guam, Samoa, or other Pacific Islands.

White. A person having origins in any of the original peoples of Europe, the Middle East, or North Africa.

Respondents shall be offered the option of selecting one or more racial designations. Recommended forms for the instruction accompanying the multiple response question are "Mark one or more" and "Select one or more."

2. Data Formats

The standards provide two formats that may be used for data on race and ethnicity. Self-reporting or self-identification using two separate questions is the preferred method for collecting data on race and ethnicity. In situations where self-reporting is not practicable or feasible, the combined format may be used.

In no case shall the provisions of the standards be construed to limit the collection of data to the categories described above. The collection of greater detail is encouraged; however, any collection that uses more detail shall be organized

in such a way that the additional categories can be aggregated into these minimum categories for data on race and ethnicity . . .

a. Two-Question Format
To provide flexibility and ensure data quality, separate questions shall be used
wherever feasible for reporting race and ethnicity. When race and ethnicity are
collected separately, ethnicity shall be collected first. If race and ethnicity are
collected separately, the minimum designations are:

Race:
—American Indian or Alaska Native
—Asian
—Black or African American
—Native Hawaiian or Other Pacific Islander
—White

Ethnicity:
—Hispanic or Latino
—Not Hispanic or Latino

When data on race and ethnicity are collected separately, provision shall be
made to report the number of respondents in each racial category who are Hispanic or Latino.

When aggregate data are presented, data producers shall provide the number of respondents who marked (or selected) only one category, separately for
each of the five racial categories. In addition to these numbers, data producers
are strongly encouraged to provide the detailed distributions, including all possible combinations, of multiple responses to the race question. If data on multiple responses are collapsed, at a minimum the total number of respondents reporting "more than one race" shall be made available.

b. Combined Format
The combined format may be used, if necessary, for observer-collected data on
race and ethnicity. Both race (including multiple responses) and ethnicity shall
be collected when appropriate and feasible, although the selection of one category in the combined format is acceptable. If a combined format is used, there
are six minimum categories:

   —American Indian or Alaska Native
   —Asian
   —Black or African American
   —Hispanic or Latino
   —Native Hawaiian or Other Pacific Islander
   —White

When aggregate data are presented, data producers shall provide the number of respondents who marked (or selected) only one category, separately for each of the six categories. . . .

3. Use of the Standards for Record Keeping and Reporting

The minimum standard categories shall be used for reporting as follows:

a. Statistical Reporting

These standards shall be used at a minimum for all federally sponsored statistical data collections that include data on race and/or ethnicity, except when the collection involves a sample of such size that the data on the smaller categories would be unreliable, or when the collection effort focuses on a specific racial or ethnic group. . . .

b. General Program Administrative and Grant Reporting

These standards shall be used for all Federal administrative reporting or record keeping requirements that include data on race and ethnicity. Agencies that cannot follow these standards must request a variance from OMB. . . .

c. Civil Rights and Other Compliance Reporting

These standards shall be used by all Federal agencies in either the separate or combined format for civil rights and other compliance reporting from the public and private sectors and all levels of government. . . .

4. Presentation of Data on Race and Ethnicity

Displays of statistical, administrative, and compliance data on race and ethnicity shall use the categories listed above. The term "nonwhite" is not acceptable for use in the presentation of Federal Government data. It shall not be used in any publication or in the text of any report. . . .

5. Effective Date

The provisions of these standards are effective immediately for all *new* and *revised* record keeping or reporting requirements that include racial and/or ethnic information. All *existing* record keeping or reporting requirements shall be made consistent with these standards at the time they are submitted for extension, or not later than January 1, 2003.

Senator Daniel Inouye, Speech on Filipino World War II Veterans, May 13, 1998

Inouye, a Japanese American World War II army veteran and a recipient of the Congressional Medal of Honor, knows he is in a perfect position to advocate for fair treatment of the Filipinos and Filipino Americans who joined America's war efforts against the Japanese in the Pacific. This speech, delivered at the State Department in Washington, DC, provides important details about their historical service and the sorry record of American treatment of these veterans.

Reprinted with permission from Senator Daniel Inouye.

Open Forum

Asian Pacific American Federal Foreign Affairs Council
"Conference on U.S.-Philippine Relations"
Senator Daniel K. Inouye (D, Hawaii)
U.S. Department of State
May 13, 1998

Many Americans unfortunately share a common weakness. We tend to forget the great events beyond our recent memory, especially those that did much to shape the very future of our country. In fact, I doubt if too many of our young men and women are aware of the events that led up to the commencement of World War II. Do the names of Benito Mussolini, Hideki Tojo, or Adolph Hitler mean anything to them? Far too many are simply not aware of these names and the important roles that they played. The days of the 1940s were terrible ones, yet we have very short memories.

Similarly, I believe that too many Americans are not aware of, or have forgotten the sacrifices of our Filipino friends. In the spring of 1942, the Japanese 14th Army overran the Bataan Peninsula and after a heroic but futile defense, nearly 80,000 American and Filipino troops were captured. From April 9, 1942 through May of that year, the infamous Bataan Death March continued. Many ill and seriously wounded prisoners of war were forced to make the devastating march of 65 to 70 miles on foot, without medicine or water. Others were packed into railroad cattle cars, one hundred per car. Is it any wonder that nearly 10,000 died en route? Even today, the many reports of brutality and deprivation remain unsurpassed in modern times. There was not rest, no food, rampant infections, no hope. Those who straggled behind often in their delirium were summarily executed. In restrospect, it is miraculous that so many survived and live today.

Filipinos residing in the United States wanted to show their loyalty to America by enlisting in the Armed Forces of the United States. Although the Philippines were a U.S. territory, they were initially denied enlistment because of the Tydings-McDuffie Act, which designated Philippine-born residents as aliens and restricted their immigration quota to 50 immigrants a year. However, on December 20, 1941, President Franklin Roosevelt signed the Selective Training and Service Amendments Act, Public Law 77–360, which, among other things, allowed Filipinos in the United States to enlist, and also provided them with the opportunity to become United States citizens by virtue of the fact that they were serving in the military.

The mobilization of forces included the activation and assumption of command of the First Filipino Infantry Battalion on April 1, 1942 at Camp San Luis Obispo with four officers and twelve enlisted personnel. There were so many recruits, orders were issued to activate the First Filipino Infantry Regiment and Band at Salinas, California, effective July 13, 1942, with 143 officers, 6 warrant officers, and 3,019 enlisted men. The Second Filipino Infantry Regiment was activated on November 21, 1942 at Fort Ord, California. In all, approximately 7,000 Filipinos and Filipino Americans fought in the U.S. Army 1st and 2nd Filipino Infantry regiments.

When General Douglas MacArthur was forced to flee the Philippines in 1942, he vowed to return but needed intelligence behind enemy lines. More than 800 handpicked volunteers from the 1st and 2nd Filipino Infantry Regiments were assigned to supply intelligence in the 1st Reconnaissance Battalion in the Japanese-occupied Philippines. By the end of the war, the unit's casualties totaled 164 killed, 6 wounded, 178 missing and 75 captured. More than half of the battalion received the Bronze Star for heroic service. Soldiers of the 1st and 2nd Filipino Infantry Regiments participated in the bloody combat and mop-up operations at New Guinea, Leyte, Samar, Luzon and the Southern Philippines. Members of the 1st Regiment were also attached to the U.S. 6th Army Alamo Scouts, a reconnaissance group that traveled 30 miles behind enemy lines to free Allied prisoners from the Cabanatuan death camp on January 30, 1945.

President Roosevelt also issued an Executive Order calling members of the Philippine Commonwealth Army into the service of the United States Armed Forces of the Far East (USAFFE). More than 100,000 Filipinos volunteered for the Philippine Commonwealth Army and fought alongside the United States armed forces. These loyal and valiant men fought, suffered, and in many instances, died in the same manner and under the same commander as other members of the United States Armed Forces during World War II.

In March 1942, the Congress amended the Nationality Act of 1940, and granted our Filipino allies the privilege of becoming United States citizens for having served in the USAFFE. The law expired at the end of 1946, but not before the United States withdrew the naturalization examiner from the Philippines for a nine-month period. This effectively denied Filipino veterans the opportunity to become citizens.

Furthermore, under President Roosevelt's prior Executive Order, Filipinos were entitled to full veterans' benefits. Yet, on February 18, 1946, the Congress betrayed the Filipino veterans by enacting the Rescission Act of 1946, which declared the service performed by the Philippine Commonwealth veterans as not active service, thus denying them many benefits to which they were entitled.

Legislation which I authored allowed Filipino veterans of World War II to apply for naturalization. Under the Immigration Act of 1990, certain Filipino veterans who served during World War II became eligible for United States citizenship. Between November 1990 and February 1995, approximately 24,000 veterans took advantage of this provision and became United States citizens. However, this law did not confer veterans' benefits on these American citizens. I believe the final taint must be removed to uphold the promise made, and the promise which the Filipino veterans relied upon, in 1942.

When the war was over, because of the geopolitical situation of that time, we decided that the best interests of the United States and the Western World would be served by building up Japan. So, while we were spending billions in Japan, our friends in the Philippines, those who sacrificed themselves, were waiting on the sidelines. Manila had been destroyed. Luzon had been destroyed. And we gave them a pittance.

In the treaty that we agreed upon with the Philippines, we told our Filipino brothers, since you have lived with us for a long time under our flag, we would like you to have the opportunity of serving in our Armed Forces, provided you serve as a steward in the Navy. Filipinos were exclusively assigned to steward duties as cooks, waiters, pantrymen, dishwashers, custodians, bed makers, and valets. Many Filipino enlisted men provided valet services to Navy captains and admirals. It was only in the early 1970s that the United States Navy changed its policies and granted Filipino enlistees the right to enter any occupational rating. Today, they still provide support duties to the White House and White House Staff Mess.

In October 1979, President Jimmy Carter asked me to fly to the Philippines as his special representative and meet with President Ferdinand E. Marcos. At that time, the United States and the Philippines were renegotiating the military base agreements for Clark Air Force Base and Subic Bay, which were due to expire. President Marcos had recalled his representatives and the negotiations were at a standstill. President Marcos felt slighted that our government would not agree to having the Philippine flag flown together with the American flag on these bases. Our military bases were on Philippine soil. We refused our Filipino allies, while at the same time, we allowed the Japanese, Greek, British, Panamanian and Italian flags to be flown together next to American flags at our military installations in Japan, Greece, Great Britain, Panama, and Italy. I apologized for our country's insensitivities and asked President Marcos if we could fly our flag next to the Philippine flag.

President Marcos also took it personally that the United States drastically reduced our commitment to provide payments for the hospital care, medical services, and nursing home care for eligible Commonwealth Army veterans and World War II Philippine scouts. These were men who served in the war alongside the United States Armed Forces. The Congress ultimately eliminated funding for the Philippine Veterans Memorial Hospital.

How many of us can recall the contributions and sacrifices of those Filipinos who came to North America over 400 years ago and helped to shape the development and advancement of this nation. Filipinos became an integral part of the American work force since the first settlement in the bayous of Louisiana in 1763. From the sugar cane plantations of Hawaii, to the agricultural fields of California, to the fish canneries of Alaska, Filipinos cleaned, cooked, planted, tilled, and harvested for America.

Filipinos helped to develop Hawaii into what it is today. Unlike other ethnic groups, the Filipinos who first arrived were, for the most part, prohibited from bringing their wives and families to Hawaii. Furthermore, as the plantation records indicate, illiterate men were favored over literate ones. Despite these imposed handicaps, they did well. They helped to make sugar in Hawaii the major source of income for these islands. They were industrious, patient, and very hard working. The road they traveled was a difficult one. Many were victims of ethnic exploitation. Discrimination was widespread. For most, life was a lonely existence.

Despite these extreme hardships, some were able to begin families in Hawaii and today we benefit from their talents and services. The first Governor of Filipino ancestry is now serving the State of Hawaii. The first federal judge of Filipino ancestry served the Commonwealth of the Northern Mariana Islands. There are a number of distinguished Filipino legislators serving the State of Hawaii. The legal profession has a number of distinguished Filipino names. These are the Filipinos who made it easier for the succeeding waves of Filipino immigrants to make good in Hawaii and elsewhere. These early pioneers and their children laid a good foundation for today's new Filipinos. We should never forget them.

142

Statement at Official Close of Japanese American Redress Office, September 10, 1998

Sox Kitashima was one of the most spirited leaders of the movement to secure re-dress for Japanese Americans who had been interned during World War II. The Office of Redress Administration (ORA), housed in the Justice Department, did a superb job of locating Japanese American survivors and providing letters of apol-ogy and checks for $20,000 to those alive when President Reagan signed the Civil Liberties Act of 1988. Bob Bratt directed the effort and incorporated hundreds of staff and volunteers from the Japanese American community. In spite of a few se-rious gaps, such as that of the Japanese in Latin America who had been kid-napped and transported to America's camps and who remained uncompensated for many years, the ORA received high marks for diligence and effectiveness in this unparalleled instance of government reparations for wrongdoing. Kitashima's remarks at the ceremonies were especially moving. Her eloquence provided ap-propriate closure to this phase of that difficult history. The NCRR to which she refers was the National Coalition for Redress/Reparations, one of three major or-ganizations leading the effort to secure redress.

Reprinted with permission from Sox Kitashima. Washington, DC, Justice Depart-ment, September 10, 1998.

Good morning Attorney General Janet Reno—members of Congress—distin-guished guests and friends. Senator "Sparky" Matsunaga is here with us in spirit.

I was asked to speak briefly about my experience.

On May 9, 1942—I became citizen 21373. My mother, 3 adult brothers and I were evacuated to Tanforan Racetrack where we were greeted by armed guards and surrounded with barbed wire fences. We were physically searched like criminals. In the process, our neatly packed suitcases were tipped over in search of contrabands.

Our first meal consisted of discolored cold cuts, overcooked swiss-chard and moldy bread. I refused it.

A horsestall 20 x 9 feet with manure on the floor was assigned to us. We were ordered to fill sacks with straw for our mattress.

That night, I cried myself to sleep and said to myself—I can't believe I'm in America.

A three-sided makeshift toilet, with no door, was situated on the pathway to the messhall. A gentleman donated his precious underwear that covered us from the waist up. Some camps had raw sewage running in front of their stable.

After 4 months—an old dusty gas lamped train took us to Topaz, Utah—a desolate sagebrush camp. Shades were drawn throughout our trip until we reached Salt Lake.

Topaz, Utah was to be our home for an indefinite time. We were shocked to see there were no doors in the latrines. No privacy—no partitions in our barracks—no furnitures. A potbelly stove and one naked light bulb served the entire family.

We were fed innards of animals until we complained. We again suffered psychological stress of confinement.

For many young people—life stopped in mid-career. They were immobilized for lack of purpose. Traditionally strong family ties were broken. Parents lost control of their children. Father lost his status. He was not the breadwinner.

We endured over 100 degrees in the summer and 10-20 degrees below in the winter.

The camps went smoothly—until the loyalty questionnaire #27 and #28 were issued, a proof of loyalty to serve on combat duty wherever ordered. Internees were outraged. Those who resisted wanted their Constitutional Rights restored, their families released from camp. Mothers cried and begged their sons not to go: "We lost everything to evacuation—we are too old to begin life anew without you." It was a trying period for all concerned. They said, "but if you must go—don't try to be a hero—and do not bring shame to the family." Japanese Americans served with distinction.

NCRR's first lobbying was in 1984—we were nervous—we knew nothing about lobbying. But Congressman Barney Frank gave us a much needed shot in the arm when he said—"Don't waste your time on me—I'm for it—go after the others."

Our efforts intensified. Over 25,000 letters and over 400 mailgrams were sent to Congress and the President.

We had many ups and downs—but we persevered.

Finally—on August 10, 1988—the Civil Liberties Act of 1988, enacted by Congress and signed into law by President Ronald Reagan acknowledged the fundamental injustice of the World War II incarceration of Japanese Americans.

But the appropriation was inadequate—we leaned heavily on our Japanese American Congressional Representatives for encouragement. They gave us strength to continue our fight. We were losing so many internees so fast.

Our efforts were not in vain.

Finally—on October 9, 1990, I witnessed the first check presentation by Attorney General Richard Thornburgh—who said to each of the 9 recipients—"I'm sorry it took so long."

Congress apologized on behalf of the nation—America had shown its greatness.

We thank the Commission on Wartime Relocation and Internment of Civilians for providing us the opportunity to prove our right to redress.

Our thanks to the Office of Redress Administration—Bob Bratt, the first Administrator, who left his footprints in our hearts—to Paul Suddes, Alicie Simpson, DeDe Greene, Joanne Kiedi, Lisa Johnson, Tink Cooper and Emi Kuboyama for their cordial assistance with redress cases—the homeless—cases in Japan—the physically impaired that required special attention—color code forms to avoid confusion and many, many situations beyond the call of duty.

We owe a debt of gratitude for the endless support from the community—from people of all races—and all walks of life. You made redress a reality.

The closure of the camps created resettlement problems—far greater than the evacuation. No home to go back to and only what you brought with you from the camp. Storages were ransacked—ugly signs greeted us. Our parents, who suffered the most, took it on the chin,—shared tiny rooms with others, lived in storefronts—church auditorium. Frightening night riders targeted those who returned to their homes.

Perhaps it was these stories that roused the conscience of the 3rd generation to seek restitution for their parents and grandparents who were traumatized.

WE CANNOT UNDO HISTORY—BUT LET US CONTINUE TO MAKE THE LESSONS OF THE PAST SERVE AS A BEACON TO PROTECT CIVIL RIGHTS FOR ALL AND THAT THE CIVIL LIBERTIES PUBLIC EDUCATION FUND GRANT PROGRAM WILL CONTINUE TO ILLUMINATE THE TRUE AND ACCURATE HISTORY SURROUNDING THE EXCLUSION, FORCED REMOVAL AND INTERNMENT OF JAPANESE AMERICANS DURING WORLD WAR II.

I AM TRULY HUMBLED—THANK YOU FOR THIS PRIVILEGE AND FOR ALLOWING ME TO SHARE IN YOUR GLORY.

I LOVE YOU ALL!

143

Vu Nguyen, "Why I Hate Ho Chi Minh," February 19–25, 1999

The population of Vietnamese in the United States zoomed from 245,025 in 1980 to 614,547 in 1990, an increase of 150 percent. The total will probably approach 1 million soon. Many are here as refugees from war-torn Vietnam, having escaped as "boat people" and via harrowing experiences in various temporary camps sometimes lasting for years. The United States assumed some responsibility for economic and political refugees and dispersed them throughout the country to avoid unusual population concentrations. But many eventually resettled in California; one of the major centers is now located in Orange County, where significant economic, cultural, and social networks of Vietnamese Americans have developed. Most are neutral or hostile to North Vietnam, communism, and Ho Chi Minh as symbols of the tragedies they were forced to endure. Thus, Vietnamese who supported any of these have faced intense hostility. In this article, Vu Nguyen tries to explain why the feelings continue to be so intense. The precipitating event, an attempt by owner Truong Van Tran to post a portrait of Ho Chi Minh in his shop in February 1999, caused an uproar and a riot. Tran was forced to close his shop. The controversy continues.

Vu Nguyen, "Why I Hate Ho Chi Minh." *Orange County Weekly*, February 19–25, 1999, 18.

Why I Hate Ho Chi Minh

By Vu Nguyen

Political demonstrations are a regular feature of Little Saigon. But even by Little Saigon's hyperpolitical standards, the events of the past few weeks have been, well, hyper. The street politics culminated in a Feb. 15 demonstration when word swept through the community that shopowner Truong Van Tran would attempt to hang a poster of the late Ho Chi Minh and a flag of communist Vietnam in his Westminster video store.

It wasn't Tran's first go at building a shrine to Vietnam's most infamous communist. For several days early this month, Ho hung in the front window of Hi-Tek Video. But, following a near riot in the parking lot outside, a judge had intervened with a restraining order requiring Ho's removal. Tran's landlord moved to revoke his lease for interfering with the all-important commercial activity around his store.

But early on Feb. 10, Superior Court Judge Tam Nomoto Schumann said Tran's First Amendment right to free speech was at stake, and she dismissed protesters' charges that posting a picture of Ho was provoking the 200,000-plus Vietnamese community with "fighting words." Tran reappeared later that day, ready to rehang Ho and the flag.

I missed Tran's futile attempt to rehang them; missed the dramatic arrival of the Westminster police to escort him; and missed his scuffle with an agitated protester that included Tran's bogus fall, for which the 37-year-old shopkeeper deserves an Academy Award. I did not miss the powerful, angry reactions of scores of my neighbors to Tran's truncated political statement.

I was outside Tran's video store on Feb. 15, the day Tran had promised to try hanging Ho again. Tran was a no-show, but when 150 police in riot gear with batons faced off against 500 anti-Tran protestors, the city declared an end to Orange County's brief experiment in free-for-all political debate. Police Chief James Cook warned Tran that any attempt to rehang Ho would land the businessman in jail.

To many Americans, images of Ho and the flag of Vietnam evoke bitter memories. To many others—like those who called KROQ's *Kevin and Bean Show* the following morning—Vietnamese outrage is incomprehensible. Between jokes about bad Asian drivers and calls for Vietnamese-Americans to "just get over it," two callers expressing the therapeutic politics of the day defended Tran's speech rights by attacking the rights of his critics to respond angrily. Free speech apparently now means the right to monologue.

But I look at Tran's shrine to Ho and see my father taking his wife, his brother and me—his 2-month-old son—in a military Jeep through sniper fire and past the bodies of unlucky friends and relatives to get to Tan Son Nhut Airport in April 1975.

I see my mother carrying me over barbed-wire fences while being shot at by communist troops as her husband prepares to take off in a stolen cargo plane, cramming in as many people as possible, to escape certain execution.

I see my parents trying to adjust to their new surroundings without being able to speak a lick of English.

I see my dad taking a job in Arlington, Texas, killing rats beneath people's homes just to make ends meet.

I see my family driving to Orange County in 1979 because the eternal summers remind my mom of home.

I see my parents—too proud to take food stamps and welfare checks—struggling every day to put my brother and me through Catholic school.

I see Thai pirates dangling my 2-year-old cousin Anh Tho by her ankles over shark-infested waters, her body used as collateral to loot the tiny boat of half-starved refugees in 1978.

I see the look of distress on my dad's face as his father lay dying in Vietnam in 1997 because he couldn't go home to say goodbye for fear of being jailed—or worse—by the Vietnamese government.

America has been good to our family. Mom owns a successful business in Garden Grove; Dad serves on the cabinet of a local state senator. This country welcomed us, and we have prospered. But Dad never lets me forget where we came from. I came to political consciousness attending raucous demonstrations in Los Angeles, Westminster and other scattered places for as long as I can remember to, as he puts it, "preserve the cause."

Most Americans live with luxury—not just material, mind you, but also the luxury of historical amnesia. With the exception of veterans and their families, perhaps, most Americans can forget—have forgotten—Vietnam. People in Orange County can generally move on and not have to worry about something that happened more than 24 years ago. It's dated, and to the average American, it matters less than that other cultural signifier from the era, *The Brady Bunch*.

I don't have that luxury.

My family—like many Vietnamese-American families—can't forget why we are here. We are refugees from a regime Ho has come to symbolize, a regime that brutalized and murdered our people because of our beliefs.

This is why letting Tran hang his portrait of Ho Chi Minh and the flag of communist Vietnam meets with such rage, such intemperate displays of political passion. The shrine is a constant reminder of our failure to preserve democracy in a country that was stolen from us. We still fight the war every day.

144

Le Ly Hayslip Commentary, February 24, 1999

The protests generated by the attempt of Truong Van Tran, the video store owner in Orange County, California's "Little Saigon," to display a portrait of Vietnamese Communist leader Ho Chi Minh and the Communist flag, inspired considerable commentary. Because most of the Vietnamese American community in Southern California and the rest of the nation blames the Communists for their forced exile, feelings run very high. But anti-Communist protests are encountering more resistance as increasing numbers of younger Vietnamese Americans take a broader view of their history. They are supported by individuals like Le Ly Hayslip, the author whose work became an acclaimed film directed by Oliver Stone. Hayslip's comments reflect unusual courage in the face of widespread community hostility but also indicate a gradual softening of rigid ideological stances.

Le Ly Hayslip, "Being Free in America Means Letting Other People Speak Out," *Los Angeles Times*, February 24, 1999, B-4.

Being Free in America Means Letting Other People Speak Out

Culture: Vietnamese refugees fled their homeland for the very right they now wish to silence in Little Saigon.

By Le Ly Hayslip

When I was a young girl growing up in my little village in Vietnam during the civil war between North and South Vietnam, at different times, soldiers from both sides appeared and ordered all the villagers to come out and protest against the other side. And they said that anyone who didn't would be shot on the spot.

Like most villages then, ours had no electricity. So it was always very dark and frightening when we would stumble out and follow orders to march up and down, shouting slogans against the other side. But between life and death we did what we were told, without the freedom to think and decide which side we belonged to. Such villagers were victims who could not read, write and decide, but only take orders from whichever side brings the guns. And don't forget that by the end of the war, more than 2 million Vietnamese had been killed.

Like so many others around the world, many of my fellow Vietnamese tried hard to get out of that country and find freedom in the U.S., where some have lived now almost 30 years. With the Vietnam War over for almost 25 years, I thought I had found freedom here in the U.S. But for the past 10 years, I have been protested against by my fellow Vietnamese in the U.S.—sometimes in large, organized demonstrations—because they keep insisting I am a Communist. This is because I have often said the struggle should be over, that the suffering should end, that I would like to see reconciliation among all Vietnamese.

In the meantime, some of the sons and daughters of the protesters and those like them often have worked hard for me to come to their colleges and universities to give lectures about these issues. How sad it is that on some of those campuses, organized protesters from the Vietnamese community were demonstrating against me outside the lecture hall while inside their sons and daughters had gathered to listen and learn. This younger generation of Vietnamese Americans has been educated about American culture and American freedom of speech. Most of them understand that I have the right to tell my experiences and my thoughts, and that when their parents threaten me and disrupt my lectures, they are actually destroying the very freedom they sought when they came to the United States.

There is no freedom among us Vietnamese in the U.S. when these things happen. Why bother to come to the country of freedom if some Vietnamese have no right to put up pictures in their homes and shops, or to speak out their ideas, including ideas that are unpopular.

What is happening in Little Saigon now—the attacks on the owner of the video store who displays the Communist Vietnamese flag and a portrait of the late Communist leader Ho Chi Minh in his window—shows that some members of the older generation of Vietnamese still don't understand about the freedom of the U.S., the country that gives equal rights of free speech to even those who say the most obnoxious or unpopular things. To seek that freedom for their families was why hundreds of thousands of Vietnamese fled, many even drowning in the sea as boat people in that attempt.

In the kind of Vietnamese village where I grew up, there was no education or free newspapers for Vietnamese to learn about their rights or express them. But here in America, we have those things. So everyone who comes to America should learn about freedom of speech in the U.S.? I have never met the shop owner, Truong Van Tran, but I see that he understands about his freedom of speech. I hope there are other Vietnamese living here who also understand and who will let every one among us live out the freedom we struggled so hard to find without being hurt or threatened.

Le Ly Hayslip is the author of two books, including "When Heaven and Earth Changed Places," on which a movie by Oliver Stone was based.

145

Executive Order 13125, June 7, 1999

*The first presidential Executive Order focusing on Asian Americans since EO
9066 in 1942, this directive established a federal interagency team and a President's Advisory Commission on Asian Americans and Pacific Islanders in the Department of Health and Human Services. Former Congressman Norman Mineta
chaired the commission until he stepped down when named Secretary of Commerce in fall 2000, becoming the first Asian American to serve in any presidential
Cabinet. Because it asked for data supporting ways in which federal agencies
might assist underserved Asian Pacific American communities, this EO was a significant step toward dispelling "model minority" stereotypes.*

Executive Order, White House, Office of the Press Secretary. Washington, DC, June
7, 1999.

Executive Order 13125

Increasing Participation of Asian Americans
and Pacific Islanders in Federal Programs

By the authority vested in me as President by the Constitution and the laws of
the United States of America, including the Federal Advisory Committee Act,
as amended (5 U.S.C. App.), and in order to improve the quality of life of Asian
Americans and Pacific Islanders through increased participation in Federal programs where they may be underserved (e.g., health, human services, education,
housing, labor, transportation, and economic and community development), it
is hereby ordered as follows:

Section 1. (a) There is established in the Department of Health and Human
Services the President's Advisory Commission on Asian Americans and Pacific
Islanders (Commission). The Commission shall consist of not more than 15
members appointed by the President, one of which shall be designated by the

President as Chair. The Commission shall include members who: (i) have a history of involvement with the Asian American and Pacific Islander communities; (ii) are from the fields of health, human services, education, housing, labor, transportation, economic and community development, civil rights, and the business community; (iii) are from civic associations representing one or more of the diverse Asian American and Pacific Islander communities; and (iv) have such other experience as the President deems appropriate.

(b) The Secretary of the Department of Health and Human Services (Secretary) shall appoint an Executive Director for the Commission.

Sec. 2. The Commission shall provide advice to the President, through the Secretary, on: (a) the development, monitoring, and coordination of Federal efforts to improve the quality of life of Asian Americans and Pacific Islanders through increased participation in Federal programs where such persons may be underserved and the collection of data related to Asian American and Pacific Islander populations and sub-populations; (b) ways to increase public-sector, private-sector, and community involvement in improving the health and well-being of Asian Americans and Pacific Islanders; and (c) ways to foster research and data on Asian Americans and Pacific Islanders, including research and data on public health.

Sec. 3. The Department of Health and Human Services shall establish the White House Initiative on Asian Americans and Pacific Islanders (Initiative), an interagency working group (working group) whose members shall be appointed by their respective agencies. The Executive Director of the Commission shall also serve as the Director of the Initiative, and shall report to the Secretary or the Secretary's designee. The working group shall include both career and non-career civil service staff and commissioned officers of the Public Health Service with expertise in health, human services, education, housing, labor, transportation, economic and community development, and other relevant issues. The working group shall advise the Secretary on the implementation and coordination of Federal programs as they relate to Asian Americans and Pacific Islanders across executive departments and agencies.

Sec. 4. The head of each executive department and each agency designated by the Secretary shall appoint a senior Federal official responsible for management or program administration to report directly to the agency head on activity under this Executive order, and to serve as a liaison to the Initiative. The Secretary also may designate additional Federal Government officials, with the agreement of the relevant agency head, to carry out the functions of the Initiative. To the extent permitted by law and to the extent practicable, each executive department and designated agency shall provide any appropriate information requested by the working group, including data relating to the eligibility for and participation of Asian Americans and Pacific Islanders in Federal programs. Where adequate data are not available, the Initiative shall suggest the means of collecting such data.

Sec. 5. Each executive department and designated agency (collectively, the "agency") shall prepare a plan for, and shall document, its efforts to improve the quality of life of Asian Americans and Pacific Islanders through increased participation in Federal programs where Asian Americans and Pacific Islanders may be underserved. This plan shall address, among other things, Federal efforts to: (a) improve the quality of life for Asian Americans and Pacific Islanders through increased participation in Federal programs where they may be underserved and the collection of data related to Asian American and Pacific Islander populations and sub-populations; (b) increase public-sector, private-sector, and community involvement in improving the health and well-being of Asian Americans and Pacific Islanders; and (c) foster research and data on Asian Americans and Pacific Islanders, including research and data on public health. Each agency's plan shall provide appropriate measurable objectives and, after the first year, shall assess that agency's performance on the goals set in the previous year's plan. Each plan shall be submitted at a date to be established by the Secretary.

Sec. 6. The Secretary shall review the agency plans and develop for submission to the President an integrated Federal plan (Federal Plan) to improve the quality of life of Asian American and Pacific Islanders through increased participation in Federal programs where such persons may be underserved. Actions described in the Federal Plan shall address improving access by Asian Americans and Pacific Islanders to Federal programs and fostering advances in relevant research and data. The Secretary shall ensure that the working group is given the opportunity to comment on the proposed Federal Plan prior to its submission to the President. The Secretary shall disseminate the Federal Plan to appropriate members of the executive branch. The findings and recommendations in the Federal Plan shall be considered by the agencies in their policies and activities.

Sec. 7. Notwithstanding any other Executive order, the responsibilities of the President that are applicable to the Commission under the Federal Advisory Committee Act, as amended, except that of reporting to the Congress, shall be performed by the Secretary in accordance with the guidelines and procedures established by the Administrator of General Services.

Sec. 8. Members of the Commission shall serve without compensation, but shall be allowed travel expenses, including per diem in lieu of subsistence, as authorized by law for persons serving intermittently in the Government service (5 U.S.C. 5701–5707). To the extent permitted by law and appropriations, and where practicable, agencies shall, upon request by the Secretary, provide assistance to the Commission and to the Initiative. The Department of Health and Human Services shall provide administrative support and funding for the Commission.

Sec. 9. The Commission shall terminate 2 years after the date of this Executive order unless the Commission is renewed by the President prior to the end of that 2-year period.

Sec. 10. For the purposes of this order, the terms: (a) "Asian American" includes persons having origins in any of the original peoples of the Far East, Southeast Asia, or the Indian subcontinent; and

(b) "Pacific Islander" includes the aboriginal, indigenous, native peoples of Hawaii and other Pacific Islands within the jurisdiction of the United States.

[signature of William J. Clinton]

The White House,

June 7, 1999.

146

Senator Daniel Inouye Introduces
General Eric Shinseki, June 9, 1999

Eric Shinseki, a third-generation (sansei) *Japanese American, became the 34th Chief of Staff of the U.S. Army. Inouye (D-HI) introduced him to his Senate colleagues at confirmation hearings. In his remarks, the senator noted the irony of the occasion. In 1942, the year Shinseki was born in Hawai'i, Inouye was blocked from volunteering for the army because Japanese Americans were considered 4C, enemy aliens. It would have been an enormous stretch of the imagination for Inouye, later a recipient of the Congressional Medal of Honor for battlefront valor in Italy during World War II, to have foreseen this Senate event a half century later.*

Statement from Senator Inouye. Reprinted with permission. Washington, DC, June 9, 1999.

Statement of the Honorable Daniel K. Inouye
U.S. Senator from Hawaii
Nomination of General Shinseki as the 34th
Chief of Staff of the United States Army
June 9, 1999

Thank you very much, Mr. Chairman, for this opportunity to say a few words on behalf of our President's nominee for the 34th Chief of Staff of the United States Army. General Shinseki began his military career as a commissioned officer 34 years ago, almost exactly, on June 9, 1965. He received his commission as a Second Lieutenant after receiving a baccalaureate degree from the United States Military Academy at West Point.

After a few weeks of preparation, he was sent to Vietnam. On his first tour of duty there he distinguished himself, and he received his first Purple Heart. He was sent back to the States to be hospitalized, and a few years later he was back in Vietnam. On his second tour of duty there as a captain, he once again distinguished himself, but he was wounded very seriously, losing part of his foot.

Notwithstanding that, he applied for a waiver and requested that he be given the opportunity to continue his service to our Nation. This was granted, and he continued his illustrious career, and in 1997 became a four-star General. As Chairman Warner indicated, in March of 1994, he was made Commanding General of the First Cavalry Division.

In July 1997, he became Commander-in-Chief of the United States Army in Europe, and Commander-in-Chief of the Seventh Army. He was also Commander of the Stabilization Force on Bosnia.

As indicated by Chairman Warner, there is no question that General Shinseki is eminently qualified for this appointment, and if I may at this juncture be a bit more personal because this is a special day for many of us in the United States. In February of 1942, the United States Selective Service System directed that, because of the hysteria of that time, all Japanese, citizens or otherwise, be designated 4C. 4C, as you know Mr. Chairman, is the designation of an enemy alien.

It was a day of shame for many of us, although it was not deserved, and we petitioned the Government to permit us to demonstrate ourselves and a year later, President Roosevelt declared that "Americanism is a matter of mind and heart. Americanism is not, and has never been, a matter of race or color," and authorized the formation of a special Japanese-American combat unit, and the rest is history.

But what I wish to point out is that this young man sitting to my right was born in November of 1942. At the time of his birth, he was an enemy alien, and today, to the great glory of the United States, I have the privilege of presenting him as the 34th Chief of Staff, Army nominee. This, Mr. Chairman, can only happen in the United States. I cannot think of any other place where something of this nature can happen.

He is the grandson of a Japanese laborer from Hiroshima who arrived in Hawaii in the late 1800's, about 1888, raised his children, and raised his grandson to love America, and I believe he succeeded eminently.

Mr. Chairman, on this day, the shame that has been on our shoulders all these years has been clearly washed away by this one action, and for that I am very grateful to this Nation. I am grateful to the President, and I believe that we have before us one of the great illustrious warriors of our Nation. And I hope that this committee will vote to approve his nomination as the 34th Chief of Staff of the U.S. Army.

It is my pleasure, Mr. Chairman, to present to the Committee, General Shinseki.

147

Quang X. Pham, Vietnamese Recognition Luncheon Speech, August 1999

Houston, Texas, boasts one of the largest Vietnamese American communities. It holds an annual recognition luncheon to honor graduating high school valedictorians or salutatorians from that ethnic group. In 1999 there were eleven. Perhaps that alone would be sufficient to demand attention. Quang Pham was invited to address the group because of his reputation as a speaker and writer, because he had served in the U.S. Marines as a helicopter pilot, and because he had become a top sales specialist for a leading biotech firm. But his speech was more than motivational; it revealed that the Vietnamese had been in combat mode for decades and that many were in America because they had fought as allies against the Communists. Nonetheless, as Pham points out, anti-Asian racism could rear its ugly head in Officer Candidates School, where drill instructors used gratuitous racial harassment—now contrary to established policy.

In a similar case from the same time period, Bruce Yamashita endured identical slurs only to be told, after excelling in all the tests, that he was washed out a day before completing training because he "lacked leadership qualities." A decade later, after lengthy investigation, Yamashita was reinstated at the rank of captain. Yamashita's lesson was that challenging the practice would assist others in the future. Pham's moral to his story was that endurance would pave the way for other Vietnamese Americans in the future. Both no doubt made a difference, and both were deeply concerned about implications of their actions for their ethnic/racial communities. And, as the speech spells out, they had a growing sense that their fathers' generation's profound anticommunist ideology must be nudged aside, however gently.

Quang X. Pham, "Vietnamese-Americans 2000: Getting Beyond the War and its Aftermath." Speech to Vietnamese Culture and Science Association Annual Youth Recognition Luncheon. Houston, Texas. Reprinted with permission.

Vietnamese-Americans 2000: Getting Beyond the War and Its Aftermath

by Quang X. Pham

Greetings to the parents, families, friends and the 11 young scholars honored here today and to members of the Vietnamese Culture & Science Association. It is a privilege for me to be with all of you and thank you for your kind hospitality. . . .

Before I begin, I'd like to introduce two special guests of mine today: my father, Pham Van Hoa, my inspiration and my favorite pilot. He is a former Lieutenant Colonel in the Vietnamese Air Force and a survivor of Communist re-education and hard labor camps. Also here with us is Brad Larkin, a college classmate of mine from UCLA and a former U.S. Marine Corps infantry officer who also served in Desert Storm and Bangladesh. . . .

My hometown is Saigon. I grew up in California, but Texas will always be a part of my family. The first time I visited Houston was July 1989. I was a young, inexperienced Marine Corps student aviator flying in a T-34 trainer from Naval Air Station Corpus Christi. I was always proud to proclaim that I was from the South—South Vietnam! It was as hot and humid then, maybe just a little hotter in the cockpit, as I landed at nearby Ellington Field on my way to a baseball game at the Astrodome. Thirty years earlier, in 1959, my father had also flown over this great state as he learned to fly at Reese Air Force Base in Lubbock. He would return to fly in a war back home in Southeast Asia. Little did I know in 1989 I would venture to a war in the Arabian Gulf just a short year later.

That cross-country flight, along with dozens of others over this great state, was the beginning of a journey for me—one that I had dreamed about as a child growing up in Vietnam watching my father and his colleagues at Tan Son Nhut air base in Saigon. It was a childhood dream and a life-long passion with airplanes soaring above the earth and about putting on the uniform to serve one's country. I thought that dream had vanished on April 24, 1975, when my family boarded a crammed aircraft under the cover of darkness and fled our homeland. I never realized I could achieve that dream in America, only a mere decade removed the end of our longest and most controversial conflict.

However, that dream was not fulfilled without paying a price—a toll on the soul, a journey within. The road on becoming an officer and a pilot in the U.S. Marines was treacherous, for any young American, let alone a Vietnamese 11 years after the war had ended. The odds were high, the obstacles were tough to hurdle physically, but more so emotionally. The feeling of insecurity was the greatest, one of not belonging, probably stemming from the loss of our homeland and a lack of English fluency, especially when faced with extreme combat simulations. From the time I stepped off that airplane in America, just like your parents and mine, or like others who got off the boat, our identity forever changed. Or was it our loss of identity or self-esteem? Or was it a shame how we lost our country?

I was not unique or alone. Despite the achievements of Vietnamese-Americans, there remain many problems. According to the Vietnamese Community of Orange County Inc., a private, non-profit social and cultural services agency, many of the problems—in older refugees and in young people born or raised in America—and the events in our community, could be traced to a lack of self-esteem and a feeling of insecurity. Some people still don't know where they are or who they are. I still deal with that. As we approach the new millennium, one of our greatest challenges is how we will face our past and deal with our identity crisis. Will we forever label ourselves as refugees and not immigrants, as Viet-kieus, as a community living in exile waiting for the day of revenge to take back our homeland? Do we expect or want our younger generation to carry on the torch of freedom. Or will we face our past, share with the younger generation about our journey and look forward, with hope and confidence, to the future—all of you—right here in America.

Remember we are not alone. Millions of others around the world at this age of uncertainty, the post-Cold War era, face the same identity crisis-most recently the people of Kosovo. We can all identify with the story of Rip Van Winkle and its universal theme of exile, journey and return.

How do you deal with this identity crisis when you face it? I did it and you can too. You do it by looking to your parents as your role models and by going after your dreams and passions. That's who you are. You are made of Vietnamese family values and passions and dreams. Often, we look at stars, celebrities and big-name people. We strive to be like them without realizing our best role models, those who showed us how to love, to care, to sacrifice, to focus, to give back. They are closest to our hearts and our minds, our parents. They have suffered yet they have been strong, for you and me. They gave up their dreams and hopes, left their native land, abandoned their possessions, to reach freedom, for you and me. Their lives were turned up side down, their societal roles reversed. They are still being asked and judged about their lives in the old country. Yet they have survived and thrived, for you and me. And they are here today, to celebrate and cherish this moment, for you and me. Let's give a round of applause for all the parents.

Take the journey. It can only be done in America. Where all passions can be pursued and realized. Where duty, honor, and service to community reflect great qualities also found in our Vietnamese heritage. However, there is no free lunch. You may be shown the path or the door to the food line. No one will open the door for you or move you to the front of the line. You have to earn it yourself like you have done already, by graduating as salutatorians and valedictorians. Remember the tougher the road, the greater the internal reward.

William Faulkner once said "The end of wisdom is to dream high enough not to lose the dream in the seeking of it."

Before I tell you a little about my journey, I'd like to talk about three young Vietnamese Americans, two whom I know well and one I am huge fan of. Any of them could be here speaking to you instead of me. For they have traveled the tough roads and have broken barriers in their own right, before anyone else from our heritage. They are also in non-traditional career paths and they have done well. None of them became doctors, engineers, or lawyers. But they have contributed much to our culture and have placed us on the mainstream radarscope. Across America, there are many successful Vietnamese. But we hardly hear of them because the legacy of Vietnam and our own insecurities prevent us from looking beyond the war and its aftermath, in the Vietnamese-American community and in mainstream society.

Andrew Lam was a schoolmate of mine from Le Qui Don back in Saigon. An editor and a writer for Pacific News in San Francisco, Andrew has written extensively on the Vietnamese people in the U.S. and in Vietnam. His writing is truthful, painful and scholarly.

Quynh-Trang Nguyen is the general manager of Vietnamese Broadcasting Network in New Jersey and founder and anchor of Little Saigon Radio & Television in Orange County. She was named in top 25 Americans in Orange County and among the most influential Asian women in America. She brought daily news to the Vietnamese community with integrity and deep passion unseen before.

Dat Nguyen, whom I have never met, played college football at Texas A & M and became the all-time leading tackler in the Big 12 Conference. Drafted by the Dallas Cowboys last April, he is also the biggest Vietnamese I've ever seen on television!

Thirty years ago, as a young five-year old Vietnamese boy living in Saigon, I distinctively recall watching with my father the Apollo 11 moon landing broadcast on Armed Forces Television. I was amazed at the sight of humans actually stepping onto the scarred lunar surface. Years later, I would learn about the space program and astronauts and their training. I discovered many of the test-pilots and astronauts came from the military where they learned how to fly fighter aircraft: Neil Armstrong, John Glenn and even our greatest test-pilot who never orbited the Earth, Chuck Yeager. They had the right stuff. They were my heroes. I wanted to have the right stuff and I knew I had go through the military for training. I loved the uniform, the airplanes and the camaraderie like I had dreamed about as a child in Vietnam.

But I didn't have to look far or at the American pilots. In the back of mind was my number one inspiration, my favorite pilot—my father, who was still in Communist re-education and hard labor camps while I was in high school in the early 80s. For a long time, I wondered why he did not leave Vietnam when his colleagues did. Some of them were on the same airplane we were, dressed in civilian gear. For a long time, I missed his presence, his humor, his support, and the fishing trips we took together in Vietnam. For a long time, growing up in a house full of women, my three sisters and my mother, I missed having a man around. For a long time, I felt like an outsider to the Vietnamese community because our old friends had both parents and were moving on with their lives. For a long time, I stayed away from our community.

When you are a 5' 6", 125-pound high school junior, struggling to fit in, to speak proper English and survive the basketball team tryout, the right stuff seemed so far-fetched. Even after I made the basketball team, earned the scholar athlete award and team captain for one season, I never was offered a chance to pursue my dream. My high school counselor approached one of my best friends, Jimmy, to offer him a congressional recommendation for the Naval Academy. Jimmy was an All-American boy, 6' 2", blond and athletic. And he had absolutely no interest in the military at that time. We ended up in college together but I never forgot the incident. No one opened the door for me then.

A few years later, I discovered another entry into military flight training. It was the old-fashion way—Officer Candidates School (OCS). It was a ticket to Pensacola, the cradle of naval aviation, but the first stop was Quantico, Virginia. I am going to summarize my military experience by revisiting my first summer in Quantico. Flight school was a lot easier. Desert Storm and Somalia were much more rewarding and fulfilling. But OCS was definitely the ultimate test of my mettle. You will face your own defining moment. Be ready when it comes and give it your all! No one asked me but I carried the burden of our loss in Vietnam on my shoulders throughout that summer at OCS. The lingering belief of South Vietnamese as inept soldiers and the way we lost our country were in the minds of the OCS staff. "Hey Candidate Chong, Fang, Fong, whatever your bleeping name is, get down and give me 20 bends and thrusts!"

Another drill sergeant shouted "What are you doing here in my Marine Corps? Are you a Viet Cong spy?"

There were numerous times when my arms and legs could no longer carry the 80-pound pack and M-16 rifle and my skinny neck could no longer don the Kevlar helmet in the 90 degree heat and 90% humidity. It was during those moments when I was to ready to forgo the honor of an officer's commission and suffer the ridicule of the DIs. Ask for a Drop on Request (DOR) or risk getting kicked out after a long summer.

I thought about the next Vietnamese to go through OCS. The staff would dismiss him too. I thought about all the Vietnamese soldiers who died for our freedom. I thought about their long years of fighting and their families who suffered their losses. I only had to survive 10-weeks of simulated combat, nothing compared to the years and agony suffered by our South Vietnamese soldiers. I thought about my father, who by 1986, had been locked up for 11 years. During those lonely and humid nights in the Quantico barracks, I lied awake thinking about my dream, my passion and my life. I got angry and became eager to wake up the next day of training to prove the staff wrong. I wanted to scream back but I could not. You have to chose your battle wisely and cannot cry wolf every time about discrimination or we will never catch up let alone get ahead. I bit my tongue and swallowed my pride. I took the respectful, silent and subdued Asian approach. I wanted to shout back at the DIs "You lost 58,000 Americans in Vietnam. We lost over two million people. You served one tour of duty in combat. My father and his colleagues fought the Commies for nearly 20 years! And you think we (I) cannot make your military?"

The Vietnamese people and my parents, inspired me without even being there, to march that extra mile in the woods, to swim that extra 15 feet, to grit my teeth and bear the harassment, to prove Vietnamese can belong in America and in the U.S. Marines.

When I entered in the Marines, I was merely after my passion of flying and becoming a military officer. I was fascinated by the uniform and the glory. I made a lot of friends, traveled the world, and was very fortunate to come home alive. I learned about the suffering and losses from the American perspectives, from Vietnam Veterans I befriended and served alongside and their families. What I never expected to learn in the Marines was a lesson of life—about duty, honor and commitment to country and community, like my father had demonstrated. But I already knew those characteristics—from my father early on.

While my father served as my inspiration, my mother was my day-to-day role model. She taught me about personal sacrifice and love. After the day my father drove us to the airport to leave Vietnam, my mother took charge and raised four young children in a strange land without any money to start and without any English. She too had wanted me to be a doctor, an engineer or a lawyer. But she knew my obsession with flying. It was very difficult for her when I told her my desire to serve in the Marines. Her first words were "Why the Marines? Go to the Air Force or the Navy. They're much easier." She never discouraged me from joining yet it was extremely difficult for her to send me off to war like she had seen my father leave so many times before. Even though my mother is not here today, she is always supportive in spirit.

The legacy of Vietnam still lingers on. I refer to it as the American conflict in Vietnam, not the Vietnam War, because Vietnam has been in a war of some sort during its entire history. Against the Chinese, the French, among ourselves, the Americans, and now against change and the new millennium. But Americans prefer to call the "Vietnam War" as its own sort of war, a lingering sore, an open wound that would not heal, even 24 years later.

For the Vietnamese who left the country in a mass exodus, the legacy, pain and anger continue onto life in America and the next generation. Coming to terms with our past, your past, have not been easy. In some ways for me, it was as hard at OCS in 1986 as it has been this year in Orange County, California.

We've come a long way but we're still mourning an irretrievable past. Next year, 25 years after the war ended, will be the silver anniversary of our arrival in America. But so far in 1999, our community in Orange County has faced its past with much disparity. First there was the video store demonstration for 60 days. Then the April 30th celebration conflicts. Last month, the Bowers Museum started hosting a controversial art exhibit from Vietnam, the same one that was on display at Plano last summer. I wonder how the community will react when the popular Broadway play "Miss Saigon" will come in September. Our community is going through a maturation process and growing pains just like other immigrant groups previously had done. We must resist the temptation to forever label ourselves as refugees and war victims of the Communists. Letting go of our haunting past can only help the next generation achieve their full potential without the hinder of the ghosts of Vietnam.

Young Vietnamese-Americans today face far greater expectations than those of my generation—those born in Vietnam and grew up America. The bar has been raised. The expectations for you are enormous because we, the Vietnamese, have been here longer now. You are expected to study and excel and pay back the sacrifices your parents made. You are expected to maintain your cultural heritage and Vietnamese fluency. You are expected to play the violin or piano well. You are expected to be well-rounded yet focused on getting into a top-notch university. You are expected to take care of your family and the people of Vietnam. Soon, you will move to your respective college dormitories and live among students from different cultures and regions. Take advantage of this period of learning in your life. Seek to understand those around you and yourself. Show compassion and tolerance. Go after your dreams, what ever they may be. Don't let anyone tell you no. Put your face and your body in the uniform, suit, lab coat or in the executive chair. Don't rely on anyone to open the door for you. Charge it at full speed and knock it down! Dream, pursue and realize your passions and don't stop until you do. They may change but you will enjoy the journey wherever your destination may be in life.

Whether this year or next or when you are ready, do come back to contribute to our community, in your own way. Don't wait as long as I did. Vietnamese-Americans can have a voice in mainstream as we do have an elected official in Orange County, a councilman in Westminster, one of our own. Protesting in the streets with 15,000 people is another way to make the headline news. But hosting a celebration luncheon like this one is much more effective and meaningful. Congratulations to the members of the Vietnamese Culture and Science Association for a job well-done, and best wishes to Houston's cream of the crop—the 11 young scholars honored here today.

Thank you and god bless all of you.

148

Hmong Veterans Naturalization Act
(Public Law 106–207), May 26, 2000

Public Law 106–207 allowed refugee veterans from Laos an exemption from English language requirements for citizenship and provides for qualified translators during special civics tests usually permitted only for elderly permanent residents. Long overdue, the law recognizes the extraordinary risks taken by largely preliterate tribespeople who were recruited into irregular or guerrilla forces by American operatives between 1961 and 1978. Spouses are eligible for the exemption if they were married to the veterans on the day they applied for admission into the United States and if they too were Laotian refugees. About 45,000 Hmong people were estimated to have been eligible to take advantage of this narrow window for naturalization until November 26, 2001. As with some immigration and naturalization exemptions, this law recognized the responsibility of the U.S. government in creating relationships that resulted in undue hardship. There are many other cases that remain unresolved.

Weekly Compilation of Presidential Documents, Vol. 36 (2000). Washington, DC: Government Printing Office, 2000.

Public Law 106–207
106th Congress
An Act
To facilitate the naturalization of aliens who served with
special guerrilla units or irregular forces in Laos

Be it enacted by the Senate and House of Representatives of the United States of America in Congress assembled,

Section 1. Short Title

This Act may be cited as the "Hmong Veterans' Naturalization Act of 2000."

Sec. 2. Exemption from English Language Requirement for Certain Aliens Who Served with Special Guerrilla Units or Irregular Forces in Laos

The requirement of paragraph (1) of section 312(a) of the Immigration and Nationality Act (8 U.S.C. 1423 (a)(1)) shall not apply to the naturalization of any person—

 (1) who—

  (A) was admitted into the United States as a refugee from Laos pursuant to section 207 of the Immigration and Nationality Act (8 U.S.C. 1157); and

  (B) served with a special guerrilla unit, or irregular forces, operating from a base in Laos in support of the United States military at any time during the period beginning February 28, 1961, and ending September 18, 1978; or

 (2) who—

  (A) satisfies the requirement of paragraph (1)(A); and

  (B) was the spouse of a person described in paragraph (1) on paragraph (1) on the day on which such described person applied for admission into the United States as a refugee.

Sec. 3. Special Consideration Concerning Civics Requirement for Certain Aliens Who Served with Special Guerrilla Units or Irregular Forces in Laos

The Attorney General shall provide for special consideration, as determined by the Attorney General, concerning the requirement of paragraph (2) of section 312(a) of the Immigration and Nationality Act (8 U.S.C. 1423(a)(2)) with respect to the naturalization of any person described in paragraph (1) or (2) of section 2 of this Act.

Sec. 4. Documentation of Qualifying Service

A person seeking an exemption under section 2 or special consideration under section 3 shall submit to the Attorney General documentation of their, or their spouse's, service with a special guerrilla unit, or irregular forces, described in section 2(1)(B), in the form of—

 (1) original documents;

 (2) an affidavit of the serving person's superior officer;

 (3) two affidavits from other individuals who also were serving with such a special guerrilla unit, or irregular forces, and who personally knew of the person's service; or

 (4) other appropriate proof.

Sec. 5. Determination of Eligibility for Exemption and Special Consideration

(a) In determining a person's eligibility for an exemption under section 2 or special consideration under section 3, the Attorney General—

(1) shall review the refugee processing documentation for the person, or, in an appropriate case, for the person and the person's spouse, to verify that the requirements of section 2 relating to refugee applications and admissions have been satisfied;

(2) shall consider the documentation submitted by the person under section 4;

(3) may request an advisory opinion from the Secretary of Defense regarding the person's, or their spouse's, service in a special guerrilla unit, or irregular forces, described in section 2(1)(B); and

(4) may consider any documentation provided by organizations maintaining records with respect to Hmong veterans or their families.

(b) The Secretary of Defense shall provide any opinion requested under paragraph (3) to the extent practicable, and the Attorney General shall take into account any opinion that the Secretary of Defense is able to provide.

Sec. 6. Deadline for Application and Payment of Fees

This Act shall apply to a person only if the person's application for naturalization is filed, as provided in section 334 of the Immigration and Nationality Act (8 U.S.C. 1445), with appropriate fees not later than 18 months after the date of the enactment of this Act.

Sec. 7. Limitation on Number of Beneficiaries

Notwithstanding any other provision of this Act, the total number of aliens who may be granted an exemption under section 2 or special consideration under section 3, or both, may not exceed 45,000.

Approved May 26, 2000.

149

"On Behalf of Lesbian, Gay, Bisexual, and Transgender [LGBT] Asian Pacific Islander Individuals and Organizations," September 18, 2000

This statement, crafted by Pauline Park and Christine Lipat, was submitted to the Presidential Advisory Commission on Asian Americans and Pacific Islanders/White House Initiative on Asian Americans and Pacific Islanders, established by Executive Order 13125. It was received by the commission at one of its regional "Town Hall" meetings in New York City. Asian American communities have long-standing commitments to civil and human rights regardless of class, gender, region, language, religious, ideological or other factors. More recently, sexual orientation in the form of gay/lesbian/bisexual lifestyles has become an issue, with mixed reception from the Asian American communities. Rarely, however, have these communities addressed transgendered and gender-variant people, and it appears that wider parameters for sexual self-determination will be an important item on the agenda. This statement takes several path-breaking steps: first, it stakes a claim for this cause across many boundaries, regional, ethnic, gender, and political; second, it correctly asserts the historical existence of LGBT individuals in traditional Asian societies; third, it demonstrates the concrete ways in which these individuals are denied access to agencies and support routinely provided to others; and fourth, it suggests that there are many who "do not have the luxury of separating issues of sexuality and gender identity from those of race, ethnicity, national origin and citizenship status."

"Statement of Pauline Park and Christine Lipat: On Behalf of Lesbian, Gay, Bisexual, and Transgender Asian Pacific Islander Individuals and Organizations" to Presidential Advisory Commission on Asian Americans and Pacific Islanders. New York City, September 18, 2000. Printed with permission of the authors.

Statement of Pauline Park and Christine Lipat on Behalf of Lesbian,
Gay, Bisexual, and Transgender Asian Pacific Islander Individuals
and Organizations

*Before the Presidential Advisory Commission on Asian Americans & Pacific
Islanders White House Initiative on Asian Americans & Pacific Islanders*

My name is Christine Lipat, and I am a board member of the Audre Lorde Project, a community center for lesbian, gay, bisexual, and transgendered (LGBT)
people of color and a founding member of Kilawin Kolektibo, a Filipina LBT
collective, both based in New York City. I am also senior program officer of Astraea Lesbian Action Foundation, directing all our grants programs supporting
progressive, grassroots lesbian organizing, and overseeing Astraea's International Fund for Sexual Minorities, the only fund in the United States that exclusively supports LGBT organizing in Asia and other developing regions.

My name is Pauline Park. I am a member of the political committee of the
Gay Asian & Pacific Islander Men of New York (GAPIMNY), a founding member of Iban/Queer Koreans of New York (Iban/QKNY) and co-founder of the
New York Association for Gender Rights Advocacy (NYAGRA). Currently, I am
leading a campaign for a transgender anti-discrimination bill pending in the
New York City Council. . . . As a transgendered Korean adoptee, I do not have
the luxury of separating issues of sexuality and gender identity from those of
race, ethnicity, national origin and citizenship status.

In our work, we see very clearly the complex roots of the multiple oppressions that LGBT people of color labor under in this city and in this country. We
are here representing a consortium of LGBT Asian Pacific American organizations in the northeast, in collaboration with national LGBT API networks, and
it is our distinct privilege and high honor to speak on behalf of a community
that until recently has been among the most invisible and the most marginalized in this society.

In every pre-modern Asian culture, there were individuals whom we would
identify as lesbian, gay, bisexual, transgendered, or intersexual, though they would
have identified themselves not as LGBT but rather as *bakla* (in Tagalog),
shamakhami (in Bengali), *hijra* (in Hindi), *waria* (in Javanese), or *paksu mudang*
(in Korean). And in every Asian immigrant community, there are LGBT people
whose sexuality or gender identity sets them apart from their community of origin. The challenge of full LGBT inclusion is nowhere better illustrated than by
the recent decision to allow the South Asian Gay & Lesbian Association (SALGA)
to march in the India Day parade for the first time since 1992, after eight years of
fighting to get back into the event.

As Asian Pacific Americans, we need to recognize that barriers to accessing
health and social services and to full participation in this society are based not

only on race and ethnicity, but also on homophobia and transgenderphobia. Many API lesbian, bisexual, and transgendered women are especially disadvantaged by their invisibility in attempting to access health and social services. For example, if a Korean-speaking lesbian recently arrived in New York, she might be extremely reluctant to approach a Korean social service agency for fear of exposure as a lesbian; however, she might not even be aware of the existence of LGBT social service providers; and even if she were able to locate the Lesbian & Gay Community Services Center, she would find no Korean-speaking staff and no culturally appropriate services. There are also no Korean LGBT organizations in New York that have the capacity to provide social services. Mental health professionals and other social service providers are generally ill-equipped to address the multiple oppressions that we face based on sexuality and gender identity as well as race, ethnicity and class. We therefore encourage this Commission as well as API organizations to acknowledge the presence of LGBT people in our communities, including through the use of LGBT-inclusive language and imagery in all their communications. We also encourage API communities as a whole to appreciate the valuable contributions that LGBT coworkers, friends and relatives make in their communities of origin.

In the last few years, the concerns of the bisexual and transgender communities have increasingly become integral to the lesbian and gay movement. Similarly, API initiatives that include sexual orientation should also include the language of gender identity and expression. For example, the fear of persecution based on sexual orientation is now recognized as cause for political asylum; however, the term 'sexual orientation' does not necessarily include the transgendered and gender-variant. A statement from the Commission in favor of the addition of 'gender identity or expression' to political asylum law would therefore help address the problem of pervasive discrimination and violence that our transgendered brothers and sisters face in many Asian countries.

In conclusion, the following recommendations are among the more detailed recommendations included in our national written testimony, to be submitted by October 2, 2000:

First, we call upon the Commission to recommend LGBT inclusion in all API-specific government-funded programs; and we also call upon the Commission to recommend funding specifically for LGBT API organizations and for organizations that serve LGBT Asian Pacific Americans.

Second, we call upon the Commission to recommend the initiation of a major federally-funded research project to assess the needs of the LGBT Asian Pacific American community and the state of services currently available to us, including the full range of social, economic, political, and environmental justice issues facing our communities.

Third, we call upon the Commission to recommend that the Department of Justice and other federal agencies document hate crimes and domestic violence in a way that is specific and detailed enough by sexual orientation and gender identity to be useful to our API communities as well as to law enforcement; we also call upon the Commission to recommend the funding of programs of education and prevention in this area.

Fourth, we hope that the invitation that you extended to us to give testimony here today is just the beginning of an ongoing dialogue on LGBT inclusion in API-specific initiatives; and therefore we call upon the Commission to hold hearings specifically on the concerns of LGBT Asian Pacific Americans.

Finally, we would like to express our solidarity with Wen Ho Lee and add our voices to those within the API community who have spoken out against the disturbing and apparently racially discriminatory treatment to which he has been subjected. For LGBT people of Asian and Pacific origin, we look forward to the day when this country affords all APIs not only opportunities for full participation in the economic and political life of the nation, but the genuine promise of self-determination in sexuality and gender expression that is a basic human right.

150

Celebrating South Asians, September 21, 2000

About two million Americans from South Asia, primarily India, Pakistan, Sri Lanka, and Bangladesh, have become a crucial part of the American social fabric. They are hotel/motel owners, high-tech scientists and entrepreneurs, taxicab drivers, artists, scholars, and exploited low-wage workers. Sreenath Sreenivasan, journalism professor at Columbia University and cofounder of the South Asian Journalists Association, delivered this keynote at a function honoring "South Asian Culture and Heritage" organized by the office of the Comptroller of New York City. His speech discusses the pros and cons of using the generic "South Asian" identity versus specific national origin. He also usefully makes reference to the fact that some South Asians enter the United States from Fiji, in the Pacific, or islands in the Caribbean. He might have mentioned South America or Africa and Europe as well. Sreenivasan also references the lack of realistic images in film and on TV, by implication also critiquing the caricatures and stereotypes that do appear. By the time of his speech, there was, however, solid indication of fairly widespread appreciation of South Asian American writers among American readers. The South Asian identity question is a subset of the larger "Asian American" or "Asian Pacific American" identifications that continue to be defined and debated.

"Celebrating South Asians," keynote speech by Sreenath Sreenivasan at Comptroller of New York City function honoring South Asians and South Asian culture and heritage. New York, September 21, 2000. Printed with permission of the author.

It's a singular honor for me to address you tonight. And a pleasure to see so many South Asians—or "desis," as many of us like to call ourselves—gathered here. This is surely the largest total at City Hall in history. Perhaps we can lobby for something big—how about replacing the bagel as the official food of Queens with the samosa?

As you may know, journalists like me can seize on a particular topic and cling to it with a ferocity that would make the most nasty New York rotweiller blush. Just ask some of politicians in Washington—or even right here in Manhattan. But give us carte blanche—as the comptroller's office did when I asked about a topic for today—we are often at a loss.

But the theme of today's ceremony—"celebrating South Asian heritage and culture"—got me thinking. About South Asia and the phrase "South Asian." What exactly does it mean, especially in the context of this extraordinary mosaic of America and New York in particular? A city where most Pakistanis will tell you they met an Indian or a Sri Lankan or a Bangladeshi for the very first time. The same goes for almost any subcontinental you ask: in South Asia, meeting someone from one of the neighoring countries—let alone working side by side—is almost unheard of.

My involvement with the South Asian Journalists Association has made me realize what a provocative phrase "South Asian" is. Those who embrace it are embracing the idea that 1.5 billion people of the subcontinent can have something in common. That close to two million folks in the U.S. share in a destiny that unites them as immigrants, children of immigrants, or as visitors. Whether you are a Mt. Sinai Hospital nurse from Kerala, a Wall Street trader from Karachi or a desi NYU student whose parents came to Kansas a lifetime ago.

There are, of course, people within the community who dislike the phrase strongly—they feel it takes away from the narrower national identity they know better . . . Indian, Pakistani, Bangladeshi. Many Indians in the US are particularly unhappy with it: they think they get drowned in this larger identity, when they dominate by virtue of their numbers and history.

A California-based columnist wrote a piece for Rediff.com, an Indian Web site, entitled "Why I am Not a South Asian." In it he slammed America's "intellectual laziness" and the "loss of branding" by those of us who use "South Asian" when talking about the diaspora. The writer, Rajeev Srinivasan (we are not related), railed against the false presumption of commonality among desis by various groups, including SAJA (we were honored to be named at the top of his list). "We lose by pushing South Asia," he declared.

I believe he is wrong about this and there are plenty of people just like him—including Pakistanis who don't like being lumped together with India.

In April, Columbia's Southern Asian Institute received an e-mail message from an Indian upset that the Institute's map of South Asia showed more than just India. "If you don't know what is India shut your mouth don't try to give some map representing all the countries . . . If you don't remove the sketch, you will face the consequences soon. Regards. . . ."

I say all this as a proud Indian—my first identity. An Indian not at all ashamed of being from India—as I have been accused of more than once. I just happen to believe that South Asian is a valid label, too. Too.

I feel I can speak authoritatively about the common experience that South Asians have and the wonderful heritage we all share. And not just because I happen to be married to a former gold medalist at the South Asian Federation Games.

I went to high school in the Fiji Islands and have gotten a first hand look at how seriously my Fiji-Indian friends—generations removed from British India—took their desi-ness, their heritage, their culture. I have also seen how proud Caribbean South Asians in New York are about their connection to an ancient and beautiful place. A place most of their grandparents have never seen.

I do understand that some of the smaller countries and cultures can get lost in the mix. I also acknowledge that there isn't a single, monolithic South Asian "community," but rather separate communities that can celebrate their differences while sharing in their commonality. By pandering to those who would keep us separate, we all lose.

These are exciting times to be a South Asian here in the U.S. From the old economy to the new economy, from popular culture to public service, desis are having an impact disproportional to their numbers. One example: when the Minneapolis Star-Tribune wrote this year about the hottest trend in American fashion, it declared that the bindi had replaced last year's hottest trend—mehndi. And then there's the bidi—the one desi trend I am not proud of.

Speaking of being proud, I want to take you specifically to one date this past spring: April 9. That Sunday, I sat transfixed as Fiji's Vijay Singh won the Masters, defeating the world's best golfers.

The next afternoon, I was at a small announcement ceremony at Columbia, where it was announced that Jhumpa Lahiri had won the Pulitzer Prize in fiction—becoming the first Asian winner of the prize. In the course of those 24 hours, South Asians had broken through in two quintessentially "American" arenas. Winning the Masters at hallowed Augusta and a Pulitzer—the wording reads: "for distinguished fiction by an American author, preferably dealing with American life."

Bathing in all the success of the community is one thing, but it is also important to acknowledge and do something about the desis being left behind in these dot-com-obsessed days. Many South Asian organizations are, in fact, fighting great odds to improve those lives, but there's a lot more that needs to be done.

We also need to look beyond our own comfortable walls and to get more involved with the city we live in, becoming active participants in the New York experience as well as the desi one.

Incidentally, it has always bothered me that there were no desis on "E.R.," the hit NBC show. What kind of hospital was that in a country where almost 10 percent of the students in medical programs are South Asian?

Well, I am pleased to tell you that a friend of mine, Purva Bedi—who is here tonight—will get to play just such a role in the new season of the show. How many times she gets to appear depends on the support the desi community shows her, by writing to NBC, by encouraging them to keep putting on diverse characters—just like hers. You see, as with little kids, decision makers in the media need positive reinforcement and feedback. That's a good lesson when it comes to articles in the press, too.

Writing to the editor when they do a responsible story is as effective as dashing off angry letters when they do an irresponsible one. There's plenty of irresponsibility to go around; that's why SAJA runs a mailing list called "Dissecting American Media Now"—or D.A.M.N.

To my way of thinking, a group needs a sense of maturity to identify itself in a broad way, and your presence here tonight—as representatives of your own nationalities and as South Asians—is an affirmation that we are mostly on the same page. And for a journalist there's no greater sense of satisfaction.

151

Association for Asian American Studies
Resolution on Wen Ho Lee, May 26, 2000

This resolution, adopted at the annual meeting of the Association for Asian American Studies, describes the racial profiling case of Chinese American scientist Wen Ho Lee, who was targeted as a possible spy for China while working at the Los Alamos National Laboratory, a top-secret weapons research facility. Lee's case was marked by extraordinary controversy in the context of congressional assaults on alleged Clinton administration laxity in protecting American nuclear secrets from China. There was sufficient evidence of FBI and Department of Energy mishandling of the case to evoke protest from prominent scientific associations against his imprisonment and harsh treatment. Eventually, the government dropped all but one of 70 felony indictments, and Lee was ordered released from prison under a plea bargain allowing for additional, limited investigation. The case infuriated Chinese and other Asian American groups because it apparently singled out and scapegoated a scientist just because he was ethnically related to a country accused of stealing nuclear weapons secrets.

Resolution introduced by Professor L. Ling-chi Wang, Chair, Ethnic Studies, UC Berkeley, and adopted by the Association for Asian American Studies at its 17th National Conference. Scottsdale, AZ, May 26, 2000.

Resolution on Dr. Wen Ho Lee

Whereas, Dr. Wen Ho Lee, a Chinese American scientist, has devoted his entire professional career in science to the service of his country, the United States, at the Los Alamos National Laboratory, a weapons research facility managed by the University of California under a contract with the U.S. Department of Energy;

Whereas, Dr. Wen Ho Lee was summarily and arbitrarily dismissed from his job by the University of California and Secretary Bill Richardson of the U.S. Department of Energy without due process, immediately following an unfounded allegation published in the New York Times in March 1999 that he was responsible for leaking or transferring nuclear secrets to China;

Whereas, Dr. Wen Ho Lee was subsequently found to be a victim of racial profiling and discriminatory investigation by the U.S. Department of Energy and the FBI, including a rare public acknowledgment by both Attorney General Janet Reno and FBI Director Louis J. Freeh in late September 1999, that only he alone among hundreds of scientists and engineers was targeted for the criminal investigation that led to his dismissal on the one hand, and most recently, May 19, 2000, by a 4-volume investigation report of the U.S. Department of Justice, that concluded, among other findings, that the FBI "focused so narrowly on the Los Alamos Scientist that it may have missed other national security breaches," on the other hand;

Whereas, Dr. Wen Ho Lee was subjected to one year of improper and illegal search and seizure, harassment, and intimidation, including the deployment of 60 computer specialists and 200 FBI agents to keep him and his family, friends and colleagues, under intense 24-hour surveillance;

Whereas, Dr. Wen Ho Lee was subsequently and unjustly targeted for selective prosecution, solely on account of his race, by the U.S. Departments of Energy and Justice, even though the charges finally brought against him on December 10, 1999, the "mishandling of classified data," had nothing to do with his alleged spying for China and even though hundreds, if not thousands, of scientists working in the national labs had routinely done the same thing for which he had been charged;

Whereas, former CIA director John Deutch had been allowed to retain his security clearance and remain free from criminal prosecution, even though he had more seriously compromised the national security of the U.S. than Dr. Lee and had resigned from his position as the director of the CIA;

Whereas, since his arrest and incarceration on December 10, 1999, Dr. Wen Ho Lee had been put under solitary confinement and subjected to unprecedented cruel and unusual punishment while he awaits for his trial now scheduled to begin November 6, 2000, a day before the November 7 presidential election;

Whereas, the arrest and unusually severe punishment already imposed on Dr. Wen Ho Lee without a trial and the sweeping allegations made against all Asian Americans by the Cox Report have had a chilling effect on all Asian Americans in science and technology; and

Whereas, the National Science Foundation (NSF), the Committee of Concerned Scientists (CCS), the American Physical Society (APS), and the American Association for the Advancement of Science (AAAS), four prestigious science organizations, have strongly protested the inhumane and cruel treatment of Dr. Wen Ho Lee and expressed their concern over the adverse impact the case has had in attracting the best scientific talents for the nation's labs;

Be it therefore resolved, that the Association of Asian Americans Studies (AAAS) strongly condemns the mistreatment of Dr. Wen Ho Lee by the University of California, the U.S. Department of Energy, and the U.S. Department of Justice and the practice of racial profiling and discrimination in the national laboratories against Asian American scientists and engineers;

Be it further resolved, that the AAAS sends a letter to U.S. Attorney General Janet Reno, demanding that (1) all charges of "mishandling classified data" against Dr. Wen Ho Lee be dropped; (2) he be released immediately and unconditionally, pending completion of the FBI investigation of all lab employees and former CIA director John Deutch who had similarly mishandled classified data; (3) he be reinstated to his job at the Los Alamos National Laboratory with back pay; (4) a public apology be made to Dr. Lee and his family by Secretary Bill Richardson of the U.S. Department of Energy and Dr. Richard Atkinson, president of the University of California; and (5) the illegal practice of racial profiling of and discrimination against Asian Americans in the labs be terminated immediately;

Be it further resolved, that as long as Dr. Wen Ho Lee continues to be unfairly and unjustly prosecuted and persecuted, the AAAS joins the call made by the Asian Pacific Americans in Higher Education (APAHE) upon all Asian American scientists and engineers not to apply for jobs at the national labs operated under contracts with the U.S. Department of Energy as the most effective protest against the mistreatment of Dr. Wen Ho Lee and against the use racial profiling and discrimination in these facilities; and

Be it further resolved, that the AAAS calls upon all institutions of higher education to hold campus forums on the Wen Ho Lee case, to integrate Dr. Lee's case into the curriculum, and to assess and evaluate their attitude toward and treatment of Asian Americans in their respective campuses, making sure that racial profiling is not in use and Asian Americans are accorded equal and fair treatment in all aspects of campus life; and

Be it further resolved, that the AAAS calls upon all its members to endorse the Coalition Against Racial and Ethnic Stereotyping (CARES) and join in its call for a National Day of Action on June 8th, 2000, to protest the continuing incarceration of Dr. Wen Ho Lee.

Resolution introduced by Prof. L. Ling-chi Wang, Chair, Ethnic Studies, UC Berkeley

Co-signed by: 17 others.

152

Committee of 100: American Attitudes Toward Chinese Americans and Asian Americans, 2001

At the turn of the twenty-first century, U.S. policies contributed to the demise of the Soviet Union, and the United States began facing off with China as its major global rival. The inevitable result was heightened profiling of Chinese Americans, who were increasingly viewed as perpetual aliens and of dubious loyalty. The Committee of 100 formed in 1990 with prominent Chinese Americans as leaders. Its major mission was to intervene in the public arena to protect the rights of Chinese Americans. Because it was historically clear that the general American public would not distinguish Chinese from other Asian Americans, the committee has assumed the larger role of advocating for the entire group. As anti-China paranoia grew in the wake of ethnic Chinese contributions to the Democratic National Committee in the 1996 presidential election and the Wen Ho Lee nuclear espionage case, the Committee of 100 moved to avert a crisis by collaborating with the Anti-Defamation League and commissioning Marttila Communications Group and Yankelovitch in early 2001 to conduct focus groups and a national survey of attitudes toward Chinese Americans and Asian Americans. This excerpt comes from the Marttila focus groups sessions. More information from the national surveys conducted by Yankelovitch may be found in the original publication. The results were widely publicized in press conferences and served as a benchmark for tracking contemporary racial attitudes in this area.

"American Attitudes Toward Chinese Americans and Asian Americans: Including Conversations with Americans About Chinese Americans and Asian Americans." New York: Committee of 100, 2001.

Executive Summary

This executive summary identifies the key findings from ten focus groups that were conducted for the Committee of 100 during January 2001. Four groups were conducted in New York, four in Los Angeles and two in Chicago.

The focus groups were meant to provide insights into the thinking of key target audiences, most particularly upper-educated Americans, Asian Americans and, of course, Chinese Americans. Since Asian Americans comprise 1% of the national sample in the Yankelovich survey, their views could not be broken out for a statistically reliable analysis. Therefore, the focus groups are the primary source of information about the views of Chinese Americans and Asian Americans for this Committee of 100 research project.

General Observations

Even though the focus groups were held in three different regions of the country, the findings among non-Asian Americans and Asian Americans were very consistent.

On balance, the non-Asian focus group participants expressed a great deal of admiration for Asian Americans, who they consider to be a real asset to American life. There is a genuine regard for the hard work, family focus, ambition, commitment to education and the intellectual gifts of Asian Americans.

However, many negative and prejudicial judgments about Asian Americans also emerged during the focus groups. And many of these negative views were the flip side of the respect for Asian Americans because they were resentful reactions to their perceived success. Therefore, many focus group participants described Asian Americans as arrogant, aloof, keeping to themselves, disinterested in/and disapproving of the larger American community, not approachable, etc.

Key Findings

1. In the focus groups, the majority of non-Asian American participants could not make meaningful distinctions between Asian Americans of different national origins.

2. The focus group participants believed that African Americans face the most discrimination in the U.S. and Hispanics face only slightly less. Of the three racial groups tested, the participants believed Asian Americans faced the least discrimination.

3. A consensus existed among all focus group participants, regardless of race, regarding the roots of prejudice: the same words and terms emerged in all of the focus groups. A lack of education and a lack of a "proper upbringing" were the most prevalent explanations for prejudicial views.

4. Among the non-Asian participants, the positive judgments about Asian Americans were very sharply defined. There is a genuine regard for the hard work, family focus, ambition, commitment to education and the intellectual gifts of Asian Americans.

5. The most frequently mentioned criticism in the focus groups was that Asian Americans keep to themselves. "They stick together." "They are cliquish/clannish."

6. Most focus group participants believed that the substantial increase of immigrants to the U.S. during the 1990's had exacerbated interracial tension in the country. All participants, non-Asian and Asian alike, agreed an economic slowdown could create real resentments against Asian Americans among more economically vulnerable Americans.

7. The focus group participants believed the military and/or economic power of China is a looming future threat to U.S. security, a view shared by many of the non-Chinese Asian participants. Virtually all the Asian Americans and Chinese American participants indicated that their lives could be adversely affected if there was a serious showdown between the U.S. and China.

8. Non-Asian participants saw Asian Americans as being less likely to be full participants in the entire community as other Americans. They were seen to be more inward looking.

9. A discussion about the educational success of Asian American teens indicated that this issue has the potential to create some tension among non-Asian middle-class parents with college-bound kids.

10. The Asian American focus group participants believed that too many Americans see them as foreigners, or as "permanent aliens." This perception seemed to have contributed to a lack of interest in politics among the Asian American participants: only a few of the Asian American participants were interested in politics, a surprising result from such a well-educated group.

Full Report

This report summarizes the key findings from ten focus groups that were conducted for the Committee of 100 during January 2001.

In part, these focus groups were convened to instruct the questionnaire development for the national Yankelovich survey. However, the focus groups were also meant to provide deeper insights into the thinking of key target audiences, most particularly upper-educated Americans, Asian Americans and, of course, Chinese Americans.

Since Asian Americans comprise 1% of the national sample in the Yankelovich survey, their views could not be broken out for a statistically reliable analysis. Therefore, the focus groups are the primary source of information about the views of Chinese Americans and Asian Americans for this Committee of 100 research project.

The Focus Groups

Four of the ten focus groups were conducted in New York (January 10 & 11); four in Los Angeles (January 15 & 16); and two in Chicago (January 17).

The demographic composition of the focus groups in New York and Los Angeles were identical:

one group of upper-educated (no Asian Americans);
one group of a representative cross-section (no Asian Americans);
one group of Asian Americans (including Chinese Americans);
and one group of Chinese Americans.

In Chicago, the focus groups included no Asian Americans:

one group of upper-educated;
and one of a representative cross-section.

The upper-educated participants were screened for post-graduate degrees, a record of political activity and an interest in foreign affairs. In our experience, post-graduates are the Americans who pay the greatest attention to foreign policy and who are most likely to follow political/social issues closely.

New York and Los Angeles were selected because of their sizable Asian American populations; Chicago was selected because of its comparatively small Asian American population and its heartland location.

The educational levels of both the Asian American and Chinese American groups were above the norm. After consultation with Committee of 100 leaders, we decided that more educated Asian Americans—which also meant younger participants—would be more likely to be open and forthright during our conversations. Also, the higher education levels were meant to more accurately reflect the Asian American population under forty years of age.

General Observations

The focus groups were held in three different cities but the findings among non-Asian Americans and Asian Americans were very consistent.

On balance, the non-Asian focus group participants expressed a great deal of admiration for Asian Americans, who they consider to be a real asset to American life. There is a genuine regard for the hard work, family focus, ambition, commitment to education and the intellectual gifts of Asian Americans.

However, many negative and prejudicial judgments about Asian Americans also emerged during the focus groups. And many of these negative views were the flip side of the respect for Asian Americans because they were resentful reactions to their perceived success. Therefore, many focus group participants described Asian Americans as arrogant, aloof, keeping to themselves, disinterested in/and disapproving of the larger American community, not approachable, etc.

In this regard, some of the prejudicial views about Asian Americans are similar to those about Jews, because they are reactions to perceptions of success. For example, during the past decade, prejudicial attitudes toward Jews have increasingly focused on the issue of too much Jewish power in the U.S., which is obviously an expression of resentment about Jewish success in America.

The negative perceptions about Asian Americans that were revealed in the focus groups are real concerns and they undermined the generally positive perceptions. Nevertheless, we do not believe that these negative views outweigh the very strong positive impressions about Asian Americans that were revealed in the focus groups.

On the following pages, we have identified what we believe to be the key findings from the focus groups

1. *In the focus groups, the majority of non-Asian American participants could not make meaningful distinctions between Asian Americans of different national origins. Therefore, the focus group participants had very few distinct impressions of Chinese Americans in contrast to Asian Americans of other national origins.*

The Yankelovich survey confirmed Americans' inability to distinguish between Chinese Americans and other Asian Americans.

Only a handful of non-Asian focus group participants, 50% of who were postgraduates, could make meaningful distinctions between Asian Americans of different national origins and they believed few other non-Asians could do so. To the extent they could offer impressions, the non-Asians believed the Japanese Americans were the likeliest to be successful at business, and there was some limited awareness of tension between Korean Americans and African Americans. . . .

2. *The focus group participants believed that African Americans face the most discrimination in the U.S. and Hispanics face only slightly less. Of the three racial groups tested, the participants believed Asian Americans faced the least discrimination.*

The Yankelovich national survey confirmed this rank order. However, the same poll found striking levels of anti-Asian American views.

All of the focus group participants, including Asian Americans, agreed that African Americans face the most discrimination, and that Hispanics still face considerable discrimination but less than African Americans. . . .

Many Caucasian participants believed that Asian Americans do not face a great deal of discrimination. A few younger, more well educated Asian Americans and Chinese Americans (more so in NYC) believed Asian Americans faced minimal discrimination.

The Yankelovich survey confirmed the rank order that emerged in the focus groups—but it also found significant levels of anti-Asian American prejudice: the Yankelovich survey ALSO found:

23% of Americans would be uncomfortable voting for an Asian American candidate for president.

24% of Americans would disapprove of someone in their family marrying an Asian American.

17% of Americans would be upset if Asian Americans moved into their neighborhood.

3. A consensus existed among all focus group participants, regardless of race, regarding the roots of prejudice: the same words and terms emerged in all of the focus groups. A lack of education and a lack of a "proper upbringing" were the most prevalent explanations for prejudicial views. . . .

Most of the focus group participants mentioned a lack of education, which produced a minimal understanding of, and respect for, cultural differences, as probably the most prevalent explanation for prejudicial views. . . .

A lack of "proper upbringing" was mentioned as frequently by the focus group participants. While some thought that an individual could change his/her prejudicial views over time, most thought it was very difficult to overcome a lack of proper family values. . . .

Economic insecurity was also seen to be a major factor in the formation and/or the reinforcement of discriminatory views. . . .

Ignorance: the word ignorance emerged in virtually all of the groups, and by it, participants meant a willingness to accept racial stereotypes without considering alternative views.

Fear: the word fear emerged in all of the groups. To the participants, this meant fear of the unknown, an emotional fear—not physical fear.

Personal insecurity, and a lack of self-esteem were thought to be key personal factors that breed resentment and a jealousy of others.

Finally, the focus group participants thought the lack of exposure or interaction with other groups was a major contributor to racial prejudice because it preserved prejudicial views.

4. Among the non-Asian focus group participants, the positive judgments about Asian Americans were very sharply defined and emerged without any prompting.

When considered together, these positive perceptions reveal a very clear, and ultimately, very flattering portrait of Asian Americans. . . .

Asian Americans are seen to be exceptionally hard working.

They are seen to have strong family values. They respect their elders.

The Asian American family/community places a great emphasis on education. They are seen to be people who truly believe education is the path to future success.

Asian Americans are thought to be very smart. The community produces a disproportionate share of academic superstars.

They are very ambitious and industrious. They are interested in owning their own businesses.

Asian Americans have great respect for their history and culture.

Asian Americans are talented and creative.

Finally, Asian Americans are well mannered. They are quiet. They don't cause problems and don't complain. They are not troublemakers.

5. *While clearly troublesome, the negative judgments about Asian Americans that emerged in the focus groups were less clearly defined, less top-of-the-mind than the positive views. Nevertheless, an understandable "negative portrait" emerged. . . .*

Although the negative judgments about Asian Americans were less top-of-the-mind, the same criticisms were mentioned in most of the groups and when they are considered together, they create a coherent statement:

First, unlike the prejudicial attitudes towards African Americans and Hispanics that stem from many negative judgments about the respective communities, the prejudicial views against Asian Americans are frequently resentful reactions to perceived Asian American success.

Second, the non-Asian focus group participants appeared to have a distant, and emotionally cool relationship with the Asian American community. This "emotional distance" seemed to be at the heart of many of the other criticisms. The Caucasian participants indicated that they had much less interaction with Asian Americans than they did with African Americans and Hispanics.

> The most frequently mentioned criticism in the focus groups was that Asian Americans keep to themselves. "They stick together." "They are cliquish/clannish."
> "Asian Americans have a tendency to be arrogant." "They look down on others."
> "They are not approachable." "They are not friendly."
> "Asian Americans cannot be fully trusted." "They are two-faced."
> "Asian Americans are secretive and insular." "They have a hidden agenda."
>   "They won't reveal what they are really thinking."
> "They do not speak English and don't want to."
> "They are only interested in doing business with other Asian Americans, making it very difficult for non-Asians to conduct business with them."
> "In business, they are only interested in money—and don't care about establishing enduring business relationships."
> Some participants from every focus group said they were bad drivers. Asian Americans humorously agreed. . . .

6. *Most focus group participants believed that the substantial increase of immigrants to the U.S. during the 1990's had exacerbated interracial tension in the country. All focus group participants, non-Asian and Asian alike, agreed that an economic slowdown could create real resentments against Asian Americans among more economically vulnerable Americans. . . .*

A majority of all focus group participants, non-Asian and Asian alike, believed that the explosion of immigration during the 1990's has heightened interracial tensions in the country.

The participants agreed that the economic boom of the 1990's had minimized popular resentment about the growth of the immigrant population but they believed that these resentments, coupled with an economic slowdown, could create serious problems for the Asian American community. The Asian American focus group participants certainly felt it could.

First, all participants agreed that an economic downturn could exacerbate concerns about all newly arrived immigrants competing for and taking away "American" jobs.

Second, a slowdown coupled with the perceptions about the industriousness and hard work of Asian Americans—could contribute to a specific backlash against Asian Americans.

The Asian American focus group participants in Los Angeles believed the rapidly growing number of Asian Americans in their area has focused more attention on them and has sparked concerns about their potential to compete for jobs.

We know from our previous work that xenophobic attitudes are powerful forces in prejudicial views. These anti-immigrant Americans believe that "Americans" should be taken care of before newly arrived immigrants receive any special consideration.

The Yankelovich survey found:

28% of Americans believe that influx of Asian Americans during the past decade has been BAD for America.

35% of Americans agree that "It bothers me to see immigrants succeeding more than Americans who were born here."

24% agree that "Chinese Americans are taking away too many jobs from Americans."

7. *The focus group participants believed the military and/or economic power of China is a looming future threat to U.S. security, a view shared by many of the non-Chinese Asian participants.*

Virtually all the Asian Americans and Chinese American participants indicated that their lives could be adversely affected if there was a serious showdown between the U.S. and China.

The Yankelovich survey found that two-thirds of Americans see China as a future threat to U.S. security and one-third questioned Chinese American loyalty to the U.S. . . .

Virtually all the Asian Americans and Chinese American participants indicated that their lives would be adversely affected if there was a serious showdown between U.S. and China because other Americans would call their basic loyalty to the U.S. into question. There was a strong consensus on this matter.

The Yankelovich survey found widespread concern about China. The survey also found major reservations about Chinese American loyalty to the U.S.:

Two-thirds (68%) see China as a future threat to the U.S.

61% have an unfavorable impression of the government of China.

32% of Americans agree that Chinese Americans are more loyal to China than the U.S.

8. *In the focus groups, Asian Americans were seen to be less likely to be full participants in the entire community as other Americans. They were seen to be more inward looking. . . .*

Among the non-Asian American participants, there was a strong sense that Asian Americans are more inward-looking than other Americans; that they are fundamentally less interested in the affairs of their local community than their fellow citizens. . . .

Several non-Asians said that Asian Americans only came to the U.S. to make money before they return to their native land.

Several Asian American participants acknowledged that Asian Americans were more inward looking. However, younger Asian American participants, in particular, believed that this was a natural occurrence in the assimilation of Asian Americans into U.S. life, no different than the experience of other immigrants in the past.

The Yankelovich survey found:

28% agree that Chinese Americans are hard to get close to, make friends with.

21% agree that Chinese Americans don't care what happens to any but their own kind.

9. *A discussion about the educational success of Asian America teens indicated that this issue has the potential to create some tension among non-Asian middle-class parents with college-bound kids.*

The educational success of Asian American teens was well understood in the focus groups. The participants were very much aware that Asian American teens have won a disproportionate share of college admissions at the best schools in the country.

It is also clear this is a potentially divisive issue that is slowly moving to the surface and may have already begun to create some tensions among middle-class parents with college-bound kids. Several parents of college students spoke ruefully about the experience of their own kids struggling to compete against these Asian American academic superstars; a few expressed their strong disapproval of admission policies that so strongly favored one ethnic group. . . .

On first consideration, a majority of the focus group participants were strong supporters of merit-based college admissions. However, when confronted with the reality of Asian American acceptance rates at the best schools, some of the non-Asian focus group participants became increasingly troubled about this imbalance and began to more carefully consider the merits of admission policies that also attempted to recruit racially representative classes.

Nevertheless at the end of lengthy discussions about merit-based acceptance policies verses admission policies that also strive to reflect the general population, a narrow majority of the participants continued to believe that college-based admissions should be based exclusively on merit. . . .

10. *The Asian American focus group participants believed that too many Americans see them as foreigners, or as "permanent aliens."*

This perception seemed to have contributed to a lack of interest in politics among the Asian American participants: only a few of the Asian American participants were interested in politics, a surprising result from such a well-educated group.

A clear majority (not all) of the Asian Americans and Chinese American participants believed that they are seen as foreigners or "permanent aliens" by too many non-Asian Americans.

Almost all the participants could describe disturbing or humorous incidents in which this prejudicial attitude was revealed by non-Asian Americans, most frequently through comments such as, "Where are you from?" "You speak very good English." etc. . . .

Finally, when compared to the very well developed channels of political communication in both the Jewish and African American community, the channels of political communication within the Asian American community seem very undeveloped

153

2001 Obon *Schedule in Hawai'i, May 2001*

In Japan, Obon *is a Buddhist festival celebrated each August to welcome the spirits of the departed, who are said to visit their communities at that time of year. There are religious services and dances,* bon odori, *specifically created and rehearsed for public performances. Japanese immigrant communities re-created this festival in many American neighborhoods and, like the rest of their culture,* bon odori *gradually assumed different forms from the homeland versions. Indeed, some of the dances reflect themes like the World War II heroism of Japanese American troops or sports like baseball. In Hawai'i, especially, the festivals attract devotees who tour the various sites throughout the summer for the opportunity to socialize and dance. It is possible, therefore, to interpret the perpetuation of Obon among Japanese American communities as an indication of ongoing ethnic consciousness. Since so few immigrants have arrived from Japan since 1920, the maintenance of ethnic customs has been transferred to generations increasingly separated from the homeland and immigrants. To the surprise of those who have long predicted the demise of the group through assimilation, Japanese Americans have continued and reinvigorated traditional practices. This 2001 schedule of public dances in Hawai'i illustrates the strength of the culture.*

The Hawaii Herald, May 18, 2001, A-13.

2001 OBON SCHEDULE

Big Island

Daifukujii Soto Mission (Kona)	July 14	S	7:30 P.M.	322–3524
Hamakua Jodo Mission	August 11	S	8 P.M.	775–0965
Hawi Jodo Mission	August 4	S	8 P.M.	889–5456
Higashi Hongwanji Mission	August 11	S	8 P.M.	935–8968
Hilo Honganji Mission	July 28	S	8 P.M.	935–8331

Hilo Meishoin	July 14	S	8 P.M.	935–6996
Hilo Nichiren Mission	August 18	S	7 P.M.	959–8894
Hilo Taishoji Soto Mission	July 21	S	7:30 P.M.	935–8407
Honohina Hongwanji	August 25	S	Following 7 P.M. service	963–6451
Honokaa Hongwanji Mission	July 21	S	8 P.M.	775–7232
Honomu Hongwanji Mission	June 30	S	8 P.M.	963–6032
Honpa Hongwanji Hilo Betsuin	August 3–4	F/S	Following 7 P.M. service	961–6677
Int'l Festival at Kaiko'o Mall	August 10	F	7–9 P.M.	934–0177
Kamuela Hongwanji Mission	August 18	S	8 P.M.	885–4481
Keei Hongwanji Fukyojo	June 30	S	7 P.M.	323–2993
Kohala Hongwanji Mission	July 7	S	8 P.M.	775–7232
Kohala Jodo Mission (Kapaau)	July 14	S	8 P.M.	889–6719
Kona Hongwanji Mission	July 7	S	7 P.M.	323–2993
Kona Koyasan Dalshiji Mission	Aug. 11	S	Following 6 P.M. service	324–1741
Kurtistown Jodo Mission	July 28	S	Following 7 P.M. service	966–9777
Paauilo Hongwanji Mission	July 14	S	8 P.M.	776–1369
Paauilo Kongoji Mission	August 4	S	Following 6 P.M. service	776–1474
Pahoa YBA	August 25	S	Following 7 P.M. service	966–9981
Papaaloa Hongwanji	July 28	S	Following 7 P.M. service	962–6340
Papaikou Hongwanji Mission	June 23	S	Following 7 P.M. service	964–1640
Puna Hongwanji Mission	July 7	S	Following 7 P.M. service	966–9981

Kauai

West Kauai Hongwanji Hanapepe Temple	June 29–30	F/S	8 P.M.	338–1537
Kapaa Honpa Hongwanji	August 3–4	F/S	8 P.M.	822–4667
Kapaa Jodo Mission	July 20–21	F/S	8 P.M.	822–4319
Kauai Soto Zen Temple	July 27–28	F/S	8 P.M.	335–3521
Koloa Jodo Mission	June 22–23	F/S	8 P.M.	742–6735

Lihue Honpa Hongwanji	July 6–7	F/S	8 P.M.	245–6262
Waimea Higashi Hongwanji	Aug. 10–11	F/S	8 P.M.	338–1847
West Kauai Hongwanji Waimea Temple	June 8–9	F/S	8 P.M.	338–1537
Waimea Shingon Mission	July 13–14	F/S	8 P.M.	338–1854
West Kauai Hongwanji Koloa Temple	June 15–16	F/S	8 P.M.	338–1537

Maui

Kahului Hongwanji Mission	June 29–30	F/S	8 P.M.	871–4732
Kahului Jodo Mission	Aug. 10–11	F/S	8 P.M.	871–4911
Kula Shofukuji Mission	Aug. 25	S	8 P.M.	661–0466
Lahaina Hongwanji Mission	Aug. 3–4	F/S	7:30 P.M.	661–0640
Lahaina Jodo Mission	July 7	S	8 P.M.	661–4304
Lahaina Shingon Mission	June 23	S	8 P.M.	661–0466
Makawao Hongwanji Mission	July 20–21	F/S	7:30 P.M.	572–7229
Maui Memorial Park	July 12	R	6 P.M.	242–9792
Paia Mantokuji Mission	July 13–14	F/S	8 P.M.	579–8051
Paia Rinzai Zen Mission	August 18	S	8 P.M.	579–9921
Puunene Nichiren Mission	June 16	S	8 P.M.	871–4831
Wailuku Hongwanji Mission	July 27–28	F/S	8 P.M.	244–0406
Wailuku Jodo Mission	June 22	F	8 P.M.	244–0066
Wailuku Shingon Mission	August 17	F	8 P.M.	244–3800

Oahu

Aiea Hongwanji Mission	August 25	S	7:30 P.M.	488–5685
Aiea Soto Mission Taiheiji	August 10–11	F/S	8 P.M.	488–6794
Ewa Hongwanji Mission	June 23	S	7:30 P.M.	681–5222
Haleiwa Jodo Mission	July 13–14	F/S	8 P.M.	637–4382
Haleiwa Shingon Mission	July 20–21	F/S	8 P.M.	637–4423
Hawaii Okinawa Center-Matsuri	Sept. 15	S	6 P.M.	676–5400
Higashi Hongwanji Betsuin	July 27–28	F/S	7:30 P.M.	531–9088
Honpa Hongwanji Mission	June 29–30	F/S	7:30 P.M.	536–7044
Jikoen Temple	July 27–28	F/S	7 P.M.	845–3422
Jodo Mission of Hawaii	August 17–18	F/S	7:30 P.M.	949–3995
Kahuku Hongwanji Mission	August 11	S	7:30 P.M.	293–5268
Kailua Hongwanji Mission	July 28	S	7 P.M.	262–4560
Kaneohe Higashi Hongwanji	July 6	F	7 P.M.	247–2661
Koboji Shingon Mission	July 13–14	F/S	7 P.M.	841–7033
Mililani Hongwanji Mission	Aug. 17–18	F/S	7:30 P.M.	625–0925

Moiliili Hongwanji Mission	July 6–7	F/S	7:30 P.M.	949–1659
Okinawan Festival, Kapiolani Park	September 1–2	S/Su		676–5400
Palolo Higashi Hongwanji Mission	August 3–4	F/S	7 P.M.	732–1491
Pearl City Hongwanji Mission	July 27–28	F/S	7:30 P.M.	455–1680
Rissho Kosei-Kai Hawaii Kyokai	July 20–21	F/S	7 P.M.	455–3212
Shingon Mission of Hawaii	Aug. 10–11	F/S	7 P.M.	941–5663
Shinshu Kyokai Mission	July 20–21	F/S	7:30 P.M.	973–0156
Soto Mission Betsuin	August 17–18	F/S	7:30 P.M.	537–9409
Tendai Mission of Hawaii	July 14	S	7 P.M.	595–2556
Wahiawa Hongwanji Mission	June 29–30	F/S	7:30 P.M.	622–4320
Wahiawa Ryusenji Soto Mission	July 27–28	F/S	7:30 P.M.	622–1429
Waialua Hongwanji Mission	July 7	S	7:30 P.M.	638–4895
Waianae Hongwanji Mission	July 21	S	7:30 P.M.	696–3125
Waipahu Cultural Garden Park	June 9	S	6–10 P.M.	677–0110
Waipahu Hongwanji Mission	July 13–14	F/S	7:30 P.M.	677–4221
Waipahu Soto Zen Mission	August 3–4	F/S	8 P.M.	671–3103

154

Norman Mineta, Speech at National Japanese American Memorial Foundation, June 29, 2001

A ribbon-cutting ceremony marked the opening of the National Japanese American Memorial dedicated to Japanese American patriotism during World War II. The memorial, the only one in Washington, DC, for a single ethnic group, is large and elaborate; it is strategically situated close to the nation's Capitol and to Union Station. The Japanese American community raised $14 million for its construction and pledged millions more for educational outreach by committing to partnerships with the Smithsonian Institution's Asian Pacific American Program and the Japanese American National Museum. Norman Mineta, Secretary of Transportation, delivered one of the keynote speeches at the ceremony. In it, he recalled that it was a decade since he and colleagues had introduced legislation in Congress to authorize construction of this memorial. Mineta was then a congressman from San Jose, California. As a regent at the Smithsonian, he was instrumental in the establishment of the APA Program in 1997. Mineta became the first Asian Pacific American to serve in the Cabinet, as Secretary of Commerce under President Bill Clinton. The memorial itself was controversial, as a few dissidents on the board challenged the suitability of adding the name and "creed" of then-JACL leader Mike Masaoka (reprinted in this volume). Mineta's message of triumph over adversity celebrated Japanese American military heroism and sacrifice in the face of massive injustice, and the redemptive nature of the apology and redress in 1988.

Norman Mineta, "Remarks at National Japanese American Memorial Ribbon Cutting Ceremony." Washington, DC, June 29, 2001. Printed with permission of the author.

Thanks to all of you for being here on this very historic day.

It is difficult to believe that more than 10 years have passed since the legislation authorizing the construction of this memorial was introduced in the Congress. And yet here we are on the day that the National Japanese American Memorial opens to the public.

Arriving at this day has taken tremendous leadership.

It has taken leadership in the Congress by statesmen like Senator Daniel Inouye and Congressman Bob Matsui, along with so many others. It has taken leadership by the dedicated men and women who have led the Memorial Foundation down the road to this success. . . .

This memorial commemorates a great American tragedy.

The forced evacuation and internment of more than 120,000 loyal Japanese Americans, simply on the basis of our race, stands as one of the greatest mass abrogations of civil liberties in our history.

But the message of this Memorial is not just one of tragedy. It is a message of faith in this nation, a message of hope, and ultimately a message of national redemption.

There are many reasons that I am proud to be an American of Japanese ancestry.

I am proud of the sacrifices my mother and father made to come to this country, to make it their home, and to build a bright future for their children.

And I am proud of the contributions our community has made to this great Nation.

But above all, I am proud that, even in the face of discrimination and the denial of our most basic civil rights, we did not lose faith in the promise of what America could be.

That faith was reflected in the thousands of Nisei who volunteered from Hawaii, and even directly from the camps, to put their lives on the line to defend this country, and to defend the cause of freedom, as part of the 100th Infantry Battalion and the 442nd Regimental Combat Team in the European theater of operations in World War II.

That faith was reflected in those who volunteered to serve this country in the Military Intelligence Service in the Pacific theater of operations.

That faith was reflected in those who challenged the internment in the courts and challenged the Nation to live up to the promises of our great Constitution.

And that faith was reflected in our national movement for redress—because in our hearts we believed that our fellow Americans would one day recognize the internment for the injustice that it was.

As we stand here today, we know that our faith was rewarded.

The passage of the Civil Liberties Act of 1988 brought a formal apology on behalf of the United States Government, and signaled a new national understanding of the place of the internment in American history.

The success of redress reminded all of us that the principles of our Constitution are only as strong as the commitment that we bring to them.

And it reminded us that our commitment to those principles must never waver.

The National Japanese American Memorial commemorates that story, in all its aspects.

It speaks of the injustice of the evacuation and internment.

It speaks of the sacrifices that we, as Americans of Japanese ancestry, made on behalf of this our country.

And it speaks of the redemption of our faith in our fellow Americans.

This Memorial embodies our national journey from injustice to understanding.

And that is a story worthy of celebration by all Americans on this very historic day.

155

U.S. Catholic Bishops Welcome Asian
Pacific Americans, July 2001

"Christ was born in Asia!" Thus begins the pastoral letter from the National Conference of Catholic Bishops, part of a sweeping institutional move to incorporate a more congenial attitude toward Asian Pacific American Catholics. This followed a pastoral statement adopted in 2000, "Welcoming the Stranger Among Us: Unity in Diversity," that challenged local parishes to provide a more "genuine spirit of welcome" to newcomers. The letter notes that the U.S. Immigration and Naturalization Service, as well as the Asian Synod of Bishops, includes Western Asia or the Middle East as part of Asia. Thus, all the major religions of the world—Buddhism, Islam, Christianity, Judaism, and Hinduism—emanated from this "continent," as well as other traditions such as Confucianism, Sikhism, and Taoism. This document is a part of a long tradition of religious activity targeting Asian communities in the United States and encouraging Asian American clergy and lay activists to be involved in and support particular congregations. It pulls few punches in relating the racism faced by Asians in America, including the Church's own glass-ceiling issues, and provides numerous concrete reasons and ways the Catholic Church might work to improve conditions.

Thanks to Cecile Motus for providing this document. "Asian and Pacific Presence: Harmony in Faith." Washington: United States Catholic Conference, Migration and Refugee Services, 2001.

Asian and Pacific Presence: Harmony in Faith

This "being Asian" is best discovered and affirmed not in confrontation and opposition, but in the spirit of complementarity and harmony. In this framework of complementarity and harmony, the church can communicate the Gospel in a way that is faithful both to her own tradition and to the Asian soul.

—Ecclesia in Asia, #6

I. Introduction

Dear brothers and sisters, in a spirit of heartfelt pastoral concern for the Asian and Pacific people in our midst, we bishops of the United States write this letter with loving assurance, to recognize and to affirm their presence and prominence in the Lord's house. We pray that this pastoral letter will facilitate a fuller participation of the Asian and Pacific communities in our local churches and will encourage more solicitous ministry with them to empower them to take on active leadership roles in every level of church life. . . .

In November 2000, we bishops in the pastoral statement, *Welcoming the Stranger Among Us, Unity in Diversity* marked out ways that the Church in the United States, a church of many races and cultures might become more fully a sacrament of unity and universality. As a direct application of that statement we welcome our Asian and Pacific sisters and brothers and encourage all members of the Church in the United States to do the same. . . .

Christ Was Born in Asia

Pope John Paul II begins his Apostolic Exhortation, *Ecclesia in Asia*, "The church in Asia sings the praises of the 'God of salvation' (Ps. 68:20) for choosing to initiate his saving plan on Asian soil . . . In the 'fullness of time' (Gal. 4:4) he sent his only begotten Son, Jesus Christ the Savior, who took flesh as an Asian!" He goes on to point out that, "Because Jesus was born, lived, died and rose from the dead in the Holy Land, that small portion of Western Asia became a land of promise and hope for all mankind."

Many may be surprised to hear that Jesus was born in Asia. The Asian Synod of Bishops, the Congregation for the Evangelization of Peoples, the United States Immigration and Naturalization Service and the art world describe as common practice the continent of Asia as Western Asia or the Middle East, Central Asia, South Asia, Southeast Asia and East Asia. This is broader than a commonly held understanding of Asia as South, Southeast and East Asia.

The history of the Church in Asia is as old as the Church herself. "From this land, through the preaching of the Gospel in the power of the Holy Spirit, the church went forth to 'make disciples of all nations' (Mt. 28:19)." Christianity spread from Jerusalem to Antioch, to Rome and beyond. Ancient tradition relates how in the first century, St. Thomas the Apostle preached and was martyred in India and thus the subcontinent traces its Christian roots to apostolic times. . . .

A Teaching Moment

Today, the Asian and Pacific communities in the United States, native-born and immigrants, span several generations. Many among the Chinese, Japanese, Filipino, Indian, Guamanian, Samoan and Tongan Americans trace their heritage to more than a century of migration; yet Asian and Pacific peoples have remained by and large until very recently, a nearly invisible community in the Church in the United States. The absence of Asian and Pacific Islanders in the episcopal leadership may be a factor. Some among us bishops have endeavored to become informed through a genuine pastoral love and concern, and some have responded to the generous invitation extended by Asian and Pacific episcopal conferences and individual bishops to be present at gatherings in their homelands. . . .

The beginning of the third millennium is a teaching moment because of the tremendous increase in Asian and Pacific presence across the United States. It is also a teaching moment because of the welcoming spirit to which we are called in *Ecclesia in America* and in the recent pastoral statement, *Welcoming the Stranger Among Us: Unity in Diversity*, "the Church in the United States is enjoined to offer a genuine and suitable welcome to newcomers, to share together as sisters and brothers belonging at the same table, and to work side by side to improve the quality of life for society's marginalized members. To underline the spirit of conversion, communion and solidarity with newcomers called for in *Unity in Diversity*, this pastoral letter focuses attention on the little known Asian and Pacific rooted communities as well as new immigrants that we may learn more about them and with them; and that they are acknowledged as an integral part of the Church in the United States. . . .

II. Harmony Among Diverse Realities

Homelands. Asian and Pacific Americans come from many national backgrounds, speak many different languages, and encompass a wide variety of physical and social characteristics. Their homelands include 51 Asian countries in geographic regions commonly referred to as Near East, Western Asia or Middle East, Central Asia, South Asia, Southeast Asia and East Asia . . . ; and 22 Pacific Island states . . . of three indigenous population groups—Polynesians, Micronesians and Melanesians. Within this vast continent, two-thirds of the world's population lives.

Language. Linguistically, Asian and Pacific communities are even more diverse. Each country has its own language or languages. For example, India has many languages as well as Hindi the official language, and China has over a hundred dialects, which are like distinct spoken languages. The Philippines has eight major languages and 87 dialects. Indonesia's official language is Bahasa Indonesia but many other languages are used by distinct ethnic groups such as the Dayak, Balinese, Madurese and Batak. In the Pacific Islands French and English are commonly used as well as almost a thousand indigenous languages of the islanders. Sometimes a source of division for immigrants here, these languages are a sign of unity for these people and a source of joy for them when they gather with one another.

Religion. This region is the birthplace of the great religions of the world: Hinduism, Buddhism, Judaism, Islam and Christianity. It is also the birthplace of other social and religious traditions including Taoism, Confucianism, and Sikhism.

Ecclesia. The presence of Eastern Catholic Churches brings an ecclesial diversity. They are both cultural and ecclesial minorities struggling to maintain their identities. There are twenty one Eastern Catholic Churches all of which are represented by faithful and clergy and, in many cases, hierarchies in the United States. . . .

Asian and Pacific Catholics in the United States

Many Asian and Pacific people have been present in the Church of the United States since the 1800s. The presence of Eastern Catholics in the United States is primarily the result of late nineteenth-century migration from Eastern Europe and the more recent turmoil and upheaval in the Middle East. "The first wave of immigration came especially from Western Ukraine; and then it involved the nations of the Middle East. This made it pastorally necessary to establish an Eastern Catholic hierarchy for these Catholic immigrants and their descendants. Therefore, we cannot but rejoice that the Eastern Churches have in recent times taken root in America alongside the Latin Churches present there from the beginning, thus making the catholicity of the Lord's Church appear more clear."

Among the Asian workers who toiled on the transcontinental railroad and among the agricultural workers opening up the west, some were Catholic and their Catholicism had deep roots. Joseph Sadoc Alemany, O.P., the first Archbishop of San Francisco, in 1856 invited a Chinese priest to minister to the Chinese migrant laborers. On December 9, 1884, the Paulist Fathers took over the administration of Old St. Mary's to begin a mission to the Chinese which continues to the present day. . . .

In 1912, finding no one who spoke his language, a young Japanese Catholic in Los Angeles wrote to the Bishop of Hakodate, his home town in Japan, to ask whether it was possible to confess his sins by registered mail and be pardoned in the same way. The church's pastoral care for the Japanese on the West Coast originated with this request. . . .

In the early 1920s, Archbishop Edward J. Hanna of San Francisco founded the Catholic Filipino Club in Stockton to provide hospitality to newcomers. . . .

Today, the number of Asian and Pacific Catholics in the United States is a difficult and complex question. Hard data are difficult to obtain or non-existent. . . .

III. Sharing Gifts and Promoting Harmony

From its inception, the United States of America has been enriched by the gifts brought to its shores from countries and cultures the world over. Likewise, the Catholic Church in the United States has been blessed by the traditions of Catholics from almost every nation on earth.

The contributions of Asian and Pacific communities were presented in a consultation in 1997 for the Bishops Committee On Migration which stated: "We believe strongly that this is a moment of special grace for the Catholic Church in the United States. As Asian and Pacific communities we bring a strong sense of family with a loving respect for the elderly and a profound and fervent religious faith. We contribute a spirituality which is eastern and rooted in Asian and Pacific cultures. We also seek to live in harmony with each other and with the whole of creation. We deepen and challenge our understanding of the meaning of the universal Church, enabling all of us to be a church which is complete and whole." . . .

Profound Spirituality and Religiosity

Asian and Pacific Catholic Americans and immigrants migrated with the experience and sensibilities of the great religions and spiritual traditions of the world together with Christianity: Judaism, Islam, Hinduism, Buddhism, Taoism, Confucianism, Zoroastrianism, Jainism, Sikhism and Shintoism. In its best expressions, the important values of harmonious relationship with one another, with society, and with nature; the realization of a cosmic design that gives meaning to an apparently chaotic world; the belief in salvation from the senseless sufferings in this world; the necessity of silence and contemplation, detachment from the world, simplicity, frugal living, consonance with neighbors and all of creation, respect for all life, non-violence; the spirit of hard work—all these shape the cultures of the peoples of Asia and the Pacific Islands. Their experience of the great religions and spiritual traditions teach them how to live with, and have the deepest respect for these traditions. Indeed, the Holy Father said on April 19, 1998, "We want to listen to what the Spirit says to the churches of Asia that they may proclaim Christ in the context of Hinduism, Buddhism, Shintoism and all those currents of thought and life which were already rooted in Asia before the preaching of the Gospel arrived."

Despite the fact that many Christian immigrants from Asia have suffered persecution in their homelands, we are mindful that their religiosity has roots in their Asian spiritual traditions. Their experience demonstrates the values of these religions and spiritual traditions, and how these values await their fulfillment in the revelation of Jesus Christ. . . .

The Contributions of Clergy and Religious

Asian and Pacific American communities have been accompanied to the United States by priests, religious sisters and brothers who speak the languages of their homelands. Most Asian and Pacific priests and religious serve not only their ethnic groups. They are pastors and associates in parishes, teachers and principals of Catholic schools throughout the country. In many instances, Asian and Pacific priests and religious establish religious education programs in the native language, in the parishes where they serve. Volunteer teachers are usually from particular ethnic groups. For instance, Hmong, Tongan and Samoan-speaking priests, religious and deacons work with lay leaders for family evangelization programs.

Vocations are quite high both in terms of numbers and proportions to the current population. In 1999, 9% of those ordained to the priesthood in the United States were of Asian or Pacific heritage. . . .

Some bishops have established Chinese, Korean and Vietnamese personal parishes or missions. Pastoral Centers for small ethnic communities like the Khmhu, Laotian, Cambodian, Hmong, Tongan and Samoan have been organized in several dioceses and multiple pastoral centers in different parts of the country provide ministry to the Vietnamese, Korean, Chinese, Japanese. These centers not only offer catechesis, bible studies, prayer services, and linguistically appropriate religious education materials, but also provide a place to experience one's language and culture, and affirm one's cultural and ethnic roots. Special tribute must be given to priests, religious and lay leaders from the United States who have worked hard to learn Asian languages and cultures in order to become more effective ministers.

On the part of specific Asian and Pacific Islander groups, creative and effective ways have begun in the parishes and sometimes regionally to bring together and support community development and interaction with each other and with other cultural groups. Chinese, Korean, Samoan and Tongan families gather for bible study. Korean, Laotian, Khmhu, Indonesian and Vietnamese youth hold summer camps at which catechesis is conducted in their own languages. The Samoans, Tongans, Filipinos, Koreans, Chinese and Vietnamese have vibrant music ministries and choirs.

Some Asian and Pacific ethnic communities have successfully formed national structures like the Hmong-American Catholic National Association; Federation of Vietnamese Clergy, Religious and Lay Leaders, the Korean Priests Association of America and Canada, the Indian American Catholic Association, Inc., and the National Filipino Ministry Council to help the new groups in building collective identity. Unfortunately, sometimes these communities exist side by side, mainly in isolation, with little or no connection with diocesan structures or with other ethnic and cultural communities in the Church.

We bishops hope that this pastoral letter will motivate members of the Church at every level to build on these achievements and strengthen ties to the local church. . . .

Empowering Leadership for Solidarity and Community
Clergy and Religious. Most of the Asian and Pacific clergy and religious sisters and brothers ministering in the United States received their training in their home countries. Several are on limited assignments from their home dioceses or religious congregations. The basic approaches to ministry may differ from those currently in the United States, e.g., place of the priest in the Catholic

community, the role of lay leadership (particularly the role of women), the U.S. parish structure and sense of stewardship, devotional practices, and religious organizations. Some immigrant priests and religious have difficulty integrating into their new situation and connect more with their home diocese than with their U.S. diocese, with priests and religious from their own land rather than with priests and religious in their new land. All of this requires time and is a matter of proportion.

From the perspective of the Asian and Pacific priests and religious, many have quietly experienced deep frustration in their ministry in the United States. Some express a sense of isolation and loneliness, and a lack of support from the diocese. Several Asian and Pacific priests and religious associations have been formed and meet regularly. These organizations have helped in building up morale, in strengthening a missionary spirituality and in introducing their membership to American pastoral approaches.

Lay Leadership. All lay people are missionaries; and the arena of their missionary work is the vast and complex worlds of politics, economics, industry, education, the media, science, technology, the arts and sport. "In many Asian countries, lay people are already serving as true missionaries, reaching out to fellow Asians who might never have contact with clergy and religious." The enormous potential and charisma of the laity as equal partners in the common mission of the church cannot be emphasized enough. The ultimate responsibility for ministry with one's ethnic community belongs to the community itself. Through mutual cooperation, the Asian and Pacific communities can provide religious education for youth, care for the elderly, enter into intercultural and interreligious dialogue, and care for the poor. Asian and Pacific Catholics have come of age and are not merely objects of the church's pastoral care. Rather they have and should continue to grow as participating agents and coworkers in the apostolic mission of Jesus Christ.

Structure. Each immigrant group has sought to maintain its community and for Asian and Pacific groups this is particularly important. At the beginning of the 20th century, bishops established personal parishes. During the later half of the century, many other structures were put in place. Now there are multicultural parishes, pastoral centers, ethnic liaisons or consultants, missions and chaplaincies. Sometimes space for liturgy and/or programs is provided. Where communities are small, language resources limited, the community scattered, a pastoral center or a roving chaplain provides the sense of a "home away from home." On the other hand, it is important to balance the needs of the community for its sense of security with the need for local church to experience what it truly means to be catholic.

Solidarity. A major challenge is overcoming national divisions and building an Asian and Pacific American solidarity which can be a unifying and solidifying force. Asian and Pacific groups have their own prejudices and biases among themselves and toward other ethnic groups. All need to undergo conversion. For

Asian and Pacific communities this means addressing historical animosities against former enemies within their own homelands or outside them. In the new situation the call of the Lord to a change of heart needs to be heeded by all . . .

V. Conclusion

Asian and Pacific communities rejoice that they are called to the house of the Lord. As the Bishops of the Church in the United States we rejoice in their presence. "Blessed be God for the peoples of Asia, so rich in their diversity yet one in their yearning for peace and fullness of life."

They have taught us a great deal and brought to us a more profound understanding to what it means to be truly Catholic, by being authentically Christian and truly Asian in the footsteps of Christ. They have taught the Church in the United States the meaning of harmony, the necessity of dialogue with their cultures, with other religions and with the poor, the value of family, of unity amidst diverse cultures and amidst diverse Catholic church communities, of closeness with all of God's creation.

As bishops of the Church we acknowledge the contributions of all Asian and Pacific persons, their creative initiatives which assist our ministries in our dioceses and parishes. "They are lively in faith, full of hope and vitality which only love can bring."

We hope in this third millennium with the yearning of the universal church and the foresight of the Holy Father to concretely strengthen our ties with our Asian and Pacific communities here in the United States and in their homelands. We will enable their voice to be heard among ourselves and the Church at large.

We pray that the Church can be truly a sacrament of harmony and unity, a Church that is complete and whole.

AAPA. *See* Asian-American Political Alliance

An Act Supplementary to the Acts in Relation to Immigration (1875). *See* Page Law

An Act to Prohibit the Coming of Chinese Laborers to the United States (1888). *See* Scott Act

An Act to Prohibit the Coming of Chinese Persons to the United States (1892). *See* Geary Act

An Act to Prohibit the "Coolie Trade" by American Citizens in American Vessels (1862), 24–25

An Act to Protect Free White Labor Against Competition with Chinese Coolie Labor, and to Discourage the Immigration of the Chinese Into the State of California (1862), 26–28

Afghanistan, immigration restrictions and, 162

AFL. *See* American Federation of Labor

African Americans, 6, 76; *versus* Asian Americans, 545; combat awards for, 470; discrimination and, 542, 547; labor unions and, 238; mixed marriages and, 358; naturalization of, 13; as racial category, 498–500; racist legislation and, 29; songs and, 104–108

Africans, 534; citizenship and, 181, 182; enslavement of, 127; naturalization and, 13, 46, 48, 186, 190–191, 201

Agbayani Village, 404–405

Agreement Between English Merchant and "Chinaman" (1850), 17–18

Ah Fong, 33

Ahrens, August, 122

"Ah Sin" (song; 1877), 41–45, 104

Ah Yup, 12, 46–48, 183

Aid to Families with Dependent Children (AFDC), 480

Aiiieeeee!, 6, 385–391

Ainu aborigines, 255

AJA. *See* Americans of Japanese ancestry

Alaska: Aleuts in, 419–420; canneries in, 459; relocation of natives from, 439

Alaska Natives: cannery jobs filled by, 460; racial category, 498–500; as unskilled workers, 457

Alemany, Joseph Sadoc, 561

Aleutian Islands, 420, 439–441

Aleuts: in Alaska, 419–420; personal injustice to, 423; relocation of, 439–441

Alien Land Law. *See* Webb Act

aliens: and citizenship, 200; classes of, excluded from U.S. (1917), 163; definition of term, 162; enemy, 298, 518; Filipinos as, 200–201, 232; immigration quotas and, 503; ineligible to citizenship, 192; Japanese as, 420, 440; naturalization and, 180, 182, 186; permanent, 543, 550; profiling of, 541; resident, 420, 421, 452; two classes of, 191; war veterans as, 199

Alliance Working for Asian Rights and Empowerment in Orange County, 469

"All Things Considered" (NPR radio show), 477

Almazol, Loreto, 368

Amerasians, 250, 434, 436–437

America. *See* United States

America Is in the Heart (Bulosan; 1943), 292–298

American Association for the Advancement of Science, 539

American Citizens for Justice, 425

American Federation of Labor (AFL), 129, 134, 198, 405; *see also* Congress of Industrial Organizations

American-Japanese Evacuation Claims Act, 447

American Physical Society, 539

Americans of Japanese ancestry (AJA), 317

ancestry, 287, 336, 420, 505, 556

An Ch'angho, 174–178

Ando, Taro, 132

Angel Island, 129, 148–149, 165, 223–228, 258

Aniya, Seishū, 246

Annamese, 75

annexation, 116, 122, 140

Anti-Alien Land Law (Washington State; 1921), 189

anticommunism, 7, 316, 355–356, 520

Anti-Defamation League, 541

Anti-Japanese Laundry League, 143–144, 144

API organizations, 531–533

Apollo 11 moon landing, 523

Arakaki Bukyū, 246

Armed Forces Television, 523

Armstrong, Neil, 523

Army, U.S. *See* military

art, 487–488, 490–492, 526

artists: activists, 318; Asian immigrant, 137; Vietnamese, 491, 492; Vietnamese American, 493

arts, in Hawaii, 464–466

As a Chinaman Sees Us, 388

Asia: immigration from, 318; Jesus born in, 559; and Pacific through 1900, 9–12; as racial category, 498

Asian American movement, 371–373, 374, 378–381, 495

Asian-American Political Alliance (AAPA), 372

Asian Americans, 371, 374, 376, 467–469, 534; anger of, at sentence of Chin killers, 427; educational success of, 549; at end of World War II, 250; ethnic studies and, 319; Executive Orders and, 514–517; focus groups and, 542, 543, 545, 548–549; hate crimes and, 411; immigration and, 247, 318; Korean War and, 316; languages of, 385–386; large communities of, 407; negative judgements about, 547; pluralism and, 413; and politics, 543, 550; popular notion of being, 388; positive judgements about, 546; quality of life of, 516; racial profiling and, 538, 539, 540; racist legislation and, 29; as scapegoats, 412; startling changes for, 409; studies, 392; survey of attitudes toward, 541; voting for, 545; war brides and, 312

Asian Indians: census statistics for, 409; immigration and, 128; naturalization of, 335; racial category, 498

Asian Pacific American Congressional Medals of Honor (1995), 470–472

Asian/Pacific American Heritage Week (Proclamation 4650; 1979), 413–414

Asian Pacific Americans, 413, 531; in Cabinet, 555; combat awards for, 470–472; identification, 534; LGBT, 532; and U.S. Catholic bishops, 558–565

Asian Pacific Americans in Higher Education, 540

Asians: ethnic studies and, 393; immigration and, 127–130, 197; labor unions and, 238; lack of, in Catholic church leadership, 560; languages of, 560, 563

"Asians Are Automatically Labeled Gang Members" (Tsang; 1994), 467–469
Asian Synod of Bishops, 558, 559
Asia-Pacific triangle, 335–338
Assembly Centers, 269
assimilation, 319, 409; of Asian Americans, 370, 371, 376, 410, 549; of Chinese, 36, 55; ethnic studies and, 394, 395; of Japanese, 256, 551; prevention of, 285, 287
Association for Asian American Studies, 538–540
Association of Indians in America, 498
Astraea Lesbian Action Foundation, 531
Atkinson, Richard, 540
Attu Island, 440
Auden, W. H., 424
Audre Lorde Project, 531
August Revolution (1945), 489–491

Bamboo Ridge Press, 415–418
Bangladesh, 9, 521, 534, 535
Barenblatt, Lloyd, 345
Barred Zone Act (Immigration Act; 1917), 162–164, 218, 232, 313, 335, 343–345
Barth, Gunther, 391
Basement Workshop, 318
Bataan Death March, 450, 502
Bayonet Constitution. See Hawaii Constitution
Becktell, W. G., 165–166
Bedi, Purva, 536
Bendetsen, Karl, 290
A Bend in the River (Naipaul), 485
Berlin Wall, 343
Biggers, Earl Derr, 388
Black, Hugo L., 306, 322, 345
Blackmun, Harry A., 463
Black Panther Party, 370
Black Power movement, 361
blacks, 498, 499, 500; ethnic studies and, 393, 395; grassroots struggles of, 378; as witnesses in court cases, 20; see also African Americans

Blee, Harry, 165
boat people, 477, 480–481, 484, 509, 511, 513
Bolshevik Revolution (Russia; 1917), 167
bon odori (dance festivals), 432–433, 551
Boyle, Kay, 391
The Brady Bunch, 510
Bratt, Bob, 506, 508
Brennan, William J., Jr., 463
Brewer, David, 93, 94
Bridgman, P. W., 349
Buddhism, 120–121, 432, 451, 558, 560, 562; Los Angeles temple, 432; as metaphor for "Yellow Peril," 172; Obon schedule, 551–554
Buddhists, 147, 170, 411, 432, 483
Bui Xuan Phai, 489, 491
Bulosan, Carlos, 292–298
Bureau of Immigration and Naturalization, 142
Burlingame, Anson, 31, 32
Burlingame-Seward Treaty (1868), 3, 11, 31–32, 33, 36, 62, 84, 87
Burns, John, 464
Burton, Harold H., 340
Butler, Pierce, 189, 199

Cable Act (1922), 4, 129, 179–180, 198
California, 76, 317, 333, 402, 410, 432, 485, 505; anti-Japanese racism in, 141; ethnic studies in, 361–364; exclusion laws and, 302; Filipinos in, 291; relocation center in, 303; reparation for Japanese Americans, 422; Vietnamese refugees in, 509
California Alien Land Law (1913). See Webb Act
California Commission on Peace Officer Standards and Training, 468
California Fish and Game Code, 325
California Fish and Game Commission, 323
California State Industrial Union Council, CIO, 273
California Supreme Court. See Supreme Court (California)

Cambodia, 6, 343, 407, 482–483, 499;
refugees from, 318, 412, 434–435
Canada, 137, 141–142
Carson, Ellen Godbey, 456
Carter, Jimmy, 413–414, 504
Catholic Filipino Club, 561
Catholics, 55, 411, 478, 483–484, 561,
563–564
Caucasians, 212, 220, 498, 545, 547;
naturalization and, 101–102, 181, 183,
185–187
censorship, 237, 248, 455
Central Intelligence Agency (CIA), 261,
412, 539–540
The Challenge of the American Dream
(Hsu), 389
Chan, Jeffrey Paul, 391
Chang, Diana, 387
Charlie Chan novels (Biggers),
388–390
Chavez, César, 6, 404
Chiang, Joe, 254
Chih-Kang, 32
children, 50, 60, 70–71, 72, 384,
482–483; immigration restrictions
and, 164, 165
Chin, Bing Heng, 425
Chin, Charlie, 378, 495
Chin, Frank, 391
Chin, Vincent, 411, 425–426, 427
China, 3, 9, 58, 77, 250, 499, 539, 548;
communism and, 250, 318, 339;
Cultural Revolution in, 370;
economic power of, 543, 548;
Emperor of, 84, 86, 112–114;
immigration from, 314, 318, 414;
Japanese invasion of, 247; Korean
patriotism in, 215; languages of, 560;
living in, 474–475; military power of,
543, 548; national leadership from,
174; Qing dynasty of, 51; relations
with U.S., 11; 1911 revolution of, 139;
as threat to U.S., 549; travel books
on, 388; United States treaties and,
86; war with U.S. and, 372
A Chinaman Looks at America, 388

Chinaman's Chance, 388
Chinatown, 365, 368, 370, 389
"Chinatown, My Chinatown" (song;
1910), 4, 150–154
Chinatown, U.S.A. (Coleman), 389
Chinatown, U.S.A. (Lee), 389
A Chinatown Family (Lin Yutang),
387, 389
Chinatown Inside Out (Leong Gor
Yun), 389
Chin Bow, 4, 208–210
Chin Dun, 208
Chinese, 3, 209, 211, 253, 410;
immigration of, 137, 148, 150, 162;
naturalization, 102, 191, 201, 330,
335; pejorative term for, 133; racial
profiling and, 538, 541; in San
Francisco, 49, 361–362; in schools,
212; as sociological case studies, 375
Chinese Americans, 2, 339, 347, 362,
386, 409, 411, 541, 545; focus groups
and, 542, 543; hate crimes and,
253–255; literary writings of, 385;
loyalty of, 548; marriage and, 6;
migration and, 559; as military
volunteers, 248–249; pride of, 381;
racial discrimination and, 5; radical
youth, 370; war brides and, 312
"The Chinese and the Times" (1854),
22–23
Chinese Communist Party, 315, 316, 339
Chinese Exclusion Act (1882), 1, 3, 67,
87, 97; Congressional passage of, 51;
documentary films and, 1; extension
of, 89; immigration policy and, 33,
165, 223; passage of, 57, 143; repeal of,
198, 280–281; treaty stipulations and,
62–63
Chinese in American Life (Kung), 389
Chinese laborers, 84, 85, 96, 98, 134, 135
Chinese newspapers, 22
Chinese Police Tax, 26–28
Chinese Primary School (1885), 72
Chinese Revolution (1911), 150
Chinese Welfare Council of Detroit, 425
Chino-Japanese war, 147

Chin Tong, 208
Chock, Eric, 415, 416
Chosen. *See* Korea
Choy, Christine, 425
Christianity, 23, 54, 73, 181, 558, 560, 562; freedom of religion and, 31; immigration and, 36; spread of, 559
Christians, 147, 157, 170–171
Chu, Louis, 387
CIA. *See* Central Intelligence Agency
CIO. *See* Congress of Industrial Organizations
Citizen 13660 (Okubo), 391
citizens, 29, 74–75, 165, 175, 311, 335, 423; loyal, 302, 303–304, 305, 310; privileges of, 55, 158
citizenship, 21, 127–128, 349; and alien war veterans, 199; Chinese and, 63; constitutional amendment and, 47; court decisions and, 129; denial of, 209; eligibility, 46, 160, 195, 198, 322–324, 331; English language requirements for, 527–528; exclusion of aliens and, 94; for Filipino veterans, 504; of Hawaii, 139–141; immigration and, 143, 166; Japanese American Creed and, 257; Japanese nationals and, 181; marriage and, 4, 179–180; migration and, 3; most-favored nations and, 32; naturalization and, 13–14, 200; people of African descent and, 11; renunciation of, 288, 289, 453; revocation of, 453–454; rights of, 3, 21, 209–210, 349; by serving in military, 249; Supreme Court decisions about, 4, 112–114; U.S. born Asians and, 148, 155–156; U.S. Congress and, 113; for whites, 183
Civilian Exclusion Order No. 34, 307, 430
civil liberties, 5, 440, 441, 556
Civil Liberties Act (1988), 412, 419, 439–443, 506–507, 556
Civil Liberties Education Fund, 442

civil rights, 6, 49, 118, 360, 374, 427, 455, 530; Japanese American, 273, 317, 449; organization and, 6; protection of, 508; of racial groups, 307; reforms, 319; U.S. violation of, 247
Civil Rights Act (1964), 347–349, 400–402, 457; Title VII of, 458–463
civil rights movement, 318, 361, 457, 495
Civil War, 11, 127
Clark Air Force Base, 315, 504
Clinton, William J., 470, 516, 538
Coachella-Delano, Calif., grape-pickers strike in, 404–405
Coalition Against Racial and Ethnic Stereotyping, 540
Coast Guard Service, U.S., 199, 340, 342; *see also* military
Cold War, 2, 6, 250, 315, 316, 327, 522
Cole, Bob, 105, 106
Coleman, Elizabeth, 389
Collins, Wayne, 453
colonialism, 64, 317, 488–489, 490
The Columbia Guide to Asian American History (Okihiro), 2
Combined Asian-American Resources Project, Inc., 391
Commission on Wartime Relocation and Internment of Civilians (1982), 419–424, 440–441, 448, 508
Committee of 100 (2001), 541–550
Committee of Concerned Scientists, 539
communism, 2, 315, 327, 354, 407, 523, 526; in China, 317, 339, 368; and Vietnam, 480, 513, 525; Vietnamese Americans and, 509, 520; Vietnam War and, 513
communities: Asian, 559, 564–565; Asian American, 128, 385, 530; Asian Pacific American, 514; black, 410; Catholic, 563–564; Chinese American, 426; ethnic, 318, 398, 399, 564; Japanese American, 157, 439, 551; Latino, 410; Native American, 410; notion of, 376; Pacific, 559, 564–565; South Asian, 536; Vietnamese, 524; Vietnamese American, 487

concentration camps, 198, 237, 299, 448, 506; closure of, 508; Executive Order 9066 and, 269; experience of, 376; former internees of, 381; Japanese in, 247, 249, 322; life in, 453

Conference on Emerging Programs, Second Annual, 392

Confucianism, 216, 489, 558, 561, 562

Confucius, 23, 371

Congregation for the Evangelization of Peoples, 559

Congress, U.S.: alien immigrant legislation and, 92; Chinese laborers and, 87; civil liberties and, 507; exclusion of aliens and, 94, 96; House Committee on Immigration, 172–173; House Committee on Interstate Migration (1942), 273; legislation and, 30, 37; Nationality Act (1940), 504; National Origins Act and (1924), 192; and naturalization, 181; override of Hoover veto by, 217; Public Law 503 (1942), 267; redress legislation and, 448; Roosevelt address to, 251–252; Scott Act of (1888), 87; see also individual acts of legislation

Congressional Medal of Honor, 470–472, 502, 518

Congress of Industrial Organizations (CIO), 197, 405; see also American Federation of Labor

Constitution, U.S., 29; Bill of Rights of, 305, 346; character of, 231; civil rights and, 449; education rights and, 212; international law and, 94; Japanese American creed and, 257; principles set forth in, 310–311; promises of, 556; protection of brown peoples and, 11; resident aliens and, 421; right guaranteed within, 450; treaties and, 87; violation of rights and, 78; see also particular amendments

Cook, James, 510

Coolies, Chinese invasion and, 221

Cooper, Tink, 508

Corea. See Korea

court cases: Yick Wo v. Hopkins (1886), 12, 77, 95

court decisions: coram nobis cases (1980s), 2; Dartmouth College v. Woodward, 186; Ho Ah Kow v. Matthew Nunan (1879), 51–52; Mochizuki v. United States, 439; The People v. George W. Hall (1854), 11; People v. Hall (1854), 2, 19–21; Salvador Roldan v. Los Angeles County (1933), 220–222; William Hohri, et al. v. United States (1988), 444–447

Cox Report, 539

Craig, Glen, 478

Cuba, 3, 109, 110, 315, 343, 499

cultures, 7, 395, 411, 468, 475, 476, 490, 562, 565; American, 371, 394, 409, 492, 513; Asian, 409, 563; blending of, 417; Chinese, 388; European American, 204; Hawaiian, 465; Japanese, 204; of Pacific Islanders, 562; pre-modern Asian, 531; Spanish, 499; Vietnamese, 492

Cuong, Pham, 481

Cuong, Tran, 478, 480

Cutting, Bronson, 217

Dallas Cowboys, 523

Dao, Minh Tri, 491

Davis, Horace Chandler, 345

deGuzman, Emil, 369

Delano strike, 367

democracy, 173, 206, 248, 334, 349

Democratic National Committee, 541

Democratic Party, 317, 318

Department of Energy, 538–540

Department of Health and Human Services, 514–515

Department of Justice, 539–540

deportation, 129, 208, 281, 311, 343, 439, 453

Desert Storm, 521, 524

desis, 534–536; see also South Asians

detention, 86, 285, 303–305, 308, 311,
    422, 448, 451, 456
Deutch, John, 539, 540
DeWitt, John L., 271, 276, 290, 306,
    430, 450
Didion, Joan, 485
Dinh, Cuong, 492
discrimination, 3, 29, 78, 93, 197, 283,
    287, 330, 331, 401, 431, 452, 462, 463,
    532, 539, 545, 546, 556; African
    Americans and, 542; in education,
    413; in employment, 413–414; equal
    protection and, 79–80, 325; Filipinos
    and, 366, 505; in housing, 413;
    Korean Americans and, 474, 533;
    racial, 99, 100, 285, 304, 306, 310,
    311, 332, 463; in schools, 72, 211–214;
    Vietnamese Americans and, 524; in
    the workplace, 457
diseases, 58, 59, 60, 98, 163, 313, 363
disparate-impact theory, 459, 460, 463
"Distant Shores, Common Ground"
    (1995), 487–493
Distinguished Service Cross, 470–471
doi moi (renovation), 491
Doll-Mission of Friendship, 202–203
Donovan, William, 261
Douglas, William O., 283, 286, 302, 343,
    345, 401
due process, 93, 94, 207, 286, 305, 311,
    454, 538; internment of Japanese
    Americans and, 248, 267–268;
    land ownership and, 189–191; of
    law, 29, 34, 37, 55, 78; liberty and,
    91, 155–156, 421; see also particular
    amendments
Duus, Masayo, 167

Eastern Catholic Churches, 561
East is West, 390
Eat a Bowl of Tea (Chu), 387
Ebens, Ronald, 425, 427
Ecclesia in America, 560
Ecole des Beaux-Arts de l'Indochine,
    489–490
Edsell, Harry, 155

education: after World War II, 250;
    American, 216; bilingual, 319, 402;
    commitment to, 542; compulsory,
    402; equality and, 401–403; ethnic,
    392–395, 398–399; fund for, 440;
    higher, 549–550; higher levels of,
    544; Japanese American creed and,
    257; Japanese parents and, 207; lack
    of, 542, 546; losses in, 440–441;
    political, 373; prosperity and, 158;
    public, 31, 32, 403 (see also schools);
    segregation and, 50; traditional, 397,
    400; universal, 49
Eighth Amendment, 455
emigration: of Amerasian children,
    437–438; free, 31; of Japanese to
    U.S., 159
Endo, Mitsuye, 5, 249, 288, 302–303,
    308, 454, 455
equality, 286, 323–324, 331, 332,
    401–403, 457
equal protection, 54, 76, 286, 358;
    discrimination and, 79–80, 325; Fifth
    Amendment and, 285–286, 454;
    Fourteenth Amendment and,
    323–324, 358, 402; land ownership
    and, 189–191; of law, 29, 34, 37, 51–52,
    54, 79–80, 208, 287; under law, 34,
    37, 55, 325; legislation for, 29, 51, 79
espionage, 304, 307, 309, 325, 420,
    440, 541
ethnicity, 498, 499–501, 532
ethnic studies, 318–319, 361, 365, 392,
    398, 410
Europe, 124, 499, 534
evacuation, 303, 439, 442, 449
Evacuation Claims Act, 449
Ewa Plantation (Hawaii), 122–123
exclusion, 49, 56, 202, 244, 307, 308, 309,
    326, 341, 422, 449; versus expulsion,
    93; of Filipinos, 217; of Japanese
    Americans, 448, 451–452, 508;
    permanent, 340–341
Executive Order 9066, 247, 267–268,
    269, 284, 420, 423, 430, 441, 455, 504;
    see also Roosevelt, Franklin D.

Executive Order 13125 (1999),
514–517, 530
Expatriation Act (1907), 180

farmworkers: Filipino, 367, 404–406;
Japanese immigrant, 189;
Mexican/Japanese (1903), 134–136
fascism, 247, 273, 370, 373
Father and Glorious Descendant
(Lowe), 389
Faulkner, William, 522
FBI. *See* Federal Bureau of Investigation
Federal Bureau of Investigation (FBI),
268, 289, 452, 538–539
Federal Communications
Commission, 452
Federation of Japanese Labor, 167–169
Federation of Vietnamese Clergy,
Religious and Lay Leaders, 563
Field, Stephen J., 33, 34–35, 51–52,
87, 93
Fifth Amendment, 93, 205, 207, 316–317;
equal protection and, 285–286, 454;
self-incrimination and, 343–346;
violation of, 284–285
Fifth Chinese Daughter (Wong), 389,
390, 391
Fiji, 534, 536
Filipino Americans, 5, 6, 249, 367, 381,
386, 404, 410, 457, 559; ethnic studies
and, 362–364; literary writings of, 292,
385; World War II veterans, 502–505
Filipino Federated Agricultural Laborers
Association, 198
Filipino-Mexican Americans, 470
Filipino-Mexican union, 198
Filipino Repatriation Act (1935), 234–235
Filipinos, 2, 3, 217, 254, 361–364, 367,
409, 411, 460; in California, 296–297;
housing for, 410; immigration and,
292–294; immigration and, 145, 198,
503; importation of, during sugar
strike (1909), 129–130, 167;
International Hotel and, 369; letter to
farmworkers, 404–406; Manila
galleons and, 10; marginalization of,

411; as migrant workers, 6;
naturalization and, 200, 281, 316, 330,
335; political cartoons and, 124–126;
racism and, 5; as sociological case
studies, 375; in U.S. armed forces,
315, 367, 496–497; as veterans, 6,
496–497, 502–505; *see also*
Philippines
Filipino Veterans Editorial, *Washington
Post* (Dec. 13, 1997), 496–497
Filipino Veterans Equity Act, 496
First Amendment, 345, 455, 510
Flower Drum Song (Lee), 387
Flying Tigers, 248–249
focus groups, 541–550
Fong, Hiram, 317; and children's
petition on civil rights bill (1963),
347–350
Foran, Martin, 67
Foran Act Prohibiting Contract Labor
(1885), 17, 67–69
Ford, John, 261
Foreign Miners Tax (California; 1850),
11, 15–16, 26, 49
Formosa, 371
442nd Regimental Combat Team,
veterans of, 451, 556
Fourteenth Amendment, 26, 29–30,
33–34, 37, 47, 51–52, 55, 77, 79–80,
102, 112–113; alien land laws and,
331–334; education and, 207, 402;
equality of legal privileges and,
323–324, 358, 402; interracial marriage
and, 358–360; land ownership and,
189–191; rights guaranteed by, 345;
segregation and, 213–214
Fourth Amendment, 454
France, 74, 75, 124, 250, 489, 560;
Vietnam and, 315, 356–357, 483–484
Frank, Barney, 507
Freeh, Louis J., 539
Freeman, J. H., 34
free negroes, 36
friendship dolls, 5, 202–203
Fritz, John Lee, 478
Frontiers of Love (Chang), 387

Fuller, Melville W. III, 95
Fu Manchu, 389, 390

Gay Asian & Pacific Islander Men of
     New York, 531
gay rights, 411, 530–533
Geary, Thomas, 89
Geary Act (1892), 89–90, 93
Gee, Seow Hong, 223–228
Gee, Theo Quee, 223–228
gender, 2, 335
Genghis Kahn, 356
Gentlemen's Agreement (1907), 128,
     141–142, 143, 159; National Origins
     Act and (1924), 192
Germany, 124, 198, 251, 287
Gilman, Ben A., 496
Glenn, John, 523
Goldblatt, Louis, 272–273
The Golden Hills' News, 22–23
"Gold Mountain" (metaphor for
     America), 22
Gompers, Samuel, 129, 134–136
Good Guys electronic store siege,
     477–479, 485
The Grass Roof (Kang; 1931), 215–216
Gray, Horace, 93, 112
Great Britain, 124
Great Depression, 198, 237
Greene, DeDe, 508
Greene, Graham, 490
Guam, 3, 11, 109, 110, 111, 124, 128, 252,
     410, 482, 499, 559
Gulick, Sidney L., 202–203
Gulliver's Travels (Swift), 387
Gutierrez, Fernando, 478

habeas corpus, 77, 86, 91–92, 94, 112, 155,
     208–209, 340, 449; Japanese
     American Citizens League and, 302;
     Mitsuye Endo and, 249, 288, 303,
     454, 455
Haiti, 499
Hakodate, Bishop of, 561
hakujin (Caucasians, whites), 244–245
Hall, George, 19

Hamlet, 485
Hanna, Edward J., 561
Hanoi, 489
Hanoi Museum of Fine Arts, 490
Hantover, Jeffrey, 487
haole, 129
Hare-Hawes-Cutting Act (1933), 217–219
Hartman, Sadakichi, 390
Harvey, William, 97
Hashimura Togo stories (Irwin), 388
hate crimes, 411–412, 427–428, 532
Hawaii, 3, 9, 10, 11, 82, 97, 137, 207, 247,
     317, 318, 405, 410, 411, 417, 518;
     annexation of, 3, 115–119, 140;
     Chinese in, 118; civil rights and,
     347–350; election of nobles in, 82–83;
     Filipinos in, 230, 234, 505;
     immigrants and, 128, 247, 519; and
     Japan, 4, 99, 129, 141–142, 159, 197,
     204, 251–252, 258–260, 551; labor
     unions and, 273, 327–329; legislature
     of, 82; literature from, 415–418;
     martial law in, 249; nationalities in,
     117–118; naturalization and, 180;
     Obon schedule (2001), 551–554;
     Okinawans and, 242, 245; Ozawa
     family in, 181; Patton in, 236;
     population of, 131; senator from, 470;
     sugar plantations on, 145, 167, 292,
     505; U.S. Navy and, 124; Varsity
     Victory Volunteers and, 264, 265;
     wage disputes in, 145–147; young
     volunteers in, 5; see also Pearl Harbor
Hawaiian Evangelical Association, 258
Hawaii Committee for the
     Humanities, 415
Hawaii Constitution (Bayonet
     Constitution; 1887), 81–83
Hawaii dock strike (1949), 327–329
Hawaii Hochi (Japanese language
     newspaper), 157–159
Hawaii Literary Arts Council
     (HLAC), 415
Hawaii State Foundation on Culture
     and the Arts, 415–416, 464
Hawaii State Planters Association, 145

Hawaii Writers Quarterly, 415
Hawes, Harry, 217
Hayashi, Harvey Saburo, 97–100
Hayes, Butler, 217
Hayslip, Le Ly, 512–513
Health, Education, and Welfare,
    Department of (HEW), 403
Hemenway, Charles R., 265–266
Heng Samrin regime, 438
Henning, John, 405
Herzig, Jack, 306, 429, 456
HEW. *See* Health, Education, and
    Welfare, Department of
Higa, Seikan, 244
Higher Wages Association (Zokyu kisei
    kai), 145
hinamatsuri (doll festival), 202–203
Hinduism, 186–188, 558, 560, 562
Hing, Alex, 370, 371
Hirabayashi, Gordon, 5, 7, 249,
    283–290, 306, 307, 358, 360, 412, 429,
    445–446
Hirabayashi, James, 392
Hirabayashi Ethnic Education
    Statement (1974), 398–400
hiring/promotion practices, 460
Hiroshima, 315, 519
Hispanics, 498–500, 542, 547
Hitler, Adolph, 502
HLAC. *See* Hawaii Literary Arts
    Council
Hmong-American Catholic National
    Association, 563
Hmong Veterans Naturalization Act
    (Public Law 106–207; 2000), 2,
    517–529
Ho, Ah Kow, 51
Hoang, Van Duc, 468
Ho Chi Minh, 7, 490, 509–511, 512–513
Ho Chi Minh City (Saigon), 477, 488
Hohri, William, 419, 444–447, 448
holehole bushi (sugar plantation blues),
    131–133, 170
Honda, Eryu, 120–121
Hong Kong, 252, 371, 435
Hongwanji, 173

Honolulu Advertiser, 327–329
Honomu Gijuku (private school), 170
Honomu Plantation, 170–171
Hoover, Herbert, 217
Horace, 493
Ho, Thanh Duc, 492
"The House Without a Key"
    (Biggers), 388
Howard University Press, 385
How Chew, 211
"How to Tell Japs from the Chinese"
    (*Life*; 1941), 253–255
Hsu, Francis L. K., 389
Hsu, Kai-yu, 391
Hue, 489
Huerta, Dolores, 404
Hughes, Charles E., 155
human rights, 49, 317, 319, 331–332,
    495, 530, 533
Hungary, 316
Hurley, Jennie M. A., 70–71
Hyakuna, Chōkō, 243
Hyun, Peter, 473–476
Hyun, Soon, 473

Iban/Queer Koreans of New York, 531
ICSA. *See* Inter-Collegiate Chinese
    for Social Action
identity, 375, 377, 388, 389, 416, 488,
    521–522, 531–532, 563
"If Tomorrow Comes," 390
Iijima, Chris, 378, 381, 495
ILGWU. *See* International Ladies
    Garment Workers' Union
ILWU. *See* International
    Longshoremen's and
    Warehousemen's Union
immigrants, 2, 67, 119, 409, 412, 559, 562;
    and, 526; Asian, 4, 29, 81, 215, 316,
    414; Catholic, 561; children of, 256,
    535; Chinese, 67, 89, 104, 247, 281,
    347, 366; dances of, 432–433;
    descendants of slave, 195; detention
    of, 237; family unification and, 351;
    Filipino, 247, 294, 505; increase of
    (1990s), 543, 547; Irish, 10; Japanese,

97, 100, 122, 160, 189–191, 197, 247, 253, 258, 330, 335, 366, 551; Korean, 247; living conditions of, 97; naturalization and, 6, 185; nonquota, described, 193–194, 195; numerical limitations of, 194–195; Okinawan, 243; from the Philippines, 247; quotas and, 5, 192, 194–195, 282; songs of, 131–133; from Vietnam, 487; *see also* Angel Island

immigration, 22, 33, 62, 91, 92, 179, 339; from Anglo-Saxon Europe, 316; from Asia, 6, 38, 197, 335; from China, 57, 84, 128, 316, 388; citizenship and, 11; denial of, to Japanese (1924), 181; discouragement of, 26–28; Hawaii and, 118; of Hmong people, 527; from Japan, 99, 141, 143–144, 452; legislation and, 197, 255; naturalization and, 35–36, 255; officials of, 138; Pacific, 197; pattern changes of, 2; from Philippines, 232; policy of, 33; prevention of, 55–56; prostitution and, 39; quota system and, 336–337, 354; reforms, 1, 5, 319; regulation of, 162–164, 324; restrictions on, 250; transportation costs and, 67; war brides and, 312

"Immigration," 38

Immigration Act (1917). *See* Barred Zone Act

Immigration Act (1924). *See* National Origins Act

Immigration Act (1990), 504

Immigration and Nationality Act (1965), 6, 192, 351–354, 528

Immigration and Naturalization Service, 185, 313, 558, 559

Immigration Law, 166, 413

immigration laws, 127

immigration policy reforms (1965), 401

immigration quota system, 192–195, 197, 318; *see also* National Origins Act

immigration visas, 193, 195

imperialism, 10, 64, 109, 115, 281, 317, 370, 371, 373

Inada, Lawson Fusao, 391

India, 9, 10, 162, 185, 318, 499, 534, 535, 559

India Day parade, 531

Indian American Catholic Association, 563

Indian Americans, 559

Indians, 20–21, 49, 315, 330

Indochina, 74–75, 162, 414

Indochina Migration and Refugee Assistance Act (1975), 407–408

Indonesia, 9, 411, 435, 560

Inouye, Daniel, 317, 470, 502–505, 518–519, 556

In re Ah Fong (1874), 33–37

In re Ah Yup (1878), 12, 46–48, 183

In re Saito (1894), 101–103

Inside Chinatown (Lui), 389

Insight (journal), 383

Inter-Collegiate Chinese for Social Action (ICSA), 372

Internal Security Act (1950), 344

International Fund for Sexual Minorities, 531

International Hotel (San Francisco), history of residents, 365–369

International Ladies Garment Workers' Union (ILGWU), 4, 238–239, 240–241

International Longshoremen's and Warehousemen's Union (ILWU), 273, 318, 327

International Workers of the World (Wobblies), 134

internment, 302, 308, 452; of Japanese Americans, 273, 439, 442, 445, 506–508, 508, 556

interracial marriages, 358–360, 366

In the New World: The Making of a Korean American (Hyun; 1995), 473–476

Invalidation of Queue Ordinance (1879), 51–56

Irons, Peter, 429

Irwin, Wallace, 388

Ishii, David, 391

Islam, 432, 558, 560, 562
issei, 129, 242, 451
Italy, 251

Jackson, Robert H., 306, 310
JACL. See Japanese American Citizens
    League
Jainism, 562
Japan, 9, 81, 198, 199, 251, 499, 504;
    attack on Pearl Harbor by, 251–252;
    coup against France, 489; defeat of,
    174, 215, 315; defeat of Russia, 215;
    Emperor of, 91, 172; immigration
    from, 10, 91, 117, 128, 315, 317, 414;
    and Korea, 139, 247; Meiji
    government in (1868), 10, 97, 170;
    Satsuma domain in, 242; Tokugawa
    Shogunate and, 10; and U.S., 124,
    189, 192, 496
Japanese, 3, 9, 67, 99, 118, 198, 361–362,
    375; Buddhism and, 120–121; in
    Hawaii, 117; as immigrants, 137, 144,
    146, 150, 162; naturalization and, 102,
    186, 191, 198, 200, 201, 281, 330
Japanese American Citizens League
    (JACL), 5, 249, 275, 288, 299–300,
    302, 317, 358, 386, 448
Japanese American Claims Act
    (1948), 317
"Japanese American Creed" (Masaoka),
    256–257
Japanese-American Evacuation Claims
    Act (1948), 422
Japanese American National
    Museum, 555
Japanese American Redress Office,
    506–508
Japanese Americans, 5, 128, 202, 248,
    250, 376, 390, 409, 411, 420, 470–472,
    502, 545; culture of, 386; curfew
    restrictions and, 288–289, 290; draft
    resistance (1944), 299–301; ethnic
    studies and, 362, 394; evacuation of
    Californian, 275; exclusion of,
    420–421; hate crimes and, 253; in
    Hawaii, 115; identity of, 450;
immigration pattern changes and, 2;
    improved treatment of, 316–317;
    interning of, 267–268; internment
    of, 5, 7, 247, 412, 439, 471; literary
    writings of, 385; loyalty of, 262,
    263–264, 307, 310; marriage and, 6;
    mass detention of, 2; migration
    and, 559; and military, 5, 249,
    470–472, 502, 555; monetary
    restitution for, 448; naturalization
    and, 317; as plaintiffs, 451; pride of,
    381; redress for, 506–508;
    relocation testimonies of, 419;
    restitution of positions, 423;
    second generation, 179, 464;
    underground press of, 390
The Japanese Conspiracy: The Oahu
    Sugar Strike of 1920 (Masayo
    Duus), 167
Japanese Evacuation report, 290–291
Japanese laborers, 99–100, 134
Japanese language newspapers, 97,
    157–159
Japanese Latin Americans, 439
Jesus Christ, 559, 562, 565
Jeter, Mildred, 359
job training, 441, 480
John Paul II, Pope, 559, 562, 565
Johnson, Billy, 104–106
Johnson, Lisa, 508
Johnson, Lyndon, 347, 355
Jonchère, Evariste, 489, 490
Judaism, 558, 560, 562
Judeo-Christian morality, 99

Kahunas, 117
Kaigai Kyōkai, 246
Kalakaua, King, 81
Kalihi/Palama, 465
Kalloch, I. S., 57
Kamehameha I, 116
Kamehameha V, 82
Kang, Younghill, 215–216
Karate Kid II (film), 432
Kaufman, Charles S., 425, 427–428
Kawatsu, Keizō, 243

Kearney, Denis, 57
Keene, Donald, 274
Kennedy, Edward, 357
Kennedy, John F., 318, 343, 374
Kennedy, Robert, 318, 357, 374
Khao I Dang camp, 438
Khmer Rouge, 434, 438
Kiedi, Joanne, 508
Kilawin Kolektibo, 531
Kim, Young Oak, 249
King, Carol, 272–273
King, Martin Luther Jr., 318, 374
King, Fong Yu, 425–426
Kitashima, Sox, 506–508
Knox, Frank, 452
Kodani, Masao, 432
Kona Hankyo (Kona Echo), 97
Korea, 9, 64–66, 174, 176, 247, 250,
    344, 499; immigrants from, 10, 315,
    318, 414
Korean Americans, 5, 383–384,
    473–476, 545
Korean independence movement, 174,
    177, 215, 473
Korean Priests Association of America
    and Canada, 563
Koreans, 2, 6, 128, 139, 146, 281, 375,
    409, 411
Korean War, 6–7, 312, 315, 316, 377, 383
Korematsu, Fred, 5, 7, 249, 283, 290, 302,
    306–311, 323, 325, 358, 360, 412,
    429–431, 445–447; *see also* U.S.
    District Court decisions: *Korematsu
    v. United States*
Kosovo, 522
KROQ's *Kevin and Bean Show*, 510
Kuboyama, Emi, 508
Ku-Klux-Klan, 356
Kung, S. W., 389
"Kung Fu," 391
Kuomintang, 315
Kurusu, Special Emissary, 255
Kwong Hai Chew, 339–342

labor, 10, 24, 26–28, 122, 131, 134, 273,
    366, 405; Japanese, 12, 67, 170–171;

Mexican, 367; migration and, 68;
    prohibitions against, 67–69; *see also*
    labor unions
laborers, 12, 167, 168, 457, 458, 561;
    agricultural, 273, 561; cannery, 457,
    459; Chinese, 17–18, 62–63, 67, 79,
    84–85, 90, 112–113, 143, 238; contract,
    137, 163; Filipino, 167, 197, 295, 366;
    in Hawaii, 118; Japanese, 99, 135,
    141–142, 145–147, 147, 197; Korean,
    141–142, 473; in mines, 98; sugar, 134,
    135, 171; transcontinental railroad,
    561; women, 168
labor leaders, 134, 273
labor movement, 167, 318, 457
labor unions, 4, 134–136, 198; *see also*
    American Federation of Labor;
    Congress of Industrial Organizations;
    International Ladies Garment
    Workers' Union; Retail Department
    Store Employees Union; United
    Farmworkers Union
Lahiri, Jhumpa, 536
Lai, H. Mark, 391
Lam, Andrew, 477–486, 523
land, 160, 161, 325–326, 330, 366
land laws, aliens, 330, 331–332, 452
land ownership, 160, 189–191, 250, 452
language, 76, 187, 198, 385–386, 411,
    560, 562–563, 563; Chinese, 66,
    205, 362–363, 475; English, 22,
    181, 182, 206, 401–402, 475, 477,
    480, 483, 510, 521; French, 560;
    Hawaiian, 466; in Hawaii history,
    417; Japanese, 97, 158, 198, 205, 206,
    455, 475; Korean, 205, 475, 532;
    Lakota, 495; Mandarin, 362–363;
    of Pacific Islanders, 560; racist,
    289; Russian, 475
Laos, 6, 318, 343, 407, 411, 412, 434–435,
    435, 438, 527–529
Larkin, Brad, 521
Latin America, 318, 506
Latin American, 362
Latinos, 378, 393, 500
laundries, 76–79

law, 12, 60, 78, 189–191, 213, 250, 287, 292, 317; equal protection and, 29, 34, 37, 51–52, 54, 79–80, 208; immigration, 99, 143, 203, 232, 313, 332; individual rights and, 96; Japanese American Creed and, 257; martial, 249, 308–309; of property, 210

Lee, C. Y., 387, 390

Lee, Calvin, 389

Lee, Wen Ho, 412, 533, 538–540, 541

legal defense program, 373

legislation, 6, 8, 55, 76, 330

Leong Gor Yun, 389

leprosy, 58, 61

Lesbian & Gay Community Services Center, 532

Leung, Kum Wui, 155

LGBT rights, 530–533

liberty, 31, 74–75, 91, 94, 287, 305, 308, 311, 421

Life of Kinzaburo Makino (*Hawaii Hochi*; 1965), 157, 158

lifestyles, 411, 530

Lin, Yutang, 387, 389, 390

Lincoln, Abraham, 216

Lipat, Christine, 530–531

Li, Ren Fong, 468

literature, 6, 387, 388, 416–418, 417

Little Saigon, 479, 509, 512–513

Little Saigon Radio & Television (Orange County, Calif.), 523

Lizarraras, J. M., 134

Longtime Californ': A Documentary Study of an American Chinatown (Nee; Nee), 387

Los Alamos National Laboratory, 538, 540

Louisiana Purchase (1803), 10

"Love, Money, Prison, Sin, Revenge" (Lam; 1995), 477–486

Loving, Richard, 359

Lowe, Pardee, 389

Lowry Redress Bill, 449

Luce-Celler Bill, 316

Lui, Garding, 389

Lum, Darrell, 415

Lum, Gong, 211–212

Lum, Martha, 211–213

Lund, Jeff, 468

Luzon, 504

MacArthur, Douglas, 503

Machida, Toku, 274

"Madame Sin," 390

Makino, Frederick Kinzaburo, 157

Malaya, 162, 191, 201, 220–221; Japanese attack on, 252

Malaysia, 435, 499

Malcolm X, 374

Manabe, Jody, 416

Manchu dynasty, 139, 150

Manila, 233, 504

Manilatown (San Francisco), 365–369

Man Sei!: The Making of a Korean American (Hyun; 1986), 473

Mao Tse-tung, 339, 370, 374

Marcos, Ferdinand E., 404, 504–505

Marianas Islands, 109

Marlow, William C., 356

marriage, 179, 220–221, 244–245, 250, 318, 474, 476; interracial, 179, 250, 318, 358–360, 366

Marshall, Thurgood, 463

Marttila Communications Group, 541

Marutani, William, 358

Marxism, 167

Masaoka, Mike, 5, 256–257, 330, 555

Matayoshi, Rinshō, 246

Matsui, Bob, 556

Matsunaga, Sparky, 506

Matthews, Stanley, 78

McCarran-Walter Immigration and Nationality Act (1952), 6, 162, 317, 335–338

McCarthyism, 2, 6, 327

McClatchy, Valentine, 172

McCloy, John J., 263, 290

McKinley, William, 124

McReynolds, James C., 204

Meiji Restoration (1868), 10, 97, 170

Melanesians, 560; *see also* Pacific Islanders

Memorial on Chinatown, Investigating Committee of the Anti-Chinese Council, Workingmen's Party of California (1880), 57–61
Merchant Marine, U.S., Chinese Americans in, 339–340
merchants, 49, 147, 165–166
Mexican Americans, 362
Mexicans, 129, 393, 499
Mexico, 9–10, 37, 137, 141–142
Micronesians, 560; see also Pacific Islanders
Middle East, 354, 499, 558, 559, 561
Midway Island, Japanese attack on, 252
migration, 31, 68, 127–130, 488
Migration and Refugee Assistance Act (1962), 407–408
military, 524; affairs, 175–178; decisions, loyalty and, 310; deportation program of, 311; Executive Order 9066 and, 267–268; Filipino troops in, 320; First Filipino Infantry Battalion, 503; invasion of West Coast and, 307; Japanese Americans in, 5; 100th Infantry Battalion, 556; Roosevelt call to serve in, 316; Second Filipino Infantry Regiment, 503; segregated units in, 248; U.S. Marines, 521, 525; U.S. Navy, 124, 315
Military Intelligence Service, 269, 312, 556
Mill, John Stuart, 349
Miller, Stuart, 391
Milton-Meyer Company, 367–368
Minami, Dale, 429
Mineta, Norman, 555–557
mining, 15, 63, 85, 98
Mink, Patsy Takemoto, 317
minorities, 127, 273, 362, 384, 393, 396, 398–400
miscegenation, 220–221, 292, 318, 358–360, 366
Missing Persons Act, 320
missionaries, 120–121, 147, 173, 388, 475, 564
Miyamoto, Ejun, 120

Miyamoto, Joanne (Nobuko), 378, 381, 432–433, 494–495
Model Cities Program, 465
modernism, 490–491
Modern Japanese Diaries (Keene), 275
Mongolians, 46, 47–48, 49, 50, 102, 212–213, 220, 221
Mori, Toshio, 391
Morrison, Frank, 134
most-favored nation treatment, 31–32
Mountain of Gold (Sung), 389
Munemori, Sadao, 249
Murphy, Frank, 282, 286, 302, 306, 308, 325
Murray, Hugh, 19
The Museum of Modern Art, 488
Muslims, 411
Mussolini, Benito, 502
Myer, Dillon, 273
My Life in China and America (Wing), 388

NAACP. See National Association for the Advancement of Colored People
Nagasaki, 315
Nago, Chōsuke, 243
Naipaul, V. S., 485
Nakatsuka, N., 189–191
Nakayama, Joji, 132
Nakayoshi, 244
Napoleon, 216
National Association for the Advancement of Colored People (NAACP), 427–428
National Coalition for Redress/Reparations, 448, 506–507
National Conference of Catholic Bishops, 558–565
National Council for Japanese American Redress (NCJAR), 444, 448–456
National Dollar Stores, 239, 240
National Endowment for the Arts, 464
National Filipino Ministry Council, 563
nationalism, 6, 256, 285, 315, 356
nationality, 194–195
Nationality Act (1940), 282

National Japanese American Memorial Foundation speech (2001), 555–557
National Origins Act (Immigration Act; 1924), 127–130, 192–195, 197, 202, 232, 281, 336; Asian Americans and, 351–354; immigration and, 255; quotas and, 3; war brides and, 313
National Public Radio, 477
National Science Foundation, 539
National Service Life Insurance Act (1940), 321
Native Americans, 5, 127, 162, 181, 267, 295, 378, 410; ethnic studies and, 393, 395; naturalization and, 11, 13, 101, 281; racial category, 498–500; representation for, 30
Native Hawaiians, 498–500
naturalization, 1, 47, 129, 172, 187, 198, 248, 332, 452, 504; of Chinese, 12, 112, 281, 316; citizenship and, 5, 11, 29, 324; Hindus and, 186–188; of Hmong people, 527–529; immigration and, 6, 35–36; of Japanese, 181, 182, 198, 317; land purchases and, 330; and 1802 law, 46; legislation and, 101–103, 255; of married women, 179–180; of Mongolians, 47–48; most-favored nations and, 32; petition for, 199; prohibition of, 62; race as a test for, 332; reforms in, 319; requirements for, 2; restrictions on, 250, 335; Supreme Court decisions and, 4; U.S. Congress and, 113; of World War I Asian veterans, 197
naturalization laws, 3, 13–14, 101–103, 127, 182, 186, 191
Navy. See military
Nazi Germany, 332
NCJAR. See National Council for Japanese American Redress (NCJAR)
Nee, Brett, 387
Nee, Victor, 387
Negroes, 20, 23, 101, 188, 499
New York Assocation for Gender Rights Advocacy, 531
Nguyen, Dat, 523

Nguyen, Bim Khac, 479
Nguyen, Cao Ky, 356
Nguyen, Do Cung, 489, 490
Nguyen, Gai Tri, 489
Nguyen, Khai, 492
Nguyen, Loi Khac, 478, 480–486
Nguyen, Long Khac, 478, 483, 485–486
Nguyen, Pham Khac, 478, 480, 483, 485–486
Nguyen, Quynh-Trang, 523
Nguyen, Sang, 489
Nguyen, Sao Thi, 479–480
Nguyen, Thanh Trang, 355–357
Nguyen, Thi Hop, 492
Nguyen, Trong Khoi, 492
Nguyen, Tu Nghiem, 489–491
Nguyen, Vu, 509–511
Nippu Jiji (Japanese language newspaper), 157
nisei, 129, 179, 243, 249, 261–262, 299, 300, 451, 556
Nisei Daughter (Sone), 391
Nishime, Tokutā, 243, 244
Nishimura, Ekiu, 91–92
Nitz, Michael, 425, 427
Noguchi, Thomas, 376
Noguchi, Yone, 390
Nomura, Admiral, 255
North Africa, 499
"North and South Vietnam Are Not Two Countries" (student newsletter), 355–357
North Vietnam, 318, 490, 509
nuclear weapons, 250, 540–542
Nunan, Matthew, 51

Oahu Sugar Co., 122–123
Obata, Chiura, 3, 137–138
An Ocean Apart, 492
Odo, Franklin, 374
odori (festivals), 432
Office of Management and Budget, 2, 498
Office of Redress Administration, 439, 508

Office of Strategic Services (OSS), 261, 345
Officer Candidates School, 524–525
Okabe, Jiro, 170
Okada, Dorothy, 391
Okihiro, Gary, 2
Okinawa (Ryukyu Islands), 242–246
Okinawa *kenjinkai* (Okinawan prefecture association), 246; creation of, 244
Okubo, Miné, 391
Olaa Japanese Christian Church, 259
Omatsu, Glenn, 391
omiai (arranged) marriage, 245
Omura, Jimmie, 299–301
On Gold Mountain (See), 165
Ong, Wenhao, 254
"On Liberty" (Mill), 349
opium smoking, 58–59
Orange County, Calif., 469, 510–511, 512–513, 525–526
Oriental Boys gang, 478
OSS. *See* Office of Strategic Services
Ōta, Kamado, 246
Ōta, Tamekichi, 243
Ozawa, Takao, 4

PACE. *See* Philipino-American Collegiate Endeavor
Pacific Citizen, 386
Pacific Islander Americans, 410
Pacific Islanders, 411, 413, 498, 499, 514–517, 516, 560, 563
Pacific News Service, 477
Page Law (1875), 12, 38–40
painting, 488, 489, 492–493
Pakistan, 9, 499, 534, 535
paper daughters, 148, 223
paper sons, 129, 148, 223, 250
Parisi, Linda M., 481
Park, Pauline, 530–531
Parsloe, C. T., 41–45
patriotism, 257, 263
Patton, George, 235–236
Paulist Fathers, 561
Pearl Harbor, 248–249, 253, 256, 420, 450, 452; Japanese attack on, 247,
251–252, 320, 325; Japanese internment and, 261; Japanese language schools after, 204; martial law and, 249; Minoru Yasui and, 288; U.S. and Japanese hostility and, 258
People's Republic of China, U.S. secrets and, 412
Perry, Matthew, 10
persecution, fear of, 408
Personal Justice Denied (1983), 420, 446
Peru, 269, 439
Petition from 1300 Chinese Merchants for Schools (1878), 49–50
Pham Quang X, 520–526
Pham, Van Hoa, 521, 523–525
Phelan, James, 17
Philipino-American Collegiate Endeavor (PACE), 372
Philippines, 3, 9, 124, 218, 316, 318, 366, 387, 499, 503, 504, 560; constitution of, 231–233; immigration from, 10, 128, 130, 230, 315, 318, 414; independence of, 130, 198, 217, 230–233; Japanese attack on, 247, 252; memoir of life in, 292–293, 296; protection of U.S. and, 200–201; racism and, 5; recognition of independence of, 218–219, 233; refugee camp in, 484; refugees and, 435; takeover of (1898), 217; and U.S., 11, 109, 110, 111, 124, 232, 315, 366, 503; veterans, 503–505; *see also* Filipinos
Philippines Independence Act. *See* Tydings-McDuffie Act
Philippines Veterans Rescission Act (1946), 6, 316, 320–321, 496, 504
Philippine Veterans Memorial Hospital, 505
Phillimore, Robert, 94
picture brides, 128, 157, 244–245, 250, 376
poetry, 148–149, 492–493
Polo, Marco, 9
Polynesia, 330, 560; immigration restrictions and, 162; *see also* Pacific Islanders
poverty, 360, 365, 366

Preis, Alfred, 415
President's Advisory Commission on Asian Americans and Pacific Islanders, 514–515, 530
Pribilof islands, 439–441
property, 85, 160–161, 421–422, 441
prostitution, 12, 36, 38–39, 58, 99, 133, 163, 170
Pruett, Ticia, 165–166; see also See, Fong
Public Law 199. See Chinese Exclusion Act: repeal of
Public Law 271. See War Brides Act
Public Law 503, 455
Puerto Rico, 3, 109, 110, 180, 200, 499

Quan Ho folk songs, 488
Queue Ordinance (1879), 54
quota system, 128, 192, 194–195, 197, 230, 335, 352–353, 366, 458

race, 101–103, 102, 498–501, 532, 539; classifications of, 46, 431, 498–501; intermarriage and, 358–360
race relations, 3, 347, 374, 383
Racial Integrity Act (1924), 357
racial profiling, 2, 538–540
racial stratification, 457–458, 460, 463
racism, 12, 145, 247, 308, 371, 376, 388, 389, 427; anti-African American, 5; anti-Asian, 202, 247, 250, 317, 376–377, 520; anti-Chinese, 57; anti-Filipino, 217; anti-Japanese, 120, 141, 143, 256; Asians and, 5, 128, 197, 316, 558; in California, 97, 275; ethnic studies and, 393–394, 395; evacuation program and, 304; government-sanctioned, 452; growth of, 318, 324; of immigration acts, 223; internment and, 440; Japanese and, 450; legalization of, 310; legislative, 385, 386; marriages and, 220–222; minorities and, 361–363, 362; Mongolians and, 58; naturalization and, 184, 185; resistance to, 3; in 1850s, 20–21; in schools, 211; segregated schools and, 73; shift

from, 327; Statue of Liberty fund raising and, 74–75; Third World Liberation Front and, 361; Varsity Victory Volunteers and, 265–266; xenophobic, 292
Rancho Santiago College, 468
Reagan, Ronald, 7, 412, 448, 507
The Real Chinese in America (Tow), 388
Red Cross, 438
Red Guard, 370, 371–372
Reed, Ishmael, 391
Reed, Stanley F., 325
Reese Air Force Base, 521
Refugee Act (1975), 434
Refugee Act (1980), 407
refugees, 319, 408, 414, 434, 526; from China, 317; Indochinese, 435; Laotian, 527; from Southeast Asia, 437–438; from Vietnam, 477, 479, 482, 483–484, 487, 509
Reimeikai Kyōkai, 245–246
Reimeikai (New Dawn Club), 245–246
religion, 31, 172, 560–561, 565
Reno, Janet, 539, 540
Renton, George, 122–123
Repairing America: An Account of the Movement for Japanese-American Redress (Hohri), 448
Rescission Act. See Philippines Veterans Rescission Act
Retail Department Store Employees Union, 239
Richardson, Bill, 538, 540
rights, 3, 21, 95, 96, 310, 349, 411, 441, 457
Roberts, Owen J., 302, 304
Rocky Shimpo (newspaper in Colorado), 299
Rogers, Marjorie, 220
Roldan, Salvador, 220–222
ronin supporters, 456
Roosevelt, Eleanor, 263
Roosevelt, Franklin D., 5, 198, 234, 236, 281, 302, 316, 452, 503, 519; Day of

Infamy speech (1941), 251–252; *see
    also* Executive Order 9066
Roosevelt, Theodore, 141–142
Roots: An Asian American Reader
    (UCLA; 1971), 6
Russia, 162, 215
Russo-Japanese War (1904–1905), 143
Rutledge, Wiley B., 325
Ryukyu Islands. *See* Okinawa

sabotage, 304, 308, 310, 440
Sacramento Bee, 477, 479
Saigon, 318, 355, 477, 483, 492, 521, 523
Saito, Miki, 120–121
Samoa, 3, 11, 124, 128, 410, 499, 559
San Francisco, 223, 363, 368, 370, 372
San Francisco State University,
    361–364, 364
San Francisco University, 396
Sansei, 451, 518
Sato, Tadashi, 464, 466
Saum Song Bo, 74–75
Saund, Dalip Singh, 317
Scheuch, Norman, 258
School of Ethnic Studies, 364
schools, 28, 206, 213, 248; Japanese
    language, 4, 206, 285, 289; public,
    50, 70–71, 72, 129, 213, 319, 349, 465;
    segregated, 11, 72, 73, 141–142, 212;
    separate, 49, 211–214
Schumann, Tam Nomoto, 509
Scott, William, 84
Scott Act (1888), 84–85, 86, 98
See, Fong, 165–166
See, Lisa, 165
segregation: principles of, 463; in
    schools, 11, 72, 73, 211; in U.S.
    armed forces, 248–249
Sei, Fujii, 160, 317, 330–334
Selective Service, 299, 519
Selective Training and Service
    Amendments Act (1941), 503
Seward, William H., 31, 32
Shanghai, 174–175
Shannon, John, 471
Shebata Saito case (1894), 101–103

Shibusawa, Eiichi, 202
Shida, Kotaro, 137
Shimomura, Toku, 275–279
Shimomura, Yoshitomi, 274
Shinran, 120
Shinseki, Eric, 518–519
Shintoism, 172, 562; *see also* Buddhism
Shoong, Joe, 238
Shorenstein, Walter, 367
Shufeldt, R. W., 66
Siberia, 9
Sikhism, 558, 561, 562
Silko, Leslie, 391
Silk Road, described, 9
Simpson, Alicie, 508
Singapore, 435
Singh, Vijay, 536
SITES. *See* Smithsonian Institution
    Traveling Exhibition Service
Sixth Amendment, 455
slavery, 5, 24–25, 36, 47, 58, 127,
    359, 395
Smith, Theodore E., 290, 291
Smithsonian Institution, 555
Smithsonian Institution Traveling Exhi-
    bition Service (SITES), 487–493
socialism, 131, 139, 167
Socialist Realism, 490
Socialist Republic of Vietnam, 436
Sohne, Kris, 478
Soka Gakkai, 172
Sokabe, Shiro, 170–171
Somalia, 524
Sone, Monica, 391
Song, John, 468
songs, 4, 378, 488, 495; *see also
    individual song titles*
Sons of the Gods, 390
South America, 534
South Asia, 313, 534
South Asian Americans, 2, 534
South Asian Federation Games, 535
South Asian Gay & Lesbian
    Association, 531
South Asian Journalists Association
    (SAJA), 534–537

South Asians: Caribbean, 536;
   celebrating (2000), 534–537;
   historical documents and, 2;
   immigration restrictions and, 162;
   marginalization of, 411
Southeast Asia, 162, 250, 315, 343, 374,
   407, 414
Southeast Asian Americans, 2
Southeast Asian Refugee Acts (1987),
   434–438
Southeast Asians, 411, 434
Southern California Branch of the
   Okinawa Kaigai Kyōkai (Okinawa
   Overseas Association), 246
South Korea, 174
South Vietnam, 355, 477–486, 521, 524
sovereignty, 92, 95, 116
Soviet Union, 250, 315, 327, 343, 541
Spain, 9–10, 109–111, 218, 231
Spanish-American War, 3, 109, 366
Sri Lanka, 534, 535
Srinivasan, Rajeev, 535
St. Thomas the Apostle, 559
Stalin, Josef, 327
Steinbeck, John, 261–262
Stephens, Roe, 41
Stevens, John Paul, 463
Stone, Harlan F., 284, 288
Stone, Oliver, 512–513
strikes, 145, 167, 239, 318, 361, 404;
   garment workers (1939), 240–241;
   sugar (1909), 129–130, 157, 159
Stump, Bob, 496–497
Subic Bay, 504
Subic Bay Naval Base, 315
"Subversity" (weekly radio show), 469
Suddes, Paul, 508
sugar cane leaves (holehole), 131–133, 170
sugar plantations, 122–123, 145, 158,
   170–171, 292, 473
Sumner, Charles, 102
Sun, Chia-Ku, 32
Sung, Betty Lee, 389
Sunoo, Brenda Paik, 383
Sun Yat-sen, 139–140
Supreme Court, 3, 157, 204–207

Supreme Court (California): Mamie
   Tape, an Infant, by Her Guardian Ad
   Litem, Joseph Tape v. Jennie M. A.
   Hurley, 11, 49, 70–71; women on
   steamship episode and, 35; Yick Wo
   petition and, 77–78
Supreme Court decisions: alien land
   law, 331; Barenblatt v. United States
   (360 U.S. 109), 345; Boyd v. U.S. (116
   U.S. 616, 636, 6 Sup. Ct. Rep. 535),
   95; Chae Chan Ping v. United States
   (1889), 86–88, 93; citizenship and,
   4; ex parte Mitsuye Endo (1944),
   302–305; Fong Yue Ting v. United
   States (1893), 93–96, 101; Fujii Sei
   v. State of California (1952), 160,
   317, 330–334; Gong Lum, et al. v.
   Rice, et al. (1927), 211–214; Gonzales
   v. Williams (192 U.S. 1, 13), 201;
   Gooey Hung Lee v. Johnson (1971),
   319; Griggs v. Duke Power Co. (1971),
   459; Hazelwood School Dist. v.
   United States (1977), 461; Hidemitsu
   Toyota v. United States (1925), 4–5,
   198, 199–201, 322; Hintopoulos v.
   Shaughnessy (1957), 344; Ho v. White
   (1922), 129; Japanese American
   treatment and, 5; Jay v. Boyd (1956),
   345; Kimm v. Rosenberg (1960), 316,
   343–346; Kiyoshi [Gordon] Hirabayashi v. United States (1943), 5, 7, 249,
   283–287, 288, 289, 290, 306, 307, 358,
   360, 429, 445–446; Knauff v. Shaughnessy (338 U.S. 537), 341; Korematsu
   v. United States (1944), 5, 7, 249, 283,
   302, 306–311, 323, 325, 358, 360,
   445–447; Kwock Jan Fat v. White
   (1920), 129; Kwong Hai Chew v.
   Colding, et al. (1853), 339–342;
   Lau v. Nichols (1974), 319, 401–403;
   Lee Joe v. United States (1893),
   93–96; Lee v. Johnson (1971), 401;
   Loving et ux v. Virginia (1967), 318,
   358–360; Maynard v. Hill (1888),
   360; Minoru Yasui v. U.S. Supreme
   Court (1943), 5, 249, 288–289, 290,

306, 429; *Nishimura Ekiu v. United States* (1892), 91–92; *Oyama v. California* (1948), 160, 325, 330–332; *Plessy v. Ferguson* (1896), 211, 213; regarding Japanese Americans, 1; *Skinner v. Oklahoma* (1942), 360; *Sung v. United States* (1902), 129; *Takao Ozawa v. United States* (1922), 181–184, 185, 186, 199; *Tang Tun v. Edsell* (1912), 155–156; *Teamsters v. United States* (1977), 461; *Terrace et al. v. Thompson, Attorney General of the State of Washington* (1923), 189–191; *Torao Takahashi v. Fish and Game Commission* (1948), 322–326; *United States v. Bhagat Singh Thind* (1923), 185–188; *United States v. Hohri* (1988), 444–445; *United States v. Ju Toy* (1905), 112; *United States v. Mitchell* (1983), 456; *United States v. Wong Kim Ark* (1898), 11, 112–114, 208; *Uphaus v. Wyman* (360 U.S. 72), 345; *Wallace R. Farrington, Governor of the Territory of Hawaii, et al. v. T. Tokushige, et al.* (1927), 198, 204–207; *Wards Cove Packing Company, Inc., et al. v. Atonio et al.* (1989), 457–463; *Watson v. Fort Worth Bank and Trust* (1988), 463; *Weedin v. Chin Bow* (1927), 208–210; *Wong Quan v. United States* (1893), 93–96; *Yick Wo v. Hopkins* (1886), 76–80, 190
Sutherland, George, 181, 185
Sweetheart Contracts, 405
Syngman Rhee. *See* Yi Sungman

Tachiki, Amy, 375
Taft, William H., 208, 211
Taiwan, 9, 318
Tajima, Renee, 425
Takao Ozawa, 101, 128
Talk Story, Inc., 415
"Talk Story: Words Bind, Words Set Free" (Honolulu conference; 1978), 415
Tamaki, Chōshirō, 244

Tang Tun, 129, 155–156
Taoism, 558, 561, 562
Tape, Frank, 72
Tape, Joseph, 70, 72
Tape, Mamie, 70, 72–73
Tape, Mary, 4, 70, 72–73
Tape v. Hurley (California Supreme Court; 1885), 11, 49, 70–71
Tardieu, Victor, 489
taxes, 11, 15–16, 26, 34, 49, 50, 81, 82, 129
Terminal Leave Act, 320
Texas, 115, 520–526
Thailand, 435, 437, 438, 478, 480, 499, 510
Thind, Bhagat Singh, 4, 128
Third World, 371, 373, 377, 381
Third World Liberation Front, 6, 361–364
Thirteenth Amendment, 47, 102, 455
Thomas, C. David, 487
Thornley, William H., 91
Title VII. *See under* Civil Rights Act
"To All Relations" (song; Nobuko Miyamoto; 1996), 494–495
Tocqueville, Alexis de, 388
"Togo Assists in a Great Diamond Robbery" (Irwin), 388
Tojo, Hideki, 254, 502
Tōki Higa, 243
Tolan Committee Hearings, 273
Tong, Ben R., 391
Tongan Americans, 559
Tongnip sinmun (independence), 174
To, Ngoc Van, 489
Tonquinese Chinese, 75
totalitarianism, 334
Tow, J. S., 388
Tōyama, Kyūzō, 244
Toyota, Hidemitsu, 4–5, 198, 199–201, 322
Tran, Quang Tri, 356
Treaty Between the United States and Corea: Peace, Amity, Commerce, and Navigation (1882), 64–66
Treaty of Guadalupe Hidalgo, 15
Treaty of Paris (1898), 11, 109–111

Treaty of Tientsin (1858), 11
Tri-Agency Resource Gang
    Enforcement Team, 468–469
Truax v. Raich (supra, 39), 190
Truman, Harry, 6, 317
Truong, Van Tran, 509–511, 512–513
Tsang, Daniel, 467–469
Tseang, Sing Hong, 17
Tsutsumi, Noboru, 167
Tu, Anh Tran, 467–469
Tule Lake War Relocation Center, 303
Tydings-McDuffie Act (1934), 5, 130, 197,
    198, 217, 230–233, 234, 235, 503

Uchida, Koyu, Bishop, 172–173
Uniform Guidelines on Employee
    Selection Procedures, 458
unions. *See* labor unions
United Asian-American Front (1970),
    370–373
United Farm Workers of American
    AFL-CIO, 404–405
United Farmworkers Union, 6
United Filipino Association, 367–368
United Front of Asians, 372
United Nations, 330, 336, 353, 435, 438
United States, 10, 116, 386, 451, 503–504,
    544, 561; and Asia, 127–130, 315; and
    China, 3, 11, 31–32, 35, 86, 372, 548;
    Cold War and, 315; Constitution of,
    76–77; as defendant, 450, 452;
    description of, 98; economic
    expansion of, 124; emergence of, 6;
    history of, 376; and Japan, 64, 189,
    192, 198, 247, 317, 422, 496; and
    Korea, 215; and manifest destiny
    doctrine, 11; national leadership
    from, 174; naturalization and, 180,
    332; Okinawans in, 241–245;
    Philippines allegiance to, 230;
    refugees and, 435; residents of, 200,
    209–210; and Spain, 109–111, 218, 231;
    Varsity Victory Volunteers and, 264;
    and Vietnam, 355–357, 407, 509;
    violation of rights and, 78; World
    War II and, 247, 250

United States Armed Forces of the Far
    East (USAFFE), 503–504
United States Public Health Service, 313
University of California, 6, 365, 374,
    538–540
Urata, Harry Minoru, 131
U.S. Catholic Bishops, 7, 558–565
U.S. District Court decisions: *Korematsu
    v. United States* (1984), 429–431
USAFFE. *See* United States Armed
    Forces of the Far East
Uyema, Seijūrō, 246

Varsity Victory Volunteers, 5, 263–264,
    265–266
VC. *See* Visual Communications
Veracruz, Philip, 404–406
veterans, 317, 320, 412, 496, 527–529;
    Filipino, 6, 316, 496–497, 502–505;
    Vietnam War, 510, 525
Veterans' Administration, 321
Vietcong, 318, 478, 480, 483, 524
Vietnam: artists in, 487–493; Asians in
    U.S. military and, 377; boat people
    from, 477, 480–481, 484, 509, 511, 513;
    census statistics for, 409; communism
    and, 7, 407; immigration from, 318,
    468; invasion of Cambodia by, 438;
    legacy of, 523; Orderly Departure
    Program from, 435; painting in,
    489; partition of, 490; people of,
    499; refugees from, 318, 412,
    434–435; as rural country, 488–489;
    Shinseki in, 518; villages in,
    488–489; war in, 343
Vietnamese Americans, 477, 493, 509,
    510–511, 512–513, 520, 523, 526
Vietnamese Broadcasting Network (New
    Jersey), 523
Vietnamese Community of Orange
    County, Inc., 522
Vietnamese Culture and Science
    Association, 521, 526
Vietnam War, 6, 434–435, 477–478,
    513, 525
Visual Communications (VC), 318

"The Voice of Labor in Hawaii" (pamphlet; 1920), 167–169
voting, 81, 82–83, 318, 545

Wada, Richard, 391
wages, 145–147, 273, 328
Wai'anae Nanakuli, 465
Wake Island, Japanese attack on, 252
Wang, L. Ling-chi, 540
war: anti-Japanese movies, 390; art and, 488; civil rights and, 348; constitutional guarantees in, 431; declaration of, 251–252; of independence, 178; independence campaigns and, 176; between Japan and U.S., 192; peaceful, 177–178; preparations for, 176; revolutionary, 176; in Southeast Asia, 341, 374; training for, 176; and women, 177
war brides, 250, 312
War Brides Act (1945), 312–313
War Department, 290, 299, 453
Warhol, Andy, 479
War Relocation Authority (W.R.A.), 300, 303–304, 420–421
Warren, Earl, 358
Wartime Relocation Authority, 273–274
Watanabe, Tamasaku, 258–260
"We Are the Children" (song; 1972), 6, 381
Webb Act (California Alien Land Law; 1913), 160–161, 244, 330
"The Wedding of the Chinee and the Coon" (song; 1897), 104–108
Weedin, Luther, 208–210
Welcoming the Stranger Among Us, Unity in Diversity, 559–560
Wheeler, Fred, 134
"When Heaven and Earth Changed Places" (Hayslip), 513
White, Byron R., 459
White House Initiative on Asian Americans and Pacific Islanders, 515, 530
white persons, 47–48, 183, 498–500; naturalization and, 101, 103, 186–187, 201

white supremacy, 360, 388, 389, 391, 411
Who Killed Vincent Chin (film), 425
"Why I Hate Ho Chi Minh" (Nguyen Vu; 1999), 509–511
Wing, Yung, 388
Wobblies. See International Workers of the World
Wolfe, Tom, 391
women, 6, 35, 133, 177, 179, 389, 564; Asian, 4, 12, 316; broom brigade of, 325; Chinese, 33, 41, 249, 386, 390; citizenship and, 4, 179–180; Filipino, 366, 367; immigration and, 38, 39; Japanese, 132, 133, 179–180, 269, 386; marriage and, 185, 250, 312; sexual threats to, 230; sugar cane workers, 131
Wong, Buck, 374, 376
Wong, Eddie, 374, 376
Wong, Flo Oy, 223
Wong, Jade Snow, 389, 391
Wong, Shawn Hsu, 391
Wong, Kim Ark, 3, 11, 104, 112–114, 127, 208
Woo, John, 484
Workingman's Party (California), 57
World War I, 5, 145, 167, 197, 359
World War II, 7, 172, 189, 292, 302, 313, 343, 496, 502, 503–504; Alaska natives and, 419–420; Aleuts and, 441; Asian Americans and, 7, 315–316; Asians and, 316, 377; Chinese and, 339–340; combat awards and, 470–471; concentration camps and, 269–271, 376, 448; end of, 109, 202, 250; Filipinos and, 504, 505; immigration reforms and, 5; internment and, 1, 157, 381, 412, 439–440, 442, 506–508, 508; Japanese Americans and, 2, 256, 299, 414, 444–445, 551, 555–557, 556; Japanese and, 174, 269–271, 281, 322, 390, 391, 507; Medals of Honor and, 1, 7; and Nazism, 317; songs during, 131; war brides and, 312; writers and, 261
W.R.A. See War Relocation Authority

Wright, George, 157
Writers of Hawaii: A Focus On Our Literary Heritage (Chock; Manabe), 416
Writers of Hawaii Conference (1980), 415–418

Yamashita, Bruce, 520
Yankelovitch survey, 541, 543, 545, 548–549
Yasui, Minoru, 5, 249, 288–289, 290, 306, 412, 429
Yasumoto, Jittoku, 243
Yat-sen, Sun, 3
Yeager, Chuck, 523
"Yellow Pearl" (song; 1972), 378–379
Yellow Peril image, 172
Yellow Power movement, 318
Yempuku, Ralph, 265–266

Yick Wo, 12, 77, 95
Yi Sungman (Syngman Rhee), 174
Yokohama, California (Mori), 391
Yokouchi, Masaru "Pundy," 464–466
Yoshinaga-Herzig, Aiko, 290, 306, 429, 456
Young Men's Buddhist Association, 121
Yu, Connie Young, 391
"Yuiyo Bon Odori" (1984), 432–433
Yung, Judy, 72

Zaibei Nihonjinkai (Japanese Association of America), 244
Zaibei Okinawa Seinenkai (Okinawan Young People's Association of America), 245–246
Zelenko, Benjamin, 456
Zen Buddhism, 172
Zoroastrianism, 562